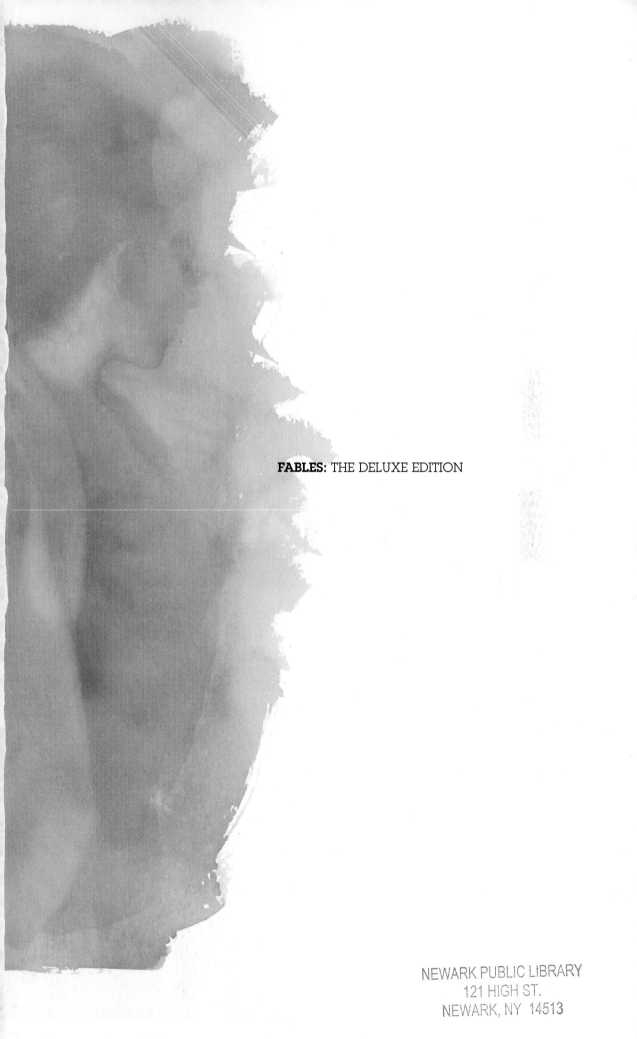

FABLES: THE DELUXE EDITION

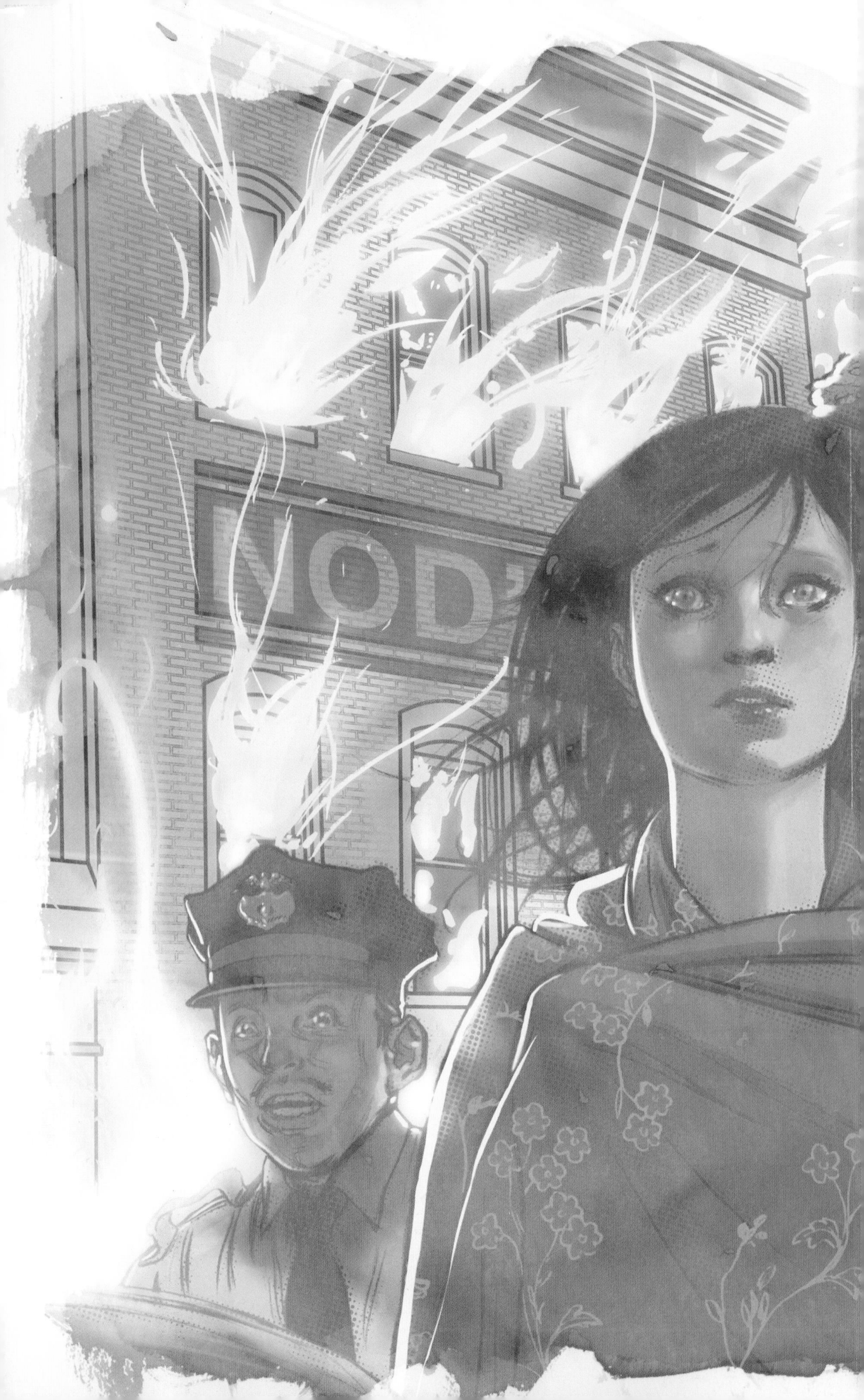
NOD

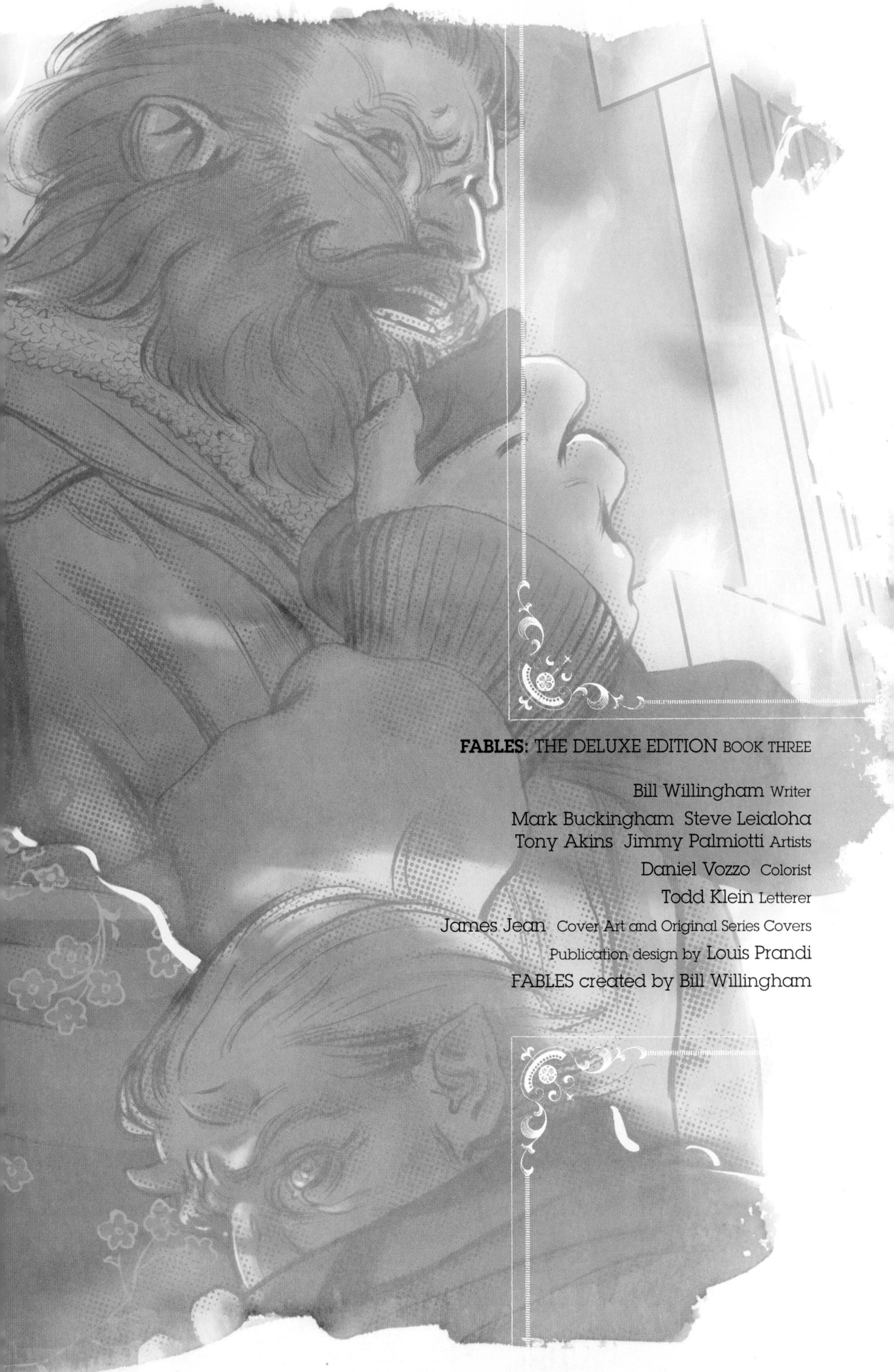

FABLES: THE DELUXE EDITION BOOK THREE

Bill Willingham Writer

Mark Buckingham Steve Leialoha
Tony Akins Jimmy Palmiotti Artists

Daniel Vozzo Colorist

Todd Klein Letterer

James Jean Cover Art and Original Series Covers

Publication design by Louis Prandi

FABLES created by Bill Willingham

These stories of war and espionage are dedicated to my MP Army buddies, particularly Bill Heck, Mike Lyons and Joe Czuchra, partners in crime, and in fighting, and in crime-fighting. Veterans of the Cold War, they stood their posts on our side of the wall, ten years before the wall came down.

— Bill Willingham

Dedicated to the memory of William and Amy, my grandparents, in whose home I drew the pages of "March of the Wooden Soldiers."

— Mark Buckingham

Shelly Bond Executive Editor – Vertigo and Editor – Original Series
Mariah Huehner Assistant Editor – Original Series
Scott Nybakken Editor
Robbin Brosterman Design Director – Books
Louis Prandi Publication Design

Hank Kanalz Senior VP – Vertigo and Integrated Publishing

Diane Nelson President
Dan DiDio and Jim Lee Co-Publishers
Geoff Johns Chief Creative Officer
John Rood Executive VP – Sales, Marketing and Business Development
Amy Genkins Senior VP – Business and Legal Affairs
Nairi Gardiner Senior VP – Finance
Jeff Boison VP – Publishing Planning
Mark Chiarello VP – Art Direction and Design
John Cunningham VP – Marketing
Terri Cunningham VP – Editorial Administration
Alison Gill Senior VP – Manufacturing and Operations
Jay Kogan VP – Business and Legal Affairs, Publishing
Jack Mahan VP – Business Affairs, Talent
Nick Napolitano VP – Manufacturing Administration
Sue Pohja VP – Book Sales
Courtney Simmons Senior VP – Publicity
Bob Wayne Senior VP – Sales

Logo design by Brainchild Studios/NYC

FABLES: THE DELUXE EDITION
BOOK THREE

DC Comics, 1700 Broadway,
New York, NY 10019
A Warner Bros. Entertainment Company.
Printed in Canada. Third Printing.
ISBN:978-1-4012-3097-5

Library of Congress Cataloging-in-Publication Data

Willingham, Bill.
Fables : the deluxe edition, book three/ Bill Willingham, Mark Buckingham, Steve Leialoha.
p. cm.
"Originally published in single magazine form as Fables 19-27."
ISBN 978-1-4012-3097-5 (alk. paper)
1. Fairy tales--Adaptations--Comic books, strips, etc. 2. Legends--Adaptations--Comic books, strips, etc. 3. Graphic novels. I. Buckingham, Mark. II. Leialoha, Steve. III. Title. IV. Title: Fables. Book three.
PN6727.W52 F354 2011
741.5'973–dc23

2011456010

SUSTAINABLE FORESTRY INITIATIVE
Certified Chain of Custody
Promoting Sustainable Forestry
www.sfiprogram.org
SFI-00507
This label only applies to the text section.

Table of Contents

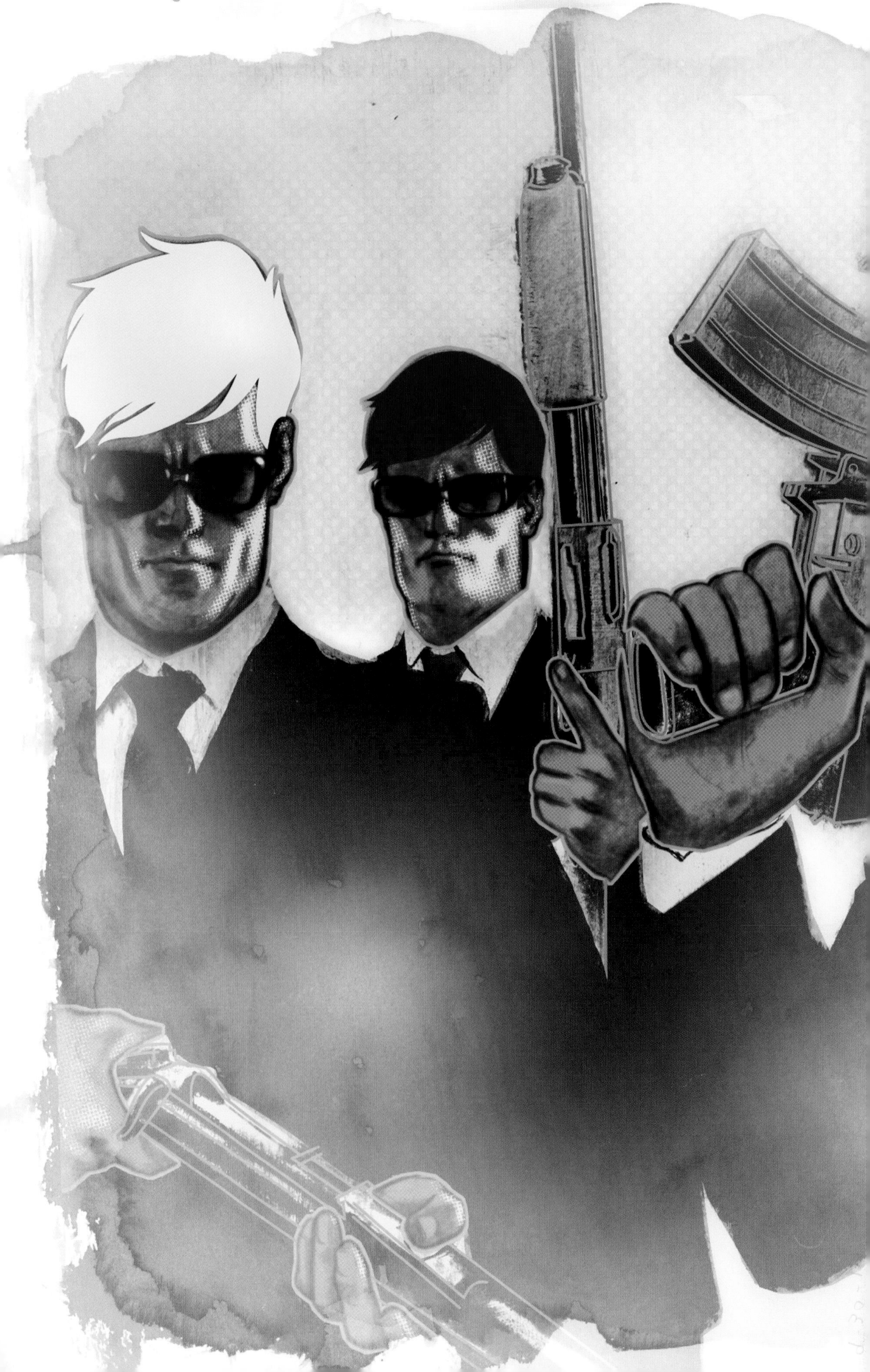

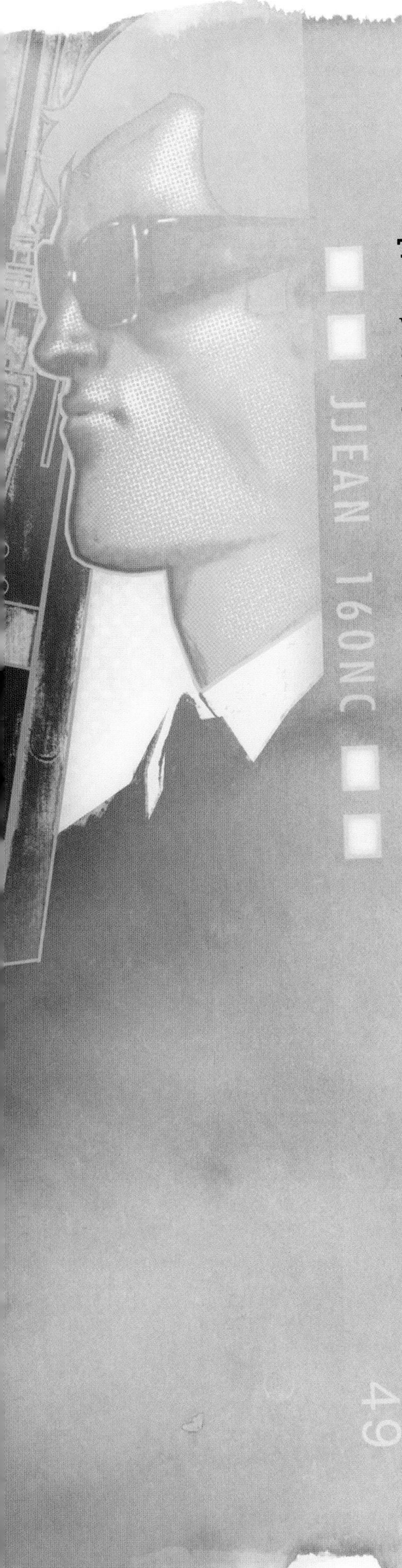
JJEAN 160NC
49

The Boy in a Bubble

The business of creating comic books is, on the whole, a solitary one. We lock ourselves away in a small office or home studio and pour everything into the pages for days or weeks at a time. Often we lose ourselves completely in that bubble of creativity, breathing life into new and fantastic worlds.

When you are on the inside of that bubble, doing all you can to add depth and vitality to your creations, it's easy to find yourself investing a lot of your own personality or elements of friends and family into the characters. As a consequence, you can find yourself getting very attached to them.

The Salvation of Fly

When I reached the end of the "Animal Farm" storyline, I knew I wanted to draw FABLES full time. Bill Willingham's wonderful writing had won me over from the first moment we worked together, but combining his work with an amazing creative and editorial team (Steve Leialoha, Todd Klein, Danny Vozzo, James Jean, Mariah Huehner and Shelly Bond) and a new fantasy world of unlimited possibilities in which to play was an irresistible combination.

My first issue in the role of regular artist came at the start of "Storybook Love." Whilst I was hesitant to risk messing with the established looks of the main cast, I couldn't resist making my three favorite supporting characters more my own, and Pinocchio, Boy Blue and Flycatcher quickly acquired the distinctive looks that they maintain to this day. Most readers, I think, were more captivated by the relationship of Snow White and Bigby Wolf, but for me the story of these three friends was key. So you can imagine my horror when Bill revealed to me his plans for "March of the Wooden Soldiers," the epic tale contained in this very volume, and the terrible things he had in store for my favorite characters.

Bill had originally intended for Flycatcher to meet his end in this story. Fly had always appeared to be a relatively limited character, perpetually cleaning the Woodland building and acting as the butt of the occasional fly-eating joke, but I'd always seen huge potential in this good-natured and noble gentleman. I couldn't bear to see him go, and begged Bill to let him live. Bill, being a supremely generous collaborator, agreed to reconsider Fly's fate, and so I inadvertently set in motion a chain of events that would culminate in the heroic adventure of "The Good Prince" three years later. In fact, all three of my favorites were soon to become key elements in the unfolding FABLES saga.

Outside the Bubble

The creative bubble is not impermeable to the impact of the real world. Most people are quick to spot creative influences in an artist's work, but it is often the highs and lows of day-to-day life that have the most profound effects.

I had begun "March of the Wooden Soldiers" at a dark time in my life. A long-term relationship had ended and I found myself living alone. Also, my grandfather had recently died and I had temporarily moved into his home and was missing him terribly. I threw myself into my work, but I knew I was missing a vital spark.

However, my circumstances were about to change dramatically. In September of 2003 I made my first trip to Spain for a comics convention, the Aviles Comics Festival in Asturias. Surrounded by friends old and new, I soon began to relish life again. Best of all, I met Irma.

When I returned to work on "March of the Wooden Soldiers" following the terrific guest issue "Cinderella Libertine" illustrated by soon-to-be JACK OF FABLES star artist Tony Akins and the equally wonderful Jimmy Palmiotti, I was a new man. My creative bubble was now pink and filled with little love hearts.

Anyone reading from issue #24 onwards will see how my love for Irma inspired some of the richest, most detailed and most elegant work I had yet produced for the series — not an easy feat considering I was jumping on an airplane every two weeks to be with her. As I mentioned before, I can never resist putting a little something of the people I love into everything I do, and Rose Red quickly began to look an awful lot like my soon-to-be wife. The eagle-eyed among you should also keep a lookout for the little Irma doll hanging from the rearview mirror of the Farm's truck.

It has been a delight to revisit these stories while writing this introduction, and I hope that "March of the Wooden Soldiers" will mean as much to you as it did to me. The FABLES team and I hope you'll continue to follow our characters for many years to come.

— Mark Buckingham

20 May 2011

Inside a bubble still filled with little love hearts

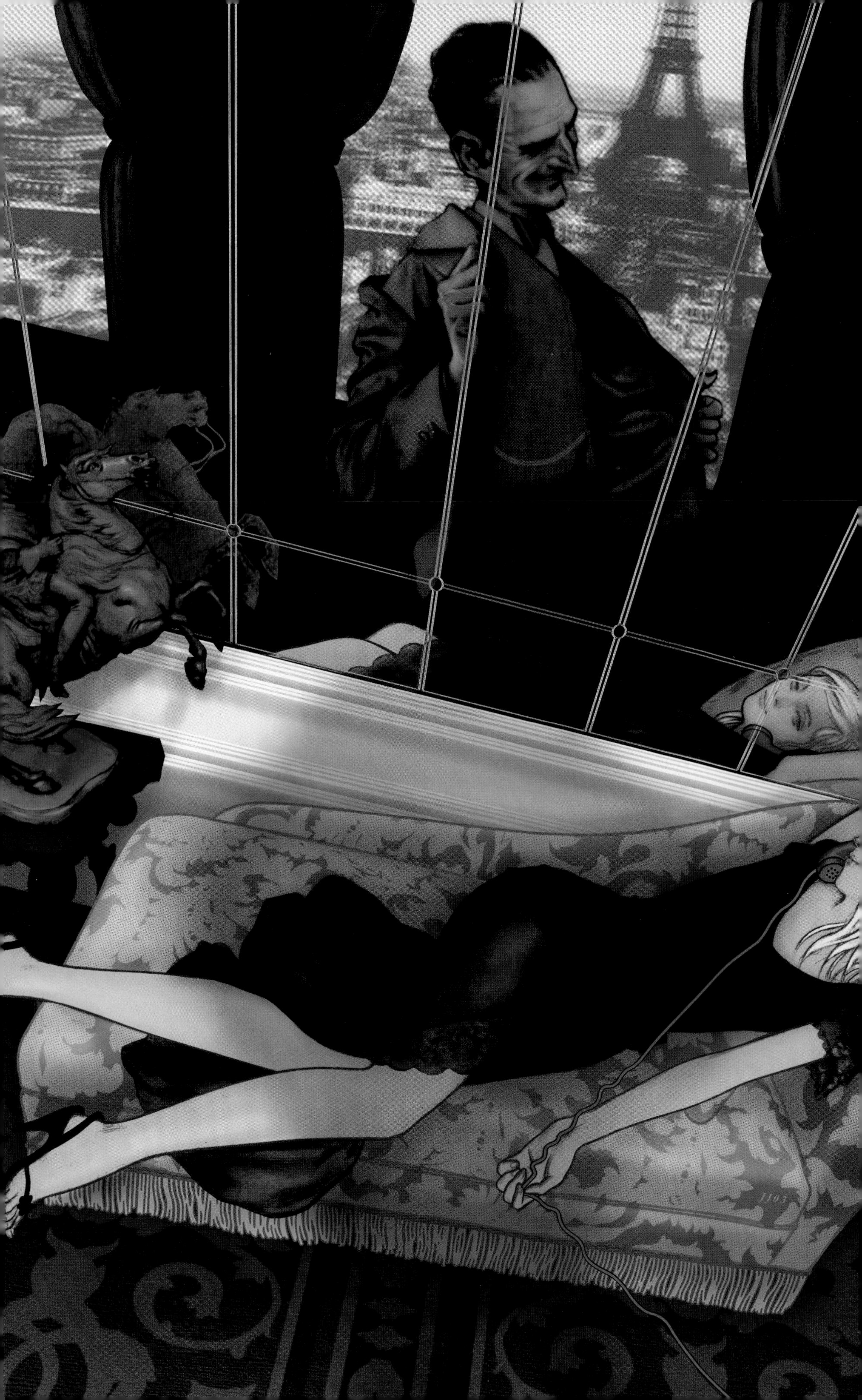

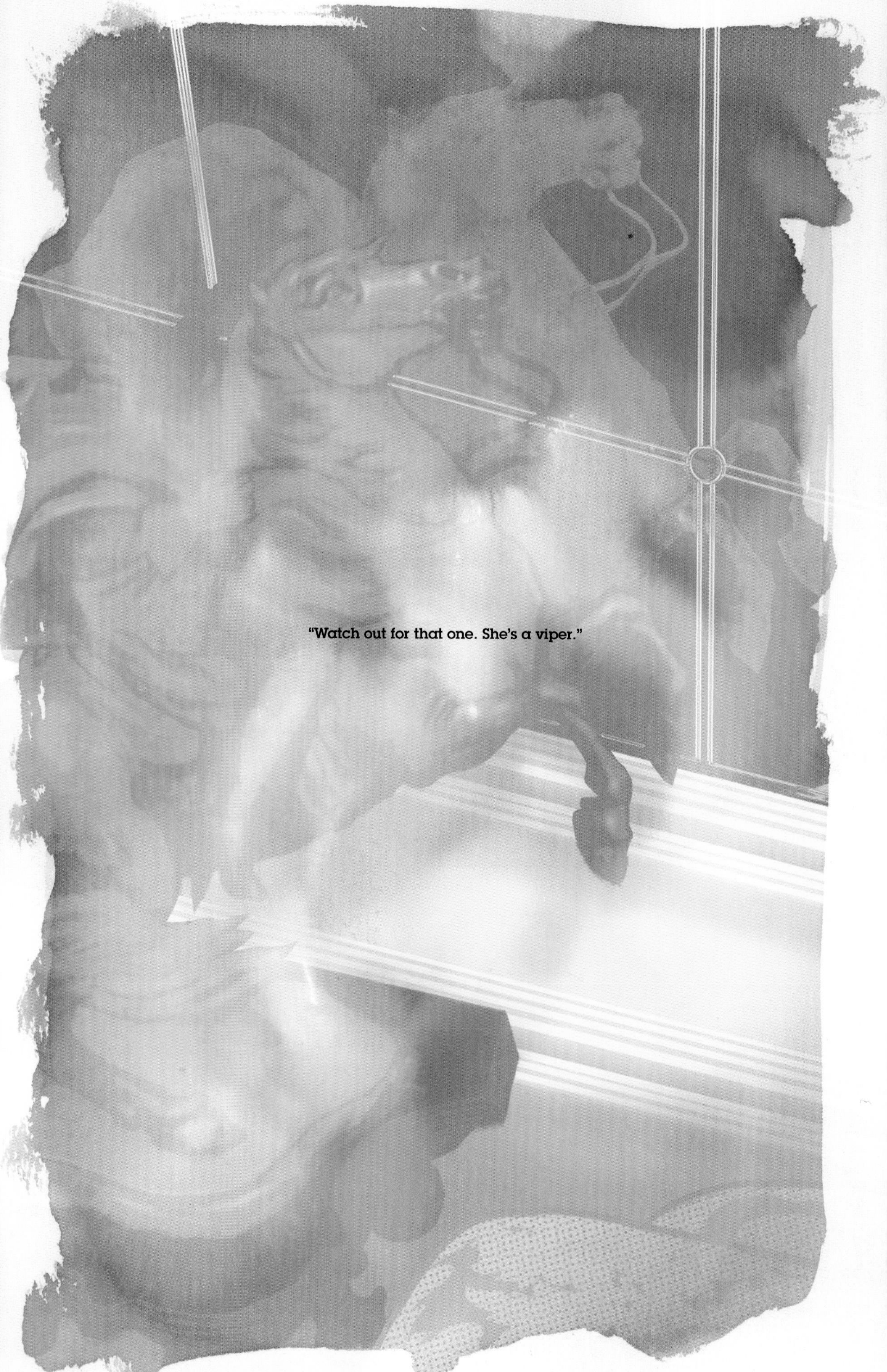
"Watch out for that one. She's a viper."

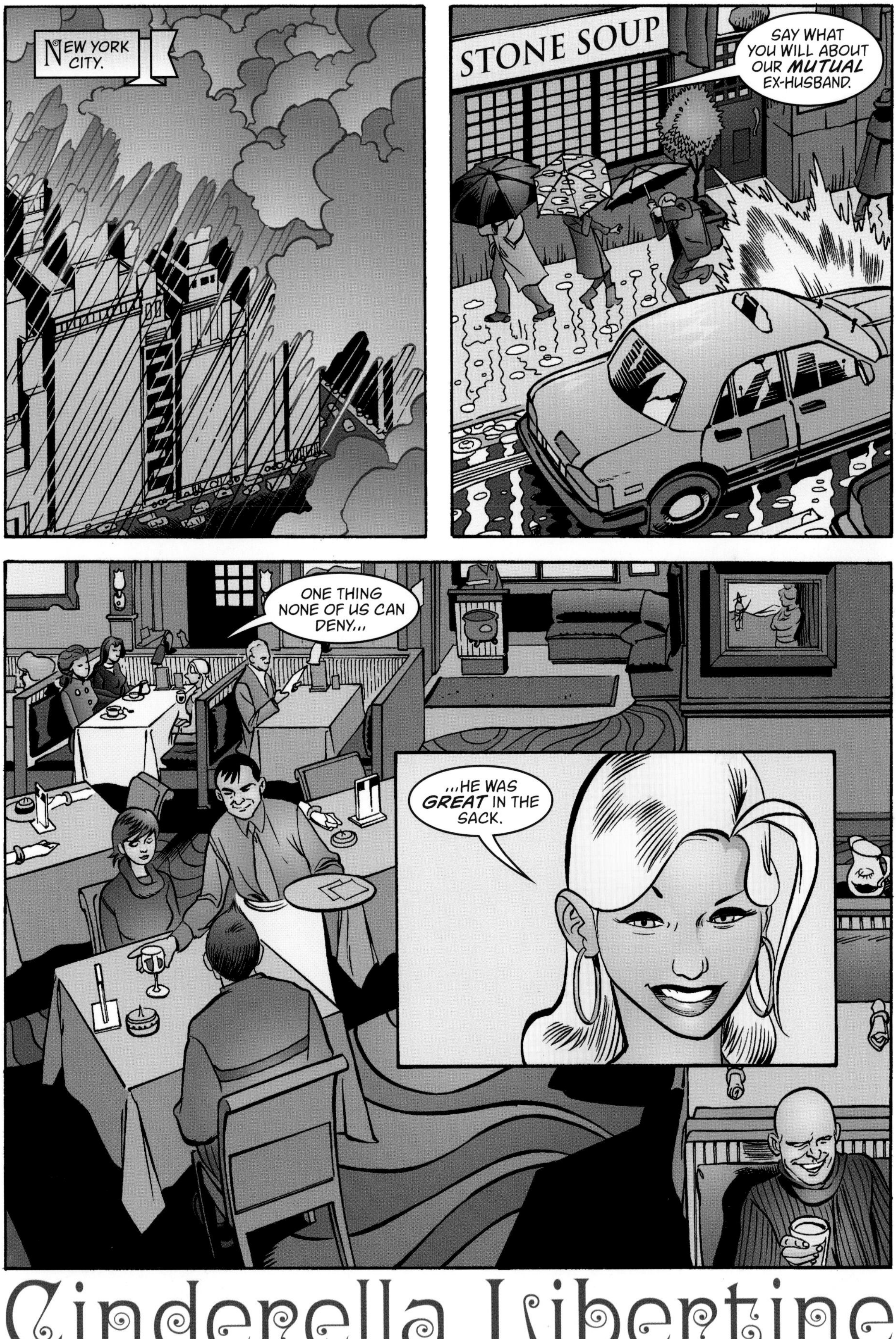
NEW YORK CITY.
STONE SOUP
SAY WHAT YOU WILL ABOUT OUR *MUTUAL* EX-HUSBAND.
ONE THING NONE OF US CAN DENY...
...HE WAS *GREAT* IN THE SACK.

Cinderella Libertine

In which we explore something of the secret life of Prince Charming's rather outspoken and rambunctious third wife.

Bill Willingham *writer/creator*
Tony Akins *guest pencils*
Jimmy Palmiotti *guest inks*
Daniel Vozzo *color/seps*
Todd Klein *letters*
James Jean *cover art*
Mariah Huehner *asst. editor*
Shelly Bond *editor*

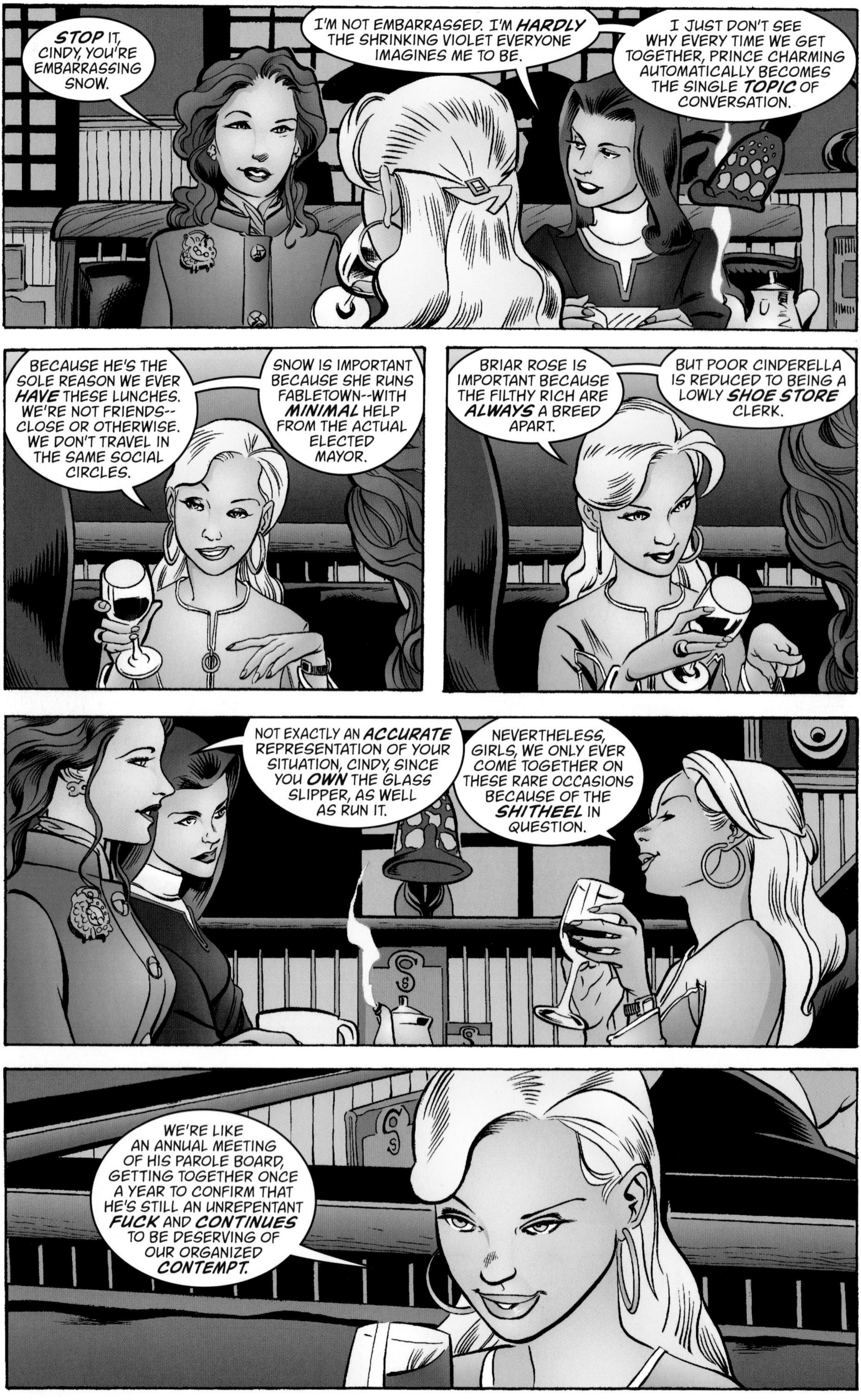
STOP IT, CINDY, YOU'RE EMBARRASSING SNOW.
I'M NOT EMBARRASSED. I'M HARDLY THE SHRINKING VIOLET EVERYONE IMAGINES ME TO BE.
I JUST DON'T SEE WHY EVERY TIME WE GET TOGETHER, PRINCE CHARMING AUTOMATICALLY BECOMES THE SINGLE TOPIC OF CONVERSATION.
BECAUSE HE'S THE SOLE REASON WE EVER HAVE THESE LUNCHES. WE'RE NOT FRIENDS--CLOSE OR OTHERWISE. WE DON'T TRAVEL IN THE SAME SOCIAL CIRCLES.
SNOW IS IMPORTANT BECAUSE SHE RUNS FABLETOWN--WITH MINIMAL HELP FROM THE ACTUAL ELECTED MAYOR.
BRIAR ROSE IS IMPORTANT BECAUSE THE FILTHY RICH ARE ALWAYS A BREED APART.
BUT POOR CINDERELLA IS REDUCED TO BEING A LOWLY SHOE STORE CLERK.
NOT EXACTLY AN ACCURATE REPRESENTATION OF YOUR SITUATION, CINDY, SINCE YOU OWN THE GLASS SLIPPER, AS WELL AS RUN IT.
NEVERTHELESS, GIRLS, WE ONLY EVER COME TOGETHER ON THESE RARE OCCASIONS BECAUSE OF THE SHITHEEL IN QUESTION.
WE'RE LIKE AN ANNUAL MEETING OF HIS PAROLE BOARD, GETTING TOGETHER ONCE A YEAR TO CONFIRM THAT HE'S STILL AN UNREPENTANT FUCK AND CONTINUES TO BE DESERVING OF OUR ORGANIZED CONTEMPT.

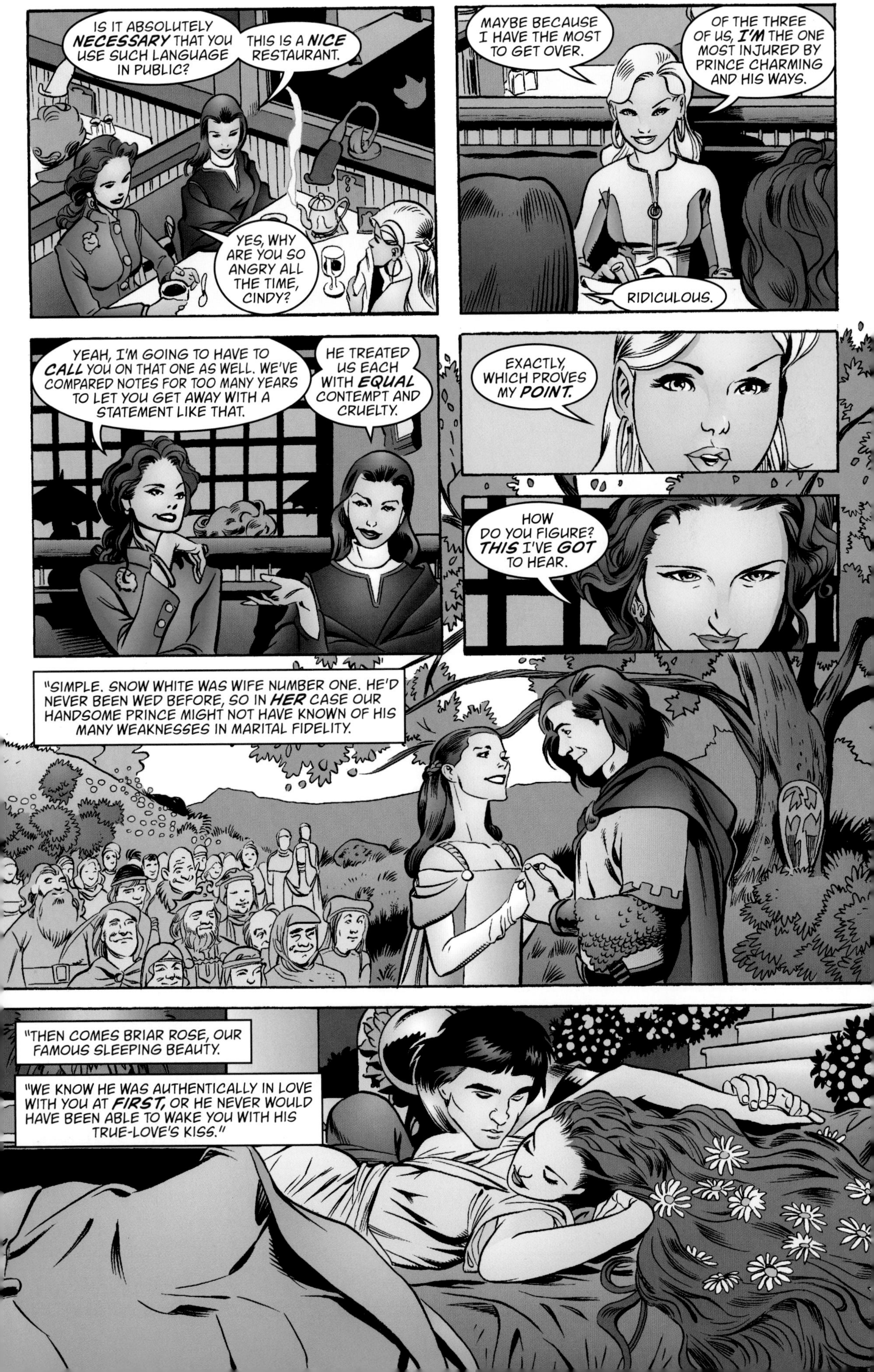

IS IT ABSOLUTELY NECESSARY THAT YOU USE SUCH LANGUAGE IN PUBLIC?
THIS IS A NICE RESTAURANT.
YES, WHY ARE YOU SO ANGRY ALL THE TIME, CINDY?
MAYBE BECAUSE I HAVE THE MOST TO GET OVER.
OF THE THREE OF US, I'M THE ONE MOST INJURED BY PRINCE CHARMING AND HIS WAYS.
RIDICULOUS.
YEAH, I'M GOING TO HAVE TO CALL YOU ON THAT ONE AS WELL. WE'VE COMPARED NOTES FOR TOO MANY YEARS TO LET YOU GET AWAY WITH A STATEMENT LIKE THAT.
HE TREATED US EACH WITH EQUAL CONTEMPT AND CRUELTY.
EXACTLY, WHICH PROVES MY POINT.
HOW DO YOU FIGURE? THIS I'VE GOT TO HEAR.
"SIMPLE. SNOW WHITE WAS WIFE NUMBER ONE. HE'D NEVER BEEN WED BEFORE, SO IN HER CASE OUR HANDSOME PRINCE MIGHT NOT HAVE KNOWN OF HIS MANY WEAKNESSES IN MARITAL FIDELITY.
"THEN COMES BRIAR ROSE, OUR FAMOUS SLEEPING BEAUTY.
"WE KNOW HE WAS AUTHENTICALLY IN LOVE WITH YOU AT FIRST, OR HE NEVER WOULD HAVE BEEN ABLE TO WAKE YOU WITH HIS TRUE-LOVE'S KISS."

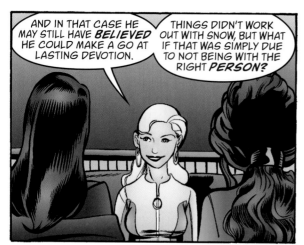

AND IN THAT CASE HE MAY STILL HAVE *BELIEVED* HE COULD MAKE A GO AT LASTING DEVOTION.

THINGS DIDN'T WORK OUT WITH SNOW, BUT WHAT IF THAT WAS SIMPLY DUE TO NOT BEING WITH THE RIGHT *PERSON?*

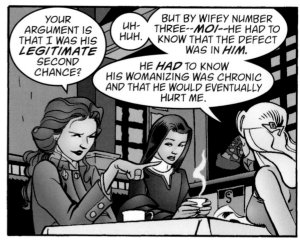

YOUR *ARGUMENT* IS THAT I WAS HIS *LEGITIMATE* SECOND CHANCE?

UH-HUH.

BUT BY WIFEY NUMBER THREE--*MOI*--HE HAD TO KNOW THAT THE DEFECT WAS IN *HIM.*

HE *HAD* TO KNOW HIS WOMANIZING WAS CHRONIC AND THAT HE WOULD EVENTUALLY HURT ME.

BY THE TIME IT WAS *MY* TURN, HE KNEW WELL IN ADVANCE HE'D *DESTROY* ME, AND YET HE JUST DIDN'T *GIVE* A FLYING FUCK.

Q.E.D., LADIES. I'M *DESERVEDLY* BITTER AND I PLAN TO STAY THAT WAY.

NOW, IF YOU'LL *EXCUSE* ME, AS MUCH FUN AS THIS HAS BEEN, I'M RUNNING LATE.

I'M OFF TO THE AIRPORT, FOR A WILD AND WANTON EUROPEAN VACATION.

AGAIN? YOUR SHOE STORE MUST BE DOING BETTER THAN YOU PROFESS.

ON THE *CONTRARY*, IT'S DOING RATHER SHITTILY.

I WAS NEVER CUT OUT TO BE A FUCKING *MERCHANT.*

"AND SO NOW I'M OFF TO SPEND WHAT'S LEFT OF THE COMPANY ASSETS--

Stone Soup

"BEFORE MY CREDITORS GET WIND THAT I ABSCONDED WITH THEM."

TAXI!

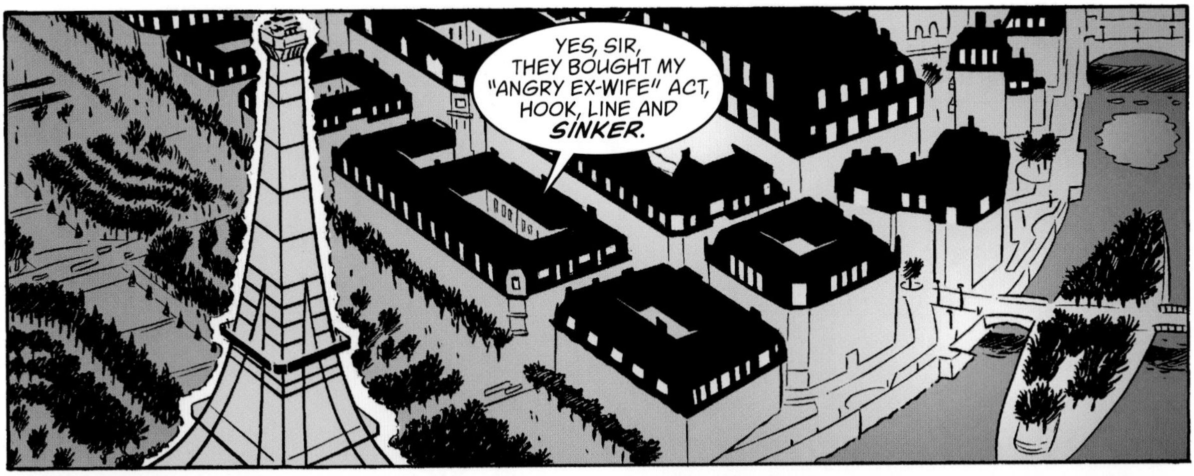
YES, SIR, THEY BOUGHT MY "ANGRY EX-WIFE" ACT, HOOK, LINE AND SINKER.

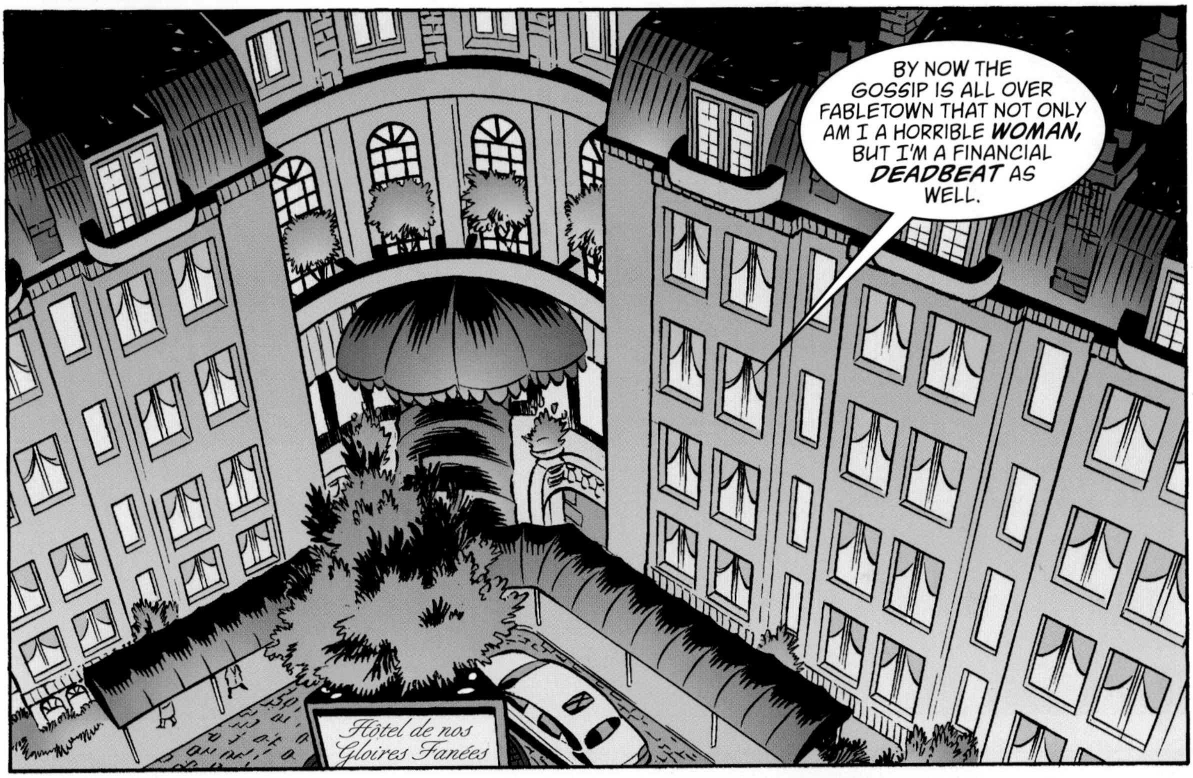
BY NOW THE GOSSIP IS ALL OVER FABLETOWN THAT NOT ONLY AM I A HORRIBLE WOMAN, BUT I'M A FINANCIAL DEADBEAT AS WELL.
Hôtel de nos Gloires Fanées

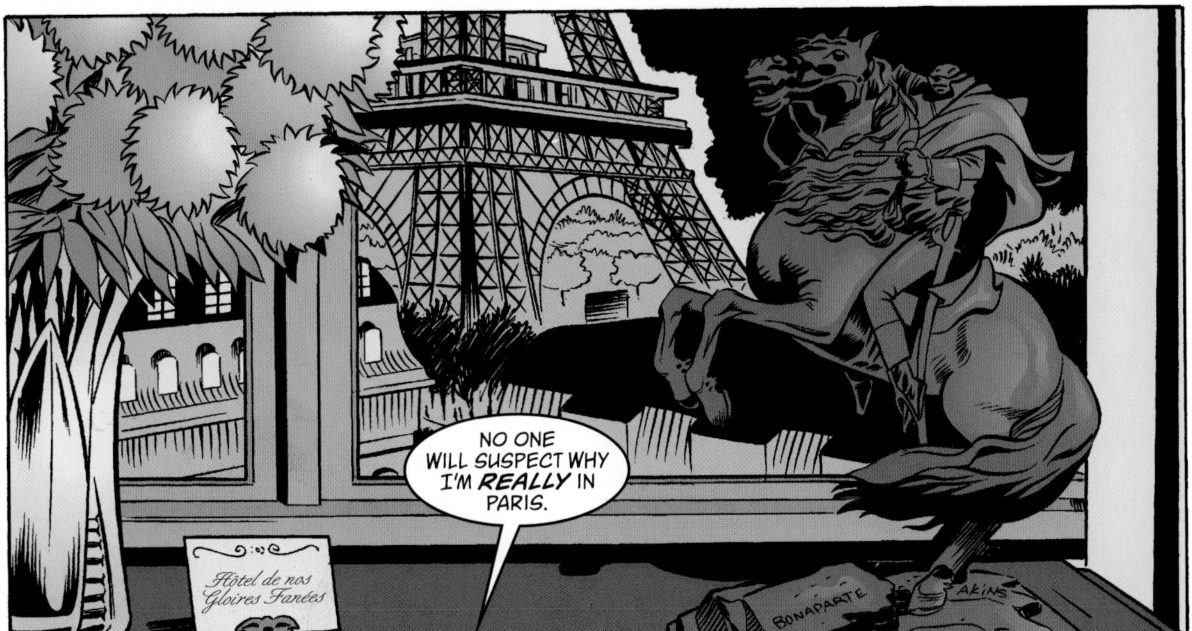
NO ONE WILL SUSPECT WHY I'M REALLY IN PARIS.
Hôtel de nos Gloires Fanées
BONAPARTE
AKINS

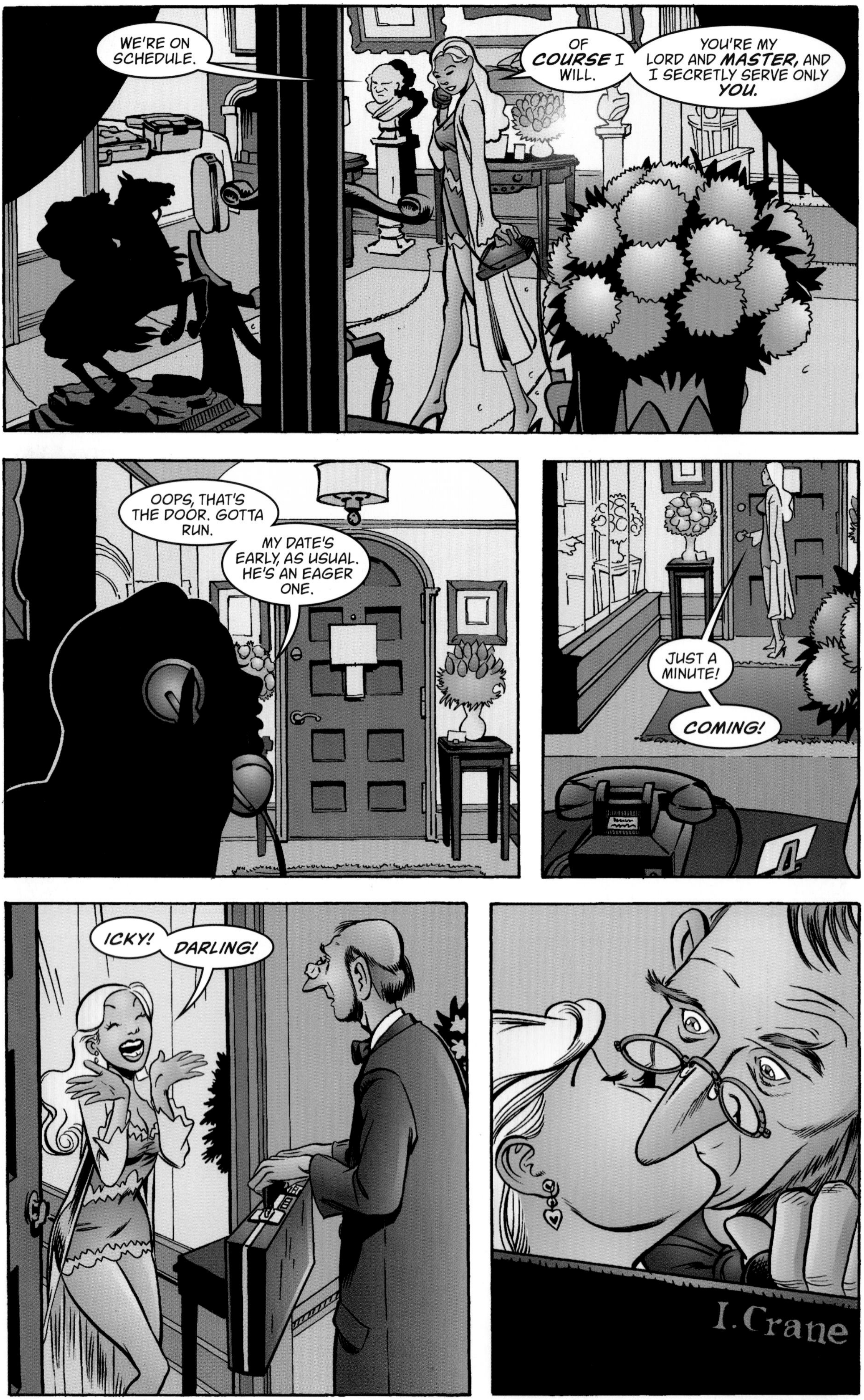

WE'RE ON SCHEDULE.
OF COURSE I WILL.
YOU'RE MY LORD AND MASTER, AND I SECRETLY SERVE ONLY YOU.
OOPS, THAT'S THE DOOR. GOTTA RUN.
MY DATE'S EARLY, AS USUAL. HE'S AN EAGER ONE.
JUST A MINUTE!
COMING!
ICKY!
DARLING!
I. Crane

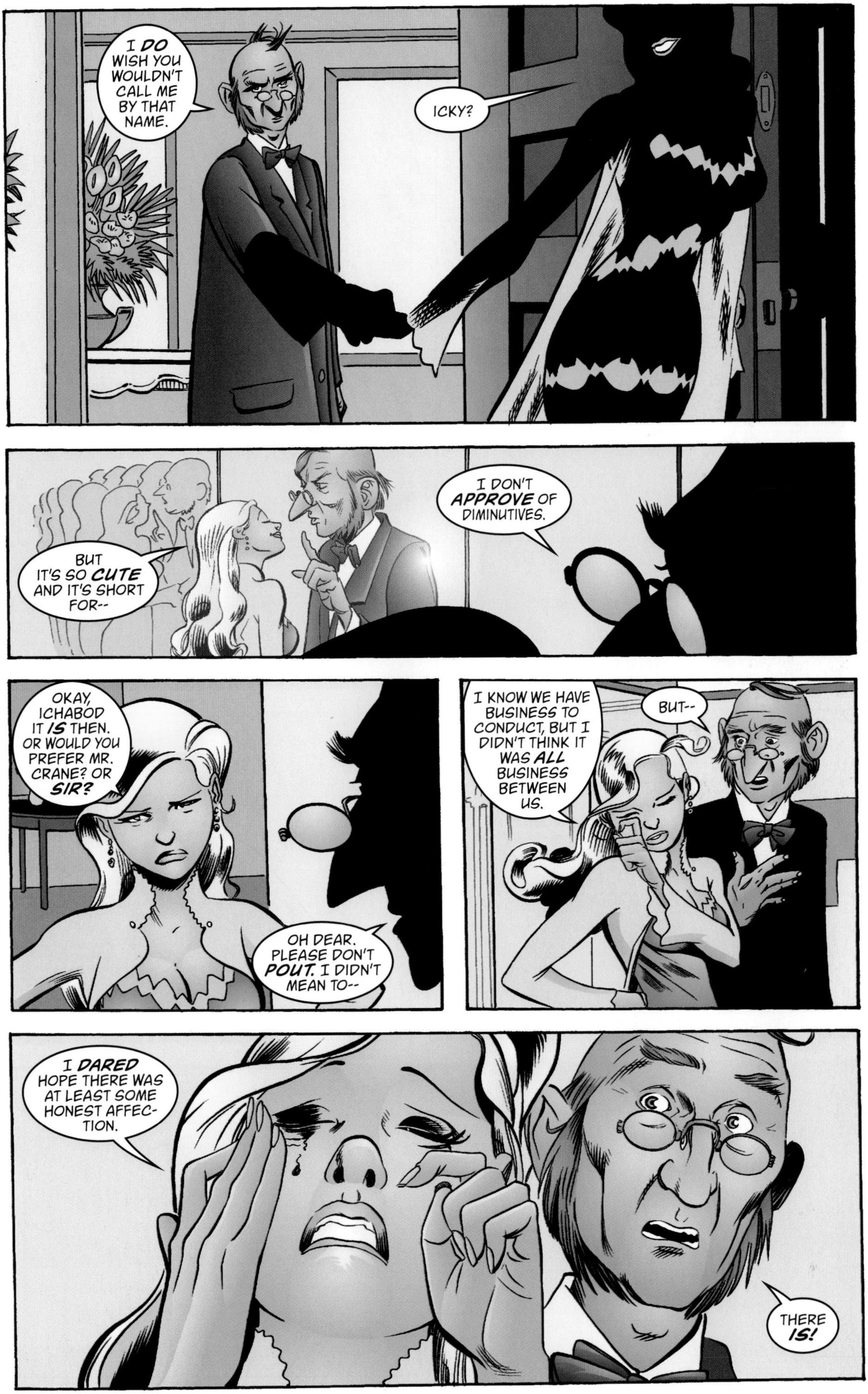
I DO WISH YOU WOULDN'T CALL ME BY THAT NAME.
ICKY?
BUT IT'S SO CUTE AND IT'S SHORT FOR--
I DON'T APPROVE OF DIMINUTIVES.
OKAY, ICHABOD IT IS THEN. OR WOULD YOU PREFER MR. CRANE? OR SIR?
OH DEAR. PLEASE DON'T POUT. I DIDN'T MEAN TO--
I KNOW WE HAVE BUSINESS TO CONDUCT, BUT I DIDN'T THINK IT WAS ALL BUSINESS BETWEEN US.
BUT--
I DARED HOPE THERE WAS AT LEAST SOME HONEST AFFECTION.
THERE IS!

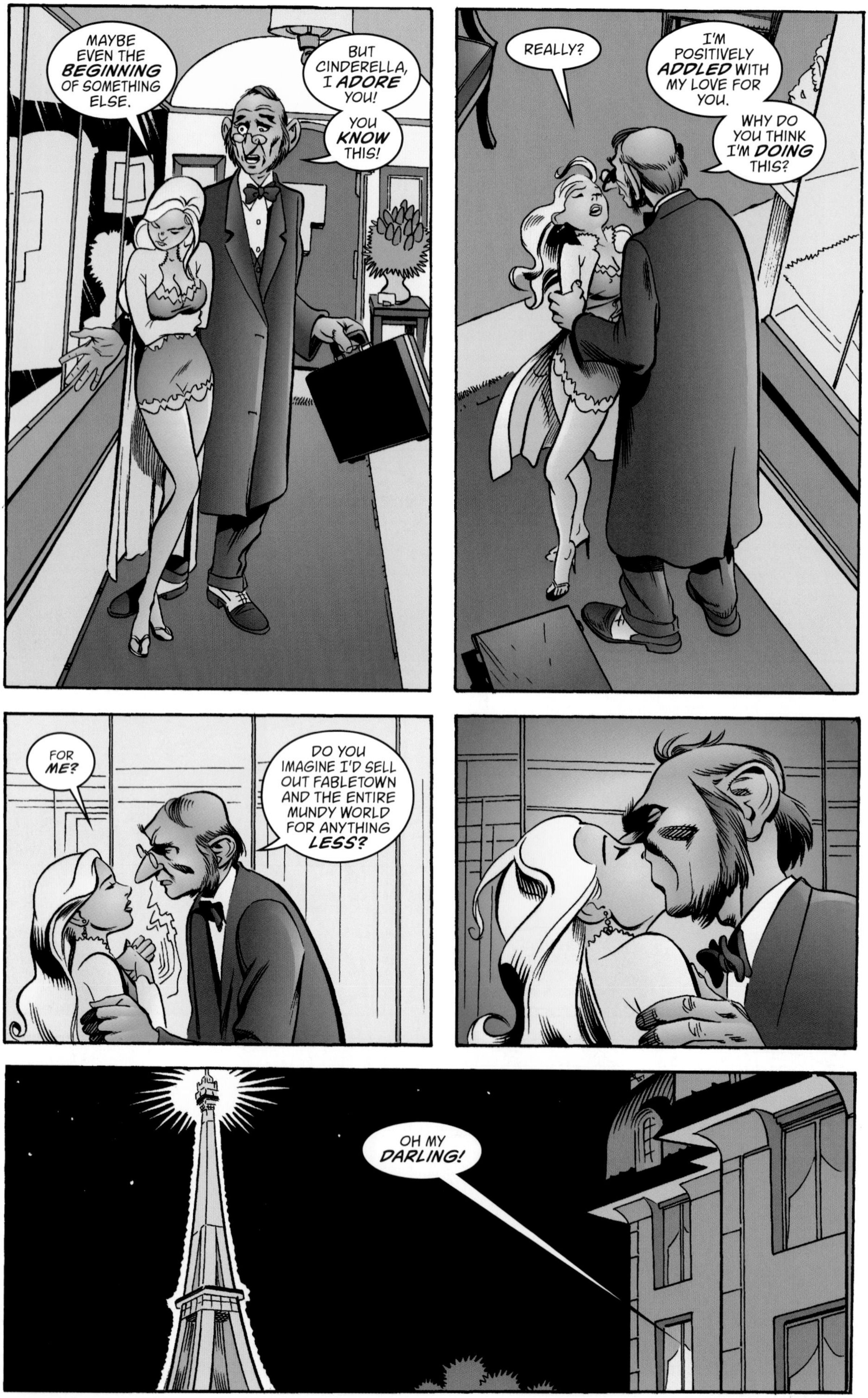
MAYBE EVEN THE BEGINNING OF SOMETHING ELSE.
BUT CINDERELLA, I ADORE YOU!
YOU KNOW THIS!
REALLY?
I'M POSITIVELY ADDLED WITH MY LOVE FOR YOU.
WHY DO YOU THINK I'M DOING THIS?
FOR ME?
DO YOU IMAGINE I'D SELL OUT FABLETOWN AND THE ENTIRE MUNDY WORLD FOR ANYTHING LESS?
OH MY DARLING!

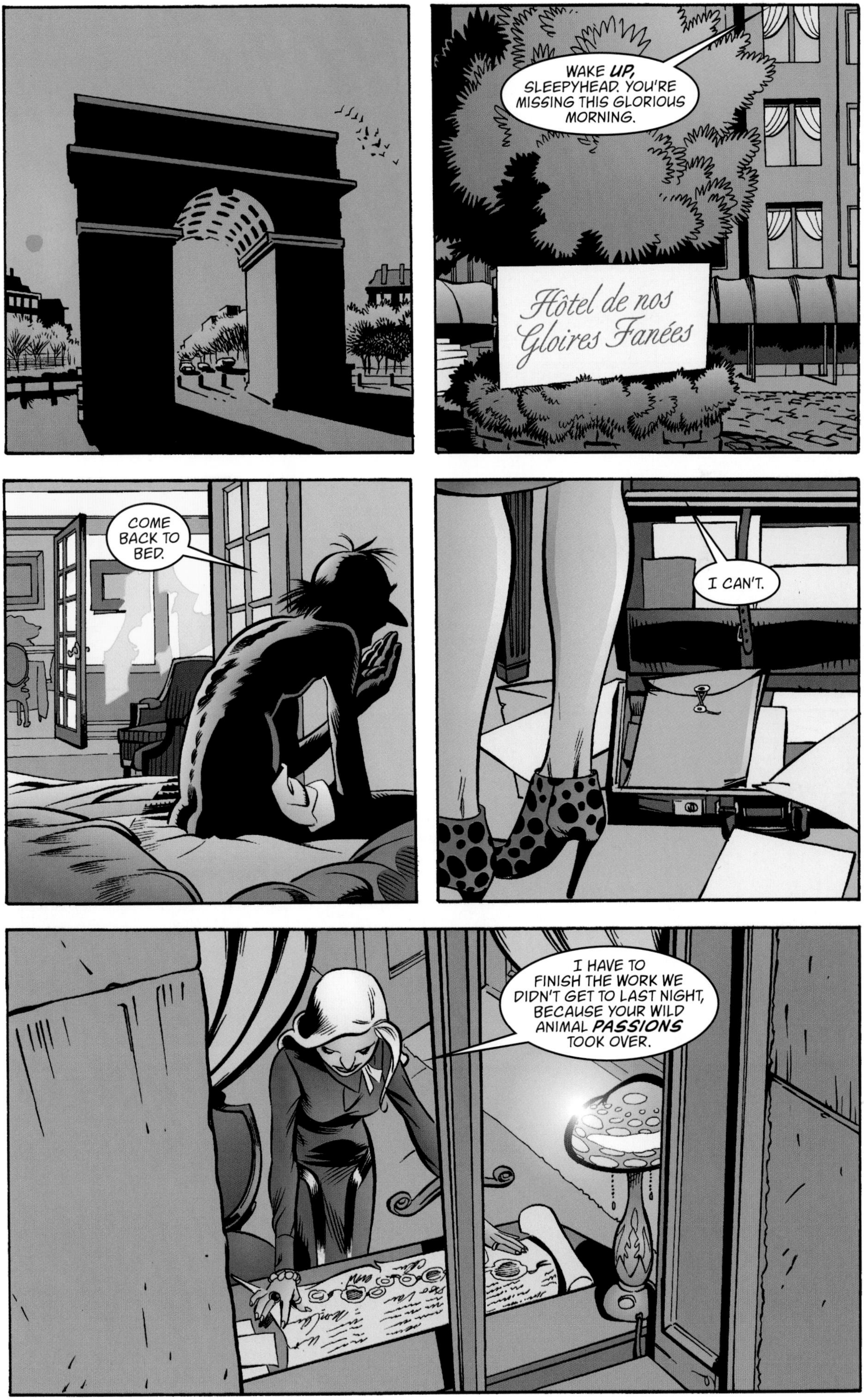
WAKE UP, SLEEPYHEAD. YOU'RE MISSING THIS GLORIOUS MORNING.
Hôtel de nos Gloires Fanées
COME BACK TO BED.
I CAN'T.
I HAVE TO FINISH THE WORK WE DIDN'T GET TO LAST NIGHT, BECAUSE YOUR WILD ANIMAL PASSIONS TOOK OVER.

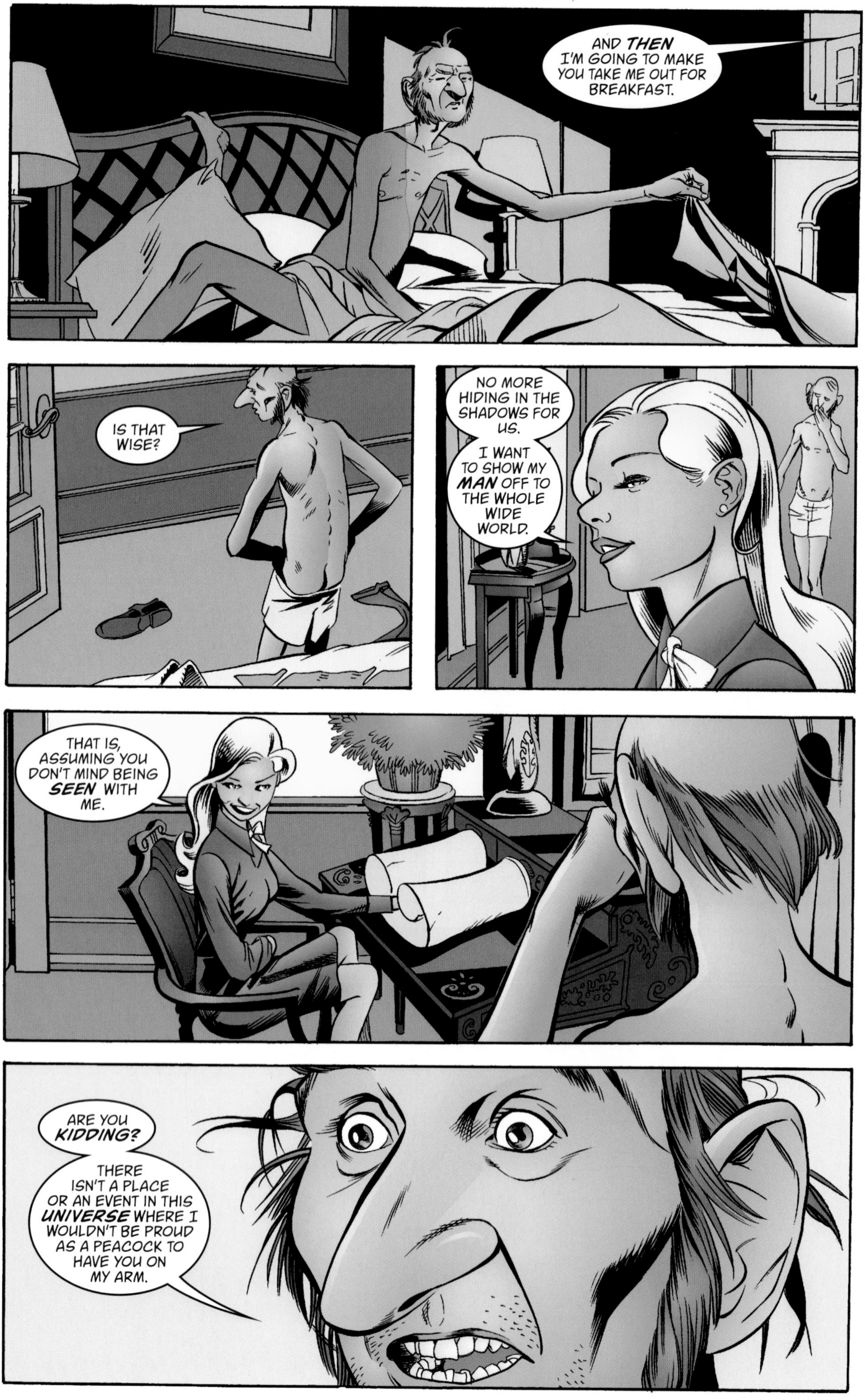

AND THEN I'M GOING TO MAKE YOU TAKE ME OUT FOR BREAKFAST.
IS THAT WISE?
NO MORE HIDING IN THE SHADOWS FOR US.
I WANT TO SHOW MY MAN OFF TO THE WHOLE WIDE WORLD.
THAT IS, ASSUMING YOU DON'T MIND BEING SEEN WITH ME.
ARE YOU KIDDING?
THERE ISN'T A PLACE OR AN EVENT IN THIS UNIVERSE WHERE I WOULDN'T BE PROUD AS A PEACOCK TO HAVE YOU ON MY ARM.

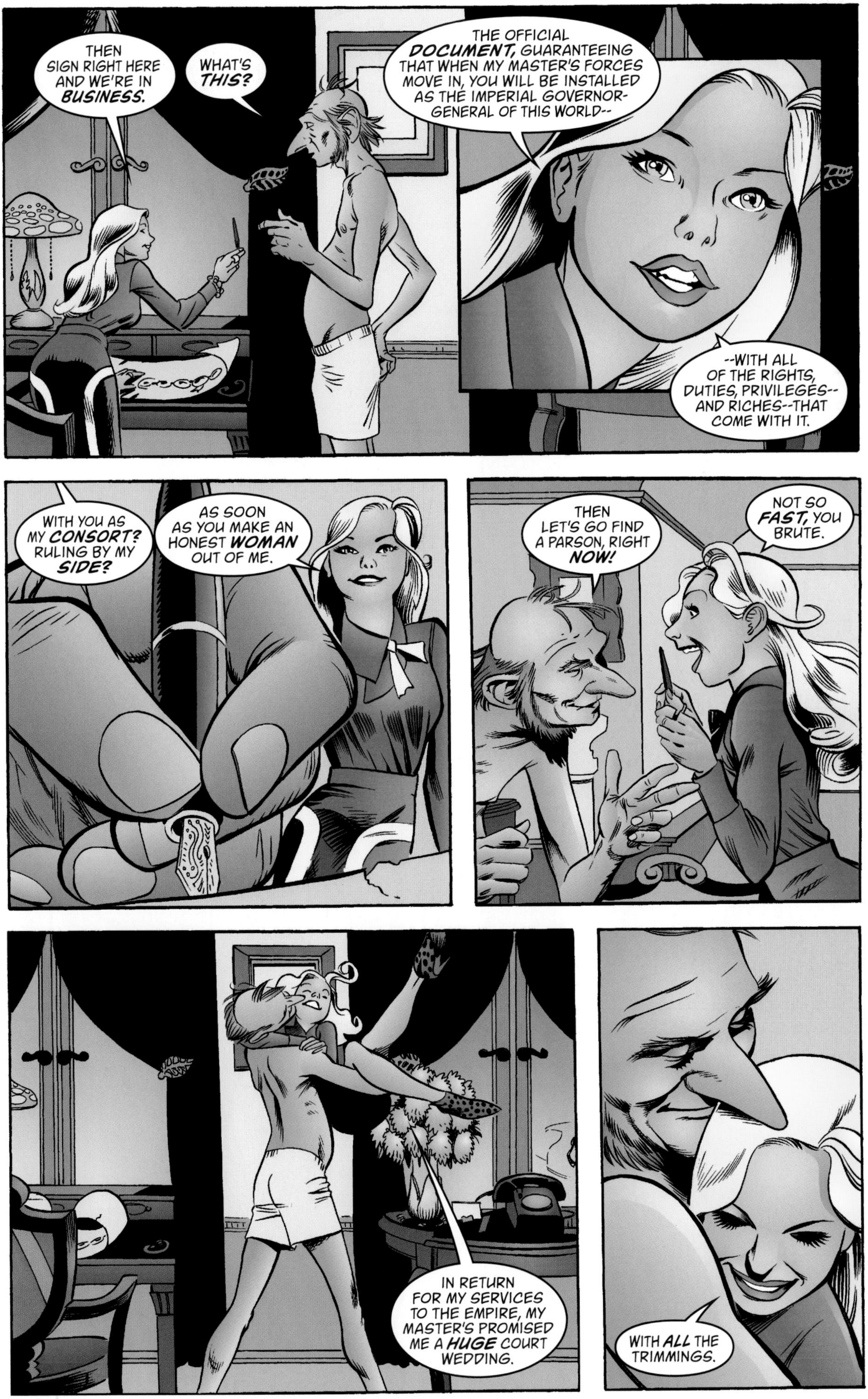
THEN SIGN RIGHT HERE AND WE'RE IN BUSINESS.
WHAT'S THIS?
THE OFFICIAL DOCUMENT, GUARANTEEING THAT WHEN MY MASTER'S FORCES MOVE IN, YOU WILL BE INSTALLED AS THE IMPERIAL GOVERNOR-GENERAL OF THIS WORLD--
--WITH ALL OF THE RIGHTS, DUTIES, PRIVILEGES--AND RICHES--THAT COME WITH IT.
WITH YOU AS MY CONSORT? RULING BY MY SIDE?
AS SOON AS YOU MAKE AN HONEST WOMAN OUT OF ME.
THEN LET'S GO FIND A PARSON, RIGHT NOW!
NOT SO FAST, YOU BRUTE.
IN RETURN FOR MY SERVICES TO THE EMPIRE, MY MASTER'S PROMISED ME A HUGE COURT WEDDING.
WITH ALL THE TRIMMINGS.

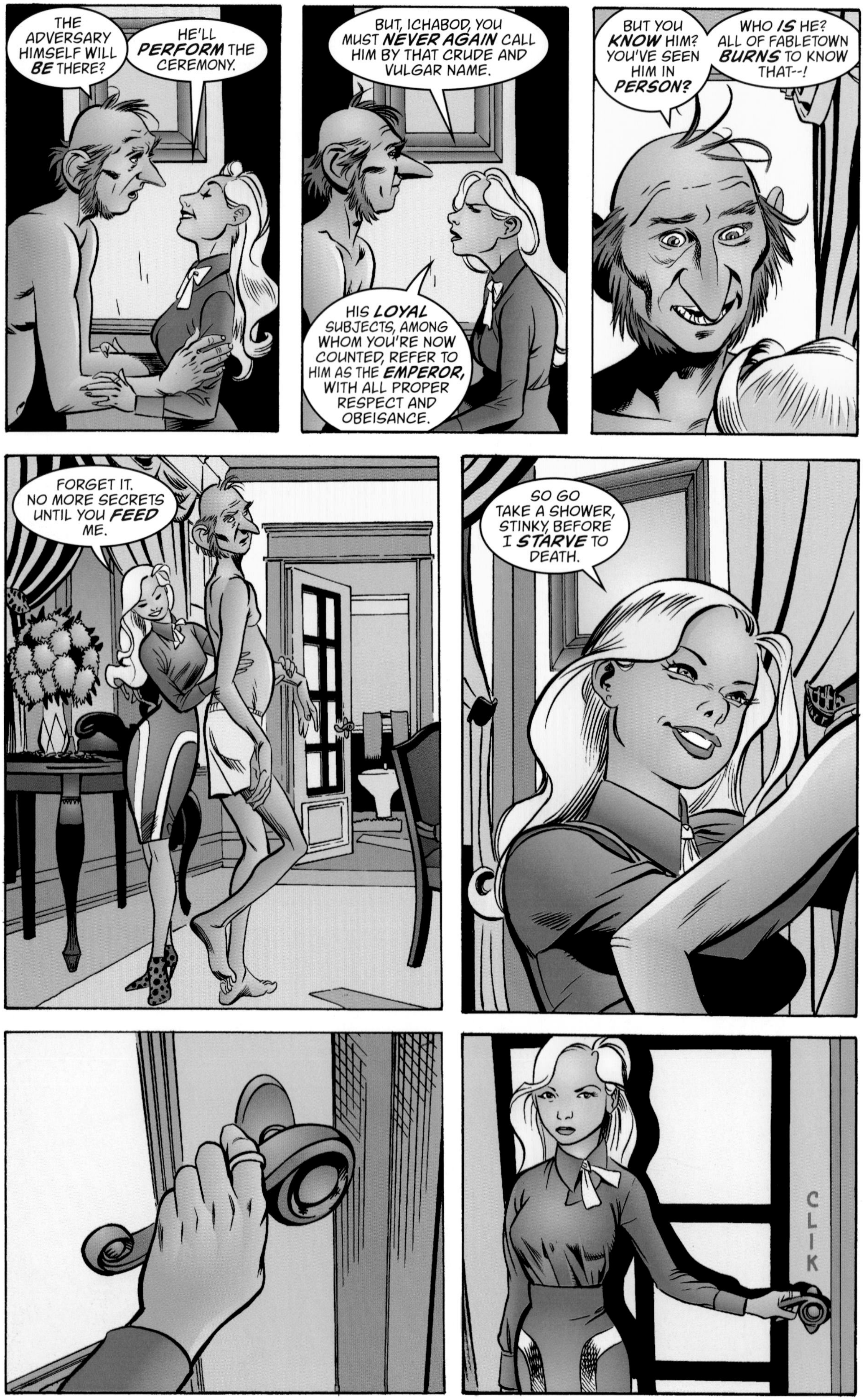
THE ADVERSARY HIMSELF WILL BE THERE?
HE'LL PERFORM THE CEREMONY.
BUT, ICHABOD, YOU MUST NEVER AGAIN CALL HIM BY THAT CRUDE AND VULGAR NAME.
HIS LOYAL SUBJECTS, AMONG WHOM YOU'RE NOW COUNTED, REFER TO HIM AS THE EMPEROR, WITH ALL PROPER RESPECT AND OBEISANCE.
BUT YOU KNOW HIM? YOU'VE SEEN HIM IN PERSON?
WHO IS HE? ALL OF FABLETOWN BURNS TO KNOW THAT--!
FORGET IT. NO MORE SECRETS UNTIL YOU FEED ME.
SO GO TAKE A SHOWER, STINKY, BEFORE I STARVE TO DEATH.
CLIK

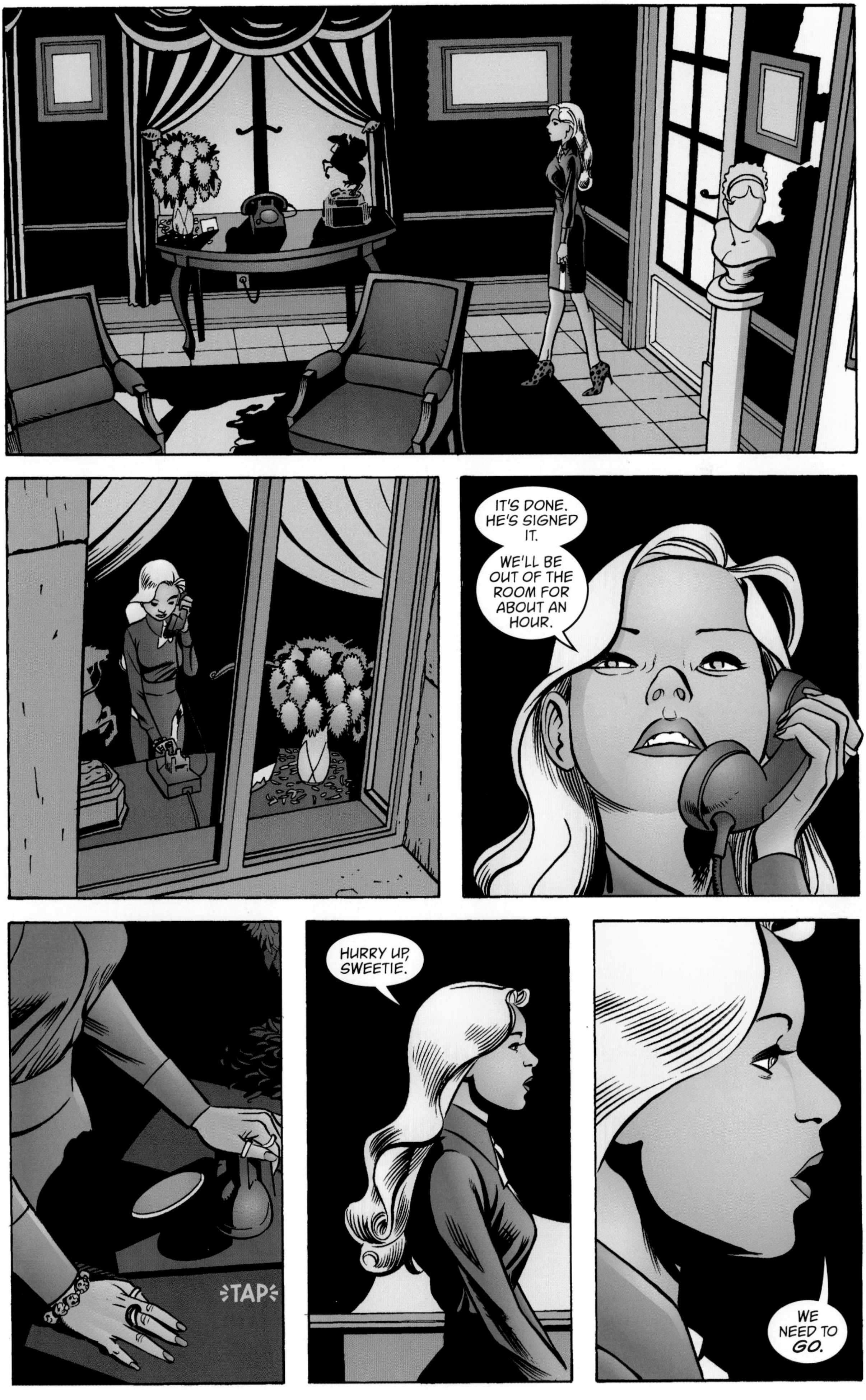

IT'S DONE. HE'S SIGNED IT.
WE'LL BE OUT OF THE ROOM FOR ABOUT AN HOUR.
TAP
HURRY UP, SWEETIE.
WE NEED TO GO.

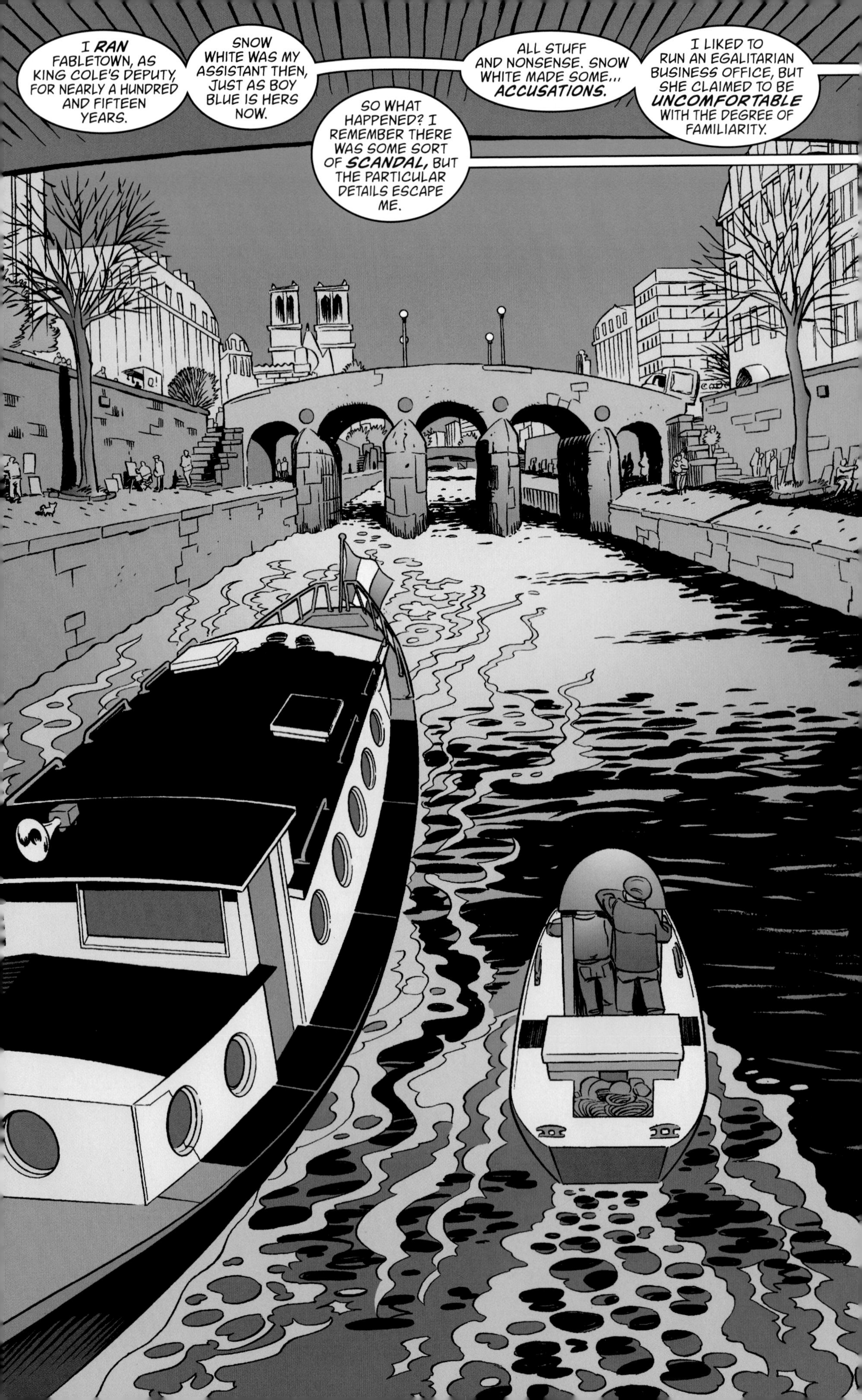

I RAN FABLETOWN, AS KING COLE'S DEPUTY, FOR NEARLY A HUNDRED AND FIFTEEN YEARS.
SNOW WHITE WAS MY ASSISTANT THEN, JUST AS BOY BLUE IS HERS NOW.
SO WHAT HAPPENED? I REMEMBER THERE WAS SOME SORT OF SCANDAL, BUT THE PARTICULAR DETAILS ESCAPE ME.
ALL STUFF AND NONSENSE. SNOW WHITE MADE SOME... ACCUSATIONS.
I LIKED TO RUN AN EGALITARIAN BUSINESS OFFICE, BUT SHE CLAIMED TO BE UNCOMFORTABLE WITH THE DEGREE OF FAMILIARITY.

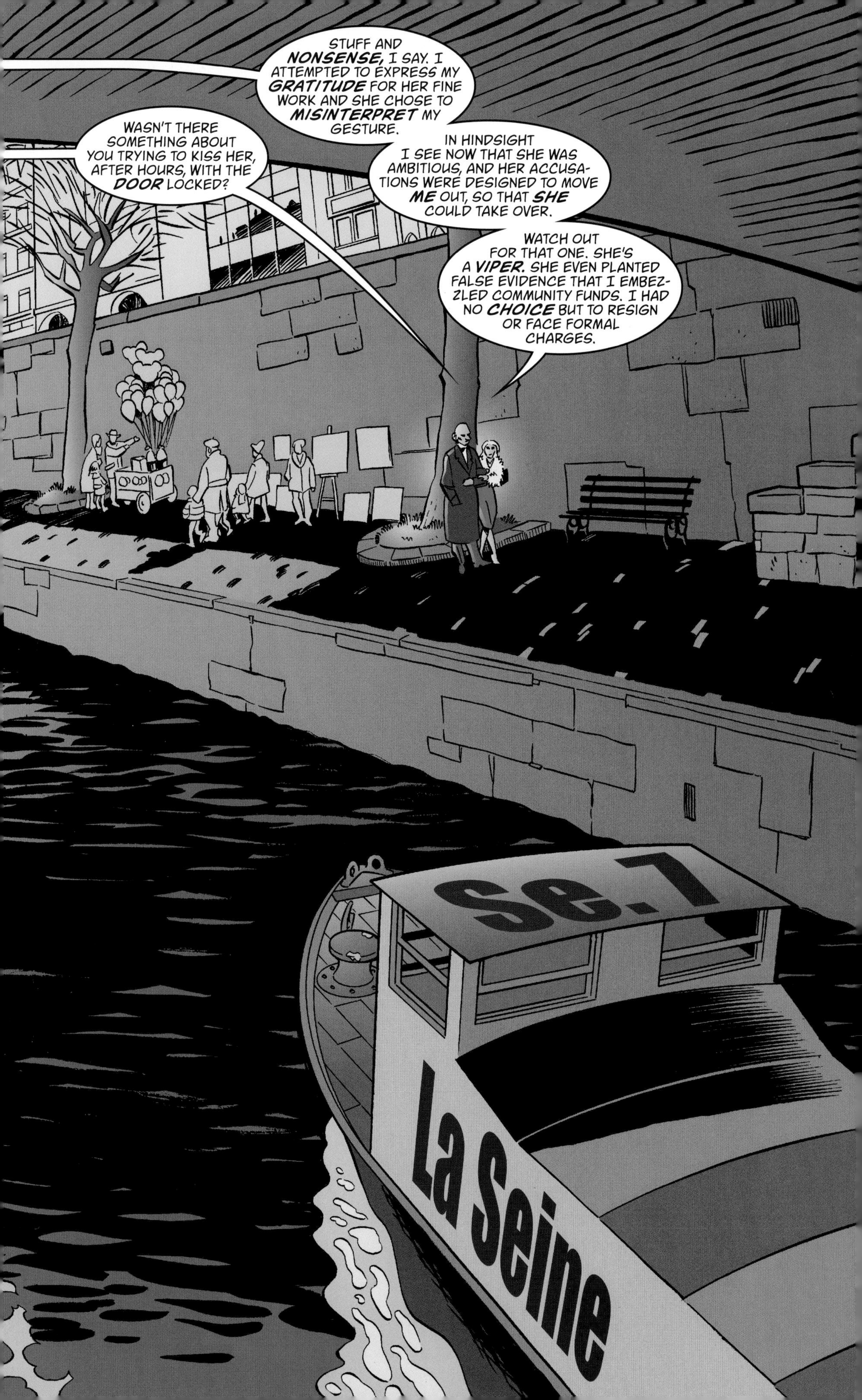
STUFF AND **NONSENSE,** I SAY. I ATTEMPTED TO EXPRESS MY **GRATITUDE** FOR HER FINE WORK AND SHE CHOSE TO **MISINTERPRET** MY GESTURE.
WASN'T THERE SOMETHING ABOUT YOU TRYING TO KISS HER, AFTER HOURS, WITH THE **DOOR** LOCKED?
IN HINDSIGHT I SEE NOW THAT SHE WAS AMBITIOUS, AND HER ACCUSATIONS WERE DESIGNED TO MOVE **ME** OUT, SO THAT **SHE** COULD TAKE OVER.
WATCH OUT FOR THAT ONE. SHE'S A **VIPER.** SHE EVEN PLANTED FALSE EVIDENCE THAT I EMBEZZLED COMMUNITY FUNDS. I HAD NO **CHOICE** BUT TO RESIGN OR FACE FORMAL CHARGES.
Se.7
La Seine

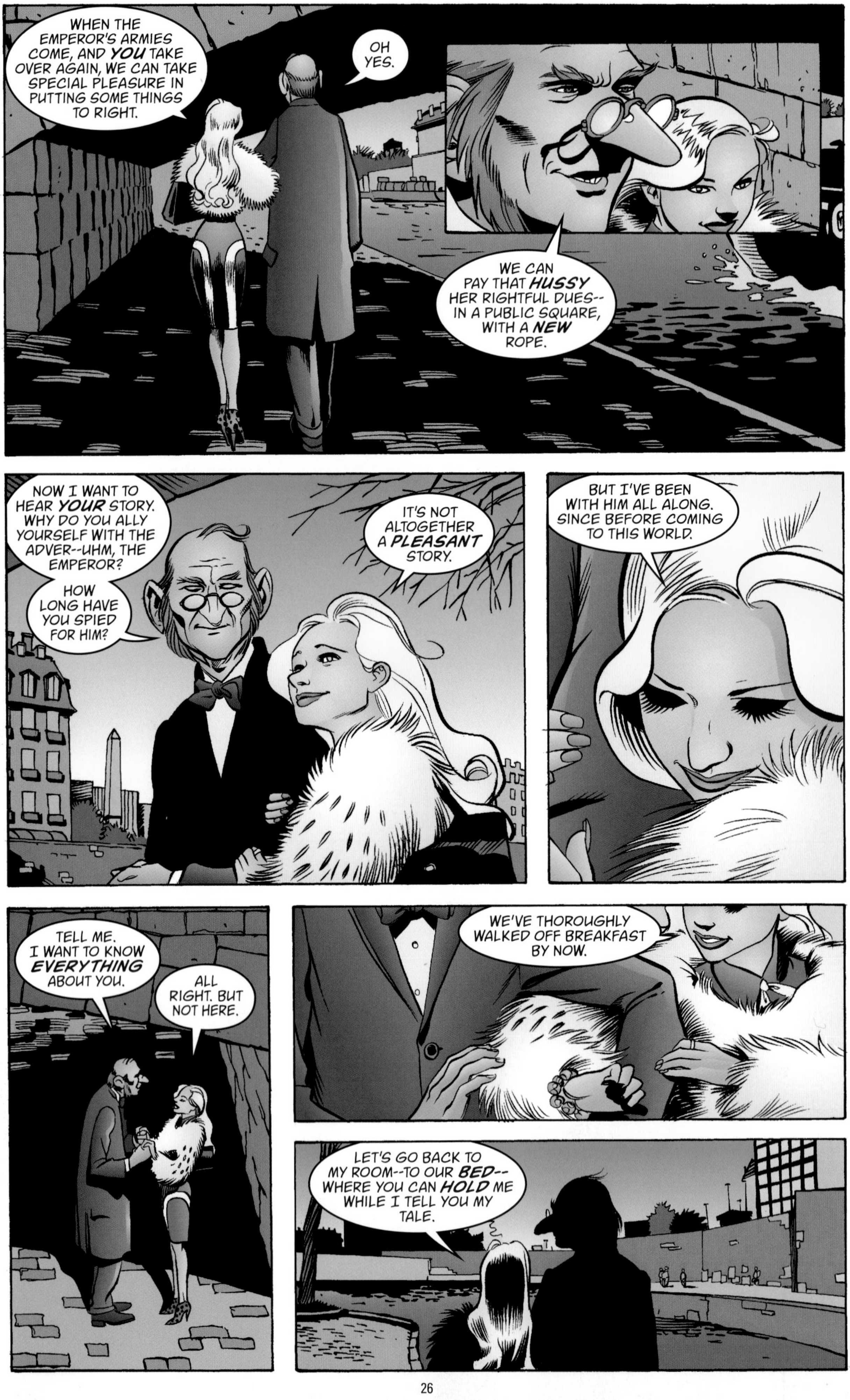
WHEN THE EMPEROR'S ARMIES COME, AND YOU TAKE OVER AGAIN, WE CAN TAKE SPECIAL PLEASURE IN PUTTING SOME THINGS TO RIGHT.
OH YES.
WE CAN PAY THAT HUSSY HER RIGHTFUL DUES-- IN A PUBLIC SQUARE, WITH A NEW ROPE.
NOW I WANT TO HEAR YOUR STORY. WHY DO YOU ALLY YOURSELF WITH THE ADVER--UHM, THE EMPEROR?
HOW LONG HAVE YOU SPIED FOR HIM?
IT'S NOT ALTOGETHER A PLEASANT STORY.
BUT I'VE BEEN WITH HIM ALL ALONG. SINCE BEFORE COMING TO THIS WORLD.
TELL ME. I WANT TO KNOW EVERYTHING ABOUT YOU.
ALL RIGHT. BUT NOT HERE.
WE'VE THOROUGHLY WALKED OFF BREAKFAST BY NOW.
LET'S GO BACK TO MY ROOM--TO OUR BED-- WHERE YOU CAN HOLD ME WHILE I TELL YOU MY TALE.

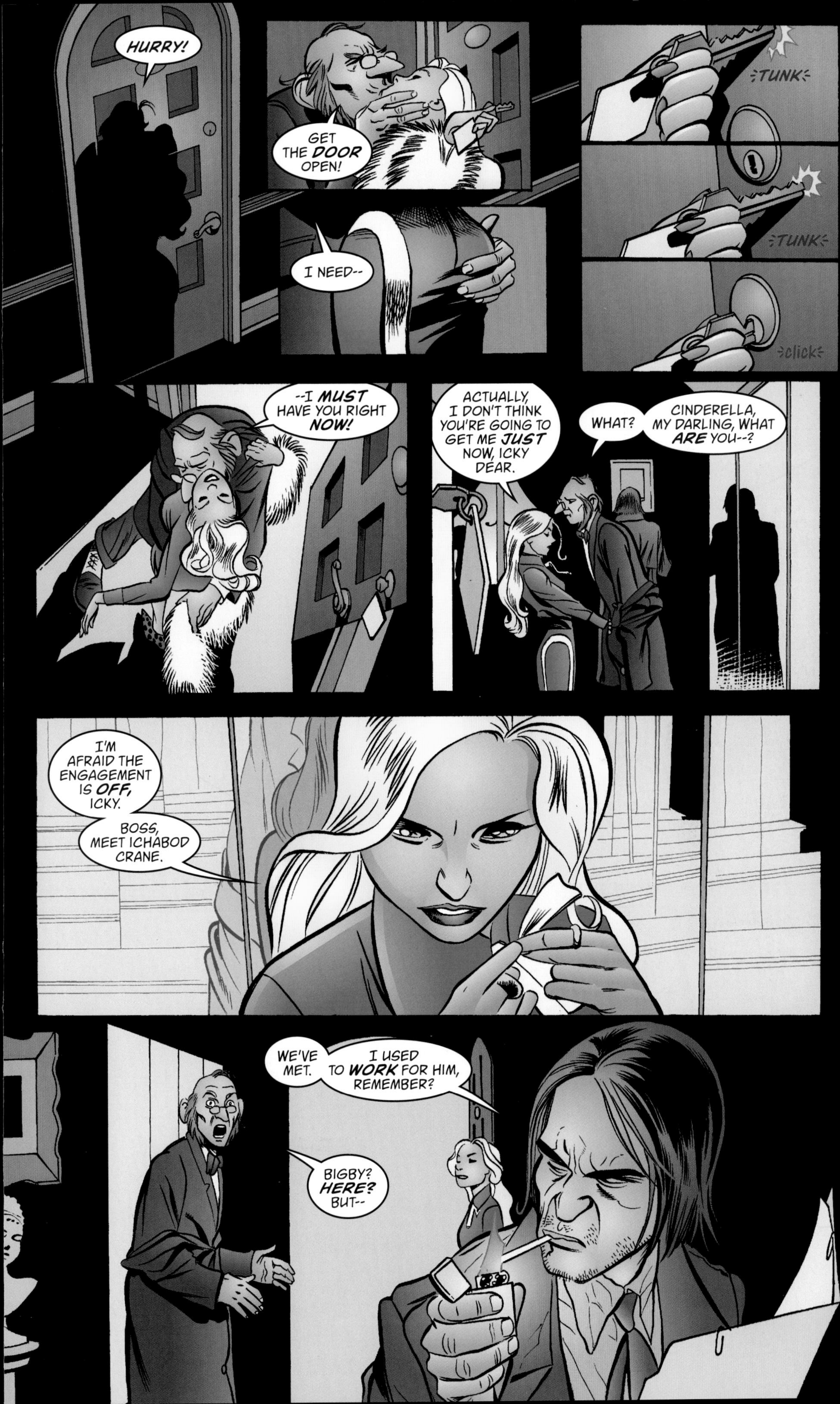
HURRY!
GET THE DOOR OPEN!
I NEED--
TUNK
TUNK
click
--I MUST HAVE YOU RIGHT NOW!
ACTUALLY, I DON'T THINK YOU'RE GOING TO GET ME JUST NOW, ICKY DEAR.
WHAT?
CINDERELLA, MY DARLING, WHAT ARE YOU--?
I'M AFRAID THE ENGAGEMENT IS OFF, ICKY.
BOSS, MEET ICHABOD CRANE.
WE'VE MET.
I USED TO WORK FOR HIM, REMEMBER?
BIGBY? HERE? BUT--

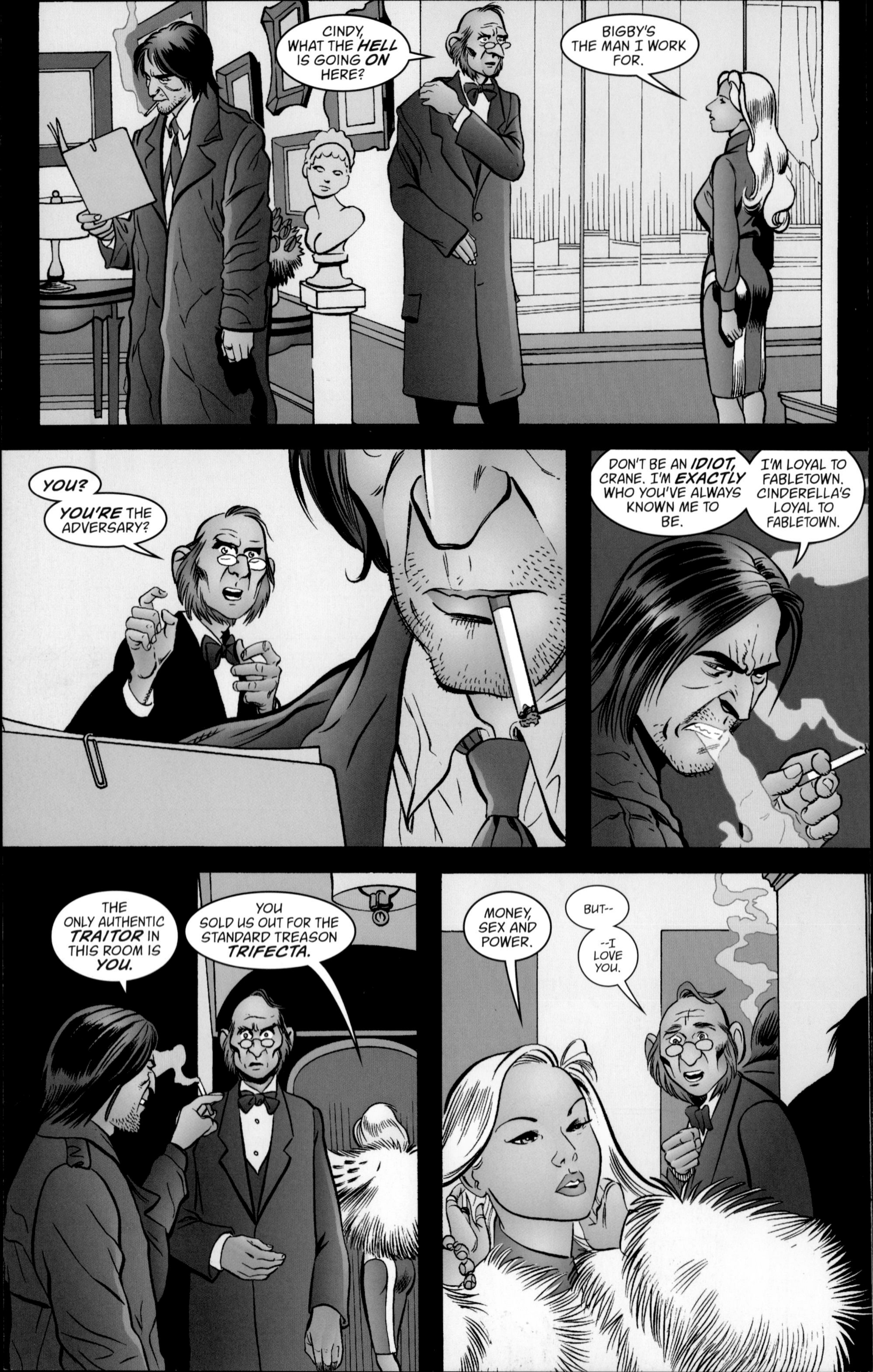
CINDY, WHAT THE HELL IS GOING ON HERE?
BIGBY'S THE MAN I WORK FOR.
YOU? YOU'RE THE ADVERSARY?
DON'T BE AN IDIOT, CRANE. I'M EXACTLY WHO YOU'VE ALWAYS KNOWN ME TO BE.
I'M LOYAL TO FABLETOWN. CINDERELLA'S LOYAL TO FABLETOWN.
THE ONLY AUTHENTIC TRAITOR IN THIS ROOM IS YOU.
YOU SOLD US OUT FOR THE STANDARD TREASON TRIFECTA.
MONEY, SEX AND POWER.
BUT--
--I LOVE YOU.

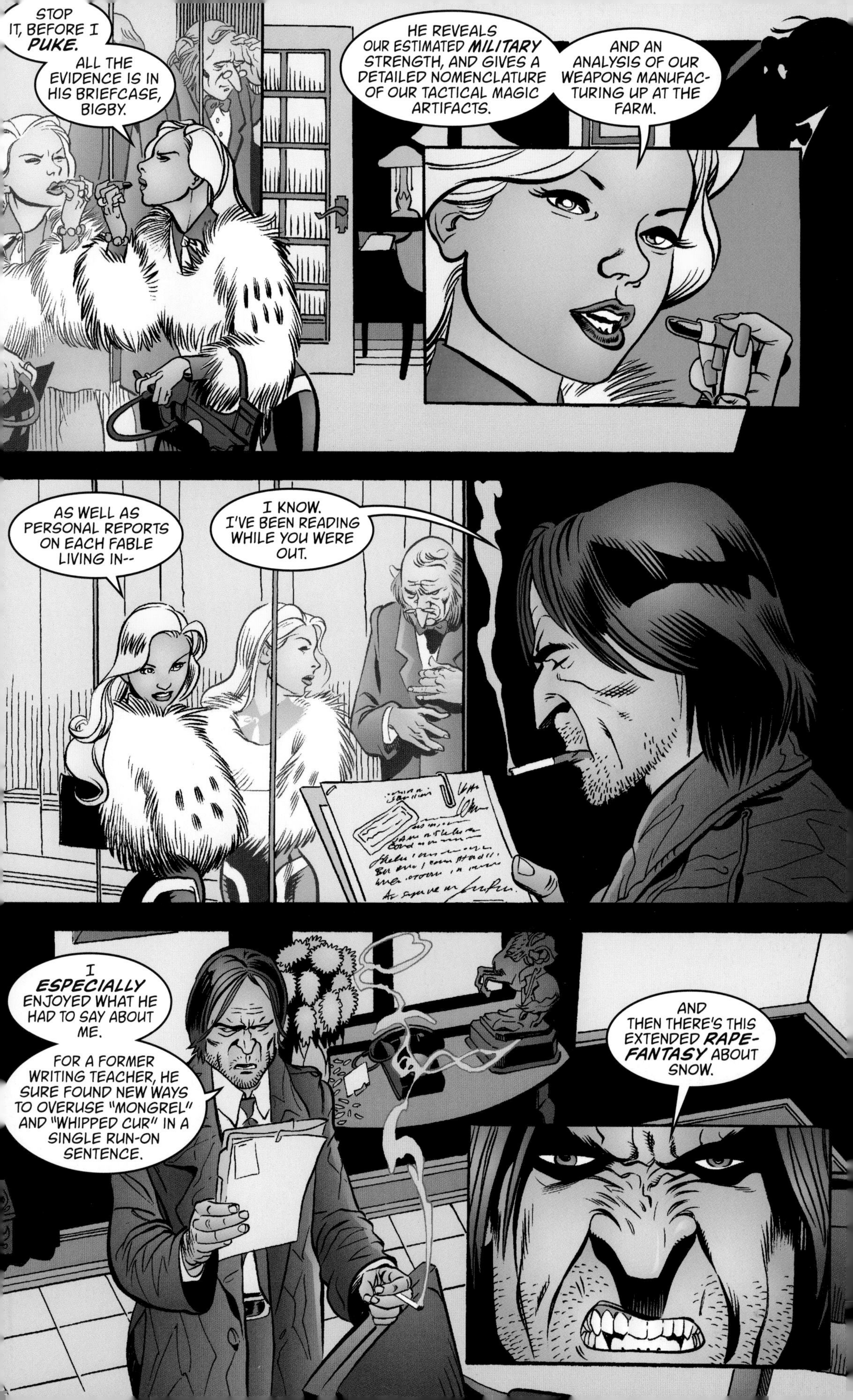

STOP IT, BEFORE I PUKE.
ALL THE EVIDENCE IS IN HIS BRIEFCASE, BIGBY.
HE REVEALS OUR ESTIMATED MILITARY STRENGTH, AND GIVES A DETAILED NOMENCLATURE OF OUR TACTICAL MAGIC ARTIFACTS.
AND AN ANALYSIS OF OUR WEAPONS MANUFACTURING UP AT THE FARM.
AS WELL AS PERSONAL REPORTS ON EACH FABLE LIVING IN--
I KNOW. I'VE BEEN READING WHILE YOU WERE OUT.
I ESPECIALLY ENJOYED WHAT HE HAD TO SAY ABOUT ME.
FOR A FORMER WRITING TEACHER, HE SURE FOUND NEW WAYS TO OVERUSE "MONGREL" AND "WHIPPED CUR" IN A SINGLE RUN-ON SENTENCE.
AND THEN THERE'S THIS EXTENDED RAPE-FANTASY ABOUT SNOW.

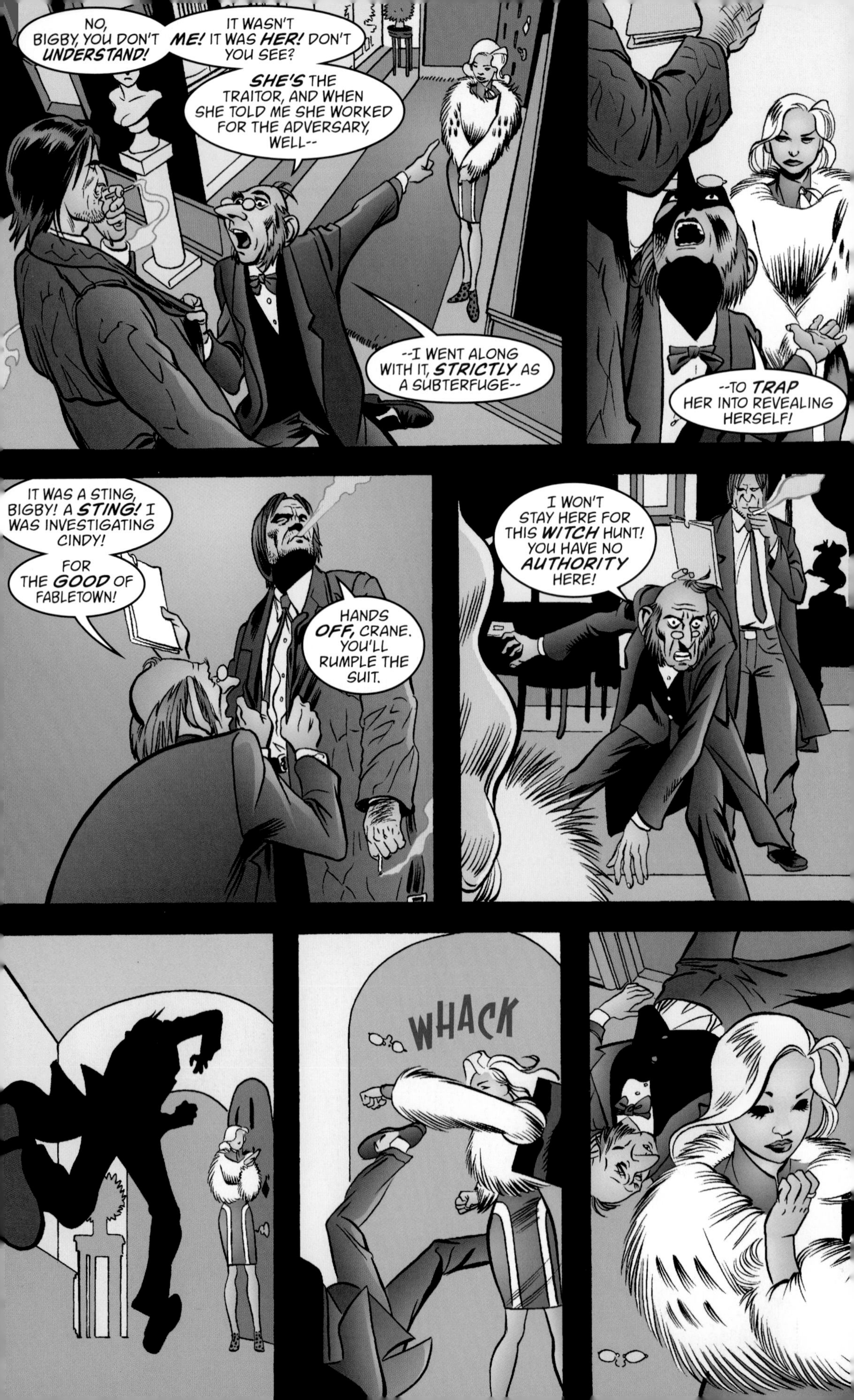
NO, BIGBY, YOU DON'T UNDERSTAND!
IT WASN'T ME! IT WAS HER! DON'T YOU SEE?
SHE'S THE TRAITOR, AND WHEN SHE TOLD ME SHE WORKED FOR THE ADVERSARY, WELL--
--I WENT ALONG WITH IT, STRICTLY AS A SUBTERFUGE--
--TO TRAP HER INTO REVEALING HERSELF!
IT WAS A STING, BIGBY! A STING! I WAS INVESTIGATING CINDY!
FOR THE GOOD OF FABLETOWN!
HANDS OFF, CRANE. YOU'LL RUMPLE THE SUIT.
I WON'T STAY HERE FOR THIS WITCH HUNT! YOU HAVE NO AUTHORITY HERE!
WHACK

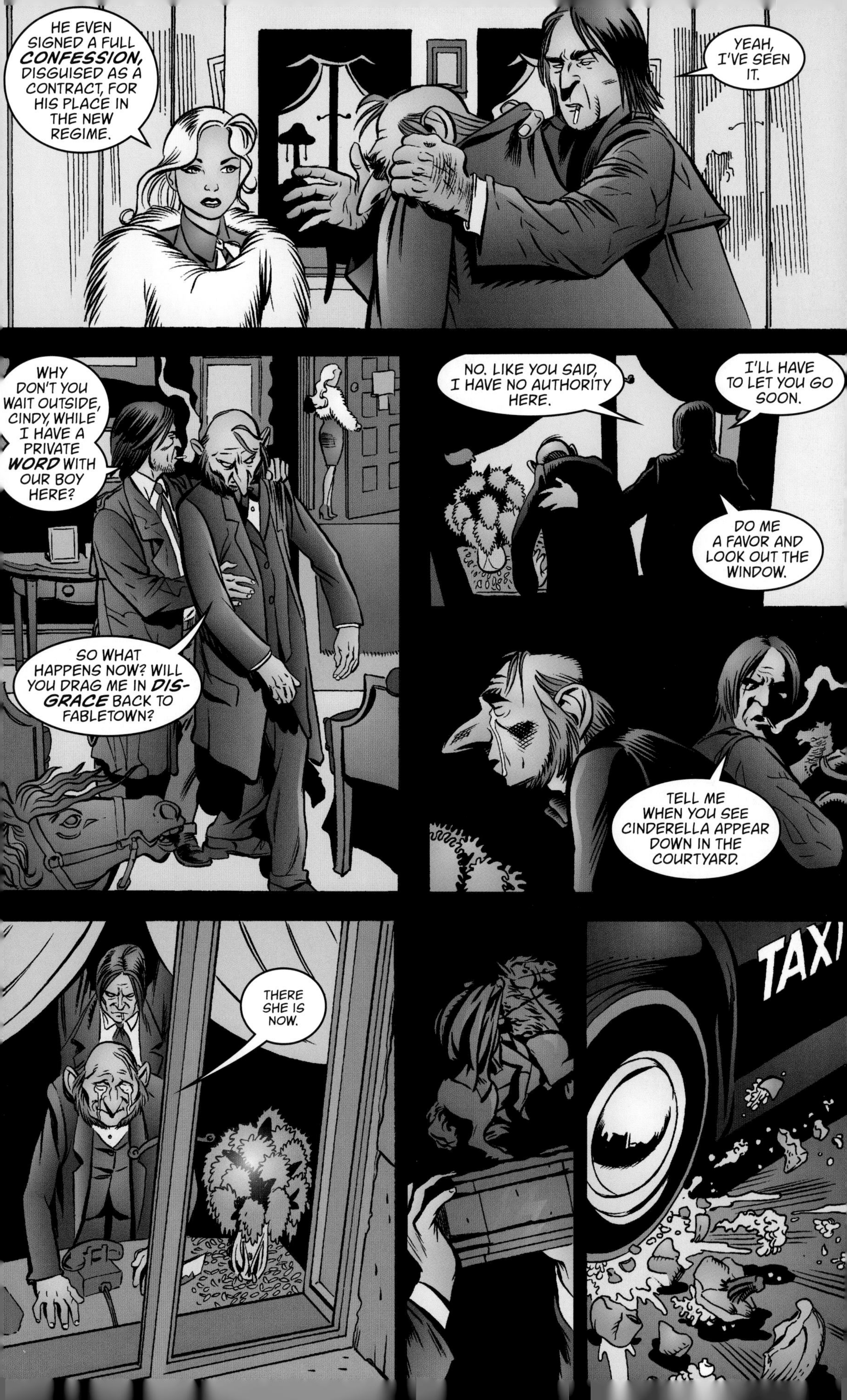
HE EVEN SIGNED A FULL CONFESSION, DISGUISED AS A CONTRACT, FOR HIS PLACE IN THE NEW REGIME.
YEAH, I'VE SEEN IT.
WHY DON'T YOU WAIT OUTSIDE, CINDY, WHILE I HAVE A PRIVATE WORD WITH OUR BOY HERE?
SO WHAT HAPPENS NOW? WILL YOU DRAG ME IN DIS-GRACE BACK TO FABLETOWN?
NO. LIKE YOU SAID, I HAVE NO AUTHORITY HERE.
I'LL HAVE TO LET YOU GO SOON.
DO ME A FAVOR AND LOOK OUT THE WINDOW.
TELL ME WHEN YOU SEE CINDERELLA APPEAR DOWN IN THE COURTYARD.
THERE SHE IS NOW.
TAXI

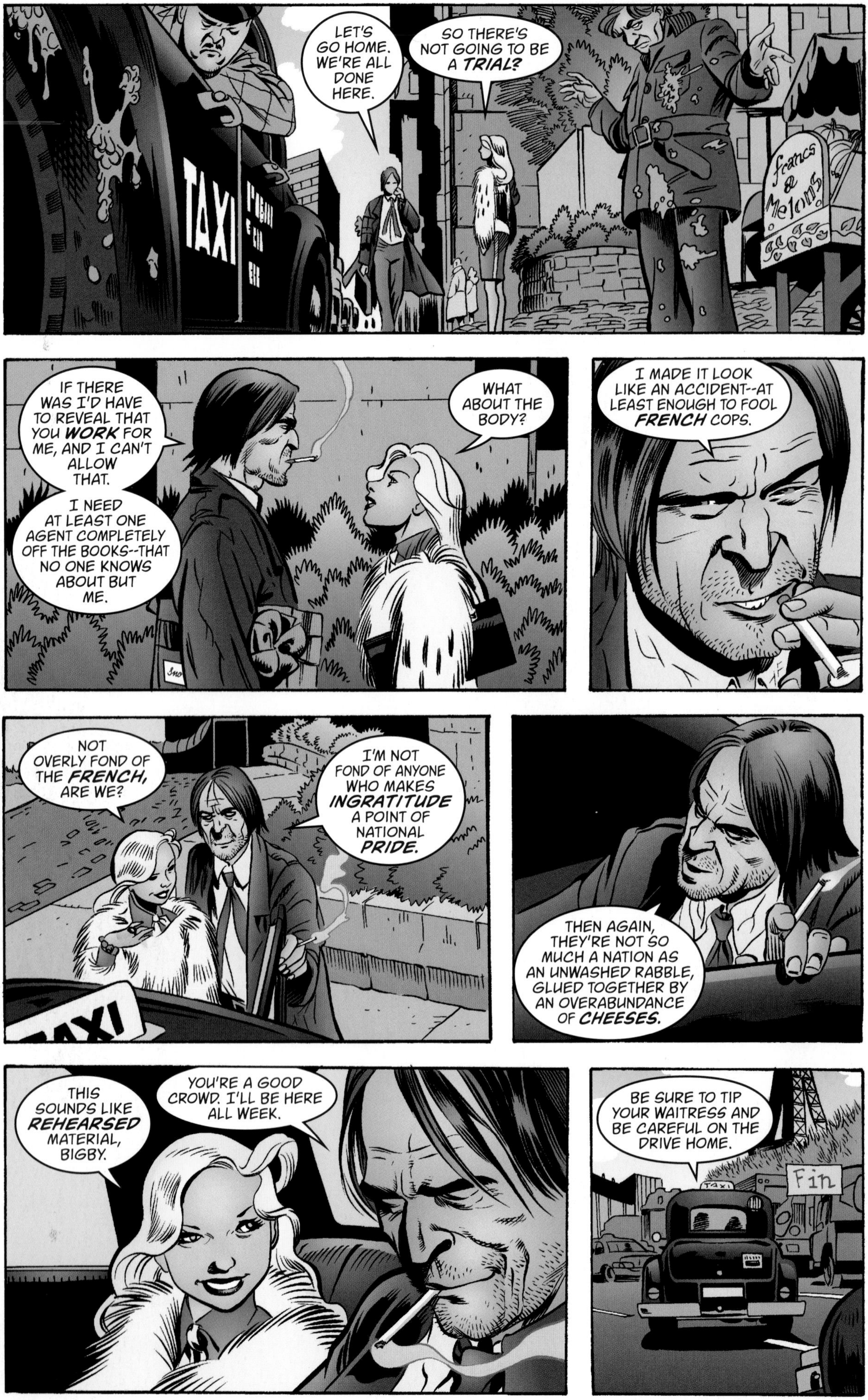
TAXI
LET'S GO HOME. WE'RE ALL DONE HERE.
SO THERE'S NOT GOING TO BE A TRIAL?
IF THERE WAS I'D HAVE TO REVEAL THAT YOU WORK FOR ME, AND I CAN'T ALLOW THAT.
I NEED AT LEAST ONE AGENT COMPLETELY OFF THE BOOKS--THAT NO ONE KNOWS ABOUT BUT ME.
WHAT ABOUT THE BODY?
I MADE IT LOOK LIKE AN ACCIDENT--AT LEAST ENOUGH TO FOOL FRENCH COPS.
NOT OVERLY FOND OF THE FRENCH, ARE WE?
I'M NOT FOND OF ANYONE WHO MAKES INGRATITUDE A POINT OF NATIONAL PRIDE.
TAXI
THEN AGAIN, THEY'RE NOT SO MUCH A NATION AS AN UNWASHED RABBLE, GLUED TOGETHER BY AN OVERABUNDANCE OF CHEESES.
THIS SOUNDS LIKE REHEARSED MATERIAL, BIGBY.
YOU'RE A GOOD CROWD. I'LL BE HERE ALL WEEK.
BE SURE TO TIP YOUR WAITRESS AND BE CAREFUL ON THE DRIVE HOME.
Fin

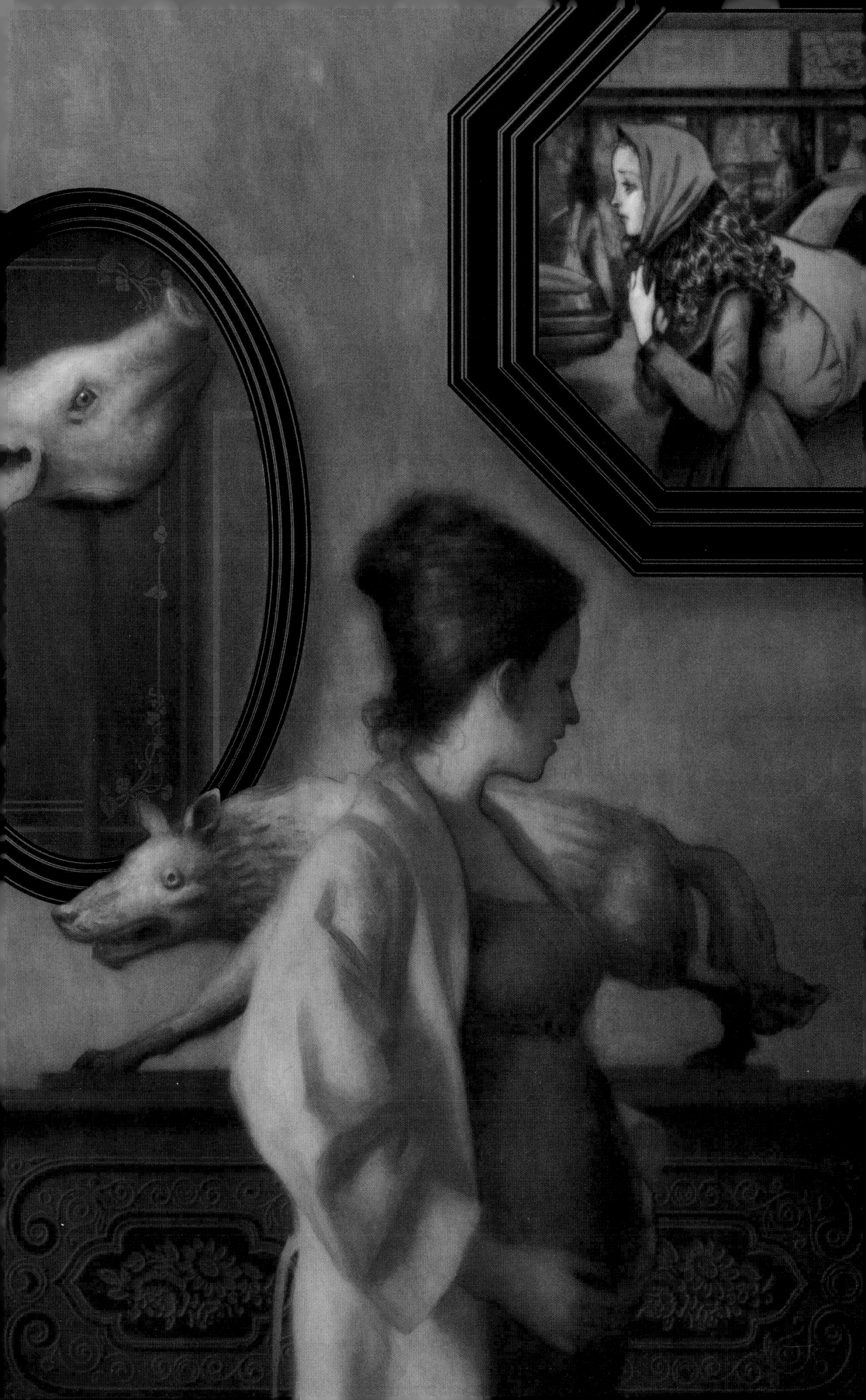

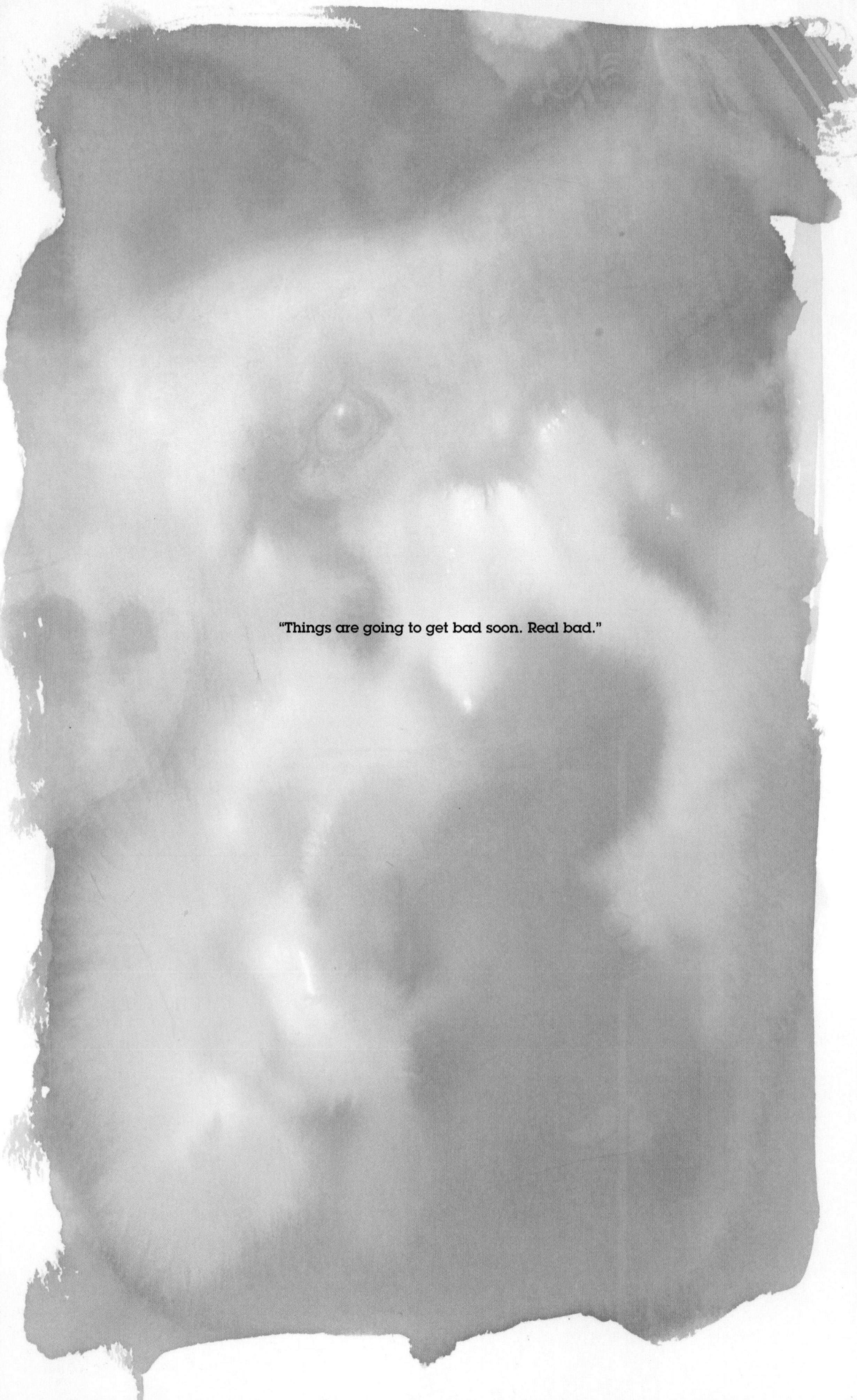

"Things are going to get bad soon. Real bad."

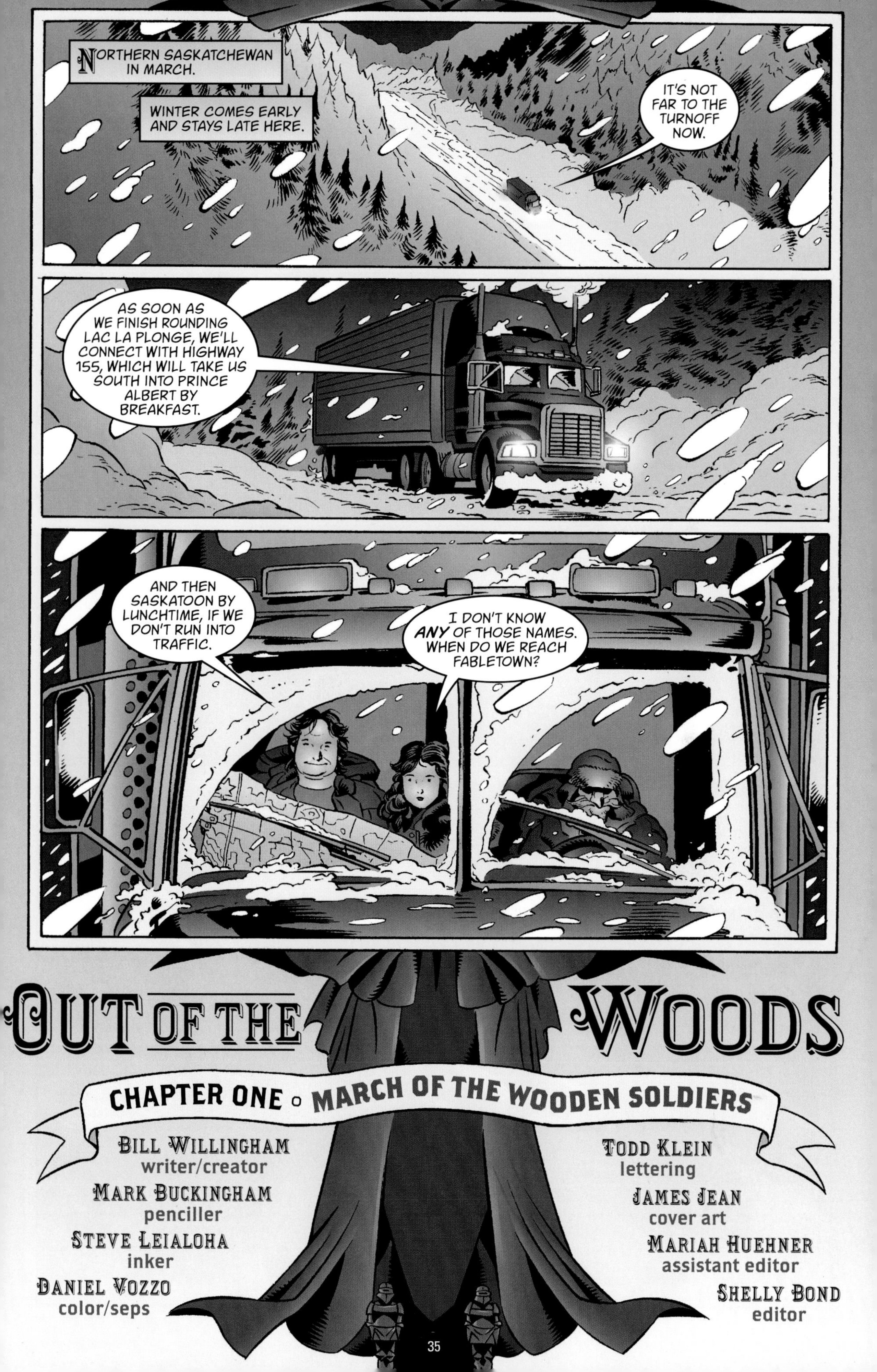
NORTHERN SASKATCHEWAN IN MARCH.
WINTER COMES EARLY AND STAYS LATE HERE.
IT'S NOT FAR TO THE TURNOFF NOW.
AS SOON AS WE FINISH ROUNDING LAC LA PLONGE, WE'LL CONNECT WITH HIGHWAY 155, WHICH WILL TAKE US SOUTH INTO PRINCE ALBERT BY BREAKFAST.
AND THEN SASKATOON BY LUNCHTIME, IF WE DON'T RUN INTO TRAFFIC.
I DON'T KNOW *ANY* OF THOSE NAMES. WHEN DO WE REACH FABLETOWN?

OUT OF THE WOODS

CHAPTER ONE • MARCH OF THE WOODEN SOLDIERS

BILL WILLINGHAM writer/creator
MARK BUCKINGHAM penciller
STEVE LEIALOHA inker
DANIEL VOZZO color/seps
TODD KLEIN lettering
JAMES JEAN cover art
MARIAH HUEHNER assistant editor
SHELLY BOND editor

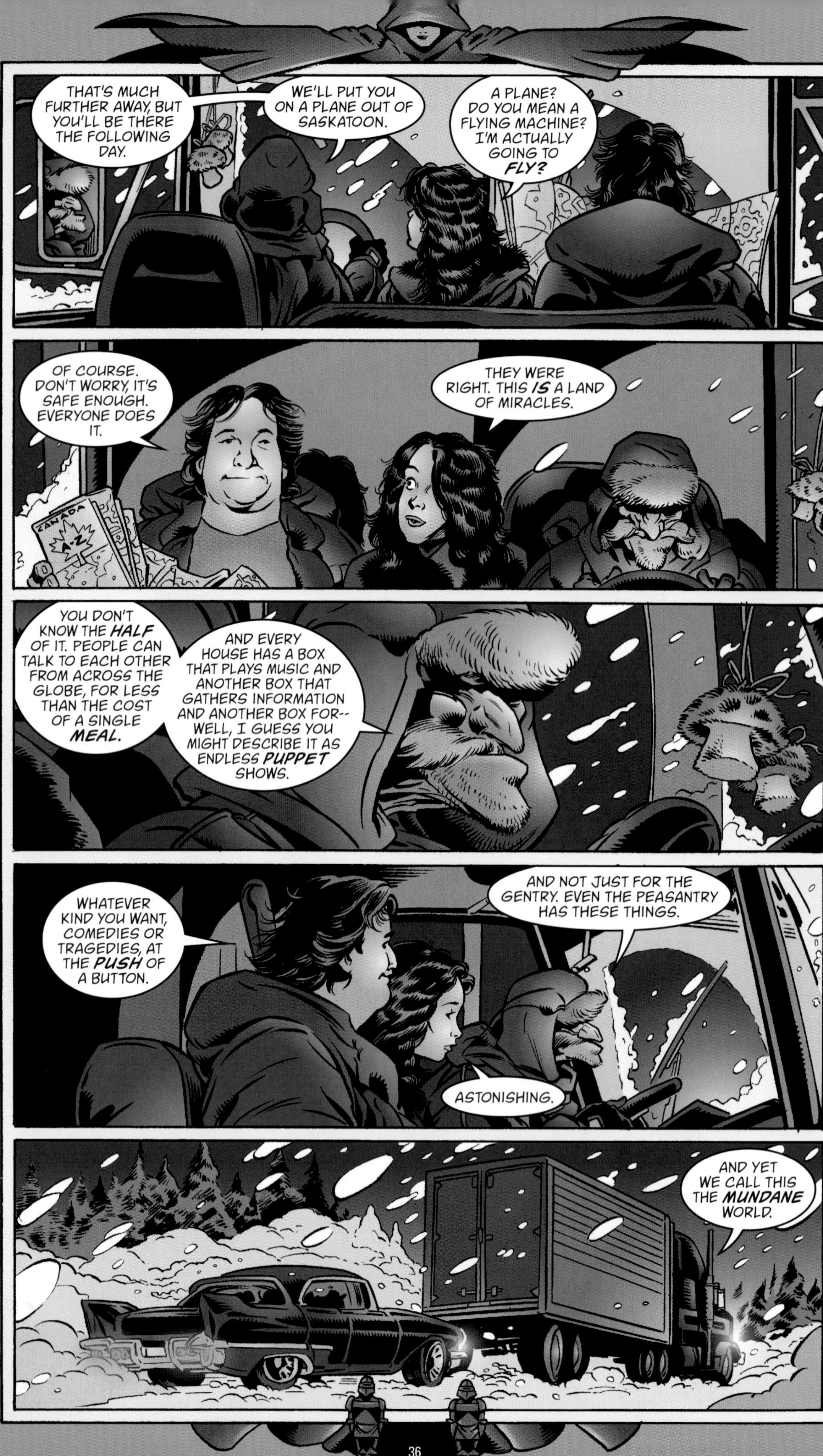
THAT'S MUCH FURTHER AWAY, BUT YOU'LL BE THERE THE FOLLOWING DAY.
WE'LL PUT YOU ON A PLANE OUT OF SASKATOON.
A PLANE? DO YOU MEAN A FLYING MACHINE? I'M ACTUALLY GOING TO FLY?
OF COURSE. DON'T WORRY, IT'S SAFE ENOUGH. EVERYONE DOES IT.
THEY WERE RIGHT. THIS IS A LAND OF MIRACLES.
CANADA A-Z
YOU DON'T KNOW THE HALF OF IT. PEOPLE CAN TALK TO EACH OTHER FROM ACROSS THE GLOBE, FOR LESS THAN THE COST OF A SINGLE MEAL.
AND EVERY HOUSE HAS A BOX THAT PLAYS MUSIC AND ANOTHER BOX THAT GATHERS INFORMATION AND ANOTHER BOX FOR-- WELL, I GUESS YOU MIGHT DESCRIBE IT AS ENDLESS PUPPET SHOWS.
WHATEVER KIND YOU WANT, COMEDIES OR TRAGEDIES, AT THE PUSH OF A BUTTON.
AND NOT JUST FOR THE GENTRY. EVEN THE PEASANTRY HAS THESE THINGS.
ASTONISHING.
AND YET WE CALL THIS THE MUNDANE WORLD.

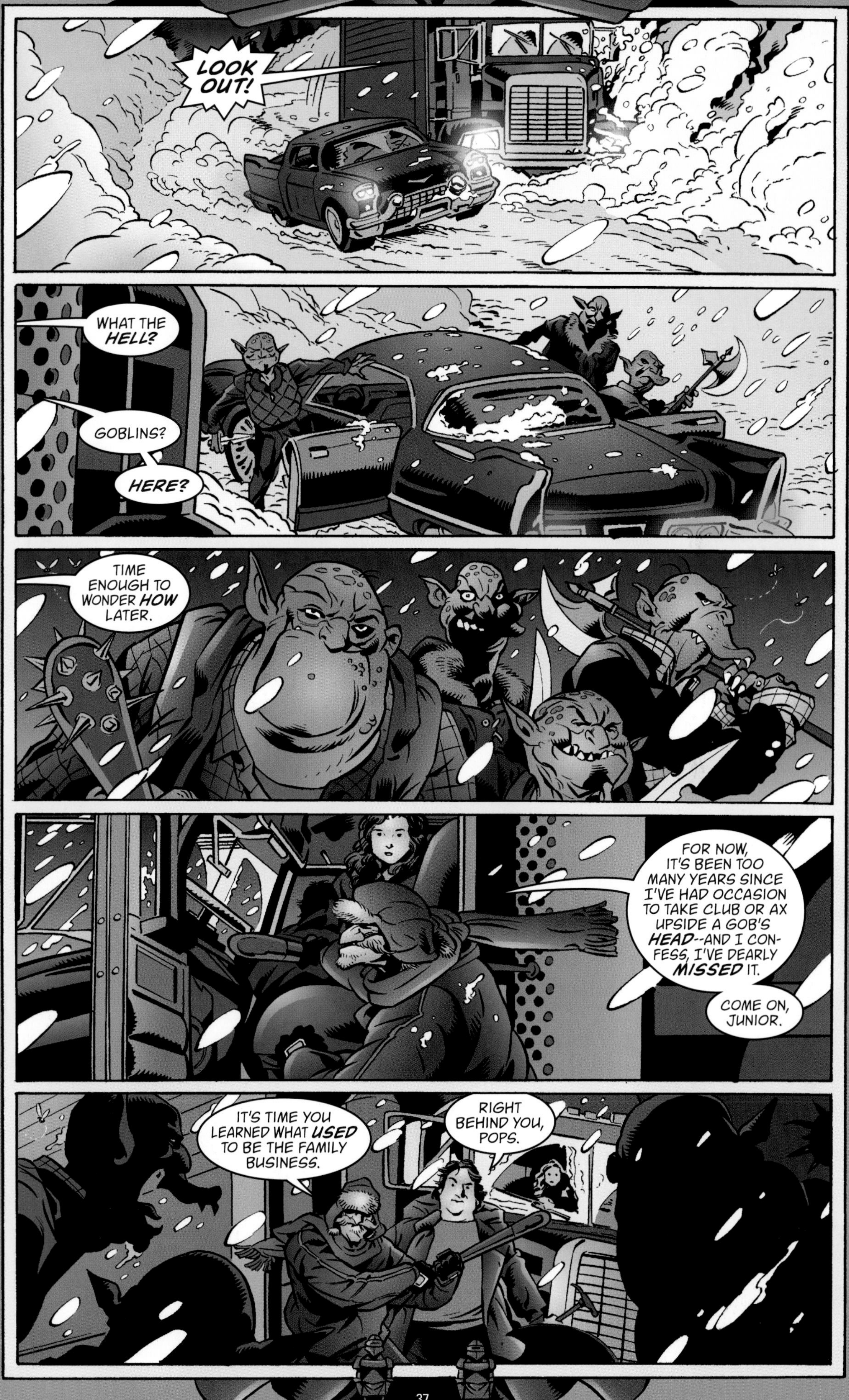
LOOK OUT!
WHAT THE HELL?
GOBLINS?
HERE?
TIME ENOUGH TO WONDER HOW LATER.
FOR NOW, IT'S BEEN TOO MANY YEARS SINCE I'VE HAD OCCASION TO TAKE CLUB OR AX UPSIDE A GOB'S HEAD--AND I CONFESS, I'VE DEARLY MISSED IT.
COME ON, JUNIOR.
IT'S TIME YOU LEARNED WHAT USED TO BE THE FAMILY BUSINESS.
RIGHT BEHIND YOU, POPS.

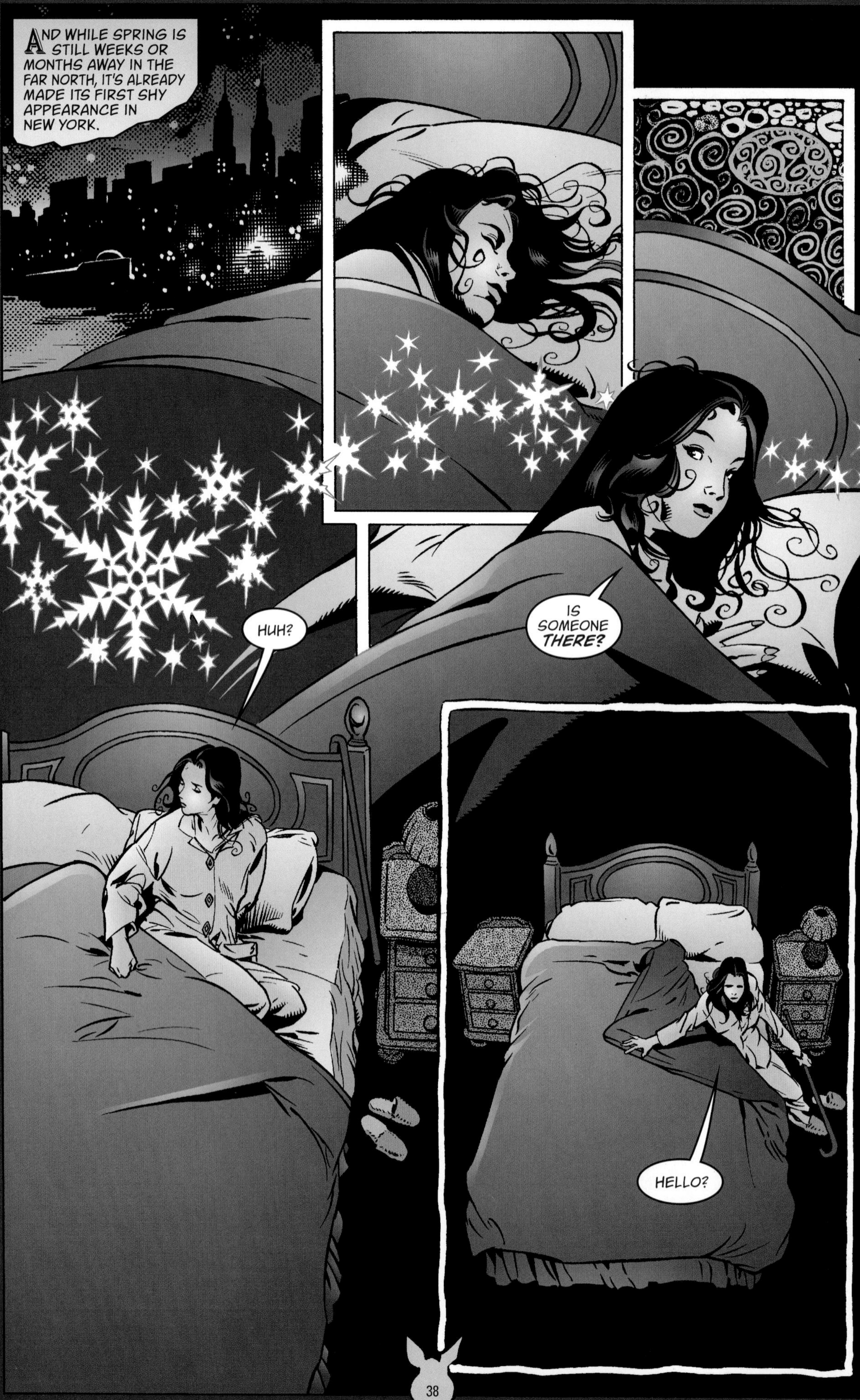
AND WHILE SPRING IS STILL WEEKS OR MONTHS AWAY IN THE FAR NORTH, IT'S ALREADY MADE ITS FIRST SHY APPEARANCE IN NEW YORK.
HUH?
IS SOMEONE *THERE?*
HELLO?

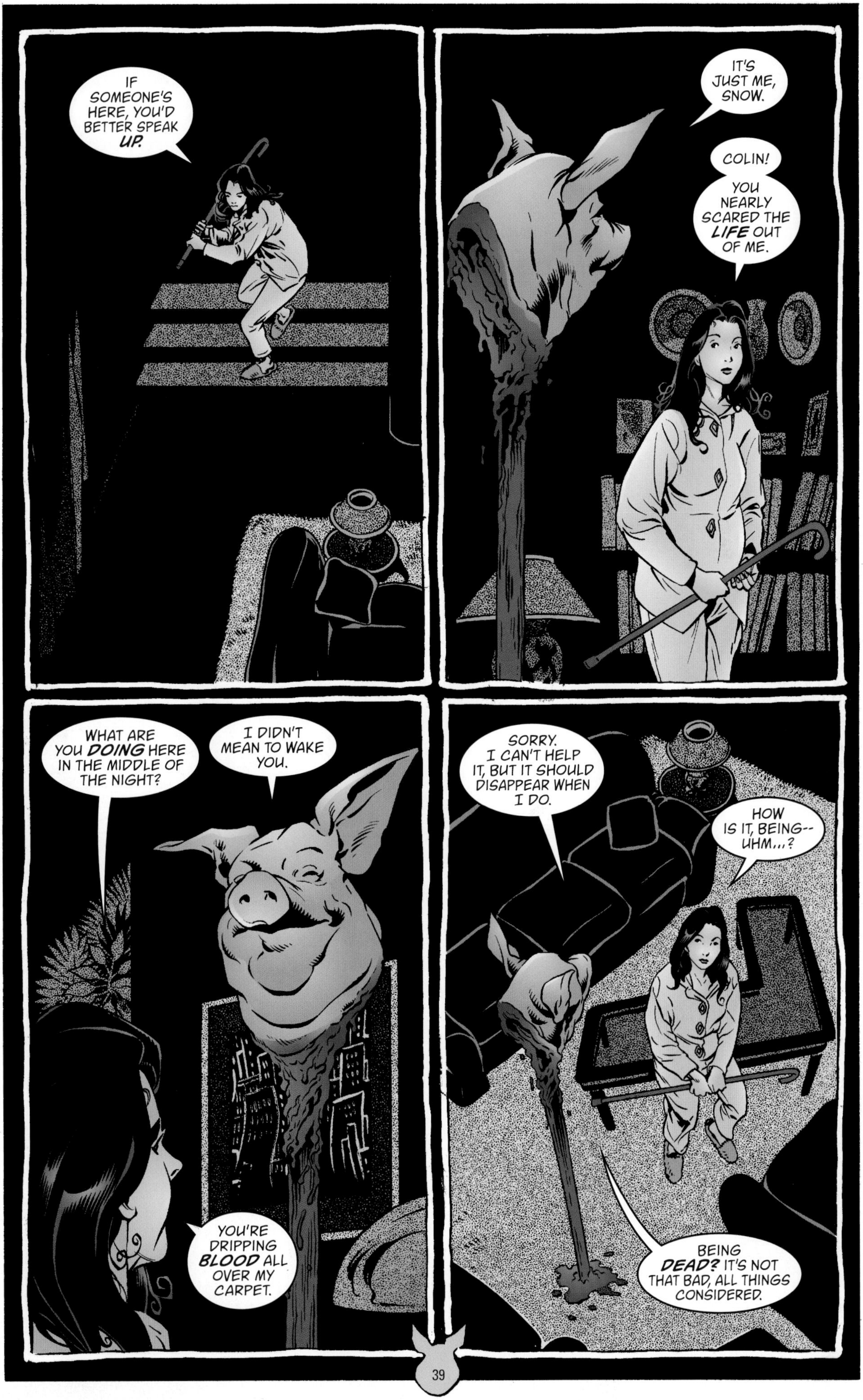

IF SOMEONE'S HERE, YOU'D BETTER SPEAK *UP.*
IT'S JUST ME, SNOW.
COLIN!
YOU NEARLY SCARED THE *LIFE* OUT OF ME.
WHAT ARE YOU *DOING* HERE IN THE MIDDLE OF THE NIGHT?
I DIDN'T MEAN TO WAKE YOU.
YOU'RE DRIPPING *BLOOD* ALL OVER MY CARPET.
SORRY. I CAN'T HELP IT, BUT IT SHOULD DISAPPEAR WHEN I DO.
HOW IS IT, BEING-- UHM...?
BEING *DEAD?* IT'S NOT THAT BAD, ALL THINGS CONSIDERED.

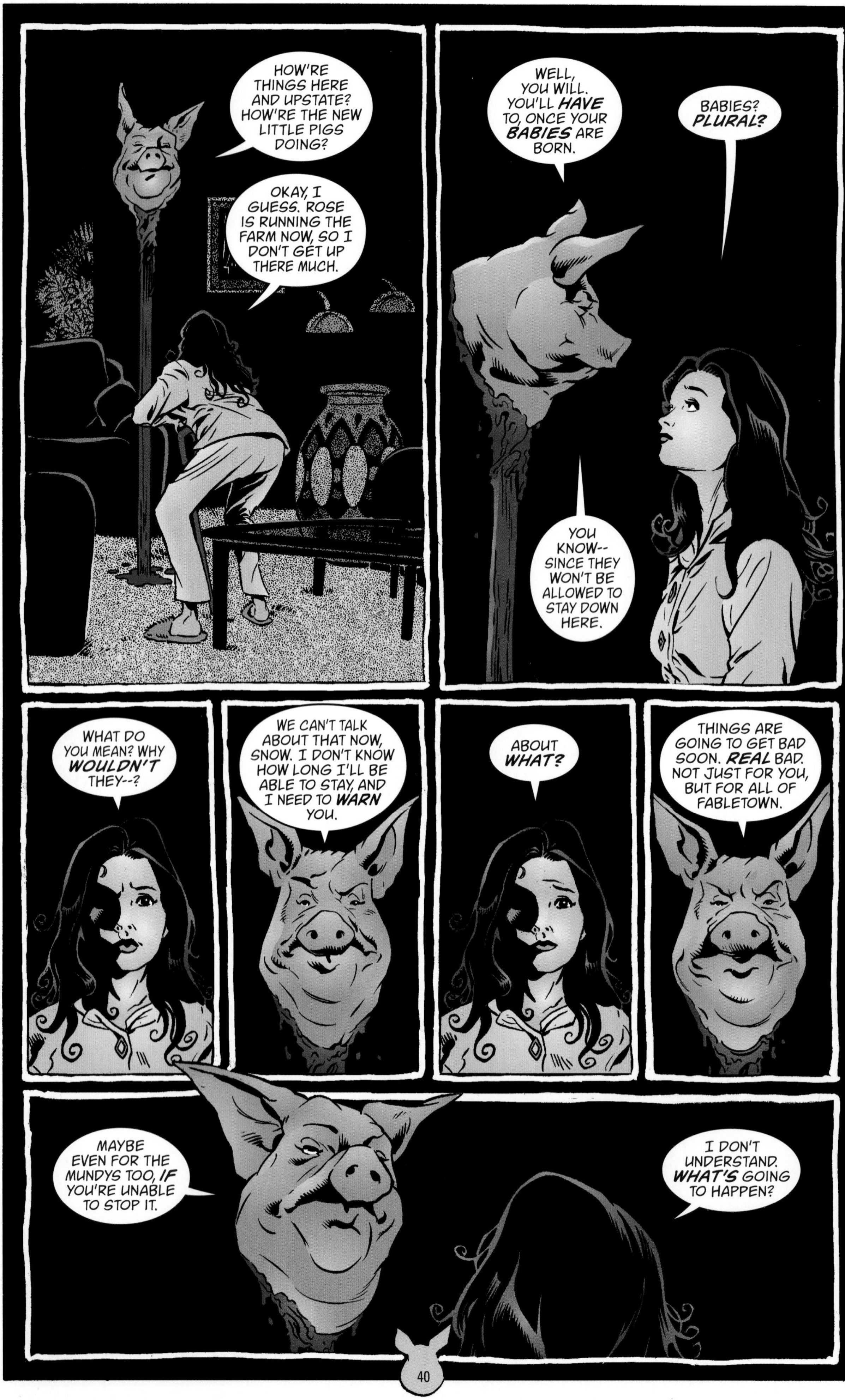
HOW'RE THINGS HERE AND UPSTATE? HOW'RE THE NEW LITTLE PIGS DOING?
OKAY, I GUESS. ROSE IS RUNNING THE FARM NOW, SO I DON'T GET UP THERE MUCH.
WELL, YOU WILL. YOU'LL HAVE TO, ONCE YOUR BABIES ARE BORN.
BABIES? PLURAL?
YOU KNOW-- SINCE THEY WON'T BE ALLOWED TO STAY DOWN HERE.
WHAT DO YOU MEAN? WHY WOULDN'T THEY--?
WE CAN'T TALK ABOUT THAT NOW, SNOW. I DON'T KNOW HOW LONG I'LL BE ABLE TO STAY, AND I NEED TO WARN YOU.
ABOUT WHAT?
THINGS ARE GOING TO GET BAD SOON. REAL BAD. NOT JUST FOR YOU, BUT FOR ALL OF FABLETOWN.
MAYBE EVEN FOR THE MUNDYS TOO, IF YOU'RE UNABLE TO STOP IT.
I DON'T UNDERSTAND. WHAT'S GOING TO HAPPEN?

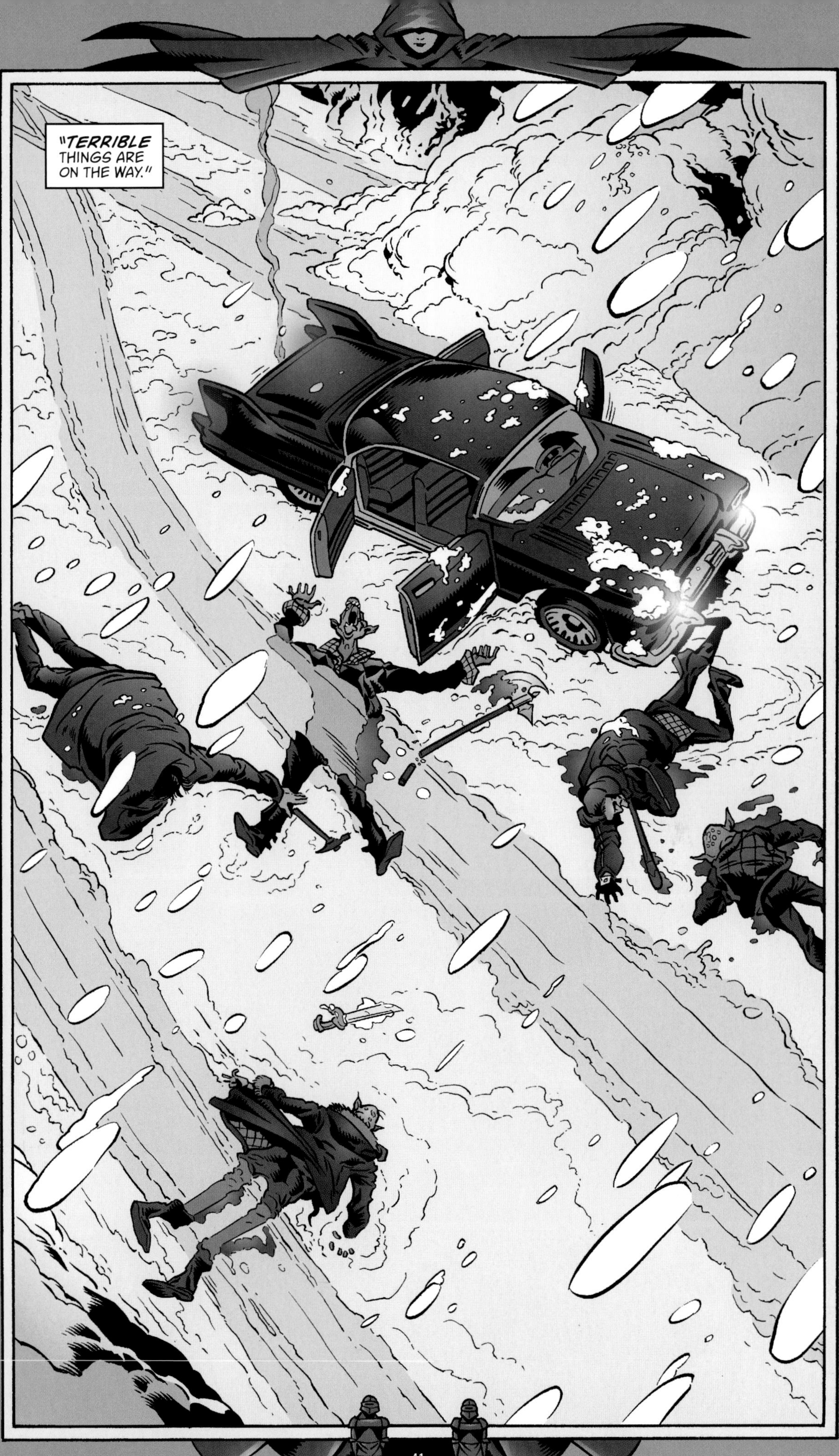
"TERRIBLE THINGS ARE ON THE WAY."

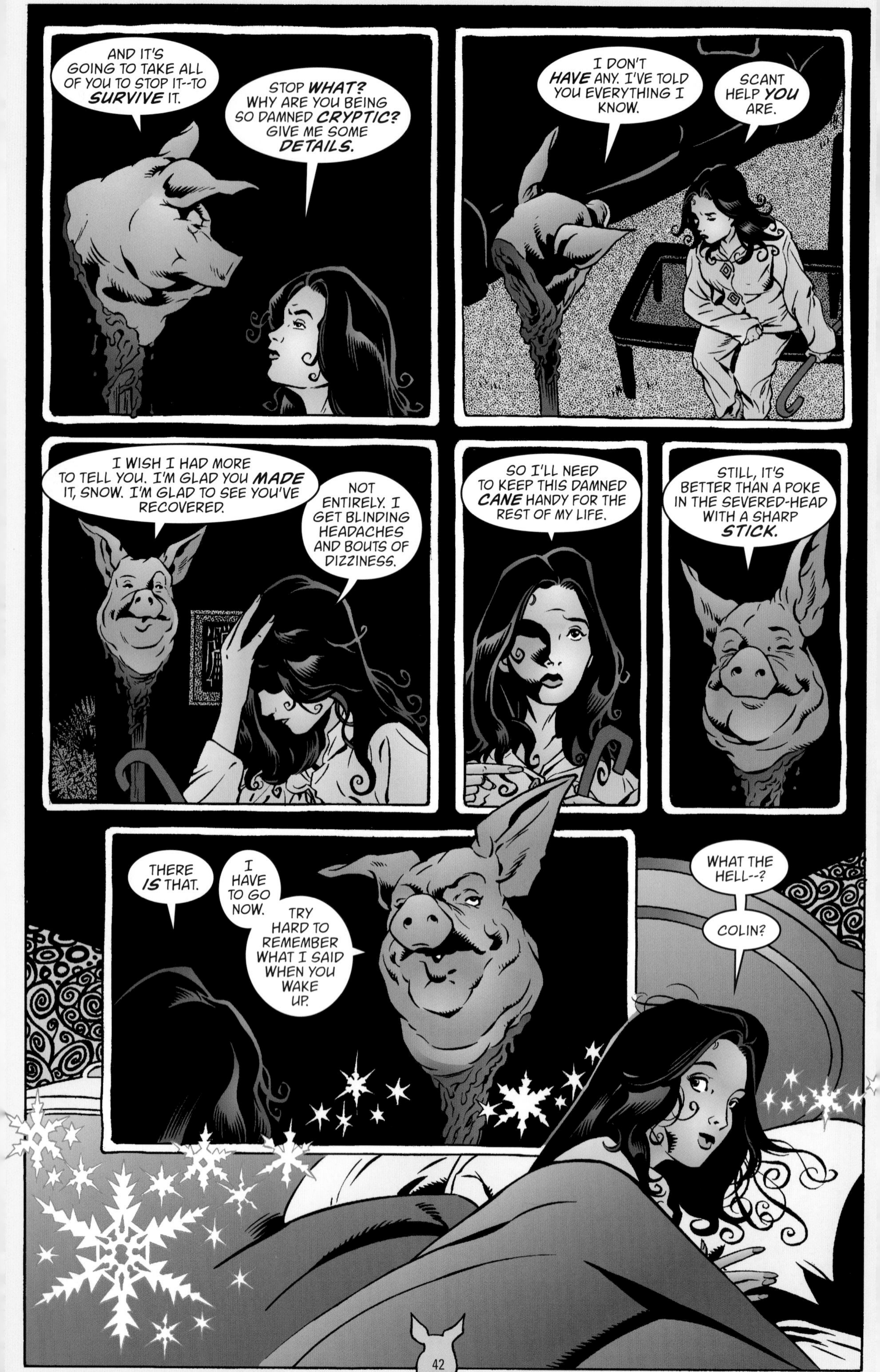
AND IT'S GOING TO TAKE ALL OF YOU TO STOP IT--TO SURVIVE IT.
STOP WHAT? WHY ARE YOU BEING SO DAMNED CRYPTIC? GIVE ME SOME DETAILS.
I DON'T HAVE ANY. I'VE TOLD YOU EVERYTHING I KNOW.
SCANT HELP YOU ARE.
I WISH I HAD MORE TO TELL YOU. I'M GLAD YOU MADE IT, SNOW. I'M GLAD TO SEE YOU'VE RECOVERED.
NOT ENTIRELY. I GET BLINDING HEADACHES AND BOUTS OF DIZZINESS.
SO I'LL NEED TO KEEP THIS DAMNED CANE HANDY FOR THE REST OF MY LIFE.
STILL, IT'S BETTER THAN A POKE IN THE SEVERED-HEAD WITH A SHARP STICK.
THERE IS THAT.
I HAVE TO GO NOW.
TRY HARD TO REMEMBER WHAT I SAID WHEN YOU WAKE UP.
WHAT THE HELL--?
COLIN?

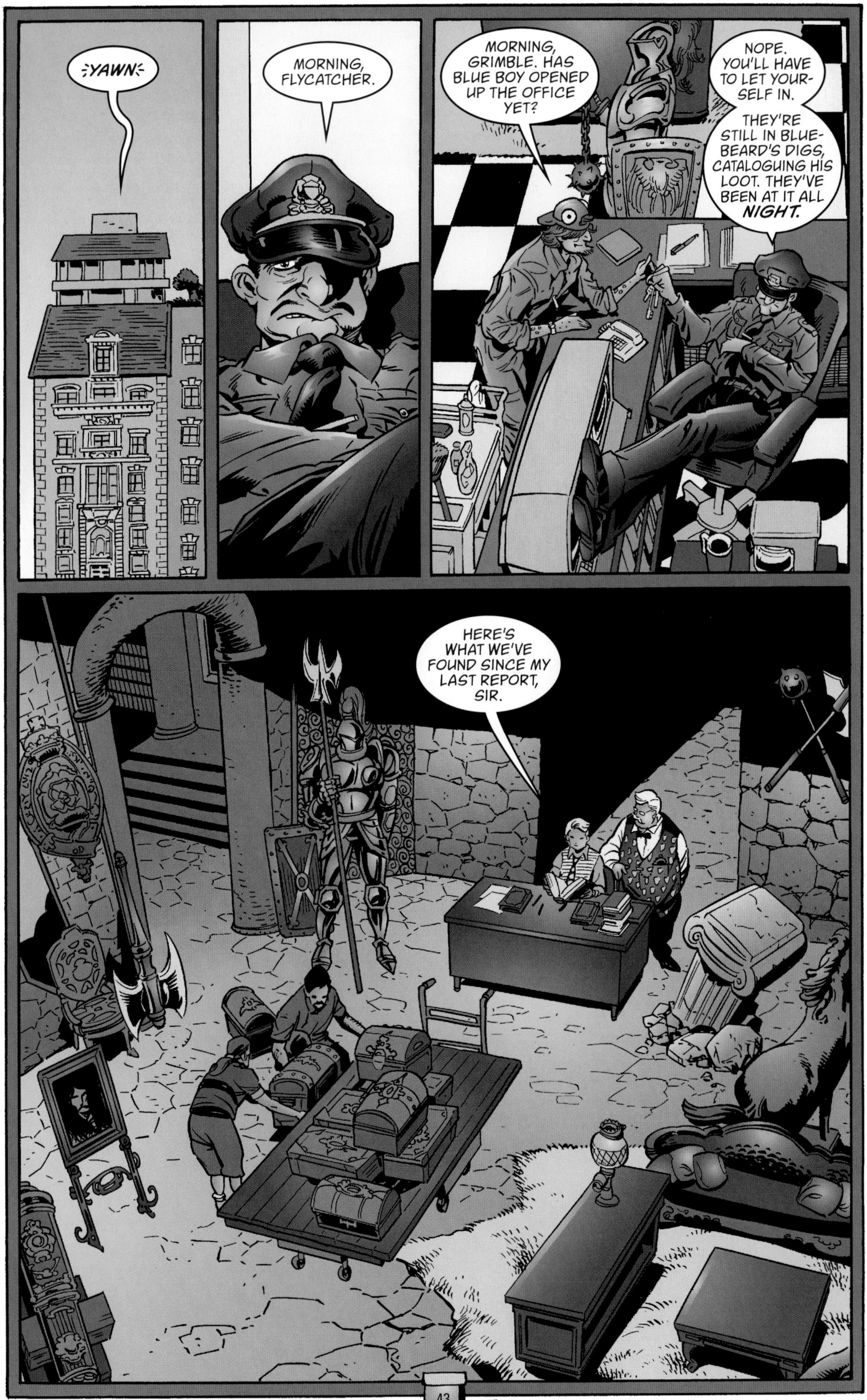

:YAWN:
MORNING, FLYCATCHER.
MORNING, GRIMBLE. HAS BLUE BOY OPENED UP THE OFFICE YET?
NOPE. YOU'LL HAVE TO LET YOURSELF IN.
THEY'RE STILL IN BLUEBEARD'S DIGS, CATALOGUING HIS LOOT. THEY'VE BEEN AT IT ALL NIGHT.
HERE'S WHAT WE'VE FOUND SINCE MY LAST REPORT, SIR.

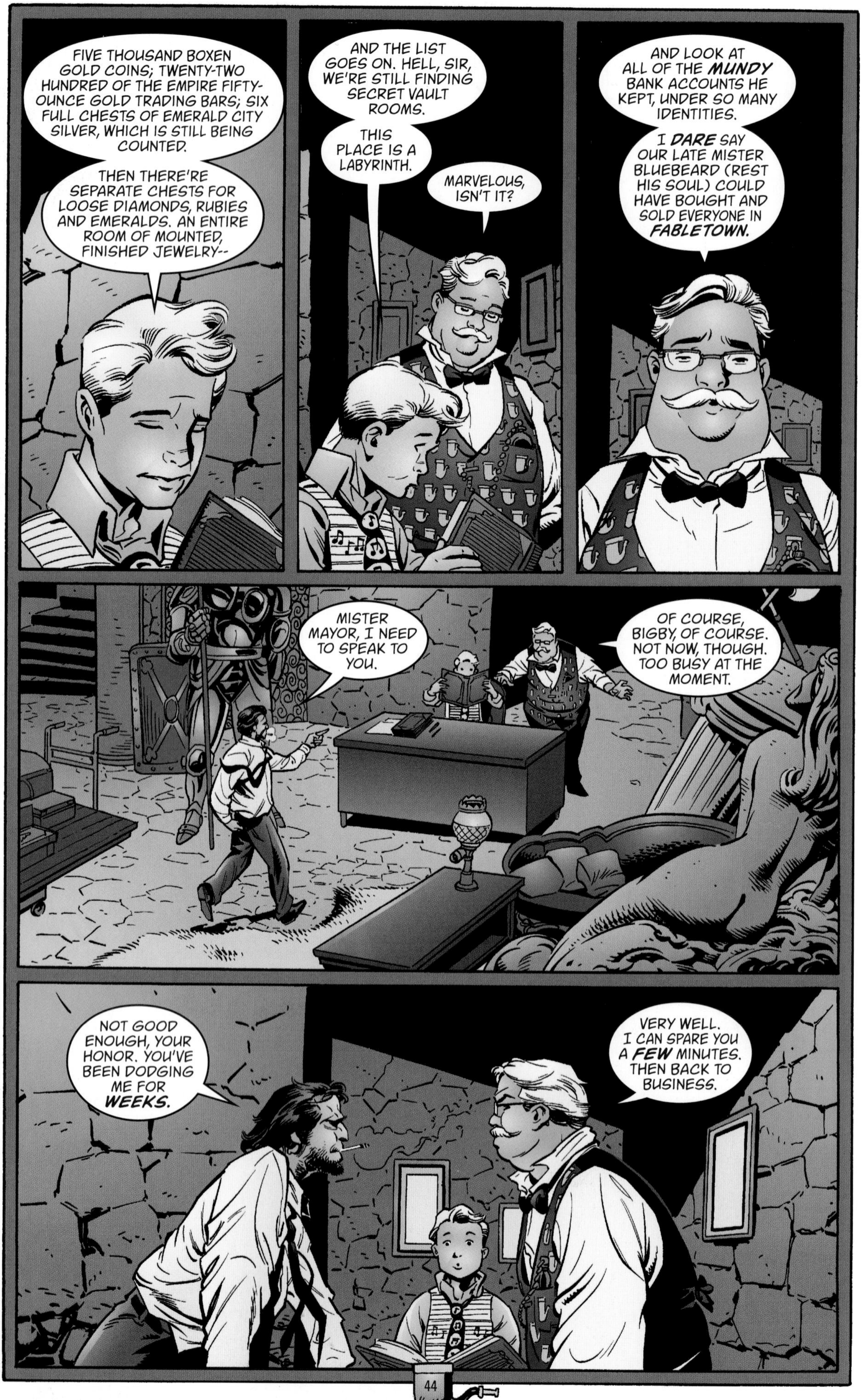
FIVE THOUSAND BOXEN GOLD COINS; TWENTY-TWO HUNDRED OF THE EMPIRE FIFTY-OUNCE GOLD TRADING BARS; SIX FULL CHESTS OF EMERALD CITY SILVER, WHICH IS STILL BEING COUNTED.
THEN THERE'RE SEPARATE CHESTS FOR LOOSE DIAMONDS, RUBIES AND EMERALDS. AN ENTIRE ROOM OF MOUNTED, FINISHED JEWELRY--
AND THE LIST GOES ON. HELL, SIR, WE'RE STILL FINDING SECRET VAULT ROOMS.
THIS PLACE IS A LABYRINTH.
MARVELOUS, ISN'T IT?
AND LOOK AT ALL OF THE MUNDY BANK ACCOUNTS HE KEPT, UNDER SO MANY IDENTITIES.
I DARE SAY OUR LATE MISTER BLUEBEARD (REST HIS SOUL) COULD HAVE BOUGHT AND SOLD EVERYONE IN FABLETOWN.
MISTER MAYOR, I NEED TO SPEAK TO YOU.
OF COURSE, BIGBY, OF COURSE. NOT NOW, THOUGH. TOO BUSY AT THE MOMENT.
NOT GOOD ENOUGH, YOUR HONOR. YOU'VE BEEN DODGING ME FOR WEEKS.
VERY WELL. I CAN SPARE YOU A FEW MINUTES. THEN BACK TO BUSINESS.

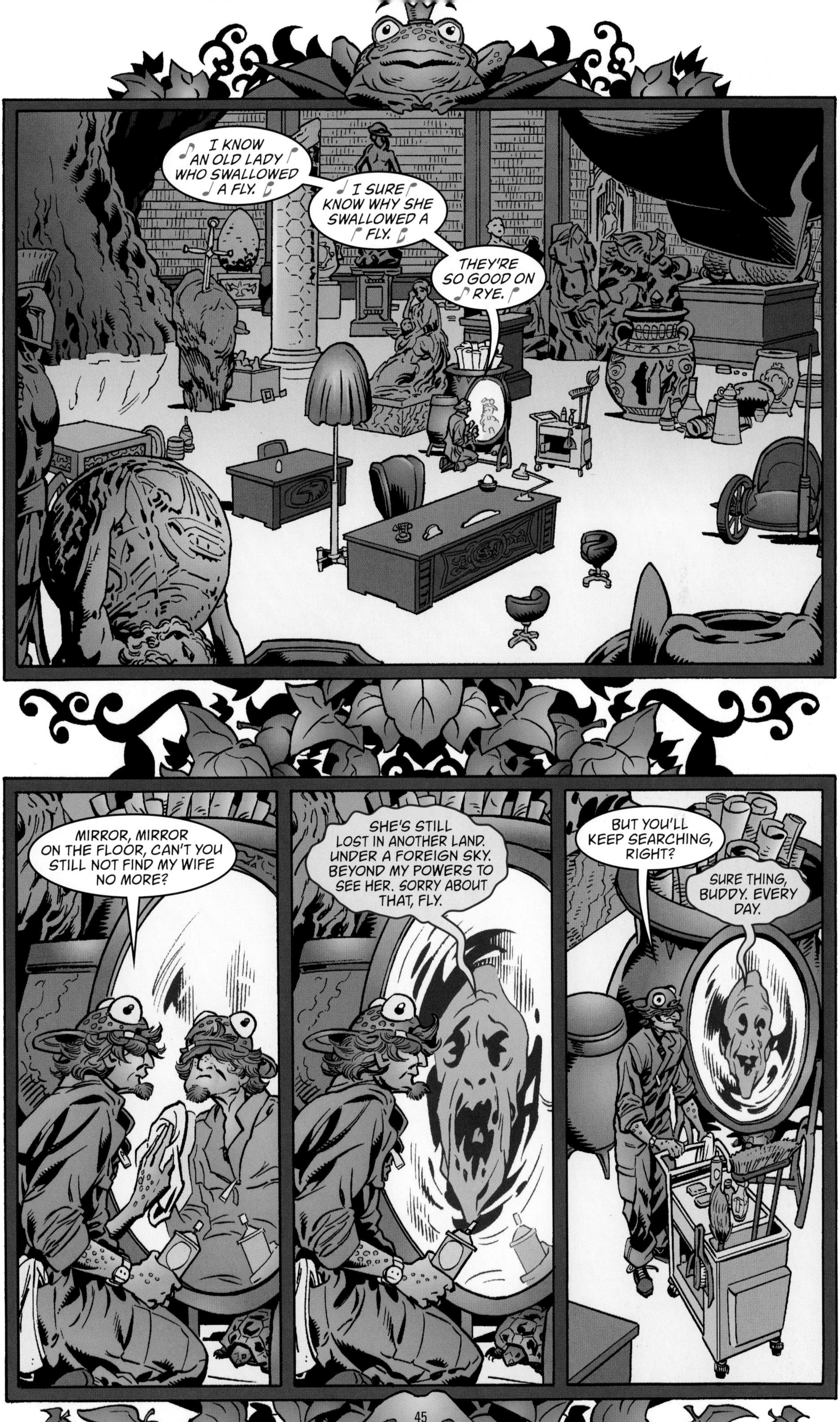

♪ I KNOW AN OLD LADY WHO SWALLOWED A FLY. ♪
♪ I SURE KNOW WHY SHE SWALLOWED A FLY. ♪
THEY'RE SO GOOD ON ♪ RYE. ♪
MIRROR, MIRROR ON THE FLOOR, CAN'T YOU STILL NOT FIND MY WIFE NO MORE?
SHE'S STILL LOST IN ANOTHER LAND. UNDER A FOREIGN SKY. BEYOND MY POWERS TO SEE HER. SORRY ABOUT THAT, FLY.
BUT YOU'LL KEEP SEARCHING, RIGHT?
SURE THING, BUDDY. EVERY DAY.

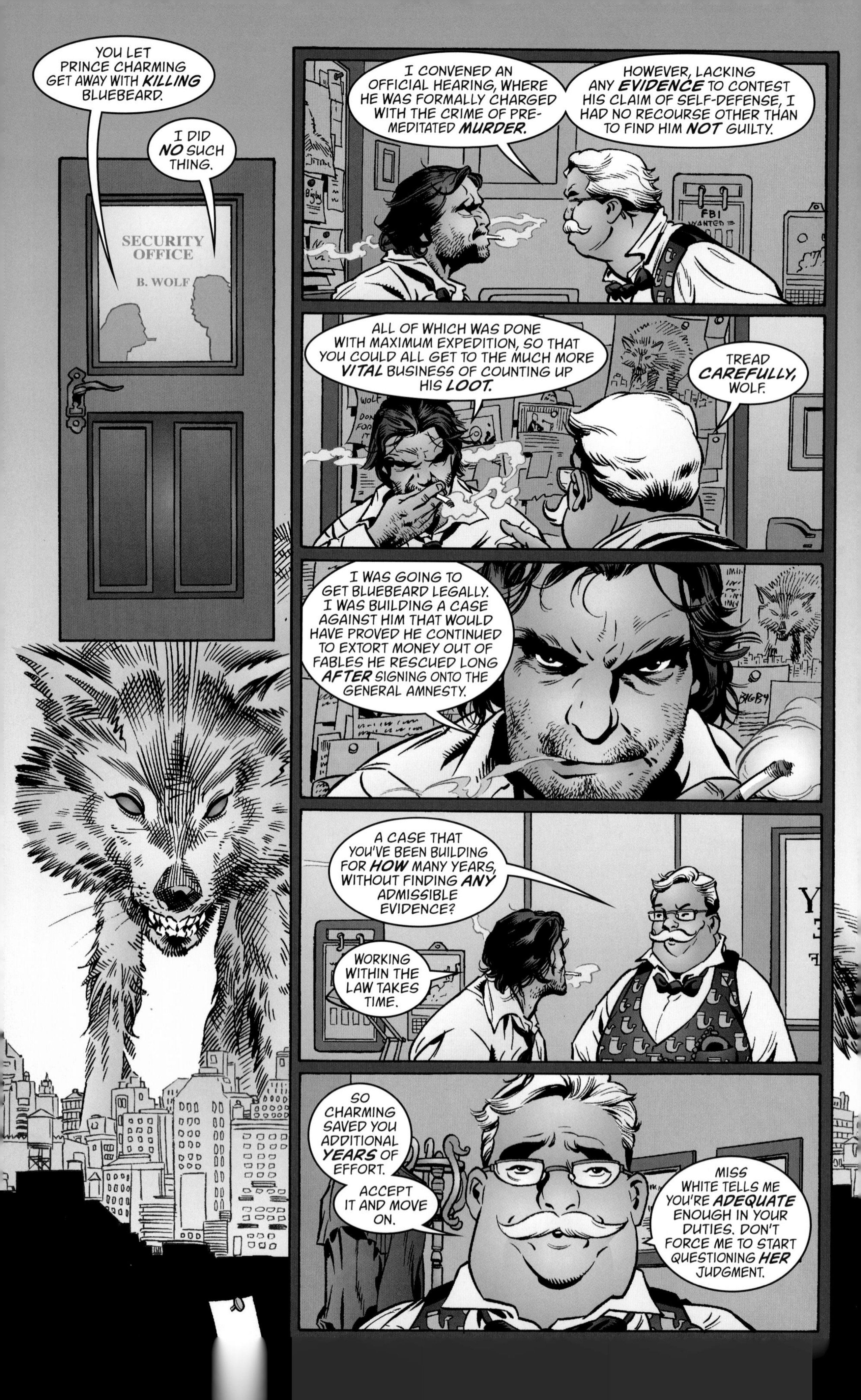
YOU LET PRINCE CHARMING GET AWAY WITH KILLING BLUEBEARD.
I DID NO SUCH THING.
SECURITY OFFICE
B. WOLF
I CONVENED AN OFFICIAL HEARING, WHERE HE WAS FORMALLY CHARGED WITH THE CRIME OF PRE-MEDITATED MURDER.
HOWEVER, LACKING ANY EVIDENCE TO CONTEST HIS CLAIM OF SELF-DEFENSE, I HAD NO RECOURSE OTHER THAN TO FIND HIM NOT GUILTY.
ALL OF WHICH WAS DONE WITH MAXIMUM EXPEDITION, SO THAT YOU COULD ALL GET TO THE MUCH MORE VITAL BUSINESS OF COUNTING UP HIS LOOT.
TREAD CAREFULLY, WOLF.
I WAS GOING TO GET BLUEBEARD LEGALLY. I WAS BUILDING A CASE AGAINST HIM THAT WOULD HAVE PROVED HE CONTINUED TO EXTORT MONEY OUT OF FABLES HE RESCUED LONG AFTER SIGNING ONTO THE GENERAL AMNESTY.
A CASE THAT YOU'VE BEEN BUILDING FOR HOW MANY YEARS, WITHOUT FINDING ANY ADMISSIBLE EVIDENCE?
WORKING WITHIN THE LAW TAKES TIME.
SO CHARMING SAVED YOU ADDITIONAL YEARS OF EFFORT.
ACCEPT IT AND MOVE ON.
MISS WHITE TELLS ME YOU'RE ADEQUATE ENOUGH IN YOUR DUTIES. DON'T FORCE ME TO START QUESTIONING HER JUDGMENT.

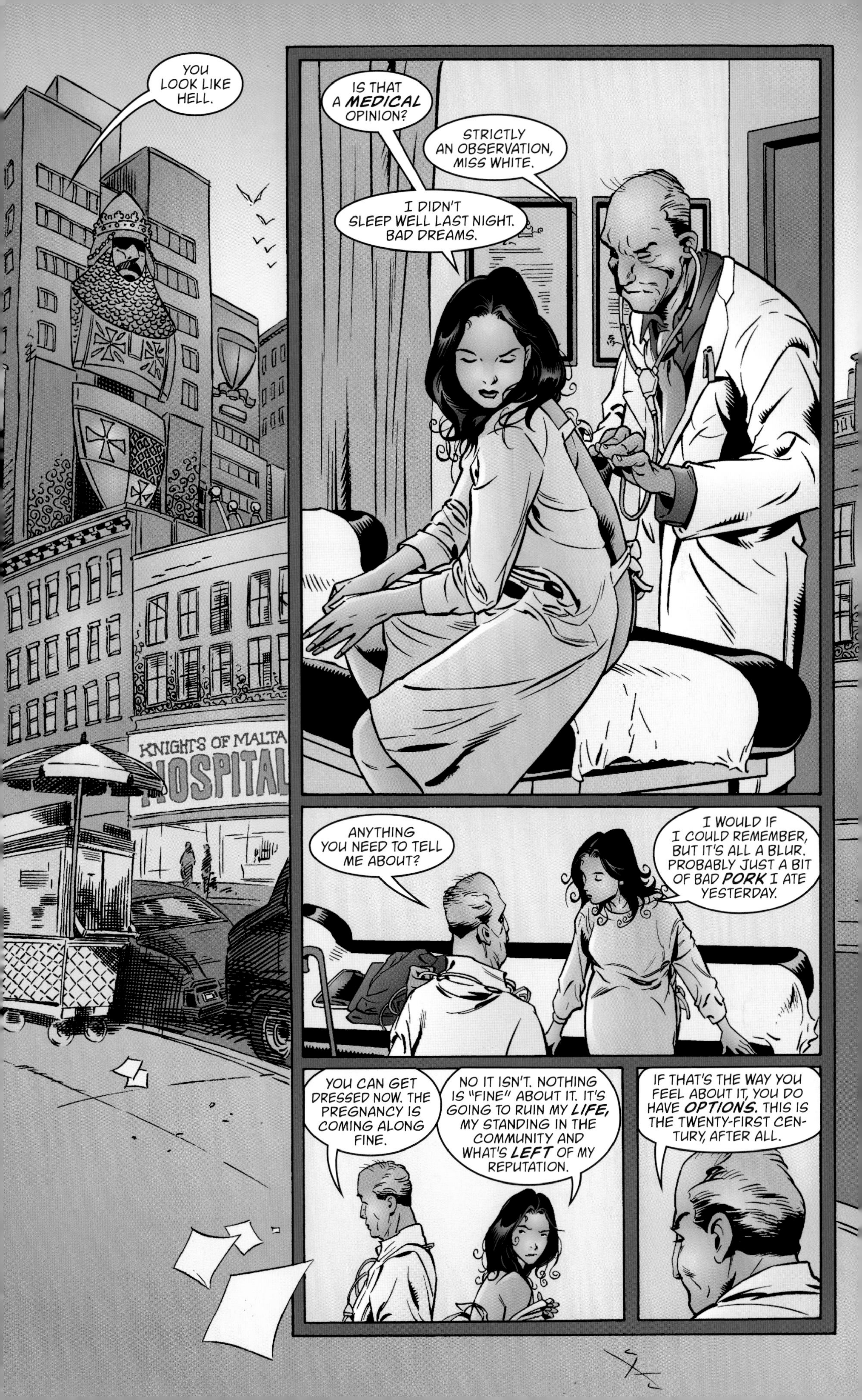
YOU LOOK LIKE HELL.
KNIGHTS OF MALTA HOSPITAL
IS THAT A MEDICAL OPINION?
STRICTLY AN OBSERVATION, MISS WHITE.
I DIDN'T SLEEP WELL LAST NIGHT. BAD DREAMS.
ANYTHING YOU NEED TO TELL ME ABOUT?
I WOULD IF I COULD REMEMBER, BUT IT'S ALL A BLUR. PROBABLY JUST A BIT OF BAD PORK I ATE YESTERDAY.
YOU CAN GET DRESSED NOW. THE PREGNANCY IS COMING ALONG FINE.
NO IT ISN'T. NOTHING IS "FINE" ABOUT IT. IT'S GOING TO RUIN MY LIFE, MY STANDING IN THE COMMUNITY AND WHAT'S LEFT OF MY REPUTATION.
IF THAT'S THE WAY YOU FEEL ABOUT IT, YOU DO HAVE OPTIONS. THIS IS THE TWENTY-FIRST CENTURY, AFTER ALL.

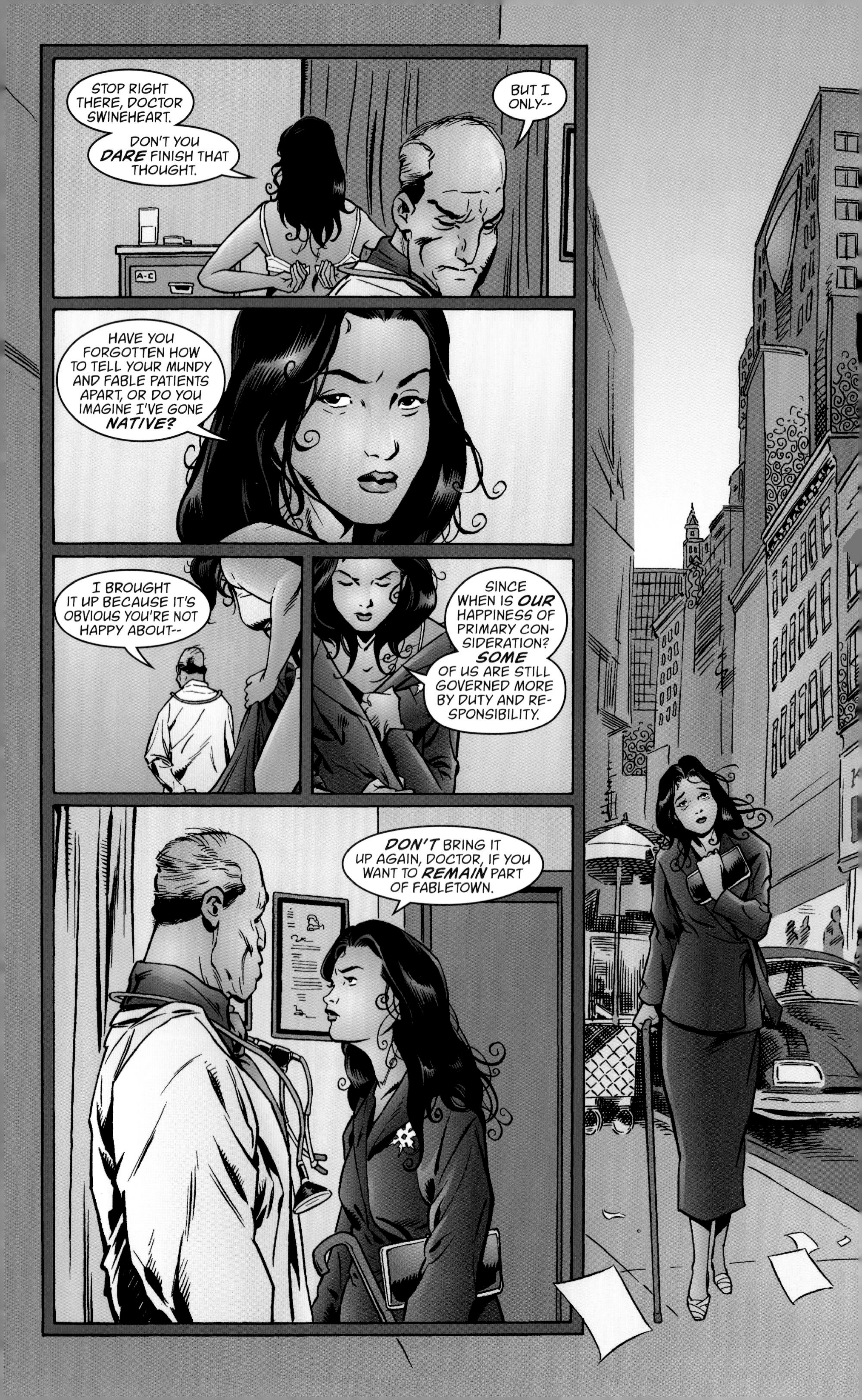
STOP RIGHT THERE, DOCTOR SWINEHEART.
DON'T YOU DARE FINISH THAT THOUGHT.
BUT I ONLY--
HAVE YOU FORGOTTEN HOW TO TELL YOUR MUNDY AND FABLE PATIENTS APART, OR DO YOU IMAGINE I'VE GONE NATIVE?
I BROUGHT IT UP BECAUSE IT'S OBVIOUS YOU'RE NOT HAPPY ABOUT--
SINCE WHEN IS OUR HAPPINESS OF PRIMARY CONSIDERATION? SOME OF US ARE STILL GOVERNED MORE BY DUTY AND RESPONSIBILITY.
DON'T BRING IT UP AGAIN, DOCTOR, IF YOU WANT TO REMAIN PART OF FABLETOWN.

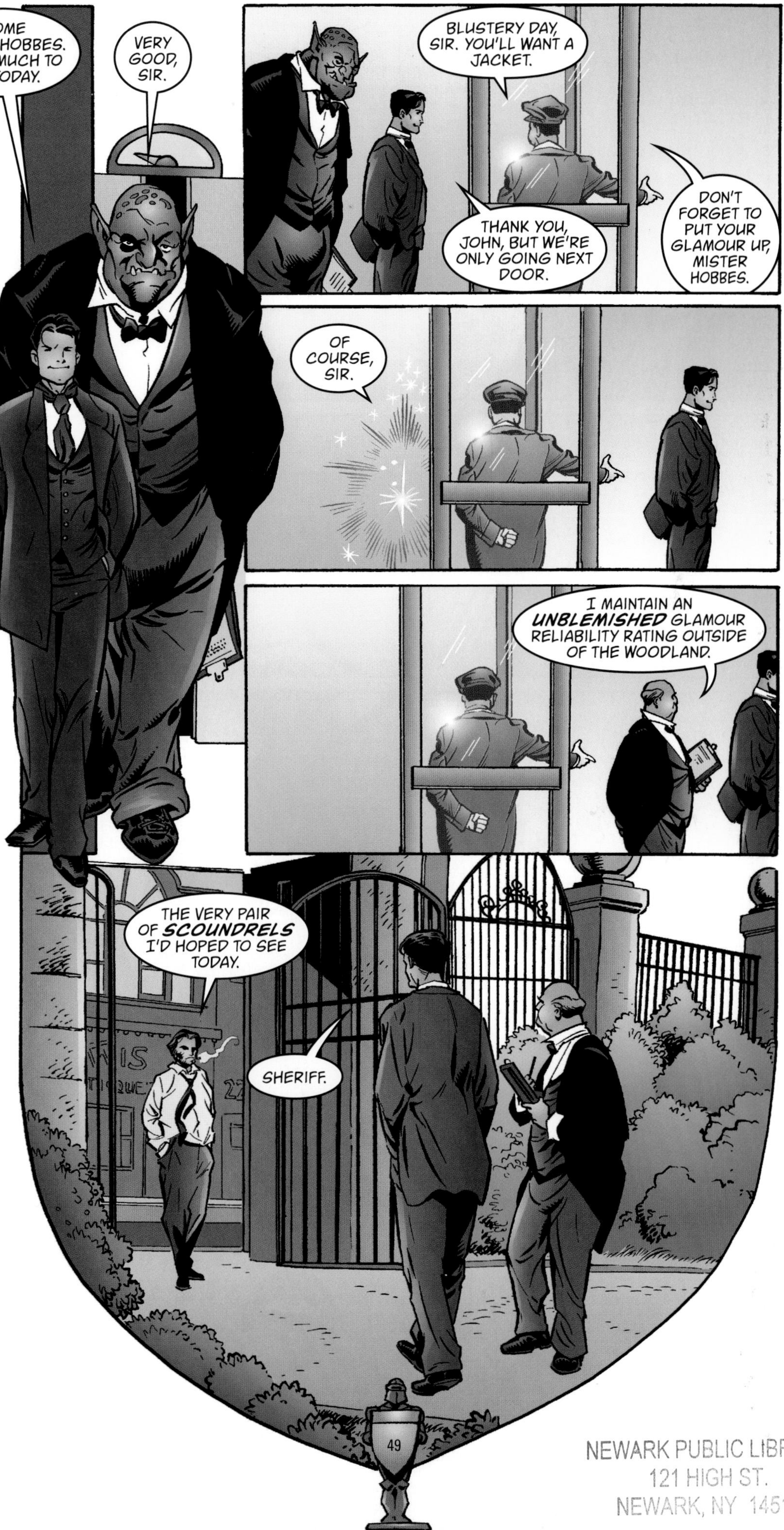
COME ALONG, HOBBES. WE'VE MUCH TO DO TODAY.
VERY GOOD, SIR.
BLUSTERY DAY, SIR. YOU'LL WANT A JACKET.
THANK YOU, JOHN, BUT WE'RE ONLY GOING NEXT DOOR.
DON'T FORGET TO PUT YOUR GLAMOUR UP, MISTER HOBBES.
OF COURSE, SIR.
I MAINTAIN AN ***UNBLEMISHED*** GLAMOUR RELIABILITY RATING OUTSIDE OF THE WOODLAND.
THE VERY PAIR OF ***SCOUNDRELS*** I'D HOPED TO SEE TODAY.
SHERIFF.

WHAT BUSINESS COULD YOU *POSSIBLY* HAVE WITH *ME?*

YOU'VE PUT BLUEBEARD BEYOND MY REACH, AND YOUR MACHINATIONS WITH OUR MAYOR HAVE MADE YOU SAFE...

...FOR NOW.

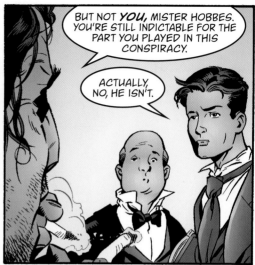

BUT NOT *YOU*, MISTER HOBBES. YOU'RE STILL INDICTABLE FOR THE PART YOU PLAYED IN THIS CONSPIRACY.

ACTUALLY, NO, HE ISN'T.

I GAVE HIM *BLANKET* AMNESTY, IN RETURN FOR HIS *INVALUABLE* HELP IN EXPOSING HIS FORMER MASTER'S *MYRIAD* DEPREDATIONS.

YOU AREN'T *AUTHORIZED* TO DO THAT.

I'M ABOUT TO BE.

HOBBES AND I ARE EMBARKING ON THE FIRST STAGES OF THAT VERY ENDEAVOR EVEN NOW.

NOW, IF YOU'LL *EXCUSE* ME, WE HAVE FIVE HUNDRED *SIGNATURES* TO COLLECT.

YOU HAVE THE VERY *BEST* OF AFTERNOONS, SHERIFF.

50

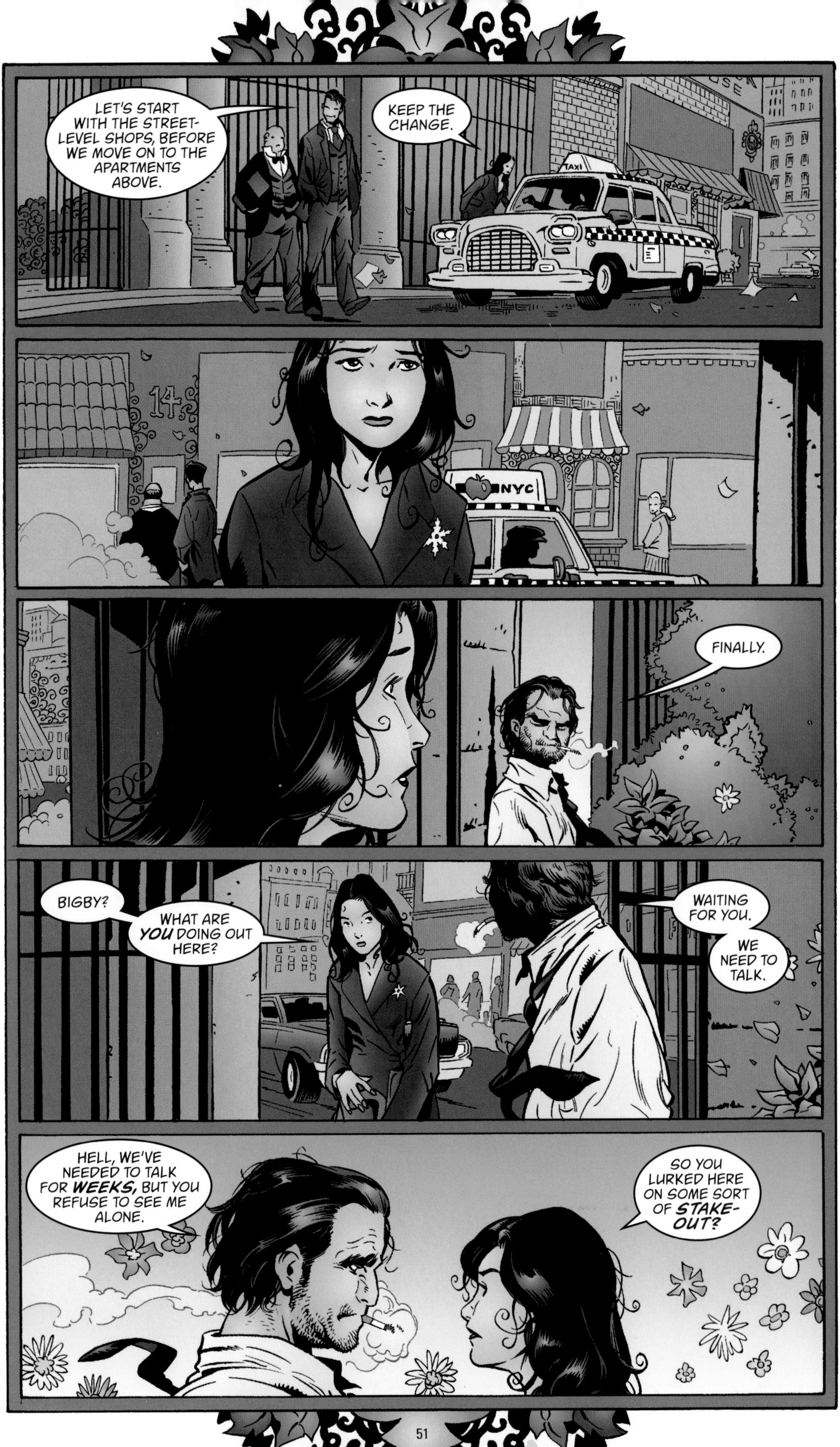
LET'S START WITH THE STREET-LEVEL SHOPS, BEFORE WE MOVE ON TO THE APARTMENTS ABOVE.
KEEP THE CHANGE.
FINALLY.
BIGBY?
WHAT ARE *YOU* DOING OUT HERE?
WAITING FOR YOU.
WE NEED TO TALK.
HELL, WE'VE NEEDED TO TALK FOR *WEEKS,* BUT YOU REFUSE TO SEE ME ALONE.
SO YOU LURKED HERE ON SOME SORT OF *STAKE-OUT?*

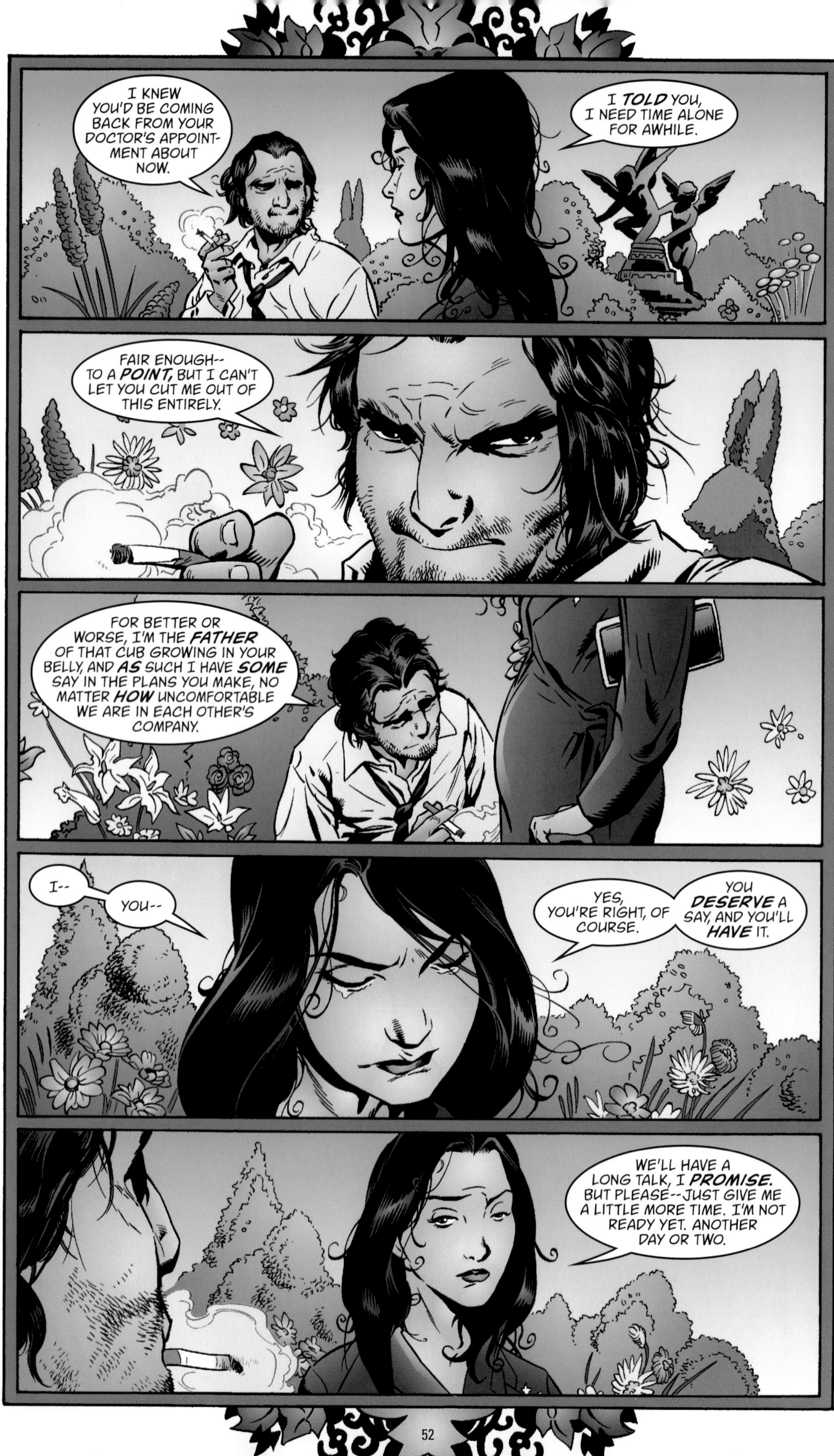
I KNEW YOU'D BE COMING BACK FROM YOUR DOCTOR'S APPOINTMENT ABOUT NOW.
I TOLD YOU, I NEED TIME ALONE FOR AWHILE.
FAIR ENOUGH-- TO A POINT, BUT I CAN'T LET YOU CUT ME OUT OF THIS ENTIRELY.
FOR BETTER OR WORSE, I'M THE FATHER OF THAT CUB GROWING IN YOUR BELLY, AND AS SUCH I HAVE SOME SAY IN THE PLANS YOU MAKE, NO MATTER HOW UNCOMFORTABLE WE ARE IN EACH OTHER'S COMPANY.
I--
YOU--
YES, YOU'RE RIGHT, OF COURSE.
YOU DESERVE A SAY, AND YOU'LL HAVE IT.
WE'LL HAVE A LONG TALK, I PROMISE. BUT PLEASE--JUST GIVE ME A LITTLE MORE TIME. I'M NOT READY YET. ANOTHER DAY OR TWO.

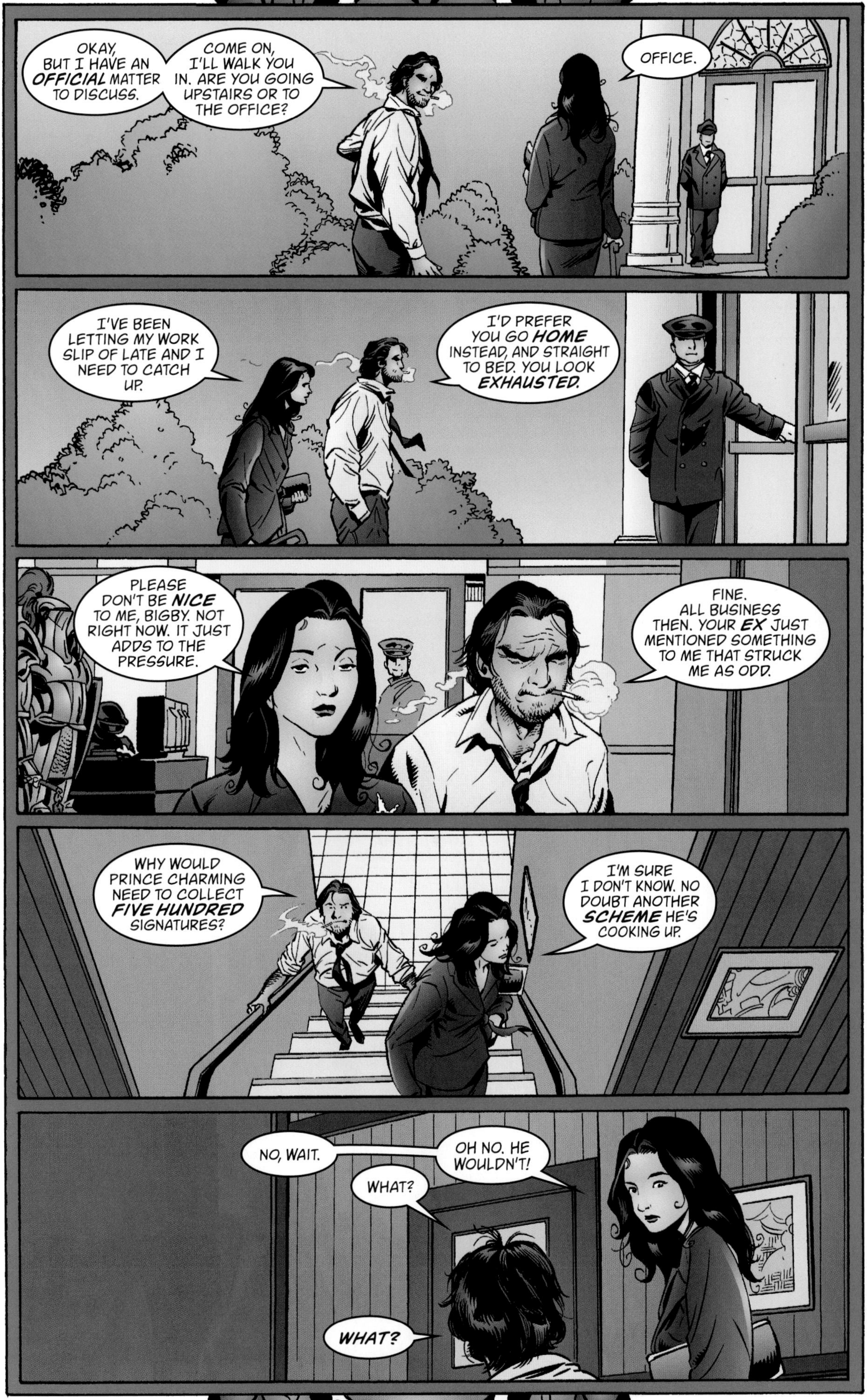
OKAY, BUT I HAVE AN OFFICIAL MATTER TO DISCUSS.
COME ON, I'LL WALK YOU IN. ARE YOU GOING UPSTAIRS OR TO THE OFFICE?
OFFICE.
I'VE BEEN LETTING MY WORK SLIP OF LATE AND I NEED TO CATCH UP.
I'D PREFER YOU GO HOME INSTEAD, AND STRAIGHT TO BED. YOU LOOK EXHAUSTED.
PLEASE DON'T BE NICE TO ME, BIGBY. NOT RIGHT NOW. IT JUST ADDS TO THE PRESSURE.
FINE. ALL BUSINESS THEN. YOUR EX JUST MENTIONED SOMETHING TO ME THAT STRUCK ME AS ODD.
WHY WOULD PRINCE CHARMING NEED TO COLLECT FIVE HUNDRED SIGNATURES?
I'M SURE I DON'T KNOW. NO DOUBT ANOTHER SCHEME HE'S COOKING UP.
NO, WAIT.
OH NO. HE WOULDN'T!
WHAT?
WHAT?

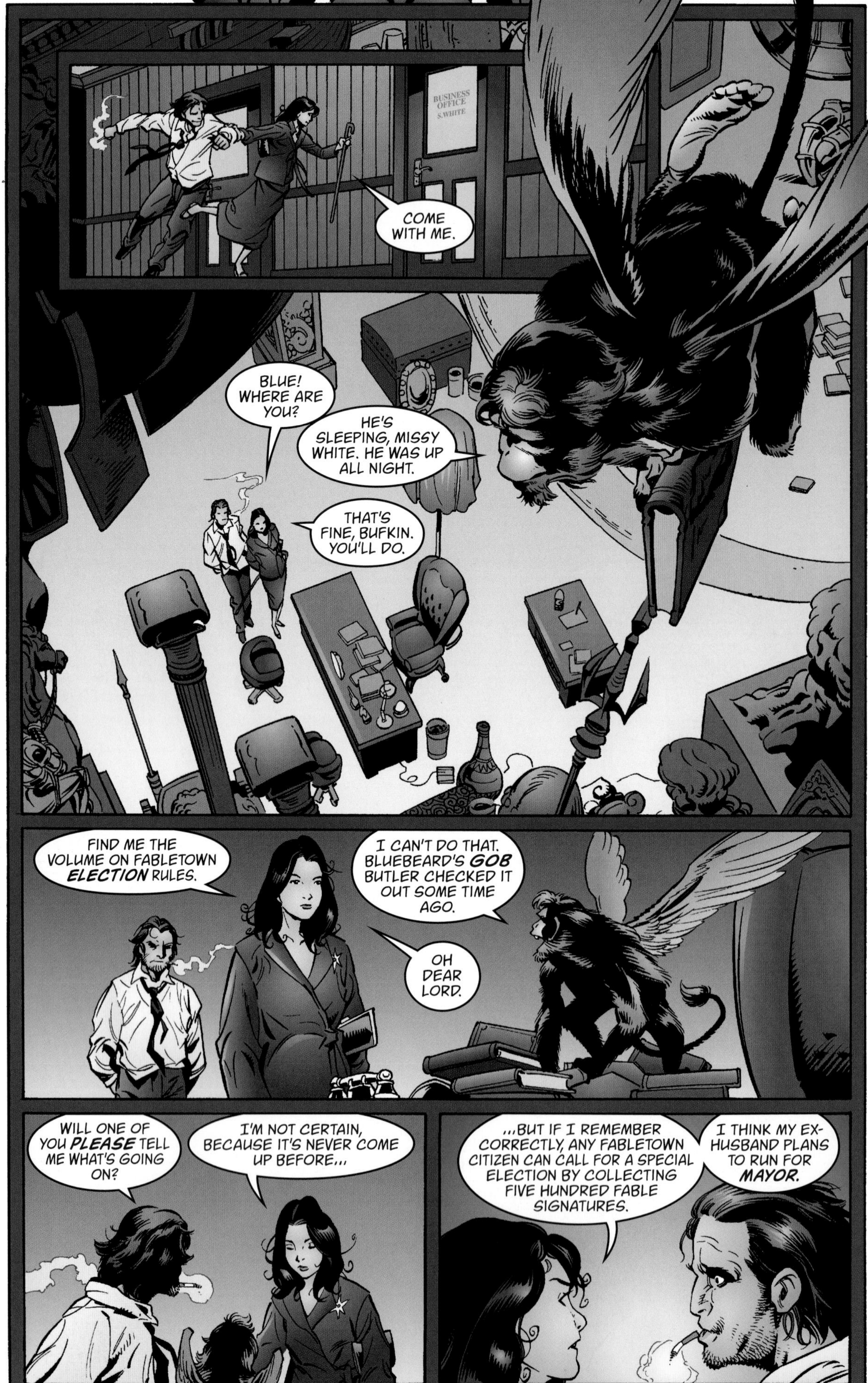
BUSINESS OFFICE S.WHITE
COME WITH ME.
BLUE! WHERE ARE YOU?
HE'S SLEEPING, MISSY WHITE. HE WAS UP ALL NIGHT.
THAT'S FINE, BUFKIN. YOU'LL DO.
FIND ME THE VOLUME ON FABLETOWN ELECTION RULES.
I CAN'T DO THAT. BLUEBEARD'S GOB BUTLER CHECKED IT OUT SOME TIME AGO.
OH DEAR LORD.
WILL ONE OF YOU PLEASE TELL ME WHAT'S GOING ON?
I'M NOT CERTAIN, BECAUSE IT'S NEVER COME UP BEFORE...
...BUT IF I REMEMBER CORRECTLY, ANY FABLETOWN CITIZEN CAN CALL FOR A SPECIAL ELECTION BY COLLECTING FIVE HUNDRED FABLE SIGNATURES.
I THINK MY EX-HUSBAND PLANS TO RUN FOR MAYOR.

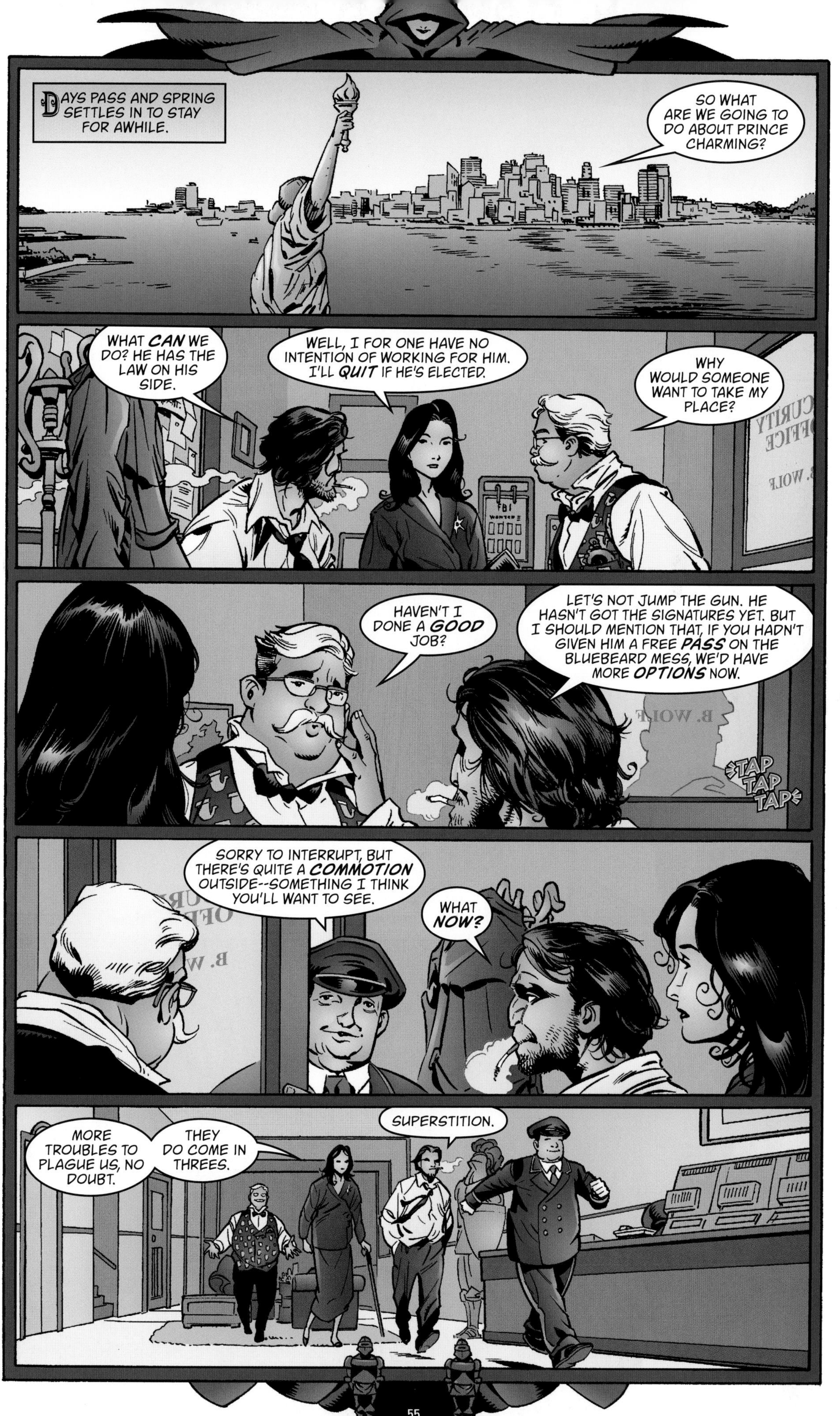
DAYS PASS AND SPRING SETTLES IN TO STAY FOR AWHILE.
SO WHAT ARE WE GOING TO DO ABOUT PRINCE CHARMING?
WHAT CAN WE DO? HE HAS THE LAW ON HIS SIDE.
WELL, I FOR ONE HAVE NO INTENTION OF WORKING FOR HIM. I'LL QUIT IF HE'S ELECTED.
WHY WOULD SOMEONE WANT TO TAKE MY PLACE?
HAVEN'T I DONE A GOOD JOB?
LET'S NOT JUMP THE GUN. HE HASN'T GOT THE SIGNATURES YET. BUT I SHOULD MENTION THAT, IF YOU HADN'T GIVEN HIM A FREE PASS ON THE BLUEBEARD MESS, WE'D HAVE MORE OPTIONS NOW.
TAP TAP TAP
SORRY TO INTERRUPT, BUT THERE'S QUITE A COMMOTION OUTSIDE--SOMETHING I THINK YOU'LL WANT TO SEE.
WHAT NOW?
MORE TROUBLES TO PLAGUE US, NO DOUBT.
THEY DO COME IN THREES.
SUPERSTITION.

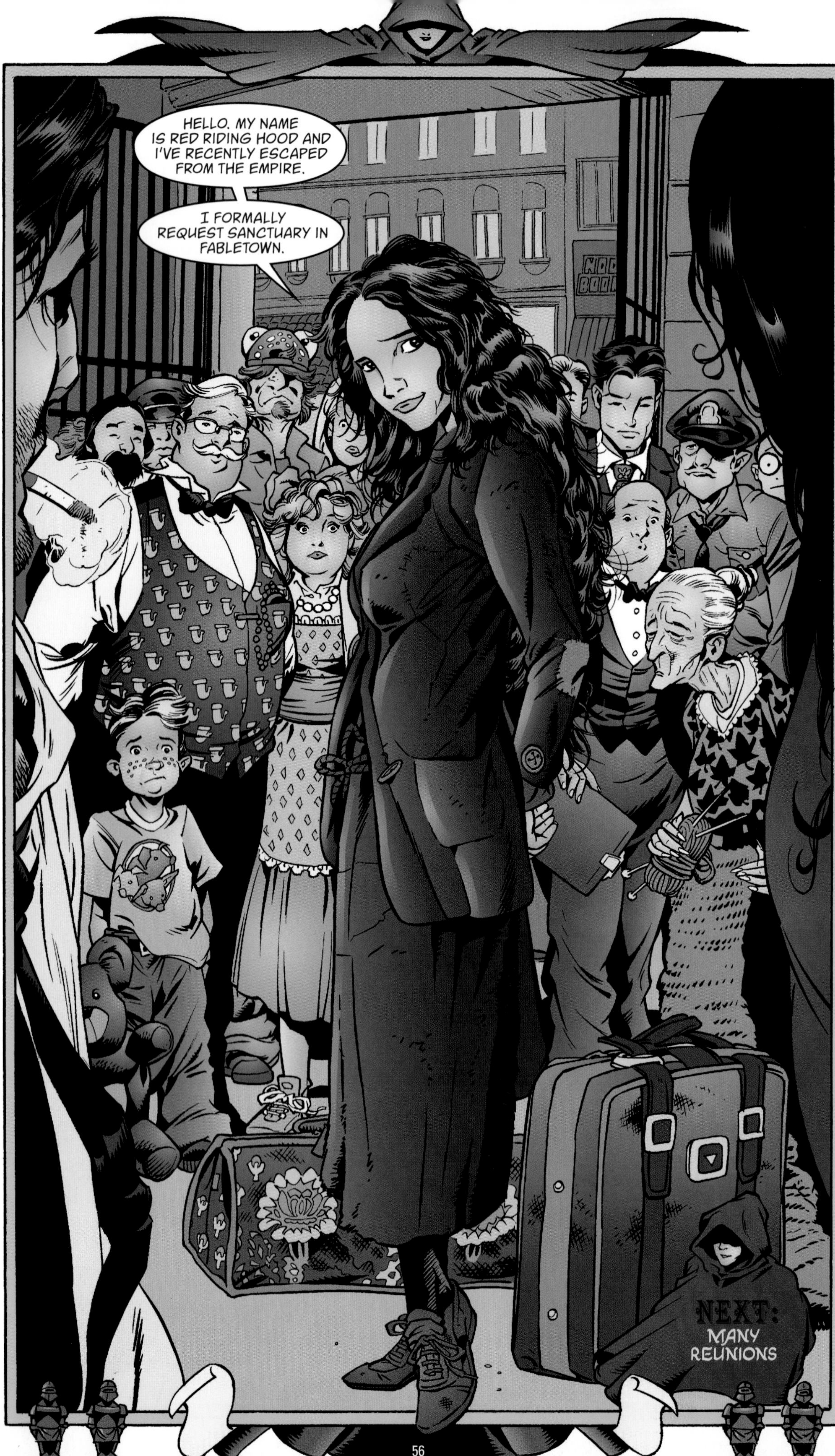
HELLO. MY NAME IS RED RIDING HOOD AND I'VE RECENTLY ESCAPED FROM THE EMPIRE.
I FORMALLY REQUEST SANCTUARY IN FABLETOWN.
NEXT: MANY REUNIONS

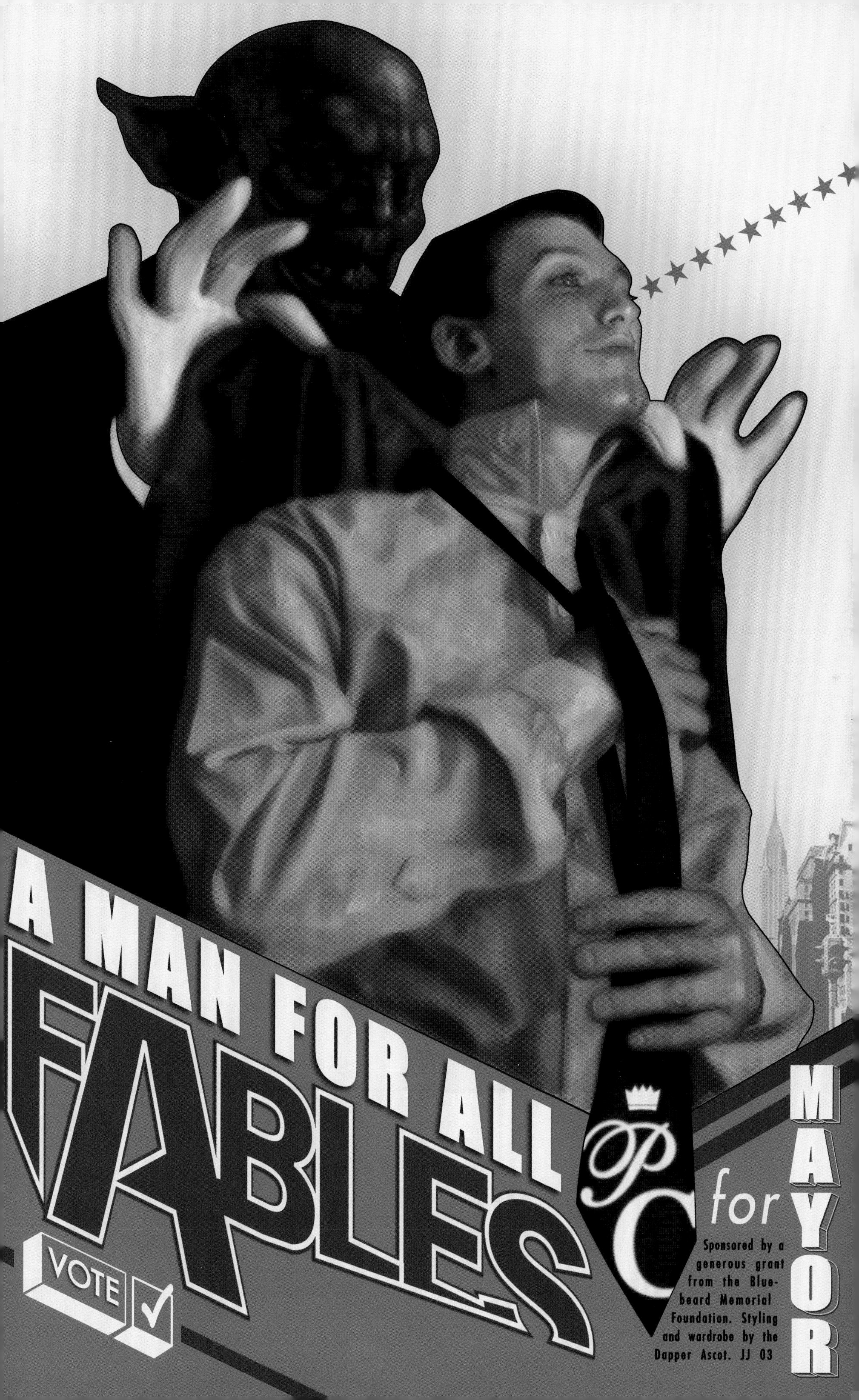
A MAN FOR ALL
FABLES
PC for MAYOR
VOTE
Sponsored by a generous grant from the Blue-beard Memorial Foundation. Styling and wardrobe by the Dapper Ascot. JJ 03

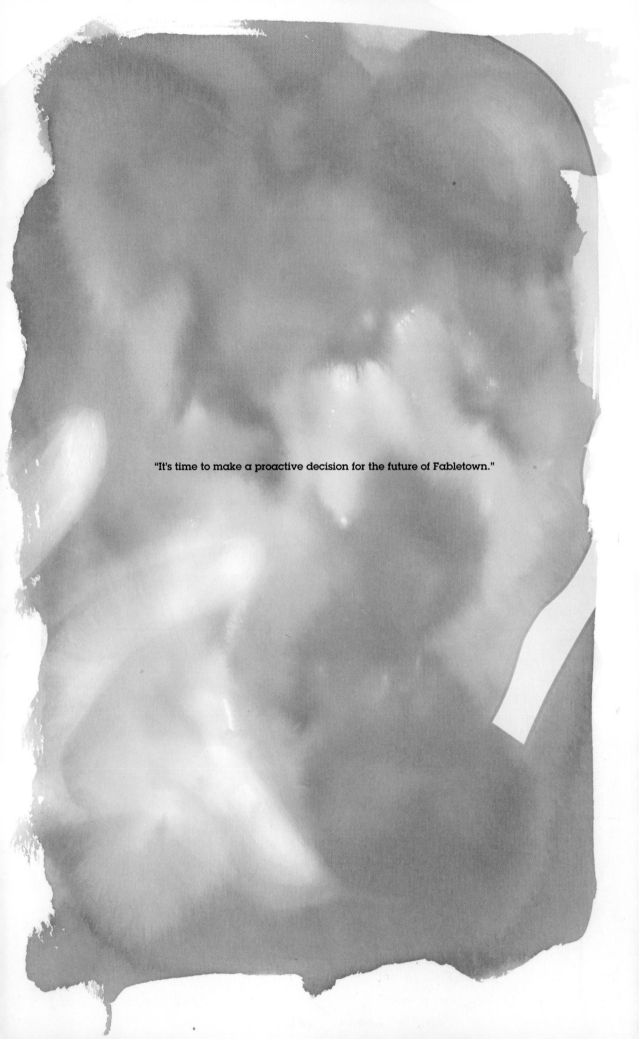

"It's time to make a proactive decision for the future of Fabletown."

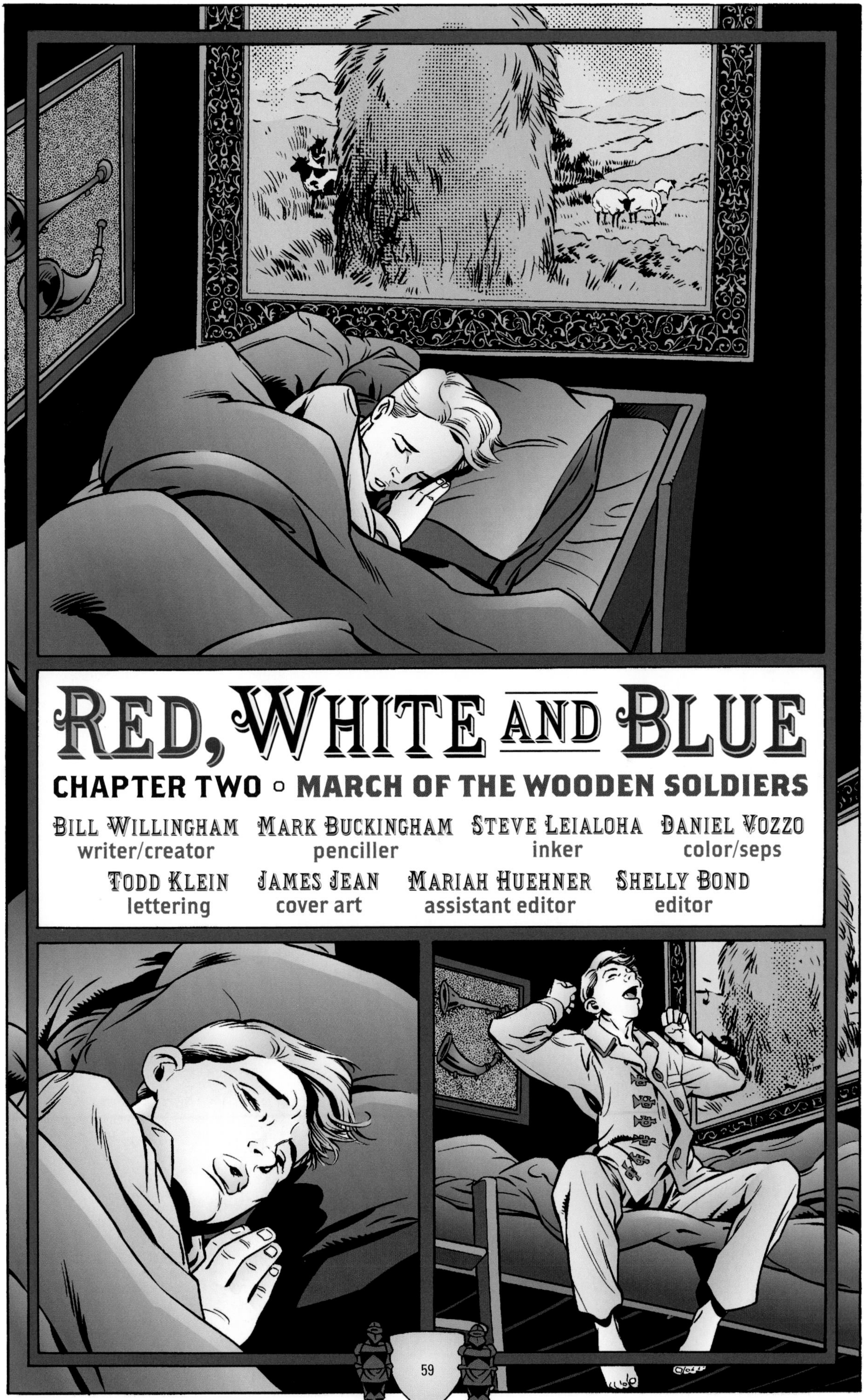
RED, WHITE AND BLUE
CHAPTER TWO ◦ MARCH OF THE WOODEN SOLDIERS
BILL WILLINGHAM writer/creator
MARK BUCKINGHAM penciller
STEVE LEIALOHA inker
DANIEL VOZZO color/seps
TODD KLEIN lettering
JAMES JEAN cover art
MARIAH HUEHNER assistant editor
SHELLY BOND editor

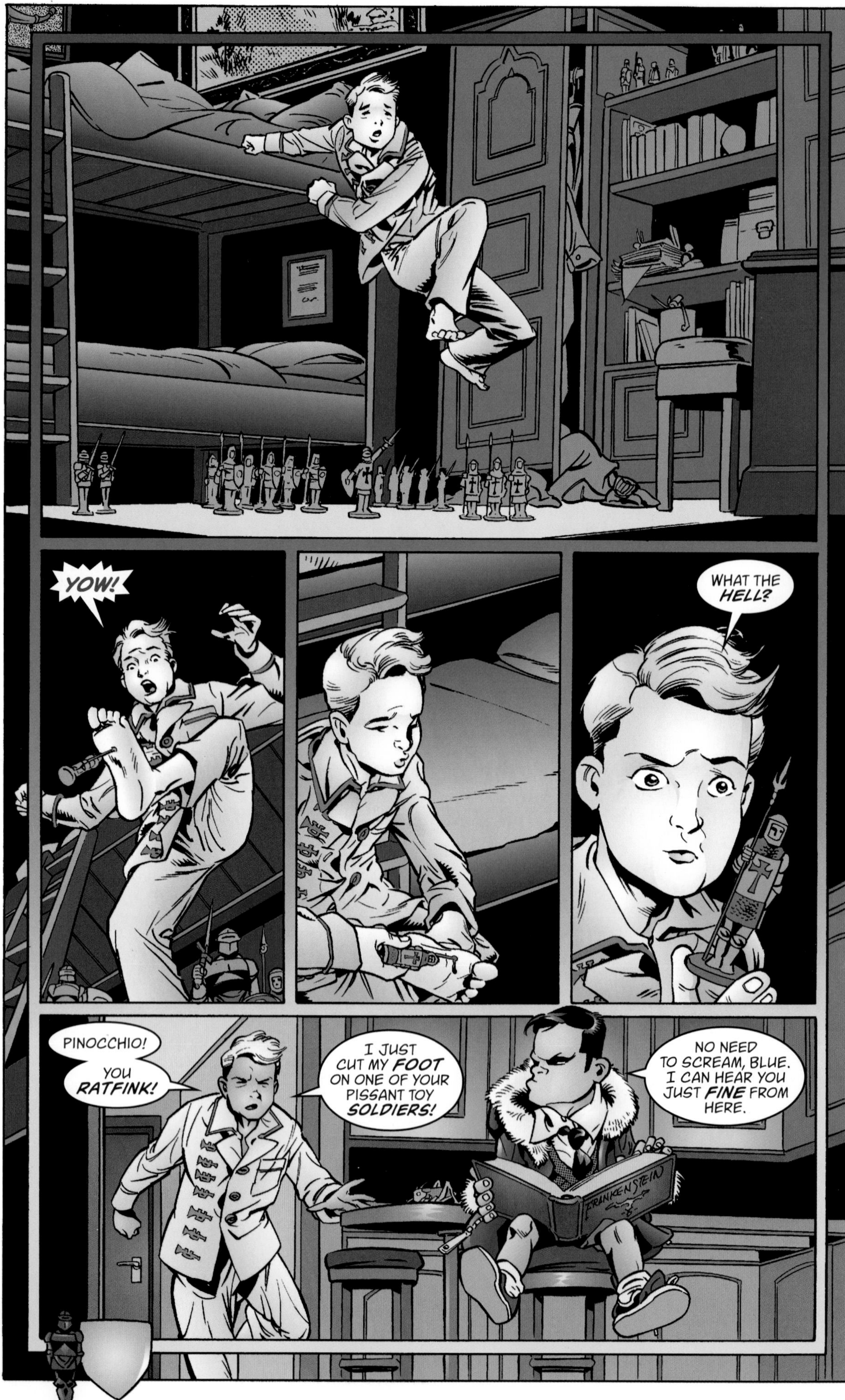

YOW!
WHAT THE HELL?
PINOCCHIO! YOU RATFINK!
I JUST CUT MY FOOT ON ONE OF YOUR PISSANT TOY SOLDIERS!
NO NEED TO SCREAM, BLUE. I CAN HEAR YOU JUST FINE FROM HERE.
FRANKENSTEIN

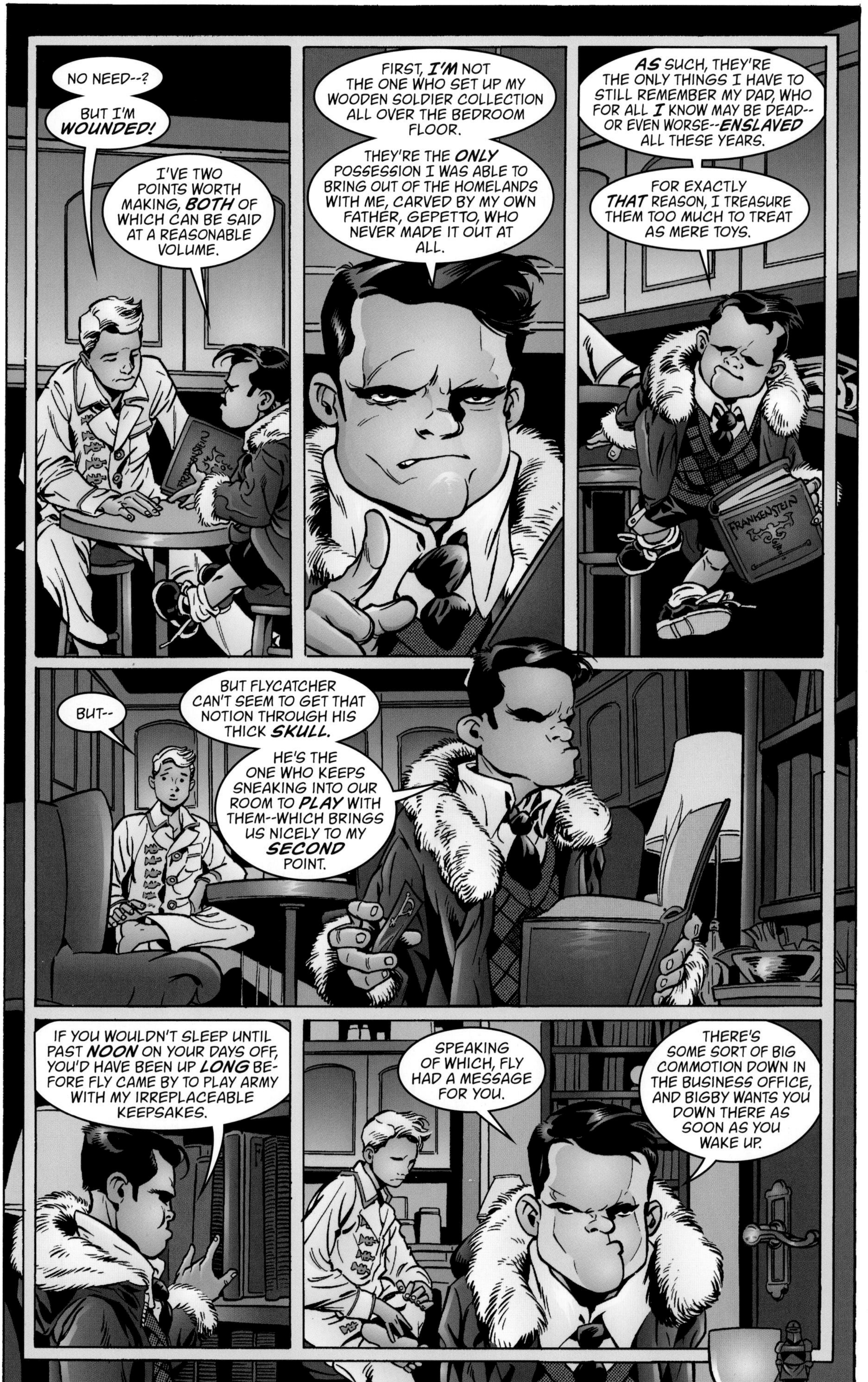
NO NEED--?
BUT I'M WOUNDED!
I'VE TWO POINTS WORTH MAKING, BOTH OF WHICH CAN BE SAID AT A REASONABLE VOLUME.
FIRST, I'M NOT THE ONE WHO SET UP MY WOODEN SOLDIER COLLECTION ALL OVER THE BEDROOM FLOOR.
THEY'RE THE ONLY POSSESSION I WAS ABLE TO BRING OUT OF THE HOMELANDS WITH ME, CARVED BY MY OWN FATHER, GEPETTO, WHO NEVER MADE IT OUT AT ALL.
AS SUCH, THEY'RE THE ONLY THINGS I HAVE TO STILL REMEMBER MY DAD, WHO FOR ALL I KNOW MAY BE DEAD--OR EVEN WORSE--ENSLAVED ALL THESE YEARS.
FOR EXACTLY THAT REASON, I TREASURE THEM TOO MUCH TO TREAT AS MERE TOYS.
FRANKENSTEIN
BUT--
BUT FLYCATCHER CAN'T SEEM TO GET THAT NOTION THROUGH HIS THICK SKULL.
HE'S THE ONE WHO KEEPS SNEAKING INTO OUR ROOM TO PLAY WITH THEM--WHICH BRINGS US NICELY TO MY SECOND POINT.
IF YOU WOULDN'T SLEEP UNTIL PAST NOON ON YOUR DAYS OFF, YOU'D HAVE BEEN UP LONG BEFORE FLY CAME BY TO PLAY ARMY WITH MY IRREPLACEABLE KEEPSAKES.
SPEAKING OF WHICH, FLY HAD A MESSAGE FOR YOU.
THERE'S SOME SORT OF BIG COMMOTION DOWN IN THE BUSINESS OFFICE, AND BIGBY WANTS YOU DOWN THERE AS SOON AS YOU WAKE UP.

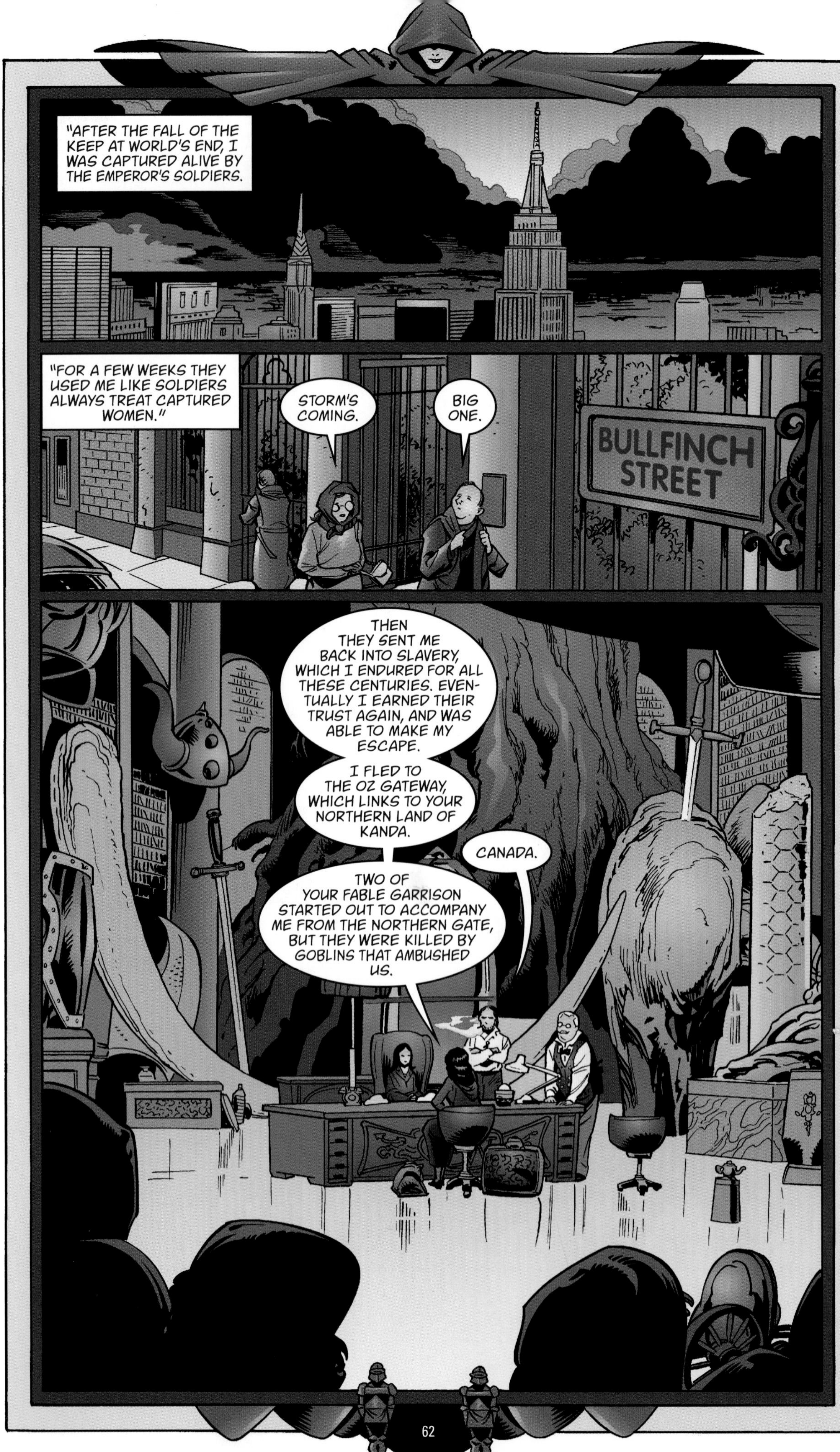
"AFTER THE FALL OF THE KEEP AT WORLD'S END, I WAS CAPTURED ALIVE BY THE EMPEROR'S SOLDIERS.
"FOR A FEW WEEKS THEY USED ME LIKE SOLDIERS ALWAYS TREAT CAPTURED WOMEN."
STORM'S COMING.
BIG ONE.
BULLFINCH STREET
THEN THEY SENT ME BACK INTO SLAVERY, WHICH I ENDURED FOR ALL THESE CENTURIES. EVENTUALLY I EARNED THEIR TRUST AGAIN, AND WAS ABLE TO MAKE MY ESCAPE.
I FLED TO THE OZ GATEWAY, WHICH LINKS TO YOUR NORTHERN LAND OF KANDA.
CANADA.
TWO OF YOUR FABLE GARRISON STARTED OUT TO ACCOMPANY ME FROM THE NORTHERN GATE, BUT THEY WERE KILLED BY GOBLINS THAT AMBUSHED US.

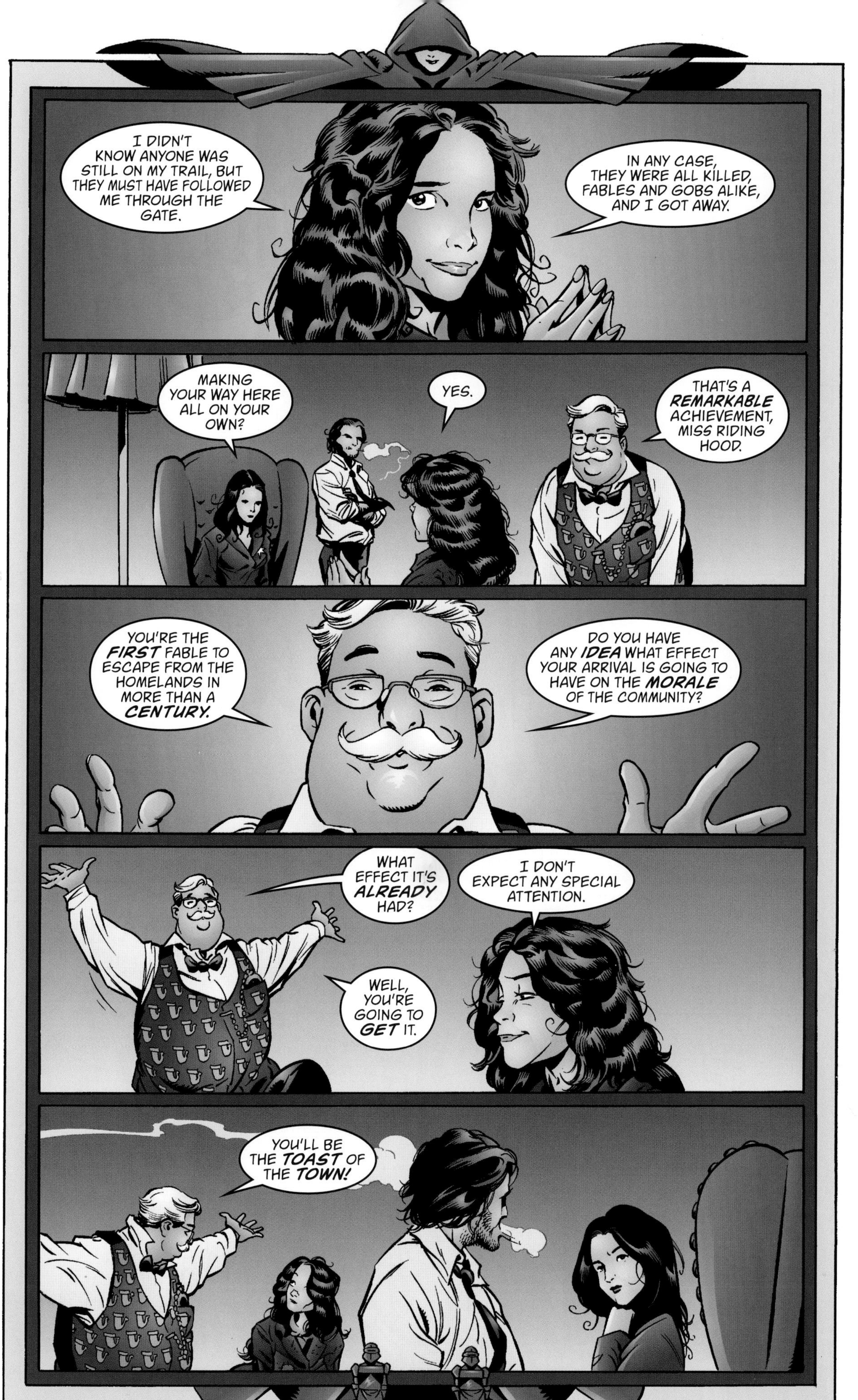
I DIDN'T KNOW ANYONE WAS STILL ON MY TRAIL, BUT THEY MUST HAVE FOLLOWED ME THROUGH THE GATE.
IN ANY CASE, THEY WERE ALL KILLED, FABLES AND GOBS ALIKE, AND I GOT AWAY.
MAKING YOUR WAY HERE ALL ON YOUR OWN?
YES.
THAT'S A REMARKABLE ACHIEVEMENT, MISS RIDING HOOD.
YOU'RE THE FIRST FABLE TO ESCAPE FROM THE HOMELANDS IN MORE THAN A CENTURY.
DO YOU HAVE ANY IDEA WHAT EFFECT YOUR ARRIVAL IS GOING TO HAVE ON THE MORALE OF THE COMMUNITY?
I DON'T EXPECT ANY SPECIAL ATTENTION.
WELL, YOU'RE GOING TO GET IT.
WHAT EFFECT IT'S ALREADY HAD?
YOU'LL BE THE TOAST OF THE TOWN!

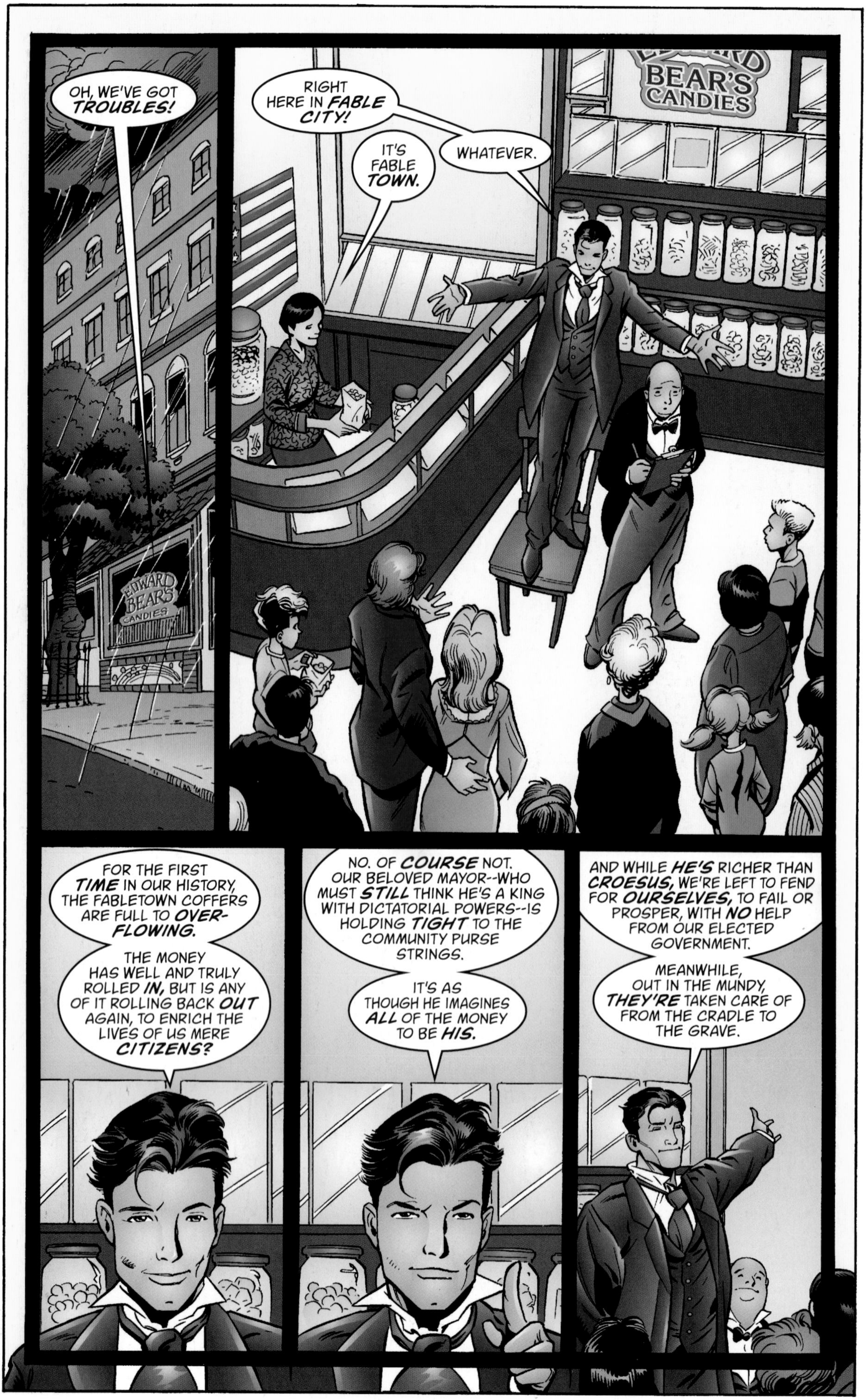
OH, WE'VE GOT TROUBLES!
BEAR'S CANDIES
RIGHT HERE IN FABLE CITY!
IT'S FABLE TOWN.
WHATEVER.
EDWARD BEAR'S CANDIES
FOR THE FIRST TIME IN OUR HISTORY, THE FABLETOWN COFFERS ARE FULL TO OVER-FLOWING.
THE MONEY HAS WELL AND TRULY ROLLED IN, BUT IS ANY OF IT ROLLING BACK OUT AGAIN, TO ENRICH THE LIVES OF US MERE CITIZENS?
NO. OF COURSE NOT. OUR BELOVED MAYOR--WHO MUST STILL THINK HE'S A KING WITH DICTATORIAL POWERS--IS HOLDING TIGHT TO THE COMMUNITY PURSE STRINGS.
IT'S AS THOUGH HE IMAGINES ALL OF THE MONEY TO BE HIS.
AND WHILE HE'S RICHER THAN CROESUS, WE'RE LEFT TO FEND FOR OURSELVES, TO FAIL OR PROSPER, WITH NO HELP FROM OUR ELECTED GOVERNMENT.
MEANWHILE, OUT IN THE MUNDY, THEY'RE TAKEN CARE OF FROM THE CRADLE TO THE GRAVE.

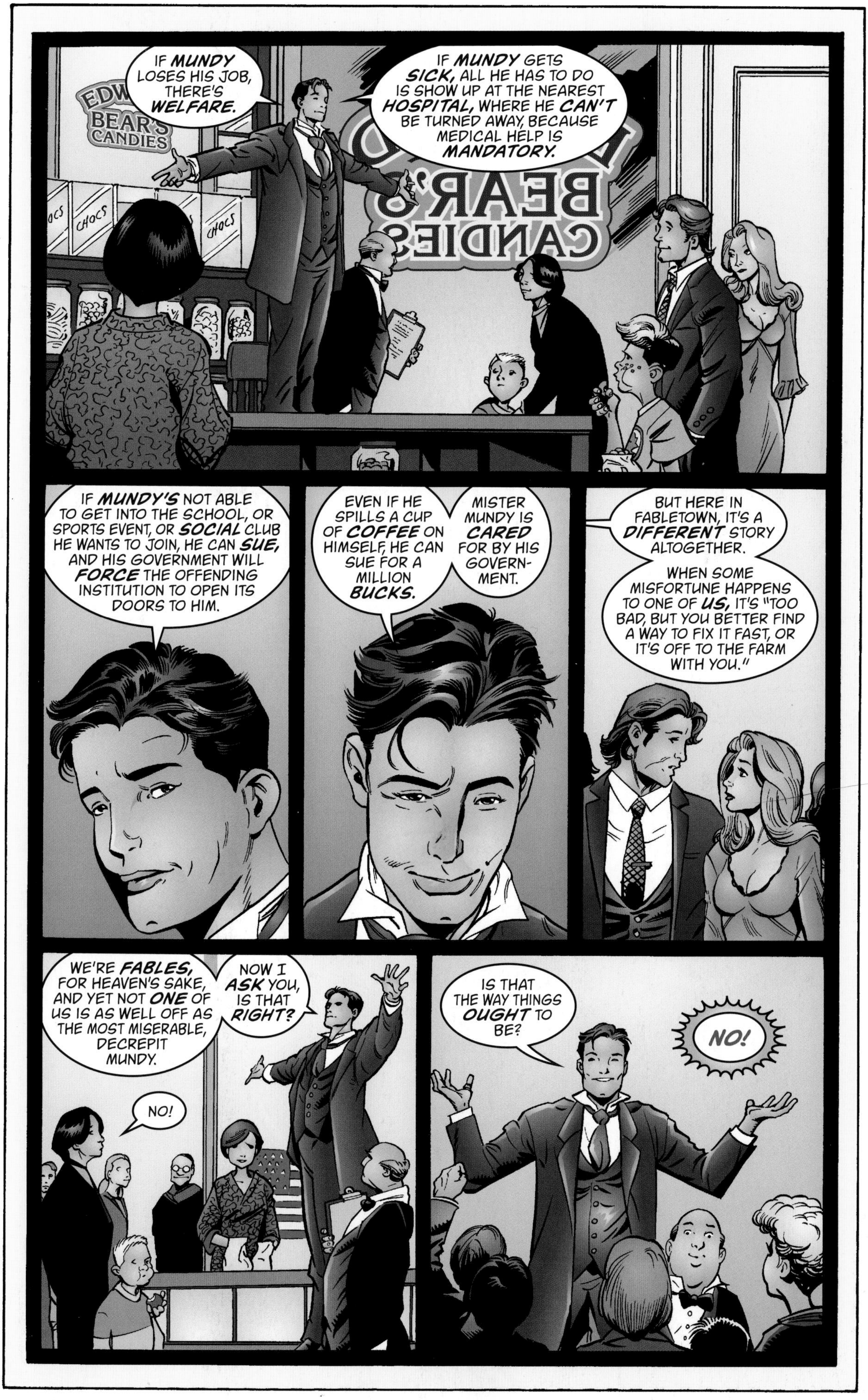
EDWARD BEAR'S CANDIES
IF MUNDY LOSES HIS JOB, THERE'S WELFARE.
IF MUNDY GETS SICK, ALL HE HAS TO DO IS SHOW UP AT THE NEAREST HOSPITAL, WHERE HE CAN'T BE TURNED AWAY, BECAUSE MEDICAL HELP IS MANDATORY.
CHOCS
CHOCS
CHOCS
BEAR'S CANDIES
IF MUNDY'S NOT ABLE TO GET INTO THE SCHOOL, OR SPORTS EVENT, OR SOCIAL CLUB HE WANTS TO JOIN, HE CAN SUE, AND HIS GOVERNMENT WILL FORCE THE OFFENDING INSTITUTION TO OPEN ITS DOORS TO HIM.
EVEN IF HE SPILLS A CUP OF COFFEE ON HIMSELF, HE CAN SUE FOR A MILLION BUCKS.
MISTER MUNDY IS CARED FOR BY HIS GOVERN-MENT.
BUT HERE IN FABLETOWN, IT'S A DIFFERENT STORY ALTOGETHER.
WHEN SOME MISFORTUNE HAPPENS TO ONE OF US, IT'S "TOO BAD, BUT YOU BETTER FIND A WAY TO FIX IT FAST, OR IT'S OFF TO THE FARM WITH YOU."
WE'RE FABLES, FOR HEAVEN'S SAKE, AND YET NOT ONE OF US IS AS WELL OFF AS THE MOST MISERABLE, DECREPIT MUNDY.
NOW I ASK YOU, IS THAT RIGHT?
NO!
IS THAT THE WAY THINGS OUGHT TO BE?
NO!

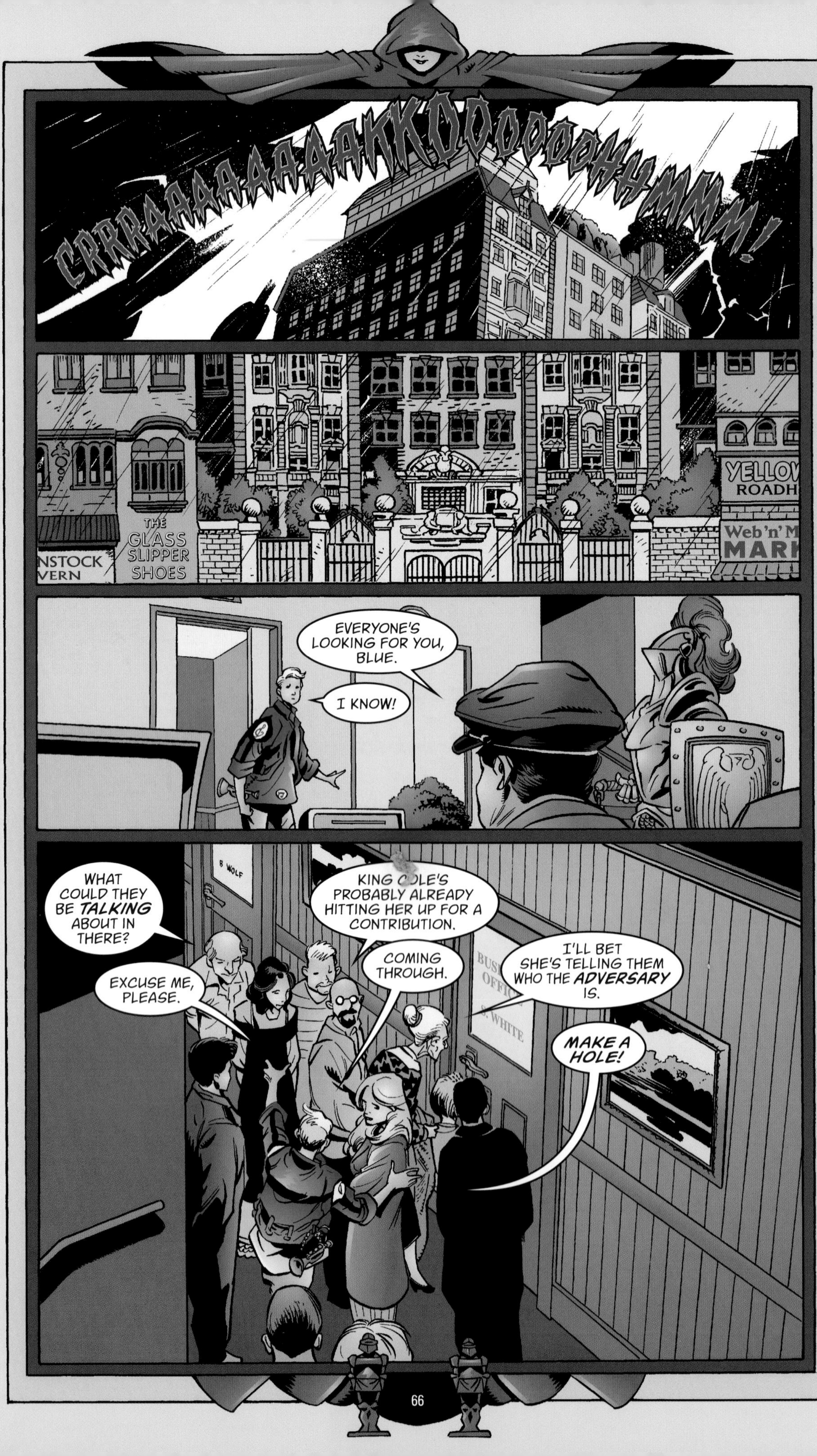
CRRAAAAAAAAAAKOOOOOOHMMM!
THE GLASS SLIPPER SHOES
NSTOCK VERN
YELLOW ROADH
Web'n'M MARK
EVERYONE'S LOOKING FOR YOU, BLUE.
I KNOW!
B WOLF
WHAT COULD THEY BE *TALKING* ABOUT IN THERE?
KING COLE'S PROBABLY ALREADY HITTING HER UP FOR A CONTRIBUTION.
EXCUSE ME, PLEASE.
COMING THROUGH.
I'LL BET SHE'S TELLING THEM WHO THE *ADVERSARY* IS.
MAKE A HOLE!

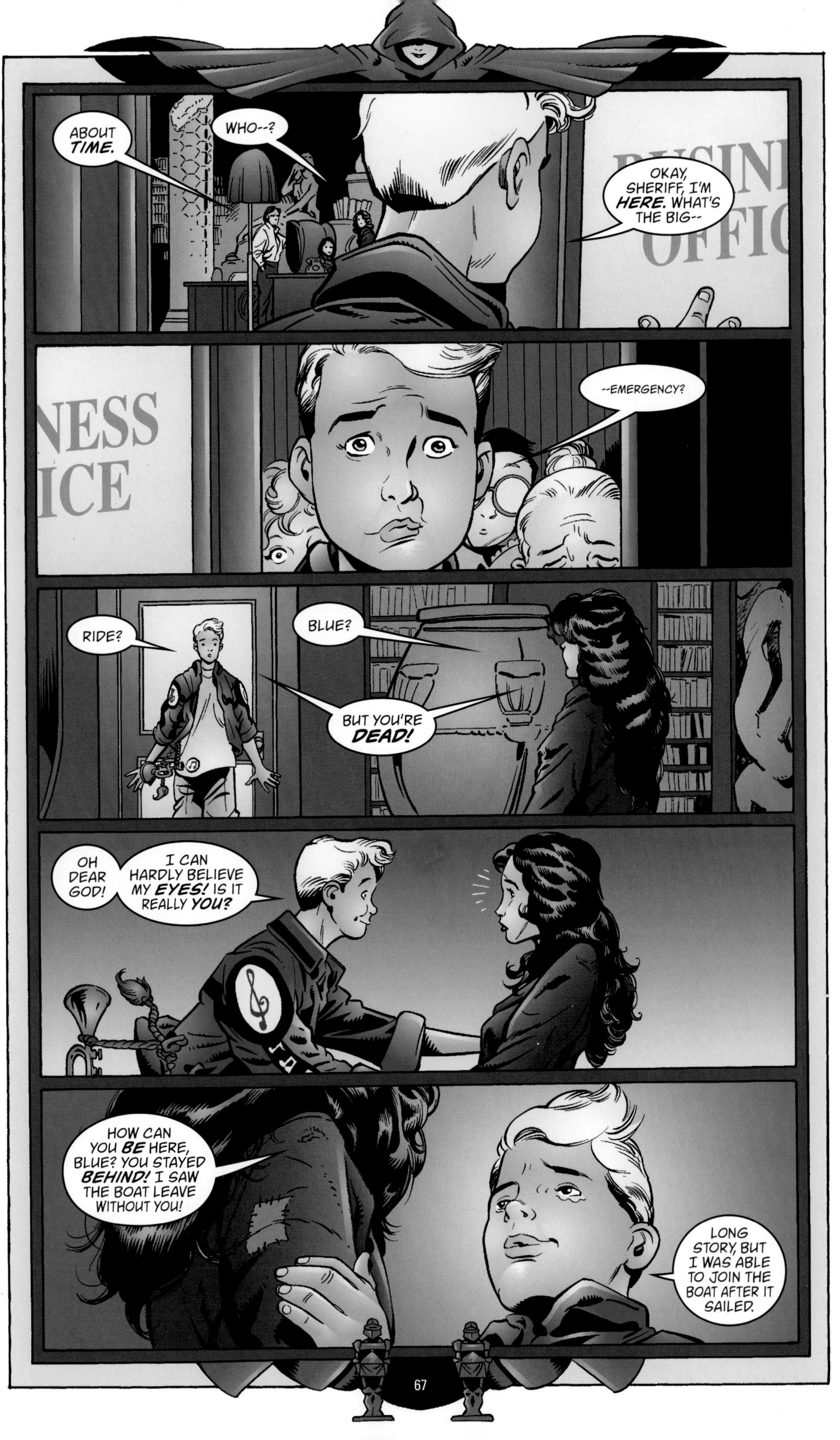

ABOUT TIME.
WHO--?
BUSINE OFFIC
OKAY, SHERIFF, I'M HERE. WHAT'S THE BIG--
NESS ICE
--EMERGENCY?
RIDE?
BLUE?
BUT YOU'RE DEAD!
OH DEAR GOD!
I CAN HARDLY BELIEVE MY EYES! IS IT REALLY YOU?
HOW CAN YOU BE HERE, BLUE? YOU STAYED BEHIND! I SAW THE BOAT LEAVE WITHOUT YOU!
LONG STORY, BUT I WAS ABLE TO JOIN THE BOAT AFTER IT SAILED.

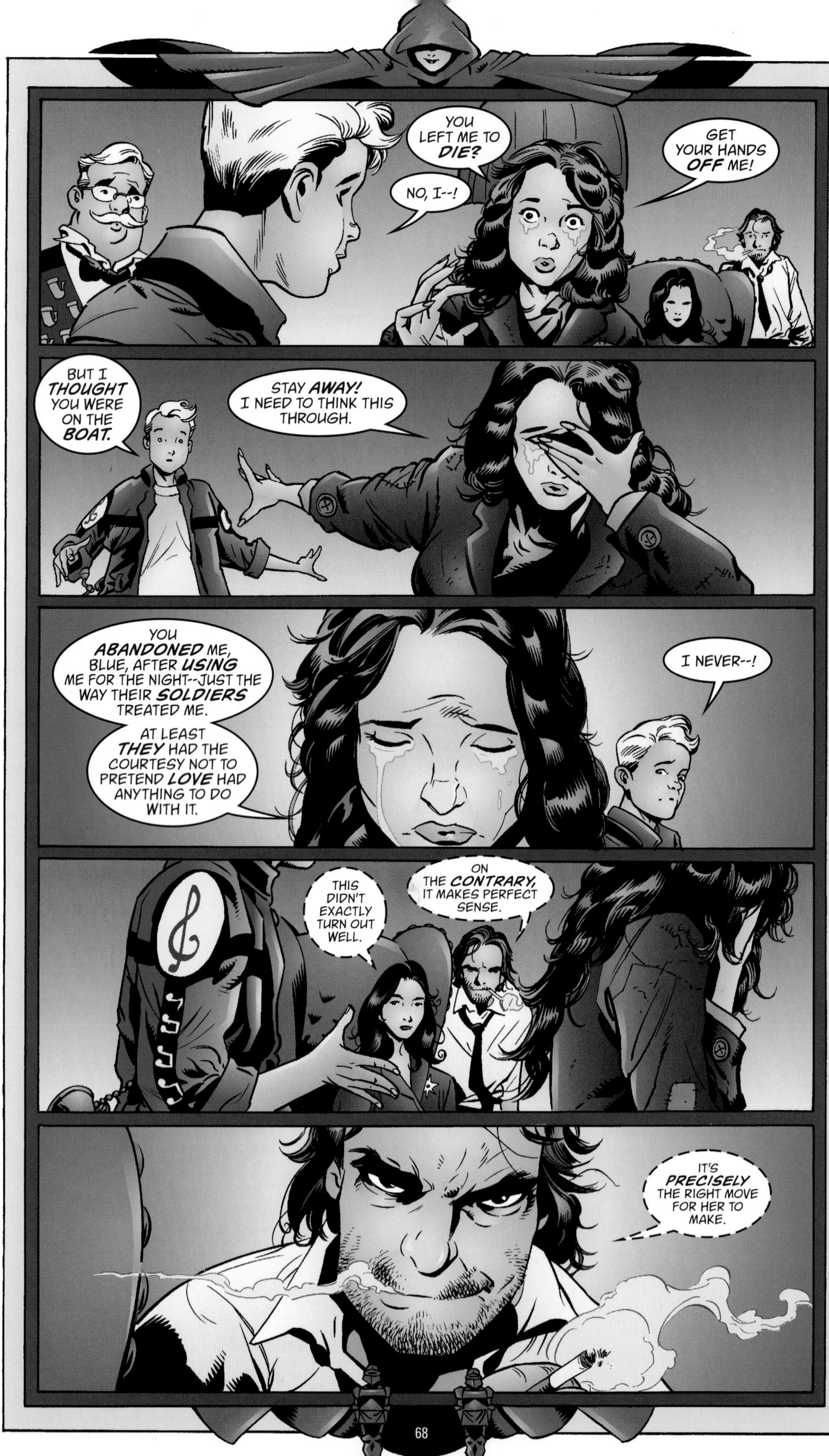

YOU LEFT ME TO DIE?
NO, I--!
GET YOUR HANDS OFF ME!
BUT I THOUGHT YOU WERE ON THE BOAT.
STAY AWAY! I NEED TO THINK THIS THROUGH.
YOU ABANDONED ME, BLUE, AFTER USING ME FOR THE NIGHT--JUST THE WAY THEIR SOLDIERS TREATED ME.
AT LEAST THEY HAD THE COURTESY NOT TO PRETEND LOVE HAD ANYTHING TO DO WITH IT.
I NEVER--!
THIS DIDN'T EXACTLY TURN OUT WELL.
ON THE CONTRARY, IT MAKES PERFECT SENSE.
IT'S PRECISELY THE RIGHT MOVE FOR HER TO MAKE.

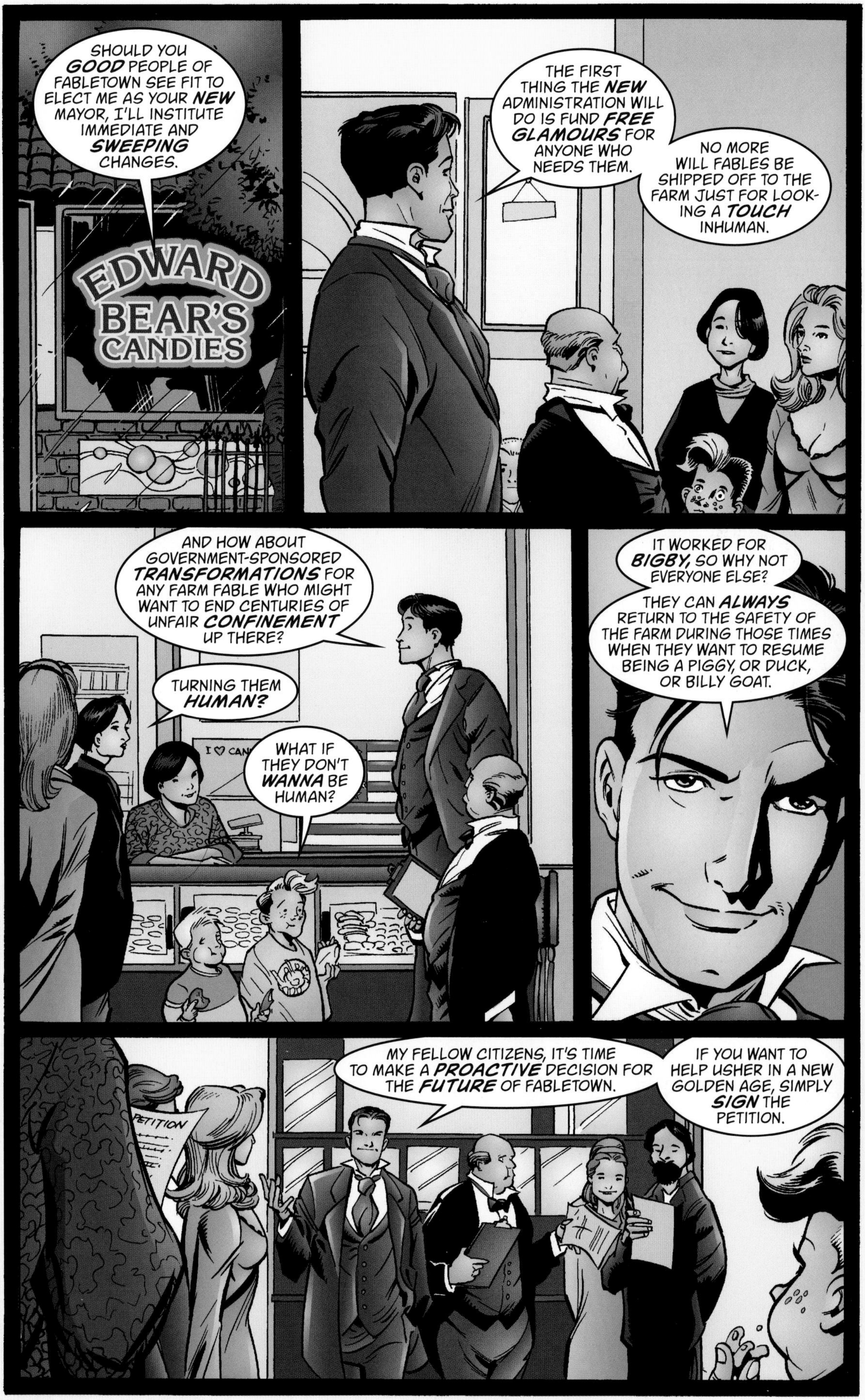

SHOULD YOU GOOD PEOPLE OF FABLETOWN SEE FIT TO ELECT ME AS YOUR NEW MAYOR, I'LL INSTITUTE IMMEDIATE AND SWEEPING CHANGES.
EDWARD BEAR'S CANDIES
THE FIRST THING THE NEW ADMINISTRATION WILL DO IS FUND FREE GLAMOURS FOR ANYONE WHO NEEDS THEM.
NO MORE WILL FABLES BE SHIPPED OFF TO THE FARM JUST FOR LOOKING A TOUCH INHUMAN.
AND HOW ABOUT GOVERNMENT-SPONSORED TRANSFORMATIONS FOR ANY FARM FABLE WHO MIGHT WANT TO END CENTURIES OF UNFAIR CONFINEMENT UP THERE?
TURNING THEM HUMAN?
WHAT IF THEY DON'T WANNA BE HUMAN?
IT WORKED FOR BIGBY, SO WHY NOT EVERYONE ELSE?
THEY CAN ALWAYS RETURN TO THE SAFETY OF THE FARM DURING THOSE TIMES WHEN THEY WANT TO RESUME BEING A PIGGY, OR DUCK, OR BILLY GOAT.
PETITION
MY FELLOW CITIZENS, IT'S TIME TO MAKE A PROACTIVE DECISION FOR THE FUTURE OF FABLETOWN.
IF YOU WANT TO HELP USHER IN A NEW GOLDEN AGE, SIMPLY SIGN THE PETITION.

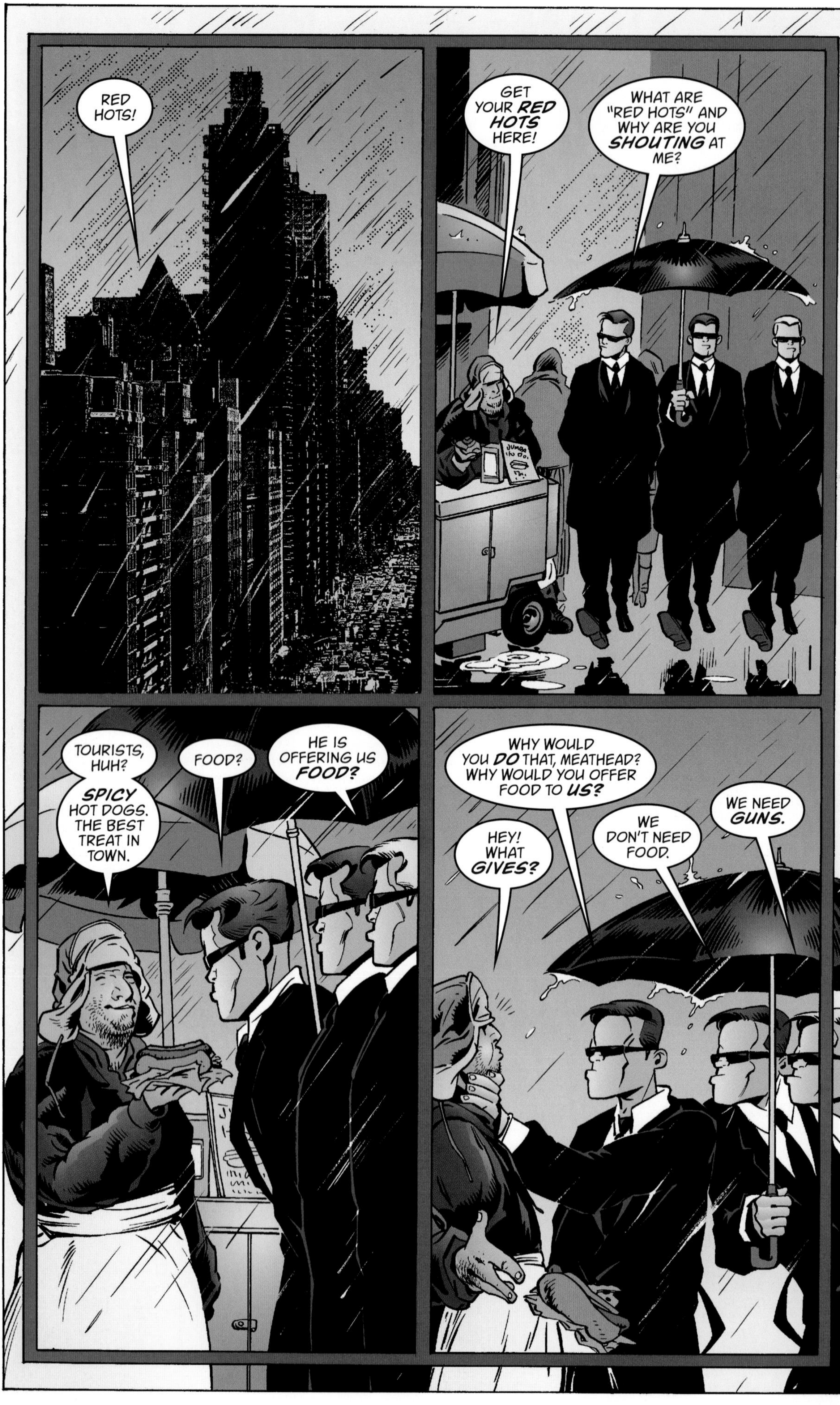
RED HOTS!
GET YOUR RED HOTS HERE!
WHAT ARE "RED HOTS" AND WHY ARE YOU SHOUTING AT ME?
TOURISTS, HUH?
SPICY HOT DOGS. THE BEST TREAT IN TOWN.
FOOD?
HE IS OFFERING US FOOD?
WHY WOULD YOU DO THAT, MEATHEAD? WHY WOULD YOU OFFER FOOD TO US?
HEY! WHAT GIVES?
WE DON'T NEED FOOD.
WE NEED GUNS.

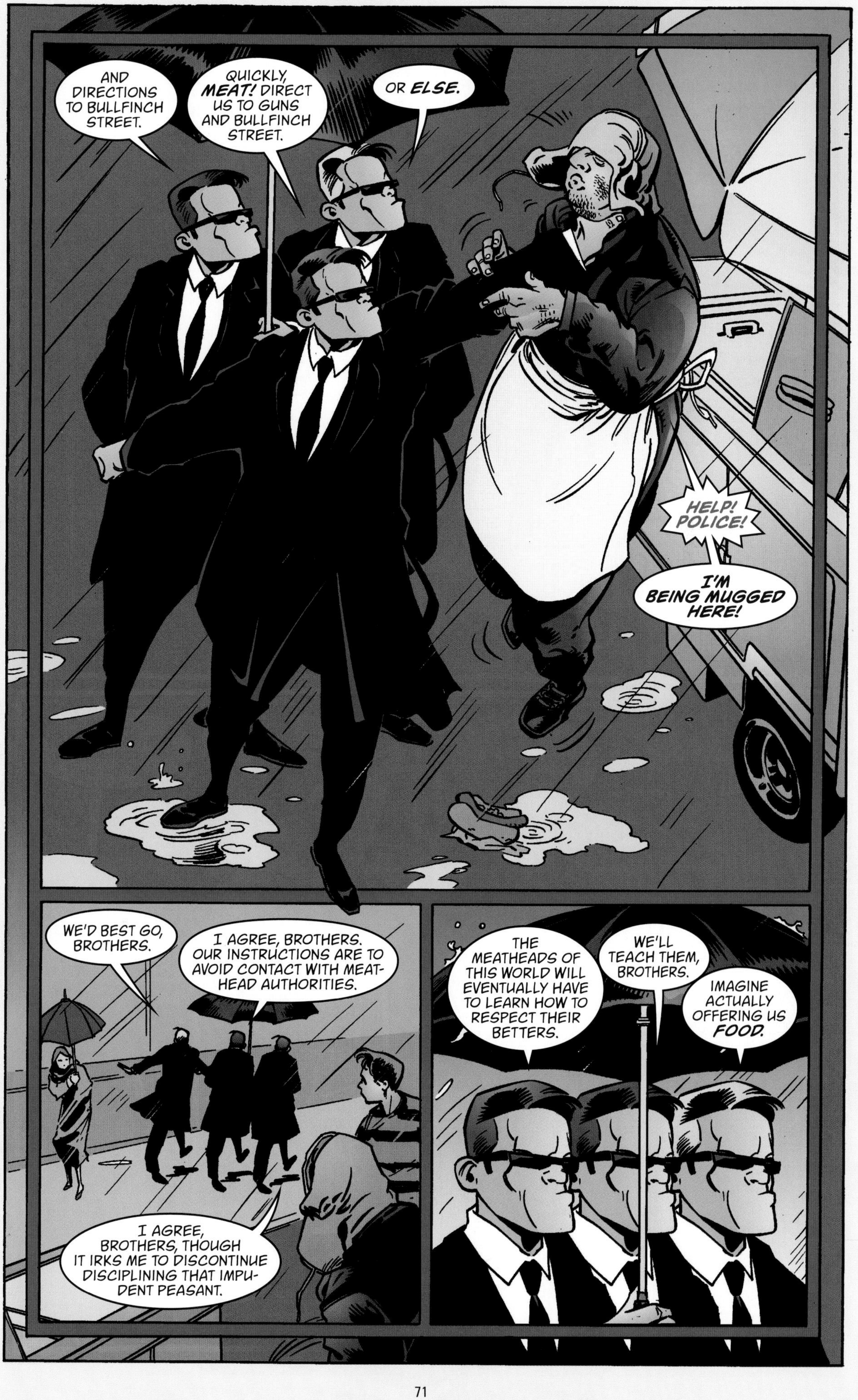
AND DIRECTIONS TO BULLFINCH STREET.
QUICKLY, MEAT! DIRECT US TO GUNS AND BULLFINCH STREET.
OR ELSE.
HELP! POLICE!
I'M BEING MUGGED HERE!
WE'D BEST GO, BROTHERS.
I AGREE, BROTHERS. OUR INSTRUCTIONS ARE TO AVOID CONTACT WITH MEAT-HEAD AUTHORITIES.
I AGREE, BROTHERS, THOUGH IT IRKS ME TO DISCONTINUE DISCIPLINING THAT IMPU-DENT PEASANT.
THE MEATHEADS OF THIS WORLD WILL EVENTUALLY HAVE TO LEARN HOW TO RESPECT THEIR BETTERS.
WE'LL TEACH THEM, BROTHERS.
IMAGINE ACTUALLY OFFERING US FOOD.

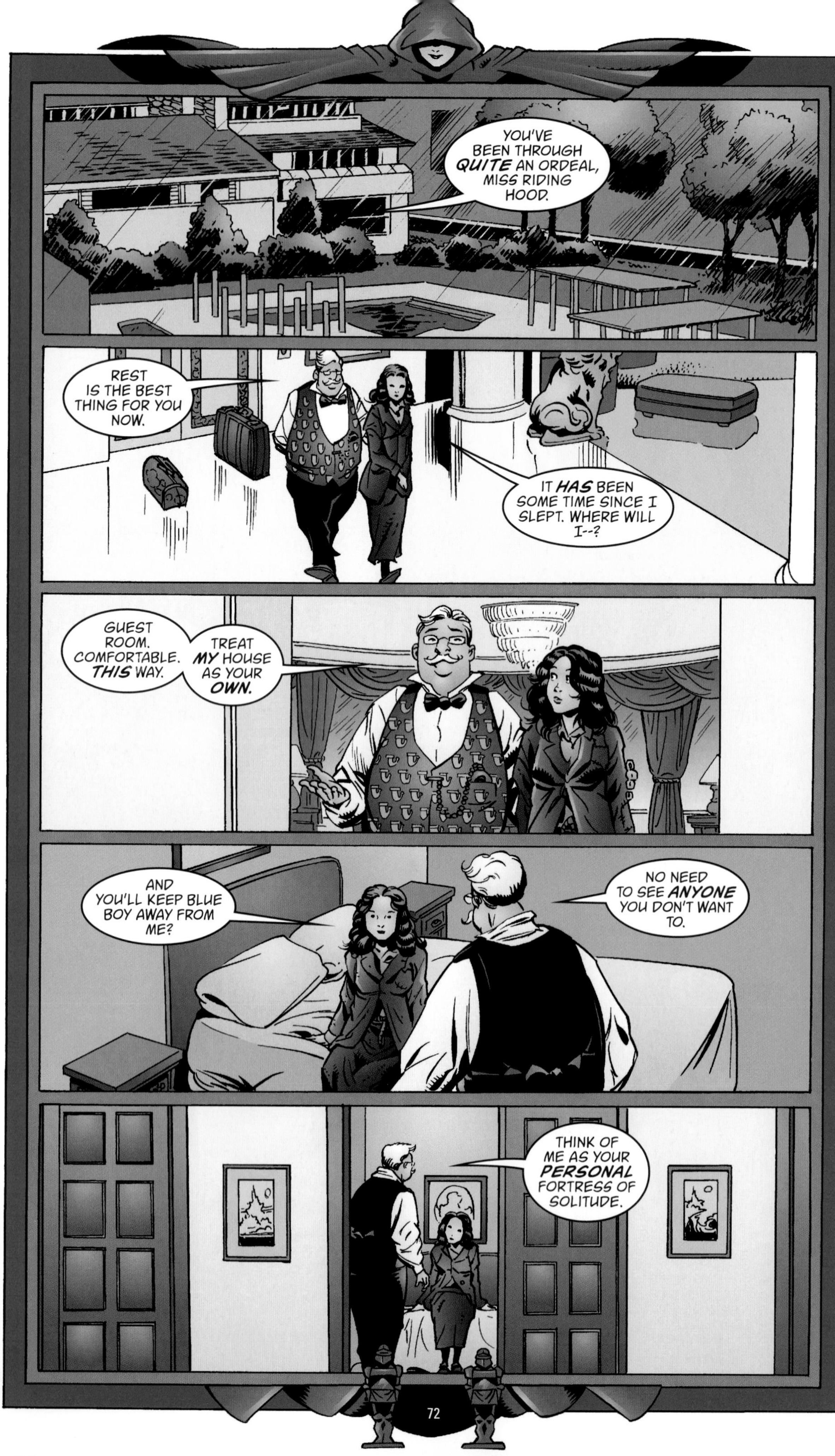
YOU'VE BEEN THROUGH QUITE AN ORDEAL, MISS RIDING HOOD.
REST IS THE BEST THING FOR YOU NOW.
IT HAS BEEN SOME TIME SINCE I SLEPT. WHERE WILL I--?
GUEST ROOM. COMFORTABLE. THIS WAY.
TREAT MY HOUSE AS YOUR OWN.
AND YOU'LL KEEP BLUE BOY AWAY FROM ME?
NO NEED TO SEE ANYONE YOU DON'T WANT TO.
THINK OF ME AS YOUR PERSONAL FORTRESS OF SOLITUDE.

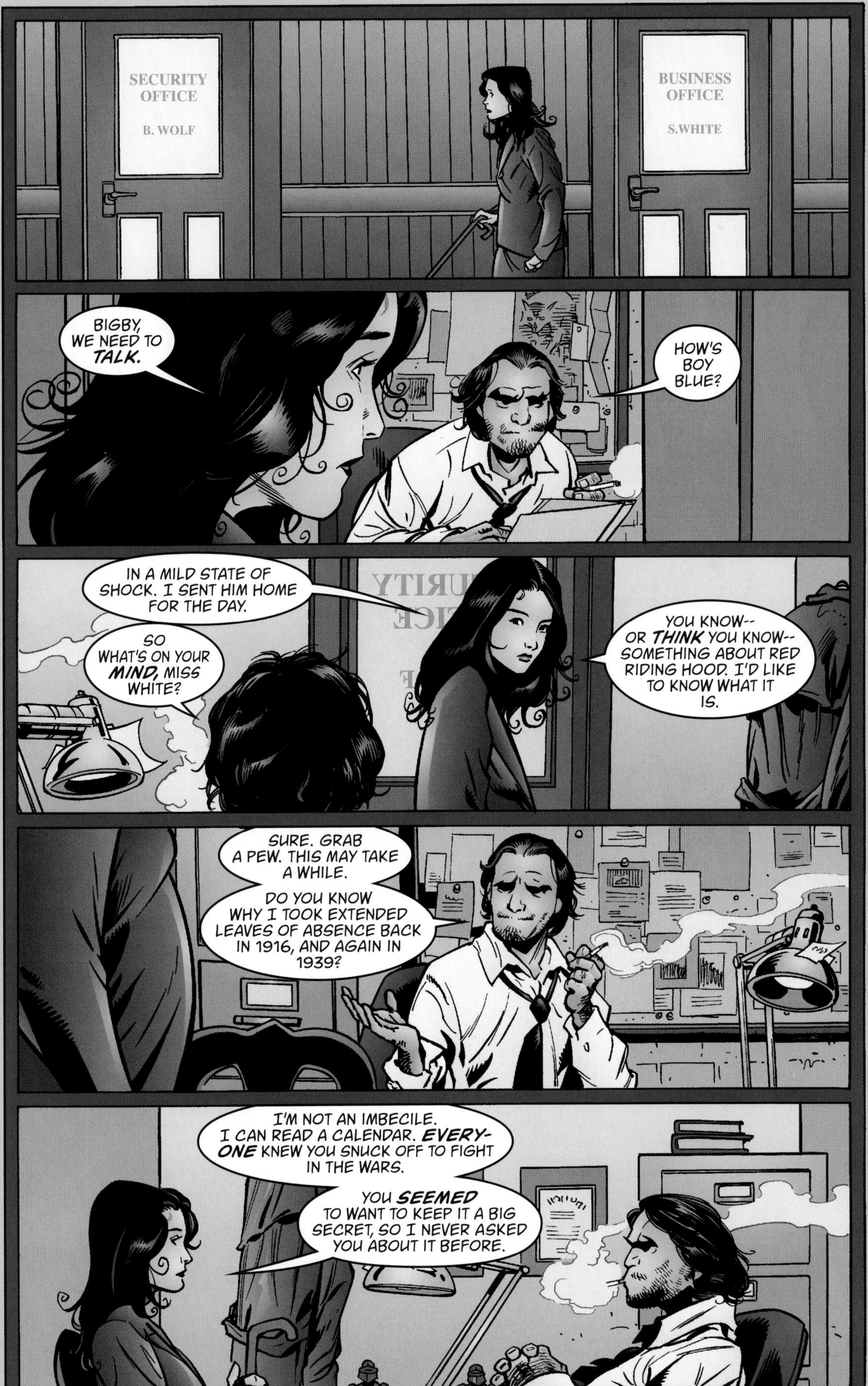
SECURITY OFFICE
B. WOLF
BUSINESS OFFICE
S.WHITE
BIGBY, WE NEED TO TALK.
HOW'S BOY BLUE?
IN A MILD STATE OF SHOCK. I SENT HIM HOME FOR THE DAY.
SO WHAT'S ON YOUR MIND, MISS WHITE?
YOU KNOW-- OR THINK YOU KNOW-- SOMETHING ABOUT RED RIDING HOOD. I'D LIKE TO KNOW WHAT IT IS.
SURE. GRAB A PEW. THIS MAY TAKE A WHILE.
DO YOU KNOW WHY I TOOK EXTENDED LEAVES OF ABSENCE BACK IN 1916, AND AGAIN IN 1939?
I'M NOT AN IMBECILE. I CAN READ A CALENDAR. EVERY-ONE KNEW YOU SNUCK OFF TO FIGHT IN THE WARS.
YOU SEEMED TO WANT TO KEEP IT A BIG SECRET, SO I NEVER ASKED YOU ABOUT IT BEFORE.

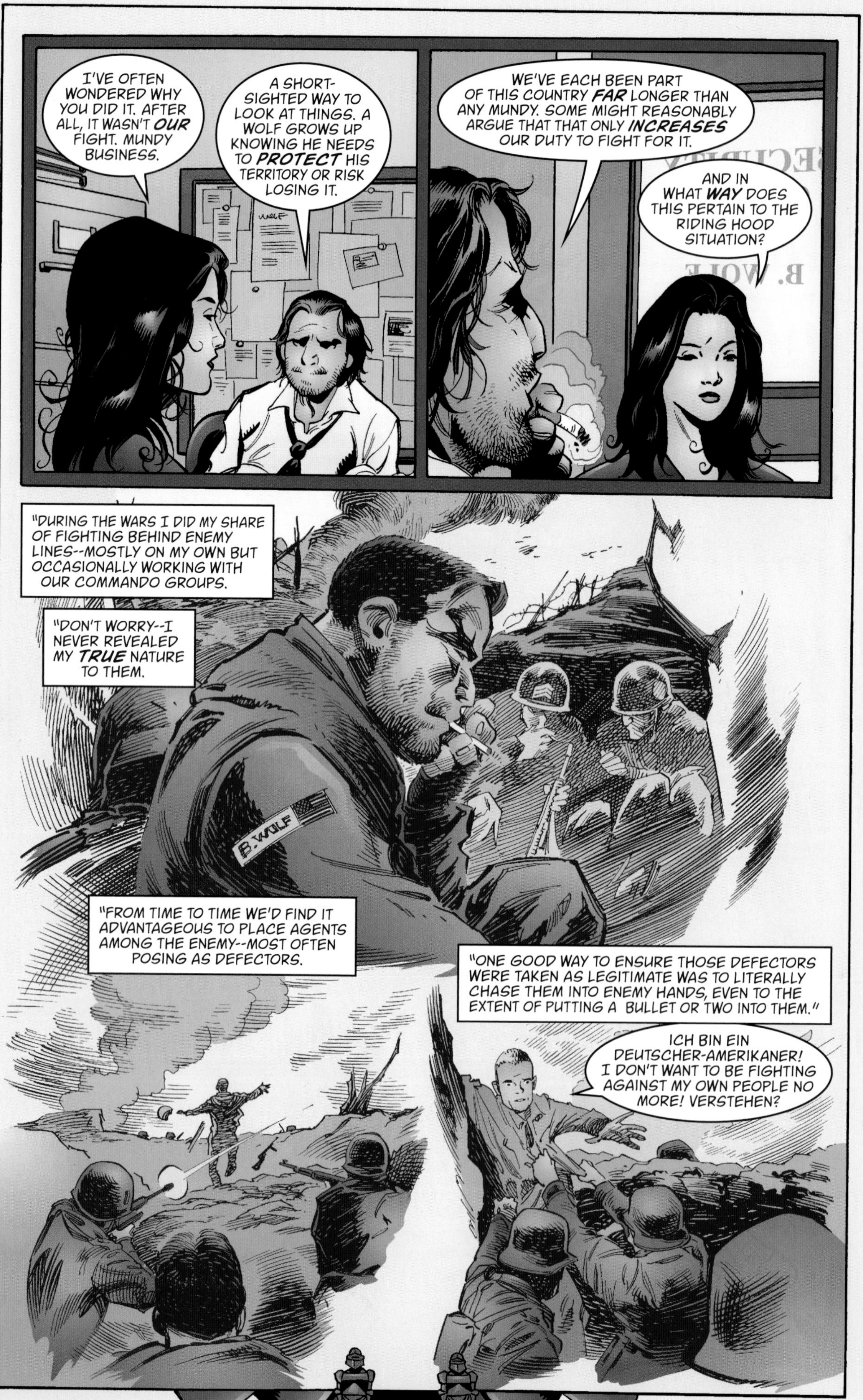
I'VE OFTEN WONDERED WHY YOU DID IT. AFTER ALL, IT WASN'T OUR FIGHT. MUNDY BUSINESS.
A SHORT-SIGHTED WAY TO LOOK AT THINGS. A WOLF GROWS UP KNOWING HE NEEDS TO PROTECT HIS TERRITORY OR RISK LOSING IT.
WE'VE EACH BEEN PART OF THIS COUNTRY FAR LONGER THAN ANY MUNDY. SOME MIGHT REASONABLY ARGUE THAT THAT ONLY INCREASES OUR DUTY TO FIGHT FOR IT.
AND IN WHAT WAY DOES THIS PERTAIN TO THE RIDING HOOD SITUATION?
"DURING THE WARS I DID MY SHARE OF FIGHTING BEHIND ENEMY LINES--MOSTLY ON MY OWN BUT OCCASIONALLY WORKING WITH OUR COMMANDO GROUPS.
"DON'T WORRY--I NEVER REVEALED MY TRUE NATURE TO THEM.
"FROM TIME TO TIME WE'D FIND IT ADVANTAGEOUS TO PLACE AGENTS AMONG THE ENEMY--MOST OFTEN POSING AS DEFECTORS.
"ONE GOOD WAY TO ENSURE THOSE DEFECTORS WERE TAKEN AS LEGITIMATE WAS TO LITERALLY CHASE THEM INTO ENEMY HANDS, EVEN TO THE EXTENT OF PUTTING A BULLET OR TWO INTO THEM."
ICH BIN EIN DEUTSCHER-AMERIKANER! I DON'T WANT TO BE FIGHTING AGAINST MY OWN PEOPLE NO MORE! VERSTEHEN?

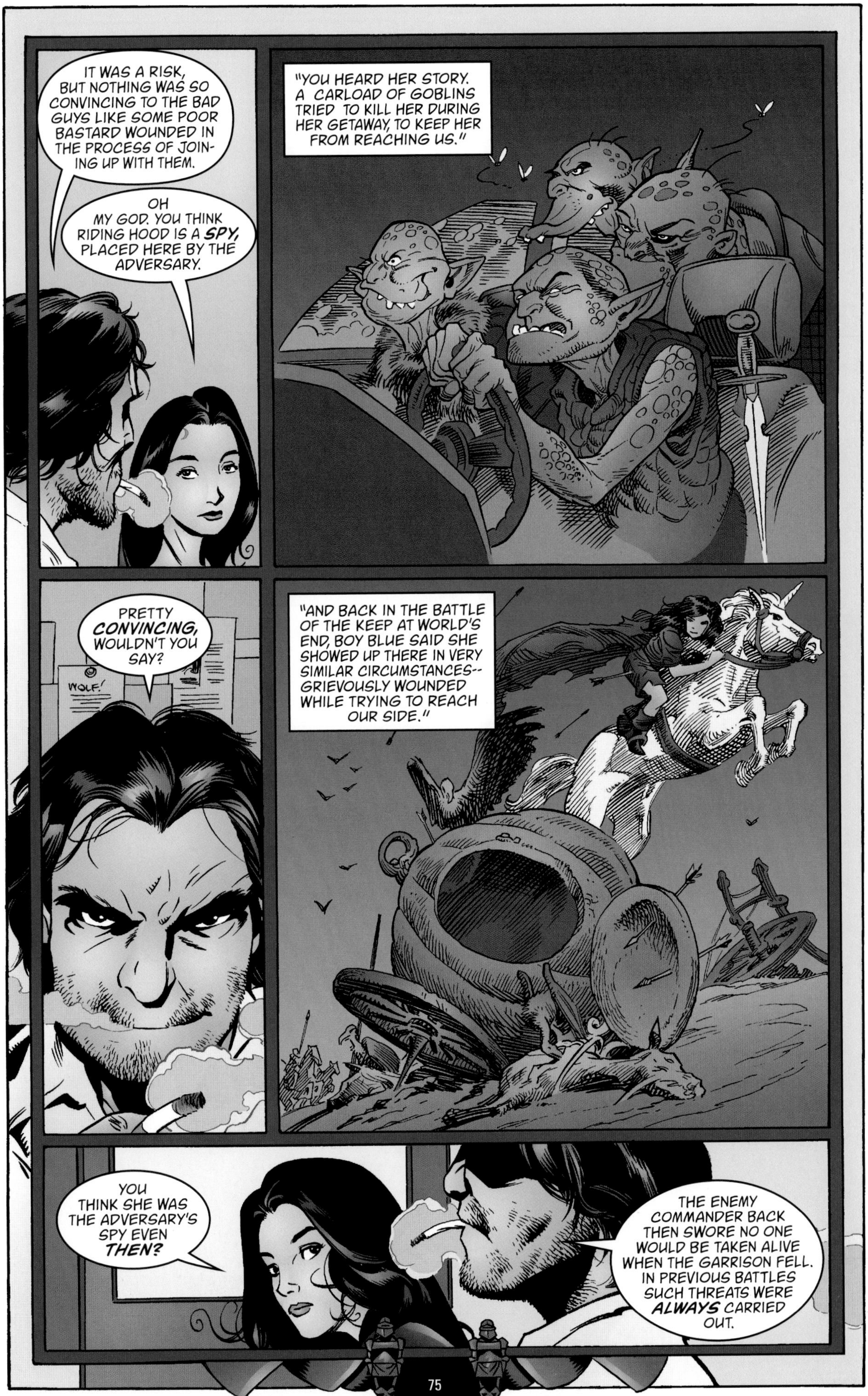
IT WAS A RISK, BUT NOTHING WAS SO CONVINCING TO THE BAD GUYS LIKE SOME POOR BASTARD WOUNDED IN THE PROCESS OF JOIN-ING UP WITH THEM.
OH MY GOD. YOU THINK RIDING HOOD IS A SPY, PLACED HERE BY THE ADVERSARY.
"YOU HEARD HER STORY. A CARLOAD OF GOBLINS TRIED TO KILL HER DURING HER GETAWAY, TO KEEP HER FROM REACHING US."
PRETTY CONVINCING, WOULDN'T YOU SAY?
WOLF!
"AND BACK IN THE BATTLE OF THE KEEP AT WORLD'S END, BOY BLUE SAID SHE SHOWED UP THERE IN VERY SIMILAR CIRCUMSTANCES-- GRIEVOUSLY WOUNDED WHILE TRYING TO REACH OUR SIDE."
YOU THINK SHE WAS THE ADVERSARY'S SPY EVEN THEN?
THE ENEMY COMMANDER BACK THEN SWORE NO ONE WOULD BE TAKEN ALIVE WHEN THE GARRISON FELL. IN PREVIOUS BATTLES SUCH THREATS WERE ALWAYS CARRIED OUT.

"SO WHY DID THEY LET HER AND **ONLY** HER LIVE? DID THEY REALLY NEED ONE MORE **SCRUB** WOMAN SO DESPERATELY?"

"ALSO, THE CANADA GATE HAS BEEN BLOCKED FOR NEARLY TWO HUNDRED YEARS, AND IT WAS CLOSED FROM THE OTHER SIDE--BY THE ADVERSARY'S FORCES, NOT OURS."

SUMMON THE COURT WARLOCKS. I WANT THIS GATE SHUT DOWN BY **NIGHT-FALL**.

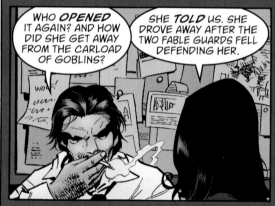

WHO **OPENED** IT AGAIN? AND HOW DID SHE GET AWAY FROM THE CARLOAD OF GOBLINS?

SHE **TOLD** US. SHE DROVE AWAY AFTER THE TWO FABLE GUARDS FELL DEFENDING HER.

YEAH, AND WHO TAUGHT HER TO **DRIVE?** AND WHO PROVIDED THE **PURSUING** GOBS WITH A CAR OF THEIR OWN?

IT WAS ALL A SETUP?

SECURITY

B. WOLF

"SOMEONE IN THE HOMELANDS CAREFULLY PREPARED EVERY PLAYER TO ACT HIS PART."

ONE PEDAL IS FOR MAKING THE MACHINE **GO.** ONE MAKES IT **STOP** AND THE THIRD IS NEEDED TO CHANGE GEARS.

WHAT'S **GEARS?**

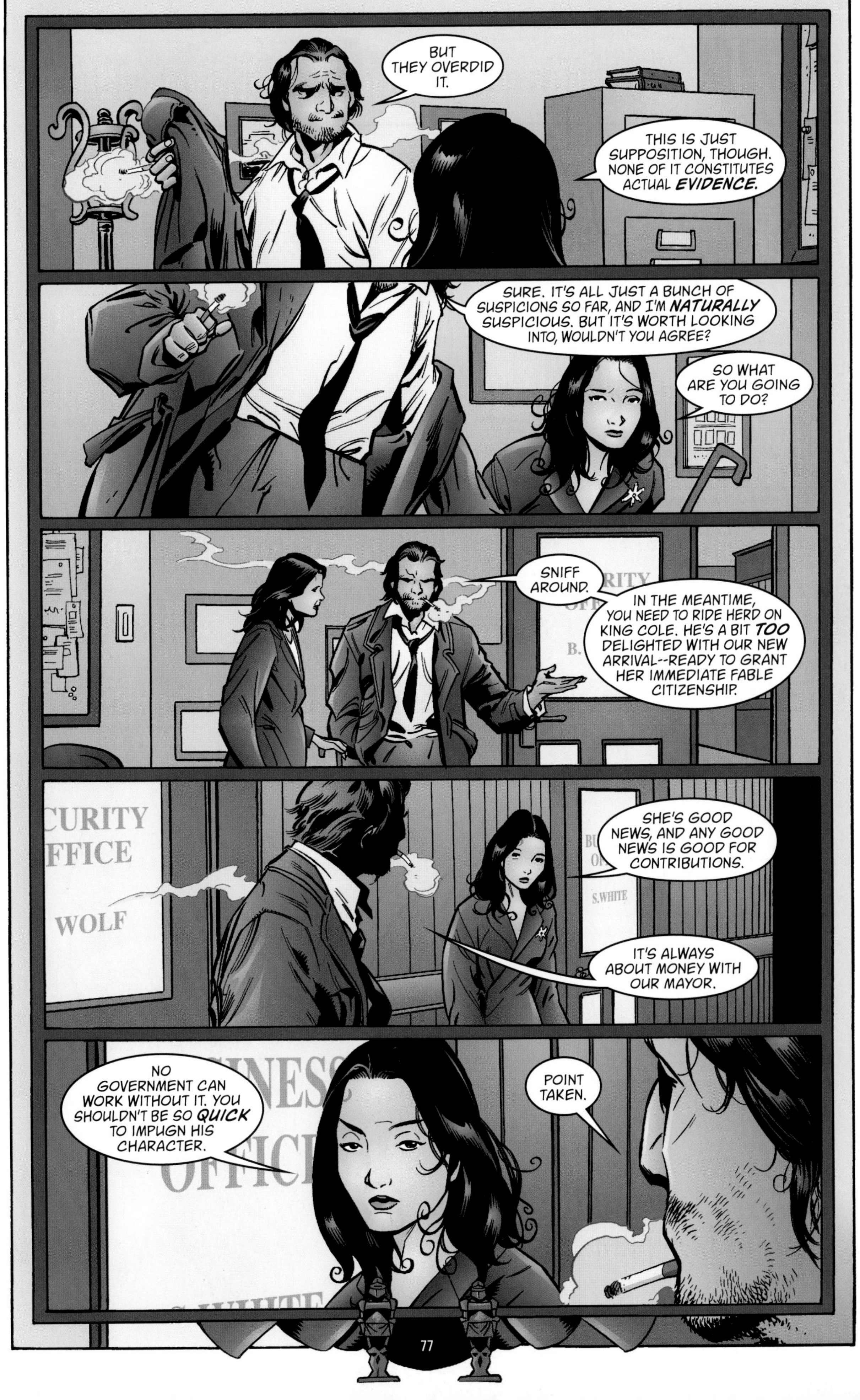
BUT THEY OVERDID IT.
THIS IS JUST SUPPOSITION, THOUGH. NONE OF IT CONSTITUTES ACTUAL EVIDENCE.
SURE. IT'S ALL JUST A BUNCH OF SUSPICIONS SO FAR, AND I'M NATURALLY SUSPICIOUS. BUT IT'S WORTH LOOKING INTO, WOULDN'T YOU AGREE?
SO WHAT ARE YOU GOING TO DO?
SNIFF AROUND.
IN THE MEANTIME, YOU NEED TO RIDE HERD ON KING COLE. HE'S A BIT TOO DELIGHTED WITH OUR NEW ARRIVAL--READY TO GRANT HER IMMEDIATE FABLE CITIZENSHIP.
CURITY
FFICE
WOLF
S.WHITE
SHE'S GOOD NEWS, AND ANY GOOD NEWS IS GOOD FOR CONTRIBUTIONS.
IT'S ALWAYS ABOUT MONEY WITH OUR MAYOR.
NO GOVERNMENT CAN WORK WITHOUT IT. YOU SHOULDN'T BE SO QUICK TO IMPUGN HIS CHARACTER.
POINT TAKEN.

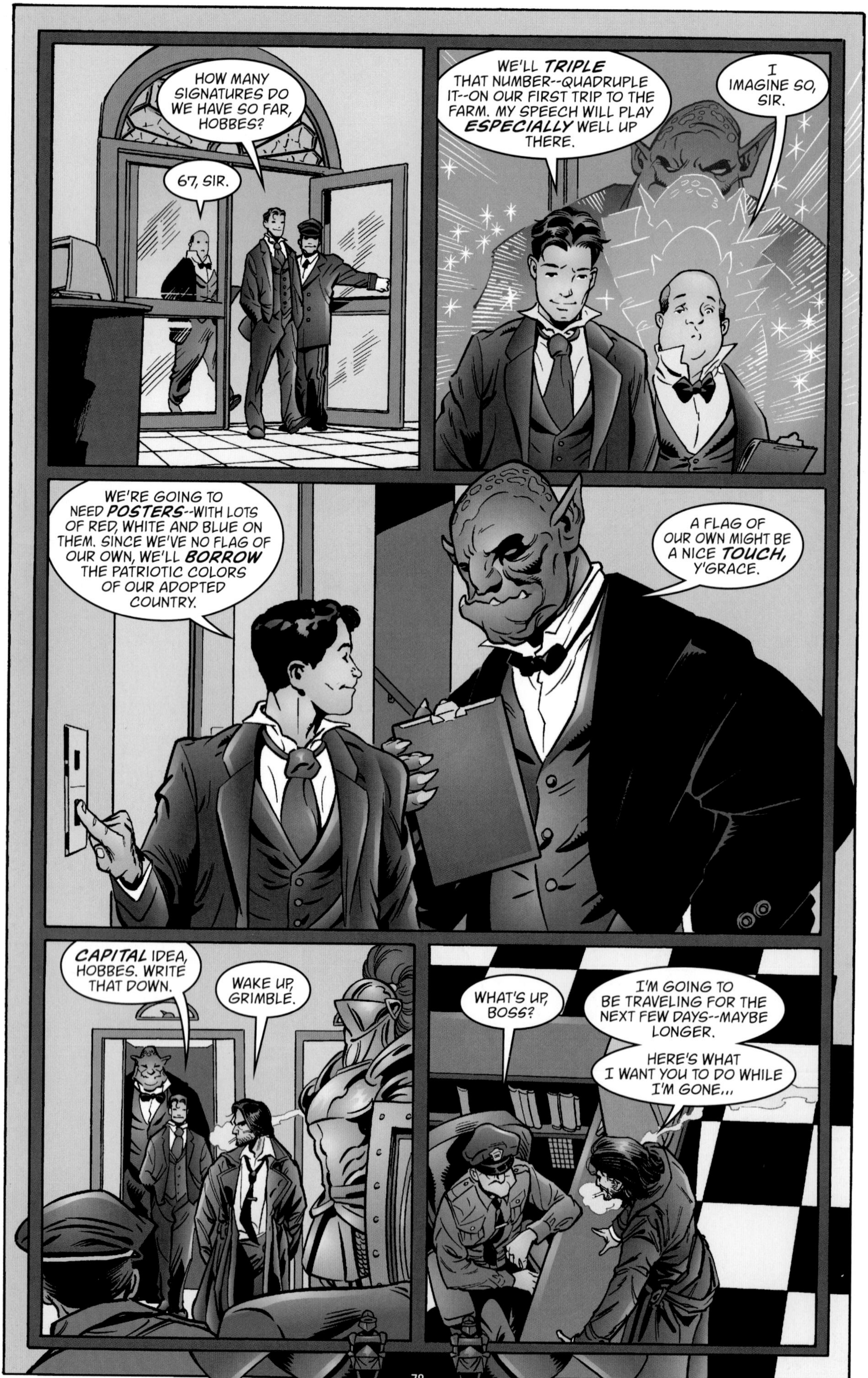
HOW MANY SIGNATURES DO WE HAVE SO FAR, HOBBES?
67, SIR.
WE'LL TRIPLE THAT NUMBER--QUADRUPLE IT--ON OUR FIRST TRIP TO THE FARM. MY SPEECH WILL PLAY ESPECIALLY WELL UP THERE.
I IMAGINE SO, SIR.
WE'RE GOING TO NEED POSTERS--WITH LOTS OF RED, WHITE AND BLUE ON THEM. SINCE WE'VE NO FLAG OF OUR OWN, WE'LL BORROW THE PATRIOTIC COLORS OF OUR ADOPTED COUNTRY.
A FLAG OF OUR OWN MIGHT BE A NICE TOUCH, Y'GRACE.
CAPITAL IDEA, HOBBES. WRITE THAT DOWN.
WAKE UP, GRIMBLE.
WHAT'S UP, BOSS?
I'M GOING TO BE TRAVELING FOR THE NEXT FEW DAYS--MAYBE LONGER.
HERE'S WHAT I WANT YOU TO DO WHILE I'M GONE...

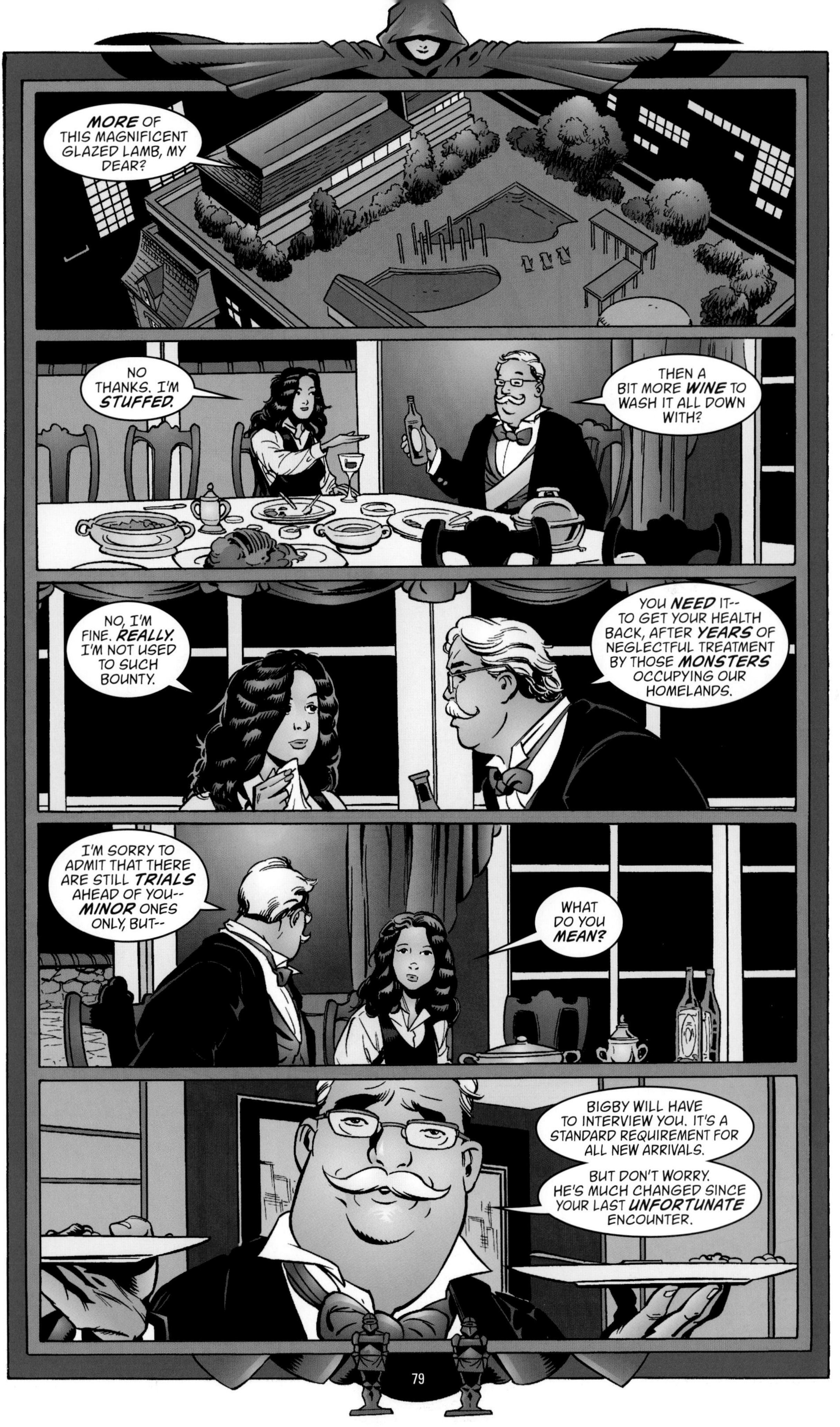
MORE OF THIS MAGNIFICENT GLAZED LAMB, MY DEAR?
NO THANKS. I'M STUFFED.
THEN A BIT MORE WINE TO WASH IT ALL DOWN WITH?
NO, I'M FINE. REALLY. I'M NOT USED TO SUCH BOUNTY.
YOU NEED IT-- TO GET YOUR HEALTH BACK, AFTER YEARS OF NEGLECTFUL TREATMENT BY THOSE MONSTERS OCCUPYING OUR HOMELANDS.
I'M SORRY TO ADMIT THAT THERE ARE STILL TRIALS AHEAD OF YOU-- MINOR ONES ONLY, BUT--
WHAT DO YOU MEAN?
BIGBY WILL HAVE TO INTERVIEW YOU. IT'S A STANDARD REQUIREMENT FOR ALL NEW ARRIVALS.
BUT DON'T WORRY. HE'S MUCH CHANGED SINCE YOUR LAST UNFORTUNATE ENCOUNTER.

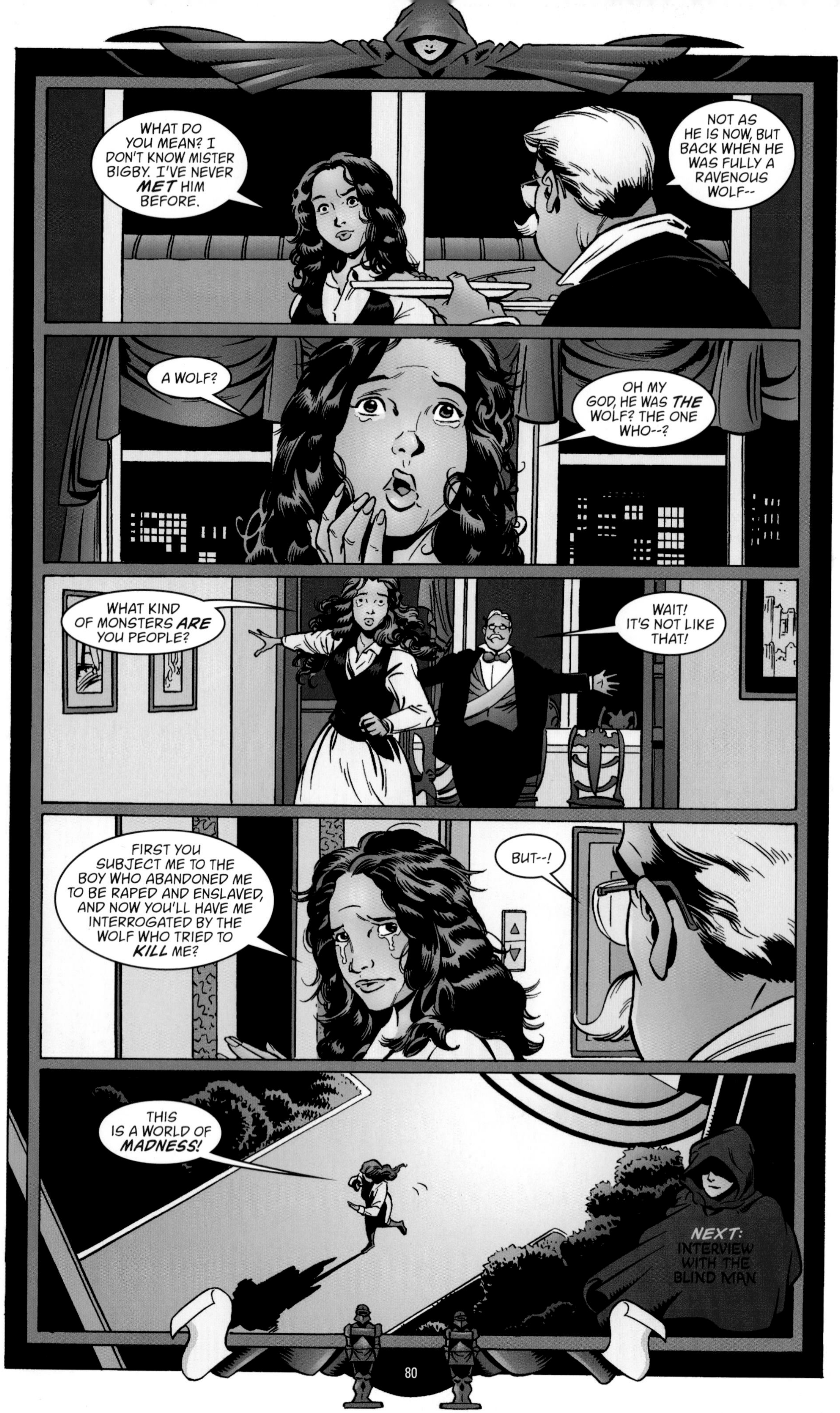
WHAT DO YOU MEAN? I DON'T KNOW MISTER BIGBY. I'VE NEVER MET HIM BEFORE.
NOT AS HE IS NOW, BUT BACK WHEN HE WAS FULLY A RAVENOUS WOLF--
A WOLF?
OH MY GOD, HE WAS THE WOLF? THE ONE WHO--?
WHAT KIND OF MONSTERS ARE YOU PEOPLE?
WAIT! IT'S NOT LIKE THAT!
FIRST YOU SUBJECT ME TO THE BOY WHO ABANDONED ME TO BE RAPED AND ENSLAVED, AND NOW YOU'LL HAVE ME INTERROGATED BY THE WOLF WHO TRIED TO KILL ME?
BUT--!
THIS IS A WORLD OF MADNESS!
NEXT: INTERVIEW WITH THE BLIND MAN

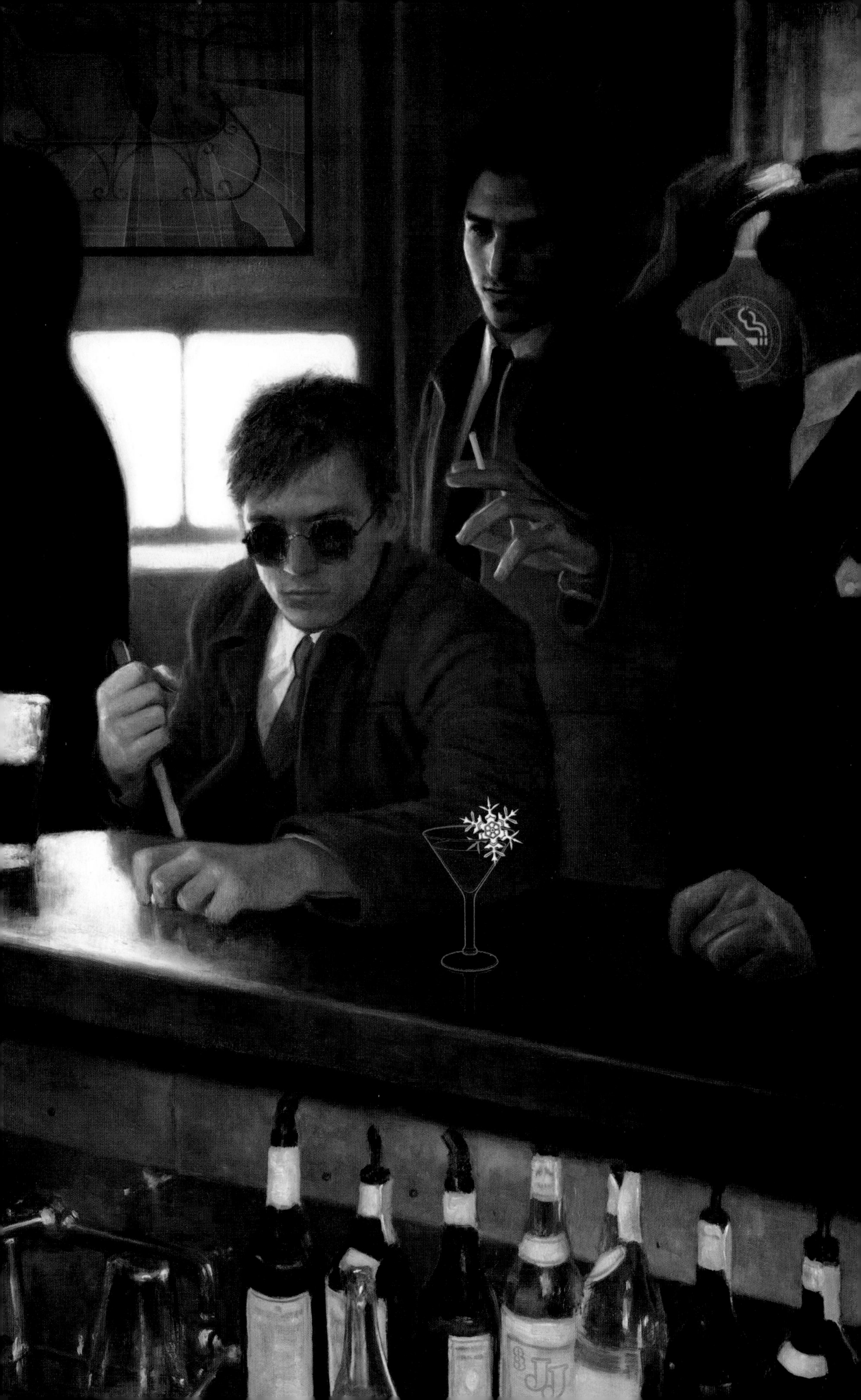

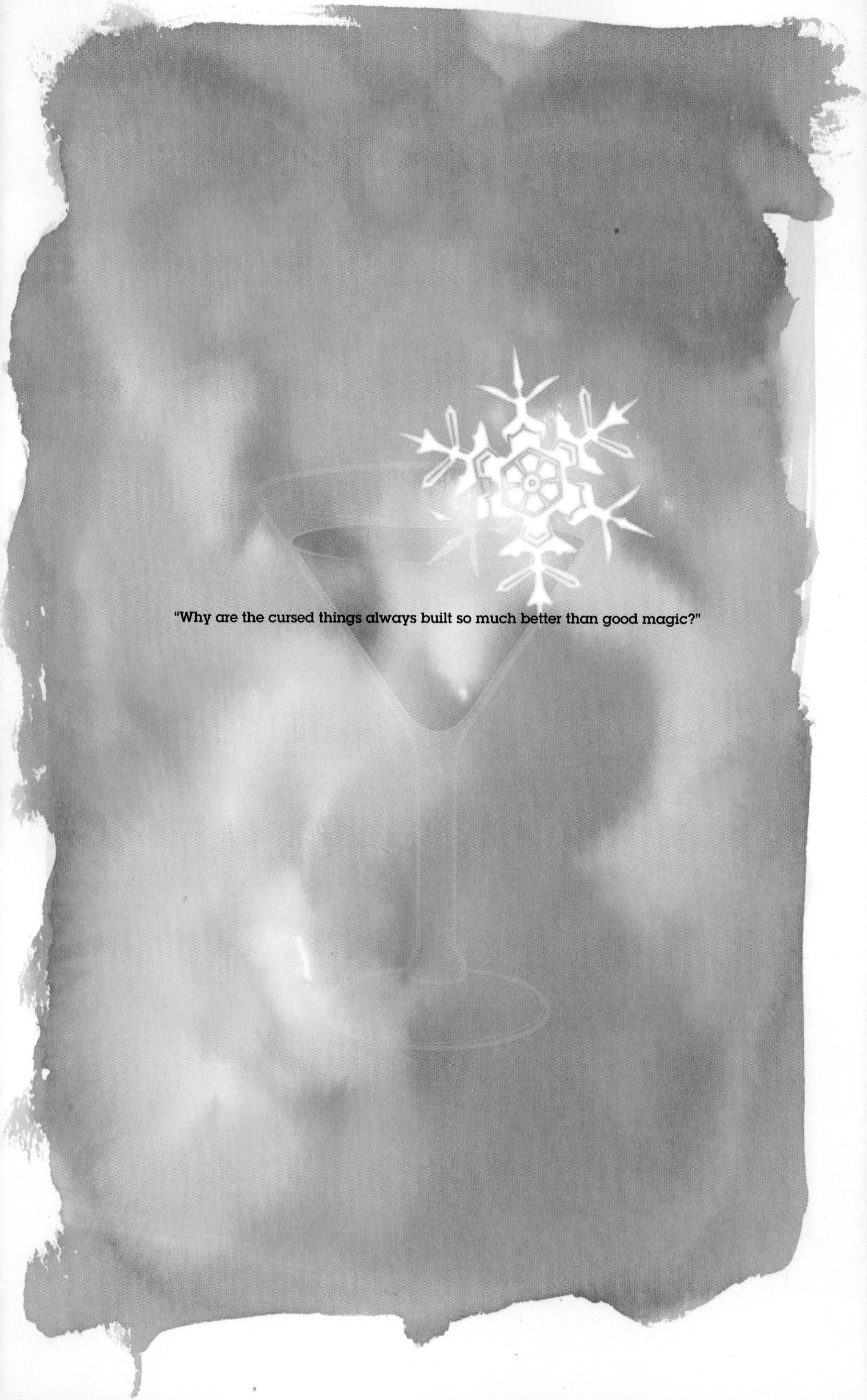
“Why are the cursed things always built so much better than good magic?”

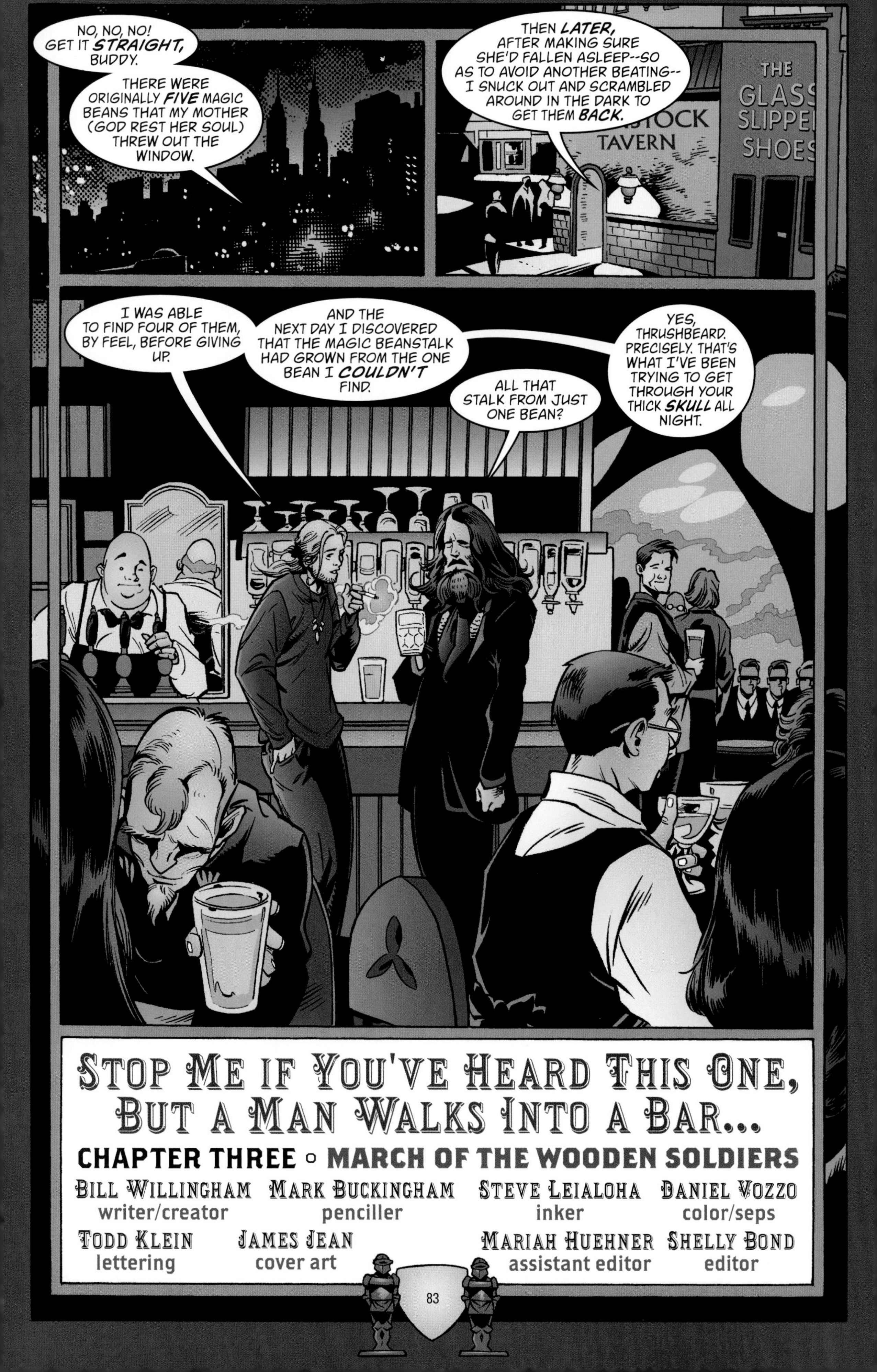
NO, NO, NO! GET IT STRAIGHT, BUDDY.
THERE WERE ORIGINALLY FIVE MAGIC BEANS THAT MY MOTHER (GOD REST HER SOUL) THREW OUT THE WINDOW.
THEN LATER, AFTER MAKING SURE SHE'D FALLEN ASLEEP--SO AS TO AVOID ANOTHER BEATING--I SNUCK OUT AND SCRAMBLED AROUND IN THE DARK TO GET THEM BACK.
TAVERN
I WAS ABLE TO FIND FOUR OF THEM, BY FEEL, BEFORE GIVING UP.
AND THE NEXT DAY I DISCOVERED THAT THE MAGIC BEANSTALK HAD GROWN FROM THE ONE BEAN I COULDN'T FIND.
ALL THAT STALK FROM JUST ONE BEAN?
YES, THRUSHBEARD. PRECISELY. THAT'S WHAT I'VE BEEN TRYING TO GET THROUGH YOUR THICK SKULL ALL NIGHT.

Stop Me if You've Heard This One, But a Man Walks Into a Bar...

CHAPTER THREE ◦ MARCH OF THE WOODEN SOLDIERS

BILL WILLINGHAM writer/creator
MARK BUCKINGHAM penciller
STEVE LEIALOHA inker
DANIEL VOZZO color/seps
TODD KLEIN lettering
JAMES JEAN cover art
MARIAH HUEHNER assistant editor
SHELLY BOND editor

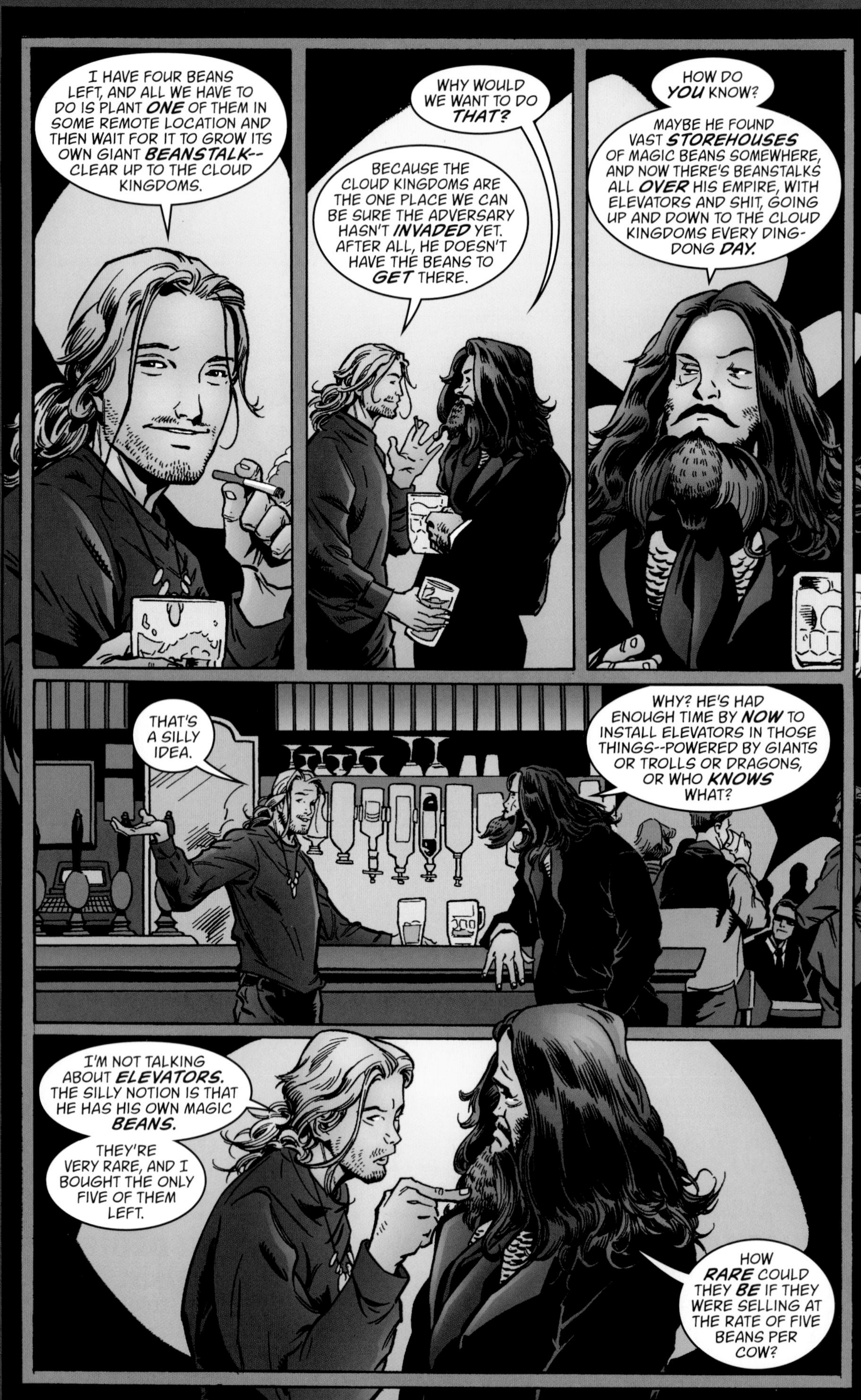
I HAVE FOUR BEANS LEFT, AND ALL WE HAVE TO DO IS PLANT ONE OF THEM IN SOME REMOTE LOCATION AND THEN WAIT FOR IT TO GROW ITS OWN GIANT BEANSTALK--CLEAR UP TO THE CLOUD KINGDOMS.
WHY WOULD WE WANT TO DO THAT?
BECAUSE THE CLOUD KINGDOMS ARE THE ONE PLACE WE CAN BE SURE THE ADVERSARY HASN'T INVADED YET. AFTER ALL, HE DOESN'T HAVE THE BEANS TO GET THERE.
HOW DO YOU KNOW?
MAYBE HE FOUND VAST STOREHOUSES OF MAGIC BEANS SOMEWHERE, AND NOW THERE'S BEANSTALKS ALL OVER HIS EMPIRE, WITH ELEVATORS AND SHIT, GOING UP AND DOWN TO THE CLOUD KINGDOMS EVERY DING-DONG DAY.
THAT'S A SILLY IDEA.
WHY? HE'S HAD ENOUGH TIME BY NOW TO INSTALL ELEVATORS IN THOSE THINGS--POWERED BY GIANTS OR TROLLS OR DRAGONS, OR WHO KNOWS WHAT?
I'M NOT TALKING ABOUT ELEVATORS. THE SILLY NOTION IS THAT HE HAS HIS OWN MAGIC BEANS.
THEY'RE VERY RARE, AND I BOUGHT THE ONLY FIVE OF THEM LEFT.
HOW RARE COULD THEY BE IF THEY WERE SELLING AT THE RATE OF FIVE BEANS PER COW?

YOU'RE MISSING THE *POINT.* THE CLOUD KINGS WERE EACH RICHER THAN MIDAS' FAVORITE WET *DREAM.*

IF WE WERE TO PLANT *ANOTHER* BEANSTALK AND CLIMB UP TO THERE, WE COULD HELP OURSELVES TO ALL THAT *LOOT.*

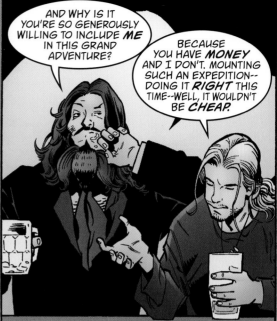

AND WHY IS IT YOU'RE SO GENEROUSLY WILLING TO INCLUDE *ME* IN THIS GRAND ADVENTURE?

BECAUSE YOU HAVE *MONEY* AND I DON'T. MOUNTING SUCH AN EXPEDITION-- DOING IT *RIGHT* THIS TIME--WELL, IT WOULDN'T BE *CHEAP.*

HERE'S THE DEAL. WE'LL BE EQUAL *PARTNERS.* I PROVIDE ONE OF THE MAGIC BEANS...

...AND YOU PUT UP THE BARE BONES MONETARY EXPENSES--LET'S SAY ABOUT THIRTEEN THOUSAND DOLLARS TO START WITH.

WHICH I WILL NEVER SEE AGAIN, ONCE I HAND THE MONEY OVER TO YOU.

FORGET IT, JACK. I'M WISE TO YOUR WAYS AND WON'T SPEND A *NICKEL* ON ANY SCHEME INVOLVING YOU OR YOUR FICTIONAL LEGUMES.

ARE YOU IMPLYING I DON'T REALLY STILL *HAVE* THE BEANS?

GOOD NIGHT, JACK.

I'VE *NEVER* LIKED YOU, THRUSHBEARD!

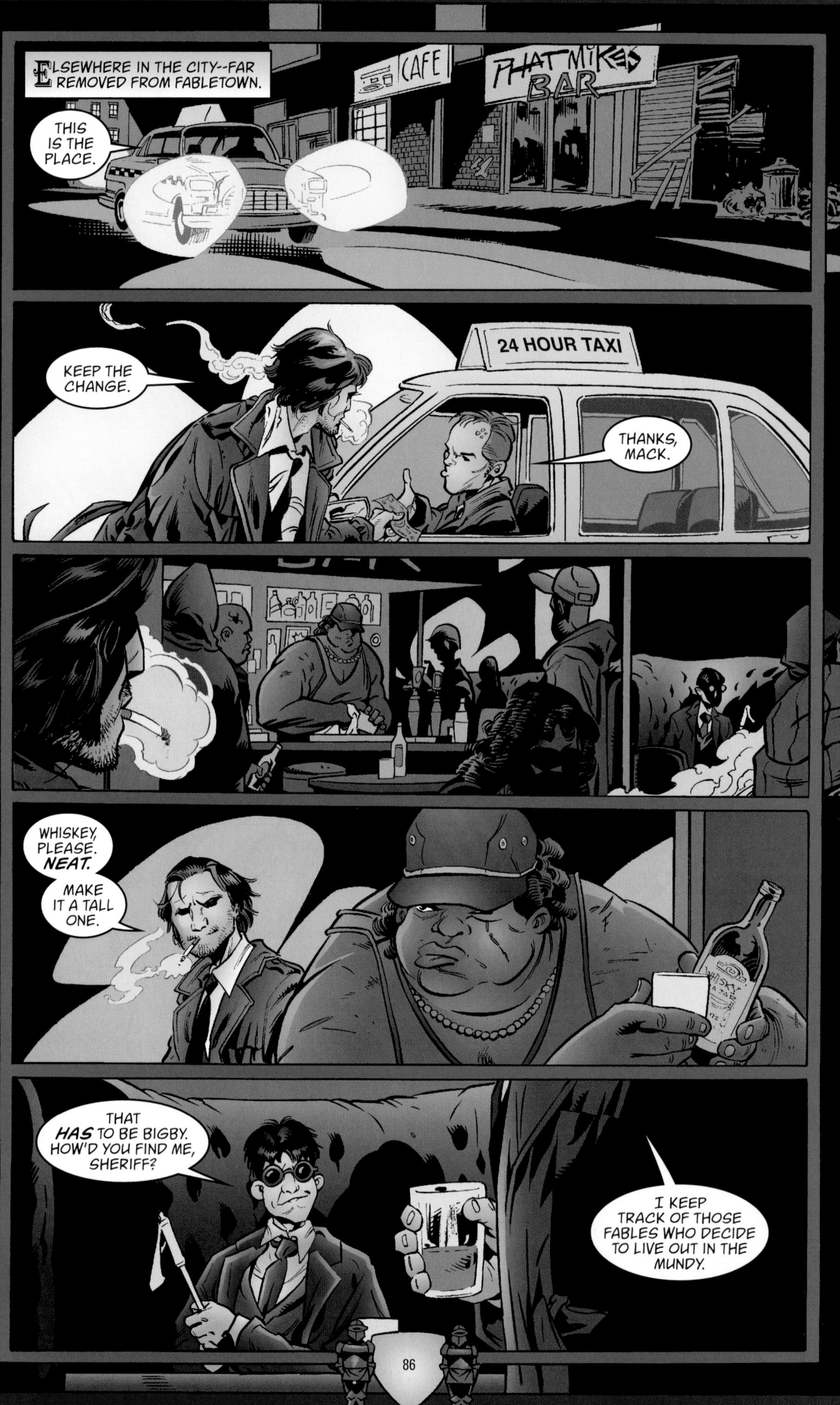
ELSEWHERE IN THE CITY--FAR REMOVED FROM FABLETOWN.
CAFE
PHAT MIKE'S BAR
THIS IS THE PLACE.
24 HOUR TAXI
KEEP THE CHANGE.
THANKS, MACK.
WHISKEY, PLEASE. NEAT.
MAKE IT A TALL ONE.
THAT HAS TO BE BIGBY. HOW'D YOU FIND ME, SHERIFF?
I KEEP TRACK OF THOSE FABLES WHO DECIDE TO LIVE OUT IN THE MUNDY.

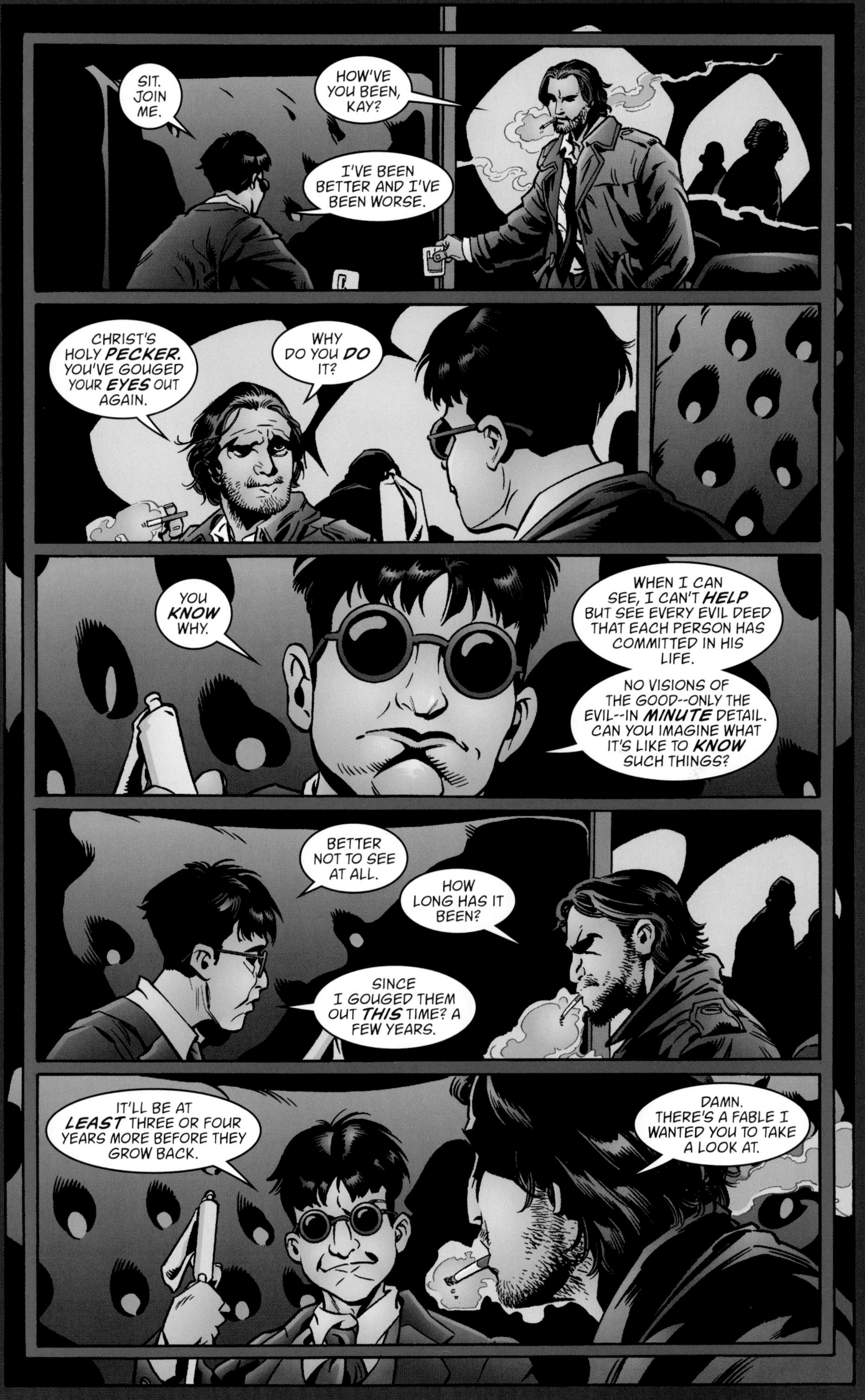
SIT. JOIN ME.
HOW'VE YOU BEEN, KAY?
I'VE BEEN BETTER AND I'VE BEEN WORSE.
CHRIST'S HOLY PECKER. YOU'VE GOUGED YOUR EYES OUT AGAIN.
WHY DO YOU DO IT?
YOU KNOW WHY.
WHEN I CAN SEE, I CAN'T HELP BUT SEE EVERY EVIL DEED THAT EACH PERSON HAS COMMITTED IN HIS LIFE.
NO VISIONS OF THE GOOD--ONLY THE EVIL--IN MINUTE DETAIL. CAN YOU IMAGINE WHAT IT'S LIKE TO KNOW SUCH THINGS?
BETTER NOT TO SEE AT ALL.
HOW LONG HAS IT BEEN?
SINCE I GOUGED THEM OUT THIS TIME? A FEW YEARS.
IT'LL BE AT LEAST THREE OR FOUR YEARS MORE BEFORE THEY GROW BACK.
DAMN. THERE'S A FABLE I WANTED YOU TO TAKE A LOOK AT.

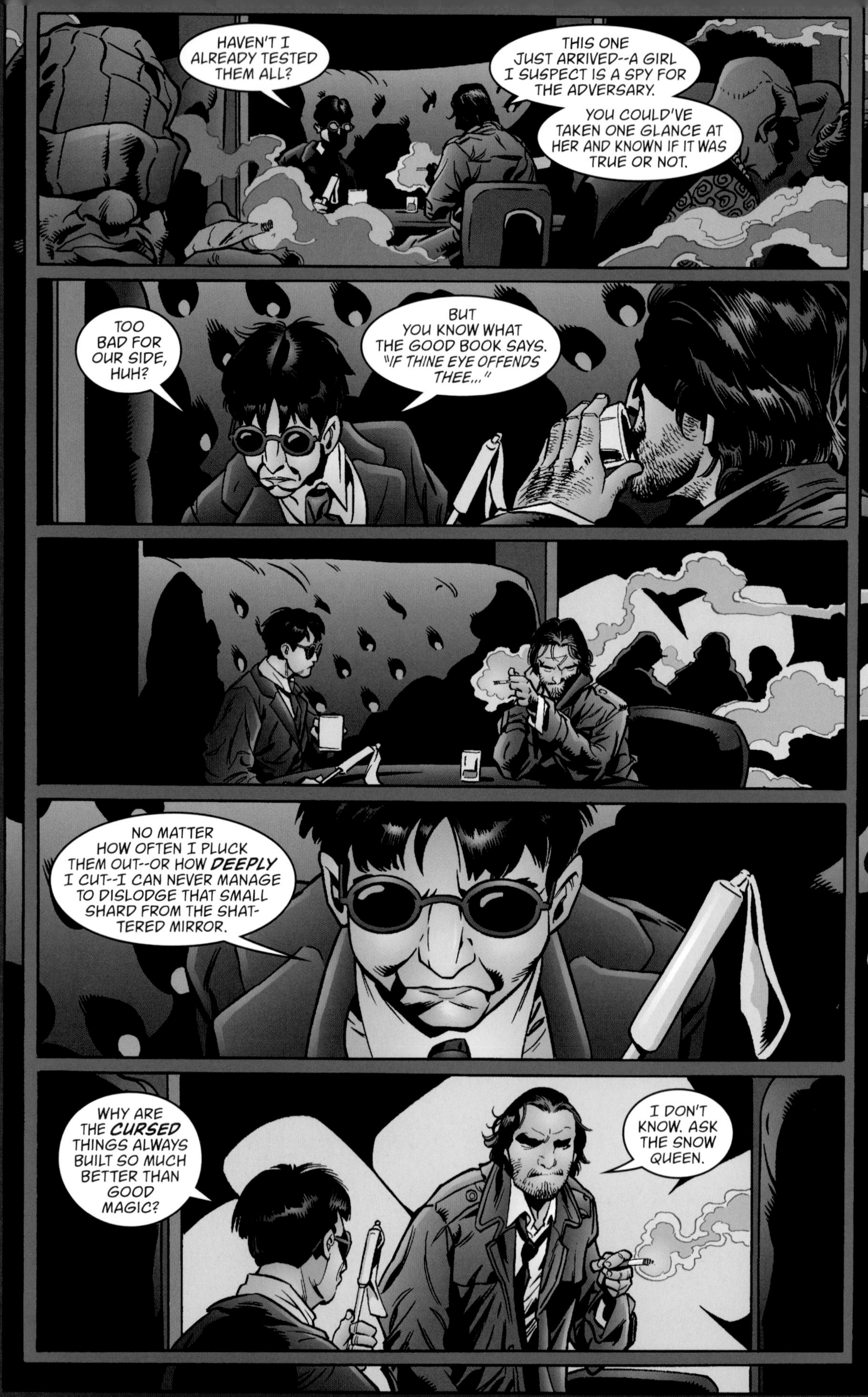
HAVEN'T I ALREADY TESTED THEM ALL?
THIS ONE JUST ARRIVED--A GIRL I SUSPECT IS A SPY FOR THE ADVERSARY.
YOU COULD'VE TAKEN ONE GLANCE AT HER AND KNOWN IF IT WAS TRUE OR NOT.
TOO BAD FOR OUR SIDE, HUH?
BUT YOU KNOW WHAT THE GOOD BOOK SAYS. "IF THINE EYE OFFENDS THEE..."
NO MATTER HOW OFTEN I PLUCK THEM OUT--OR HOW DEEPLY I CUT--I CAN NEVER MANAGE TO DISLODGE THAT SMALL SHARD FROM THE SHAT- TERED MIRROR.
WHY ARE THE CURSED THINGS ALWAYS BUILT SO MUCH BETTER THAN GOOD MAGIC?
I DON'T KNOW. ASK THE SNOW QUEEN.

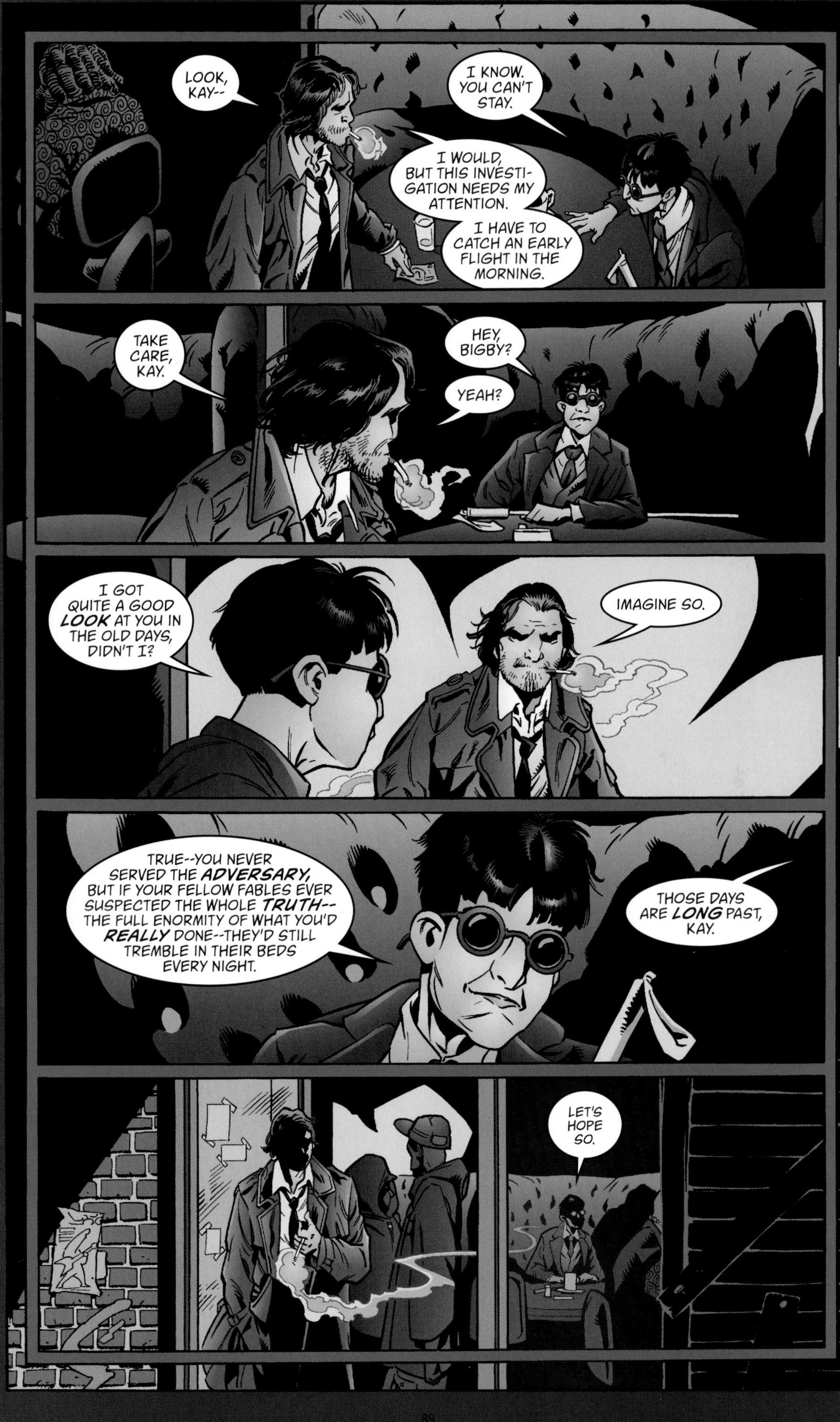

LOOK, KAY--
I KNOW. YOU CAN'T STAY.
I WOULD, BUT THIS INVESTIGATION NEEDS MY ATTENTION.
I HAVE TO CATCH AN EARLY FLIGHT IN THE MORNING.
TAKE CARE, KAY.
HEY, BIGBY?
YEAH?
I GOT QUITE A GOOD LOOK AT YOU IN THE OLD DAYS, DIDN'T I?
IMAGINE SO.
TRUE--YOU NEVER SERVED THE ADVERSARY, BUT IF YOUR FELLOW FABLES EVER SUSPECTED THE WHOLE TRUTH--THE FULL ENORMITY OF WHAT YOU'D REALLY DONE--THEY'D STILL TREMBLE IN THEIR BEDS EVERY NIGHT.
THOSE DAYS ARE LONG PAST, KAY.
LET'S HOPE SO.

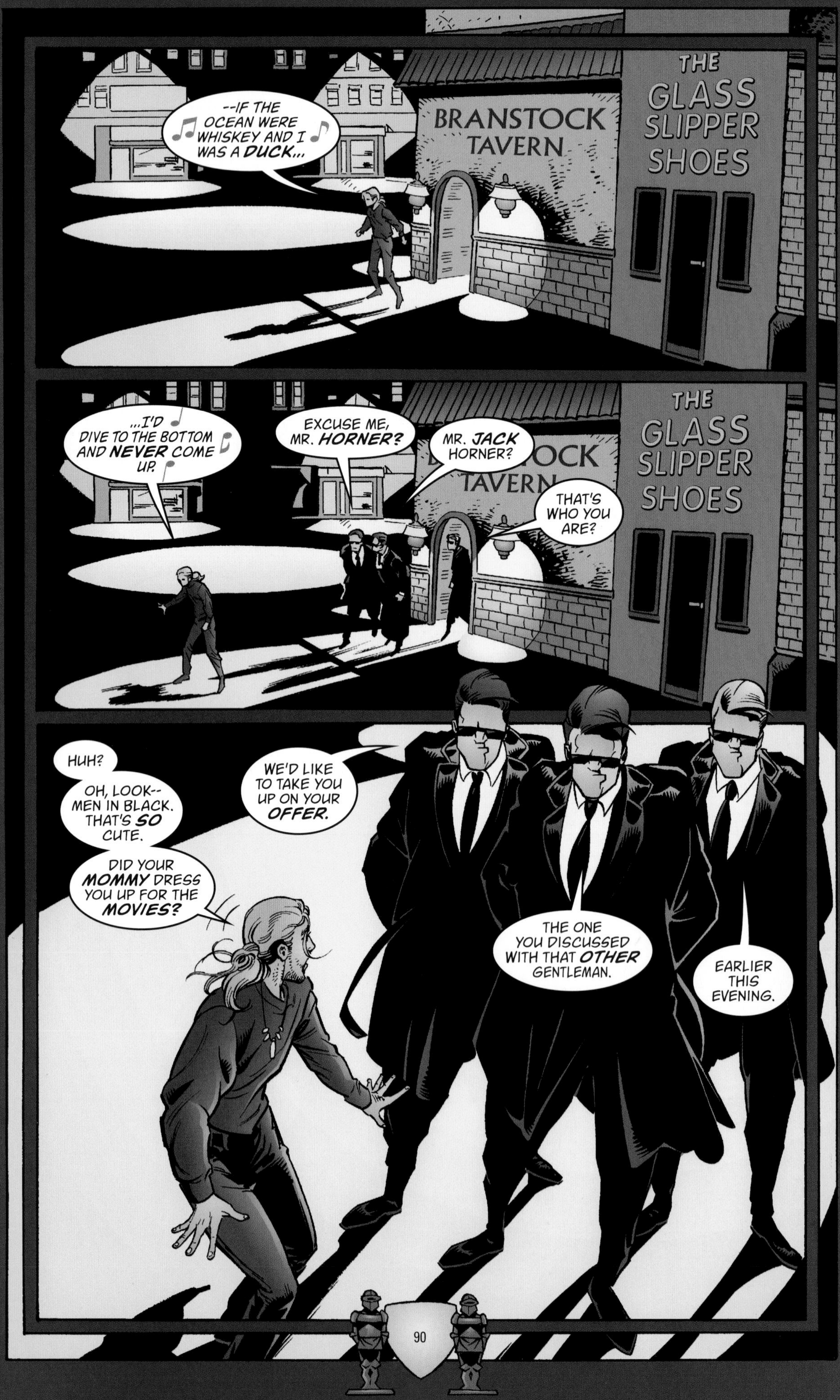

THE GLASS SLIPPER SHOES
BRANSTOCK TAVERN
--IF THE OCEAN WERE WHISKEY AND I WAS A DUCK...
...I'D DIVE TO THE BOTTOM AND NEVER COME UP.
EXCUSE ME, MR. HORNER?
MR. JACK HORNER?
THAT'S WHO YOU ARE?
HUH?
OH, LOOK-- MEN IN BLACK. THAT'S SO CUTE.
DID YOUR MOMMY DRESS YOU UP FOR THE MOVIES?
WE'D LIKE TO TAKE YOU UP ON YOUR OFFER.
THE ONE YOU DISCUSSED WITH THAT OTHER GENTLEMAN.
EARLIER THIS EVENING.

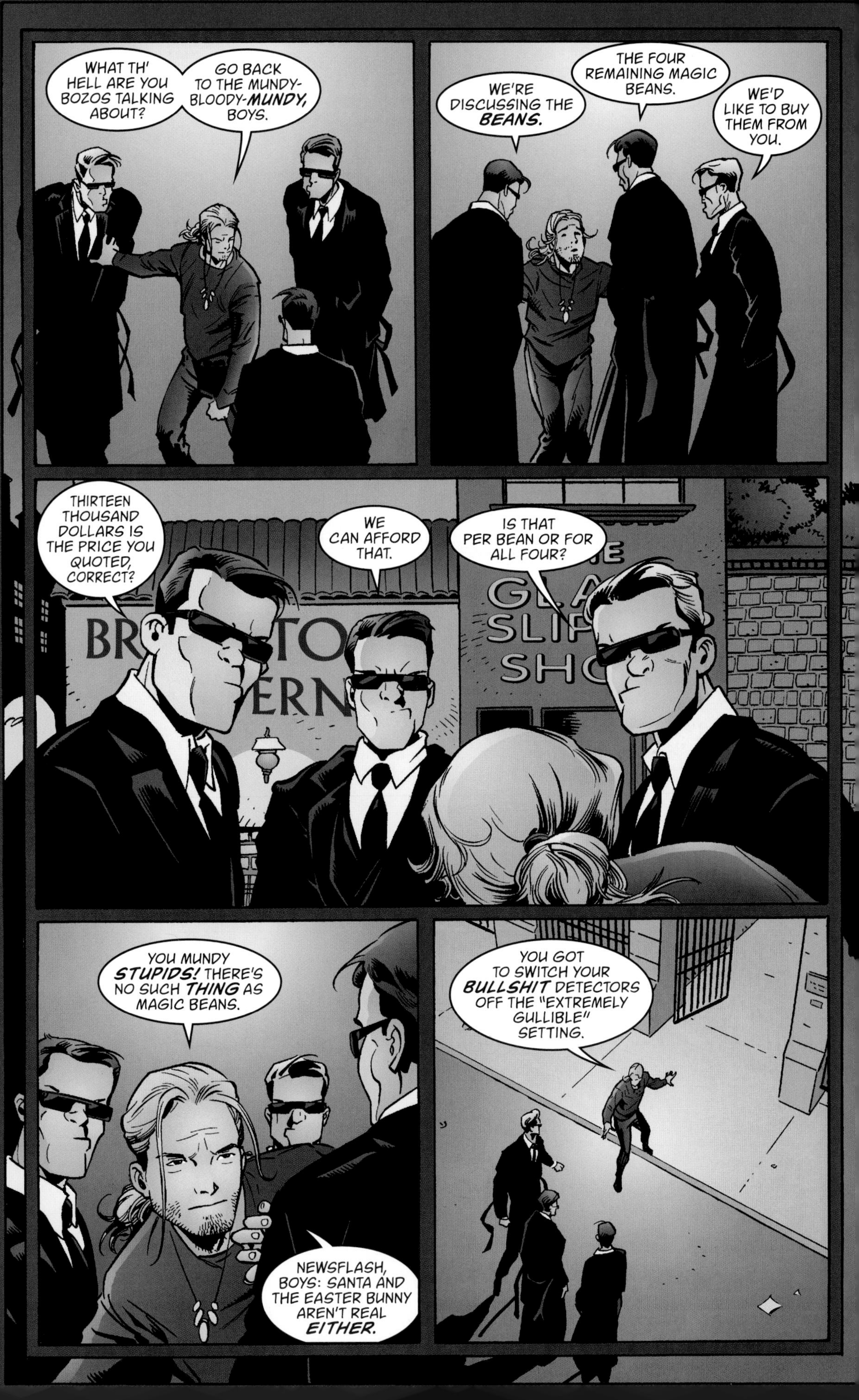
WHAT TH' HELL ARE YOU BOZOS TALKING ABOUT?
GO BACK TO THE MUNDY-BLOODY-MUNDY, BOYS.
WE'RE DISCUSSING THE BEANS.
THE FOUR REMAINING MAGIC BEANS.
WE'D LIKE TO BUY THEM FROM YOU.
THIRTEEN THOUSAND DOLLARS IS THE PRICE YOU QUOTED, CORRECT?
WE CAN AFFORD THAT.
IS THAT PER BEAN OR FOR ALL FOUR?
YOU MUNDY STUPIDS! THERE'S NO SUCH THING AS MAGIC BEANS.
NEWSFLASH, BOYS: SANTA AND THE EASTER BUNNY AREN'T REAL EITHER.
YOU GOT TO SWITCH YOUR BULLSHIT DETECTORS OFF THE "EXTREMELY GULLIBLE" SETTING.

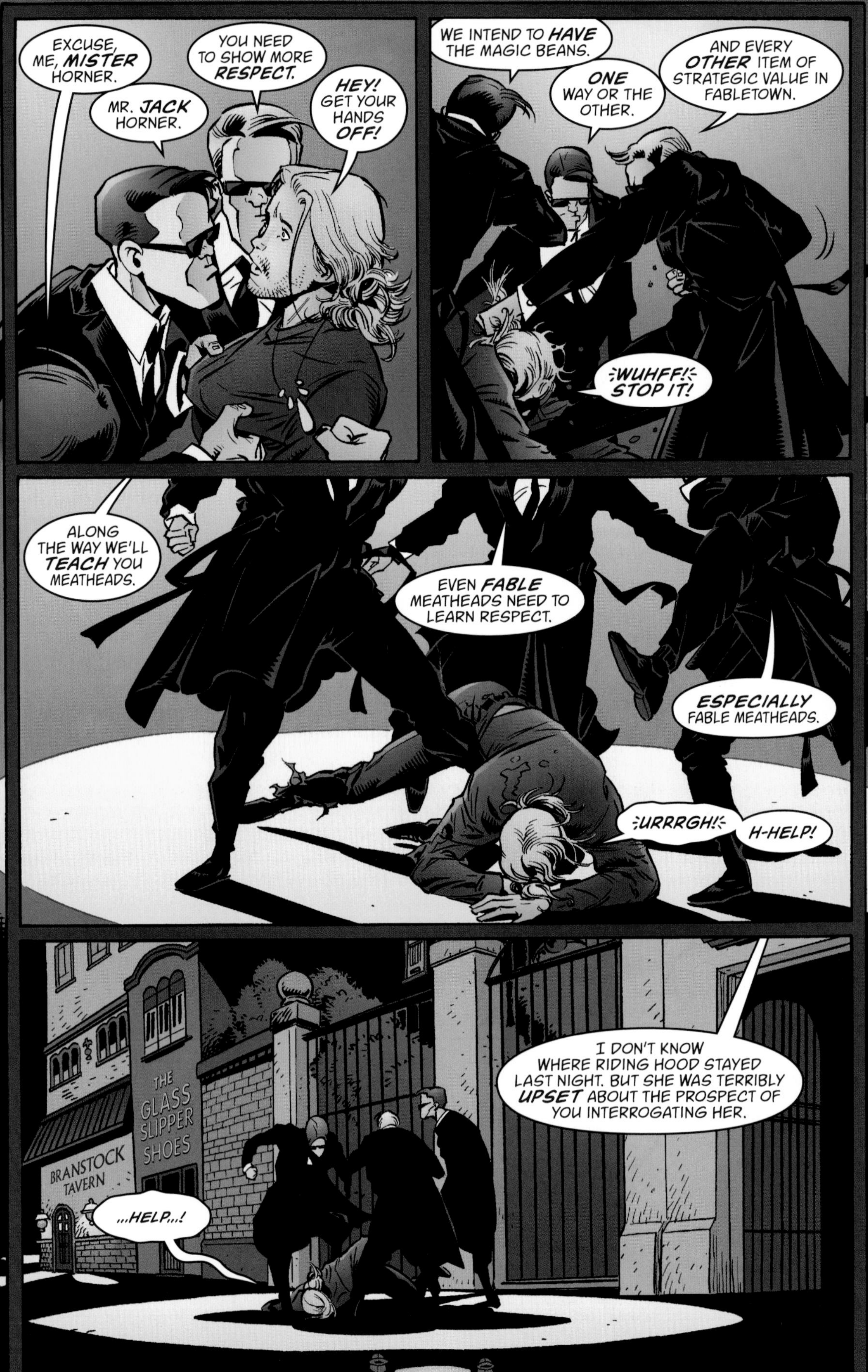
EXCUSE, ME, MISTER HORNER.
MR. JACK HORNER.
YOU NEED TO SHOW MORE RESPECT.
HEY! GET YOUR HANDS OFF!
WE INTEND TO HAVE THE MAGIC BEANS.
ONE WAY OR THE OTHER.
AND EVERY OTHER ITEM OF STRATEGIC VALUE IN FABLETOWN.
WUHFF! STOP IT!
ALONG THE WAY WE'LL TEACH YOU MEATHEADS.
EVEN FABLE MEATHEADS NEED TO LEARN RESPECT.
ESPECIALLY FABLE MEATHEADS.
URRRGH!
H-HELP!
THE GLASS SLIPPER SHOES
BRANSTOCK TAVERN
I DON'T KNOW WHERE RIDING HOOD STAYED LAST NIGHT. BUT SHE WAS TERRIBLY UPSET ABOUT THE PROSPECT OF YOU INTERROGATING HER.
...HELP...!

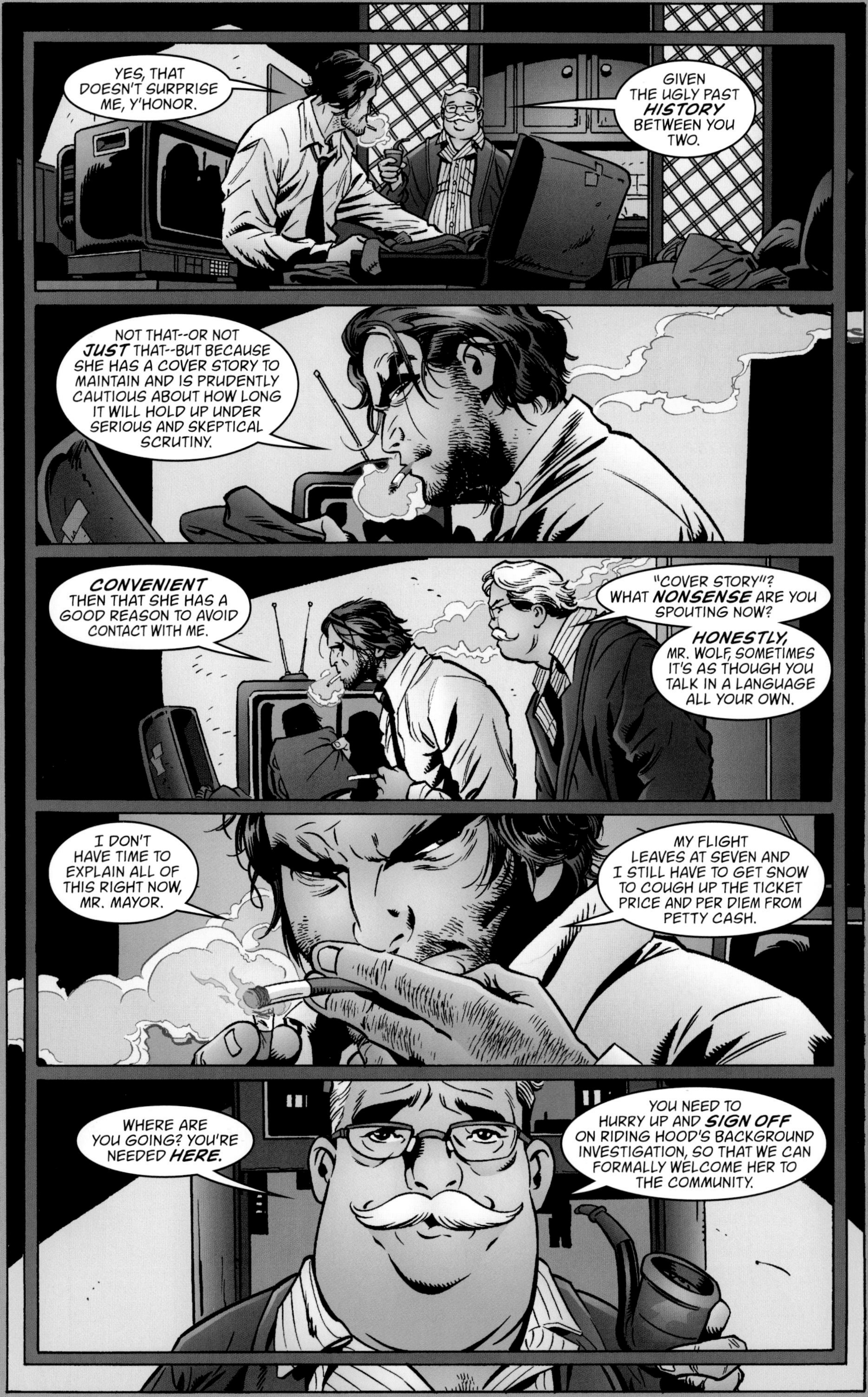
YES, THAT DOESN'T SURPRISE ME, Y'HONOR.
GIVEN THE UGLY PAST HISTORY BETWEEN YOU TWO.
NOT THAT--OR NOT JUST THAT--BUT BECAUSE SHE HAS A COVER STORY TO MAINTAIN AND IS PRUDENTLY CAUTIOUS ABOUT HOW LONG IT WILL HOLD UP UNDER SERIOUS AND SKEPTICAL SCRUTINY.
CONVENIENT THEN THAT SHE HAS A GOOD REASON TO AVOID CONTACT WITH ME.
"COVER STORY"? WHAT NONSENSE ARE YOU SPOUTING NOW?
HONESTLY, MR. WOLF, SOMETIMES IT'S AS THOUGH YOU TALK IN A LANGUAGE ALL YOUR OWN.
I DON'T HAVE TIME TO EXPLAIN ALL OF THIS RIGHT NOW, MR. MAYOR.
MY FLIGHT LEAVES AT SEVEN AND I STILL HAVE TO GET SNOW TO COUGH UP THE TICKET PRICE AND PER DIEM FROM PETTY CASH.
WHERE ARE YOU GOING? YOU'RE NEEDED HERE.
YOU NEED TO HURRY UP AND SIGN OFF ON RIDING HOOD'S BACKGROUND INVESTIGATION, SO THAT WE CAN FORMALLY WELCOME HER TO THE COMMUNITY.

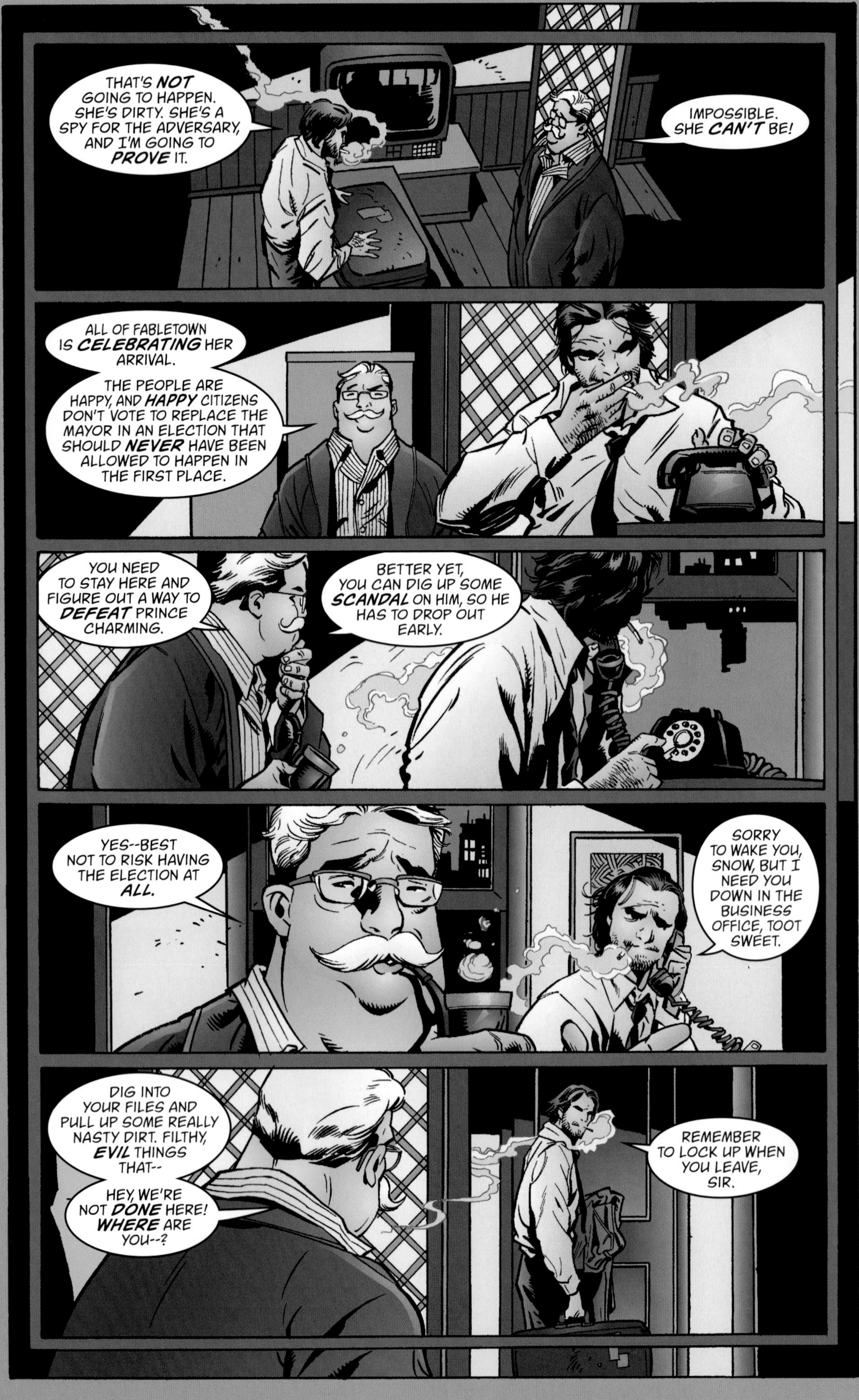
THAT'S NOT GOING TO HAPPEN. SHE'S DIRTY. SHE'S A SPY FOR THE ADVERSARY, AND I'M GOING TO PROVE IT.
IMPOSSIBLE. SHE CAN'T BE!
ALL OF FABLETOWN IS CELEBRATING HER ARRIVAL.
THE PEOPLE ARE HAPPY, AND HAPPY CITIZENS DON'T VOTE TO REPLACE THE MAYOR IN AN ELECTION THAT SHOULD NEVER HAVE BEEN ALLOWED TO HAPPEN IN THE FIRST PLACE.
YOU NEED TO STAY HERE AND FIGURE OUT A WAY TO DEFEAT PRINCE CHARMING.
BETTER YET, YOU CAN DIG UP SOME SCANDAL ON HIM, SO HE HAS TO DROP OUT EARLY.
YES--BEST NOT TO RISK HAVING THE ELECTION AT ALL.
SORRY TO WAKE YOU, SNOW, BUT I NEED YOU DOWN IN THE BUSINESS OFFICE, TOOT SWEET.
DIG INTO YOUR FILES AND PULL UP SOME REALLY NASTY DIRT. FILTHY, EVIL THINGS THAT--
HEY, WE'RE NOT DONE HERE! WHERE ARE YOU--?
REMEMBER TO LOCK UP WHEN YOU LEAVE, SIR.

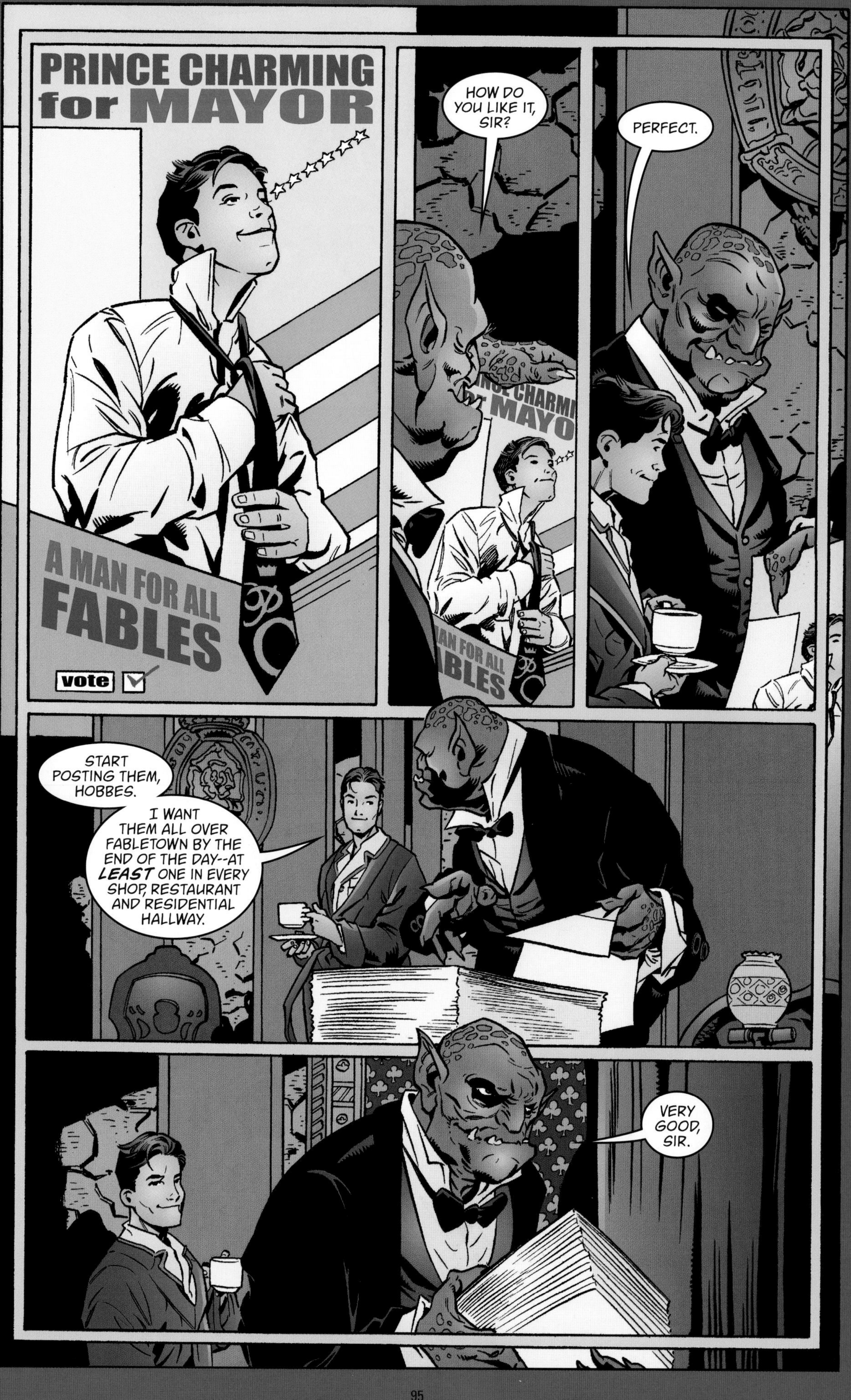
PRINCE CHARMING for MAYOR
A MAN FOR ALL FABLES
vote
HOW DO YOU LIKE IT, SIR?
PERFECT.
START POSTING THEM, HOBBES.
I WANT THEM ALL OVER FABLETOWN BY THE END OF THE DAY--AT *LEAST* ONE IN EVERY SHOP, RESTAURANT AND RESIDENTIAL HALLWAY.
VERY GOOD, SIR.

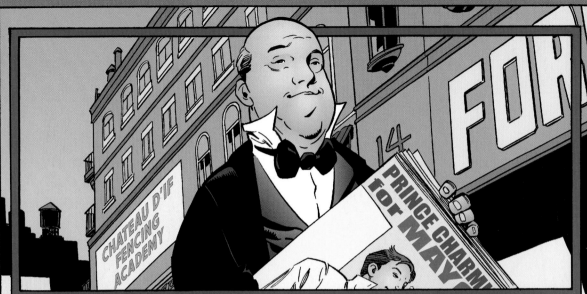

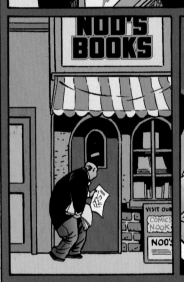

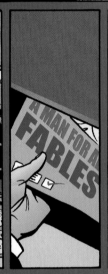

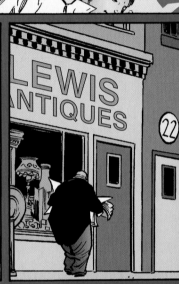

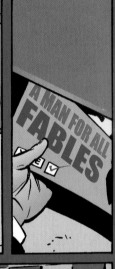

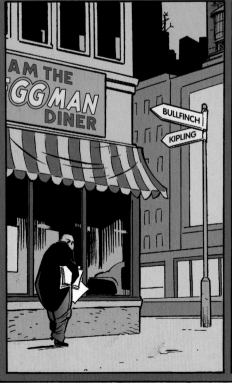

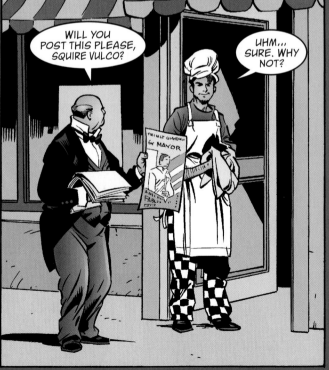

CHATEAU D'IF
FENCING
ACADEMY
14
FOR
PRINCE CHARMING
for MAYOR
NOO'S
BOOKS
VISIT OUR
COMICS
NOOK
NOO'S
A MAN FOR ALL
FABLES
LEWIS
ANTIQUES
22
A MAN FOR ALL
FABLES
AM THE
GGMAN
DINER
BULLFINCH
KIPLING
WILL YOU
POST THIS PLEASE,
SQUIRE VULCO?
UHM...
SURE. WHY
NOT?

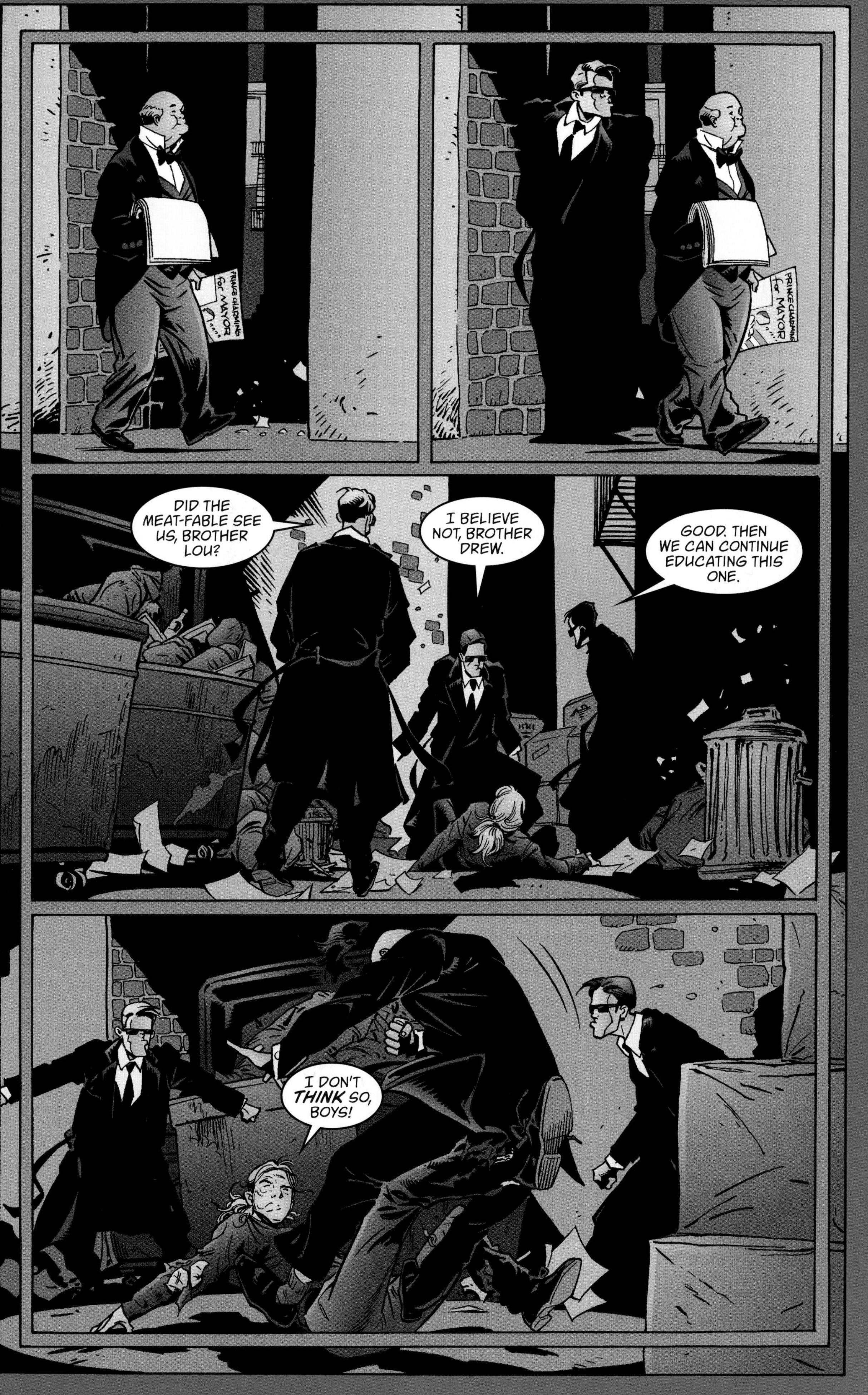
PRINCE CHARMING for MAYOR
PRINCE CHARMING for MAYOR
DID THE MEAT-FABLE SEE US, BROTHER LOU?
I BELIEVE NOT, BROTHER DREW.
GOOD. THEN WE CAN CONTINUE EDUCATING THIS ONE.
I DON'T THINK SO, BOYS!

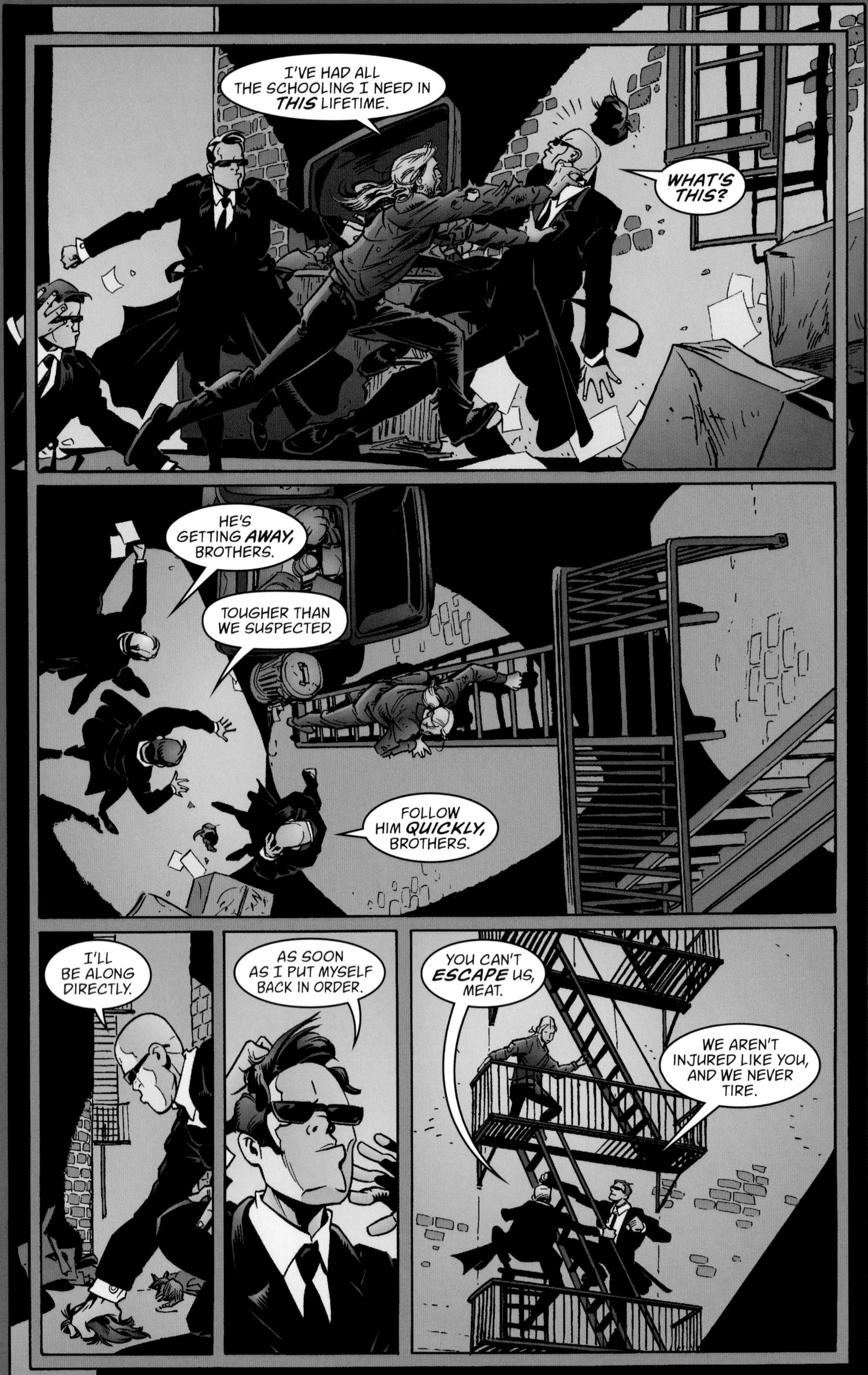
I'VE HAD ALL THE SCHOOLING I NEED IN THIS LIFETIME.
WHAT'S THIS?
HE'S GETTING AWAY, BROTHERS.
TOUGHER THAN WE SUSPECTED.
FOLLOW HIM QUICKLY, BROTHERS.
I'LL BE ALONG DIRECTLY.
AS SOON AS I PUT MYSELF BACK IN ORDER.
YOU CAN'T ESCAPE US, MEAT.
WE AREN'T INJURED LIKE YOU, AND WE NEVER TIRE.

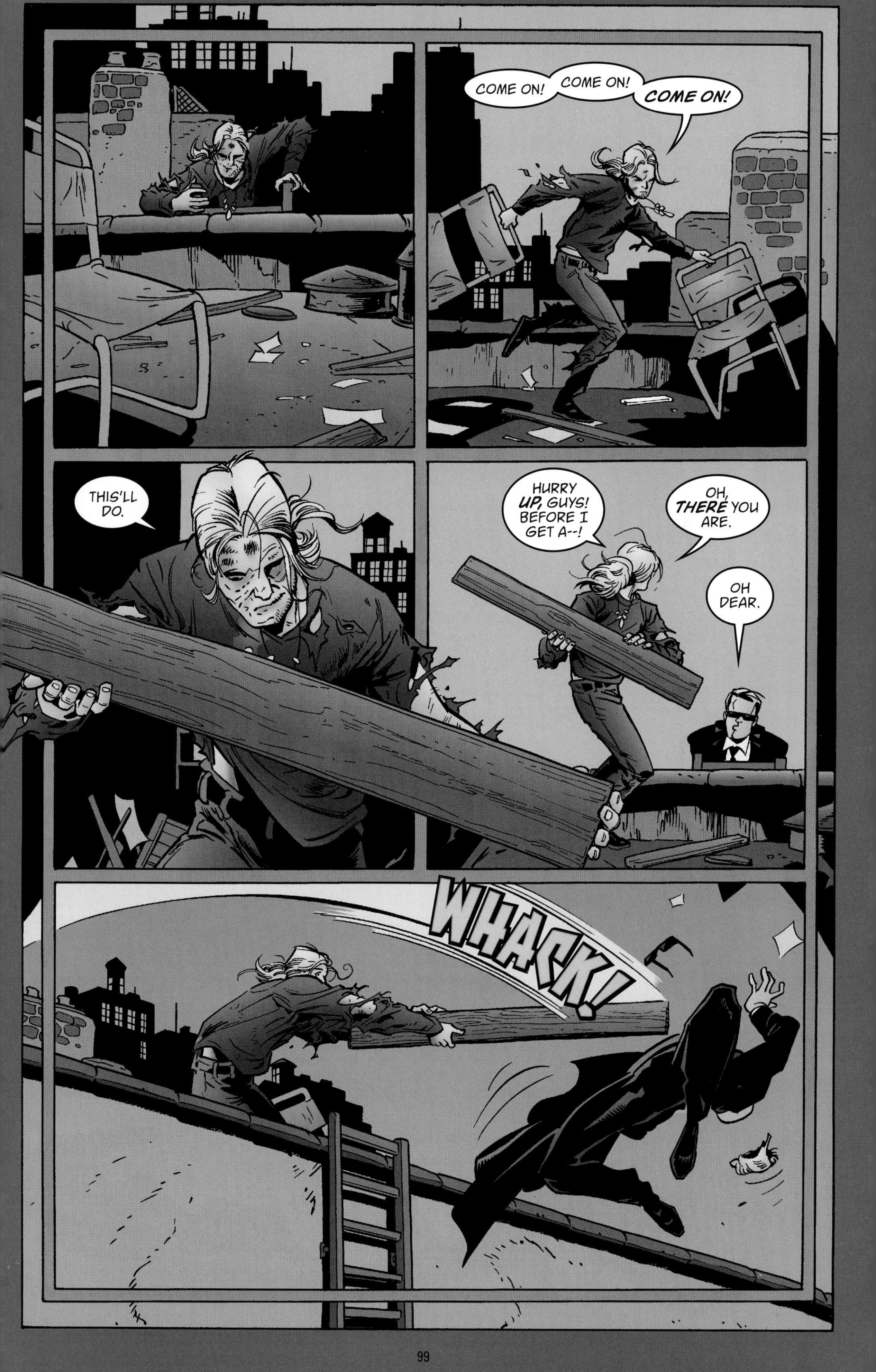
COME ON!
COME ON!
COME ON!
THIS'LL DO.
HURRY UP, GUYS! BEFORE I GET A--!
OH, THERE YOU ARE.
OH DEAR.
WHACK!

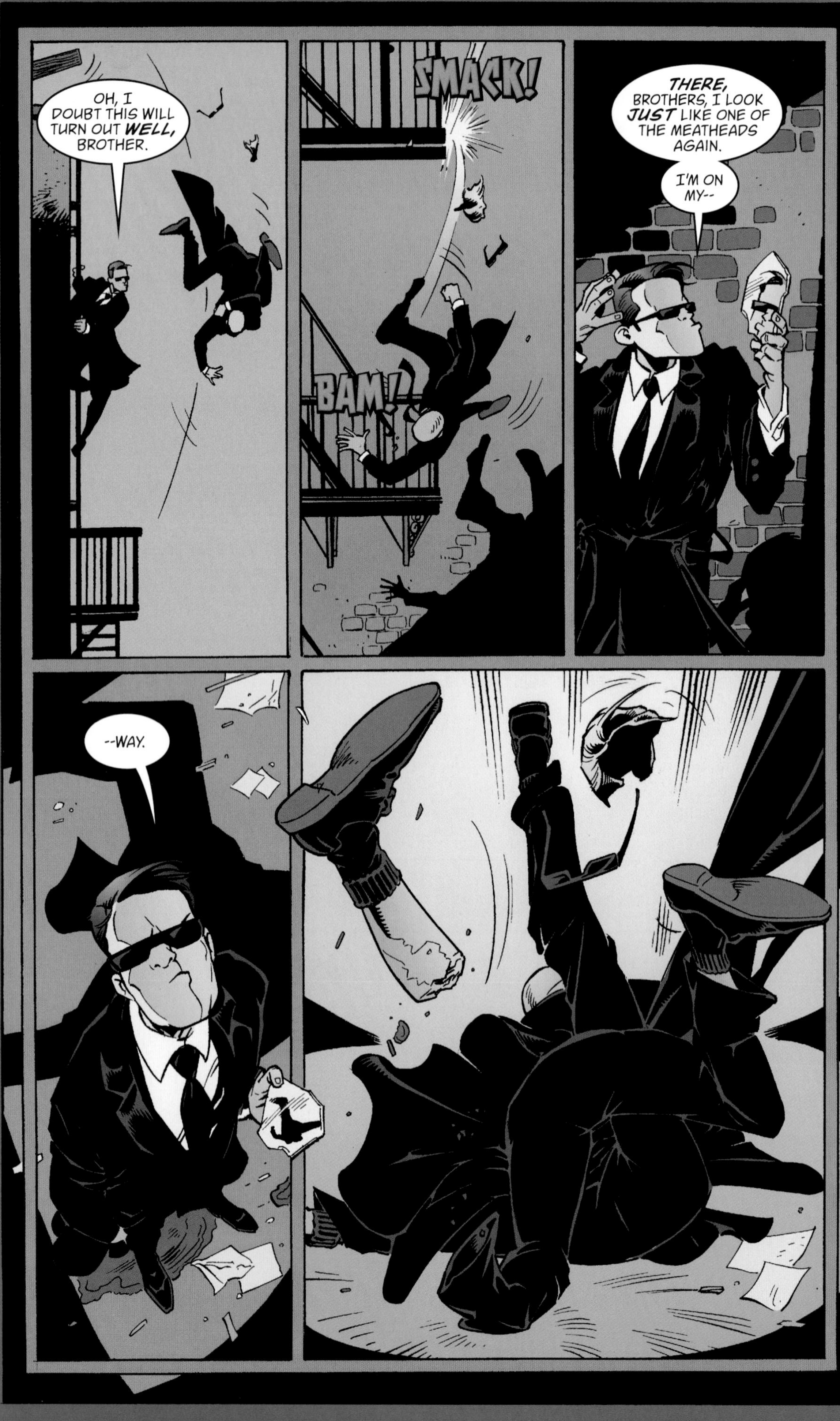
OH, I DOUBT THIS WILL TURN OUT WELL, BROTHER.
SMACK!
BAM!
THERE, BROTHERS, I LOOK JUST LIKE ONE OF THE MEATHEADS AGAIN.
I'M ON MY--
--WAY.

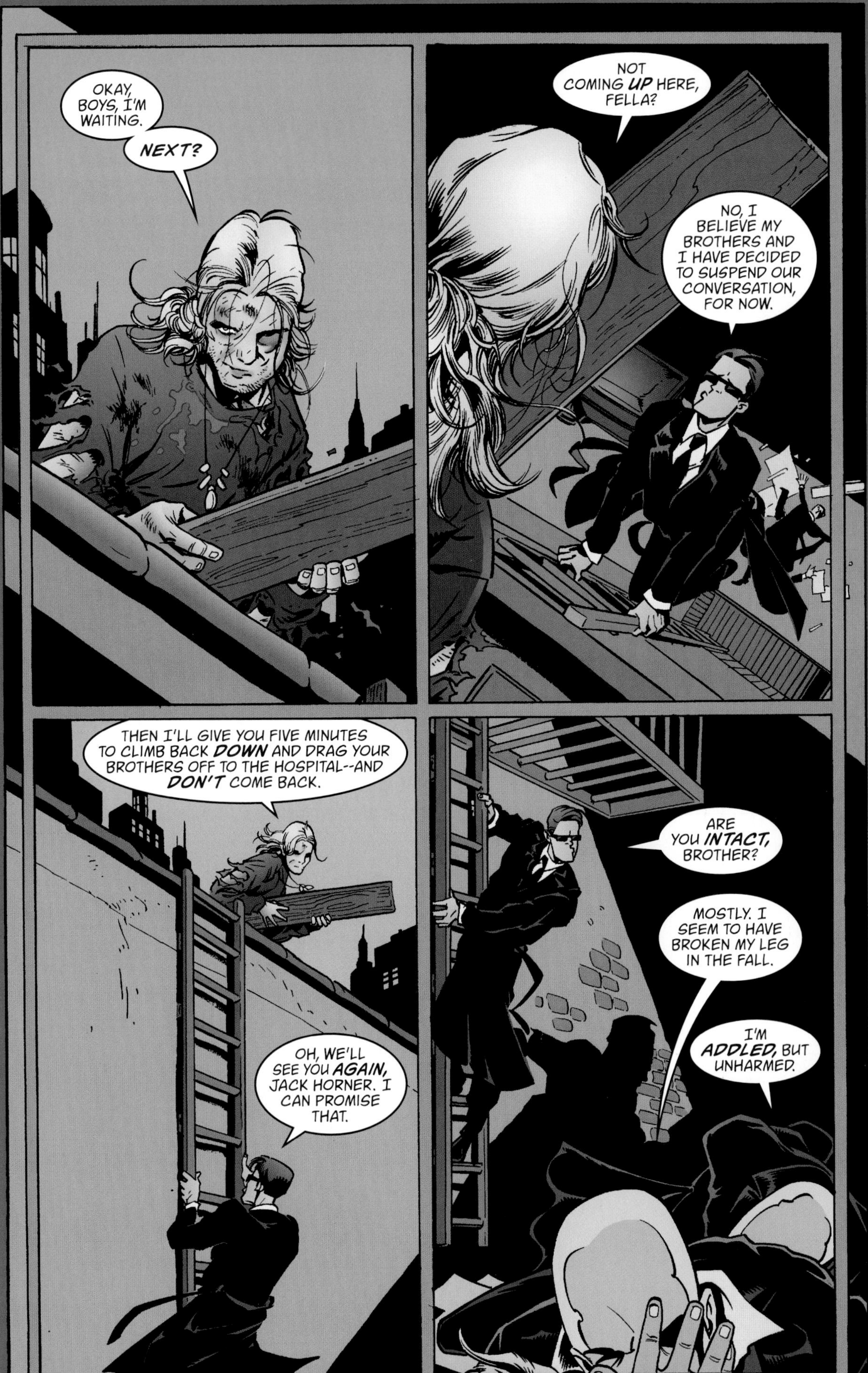
OKAY, BOYS, I'M WAITING.
NEXT?
NOT COMING UP HERE, FELLA?
NO, I BELIEVE MY BROTHERS AND I HAVE DECIDED TO SUSPEND OUR CONVERSATION, FOR NOW.
THEN I'LL GIVE YOU FIVE MINUTES TO CLIMB BACK DOWN AND DRAG YOUR BROTHERS OFF TO THE HOSPITAL--AND DON'T COME BACK.
OH, WE'LL SEE YOU AGAIN, JACK HORNER. I CAN PROMISE THAT.
ARE YOU INTACT, BROTHER?
MOSTLY. I SEEM TO HAVE BROKEN MY LEG IN THE FALL.
I'M ADDLED, BUT UNHARMED.

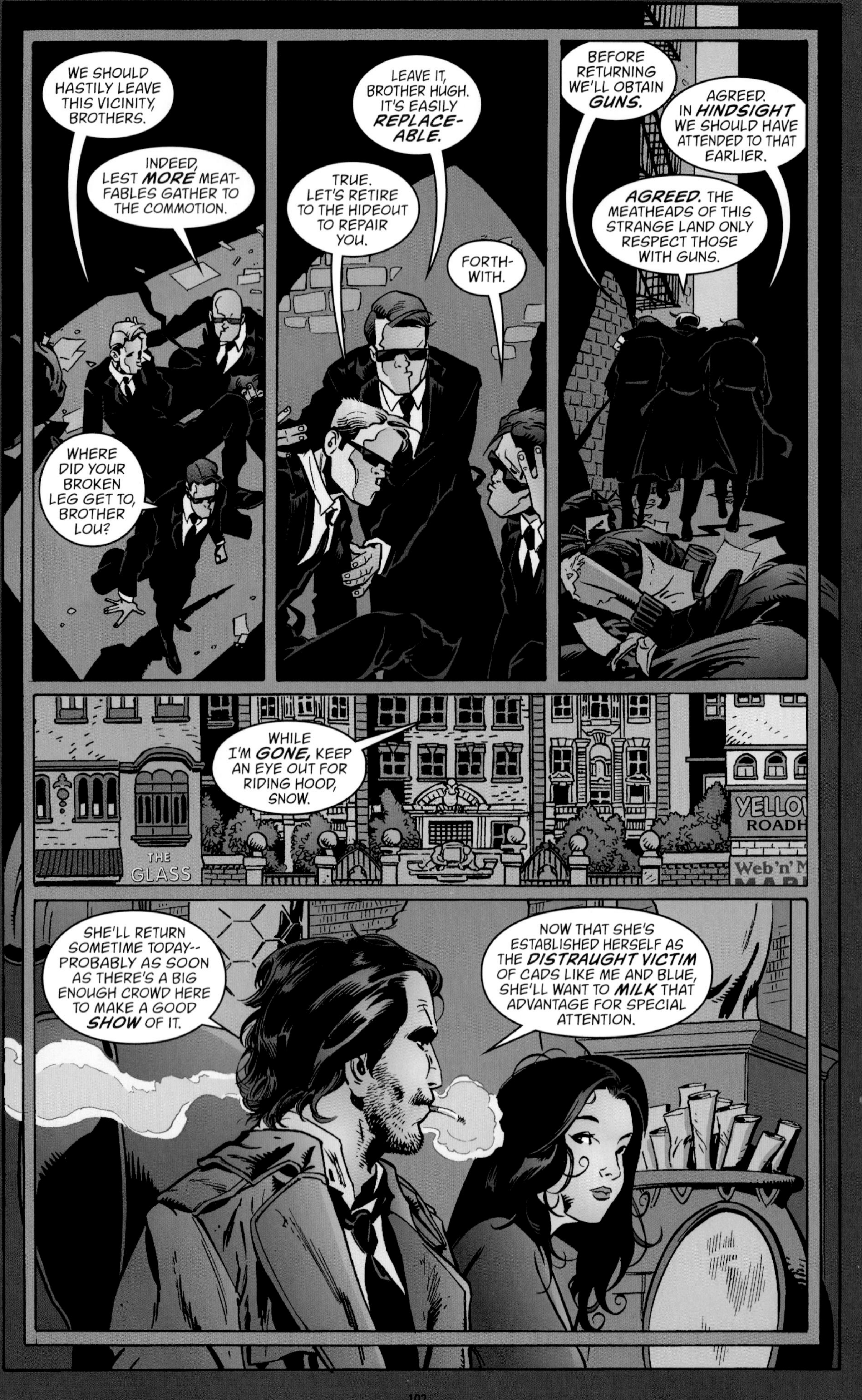
WE SHOULD HASTILY LEAVE THIS VICINITY, BROTHERS.
INDEED, LEST MORE MEAT-FABLES GATHER TO THE COMMOTION.
WHERE DID YOUR BROKEN LEG GET TO, BROTHER LOU?
LEAVE IT, BROTHER HUGH. IT'S EASILY REPLACE-ABLE.
TRUE. LET'S RETIRE TO THE HIDEOUT TO REPAIR YOU.
FORTH-WITH.
BEFORE RETURNING WE'LL OBTAIN GUNS.
AGREED. IN HINDSIGHT WE SHOULD HAVE ATTENDED TO THAT EARLIER.
AGREED. THE MEATHEADS OF THIS STRANGE LAND ONLY RESPECT THOSE WITH GUNS.
WHILE I'M GONE, KEEP AN EYE OUT FOR RIDING HOOD, SNOW.
THE GLASS
YELLOW
ROADH
Web'n'M
SHE'LL RETURN SOMETIME TODAY-- PROBABLY AS SOON AS THERE'S A BIG ENOUGH CROWD HERE TO MAKE A GOOD SHOW OF IT.
NOW THAT SHE'S ESTABLISHED HERSELF AS THE DISTRAUGHT VICTIM OF CADS LIKE ME AND BLUE, SHE'LL WANT TO MILK THAT ADVANTAGE FOR SPECIAL ATTENTION.

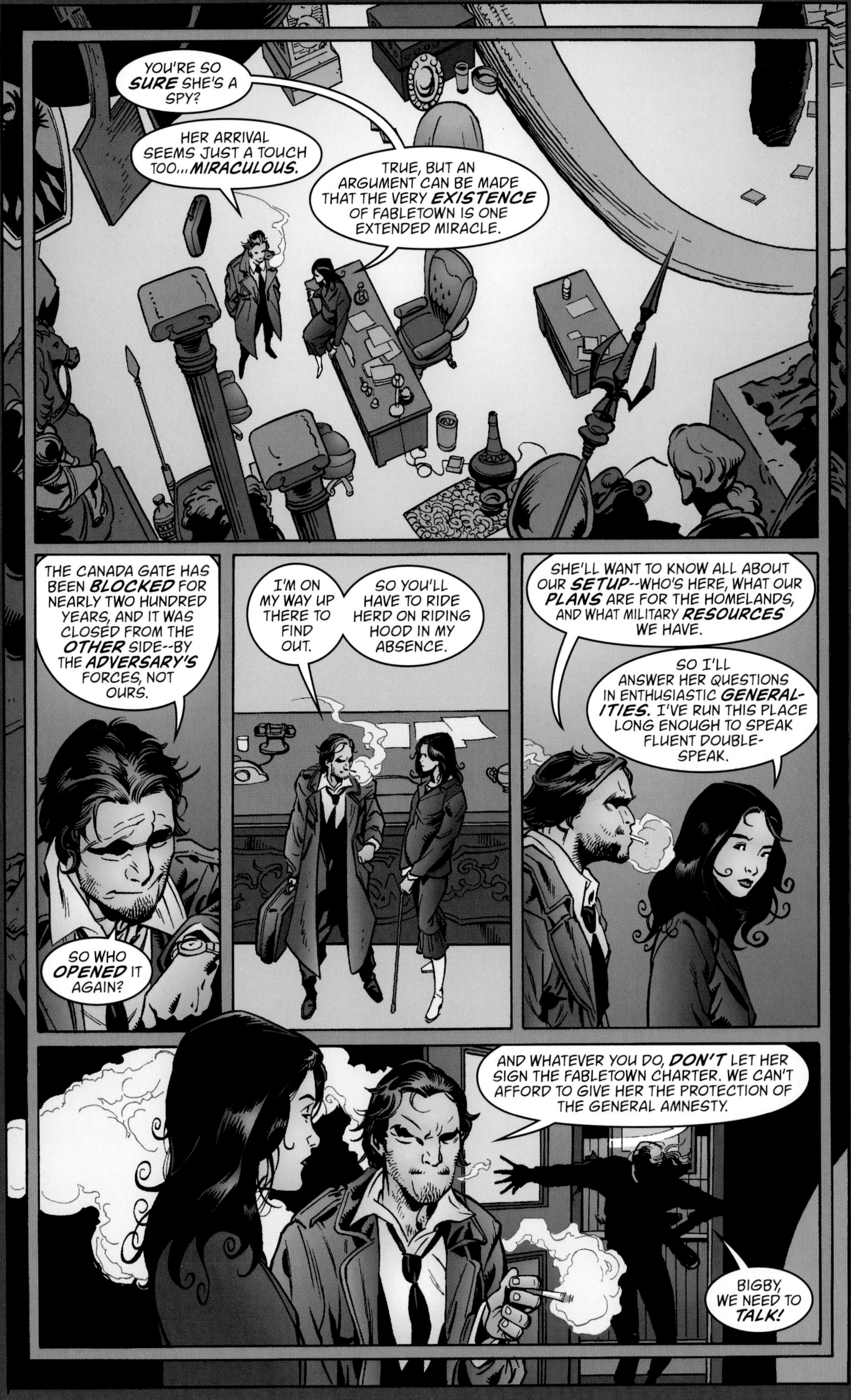

YOU'RE SO SURE SHE'S A SPY?
HER ARRIVAL SEEMS JUST A TOUCH TOO... MIRACULOUS.
TRUE, BUT AN ARGUMENT CAN BE MADE THAT THE VERY EXISTENCE OF FABLETOWN IS ONE EXTENDED MIRACLE.
THE CANADA GATE HAS BEEN BLOCKED FOR NEARLY TWO HUNDRED YEARS, AND IT WAS CLOSED FROM THE OTHER SIDE--BY THE ADVERSARY'S FORCES, NOT OURS.
SO WHO OPENED IT AGAIN?
I'M ON MY WAY UP THERE TO FIND OUT.
SO YOU'LL HAVE TO RIDE HERD ON RIDING HOOD IN MY ABSENCE.
SHE'LL WANT TO KNOW ALL ABOUT OUR SETUP--WHO'S HERE, WHAT OUR PLANS ARE FOR THE HOMELANDS, AND WHAT MILITARY RESOURCES WE HAVE.
SO I'LL ANSWER HER QUESTIONS IN ENTHUSIASTIC GENERAL-ITIES. I'VE RUN THIS PLACE LONG ENOUGH TO SPEAK FLUENT DOUBLE-SPEAK.
AND WHATEVER YOU DO, DON'T LET HER SIGN THE FABLETOWN CHARTER. WE CAN'T AFFORD TO GIVE HER THE PROTECTION OF THE GENERAL AMNESTY.
BIGBY, WE NEED TO TALK!

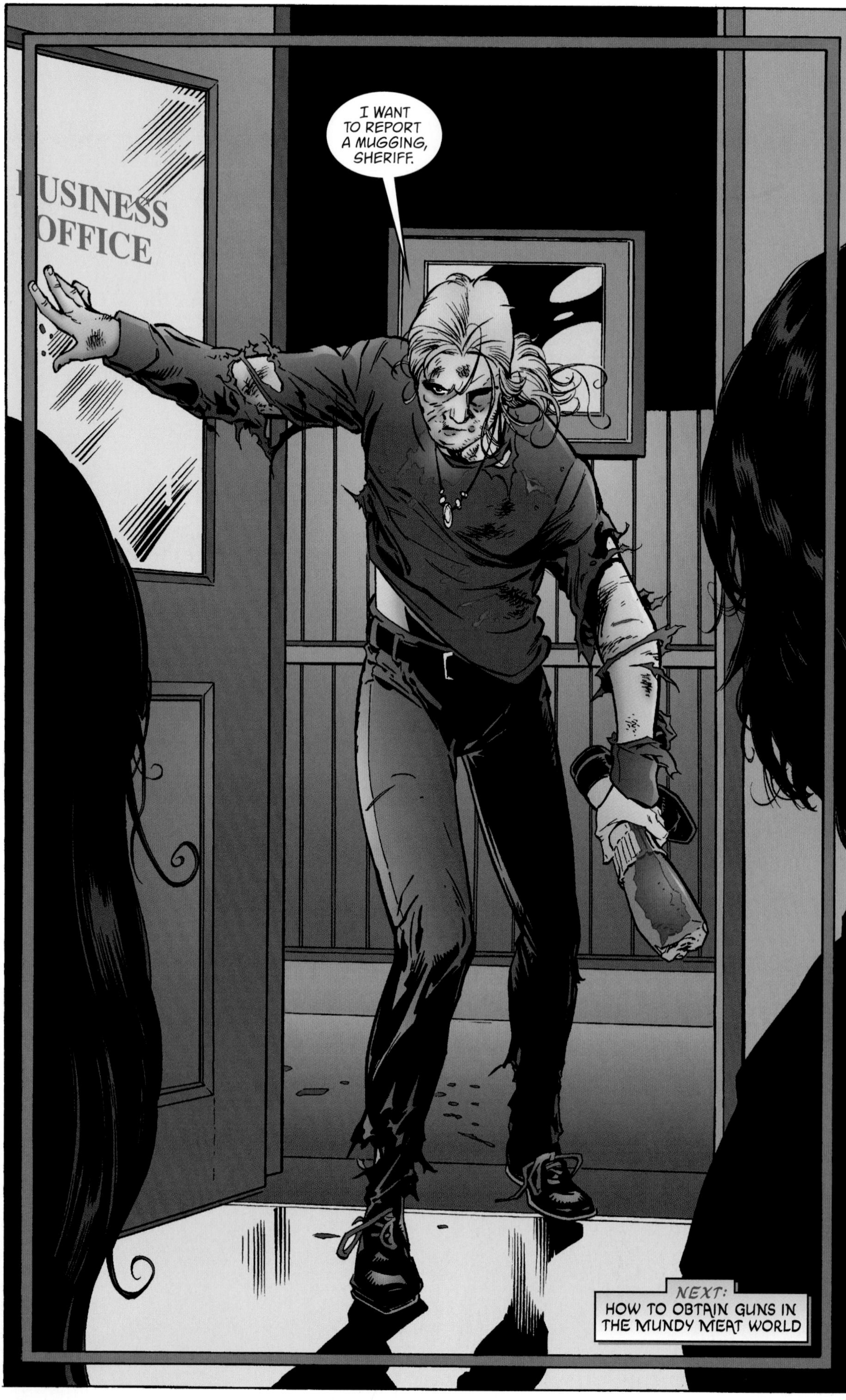

BUSINESS OFFICE
I WANT TO REPORT A MUGGING, SHERIFF.
NEXT:
HOW TO OBTAIN GUNS IN THE MUNDY MEAT WORLD

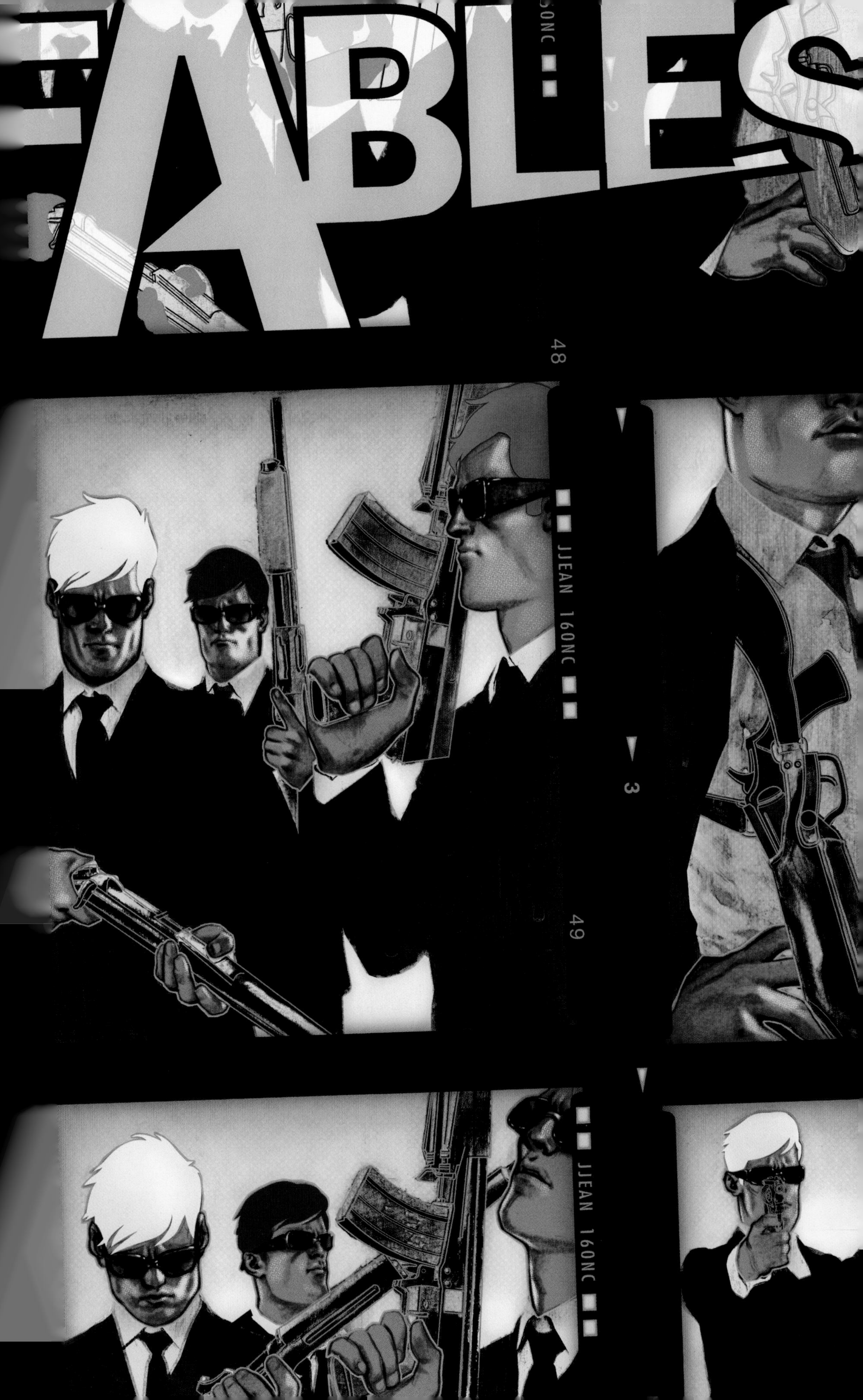
FABLES

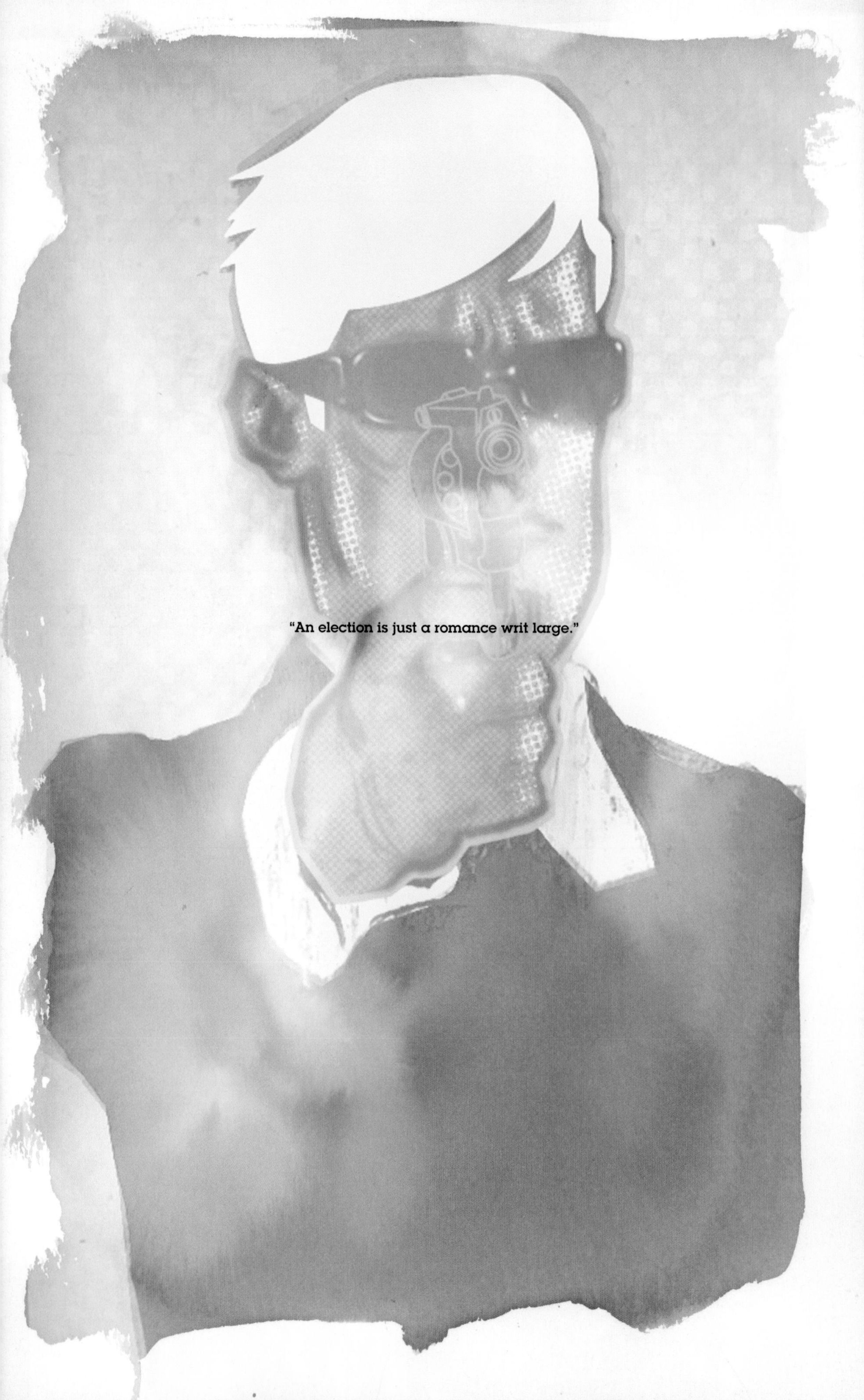
"An election is just a romance writ large."

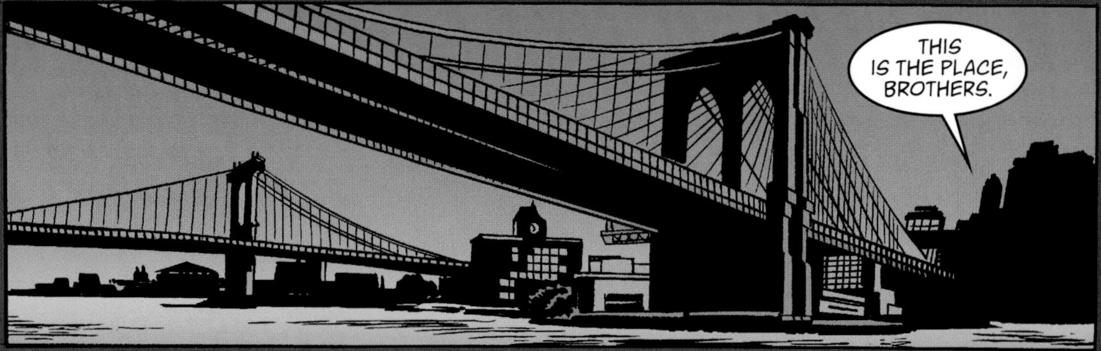
THIS IS THE PLACE, BROTHERS.

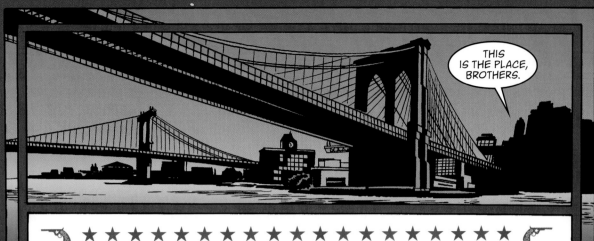

OUR SECOND AMENDMENT ISSUE

CHAPTER FOUR ○ MARCH OF THE WOODEN SOLDIERS

BILL WILLINGHAM writer/creator
MARK BUCKINGHAM penciller
STEVE LEIALOHA inker
DANIEL VOZZO color/seps
TODD KLEIN lettering
JAMES JEAN cover art
MARIAH HUEHNER assistant editor
SHELLY BOND editor

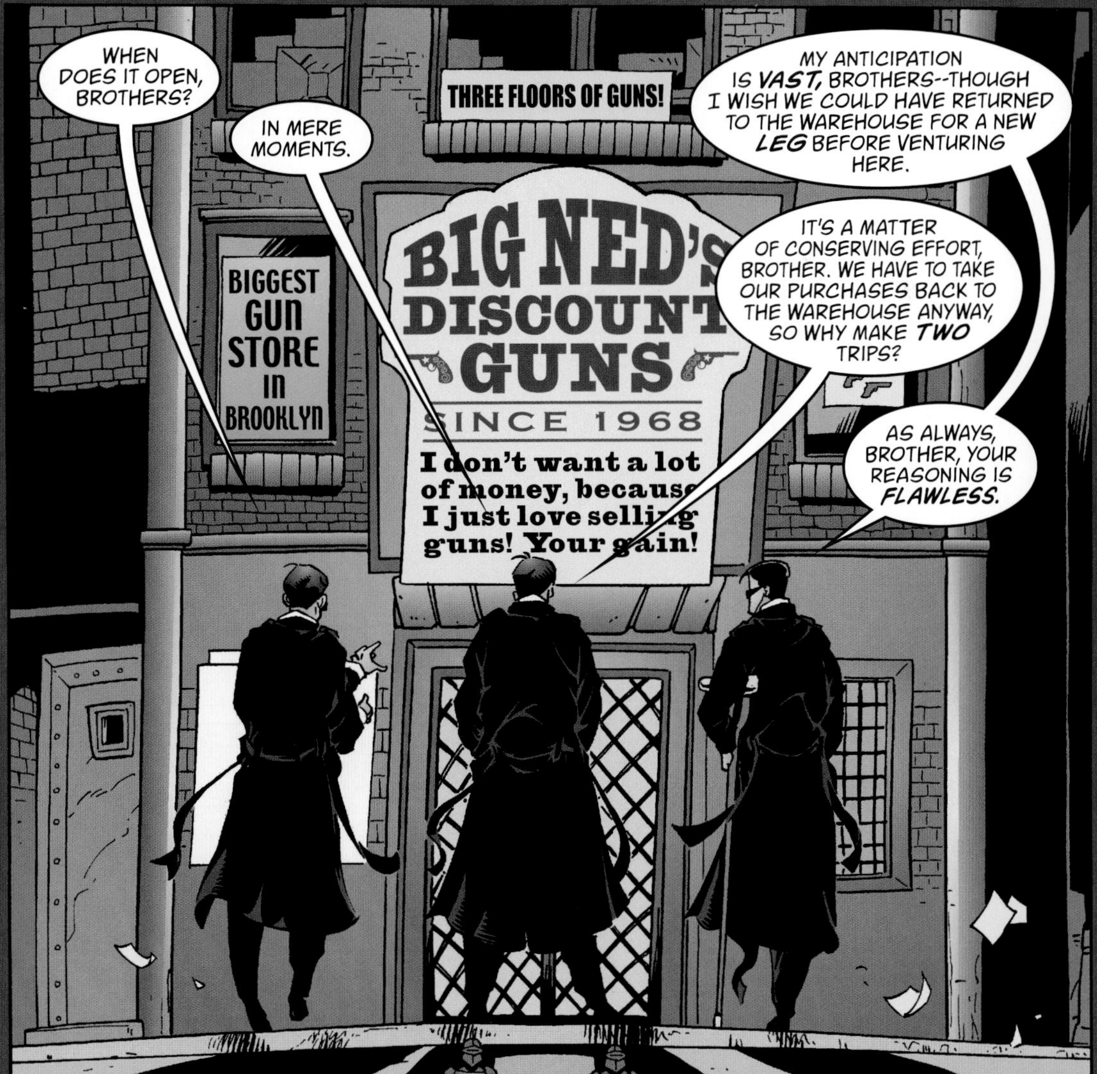
WHEN DOES IT OPEN, BROTHERS?
IN MERE MOMENTS.
THREE FLOORS OF GUNS!
MY ANTICIPATION IS VAST, BROTHERS--THOUGH I WISH WE COULD HAVE RETURNED TO THE WAREHOUSE FOR A NEW LEG BEFORE VENTURING HERE.
IT'S A MATTER OF CONSERVING EFFORT, BROTHER. WE HAVE TO TAKE OUR PURCHASES BACK TO THE WAREHOUSE ANYWAY, SO WHY MAKE TWO TRIPS?
AS ALWAYS, BROTHER, YOUR REASONING IS FLAWLESS.
BIGGEST GUN STORE IN BROOKLYN
BIG NED'S DISCOUNT GUNS
SINCE 1968
I don't want a lot of money, because I just love selling guns! Your gain!

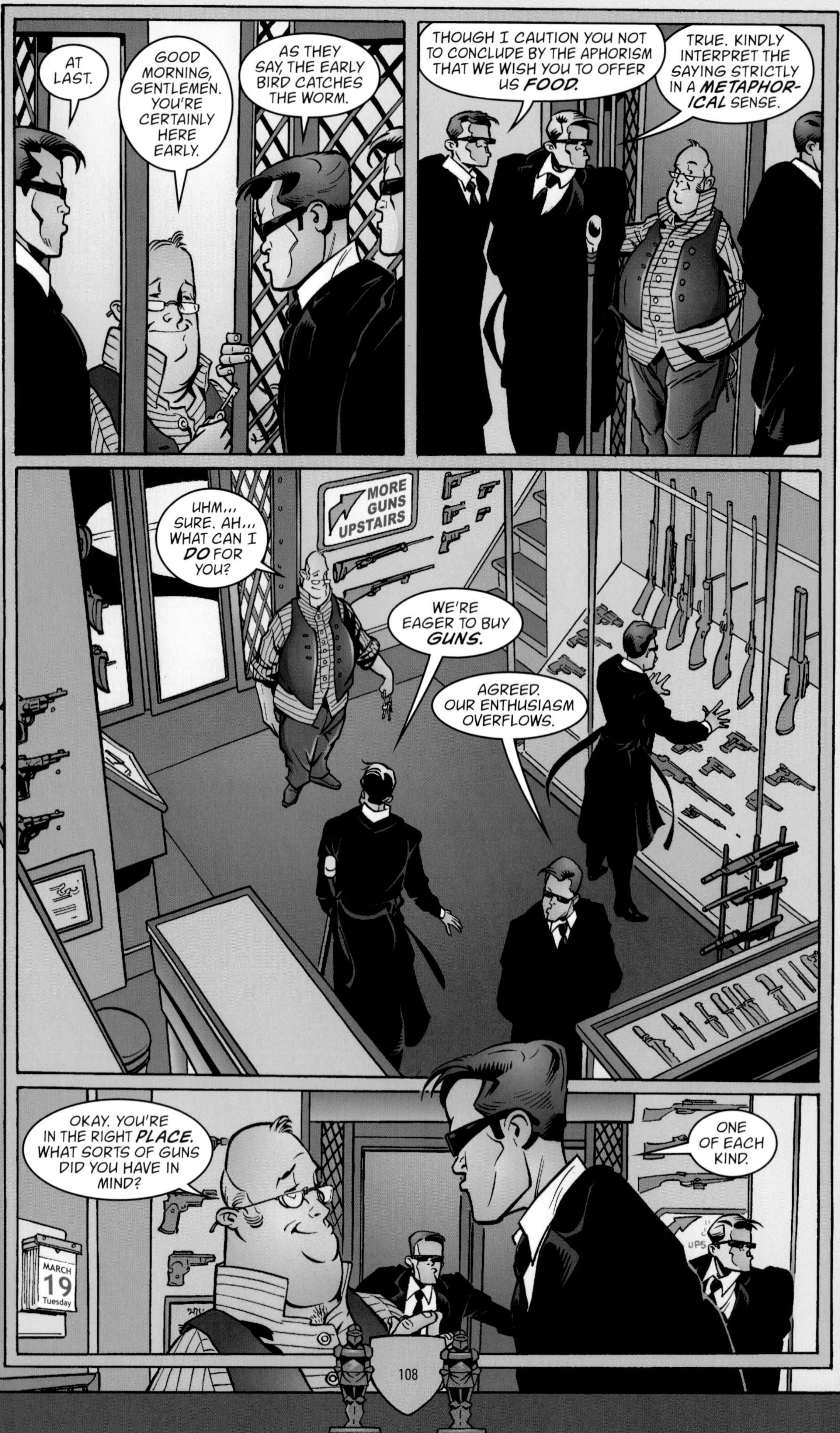
AT LAST.
GOOD MORNING, GENTLEMEN. YOU'RE CERTAINLY HERE EARLY.
AS THEY SAY, THE EARLY BIRD CATCHES THE WORM.
THOUGH I CAUTION YOU NOT TO CONCLUDE BY THE APHORISM THAT WE WISH YOU TO OFFER US FOOD.
TRUE. KINDLY INTERPRET THE SAYING STRICTLY IN A METAPHORICAL SENSE.
MORE GUNS UPSTAIRS
UHM... SURE. AH... WHAT CAN I DO FOR YOU?
WE'RE EAGER TO BUY GUNS.
AGREED. OUR ENTHUSIASM OVERFLOWS.
OKAY. YOU'RE IN THE RIGHT PLACE. WHAT SORTS OF GUNS DID YOU HAVE IN MIND?
ONE OF EACH KIND.
MARCH
19
Tuesday

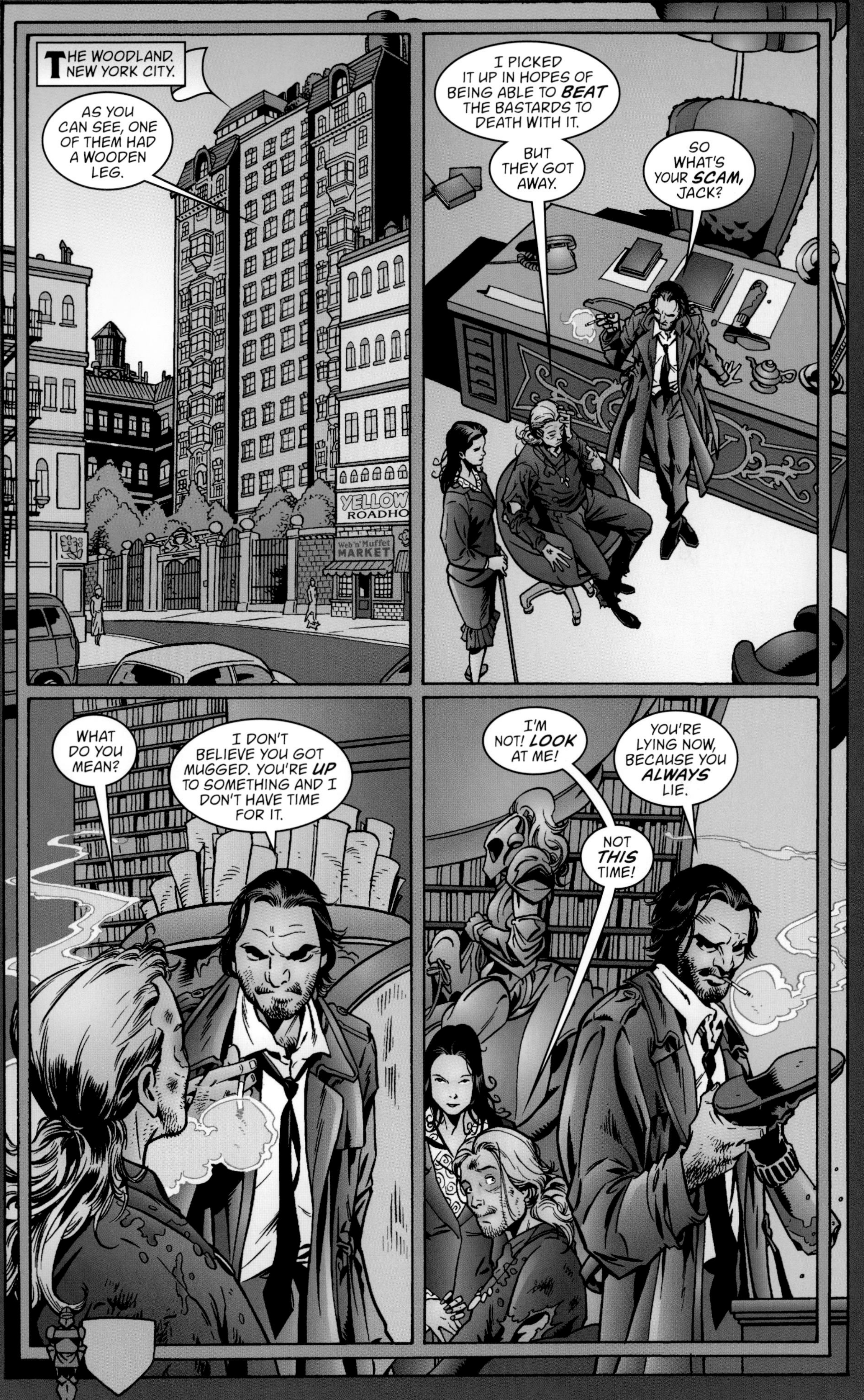
THE WOODLAND. NEW YORK CITY.
AS YOU CAN SEE, ONE OF THEM HAD A WOODEN LEG.
YELLOW ROADHO
Web 'n' Muffet MARKET
I PICKED IT UP IN HOPES OF BEING ABLE TO BEAT THE BASTARDS TO DEATH WITH IT.
BUT THEY GOT AWAY.
SO WHAT'S YOUR SCAM, JACK?
WHAT DO YOU MEAN?
I DON'T BELIEVE YOU GOT MUGGED. YOU'RE UP TO SOMETHING AND I DON'T HAVE TIME FOR IT.
I'M NOT! LOOK AT ME!
YOU'RE LYING NOW, BECAUSE YOU ALWAYS LIE.
NOT THIS TIME!

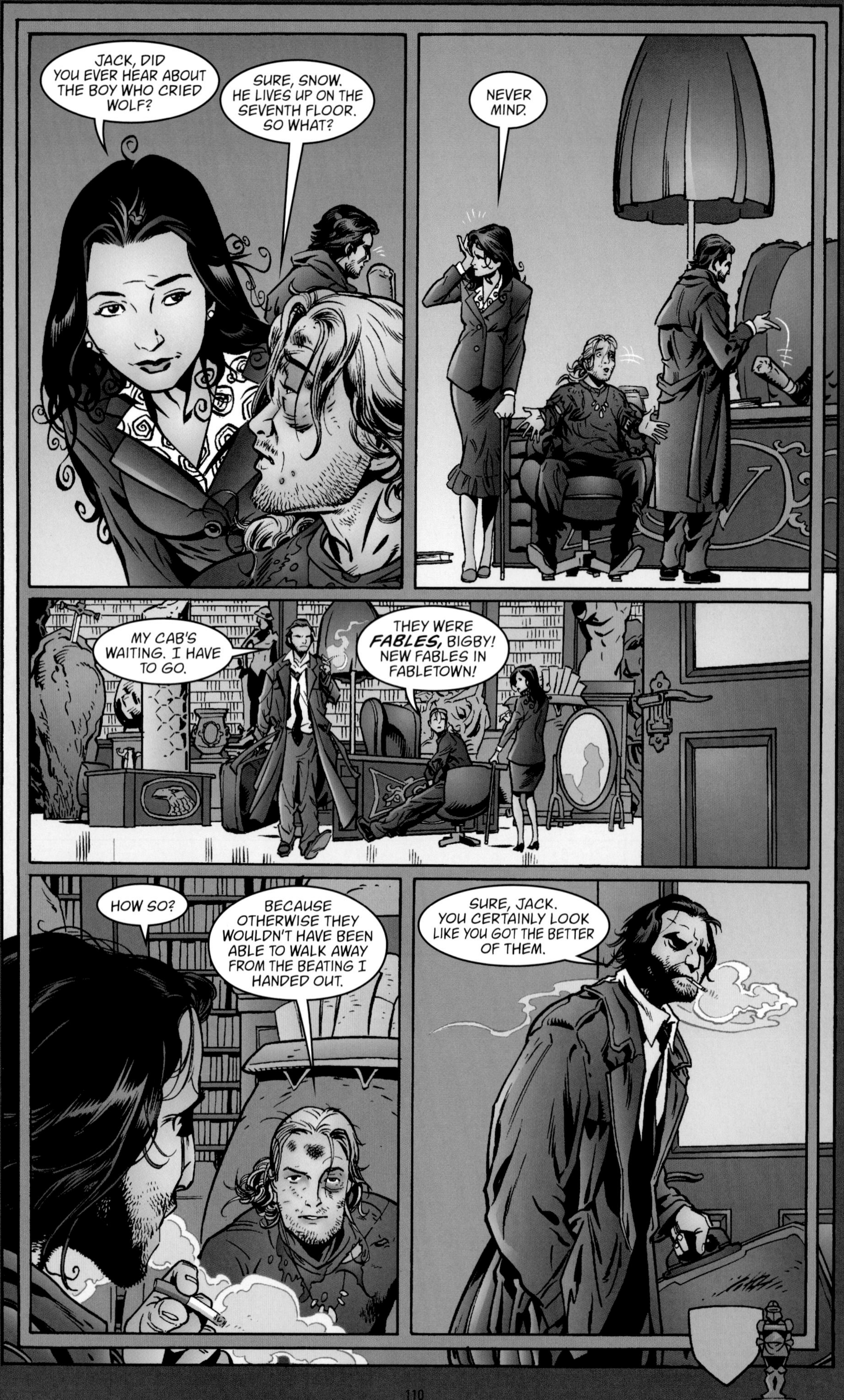
JACK, DID YOU EVER HEAR ABOUT THE BOY WHO CRIED WOLF?
SURE, SNOW. HE LIVES UP ON THE SEVENTH FLOOR. SO WHAT?
NEVER MIND.
MY CAB'S WAITING. I HAVE TO GO.
THEY WERE FABLES, BIGBY! NEW FABLES IN FABLETOWN!
HOW SO?
BECAUSE OTHERWISE THEY WOULDN'T HAVE BEEN ABLE TO WALK AWAY FROM THE BEATING I HANDED OUT.
SURE, JACK. YOU CERTAINLY LOOK LIKE YOU GOT THE BETTER OF THEM.

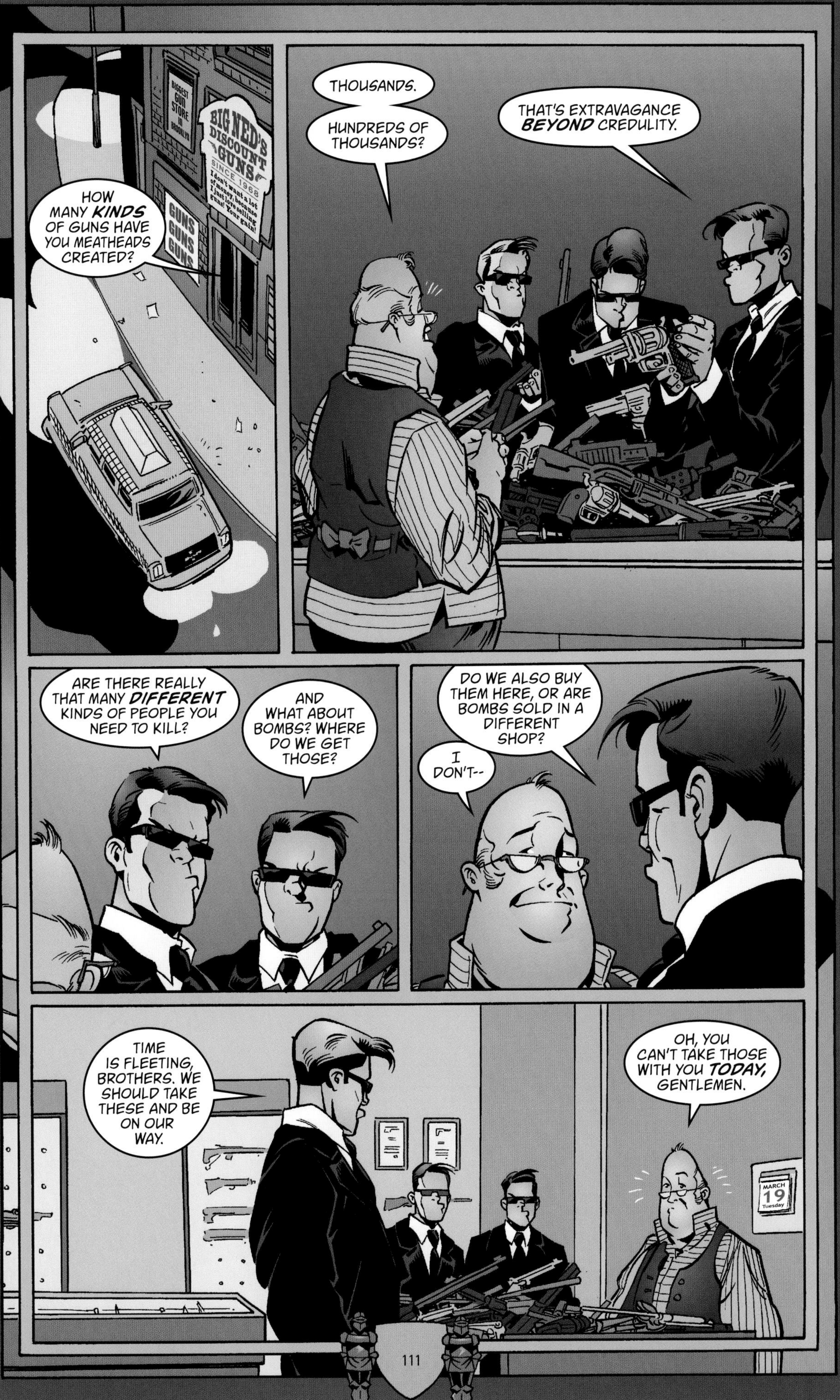
BIGGEST GUN STORE IN BROOKLYN
BIG NED'S DISCOUNT GUNS
SINCE 1968
I don't want a lot of money, because I just love selling guns! Your gain!
GUNS GUNS GUNS
HOW MANY KINDS OF GUNS HAVE YOU MEATHEADS CREATED?
THOUSANDS.
HUNDREDS OF THOUSANDS?
THAT'S EXTRAVAGANCE BEYOND CREDULITY.
ARE THERE REALLY THAT MANY DIFFERENT KINDS OF PEOPLE YOU NEED TO KILL?
AND WHAT ABOUT BOMBS? WHERE DO WE GET THOSE?
DO WE ALSO BUY THEM HERE, OR ARE BOMBS SOLD IN A DIFFERENT SHOP?
I DON'T--
TIME IS FLEETING, BROTHERS. WE SHOULD TAKE THESE AND BE ON OUR WAY.
OH, YOU CAN'T TAKE THOSE WITH YOU TODAY, GENTLEMEN.
MARCH 19 Tuesday

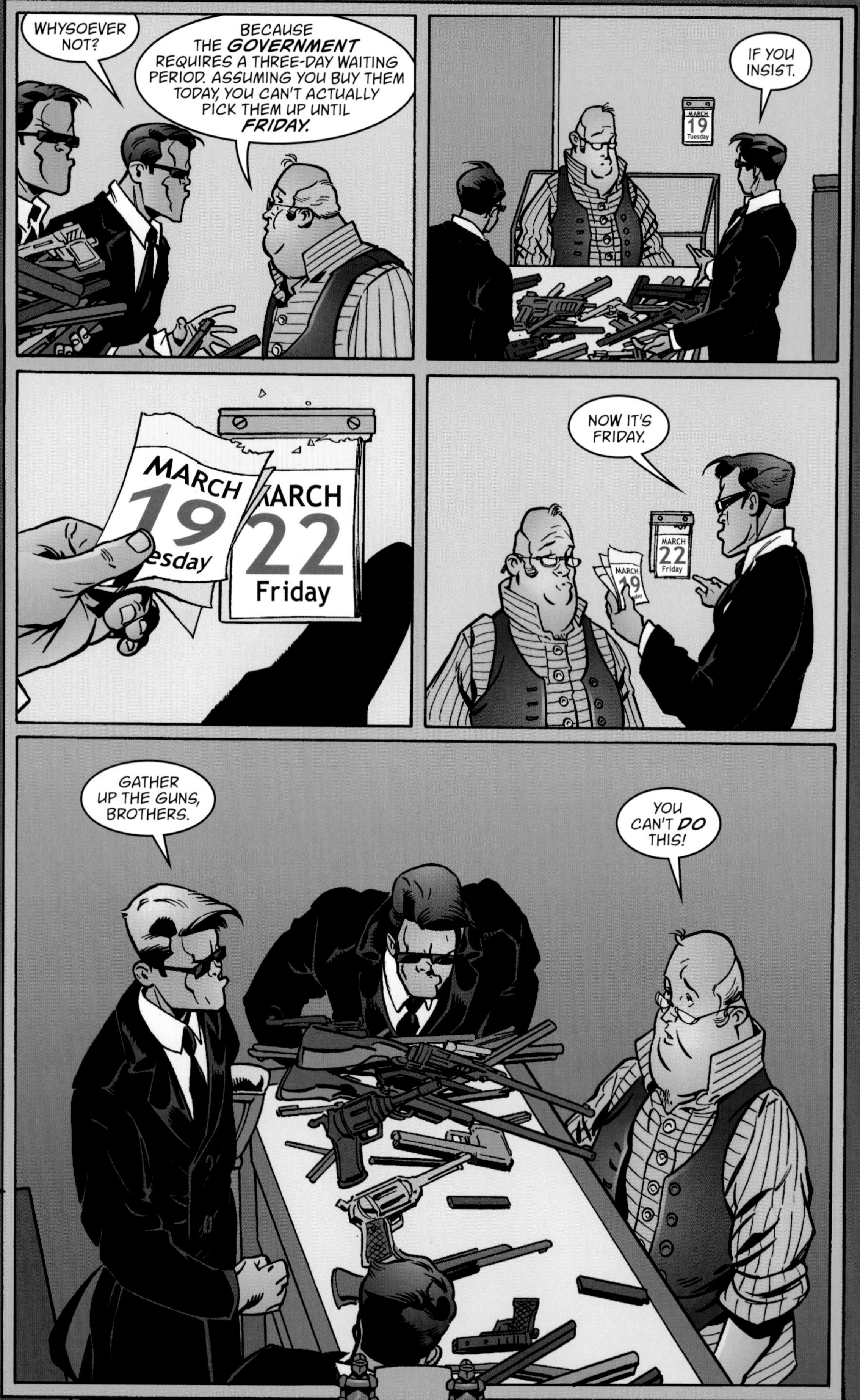
WHYSOEVER NOT?
BECAUSE THE GOVERNMENT REQUIRES A THREE-DAY WAITING PERIOD. ASSUMING YOU BUY THEM TODAY, YOU CAN'T ACTUALLY PICK THEM UP UNTIL FRIDAY.
MARCH 19 Tuesday
IF YOU INSIST.
MARCH 19 Tuesday
MARCH 22 Friday
NOW IT'S FRIDAY.
MARCH 22 Friday
GATHER UP THE GUNS, BROTHERS.
YOU CAN'T DO THIS!

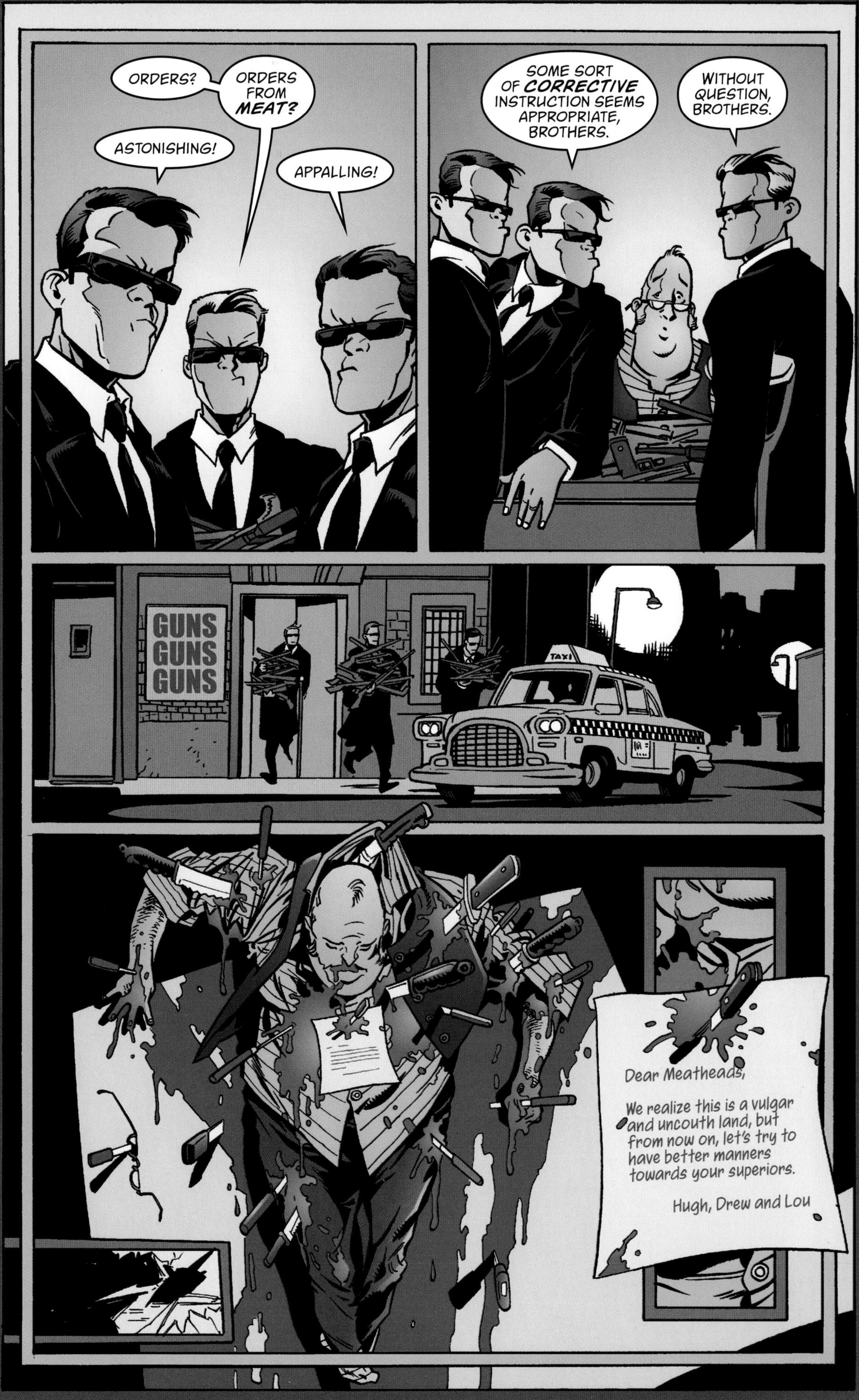
ORDERS?
ORDERS FROM MEAT?
ASTONISHING!
APPALLING!
SOME SORT OF CORRECTIVE INSTRUCTION SEEMS APPROPRIATE, BROTHERS.
WITHOUT QUESTION, BROTHERS.
GUNS GUNS GUNS
TAXI
Dear Meatheads,
We realize this is a vulgar and uncouth land, but from now on, let's try to have better manners towards your superiors.
Hugh, Drew and Lou

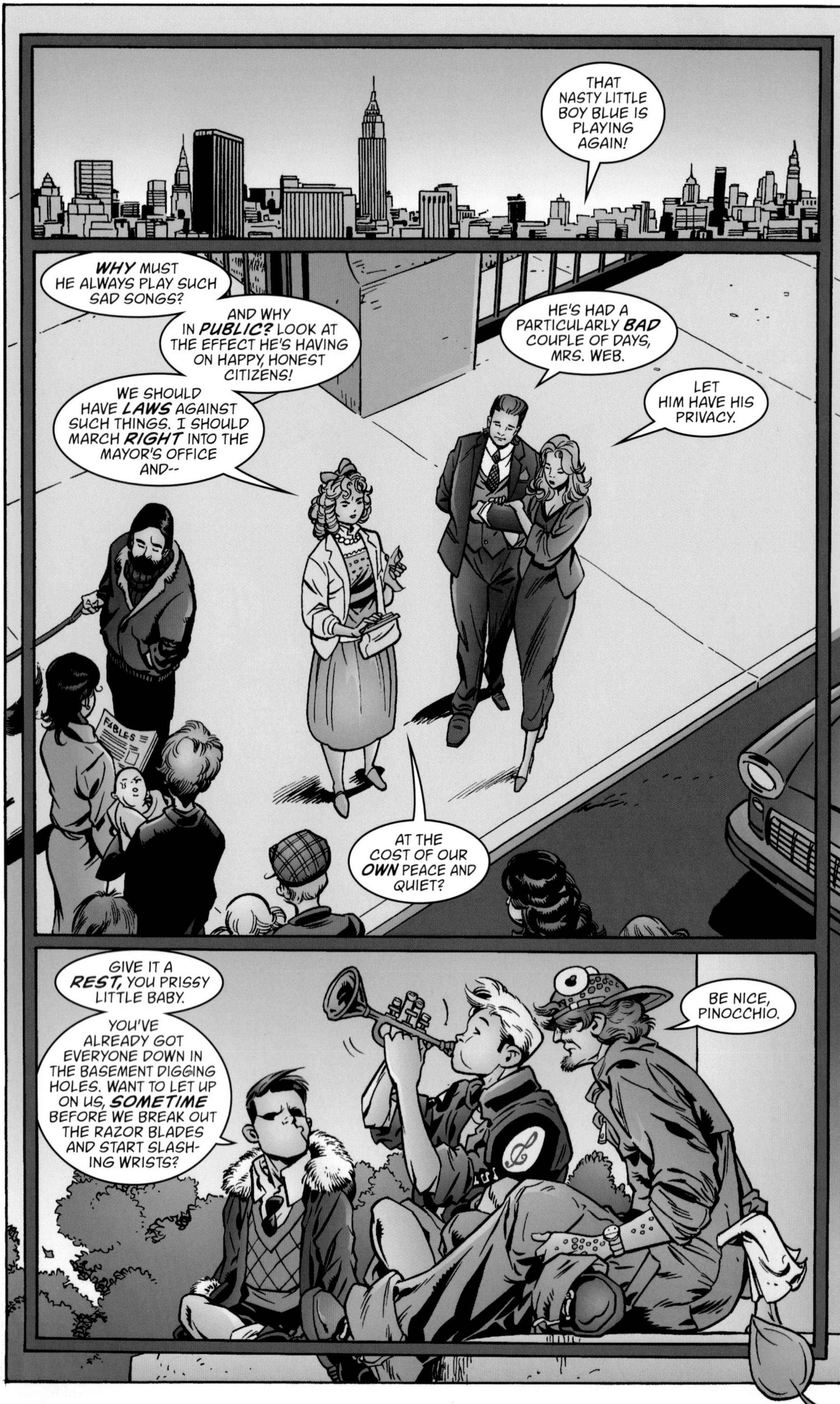
THAT NASTY LITTLE BOY BLUE IS PLAYING AGAIN!
WHY MUST HE ALWAYS PLAY SUCH SAD SONGS?
AND WHY IN PUBLIC? LOOK AT THE EFFECT HE'S HAVING ON HAPPY, HONEST CITIZENS!
WE SHOULD HAVE LAWS AGAINST SUCH THINGS. I SHOULD MARCH RIGHT INTO THE MAYOR'S OFFICE AND--
HE'S HAD A PARTICULARLY BAD COUPLE OF DAYS, MRS. WEB.
LET HIM HAVE HIS PRIVACY.
AT THE COST OF OUR OWN PEACE AND QUIET?
FABLES
GIVE IT A REST, YOU PRISSY LITTLE BABY.
YOU'VE ALREADY GOT EVERYONE DOWN IN THE BASEMENT DIGGING HOLES. WANT TO LET UP ON US, SOMETIME BEFORE WE BREAK OUT THE RAZOR BLADES AND START SLASH-ING WRISTS?
BE NICE, PINOCCHIO.

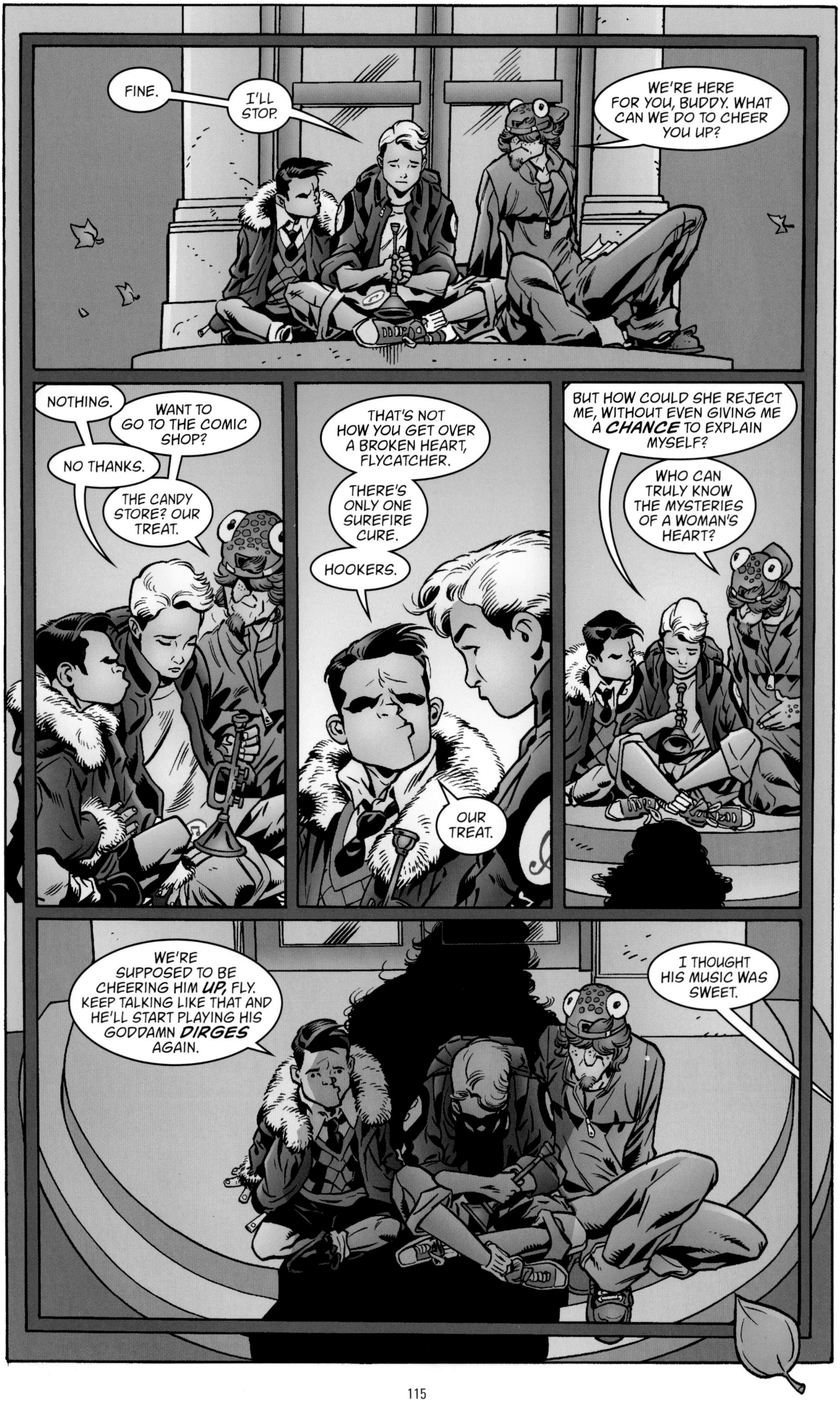
FINE.
I'LL STOP.
WE'RE HERE FOR YOU, BUDDY. WHAT CAN WE DO TO CHEER YOU UP?
NOTHING.
WANT TO GO TO THE COMIC SHOP?
NO THANKS.
THE CANDY STORE? OUR TREAT.
THAT'S NOT HOW YOU GET OVER A BROKEN HEART, FLYCATCHER.
THERE'S ONLY ONE SUREFIRE CURE.
HOOKERS.
OUR TREAT.
BUT HOW COULD SHE REJECT ME, WITHOUT EVEN GIVING ME A ***CHANCE*** TO EXPLAIN MYSELF?
WHO CAN TRULY KNOW THE MYSTERIES OF A WOMAN'S HEART?
WE'RE SUPPOSED TO BE CHEERING HIM ***UP***, FLY. KEEP TALKING LIKE THAT AND HE'LL START PLAYING HIS GODDAMN ***DIRGES*** AGAIN.
I THOUGHT HIS MUSIC WAS SWEET.

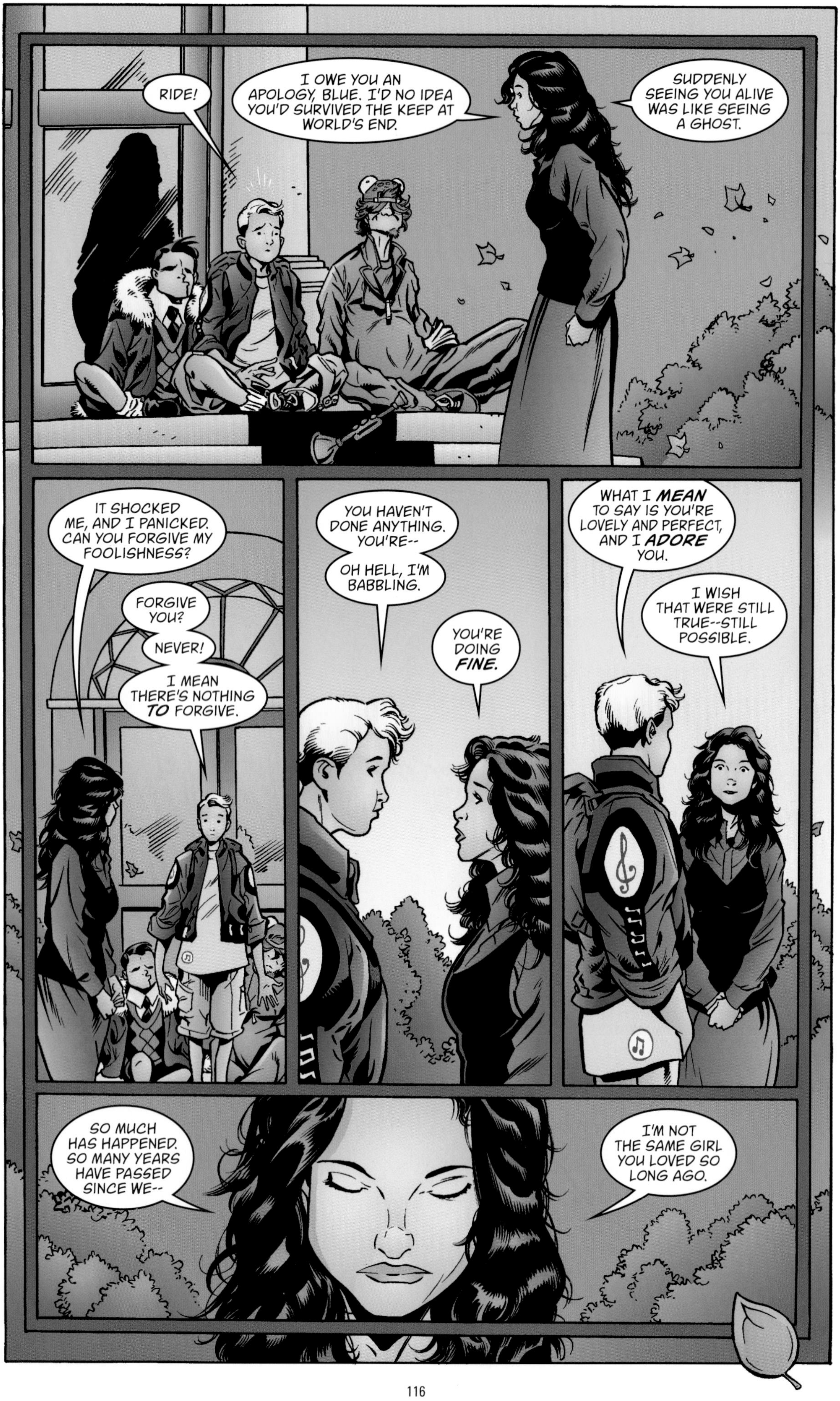
RIDE!
I OWE YOU AN APOLOGY, BLUE. I'D NO IDEA YOU'D SURVIVED THE KEEP AT WORLD'S END.
SUDDENLY SEEING YOU ALIVE WAS LIKE SEEING A GHOST.
IT SHOCKED ME, AND I PANICKED. CAN YOU FORGIVE MY FOOLISHNESS?
FORGIVE YOU?
NEVER!
I MEAN THERE'S NOTHING *TO* FORGIVE.
YOU HAVEN'T DONE ANYTHING. YOU'RE--
OH HELL, I'M BABBLING.
YOU'RE DOING *FINE.*
WHAT I *MEAN* TO SAY IS YOU'RE LOVELY AND PERFECT, AND I *ADORE* YOU.
I WISH THAT WERE STILL TRUE--STILL POSSIBLE.
SO MUCH HAS HAPPENED. SO MANY YEARS HAVE PASSED SINCE WE--
I'M NOT THE SAME GIRL YOU LOVED SO LONG AGO.

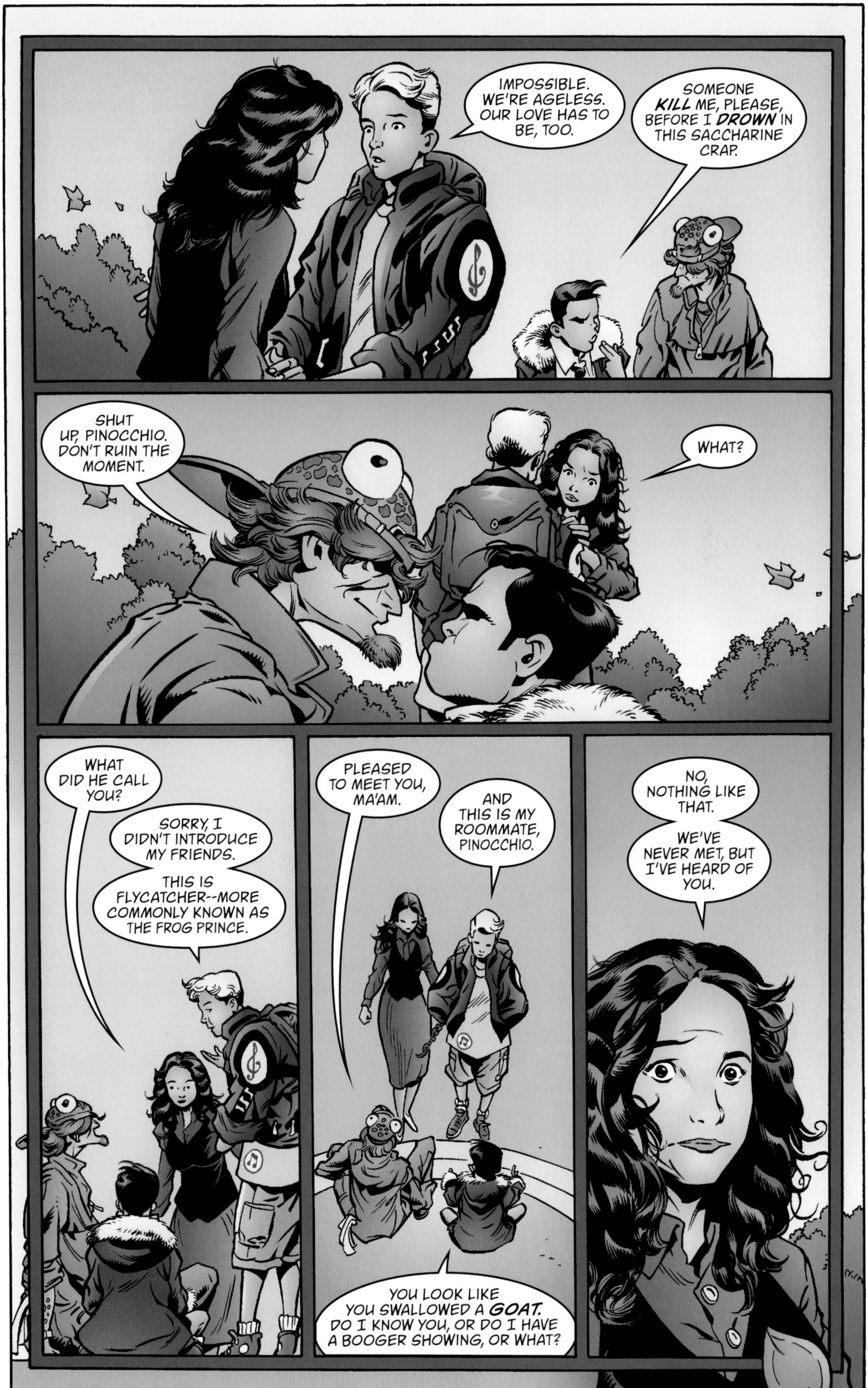

IMPOSSIBLE. WE'RE AGELESS. OUR LOVE HAS TO BE, TOO.
SOMEONE **KILL** ME, PLEASE, BEFORE I **DROWN** IN THIS SACCHARINE CRAP.
SHUT UP, PINOCCHIO. DON'T RUIN THE MOMENT.
WHAT?
WHAT DID HE CALL YOU?
SORRY, I DIDN'T INTRODUCE MY FRIENDS.
THIS IS FLYCATCHER--MORE COMMONLY KNOWN AS THE FROG PRINCE.
PLEASED TO MEET YOU, MA'AM.
AND THIS IS MY ROOMMATE, PINOCCHIO.
YOU LOOK LIKE YOU SWALLOWED A **GOAT**. DO I KNOW YOU, OR DO I HAVE A BOOGER SHOWING, OR WHAT?
NO, NOTHING LIKE THAT.
WE'VE NEVER MET, BUT I'VE HEARD OF YOU.

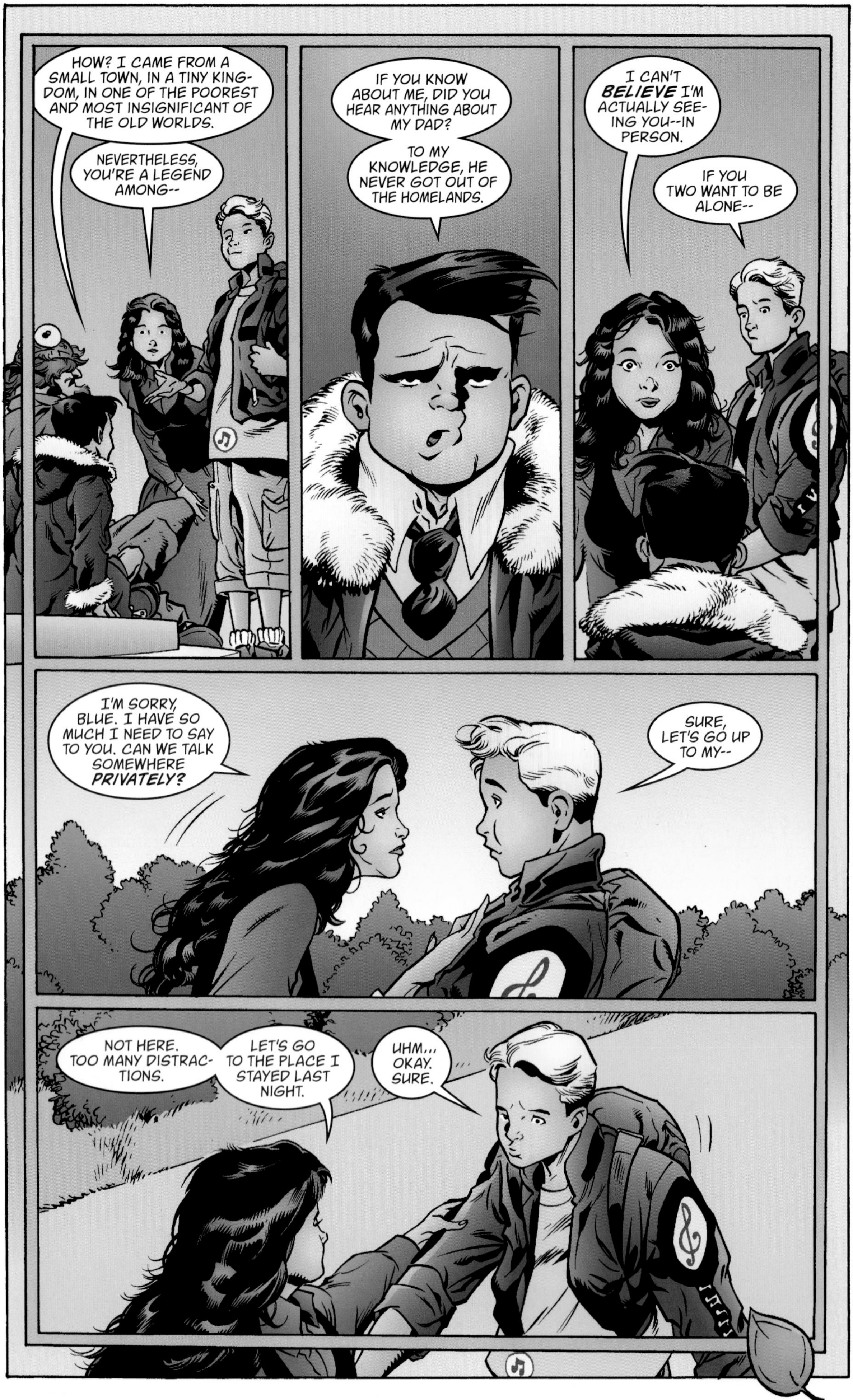
HOW? I CAME FROM A SMALL TOWN, IN A TINY KINGDOM, IN ONE OF THE POOREST AND MOST INSIGNIFICANT OF THE OLD WORLDS.
NEVERTHELESS, YOU'RE A LEGEND AMONG--
IF YOU KNOW ABOUT ME, DID YOU HEAR ANYTHING ABOUT MY DAD?
TO MY KNOWLEDGE, HE NEVER GOT OUT OF THE HOMELANDS.
I CAN'T BELIEVE I'M ACTUALLY SEEING YOU--IN PERSON.
IF YOU TWO WANT TO BE ALONE--
I'M SORRY, BLUE. I HAVE SO MUCH I NEED TO SAY TO YOU. CAN WE TALK SOMEWHERE PRIVATELY?
SURE, LET'S GO UP TO MY--
NOT HERE. TOO MANY DISTRACTIONS.
LET'S GO TO THE PLACE I STAYED LAST NIGHT.
UHM... OKAY. SURE.

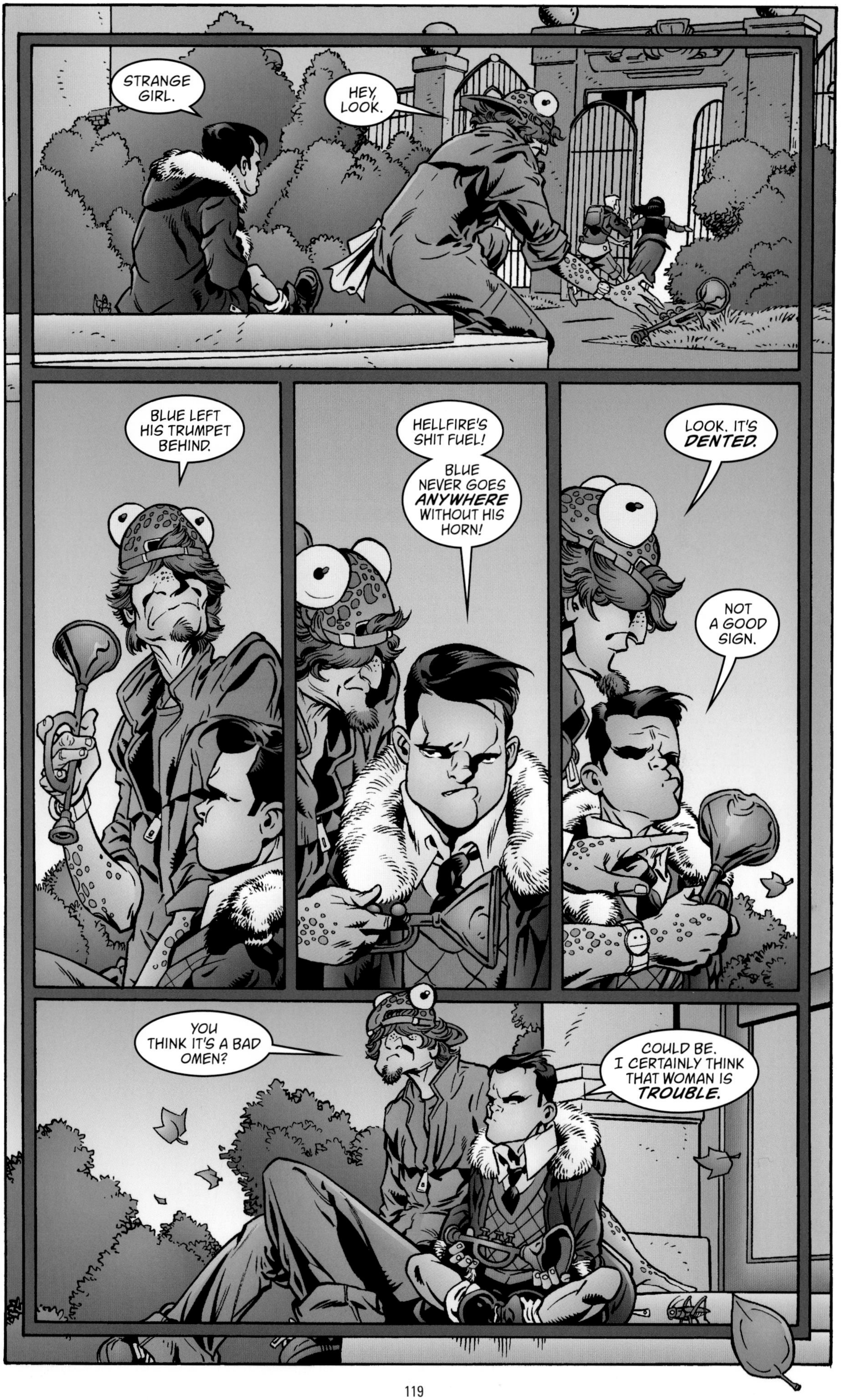
STRANGE GIRL.
HEY, LOOK.
BLUE LEFT HIS TRUMPET BEHIND.
HELLFIRE'S SHIT FUEL!
BLUE NEVER GOES ANYWHERE WITHOUT HIS HORN!
LOOK. IT'S DENTED.
NOT A GOOD SIGN.
YOU THINK IT'S A BAD OMEN?
COULD BE. I CERTAINLY THINK THAT WOMAN IS TROUBLE.

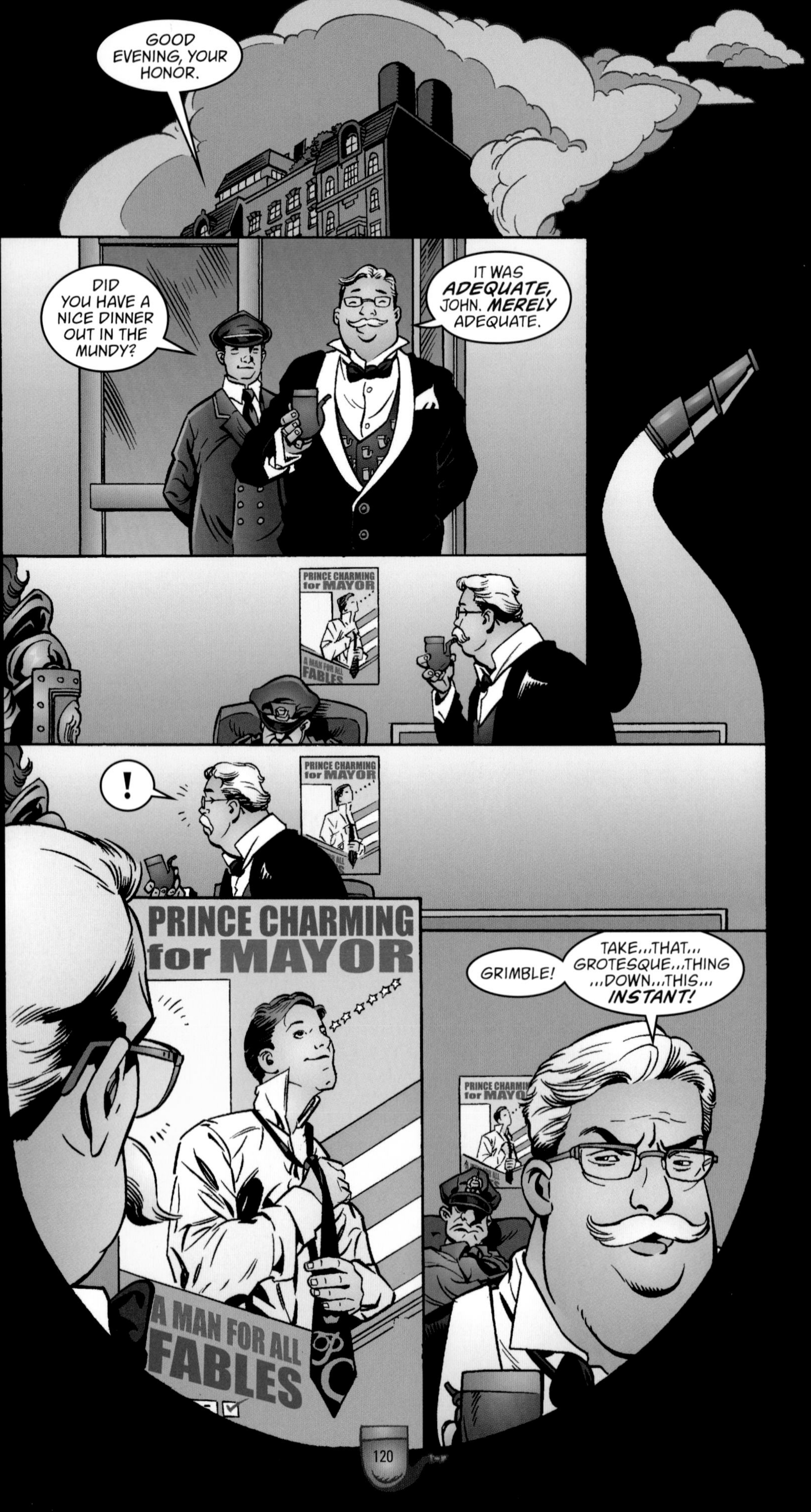
GOOD EVENING, YOUR HONOR.
DID YOU HAVE A NICE DINNER OUT IN THE MUNDY?
IT WAS *ADEQUATE,* JOHN. *MERELY* ADEQUATE.
PRINCE CHARMING for MAYOR
A MAN FOR ALL FABLES
!
PRINCE CHARMING for MAYOR
PRINCE CHARMING for MAYOR
A MAN FOR ALL FABLES
GRIMBLE!
TAKE...THAT... GROTESQUE...THING ...DOWN...THIS... *INSTANT!*

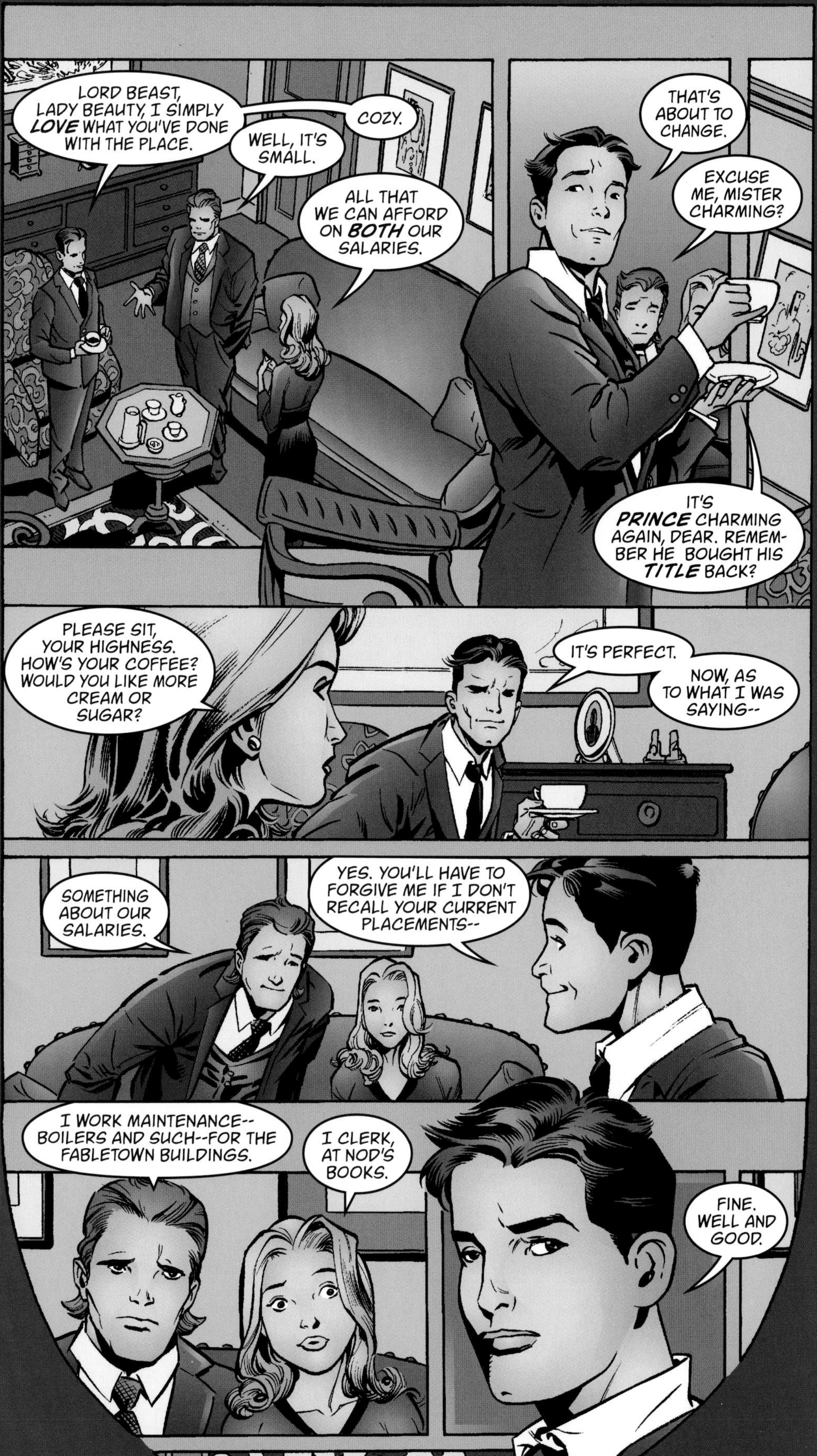
LORD BEAST, LADY BEAUTY, I SIMPLY LOVE WHAT YOU'VE DONE WITH THE PLACE.
COZY.
WELL, IT'S SMALL.
ALL THAT WE CAN AFFORD ON BOTH OUR SALARIES.
THAT'S ABOUT TO CHANGE.
EXCUSE ME, MISTER CHARMING?
IT'S PRINCE CHARMING AGAIN, DEAR. REMEMBER HE BOUGHT HIS TITLE BACK?
PLEASE SIT, YOUR HIGHNESS. HOW'S YOUR COFFEE? WOULD YOU LIKE MORE CREAM OR SUGAR?
IT'S PERFECT.
NOW, AS TO WHAT I WAS SAYING--
SOMETHING ABOUT OUR SALARIES.
YES. YOU'LL HAVE TO FORGIVE ME IF I DON'T RECALL YOUR CURRENT PLACEMENTS--
I WORK MAINTENANCE-- BOILERS AND SUCH--FOR THE FABLETOWN BUILDINGS.
I CLERK, AT NOD'S BOOKS.
FINE. WELL AND GOOD.

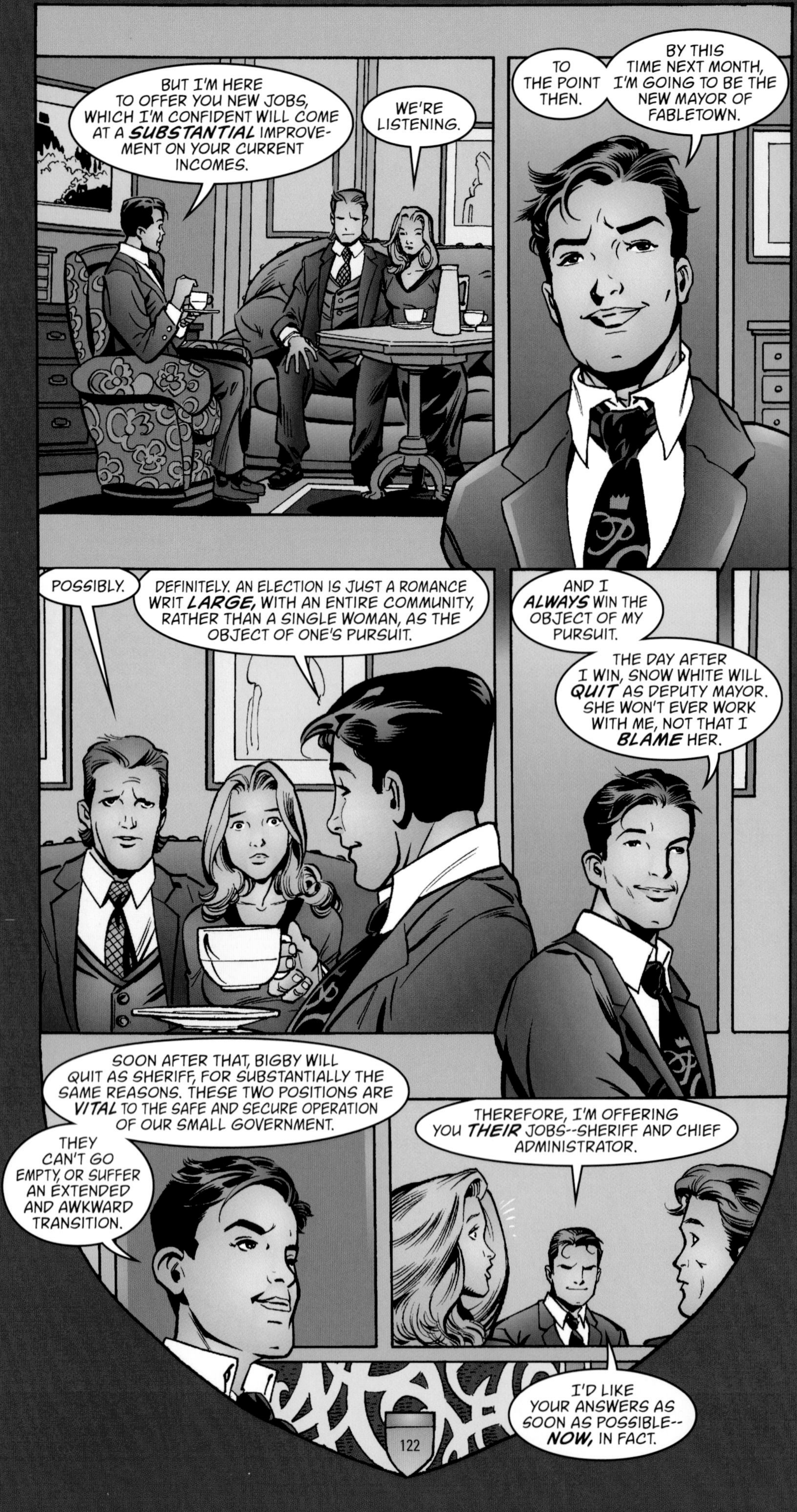
BUT I'M HERE TO OFFER YOU NEW JOBS, WHICH I'M CONFIDENT WILL COME AT A SUBSTANTIAL IMPROVEMENT ON YOUR CURRENT INCOMES.
WE'RE LISTENING.
TO THE POINT THEN.
BY THIS TIME NEXT MONTH, I'M GOING TO BE THE NEW MAYOR OF FABLETOWN.
POSSIBLY.
DEFINITELY. AN ELECTION IS JUST A ROMANCE WRIT LARGE, WITH AN ENTIRE COMMUNITY, RATHER THAN A SINGLE WOMAN, AS THE OBJECT OF ONE'S PURSUIT.
AND I ALWAYS WIN THE OBJECT OF MY PURSUIT.
THE DAY AFTER I WIN, SNOW WHITE WILL QUIT AS DEPUTY MAYOR. SHE WON'T EVER WORK WITH ME, NOT THAT I BLAME HER.
SOON AFTER THAT, BIGBY WILL QUIT AS SHERIFF, FOR SUBSTANTIALLY THE SAME REASONS. THESE TWO POSITIONS ARE VITAL TO THE SAFE AND SECURE OPERATION OF OUR SMALL GOVERNMENT.
THEY CAN'T GO EMPTY, OR SUFFER AN EXTENDED AND AWKWARD TRANSITION.
THEREFORE, I'M OFFERING YOU THEIR JOBS--SHERIFF AND CHIEF ADMINISTRATOR.
I'D LIKE YOUR ANSWERS AS SOON AS POSSIBLE-- NOW, IN FACT.

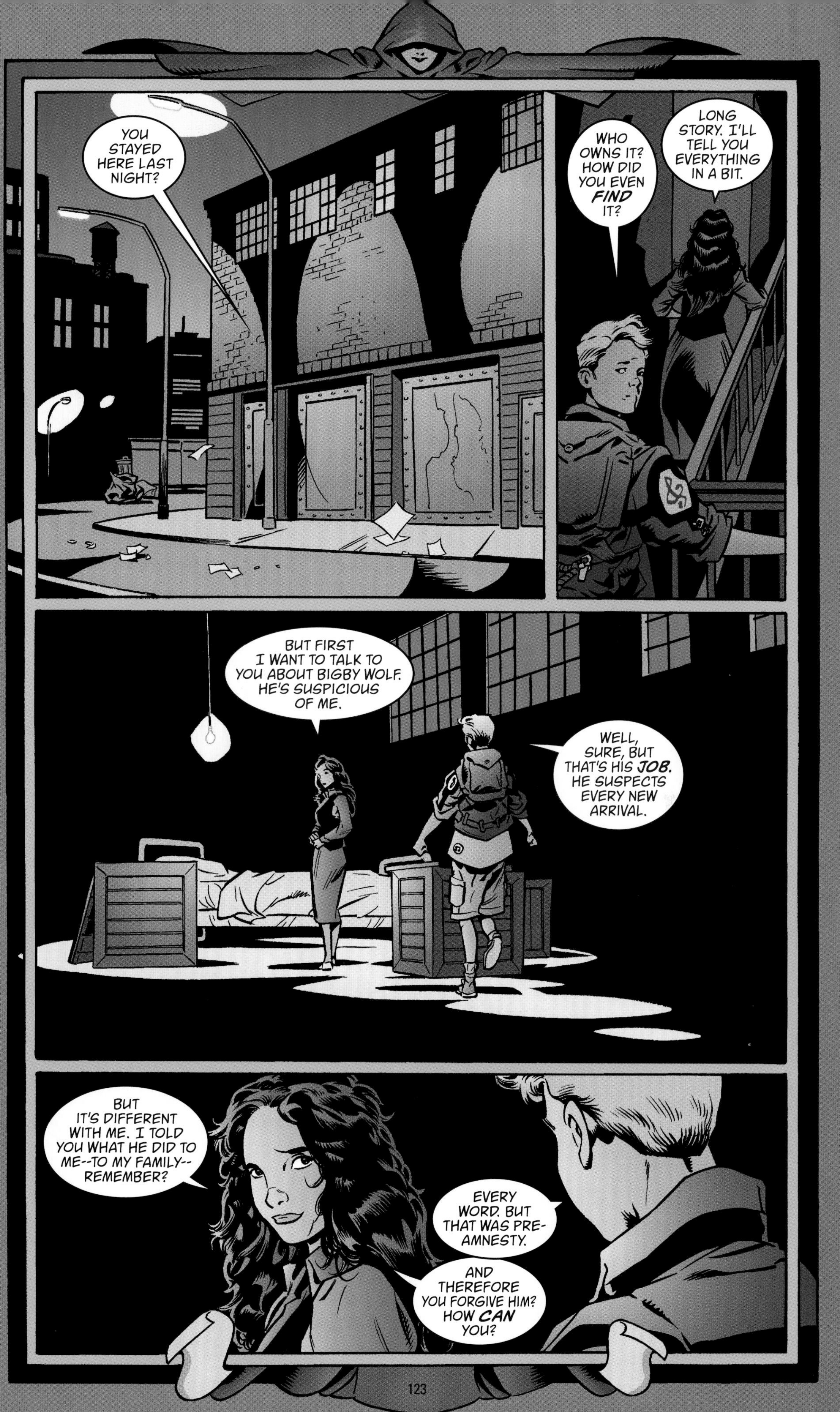

YOU STAYED HERE LAST NIGHT?
WHO OWNS IT? HOW DID YOU EVEN FIND IT?
LONG STORY. I'LL TELL YOU EVERYTHING IN A BIT.
BUT FIRST I WANT TO TALK TO YOU ABOUT BIGBY WOLF. HE'S SUSPICIOUS OF ME.
WELL, SURE, BUT THAT'S HIS JOB. HE SUSPECTS EVERY NEW ARRIVAL.
BUT IT'S DIFFERENT WITH ME. I TOLD YOU WHAT HE DID TO ME--TO MY FAMILY--REMEMBER?
EVERY WORD. BUT THAT WAS PRE-AMNESTY.
AND THEREFORE YOU FORGIVE HIM? HOW CAN YOU?

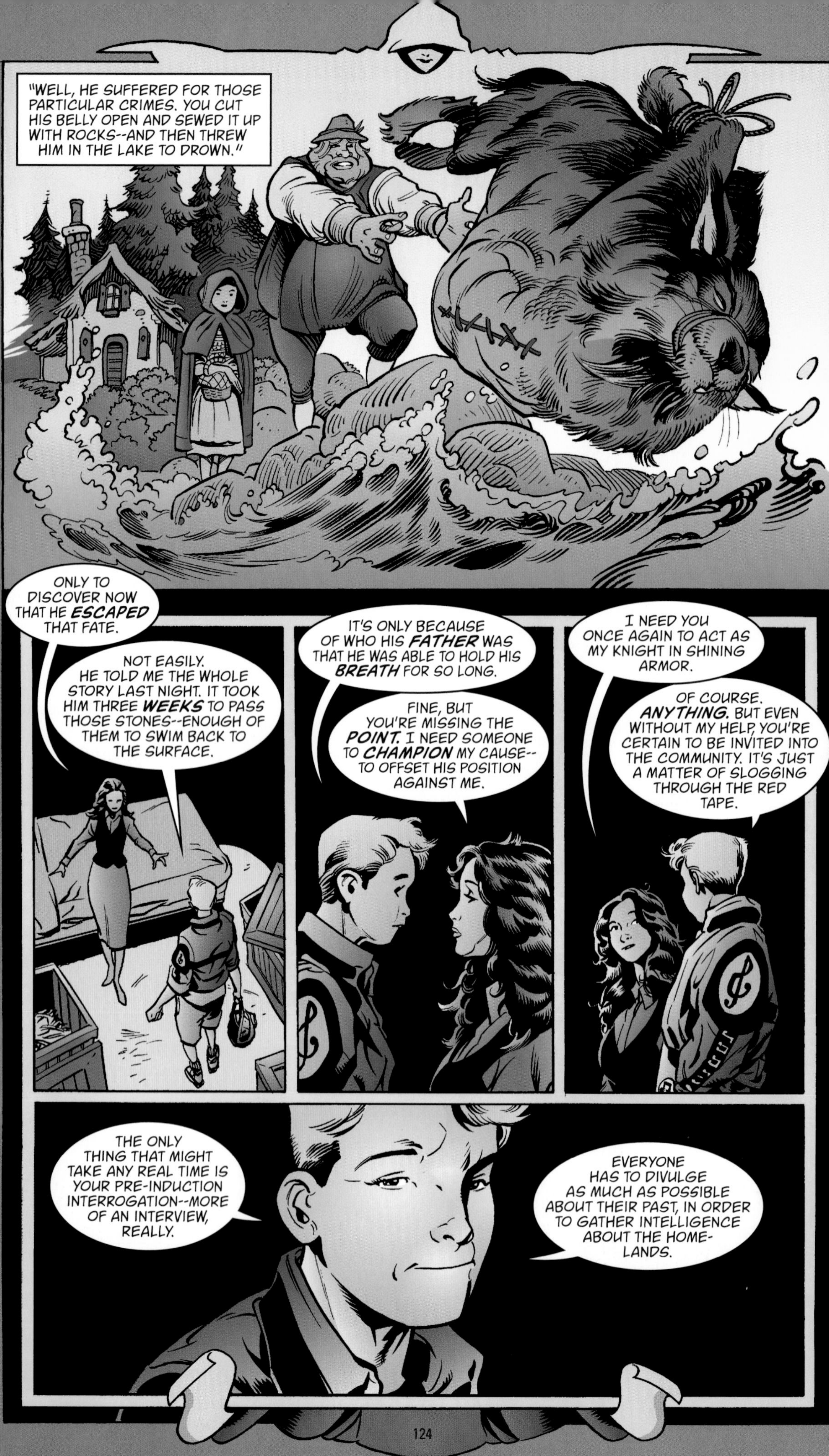
"WELL, HE SUFFERED FOR THOSE PARTICULAR CRIMES. YOU CUT HIS BELLY OPEN AND SEWED IT UP WITH ROCKS--AND THEN THREW HIM IN THE LAKE TO DROWN."
ONLY TO DISCOVER NOW THAT HE ESCAPED THAT FATE.
NOT EASILY. HE TOLD ME THE WHOLE STORY LAST NIGHT. IT TOOK HIM THREE WEEKS TO PASS THOSE STONES--ENOUGH OF THEM TO SWIM BACK TO THE SURFACE.
IT'S ONLY BECAUSE OF WHO HIS FATHER WAS THAT HE WAS ABLE TO HOLD HIS BREATH FOR SO LONG.
FINE, BUT YOU'RE MISSING THE POINT. I NEED SOMEONE TO CHAMPION MY CAUSE--TO OFFSET HIS POSITION AGAINST ME.
I NEED YOU ONCE AGAIN TO ACT AS MY KNIGHT IN SHINING ARMOR.
OF COURSE. ANYTHING. BUT EVEN WITHOUT MY HELP, YOU'RE CERTAIN TO BE INVITED INTO THE COMMUNITY. IT'S JUST A MATTER OF SLOGGING THROUGH THE RED TAPE.
THE ONLY THING THAT MIGHT TAKE ANY REAL TIME IS YOUR PRE-INDUCTION INTERROGATION--MORE OF AN INTERVIEW, REALLY.
EVERYONE HAS TO DIVULGE AS MUCH AS POSSIBLE ABOUT THEIR PAST, IN ORDER TO GATHER INTELLIGENCE ABOUT THE HOME-LANDS.

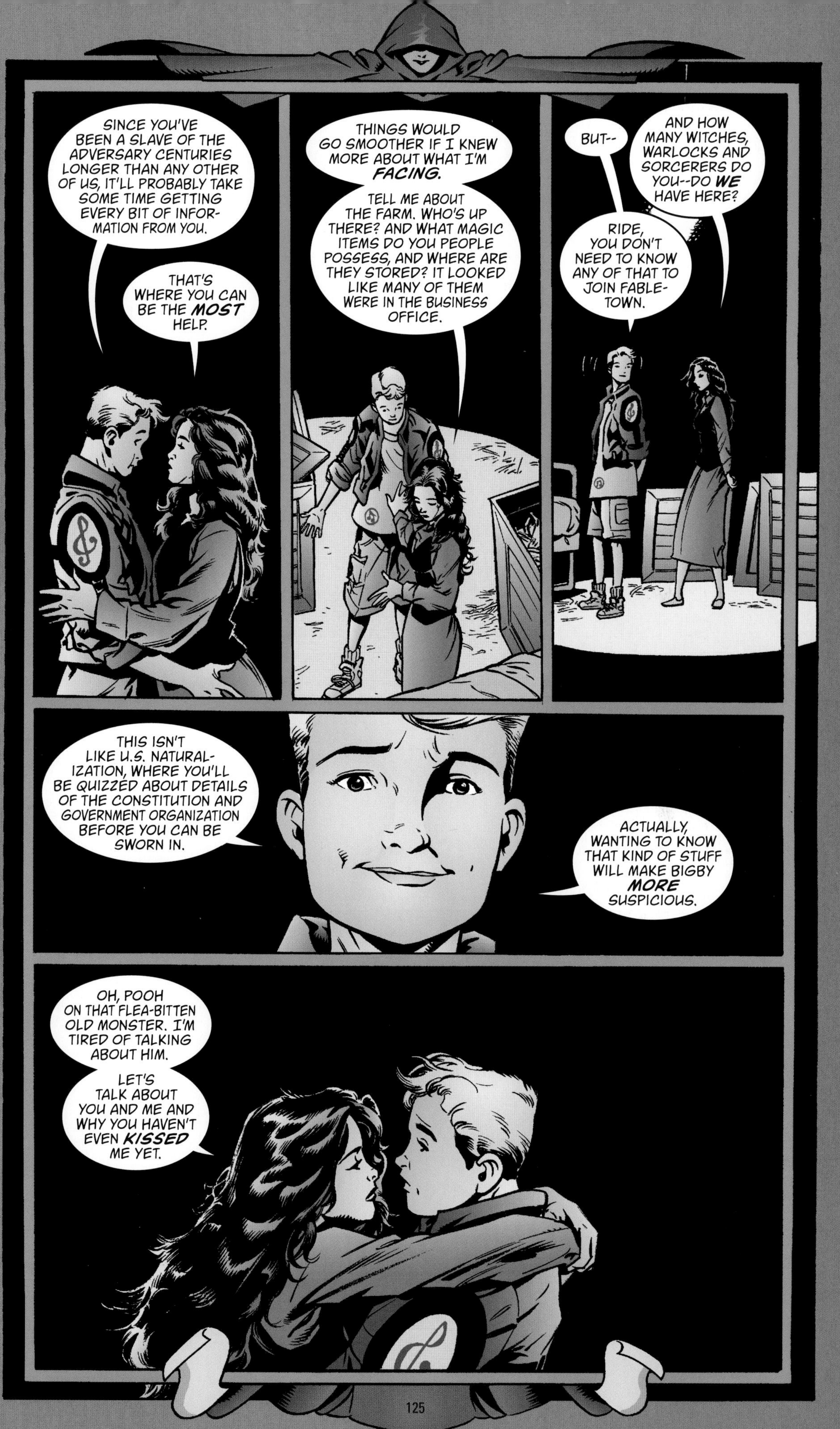
SINCE YOU'VE BEEN A SLAVE OF THE ADVERSARY CENTURIES LONGER THAN ANY OTHER OF US, IT'LL PROBABLY TAKE SOME TIME GETTING EVERY BIT OF INFORMATION FROM YOU.
THAT'S WHERE YOU CAN BE THE *MOST* HELP.
THINGS WOULD GO SMOOTHER IF I KNEW MORE ABOUT WHAT I'M *FACING.*
TELL ME ABOUT THE FARM. WHO'S UP THERE? AND WHAT MAGIC ITEMS DO YOU PEOPLE POSSESS, AND WHERE ARE THEY STORED? IT LOOKED LIKE MANY OF THEM WERE IN THE BUSINESS OFFICE.
BUT--
AND HOW MANY WITCHES, WARLOCKS AND SORCERERS DO YOU--DO *WE* HAVE HERE?
RIDE, YOU DON'T NEED TO KNOW ANY OF THAT TO JOIN FABLETOWN.
THIS ISN'T LIKE U.S. NATURALIZATION, WHERE YOU'LL BE QUIZZED ABOUT DETAILS OF THE CONSTITUTION AND GOVERNMENT ORGANIZATION BEFORE YOU CAN BE SWORN IN.
ACTUALLY, WANTING TO KNOW THAT KIND OF STUFF WILL MAKE BIGBY *MORE* SUSPICIOUS.
OH, POOH ON THAT FLEA-BITTEN OLD MONSTER. I'M TIRED OF TALKING ABOUT HIM.
LET'S TALK ABOUT YOU AND ME AND WHY YOU HAVEN'T EVEN *KISSED* ME YET.

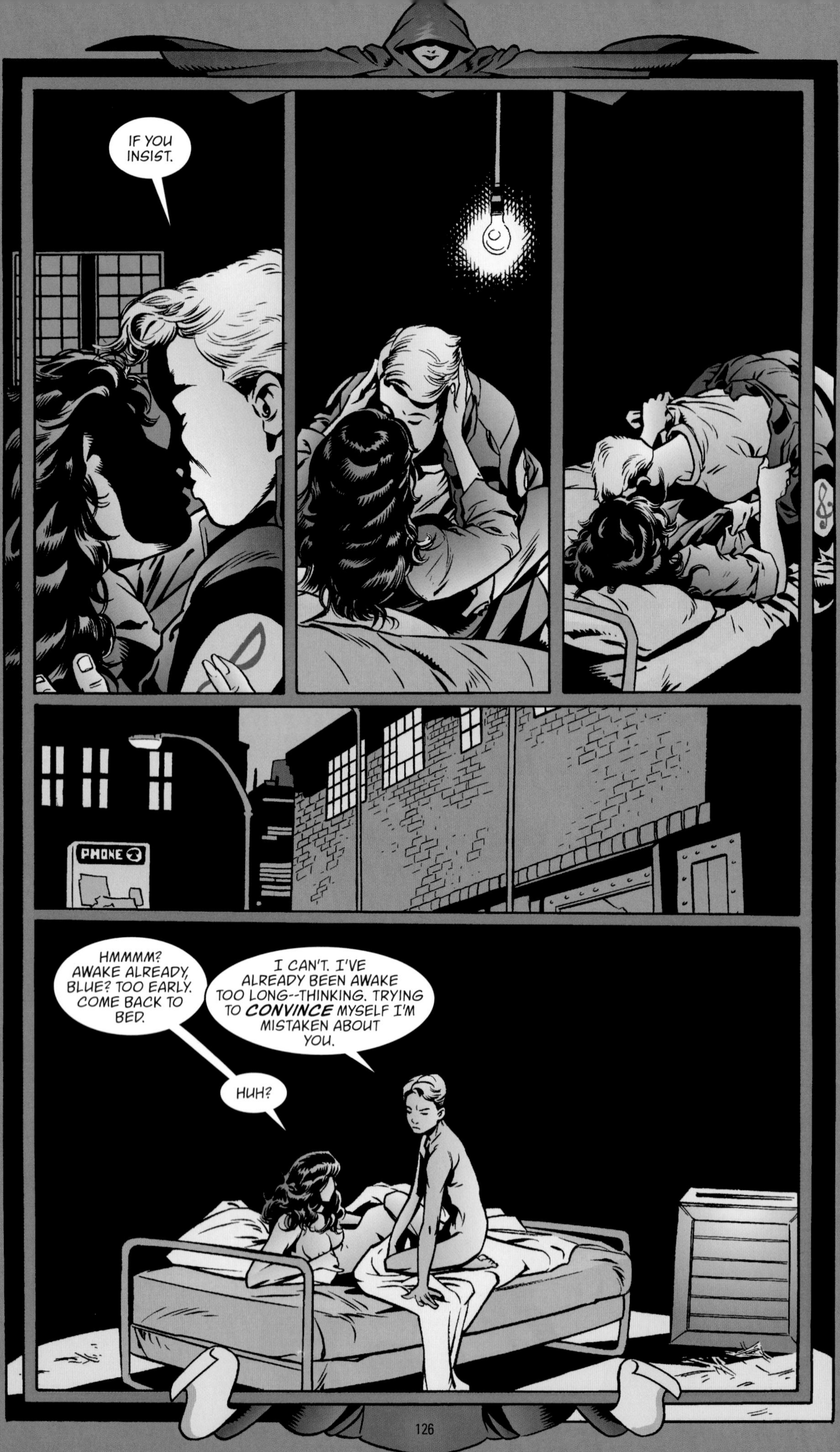
IF YOU INSIST.
PHONE
HMMMM? AWAKE ALREADY, BLUE? TOO EARLY. COME BACK TO BED.
I CAN'T. I'VE ALREADY BEEN AWAKE TOO LONG--THINKING. TRYING TO CONVINCE MYSELF I'M MISTAKEN ABOUT YOU.
HUH?

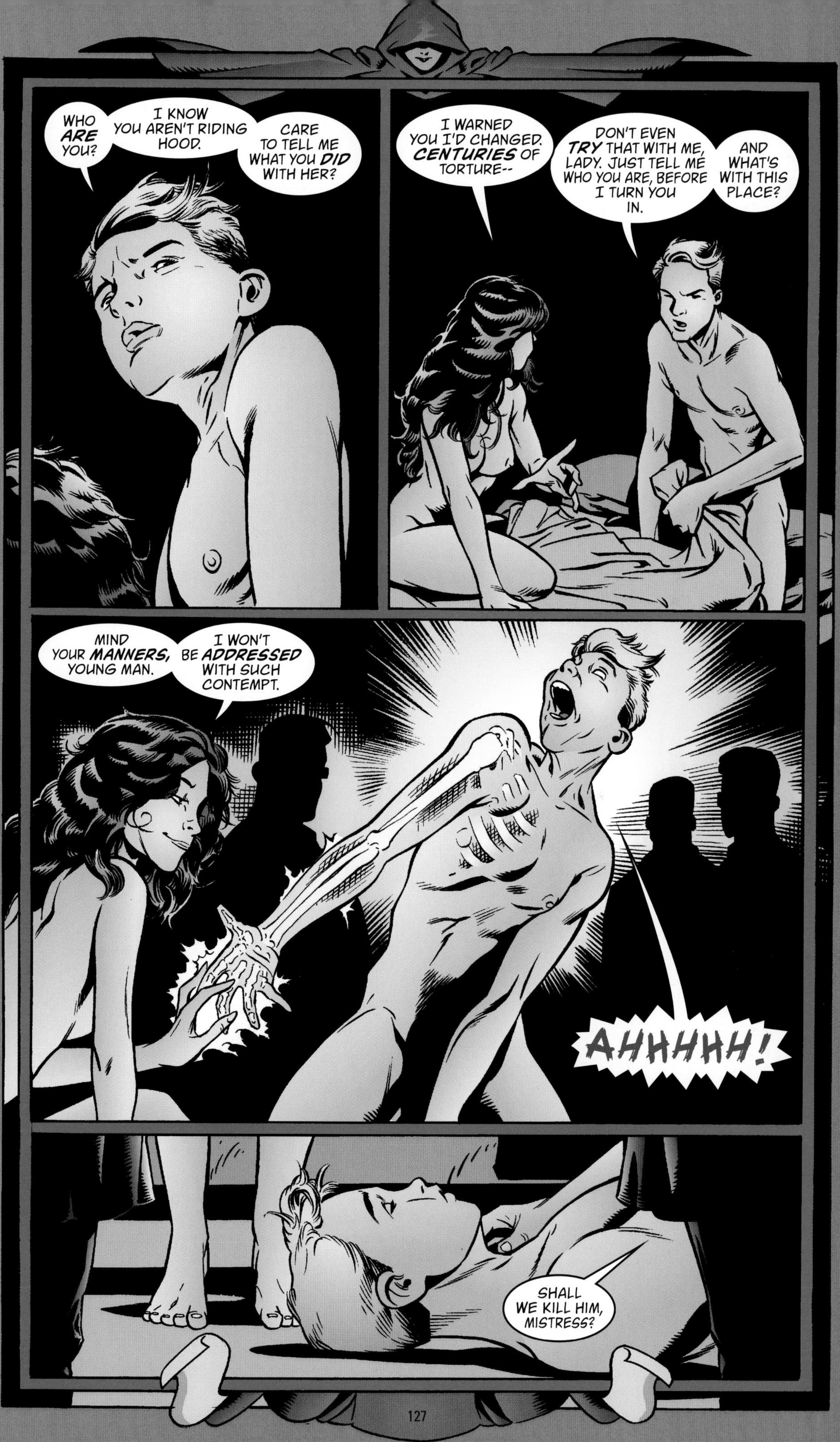
WHO ARE YOU?
I KNOW YOU AREN'T RIDING HOOD.
CARE TO TELL ME WHAT YOU DID WITH HER?
I WARNED YOU I'D CHANGED. CENTURIES OF TORTURE--
DON'T EVEN TRY THAT WITH ME, LADY. JUST TELL ME WHO YOU ARE, BEFORE I TURN YOU IN.
AND WHAT'S WITH THIS PLACE?
MIND YOUR MANNERS, YOUNG MAN.
I WON'T BE ADDRESSED WITH SUCH CONTEMPT.
AHHHHH!
SHALL WE KILL HIM, MISTRESS?

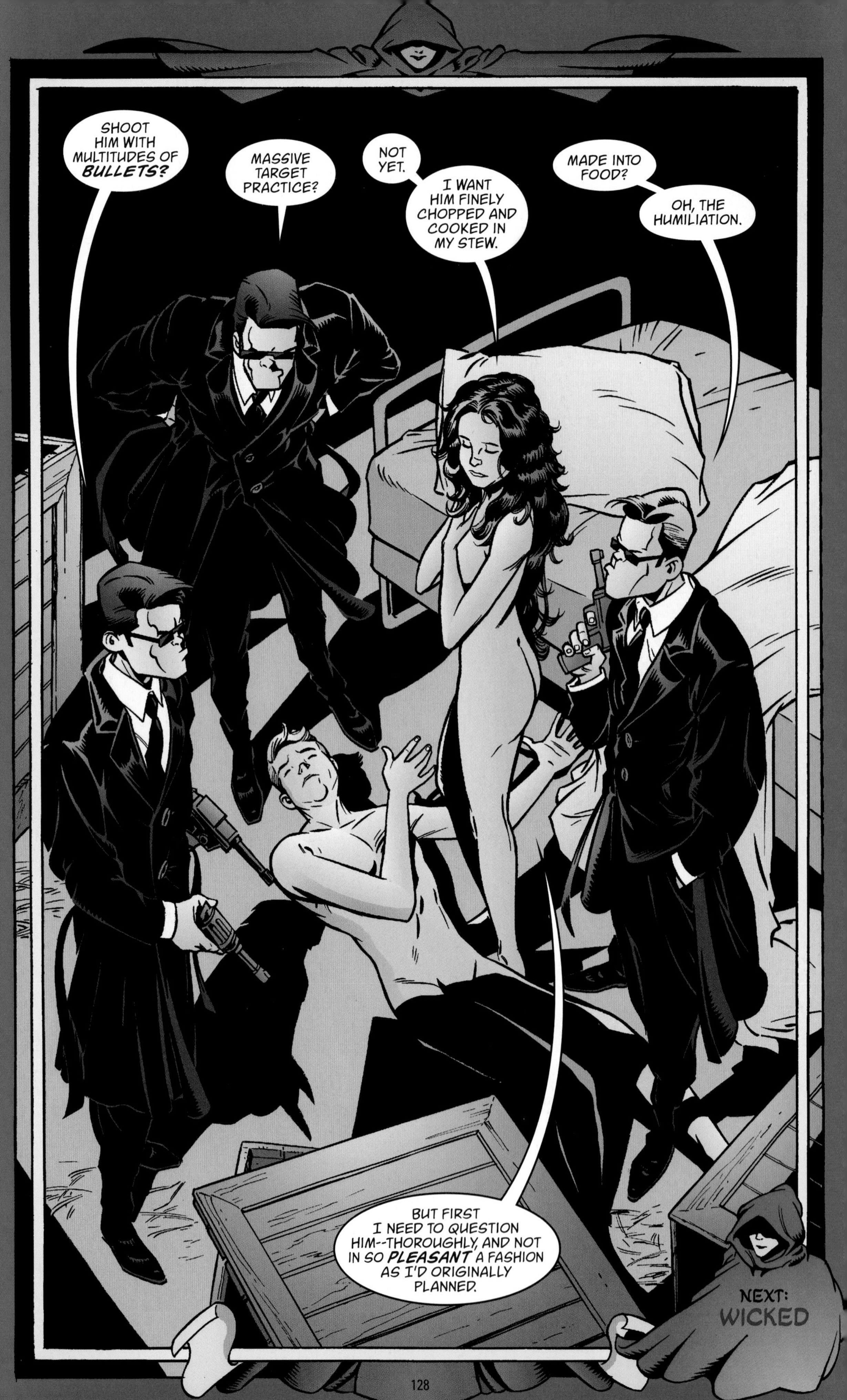
SHOOT HIM WITH MULTITUDES OF BULLETS?
MASSIVE TARGET PRACTICE?
NOT YET.
I WANT HIM FINELY CHOPPED AND COOKED IN MY STEW.
MADE INTO FOOD?
OH, THE HUMILIATION.
BUT FIRST I NEED TO QUESTION HIM--THOROUGHLY, AND NOT IN SO PLEASANT A FASHION AS I'D ORIGINALLY PLANNED.
NEXT: WICKED

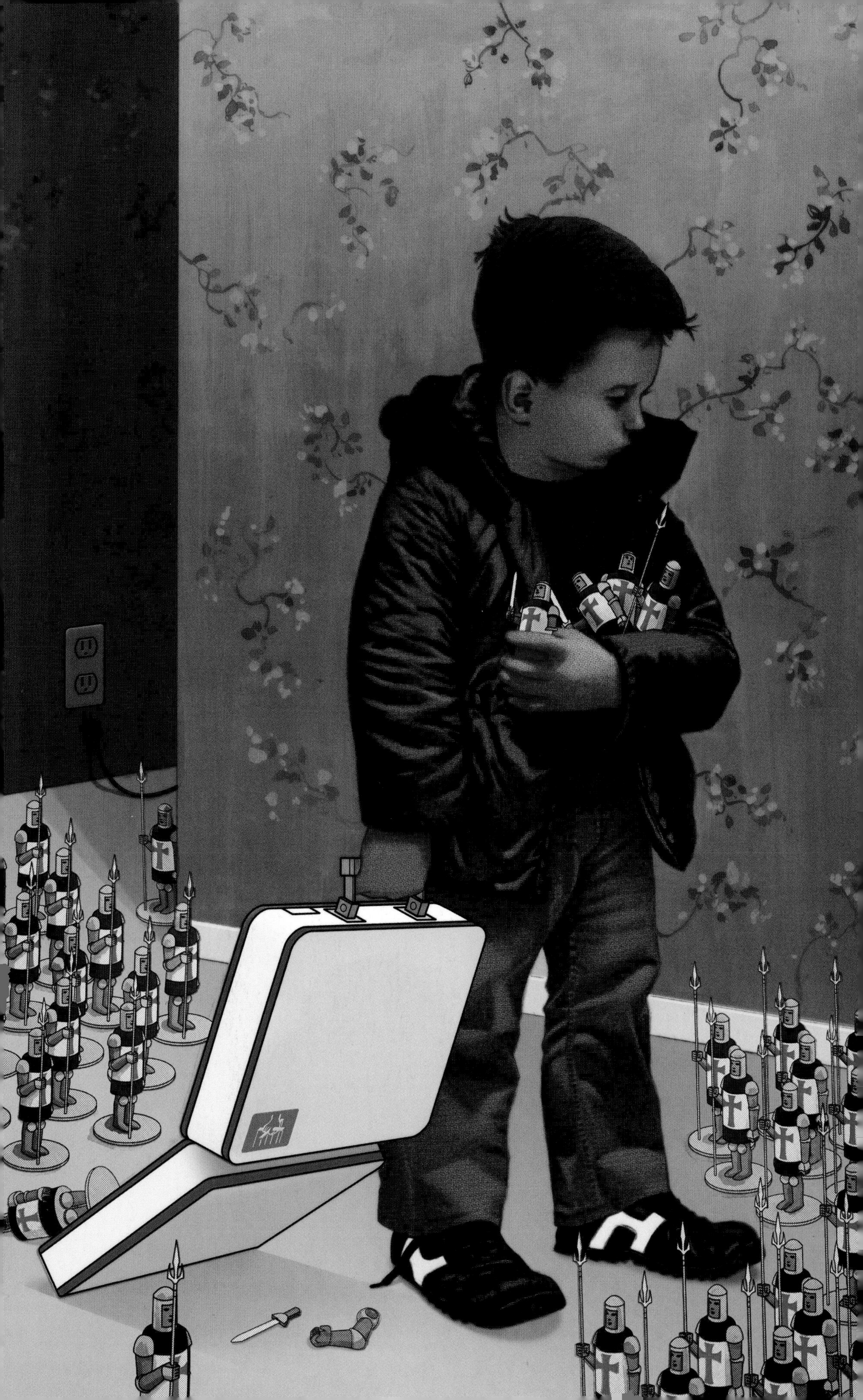

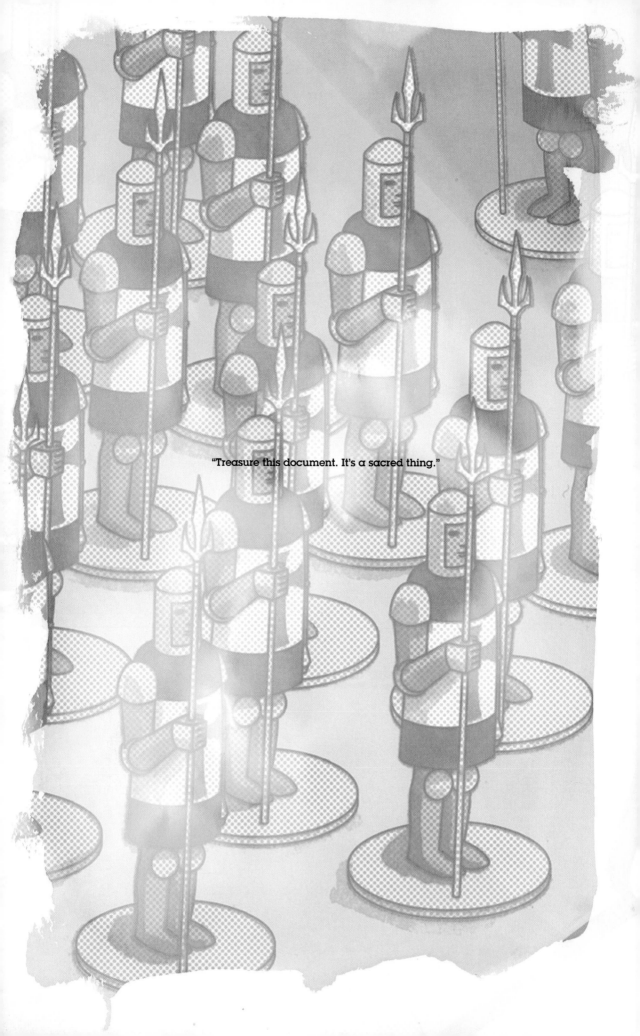

"Treasure this document. It's a sacred thing."

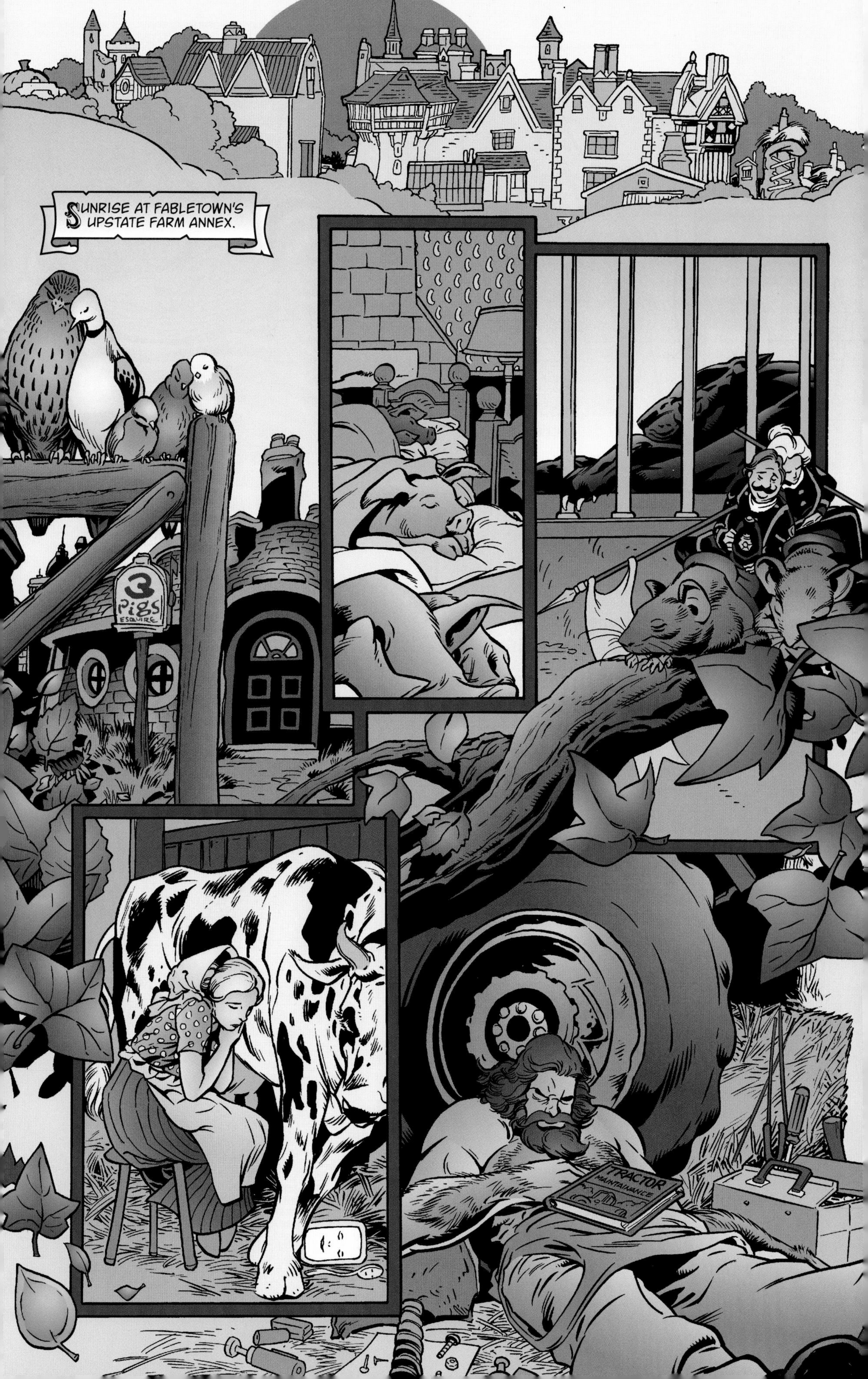
SUNRISE AT FABLETOWN'S UPSTATE FARM ANNEX.
3 Pigs ESQUIRE
TRACTOR MAINTAINANCE

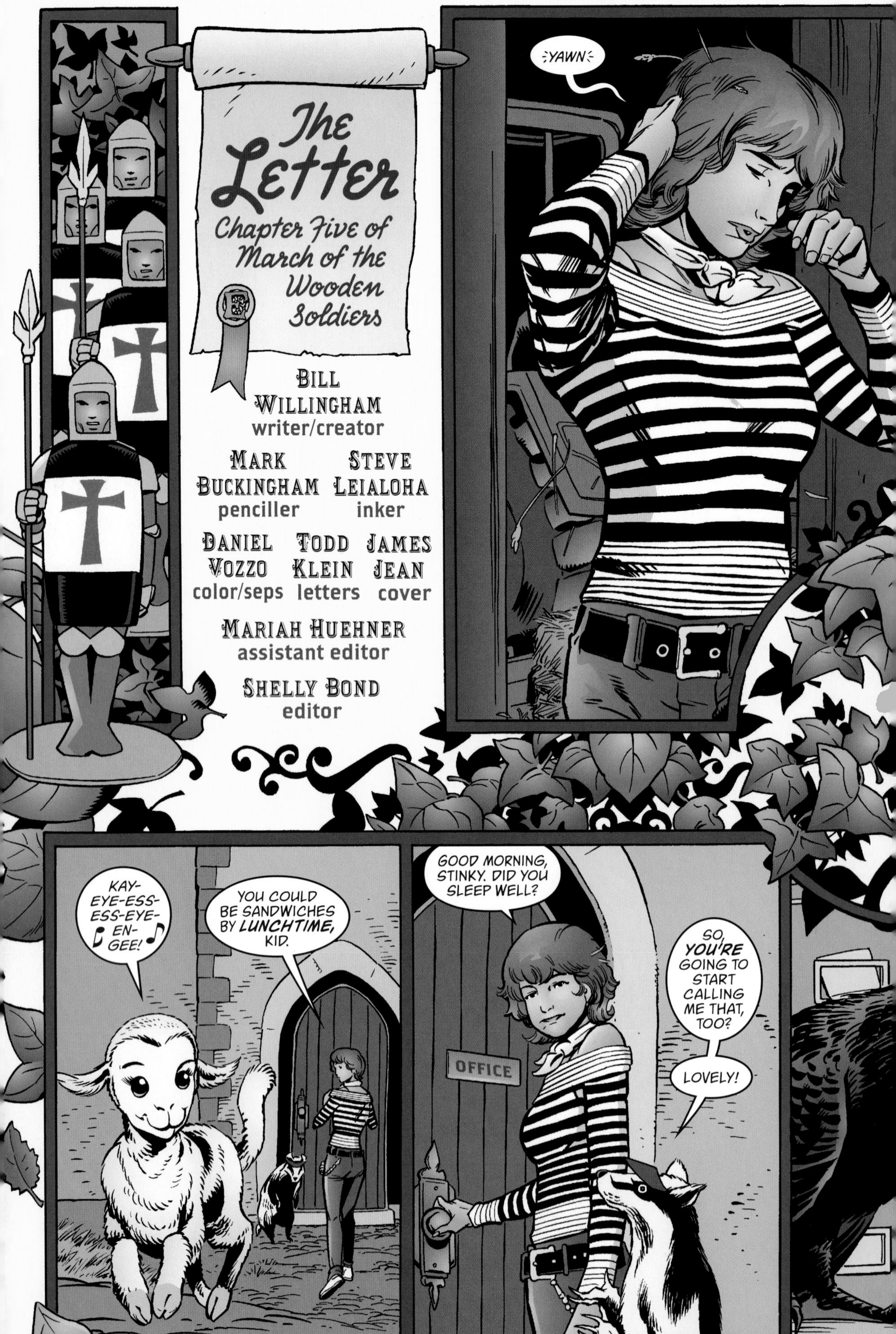

The Letter
Chapter Five of March of the Wooden Soldiers
BILL WILLINGHAM writer/creator
MARK BUCKINGHAM penciller
STEVE LEIALOHA inker
DANIEL VOZZO color/seps
TODD KLEIN letters
JAMES JEAN cover
MARIAH HUEHNER assistant editor
SHELLY BOND editor
YAWN
KAY-EYE-ESS-ESS-EYE-EN-GEE!
YOU COULD BE SANDWICHES BY LUNCHTIME, KID.
GOOD MORNING, STINKY. DID YOU SLEEP WELL?
OFFICE
SO, YOU'RE GOING TO START CALLING ME THAT, TOO?
LOVELY!

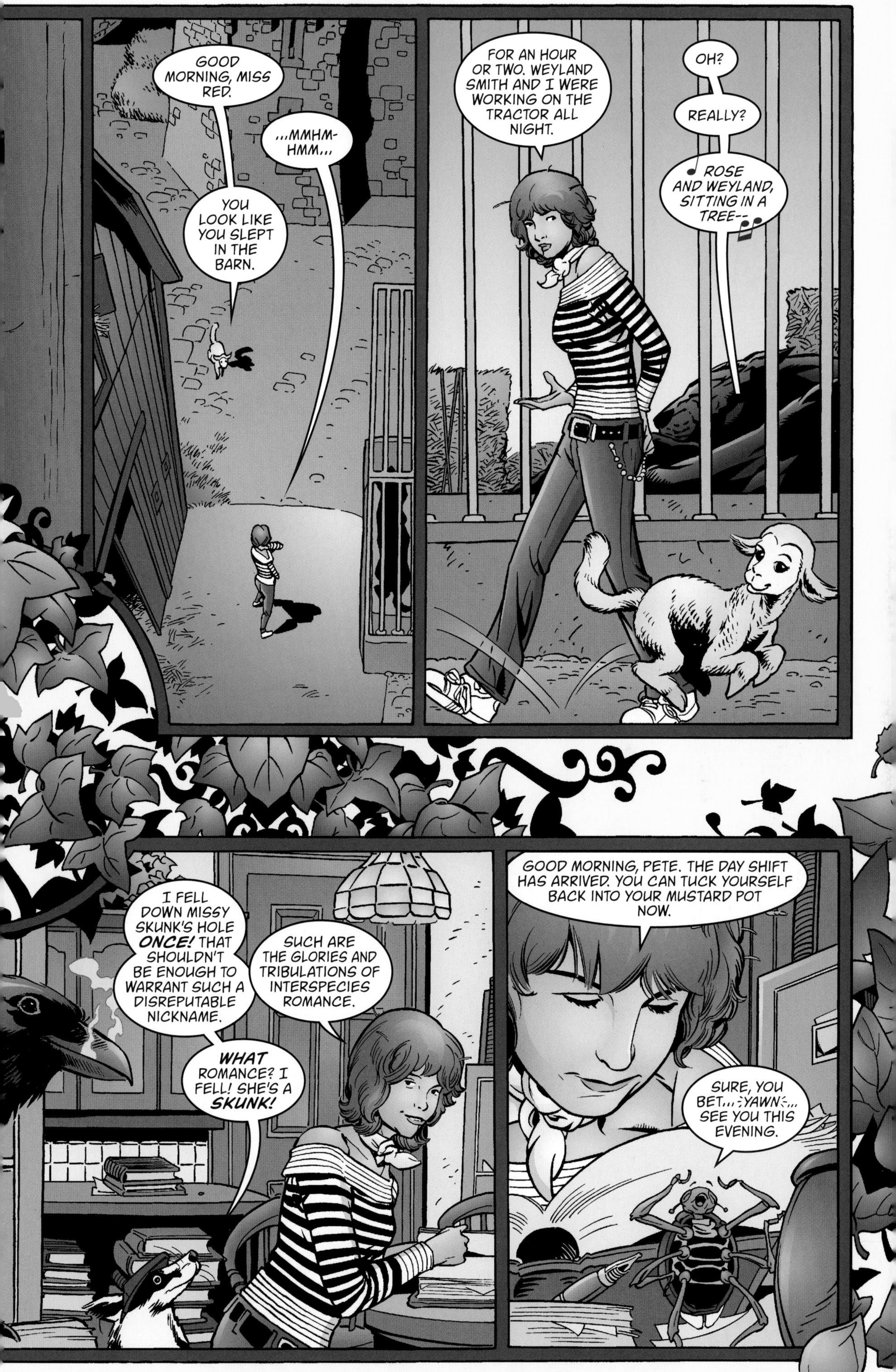
GOOD MORNING, MISS RED.
...MMHM-HMM...
YOU LOOK LIKE YOU SLEPT IN THE BARN.
FOR AN HOUR OR TWO. WEYLAND SMITH AND I WERE WORKING ON THE TRACTOR ALL NIGHT.
OH?
REALLY?
ROSE AND WEYLAND, SITTING IN A TREE--
I FELL DOWN MISSY SKUNK'S HOLE ONCE! THAT SHOULDN'T BE ENOUGH TO WARRANT SUCH A DISREPUTABLE NICKNAME.
SUCH ARE THE GLORIES AND TRIBULATIONS OF INTERSPECIES ROMANCE.
WHAT ROMANCE? I FELL! SHE'S A SKUNK!
GOOD MORNING, PETE. THE DAY SHIFT HAS ARRIVED. YOU CAN TUCK YOURSELF BACK INTO YOUR MUSTARD POT NOW.
SURE, YOU BET...YAWN... SEE YOU THIS EVENING.

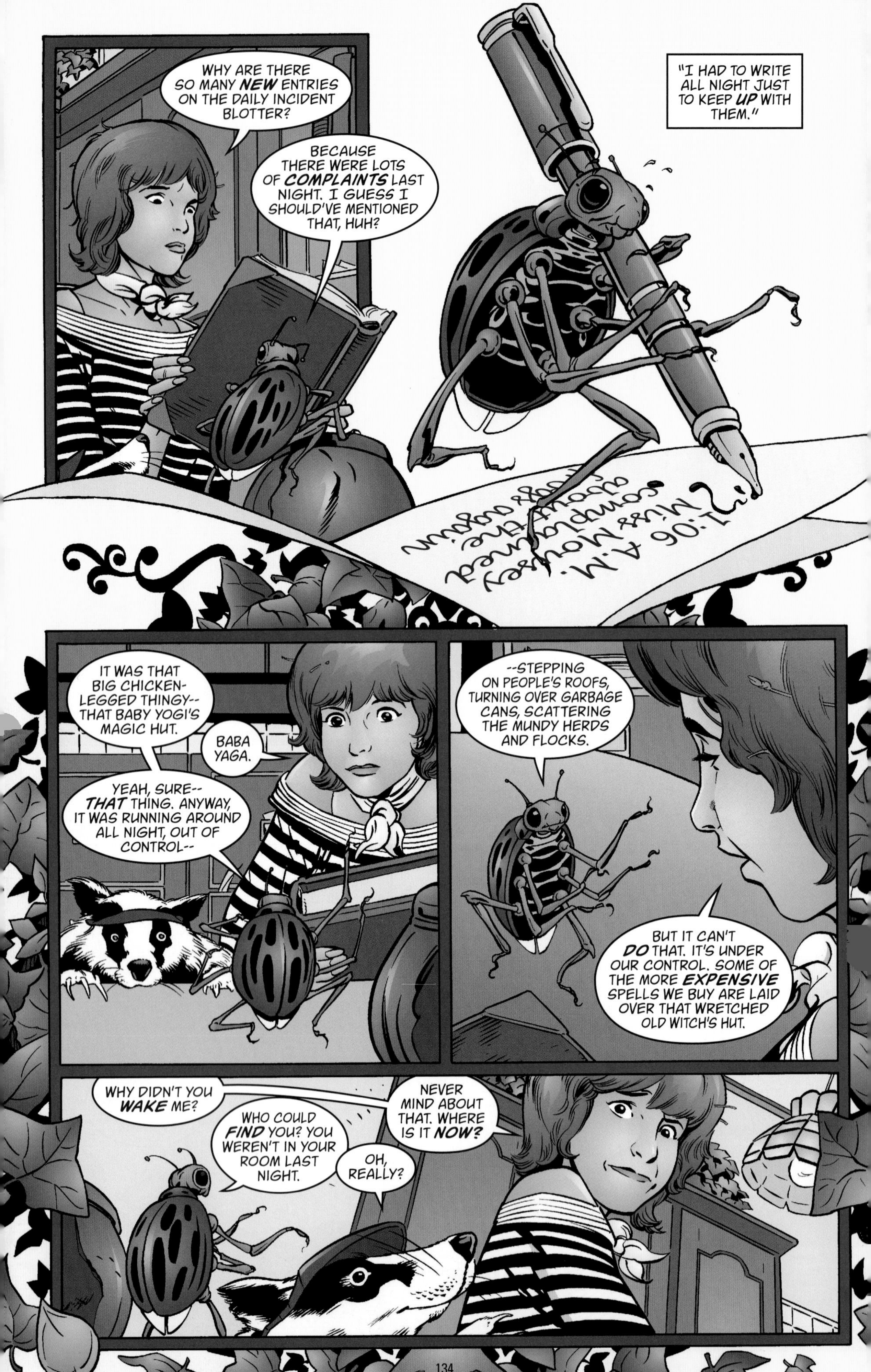
WHY ARE THERE SO MANY NEW ENTRIES ON THE DAILY INCIDENT BLOTTER?
BECAUSE THERE WERE LOTS OF COMPLAINTS LAST NIGHT. I GUESS I SHOULD'VE MENTIONED THAT, HUH?
"I HAD TO WRITE ALL NIGHT JUST TO KEEP UP WITH THEM."
1:06 A.M. Miss Mousey complained about frogs again
IT WAS THAT BIG CHICKEN-LEGGED THINGY-- THAT BABY YOGI'S MAGIC HUT.
BABA YAGA.
YEAH, SURE-- THAT THING. ANYWAY, IT WAS RUNNING AROUND ALL NIGHT, OUT OF CONTROL--
--STEPPING ON PEOPLE'S ROOFS, TURNING OVER GARBAGE CANS, SCATTERING THE MUNDY HERDS AND FLOCKS.
BUT IT CAN'T DO THAT. IT'S UNDER OUR CONTROL. SOME OF THE MORE EXPENSIVE SPELLS WE BUY ARE LAID OVER THAT WRETCHED OLD WITCH'S HUT.
WHY DIDN'T YOU WAKE ME?
WHO COULD FIND YOU? YOU WEREN'T IN YOUR ROOM LAST NIGHT.
NEVER MIND ABOUT THAT. WHERE IS IT NOW?
OH, REALLY?

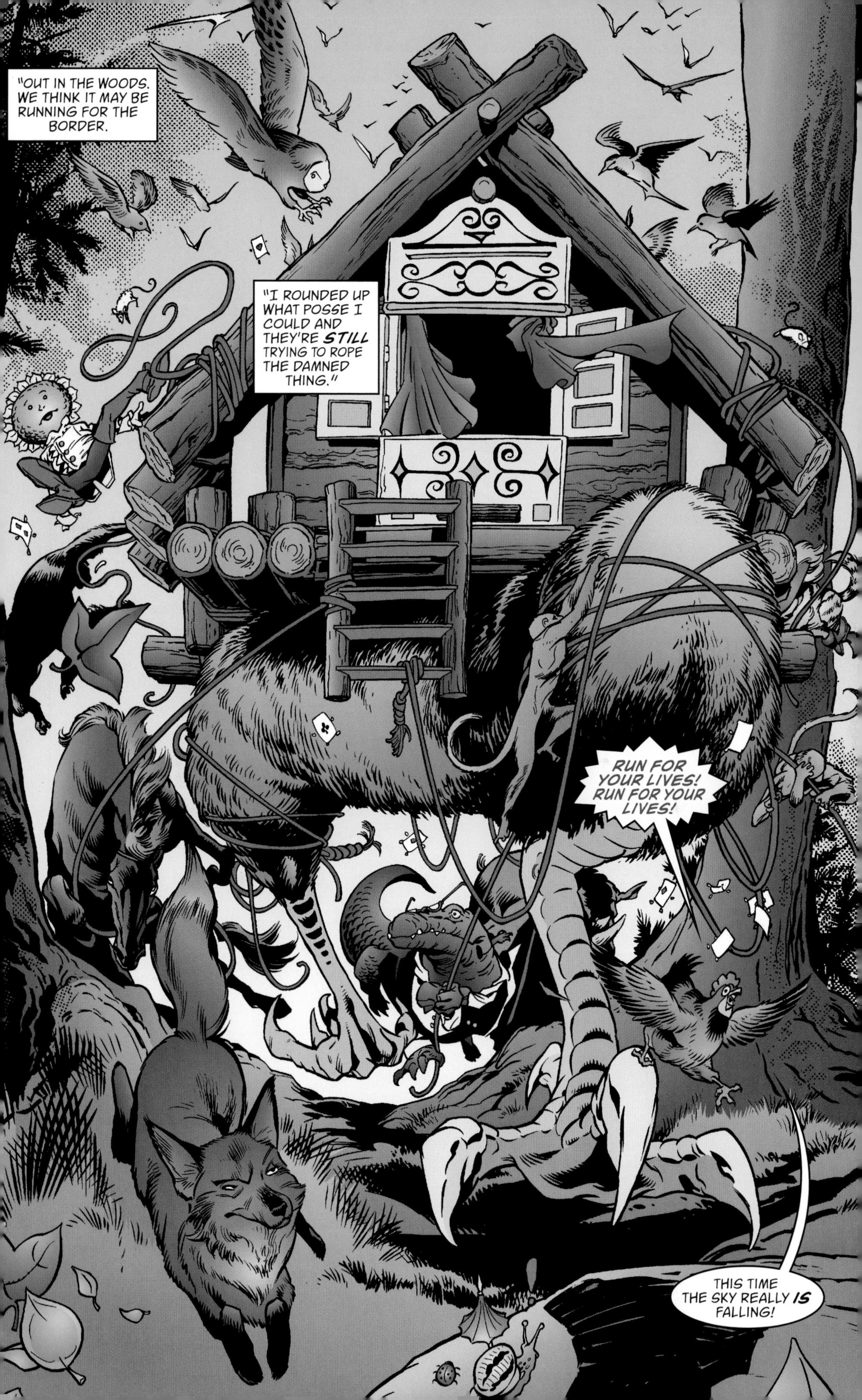
"OUT IN THE WOODS. WE THINK IT MAY BE RUNNING FOR THE BORDER.
"I ROUNDED UP WHAT POSSE I COULD AND THEY'RE *STILL* TRYING TO ROPE THE DAMNED THING."
RUN FOR YOUR LIVES! RUN FOR YOUR LIVES!
THIS TIME THE SKY REALLY *IS* FALLING!

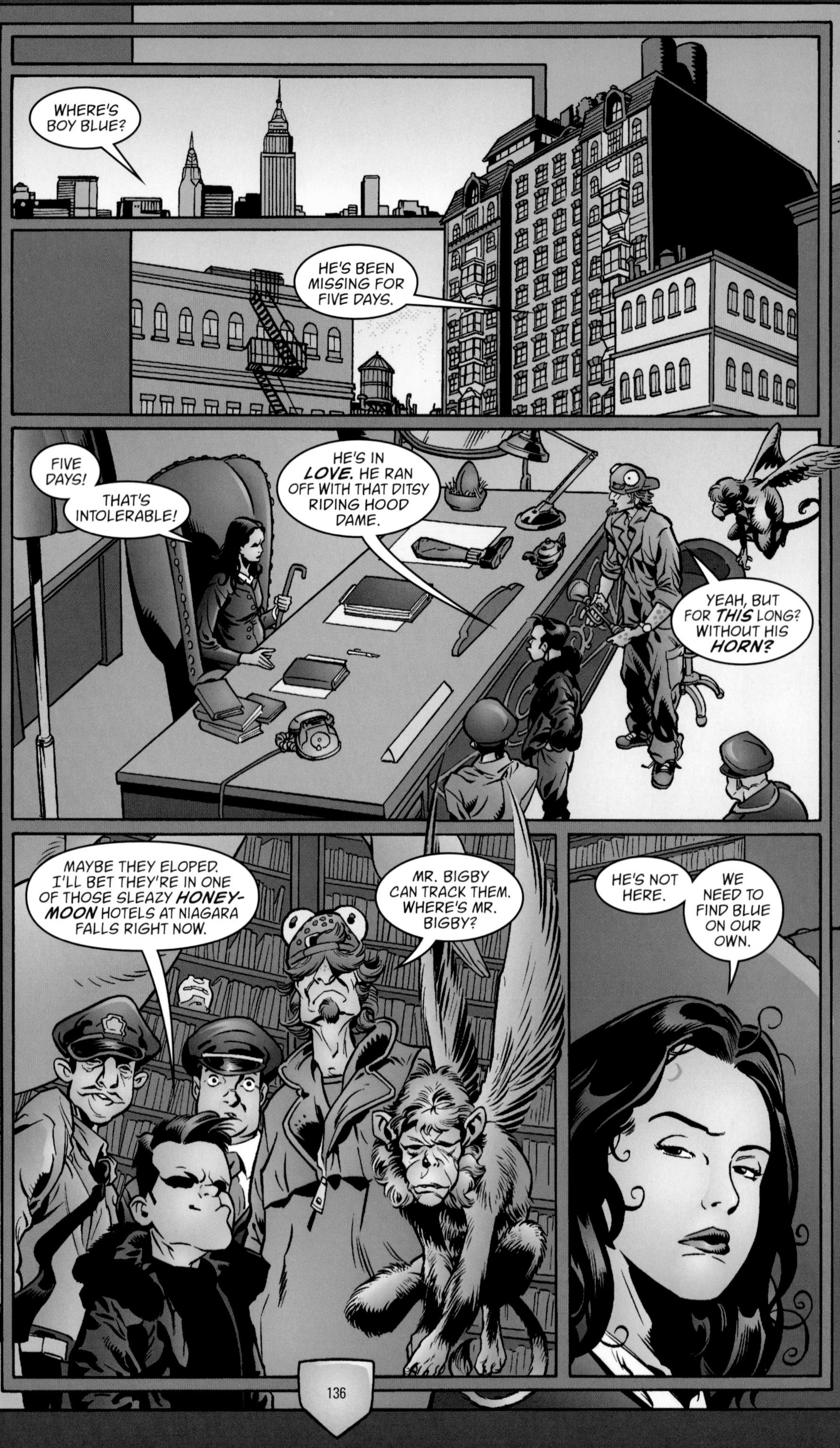
WHERE'S BOY BLUE?
HE'S BEEN MISSING FOR FIVE DAYS.
FIVE DAYS!
THAT'S INTOLERABLE!
HE'S IN LOVE. HE RAN OFF WITH THAT DITSY RIDING HOOD DAME.
YEAH, BUT FOR THIS LONG? WITHOUT HIS HORN?
MAYBE THEY ELOPED. I'LL BET THEY'RE IN ONE OF THOSE SLEAZY HONEY-MOON HOTELS AT NIAGARA FALLS RIGHT NOW.
MR. BIGBY CAN TRACK THEM. WHERE'S MR. BIGBY?
HE'S NOT HERE.
WE NEED TO FIND BLUE ON OUR OWN.

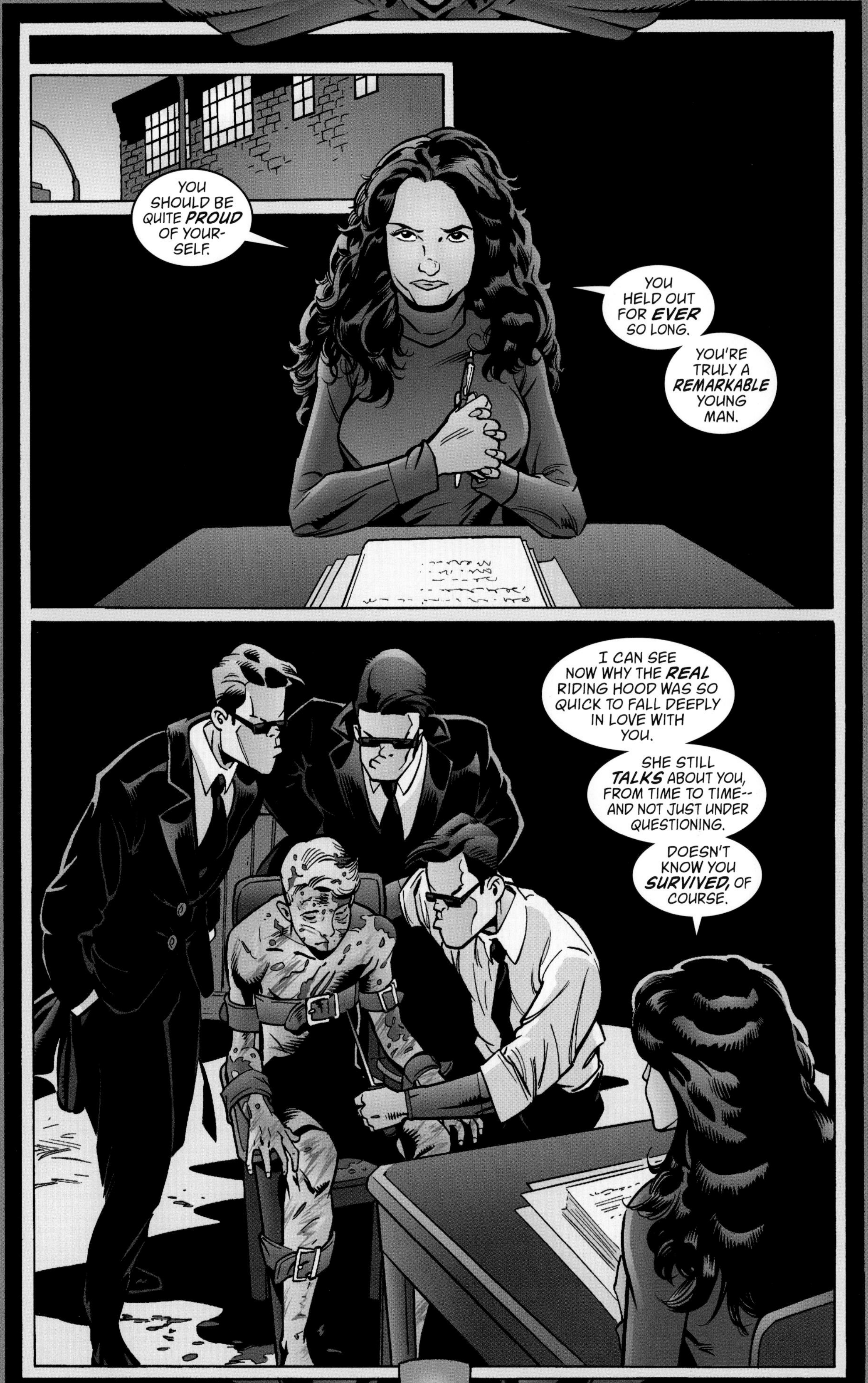

YOU SHOULD BE QUITE **PROUD** OF YOURSELF.
YOU HELD OUT FOR **EVER** SO LONG.
YOU'RE TRULY A **REMARKABLE** YOUNG MAN.
I CAN SEE NOW WHY THE **REAL** RIDING HOOD WAS SO QUICK TO FALL DEEPLY IN LOVE WITH YOU.
SHE STILL **TALKS** ABOUT YOU, FROM TIME TO TIME-- AND NOT JUST UNDER QUESTIONING.
DOESN'T KNOW YOU **SURVIVED,** OF COURSE.

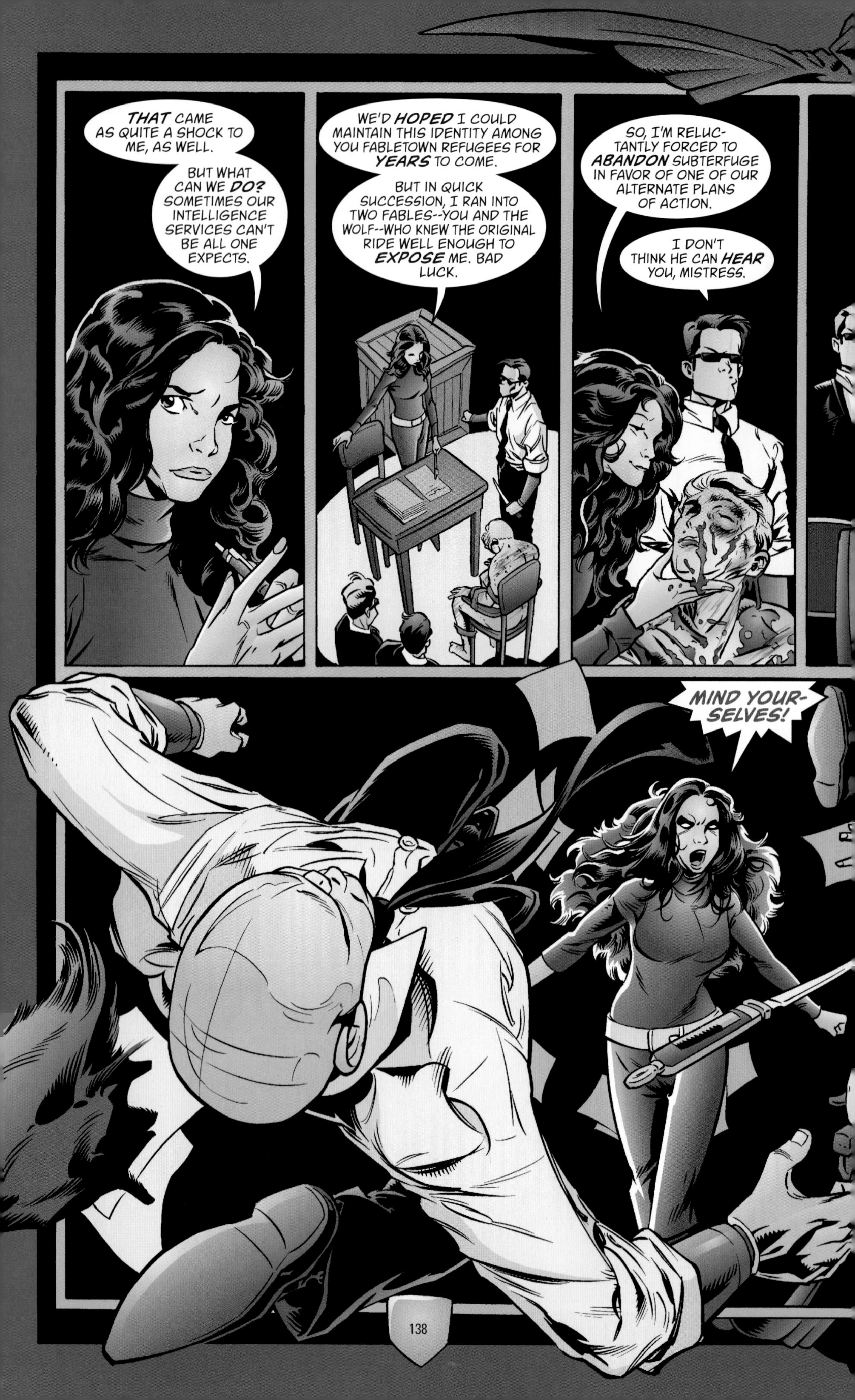
THAT CAME AS QUITE A SHOCK TO ME, AS WELL.
BUT WHAT CAN WE DO? SOMETIMES OUR INTELLIGENCE SERVICES CAN'T BE ALL ONE EXPECTS.
WE'D HOPED I COULD MAINTAIN THIS IDENTITY AMONG YOU FABLETOWN REFUGEES FOR YEARS TO COME.
BUT IN QUICK SUCCESSION, I RAN INTO TWO FABLES--YOU AND THE WOLF--WHO KNEW THE ORIGINAL RIDE WELL ENOUGH TO EXPOSE ME. BAD LUCK.
SO, I'M RELUC-TANTLY FORCED TO ABANDON SUBTERFUGE IN FAVOR OF ONE OF OUR ALTERNATE PLANS OF ACTION.
I DON'T THINK HE CAN HEAR YOU, MISTRESS.
MIND YOUR-SELVES!

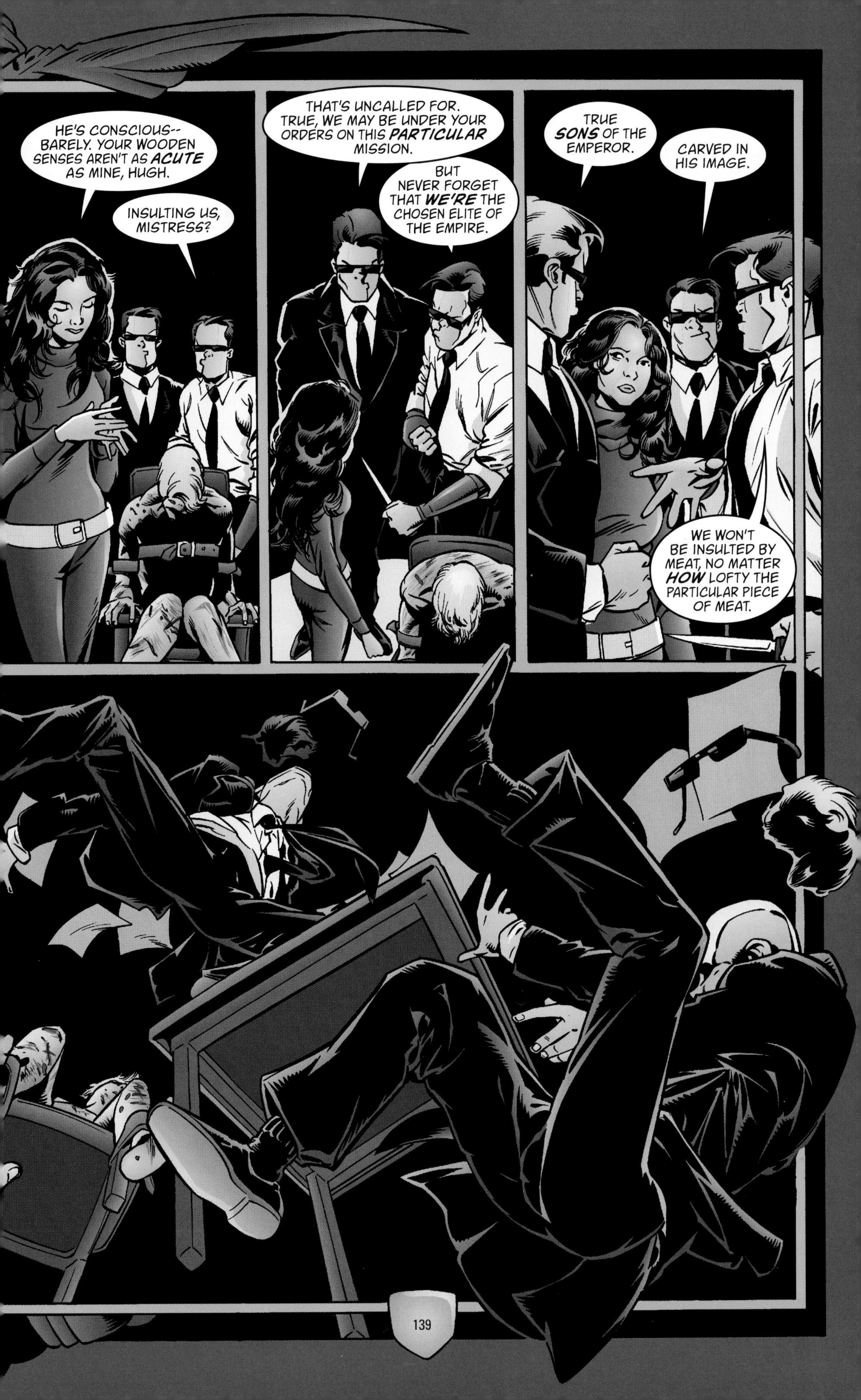

HE'S CONSCIOUS--BARELY. YOUR WOODEN SENSES AREN'T AS ACUTE AS MINE, HUGH.
INSULTING US, MISTRESS?
THAT'S UNCALLED FOR. TRUE, WE MAY BE UNDER YOUR ORDERS ON THIS PARTICULAR MISSION.
BUT NEVER FORGET THAT WE'RE THE CHOSEN ELITE OF THE EMPIRE.
TRUE SONS OF THE EMPEROR.
CARVED IN HIS IMAGE.
WE WON'T BE INSULTED BY MEAT, NO MATTER HOW LOFTY THE PARTICULAR PIECE OF MEAT.

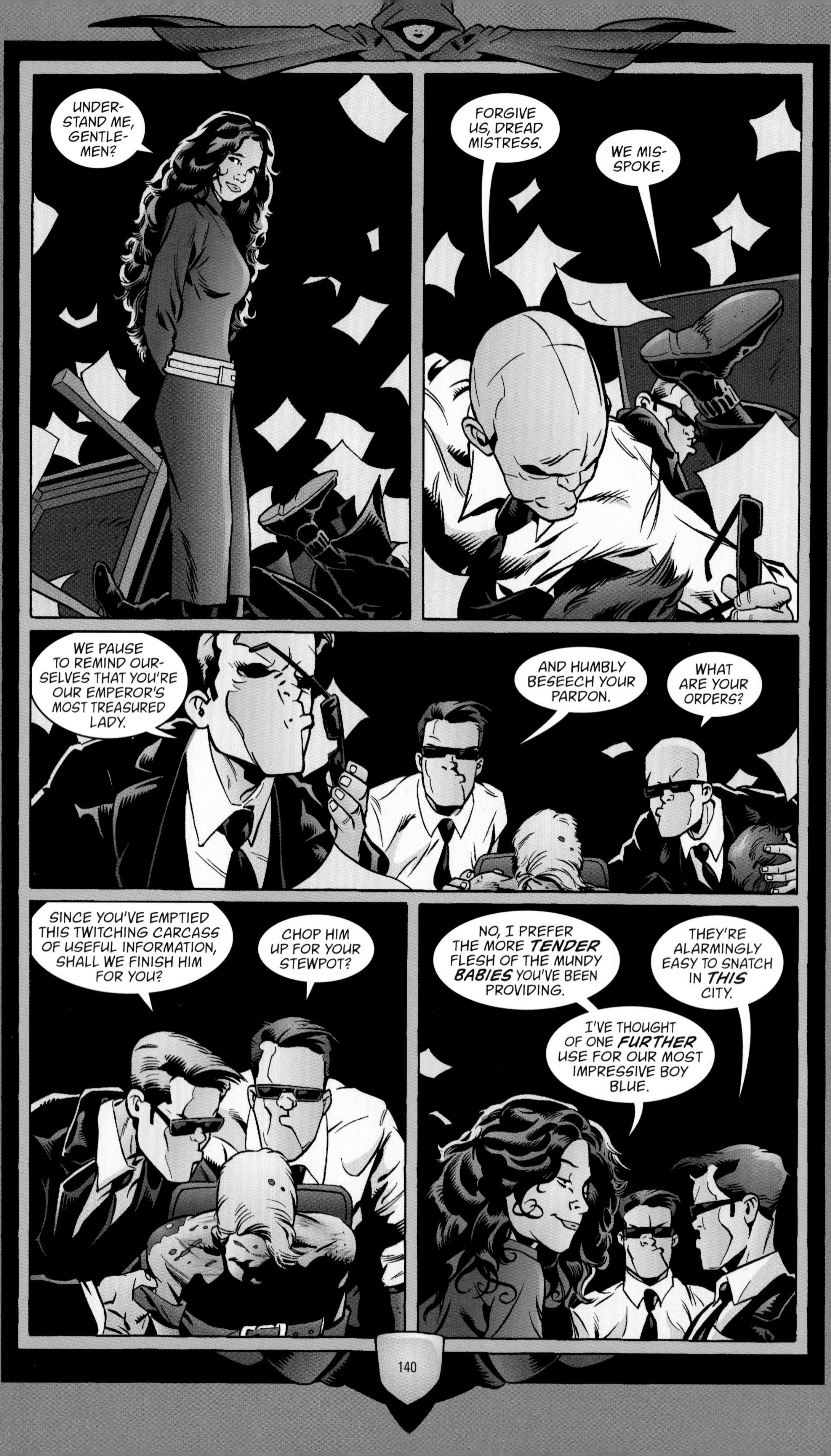
UNDER-STAND ME, GENTLE-MEN?
FORGIVE US, DREAD MISTRESS.
WE MIS-SPOKE.
WE PAUSE TO REMIND OUR-SELVES THAT YOU'RE OUR EMPEROR'S MOST TREASURED LADY.
AND HUMBLY BESEECH YOUR PARDON.
WHAT ARE YOUR ORDERS?
SINCE YOU'VE EMPTIED THIS TWITCHING CARCASS OF USEFUL INFORMATION, SHALL WE FINISH HIM FOR YOU?
CHOP HIM UP FOR YOUR STEWPOT?
NO, I PREFER THE MORE TENDER FLESH OF THE MUNDY BABIES YOU'VE BEEN PROVIDING.
THEY'RE ALARMINGLY EASY TO SNATCH IN THIS CITY.
I'VE THOUGHT OF ONE FURTHER USE FOR OUR MOST IMPRESSIVE BOY BLUE.

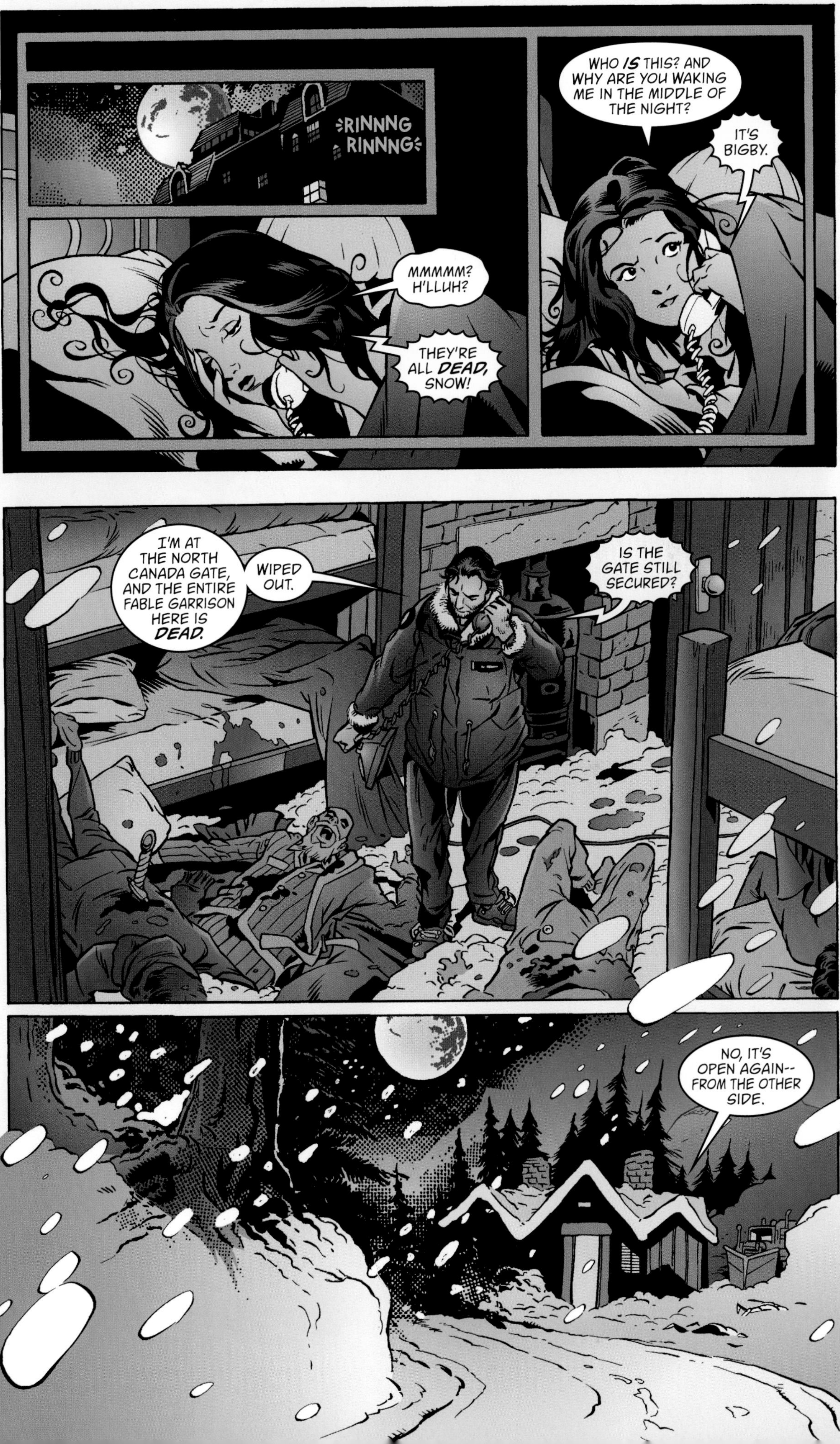
RINNNG
RINNNG
MMMMM? H'LLUH?
THEY'RE ALL DEAD, SNOW!
WHO IS THIS? AND WHY ARE YOU WAKING ME IN THE MIDDLE OF THE NIGHT?
IT'S BIGBY.
I'M AT THE NORTH CANADA GATE, AND THE ENTIRE FABLE GARRISON HERE IS DEAD.
WIPED OUT.
IS THE GATE STILL SECURED?
NO, IT'S OPEN AGAIN--FROM THE OTHER SIDE.

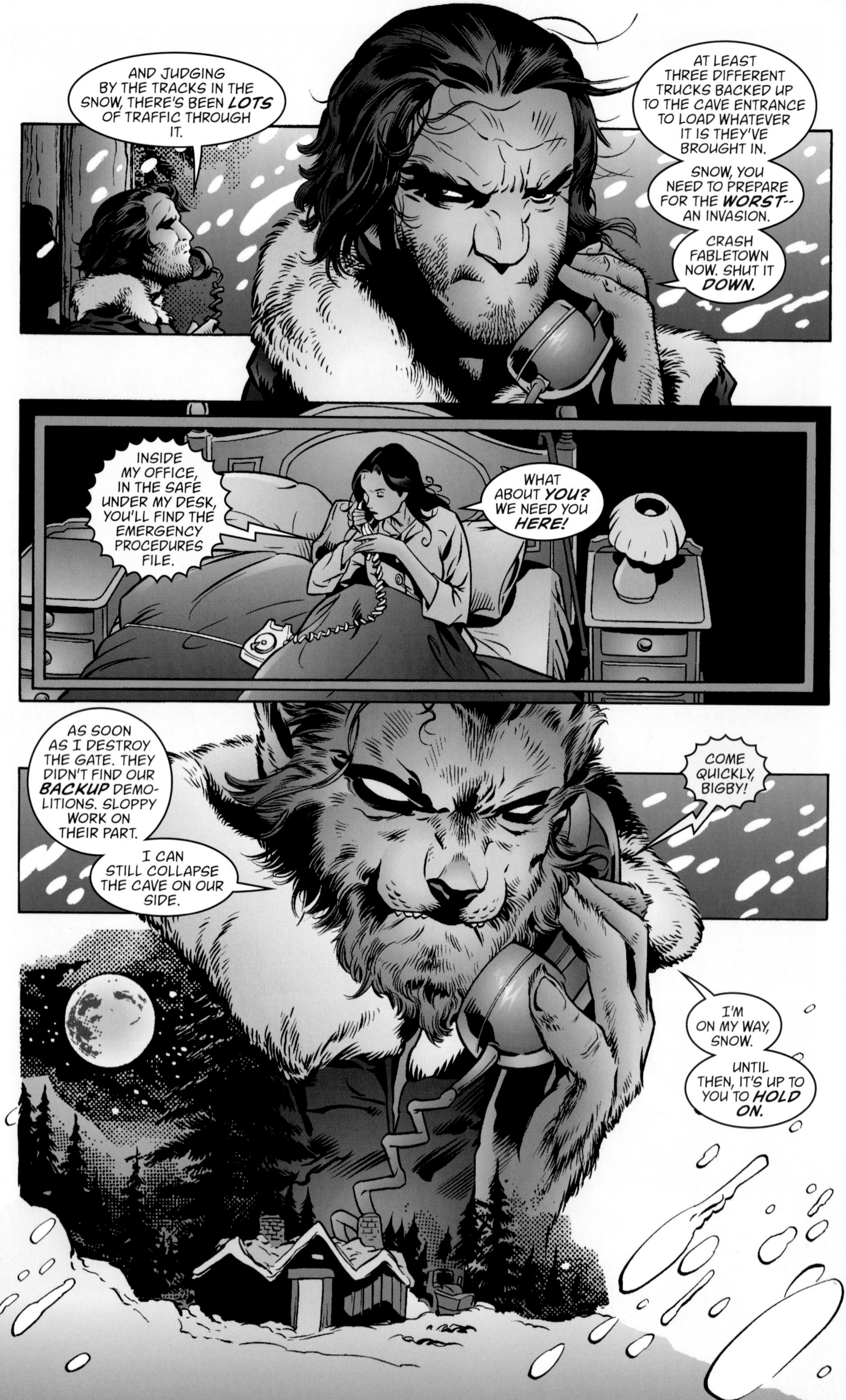
AND JUDGING BY THE TRACKS IN THE SNOW, THERE'S BEEN LOTS OF TRAFFIC THROUGH IT.
AT LEAST THREE DIFFERENT TRUCKS BACKED UP TO THE CAVE ENTRANCE TO LOAD WHATEVER IT IS THEY'VE BROUGHT IN.
SNOW, YOU NEED TO PREPARE FOR THE WORST--AN INVASION.
CRASH FABLETOWN NOW. SHUT IT DOWN.
INSIDE MY OFFICE, IN THE SAFE UNDER MY DESK, YOU'LL FIND THE EMERGENCY PROCEDURES FILE.
WHAT ABOUT YOU? WE NEED YOU HERE!
AS SOON AS I DESTROY THE GATE. THEY DIDN'T FIND OUR BACKUP DEMOLITIONS. SLOPPY WORK ON THEIR PART.
I CAN STILL COLLAPSE THE CAVE ON OUR SIDE.
COME QUICKLY, BIGBY!
I'M ON MY WAY, SNOW.
UNTIL THEN, IT'S UP TO YOU TO HOLD ON.

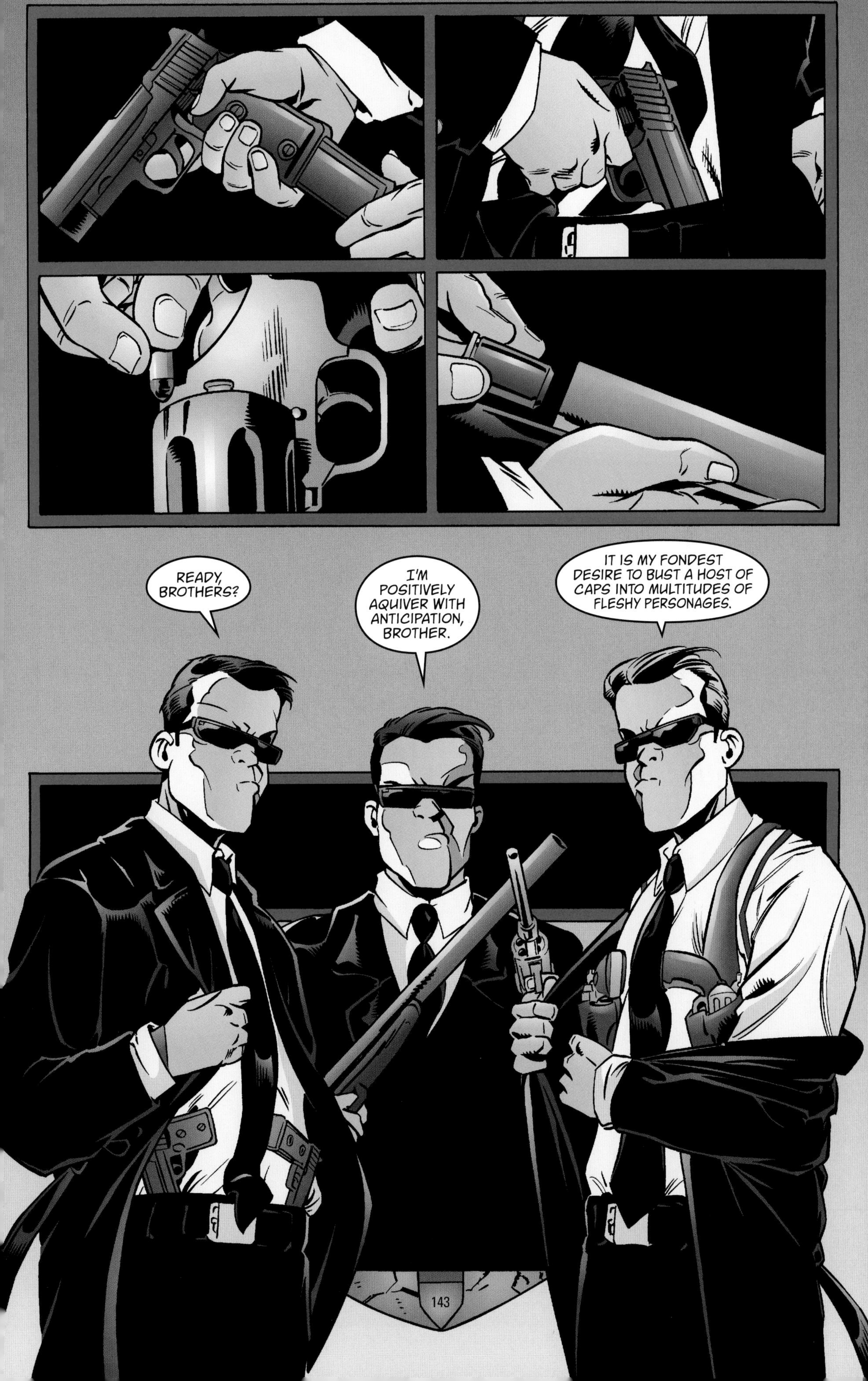
READY, BROTHERS?
I'M POSITIVELY AQUIVER WITH ANTICIPATION, BROTHER.
IT IS MY FONDEST DESIRE TO BUST A HOST OF CAPS INTO MULTITUDES OF FLESHY PERSONAGES.

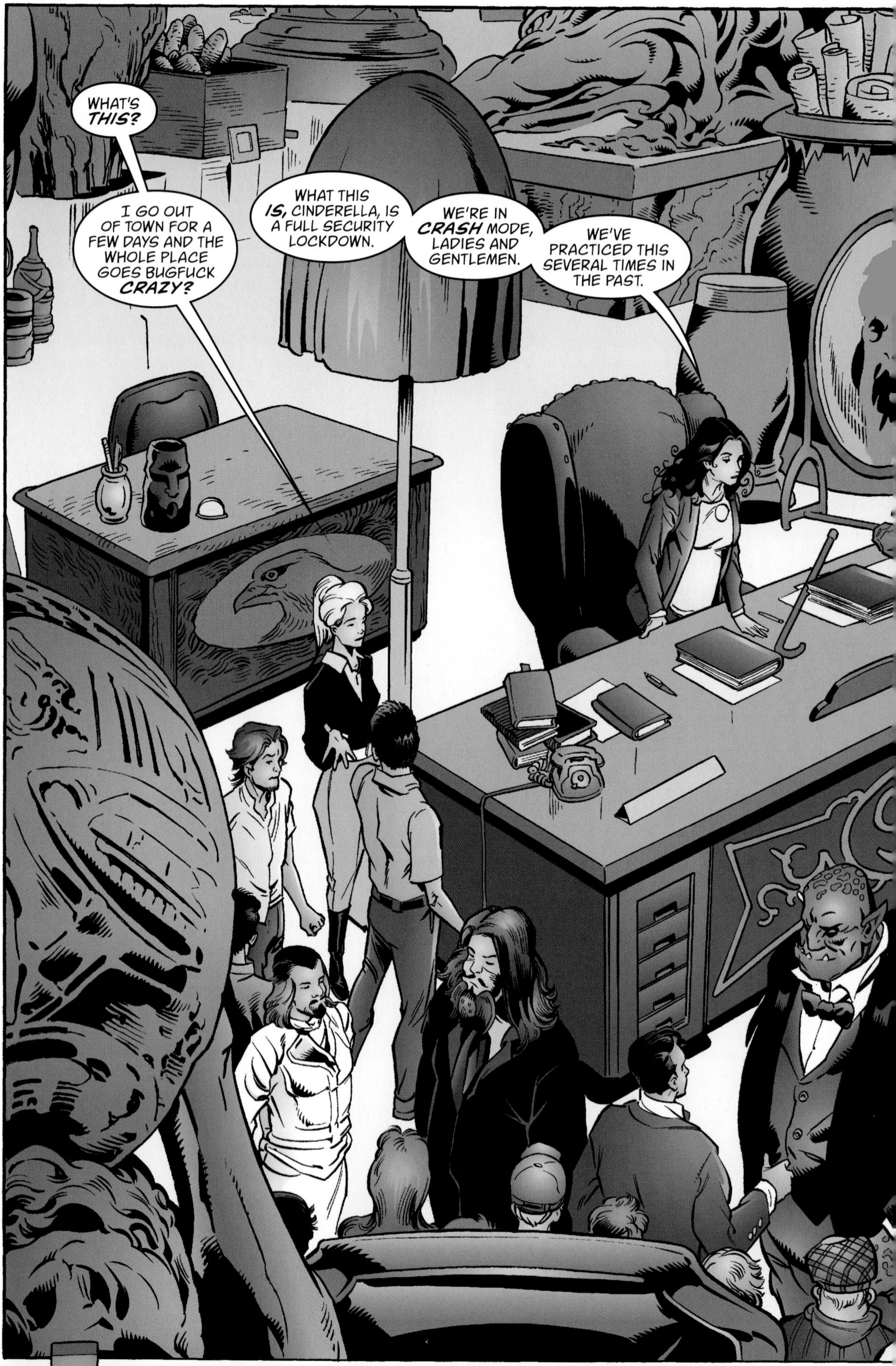
WHAT'S THIS?
I GO OUT OF TOWN FOR A FEW DAYS AND THE WHOLE PLACE GOES BUGFUCK CRAZY?
WHAT THIS IS, CINDERELLA, IS A FULL SECURITY LOCKDOWN.
WE'RE IN CRASH MODE, LADIES AND GENTLEMEN.
WE'VE PRACTICED THIS SEVERAL TIMES IN THE PAST.

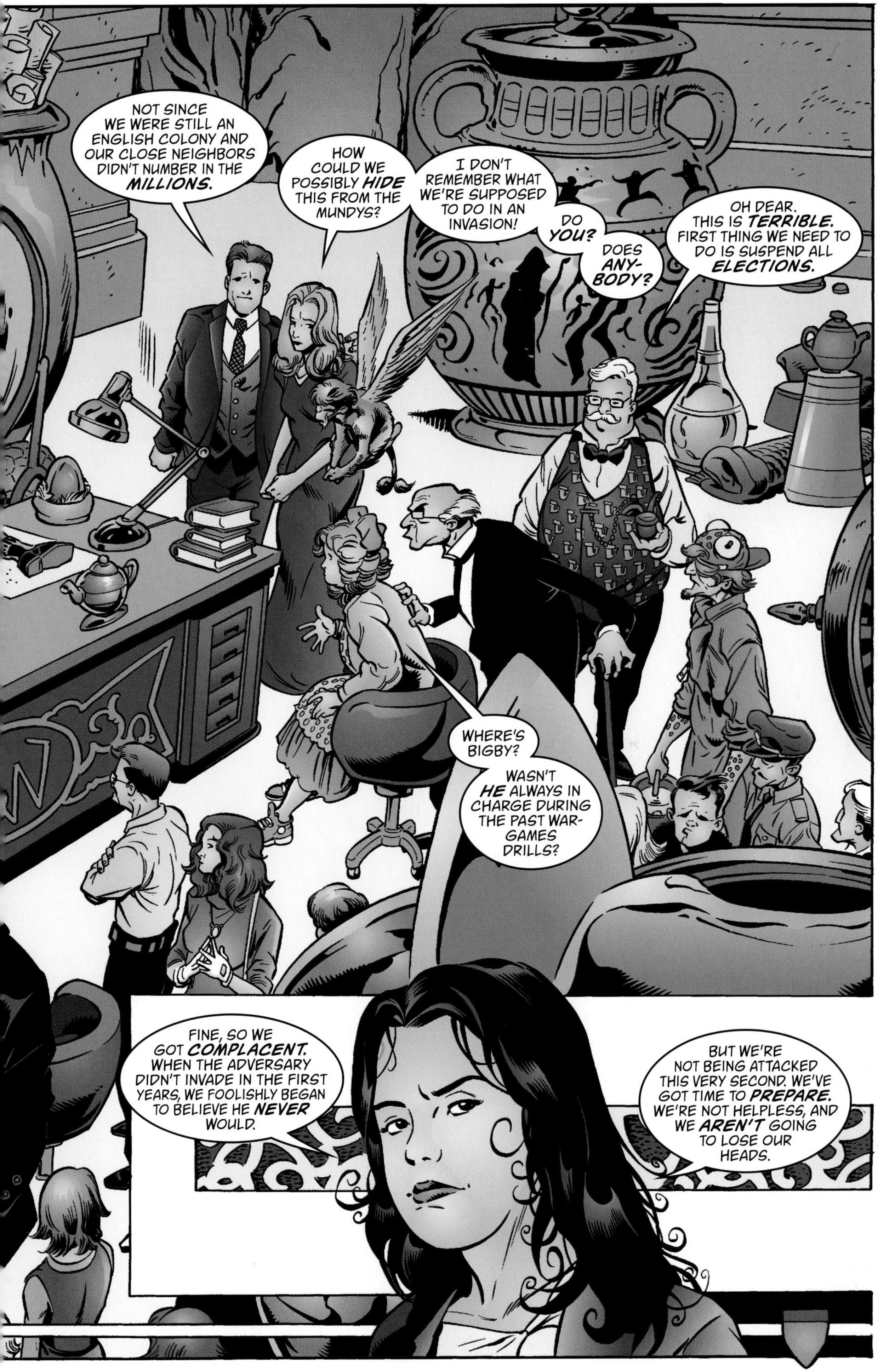

NOT SINCE WE WERE STILL AN ENGLISH COLONY AND OUR CLOSE NEIGHBORS DIDN'T NUMBER IN THE MILLIONS.
HOW COULD WE POSSIBLY HIDE THIS FROM THE MUNDYS?
I DON'T REMEMBER WHAT WE'RE SUPPOSED TO DO IN AN INVASION!
DO YOU?
DOES ANY-BODY?
OH DEAR. THIS IS TERRIBLE. FIRST THING WE NEED TO DO IS SUSPEND ALL ELECTIONS.
WHERE'S BIGBY?
WASN'T HE ALWAYS IN CHARGE DURING THE PAST WAR-GAMES DRILLS?
FINE, SO WE GOT COMPLACENT. WHEN THE ADVERSARY DIDN'T INVADE IN THE FIRST YEARS, WE FOOLISHLY BEGAN TO BELIEVE HE NEVER WOULD.
BUT WE'RE NOT BEING ATTACKED THIS VERY SECOND. WE'VE GOT TIME TO PREPARE. WE'RE NOT HELPLESS, AND WE AREN'T GOING TO LOSE OUR HEADS.

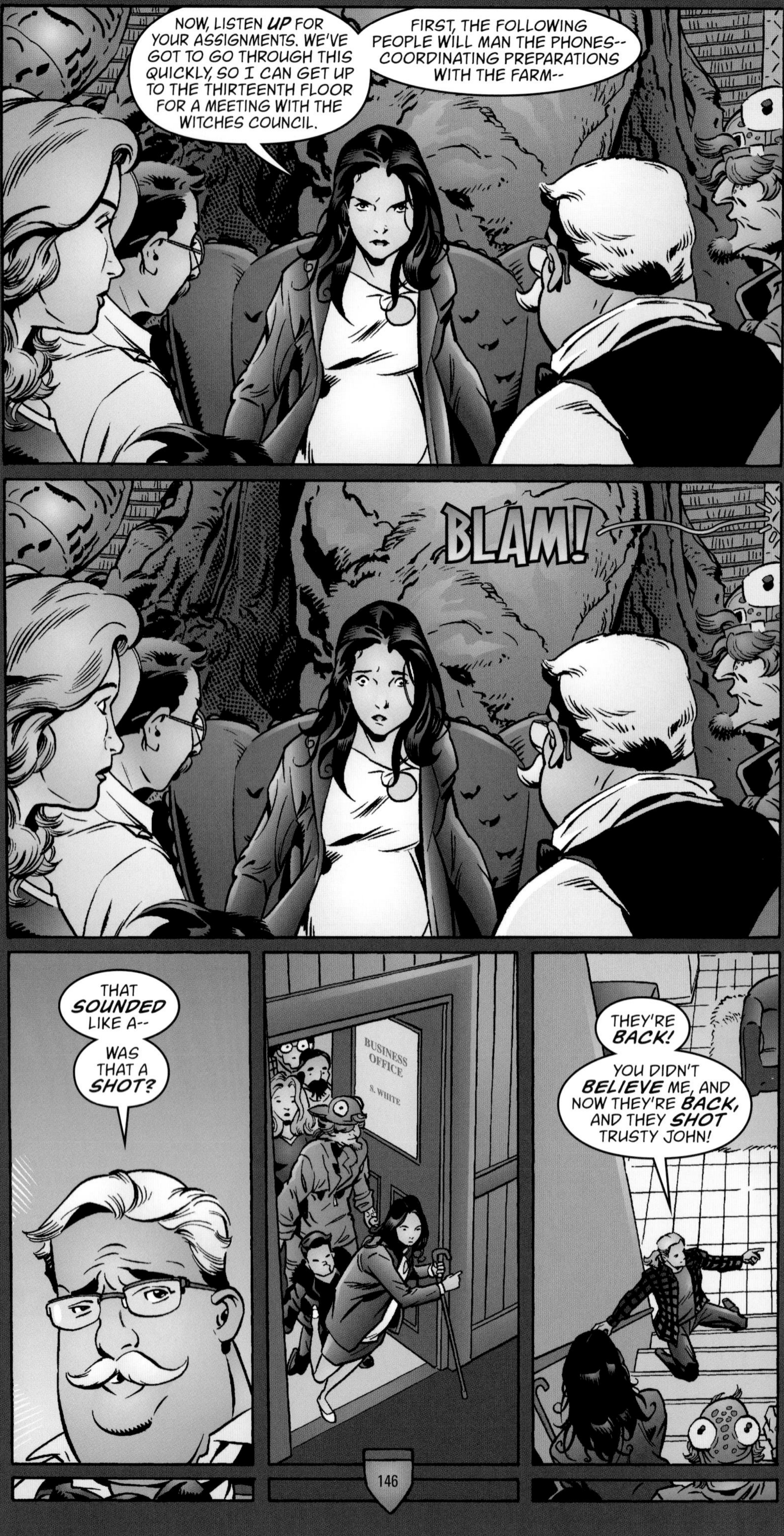
NOW, LISTEN UP FOR YOUR ASSIGNMENTS. WE'VE GOT TO GO THROUGH THIS QUICKLY, SO I CAN GET UP TO THE THIRTEENTH FLOOR FOR A MEETING WITH THE WITCHES COUNCIL.
FIRST, THE FOLLOWING PEOPLE WILL MAN THE PHONES-- COORDINATING PREPARATIONS WITH THE FARM--
BLAM!
THAT SOUNDED LIKE A--
WAS THAT A SHOT?
BUSINESS OFFICE
S. WHITE
THEY'RE BACK!
YOU DIDN'T BELIEVE ME, AND NOW THEY'RE BACK, AND THEY SHOT TRUSTY JOHN!

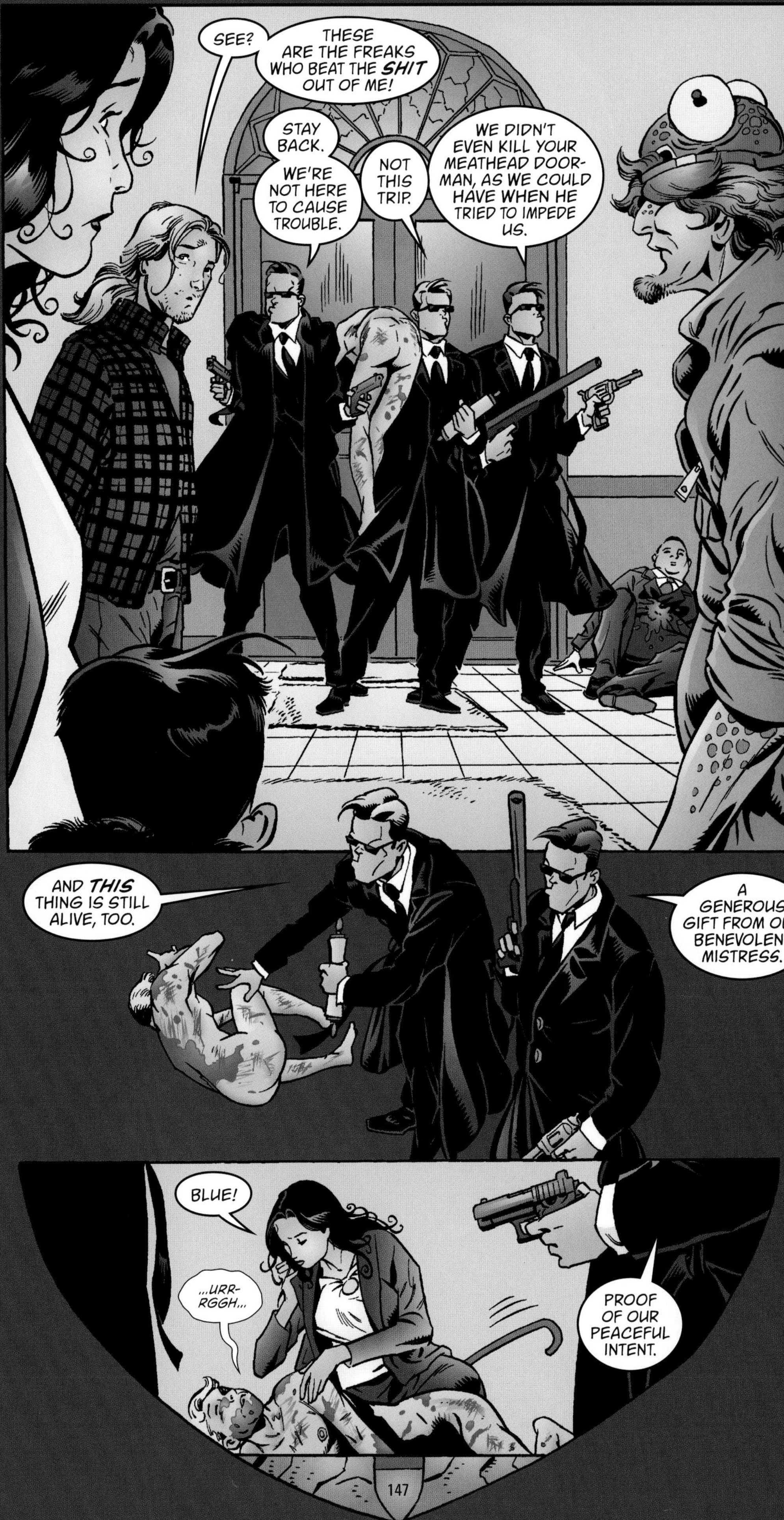
SEE?
THESE ARE THE FREAKS WHO BEAT THE SHIT OUT OF ME!
STAY BACK.
WE'RE NOT HERE TO CAUSE TROUBLE.
NOT THIS TRIP.
WE DIDN'T EVEN KILL YOUR MEATHEAD DOORMAN, AS WE COULD HAVE WHEN HE TRIED TO IMPEDE US.
AND THIS THING IS STILL ALIVE, TOO.
A GENEROUS GIFT FROM OUR BENEVOLENT MISTRESS.
BLUE!
...URR-RGGH...
PROOF OF OUR PEACEFUL INTENT.

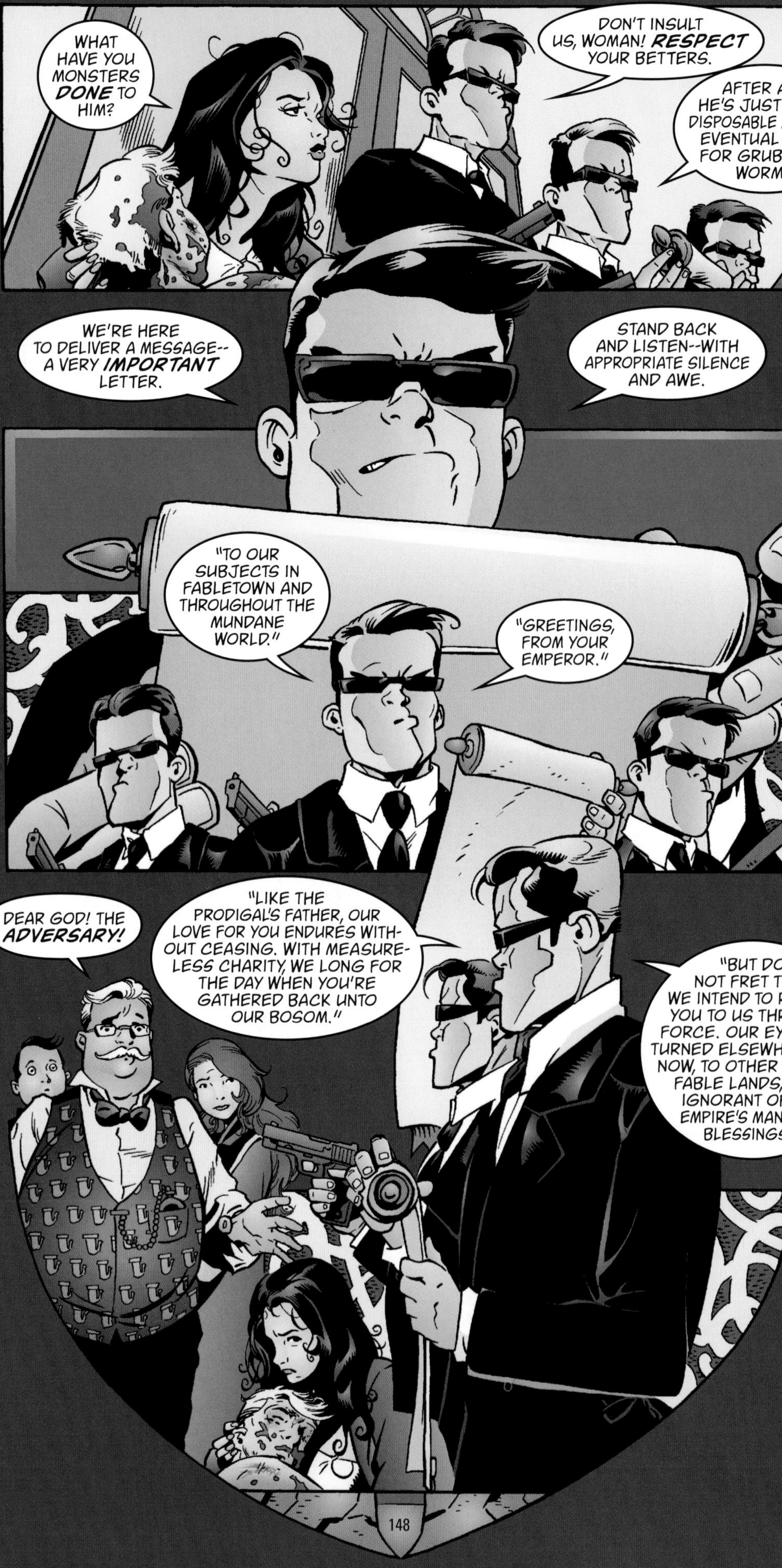
WHAT HAVE YOU MONSTERS DONE TO HIM?
DON'T INSULT US, WOMAN! RESPECT YOUR BETTERS.
AFTER ALL, HE'S JUST MORE DISPOSABLE MEAT-- EVENTUAL FOOD FOR GRUBS AND WORMS
WE'RE HERE TO DELIVER A MESSAGE-- A VERY IMPORTANT LETTER.
STAND BACK AND LISTEN--WITH APPROPRIATE SILENCE AND AWE.
"TO OUR SUBJECTS IN FABLETOWN AND THROUGHOUT THE MUNDANE WORLD."
"GREETINGS, FROM YOUR EMPEROR."
DEAR GOD! THE ADVERSARY!
"LIKE THE PRODIGAL'S FATHER, OUR LOVE FOR YOU ENDURES WITHOUT CEASING. WITH MEASURELESS CHARITY, WE LONG FOR THE DAY WHEN YOU'RE GATHERED BACK UNTO OUR BOSOM."
"BUT DO NOT FRET THAT WE INTEND TO RETURN YOU TO US THROUGH FORCE. OUR EYES ARE TURNED ELSEWHERE FOR NOW, TO OTHER DISTANT FABLE LANDS, STILL IGNORANT OF THE EMPIRE'S MANIFEST BLESSINGS."

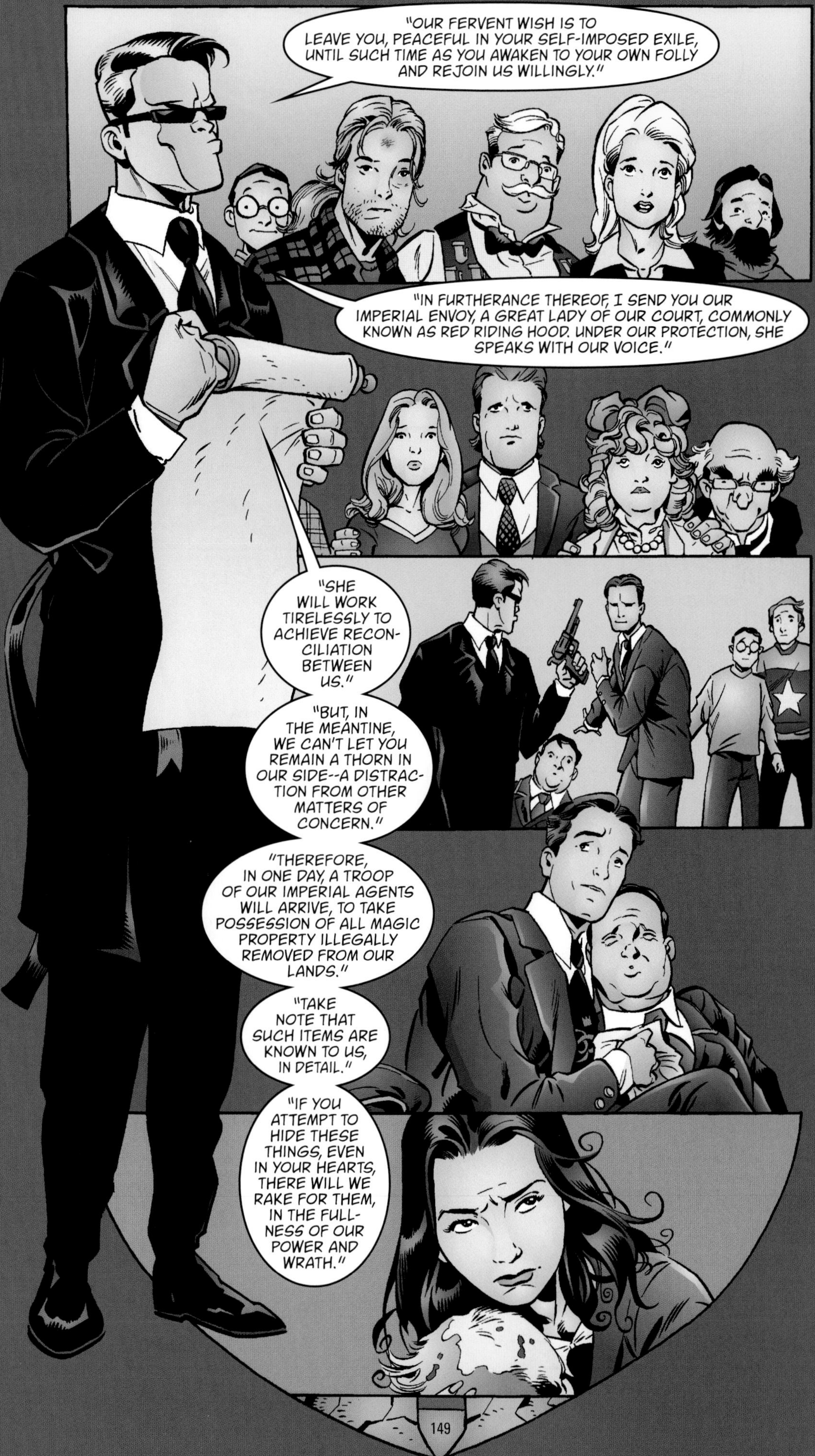
"OUR FERVENT WISH IS TO LEAVE YOU, PEACEFUL IN YOUR SELF-IMPOSED EXILE, UNTIL SUCH TIME AS YOU AWAKEN TO YOUR OWN FOLLY AND REJOIN US WILLINGLY."
"IN FURTHERANCE THEREOF, I SEND YOU OUR IMPERIAL ENVOY, A GREAT LADY OF OUR COURT, COMMONLY KNOWN AS RED RIDING HOOD. UNDER OUR PROTECTION, SHE SPEAKS WITH OUR VOICE."
"SHE WILL WORK TIRELESSLY TO ACHIEVE RECONCILIATION BETWEEN US."
"BUT, IN THE MEANTINE, WE CAN'T LET YOU REMAIN A THORN IN OUR SIDE--A DISTRACTION FROM OTHER MATTERS OF CONCERN."
"THEREFORE, IN ONE DAY, A TROOP OF OUR IMPERIAL AGENTS WILL ARRIVE, TO TAKE POSSESSION OF ALL MAGIC PROPERTY ILLEGALLY REMOVED FROM OUR LANDS."
"TAKE NOTE THAT SUCH ITEMS ARE KNOWN TO US, IN DETAIL."
"IF YOU ATTEMPT TO HIDE THESE THINGS, EVEN IN YOUR HEARTS, THERE WILL WE RAKE FOR THEM, IN THE FULLNESS OF OUR POWER AND WRATH."

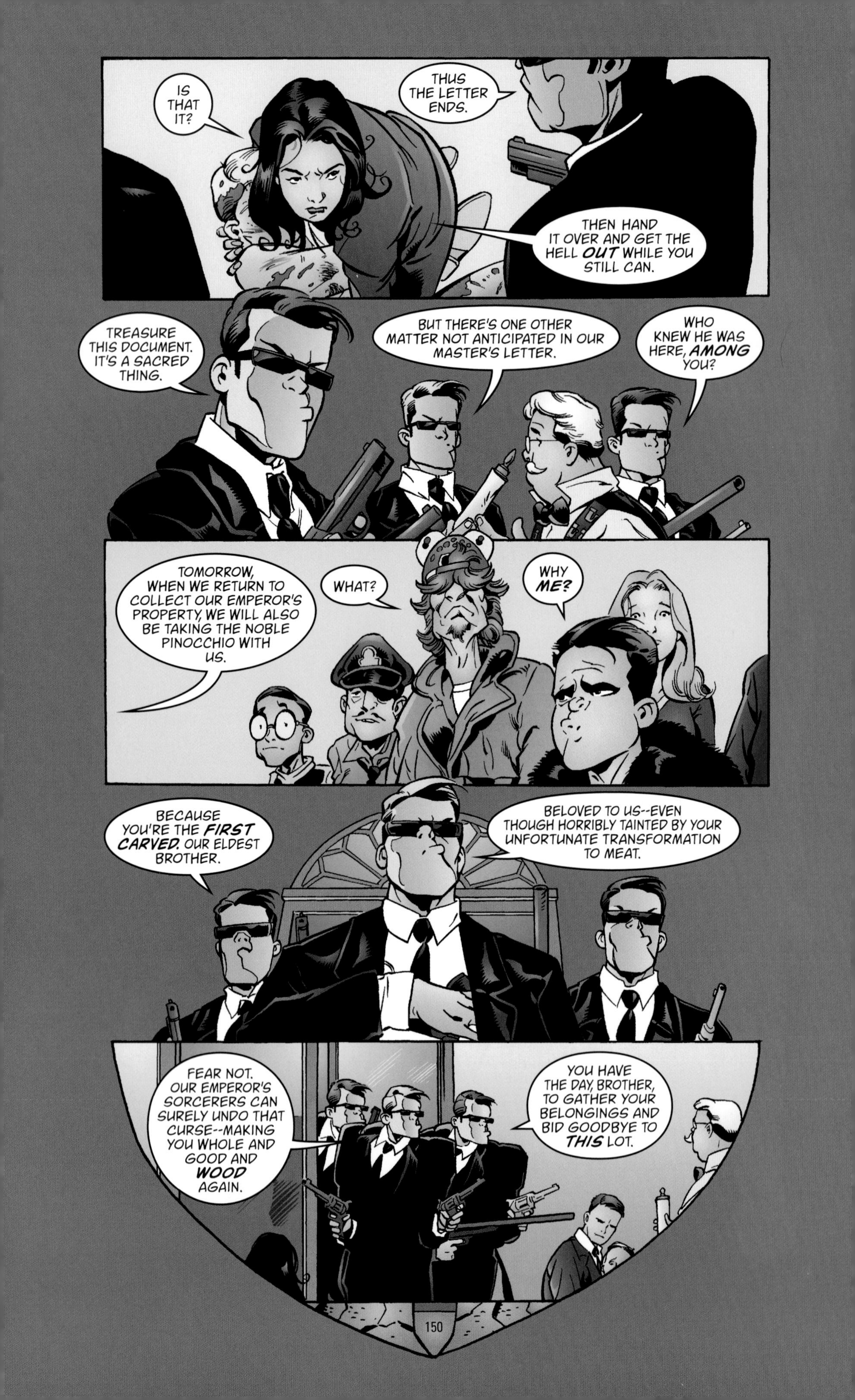
IS THAT IT?
THUS THE LETTER ENDS.
THEN HAND IT OVER AND GET THE HELL OUT WHILE YOU STILL CAN.
TREASURE THIS DOCUMENT. IT'S A SACRED THING.
BUT THERE'S ONE OTHER MATTER NOT ANTICIPATED IN OUR MASTER'S LETTER.
WHO KNEW HE WAS HERE, AMONG YOU?
TOMORROW, WHEN WE RETURN TO COLLECT OUR EMPEROR'S PROPERTY, WE WILL ALSO BE TAKING THE NOBLE PINOCCHIO WITH US.
WHAT?
WHY ME?
BECAUSE YOU'RE THE FIRST CARVED. OUR ELDEST BROTHER.
BELOVED TO US--EVEN THOUGH HORRIBLY TAINTED BY YOUR UNFORTUNATE TRANSFORMATION TO MEAT.
FEAR NOT. OUR EMPEROR'S SORCERERS CAN SURELY UNDO THAT CURSE--MAKING YOU WHOLE AND GOOD AND WOOD AGAIN.
YOU HAVE THE DAY, BROTHER, TO GATHER YOUR BELONGINGS AND BID GOODBYE TO THIS LOT.

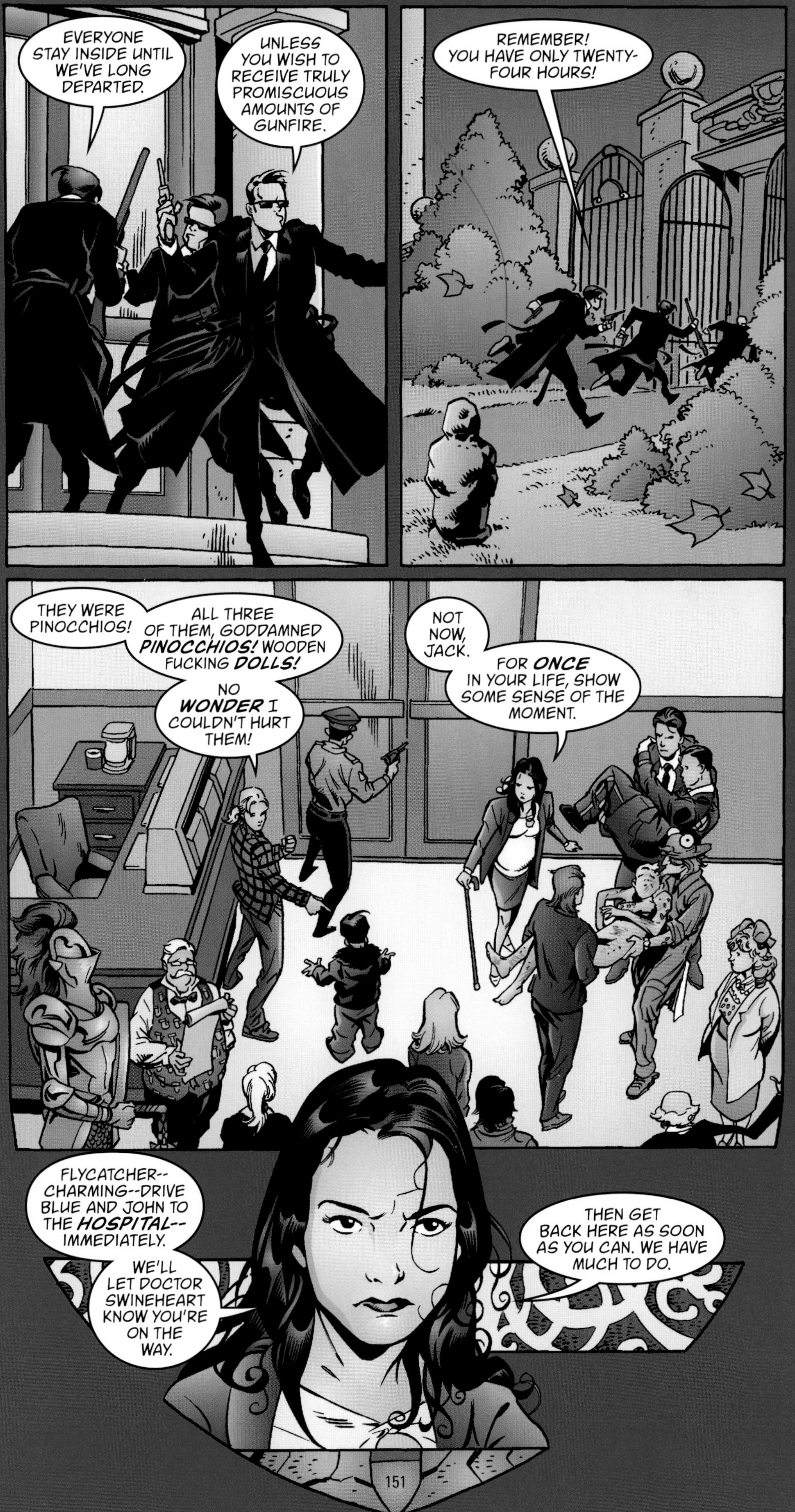
EVERYONE STAY INSIDE UNTIL WE'VE LONG DEPARTED.
UNLESS YOU WISH TO RECEIVE TRULY PROMISCUOUS AMOUNTS OF GUNFIRE.
REMEMBER! YOU HAVE ONLY TWENTY-FOUR HOURS!
THEY WERE PINOCCHIOS!
ALL THREE OF THEM, GODDAMNED PINOCCHIOS! WOODEN FUCKING DOLLS!
NO WONDER I COULDN'T HURT THEM!
NOT NOW, JACK.
FOR ONCE IN YOUR LIFE, SHOW SOME SENSE OF THE MOMENT.
FLYCATCHER--CHARMING--DRIVE BLUE AND JOHN TO THE HOSPITAL--IMMEDIATELY.
WE'LL LET DOCTOR SWINEHEART KNOW YOU'RE ON THE WAY.
THEN GET BACK HERE AS SOON AS YOU CAN. WE HAVE MUCH TO DO.

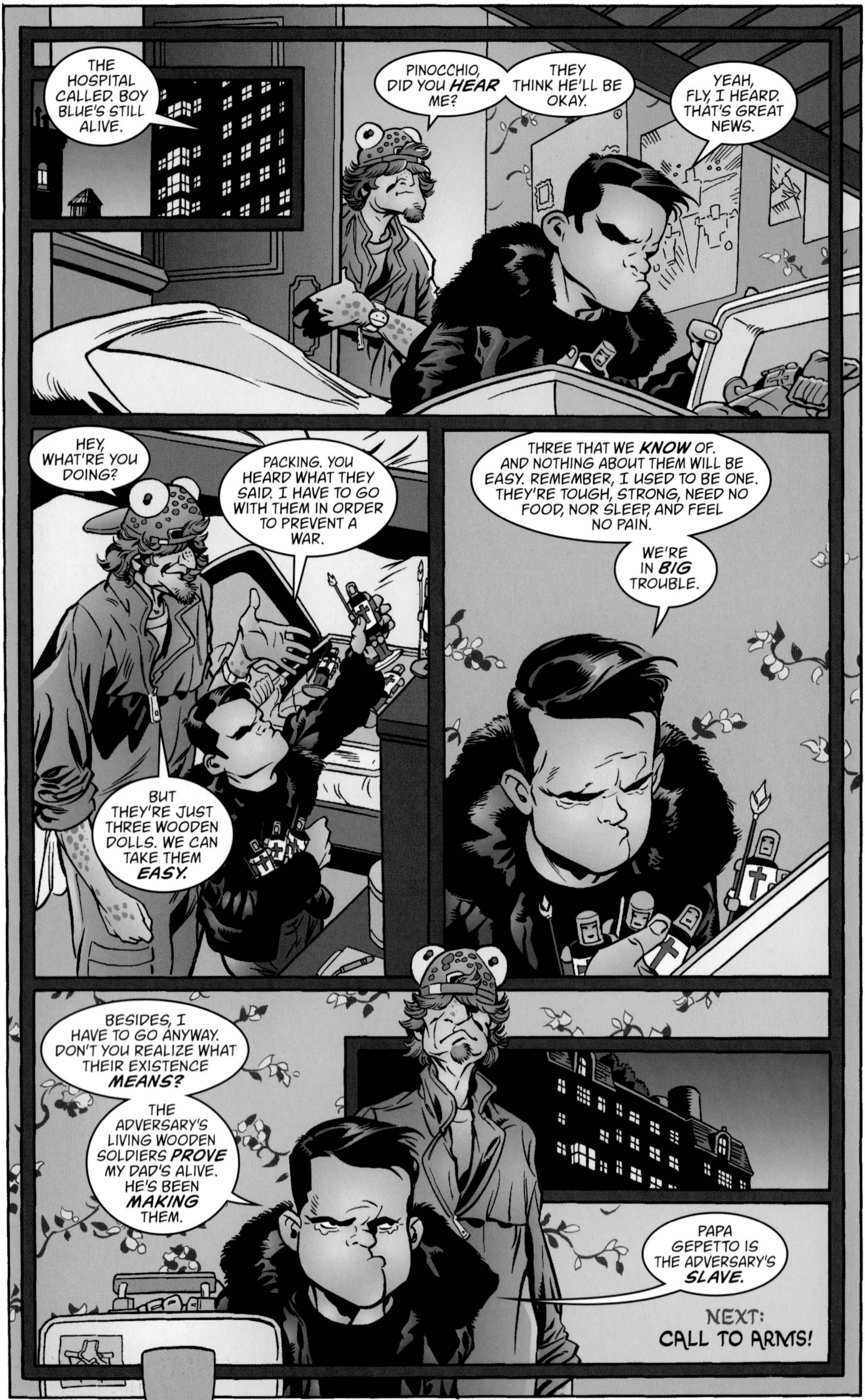
THE HOSPITAL CALLED. BOY BLUE'S STILL ALIVE.
PINOCCHIO, DID YOU HEAR ME?
THEY THINK HE'LL BE OKAY.
YEAH, FLY, I HEARD. THAT'S GREAT NEWS.
HEY, WHAT'RE YOU DOING?
PACKING. YOU HEARD WHAT THEY SAID. I HAVE TO GO WITH THEM IN ORDER TO PREVENT A WAR.
BUT THEY'RE JUST THREE WOODEN DOLLS. WE CAN TAKE THEM EASY.
THREE THAT WE KNOW OF. AND NOTHING ABOUT THEM WILL BE EASY. REMEMBER, I USED TO BE ONE. THEY'RE TOUGH, STRONG, NEED NO FOOD, NOR SLEEP, AND FEEL NO PAIN.
WE'RE IN BIG TROUBLE.
BESIDES, I HAVE TO GO ANYWAY. DON'T YOU REALIZE WHAT THEIR EXISTENCE MEANS?
THE ADVERSARY'S LIVING WOODEN SOLDIERS PROVE MY DAD'S ALIVE. HE'S BEEN MAKING THEM.
PAPA GEPETTO IS THE ADVERSARY'S SLAVE.
NEXT:
CALL TO ARMS!

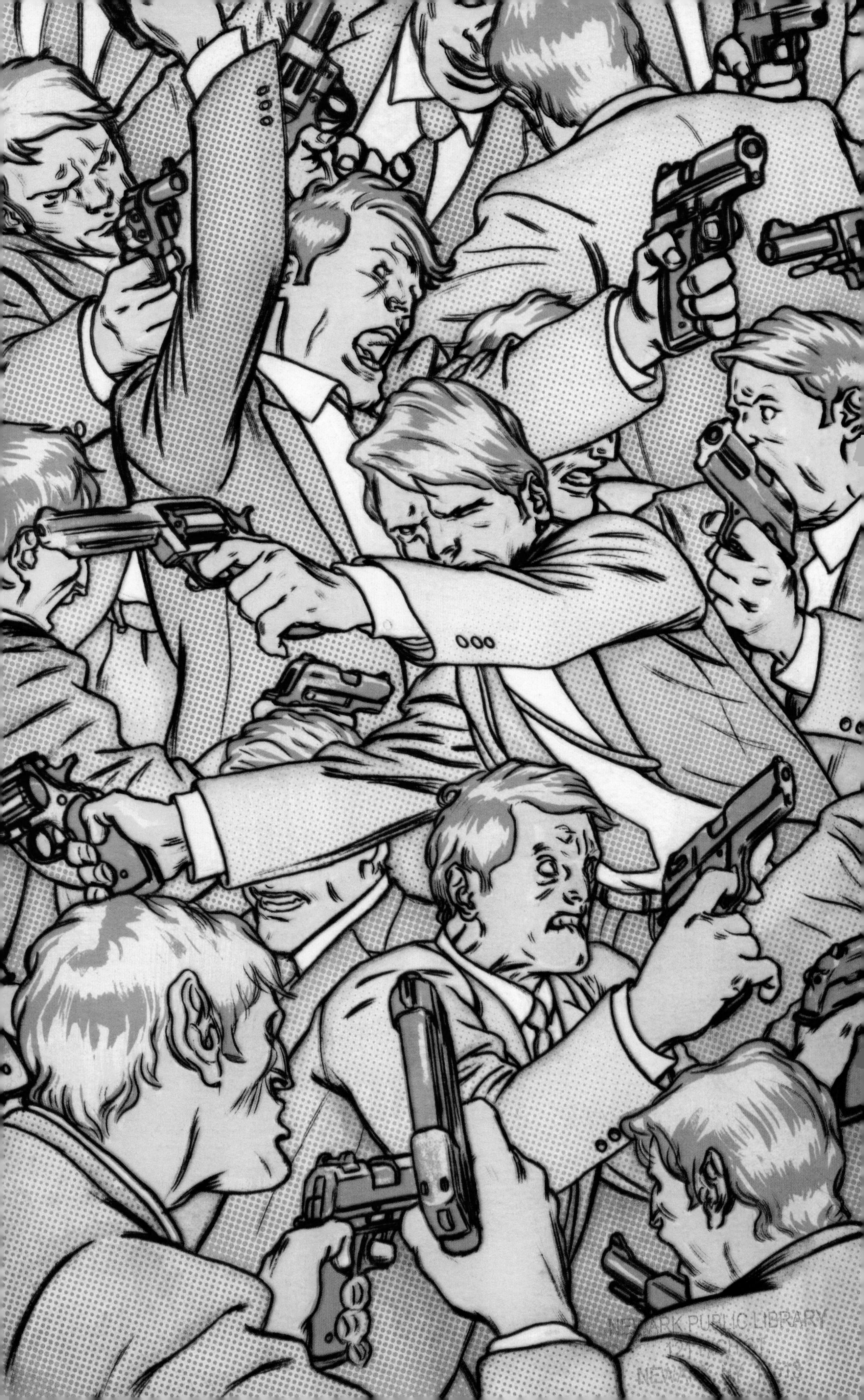

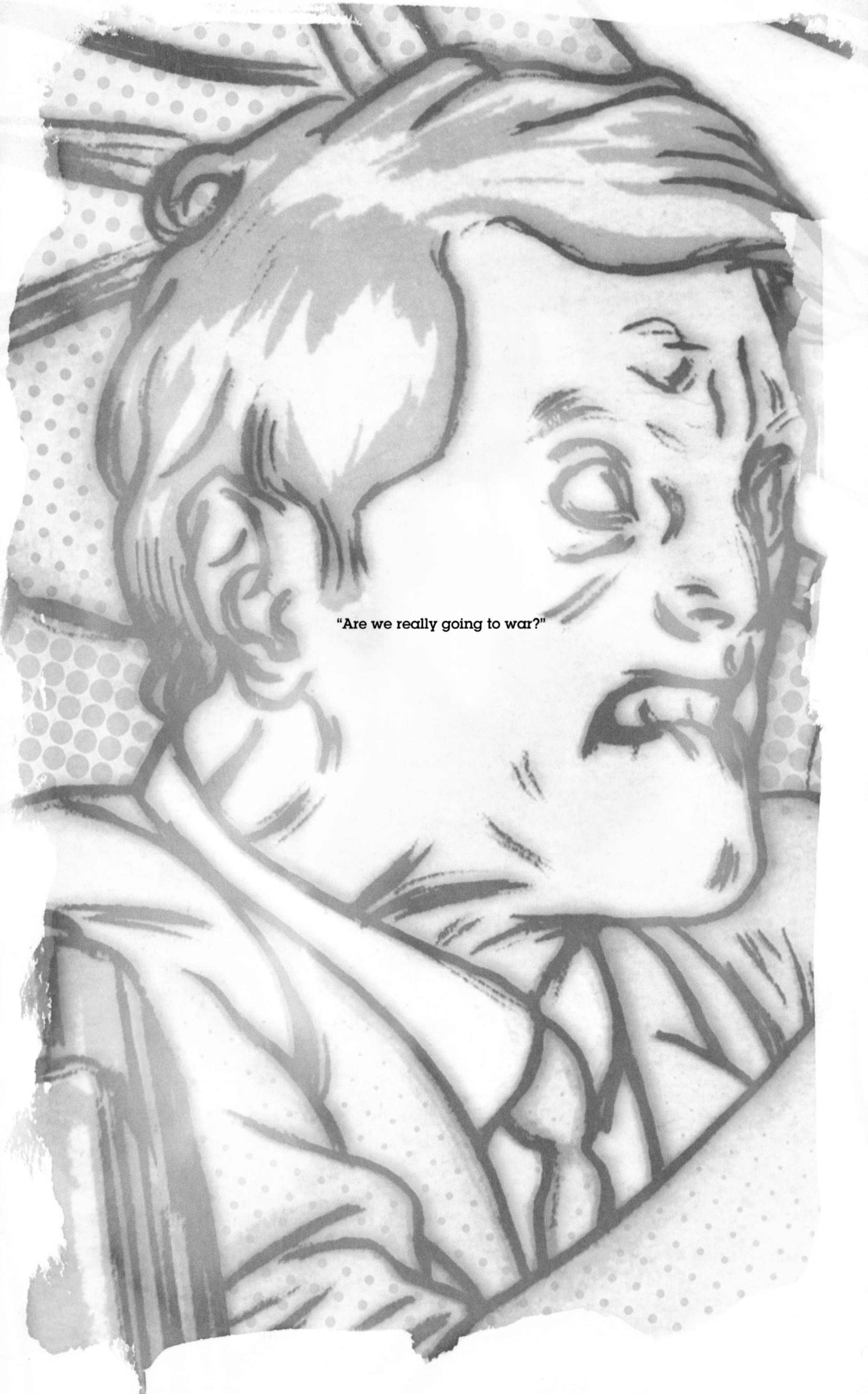
"Are we really going to war?"

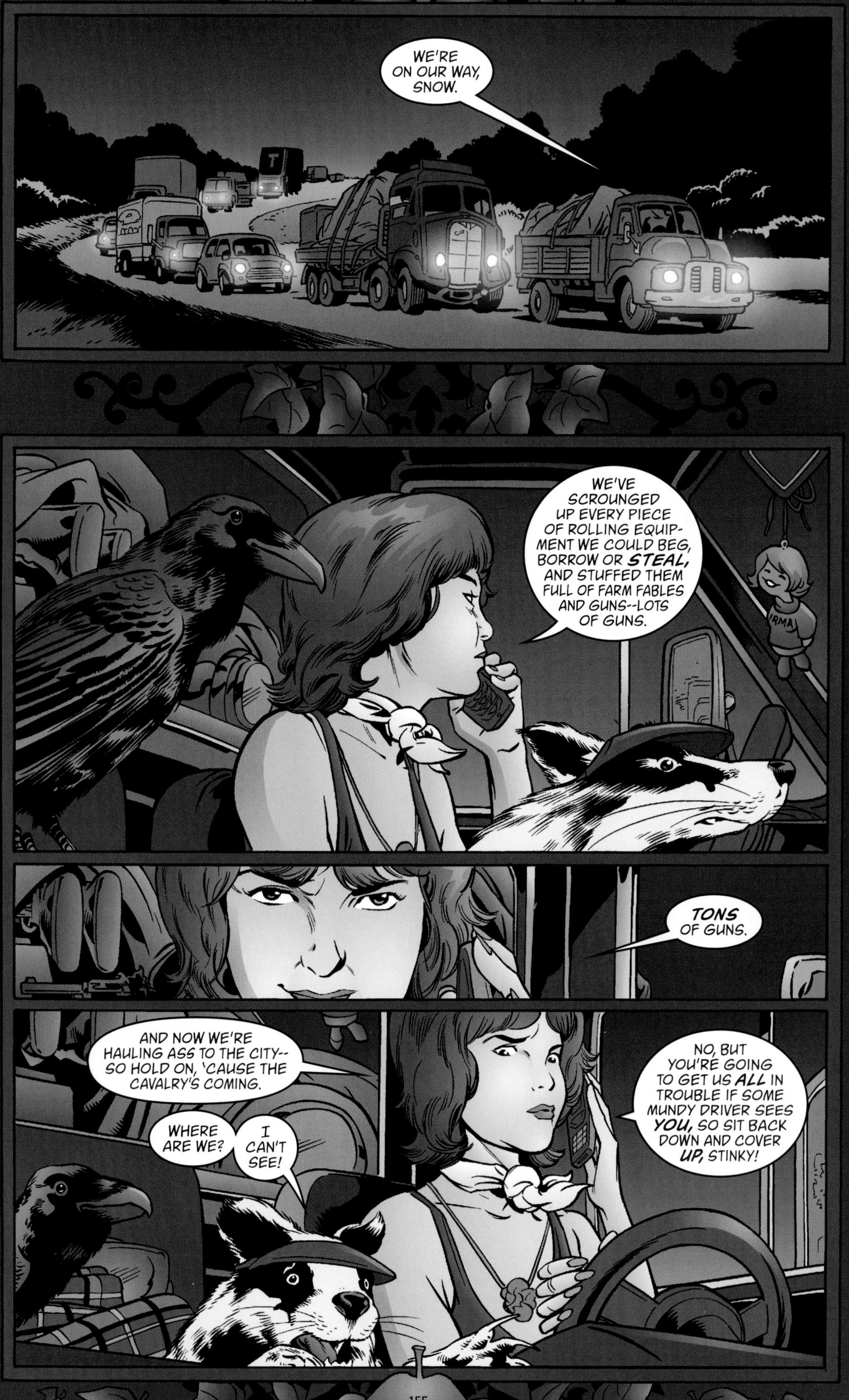
WE'RE ON OUR WAY, SNOW.
WE'VE SCROUNGED UP EVERY PIECE OF ROLLING EQUIPMENT WE COULD BEG, BORROW OR STEAL, AND STUFFED THEM FULL OF FARM FABLES AND GUNS--LOTS OF GUNS.
IRMA
TONS OF GUNS.
AND NOW WE'RE HAULING ASS TO THE CITY-- SO HOLD ON, 'CAUSE THE CAVALRY'S COMING.
WHERE ARE WE?
I CAN'T SEE!
NO, BUT YOU'RE GOING TO GET US ALL IN TROUBLE IF SOME MUNDY DRIVER SEES YOU, SO SIT BACK DOWN AND COVER UP, STINKY!

OUR RIGHT TO ASSEMBLE ISSUE

CHAPTER SIX ∘ MARCH OF THE WOODEN SOLDIERS

BILL WILLINGHAM writer/creator
MARK BUCKINGHAM penciller, inks: pp. 5-7, 16, 20-21
STEVE LEIALOHA inker
DANIEL VOZZO color/seps
TODD KLEIN lettering
JAMES JEAN cover art
MARIAH HUEHNER assistant editor
SHELLY BOND editor

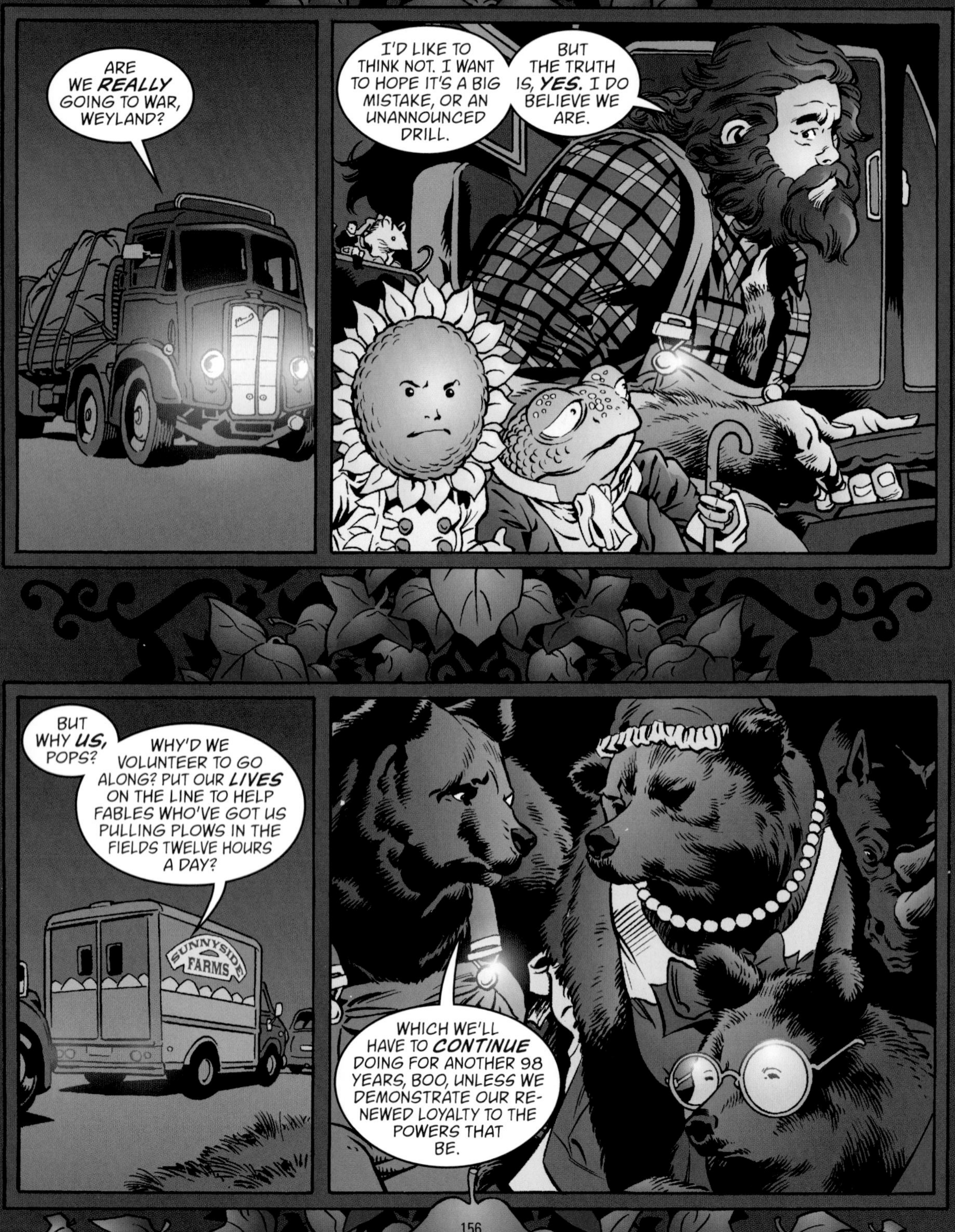

ARE WE *REALLY* GOING TO WAR, WEYLAND?
I'D LIKE TO THINK NOT. I WANT TO HOPE IT'S A BIG MISTAKE, OR AN UNANNOUNCED DRILL.
BUT THE TRUTH IS, *YES.* I DO BELIEVE WE ARE.
BUT WHY *US,* POPS?
WHY'D WE VOLUNTEER TO GO ALONG? PUT OUR *LIVES* ON THE LINE TO HELP FABLES WHO'VE GOT US PULLING PLOWS IN THE FIELDS TWELVE HOURS A DAY?
SUNNYSIDE FARMS
WHICH WE'LL HAVE TO *CONTINUE* DOING FOR ANOTHER 98 YEARS, BOO, UNLESS WE DEMONSTRATE OUR RENEWED LOYALTY TO THE POWERS THAT BE.

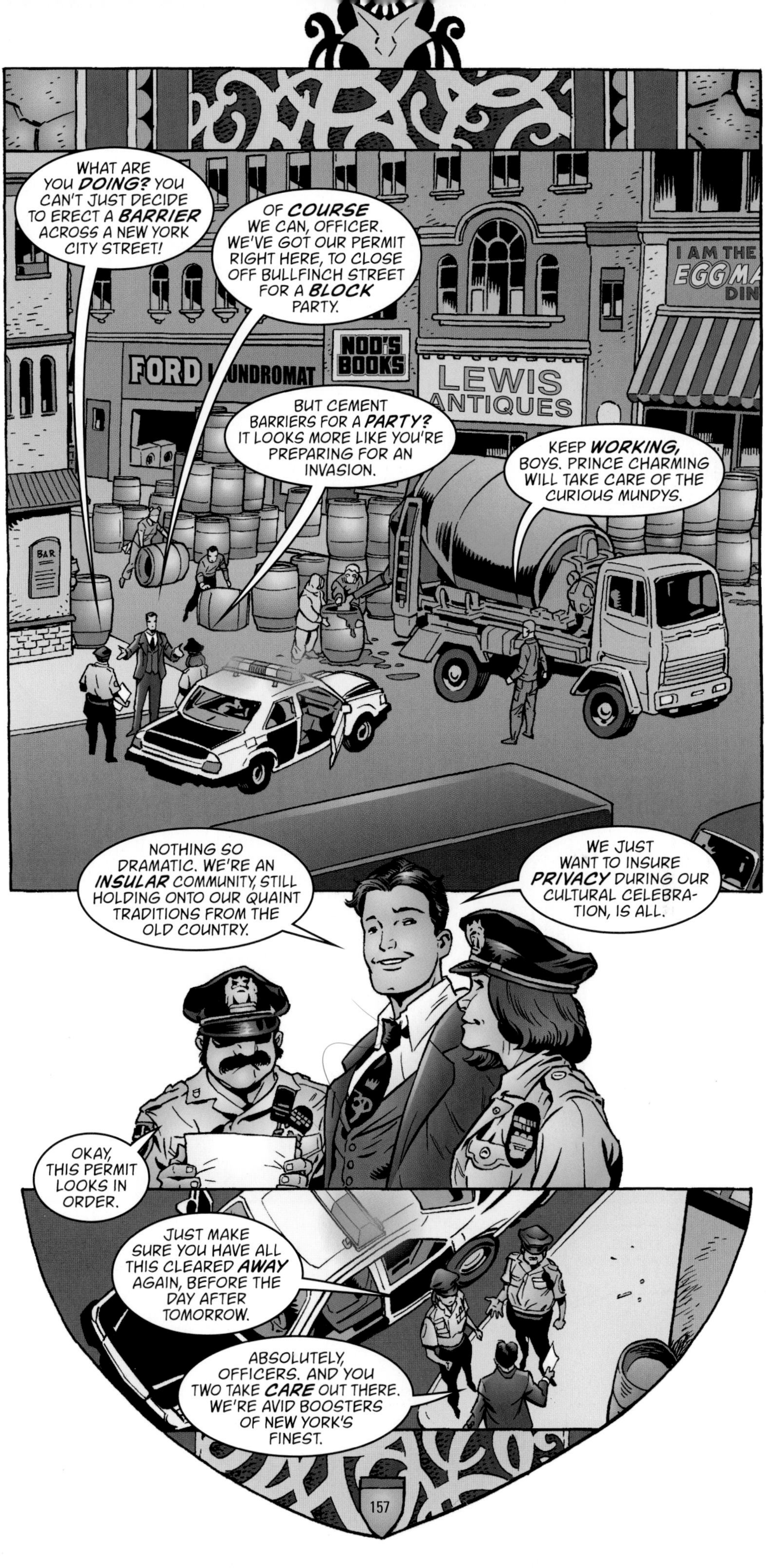
WHAT ARE YOU DOING? YOU CAN'T JUST DECIDE TO ERECT A BARRIER ACROSS A NEW YORK CITY STREET!
OF COURSE WE CAN, OFFICER. WE'VE GOT OUR PERMIT RIGHT HERE, TO CLOSE OFF BULLFINCH STREET FOR A BLOCK PARTY.
I AM THE
EGGMA
DIN
NOD'S BOOKS
FORD LAUNDROMAT
LEWIS ANTIQUES
BUT CEMENT BARRIERS FOR A PARTY? IT LOOKS MORE LIKE YOU'RE PREPARING FOR AN INVASION.
KEEP WORKING, BOYS. PRINCE CHARMING WILL TAKE CARE OF THE CURIOUS MUNDYS.
BAR
NOTHING SO DRAMATIC. WE'RE AN INSULAR COMMUNITY, STILL HOLDING ONTO OUR QUAINT TRADITIONS FROM THE OLD COUNTRY.
WE JUST WANT TO INSURE PRIVACY DURING OUR CULTURAL CELEBRATION, IS ALL.
OKAY, THIS PERMIT LOOKS IN ORDER.
JUST MAKE SURE YOU HAVE ALL THIS CLEARED AWAY AGAIN, BEFORE THE DAY AFTER TOMORROW.
ABSOLUTELY, OFFICERS. AND YOU TWO TAKE CARE OUT THERE. WE'RE AVID BOOSTERS OF NEW YORK'S FINEST.

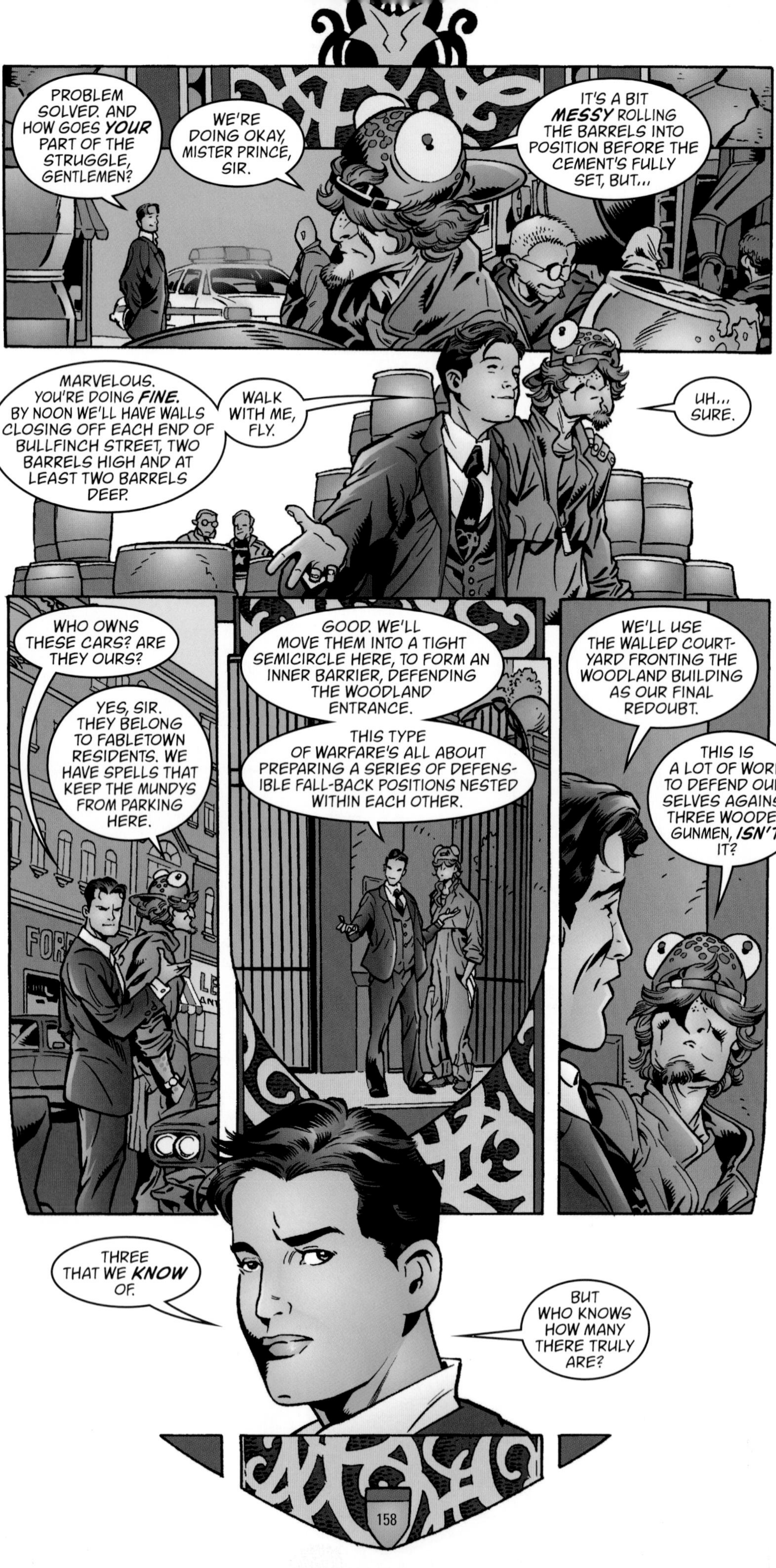
PROBLEM SOLVED. AND HOW GOES YOUR PART OF THE STRUGGLE, GENTLEMEN?
WE'RE DOING OKAY, MISTER PRINCE, SIR.
IT'S A BIT MESSY ROLLING THE BARRELS INTO POSITION BEFORE THE CEMENT'S FULLY SET, BUT...
MARVELOUS. YOU'RE DOING FINE. BY NOON WE'LL HAVE WALLS CLOSING OFF EACH END OF BULLFINCH STREET, TWO BARRELS HIGH AND AT LEAST TWO BARRELS DEEP.
WALK WITH ME, FLY.
UH... SURE.
WHO OWNS THESE CARS? ARE THEY OURS?
YES, SIR. THEY BELONG TO FABLETOWN RESIDENTS. WE HAVE SPELLS THAT KEEP THE MUNDYS FROM PARKING HERE.
GOOD. WE'LL MOVE THEM INTO A TIGHT SEMICIRCLE HERE, TO FORM AN INNER BARRIER, DEFENDING THE WOODLAND ENTRANCE.
THIS TYPE OF WARFARE'S ALL ABOUT PREPARING A SERIES OF DEFENSIBLE FALL-BACK POSITIONS NESTED WITHIN EACH OTHER.
WE'LL USE THE WALLED COURTYARD FRONTING THE WOODLAND BUILDING AS OUR FINAL REDOUBT.
THIS IS A LOT OF WORK TO DEFEND OURSELVES AGAINST THREE WOODEN GUNMEN, ISN'T IT?
THREE THAT WE KNOW OF.
BUT WHO KNOWS HOW MANY THERE TRULY ARE?
158

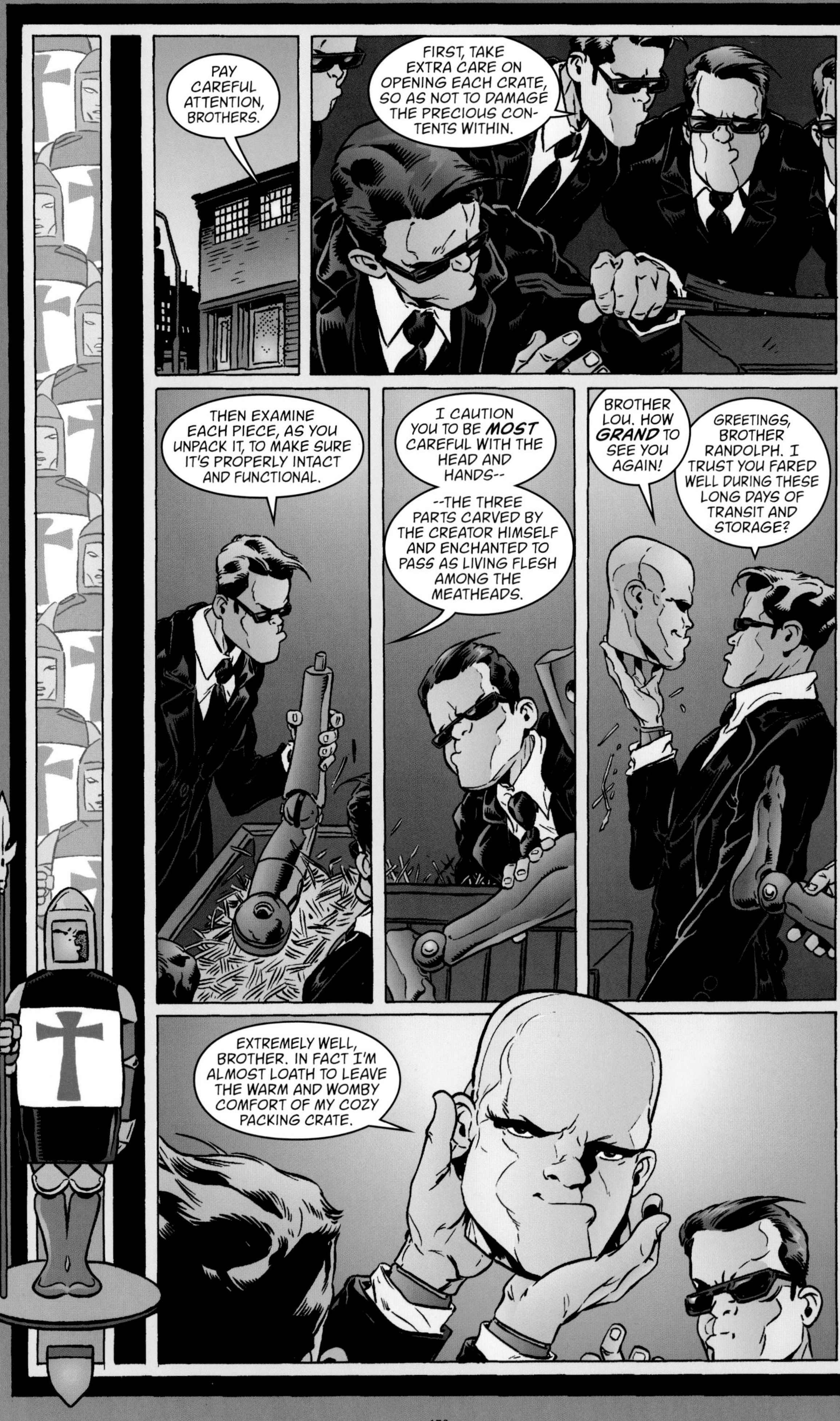
PAY CAREFUL ATTENTION, BROTHERS.
FIRST, TAKE EXTRA CARE ON OPENING EACH CRATE, SO AS NOT TO DAMAGE THE PRECIOUS CONTENTS WITHIN.
THEN EXAMINE EACH PIECE, AS YOU UNPACK IT, TO MAKE SURE IT'S PROPERLY INTACT AND FUNCTIONAL.
I CAUTION YOU TO BE ***MOST*** CAREFUL WITH THE HEAD AND HANDS--
--THE THREE PARTS CARVED BY THE CREATOR HIMSELF AND ENCHANTED TO PASS AS LIVING FLESH AMONG THE MEATHEADS.
BROTHER LOU. HOW ***GRAND*** TO SEE YOU AGAIN!
GREETINGS, BROTHER RANDOLPH. I TRUST YOU FARED WELL DURING THESE LONG DAYS OF TRANSIT AND STORAGE?
EXTREMELY WELL, BROTHER. IN FACT I'M ALMOST LOATH TO LEAVE THE WARM AND WOMBY COMFORT OF MY COZY PACKING CRATE.

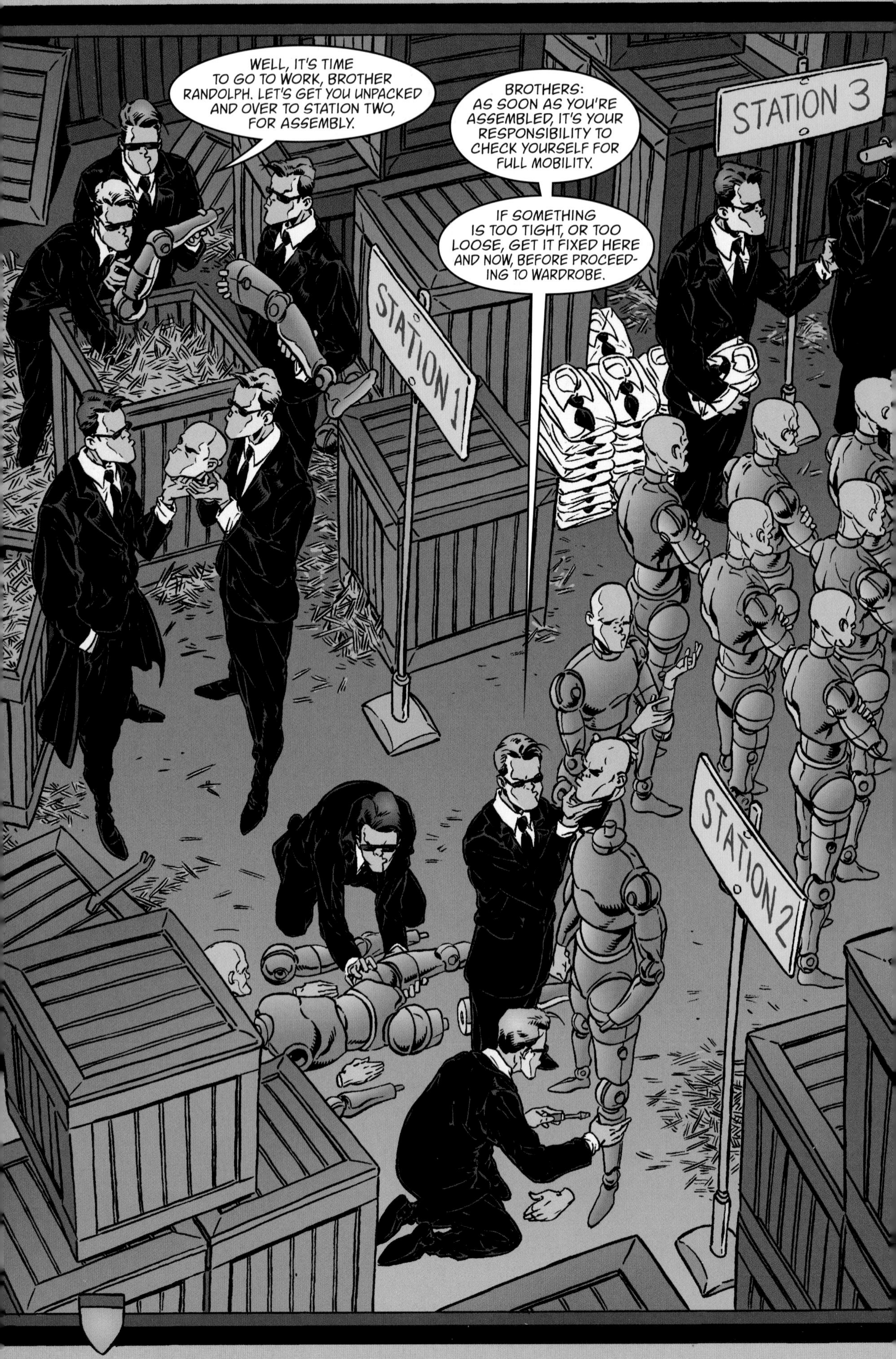
WELL, IT'S TIME TO GO TO WORK, BROTHER RANDOLPH. LET'S GET YOU UNPACKED AND OVER TO STATION TWO, FOR ASSEMBLY.
BROTHERS: AS SOON AS YOU'RE ASSEMBLED, IT'S YOUR RESPONSIBILITY TO CHECK YOURSELF FOR FULL MOBILITY.
IF SOMETHING IS TOO TIGHT, OR TOO LOOSE, GET IT FIXED HERE AND NOW, BEFORE PROCEEDING TO WARDROBE.
STATION 3
STATION 1
STATION 2

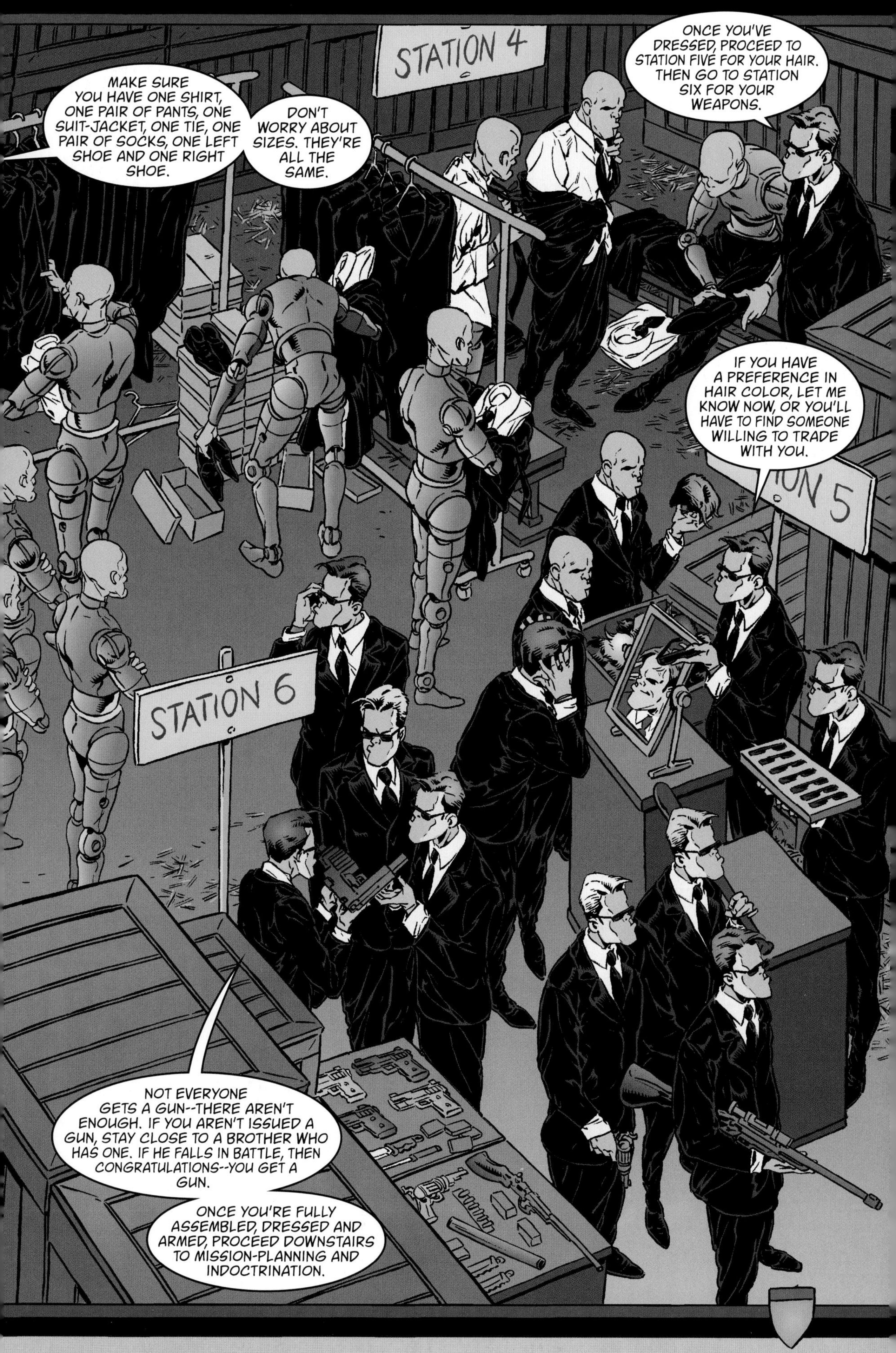
STATION 4
MAKE SURE YOU HAVE ONE SHIRT, ONE PAIR OF PANTS, ONE SUIT-JACKET, ONE TIE, ONE PAIR OF SOCKS, ONE LEFT SHOE AND ONE RIGHT SHOE.
DON'T WORRY ABOUT SIZES. THEY'RE ALL THE SAME.
ONCE YOU'VE DRESSED, PROCEED TO STATION FIVE FOR YOUR HAIR. THEN GO TO STATION SIX FOR YOUR WEAPONS.
IF YOU HAVE A PREFERENCE IN HAIR COLOR, LET ME KNOW NOW, OR YOU'LL HAVE TO FIND SOMEONE WILLING TO TRADE WITH YOU.
STATION 6
NOT EVERYONE GETS A GUN--THERE AREN'T ENOUGH. IF YOU AREN'T ISSUED A GUN, STAY CLOSE TO A BROTHER WHO HAS ONE. IF HE FALLS IN BATTLE, THEN CONGRATULATIONS--YOU GET A GUN.
ONCE YOU'RE FULLY ASSEMBLED, DRESSED AND ARMED, PROCEED DOWNSTAIRS TO MISSION-PLANNING AND INDOCTRINATION.

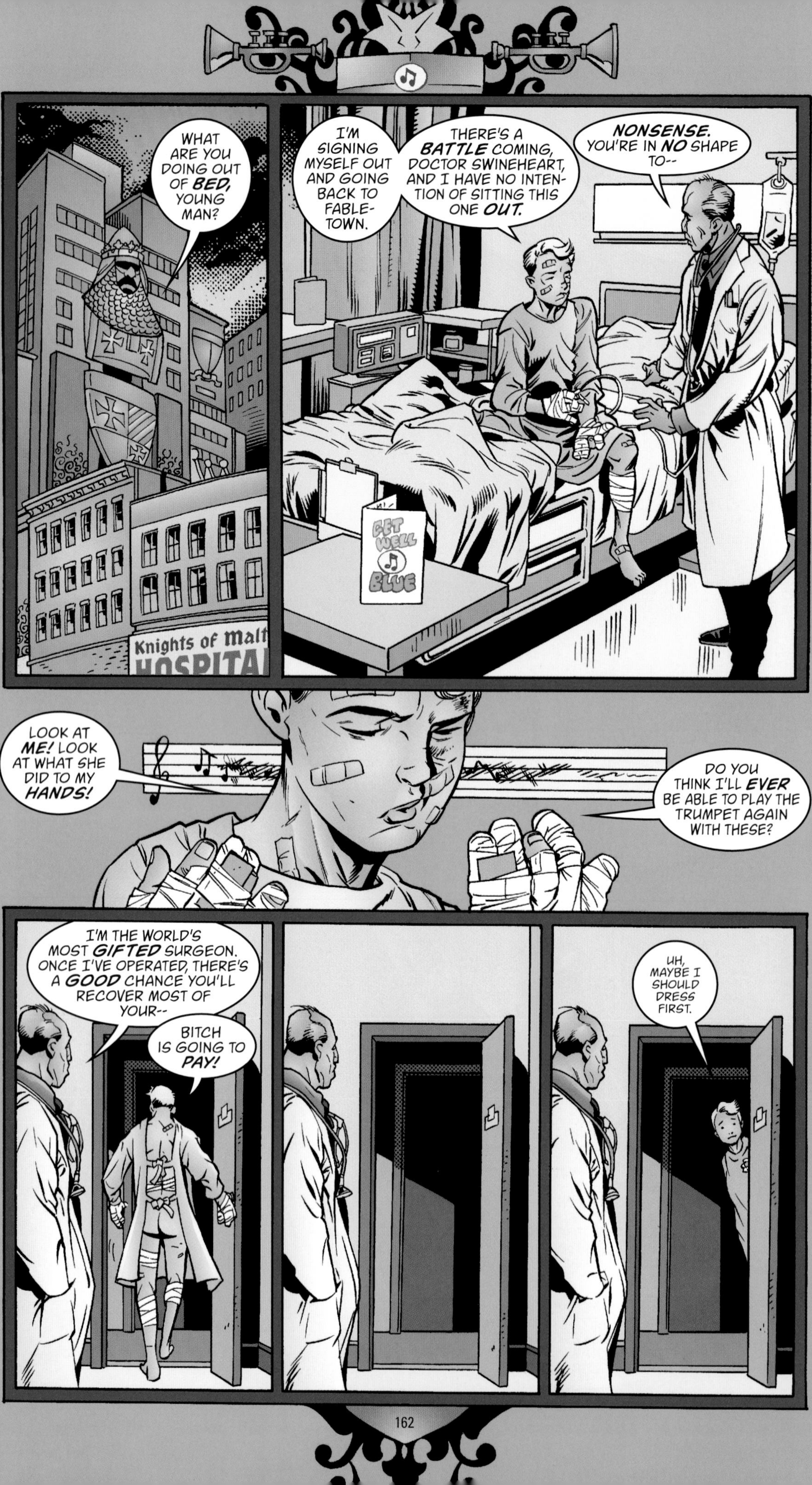
Knights of Malt
HOSPITAL
WHAT ARE YOU DOING OUT OF BED, YOUNG MAN?
I'M SIGNING MYSELF OUT AND GOING BACK TO FABLE-TOWN.
THERE'S A BATTLE COMING, DOCTOR SWINEHEART, AND I HAVE NO INTEN-TION OF SITTING THIS ONE OUT.
NONSENSE. YOU'RE IN NO SHAPE TO--
GET WELL BLUE
LOOK AT ME! LOOK AT WHAT SHE DID TO MY HANDS!
DO YOU THINK I'LL EVER BE ABLE TO PLAY THE TRUMPET AGAIN WITH THESE?
I'M THE WORLD'S MOST GIFTED SURGEON. ONCE I'VE OPERATED, THERE'S A GOOD CHANCE YOU'LL RECOVER MOST OF YOUR--
BITCH IS GOING TO PAY!
UH, MAYBE I SHOULD DRESS FIRST.

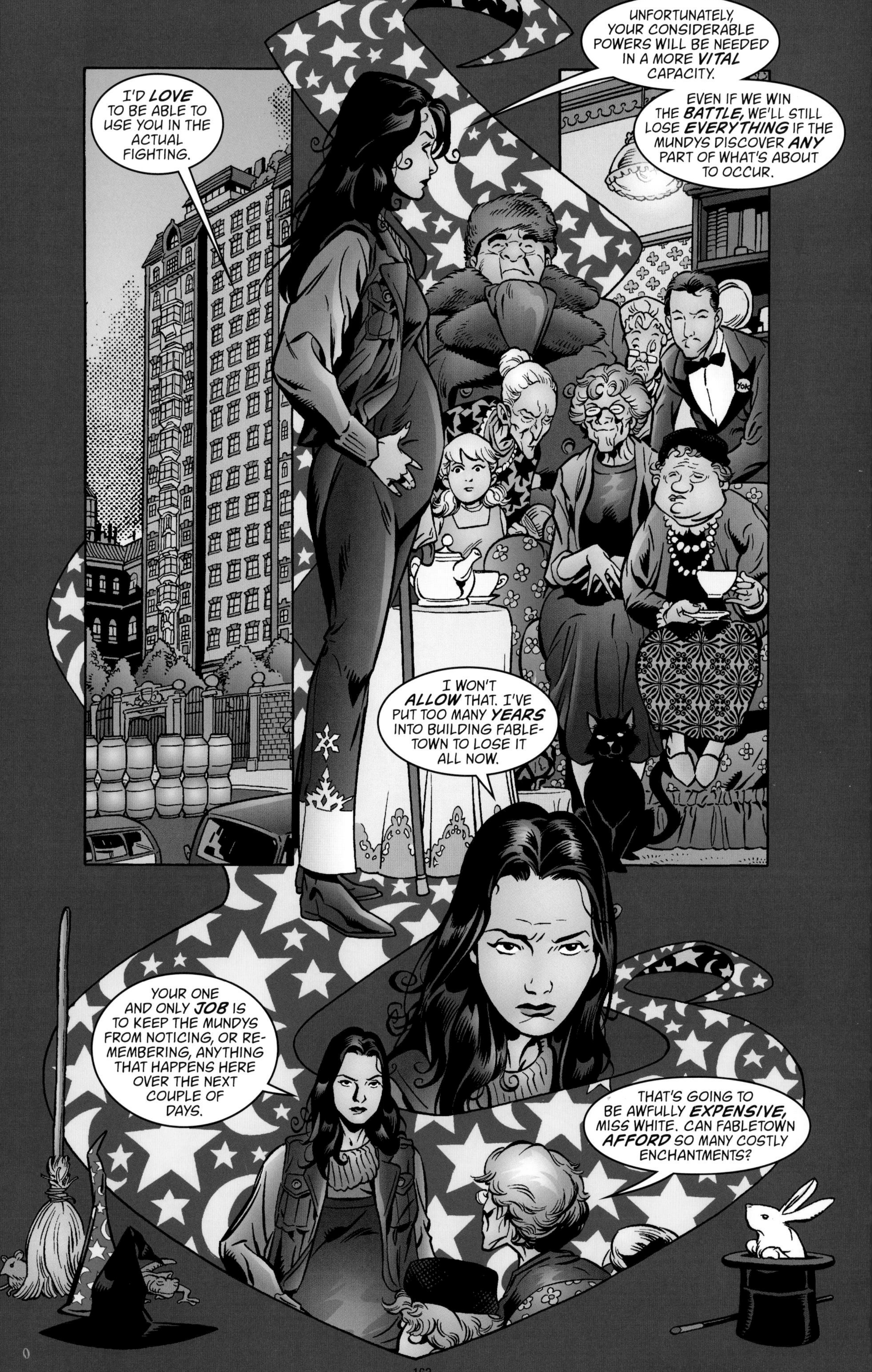
I'D LOVE TO BE ABLE TO USE YOU IN THE ACTUAL FIGHTING.
UNFORTUNATELY, YOUR CONSIDERABLE POWERS WILL BE NEEDED IN A MORE VITAL CAPACITY.
EVEN IF WE WIN THE BATTLE, WE'LL STILL LOSE EVERYTHING IF THE MUNDYS DISCOVER ANY PART OF WHAT'S ABOUT TO OCCUR.
I WON'T ALLOW THAT. I'VE PUT TOO MANY YEARS INTO BUILDING FABLE-TOWN TO LOSE IT ALL NOW.
YOUR ONE AND ONLY JOB IS TO KEEP THE MUNDYS FROM NOTICING, OR RE-MEMBERING, ANYTHING THAT HAPPENS HERE OVER THE NEXT COUPLE OF DAYS.
THAT'S GOING TO BE AWFULLY EXPENSIVE, MISS WHITE. CAN FABLETOWN AFFORD SO MANY COSTLY ENCHANTMENTS?

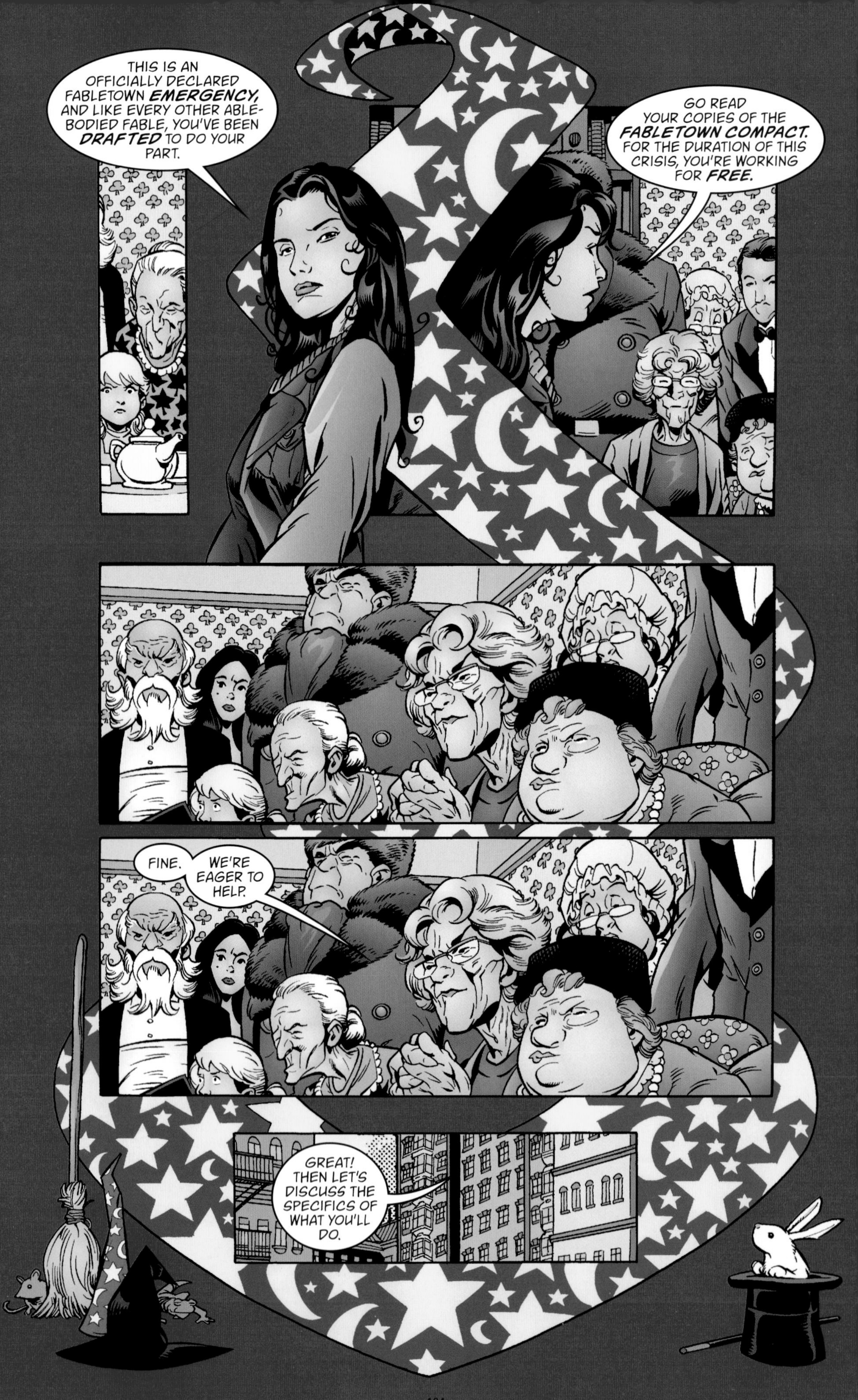
THIS IS AN OFFICIALLY DECLARED FABLETOWN EMERGENCY, AND LIKE EVERY OTHER ABLE-BODIED FABLE, YOU'VE BEEN DRAFTED TO DO YOUR PART.
GO READ YOUR COPIES OF THE FABLETOWN COMPACT. FOR THE DURATION OF THIS CRISIS, YOU'RE WORKING FOR FREE.
FINE.
WE'RE EAGER TO HELP.
GREAT! THEN LET'S DISCUSS THE SPECIFICS OF WHAT YOU'LL DO.

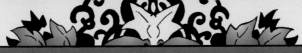

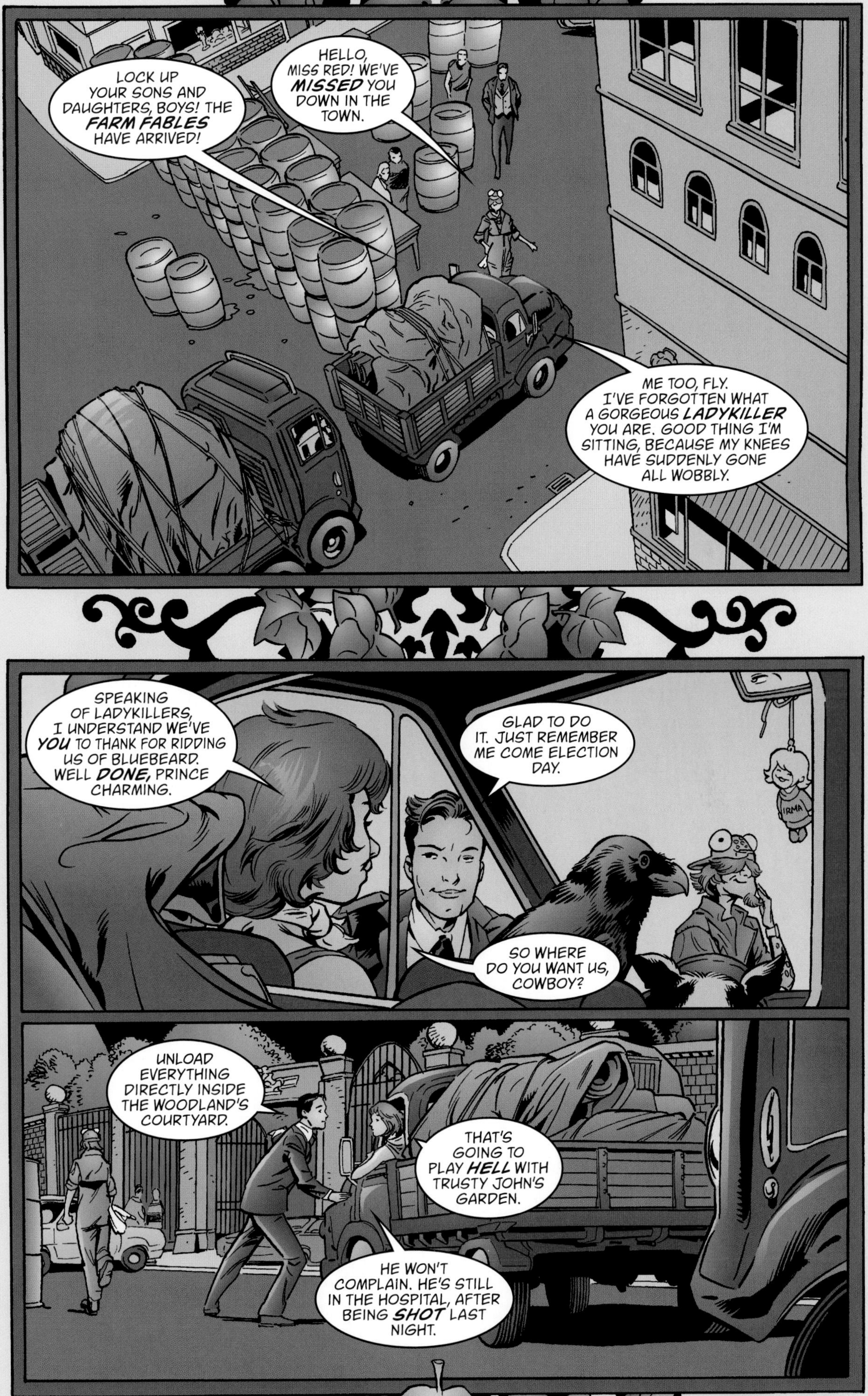
LOCK UP YOUR SONS AND DAUGHTERS, BOYS! THE FARM FABLES HAVE ARRIVED!
HELLO, MISS RED! WE'VE MISSED YOU DOWN IN THE TOWN.
ME TOO, FLY. I'VE FORGOTTEN WHAT A GORGEOUS LADYKILLER YOU ARE. GOOD THING I'M SITTING, BECAUSE MY KNEES HAVE SUDDENLY GONE ALL WOBBLY.
SPEAKING OF LADYKILLERS, I UNDERSTAND WE'VE YOU TO THANK FOR RIDDING US OF BLUEBEARD. WELL DONE, PRINCE CHARMING.
GLAD TO DO IT. JUST REMEMBER ME COME ELECTION DAY.
IRMA
SO WHERE DO YOU WANT US, COWBOY?
UNLOAD EVERYTHING DIRECTLY INSIDE THE WOODLAND'S COURTYARD.
THAT'S GOING TO PLAY HELL WITH TRUSTY JOHN'S GARDEN.
HE WON'T COMPLAIN. HE'S STILL IN THE HOSPITAL, AFTER BEING SHOT LAST NIGHT.

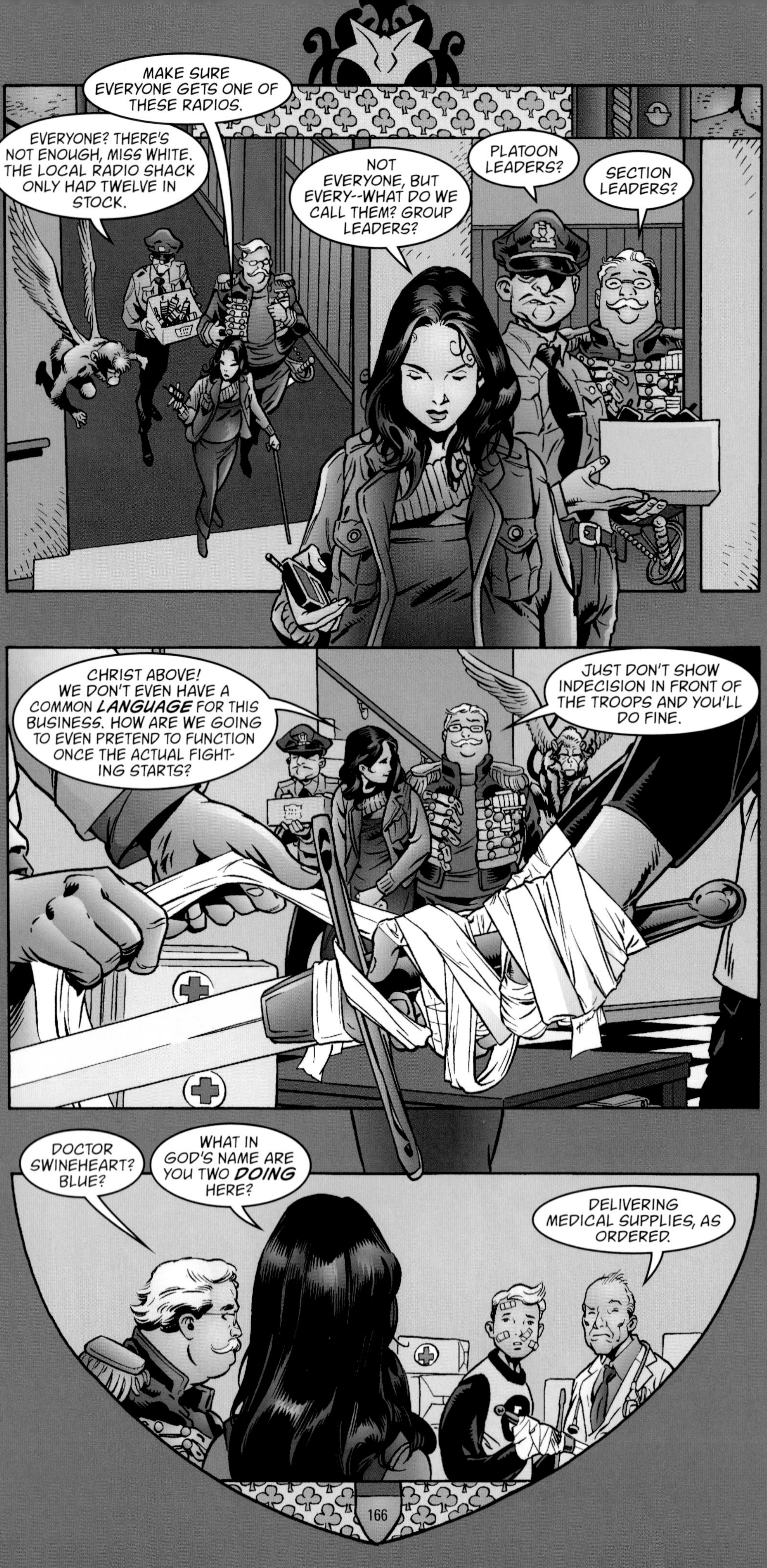
MAKE SURE EVERYONE GETS ONE OF THESE RADIOS.
EVERYONE? THERE'S NOT ENOUGH, MISS WHITE. THE LOCAL RADIO SHACK ONLY HAD TWELVE IN STOCK.
NOT EVERYONE, BUT EVERY--WHAT DO WE CALL THEM? GROUP LEADERS?
PLATOON LEADERS?
SECTION LEADERS?
CHRIST ABOVE! WE DON'T EVEN HAVE A COMMON LANGUAGE FOR THIS BUSINESS. HOW ARE WE GOING TO EVEN PRETEND TO FUNCTION ONCE THE ACTUAL FIGHTING STARTS?
JUST DON'T SHOW INDECISION IN FRONT OF THE TROOPS AND YOU'LL DO FINE.
DOCTOR SWINEHEART? BLUE?
WHAT IN GOD'S NAME ARE YOU TWO DOING HERE?
DELIVERING MEDICAL SUPPLIES, AS ORDERED.

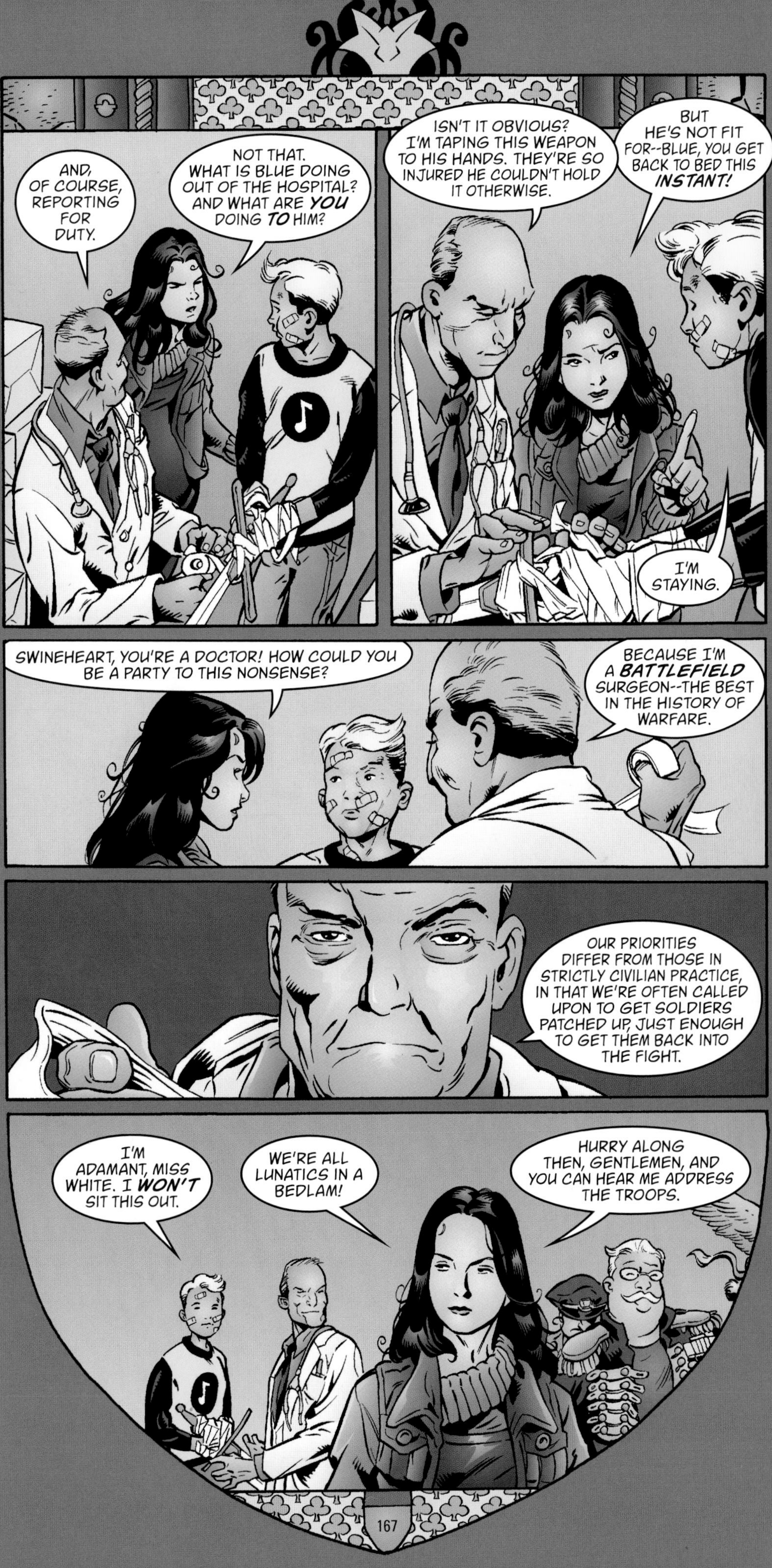
AND, OF COURSE, REPORTING FOR DUTY.
NOT THAT. WHAT IS BLUE DOING OUT OF THE HOSPITAL? AND WHAT ARE YOU DOING TO HIM?
ISN'T IT OBVIOUS? I'M TAPING THIS WEAPON TO HIS HANDS. THEY'RE SO INJURED HE COULDN'T HOLD IT OTHERWISE.
BUT HE'S NOT FIT FOR--BLUE, YOU GET BACK TO BED THIS INSTANT!
I'M STAYING.
SWINEHEART, YOU'RE A DOCTOR! HOW COULD YOU BE A PARTY TO THIS NONSENSE?
BECAUSE I'M A BATTLEFIELD SURGEON--THE BEST IN THE HISTORY OF WARFARE.
OUR PRIORITIES DIFFER FROM THOSE IN STRICTLY CIVILIAN PRACTICE, IN THAT WE'RE OFTEN CALLED UPON TO GET SOLDIERS PATCHED UP, JUST ENOUGH TO GET THEM BACK INTO THE FIGHT.
I'M ADAMANT, MISS WHITE. I WON'T SIT THIS OUT.
WE'RE ALL LUNATICS IN A BEDLAM!
HURRY ALONG THEN, GENTLEMEN, AND YOU CAN HEAR ME ADDRESS THE TROOPS.

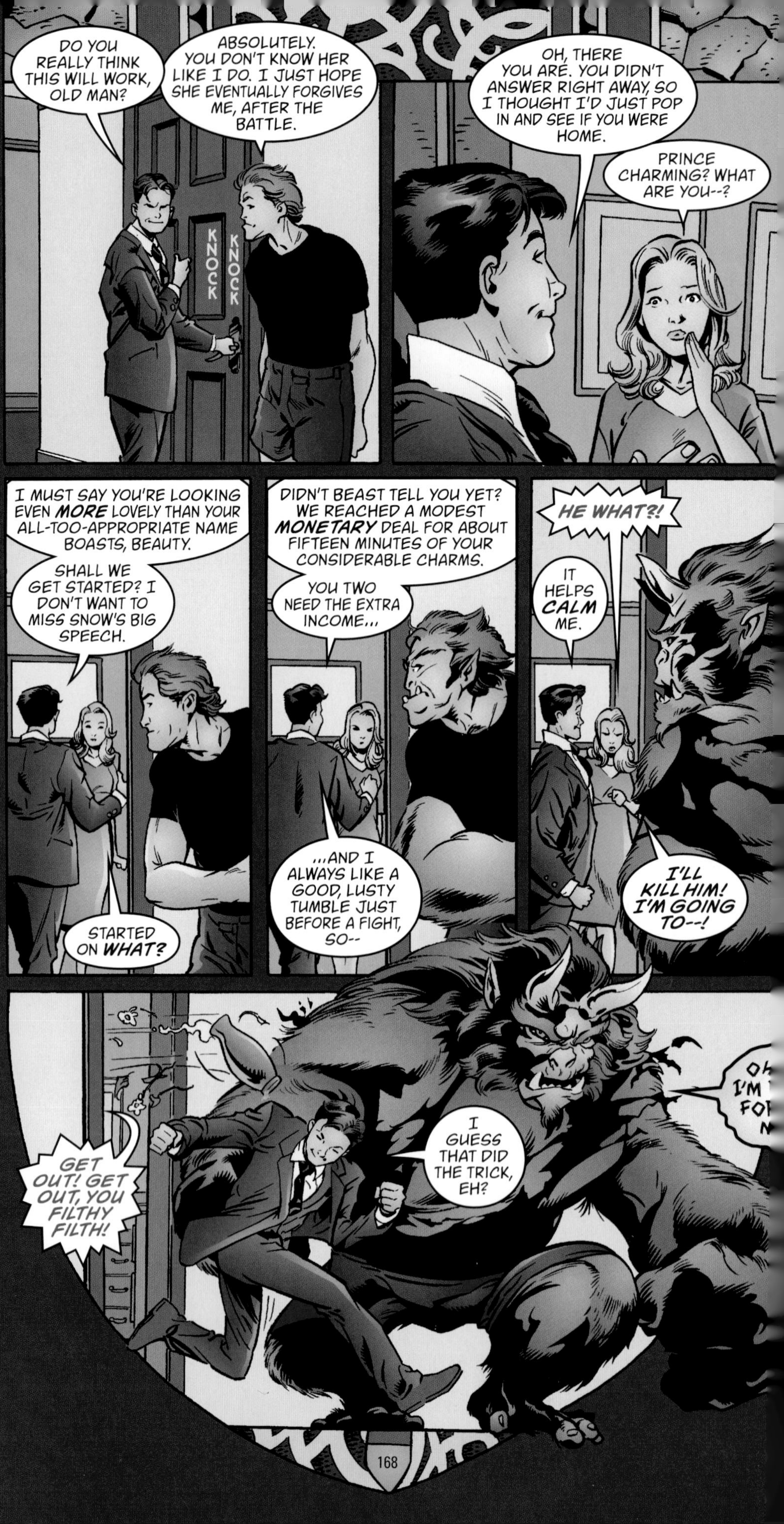
DO YOU REALLY THINK THIS WILL WORK, OLD MAN?
ABSOLUTELY. YOU DON'T KNOW HER LIKE I DO. I JUST HOPE SHE EVENTUALLY FORGIVES ME, AFTER THE BATTLE.
KNOCK
KNOCK
OH, THERE YOU ARE. YOU DIDN'T ANSWER RIGHT AWAY, SO I THOUGHT I'D JUST POP IN AND SEE IF YOU WERE HOME.
PRINCE CHARMING? WHAT ARE YOU--?
I MUST SAY YOU'RE LOOKING EVEN MORE LOVELY THAN YOUR ALL-TOO-APPROPRIATE NAME BOASTS, BEAUTY.
SHALL WE GET STARTED? I DON'T WANT TO MISS SNOW'S BIG SPEECH.
STARTED ON WHAT?
DIDN'T BEAST TELL YOU YET? WE REACHED A MODEST MONETARY DEAL FOR ABOUT FIFTEEN MINUTES OF YOUR CONSIDERABLE CHARMS.
YOU TWO NEED THE EXTRA INCOME...
...AND I ALWAYS LIKE A GOOD, LUSTY TUMBLE JUST BEFORE A FIGHT, SO--
HE WHAT?!
IT HELPS CALM ME.
I'LL KILL HIM! I'M GOING TO--!
GET OUT! GET OUT, YOU FILTHY FILTH!
I GUESS THAT DID THE TRICK, EH?

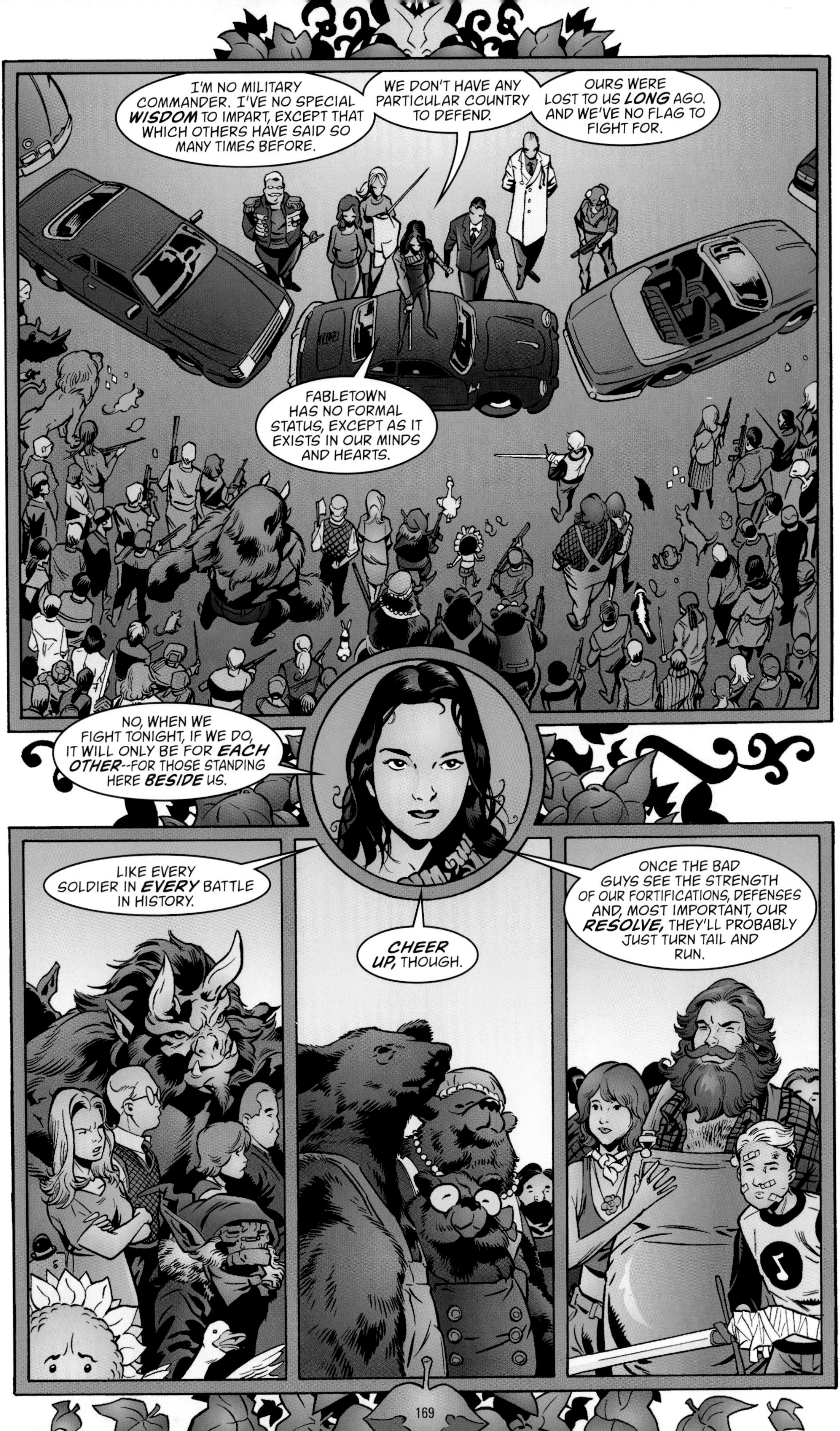
I'M NO MILITARY COMMANDER. I'VE NO SPECIAL WISDOM TO IMPART, EXCEPT THAT WHICH OTHERS HAVE SAID SO MANY TIMES BEFORE.
WE DON'T HAVE ANY PARTICULAR COUNTRY TO DEFEND.
OURS WERE LOST TO US LONG AGO. AND WE'VE NO FLAG TO FIGHT FOR.
FABLETOWN HAS NO FORMAL STATUS, EXCEPT AS IT EXISTS IN OUR MINDS AND HEARTS.
NO, WHEN WE FIGHT TONIGHT, IF WE DO, IT WILL ONLY BE FOR EACH OTHER--FOR THOSE STANDING HERE BESIDE US.
LIKE EVERY SOLDIER IN EVERY BATTLE IN HISTORY.
CHEER UP, THOUGH.
ONCE THE BAD GUYS SEE THE STRENGTH OF OUR FORTIFICATIONS, DEFENSES AND, MOST IMPORTANT, OUR RESOLVE, THEY'LL PROBABLY JUST TURN TAIL AND RUN.

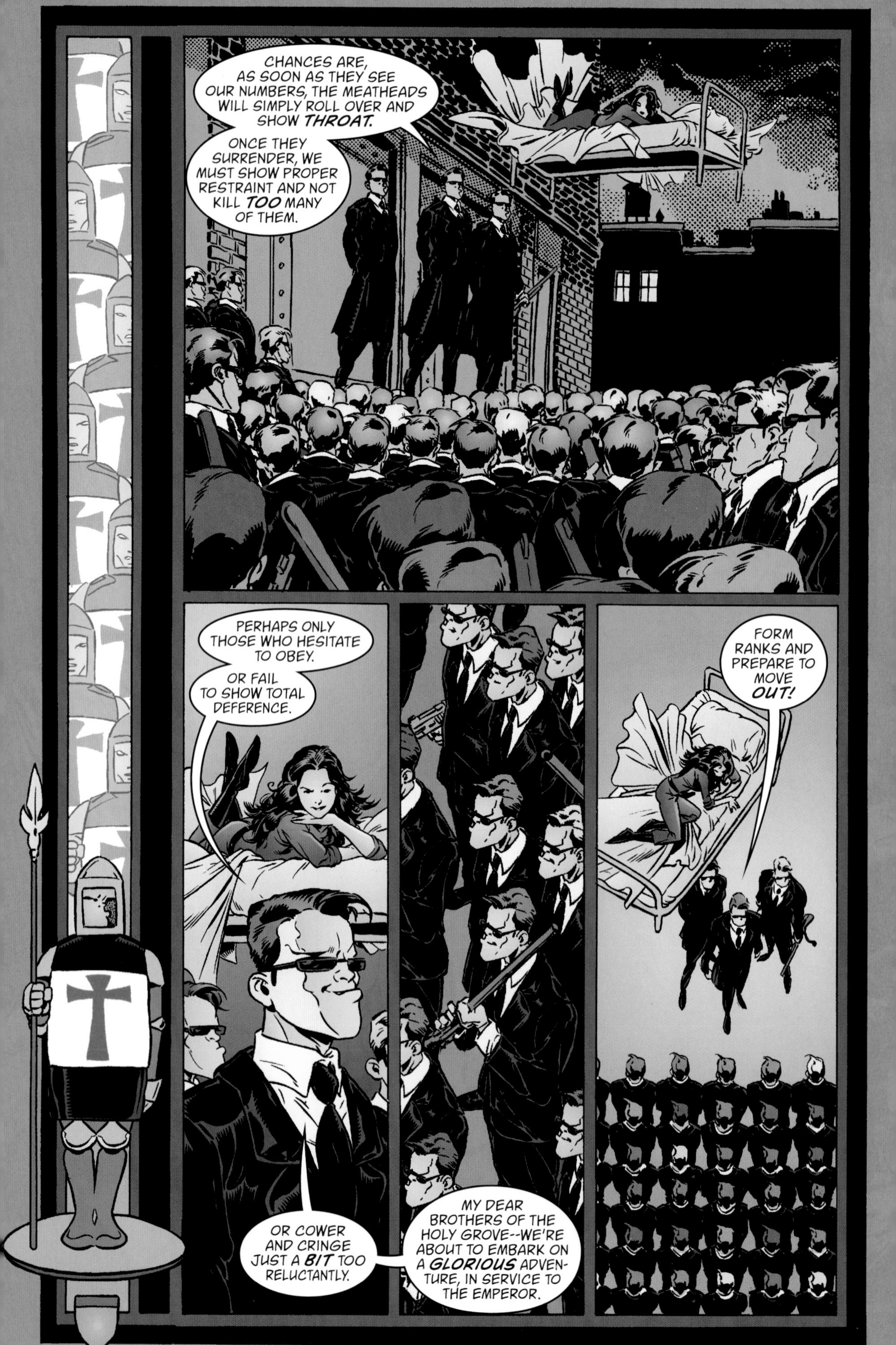
CHANCES ARE, AS SOON AS THEY SEE OUR NUMBERS, THE MEATHEADS WILL SIMPLY ROLL OVER AND SHOW THROAT.
ONCE THEY SURRENDER, WE MUST SHOW PROPER RESTRAINT AND NOT KILL TOO MANY OF THEM.
PERHAPS ONLY THOSE WHO HESITATE TO OBEY.
OR FAIL TO SHOW TOTAL DEFERENCE.
OR COWER AND CRINGE JUST A BIT TOO RELUCTANTLY.
MY DEAR BROTHERS OF THE HOLY GROVE--WE'RE ABOUT TO EMBARK ON A GLORIOUS ADVENTURE, IN SERVICE TO THE EMPEROR.
FORM RANKS AND PREPARE TO MOVE OUT!

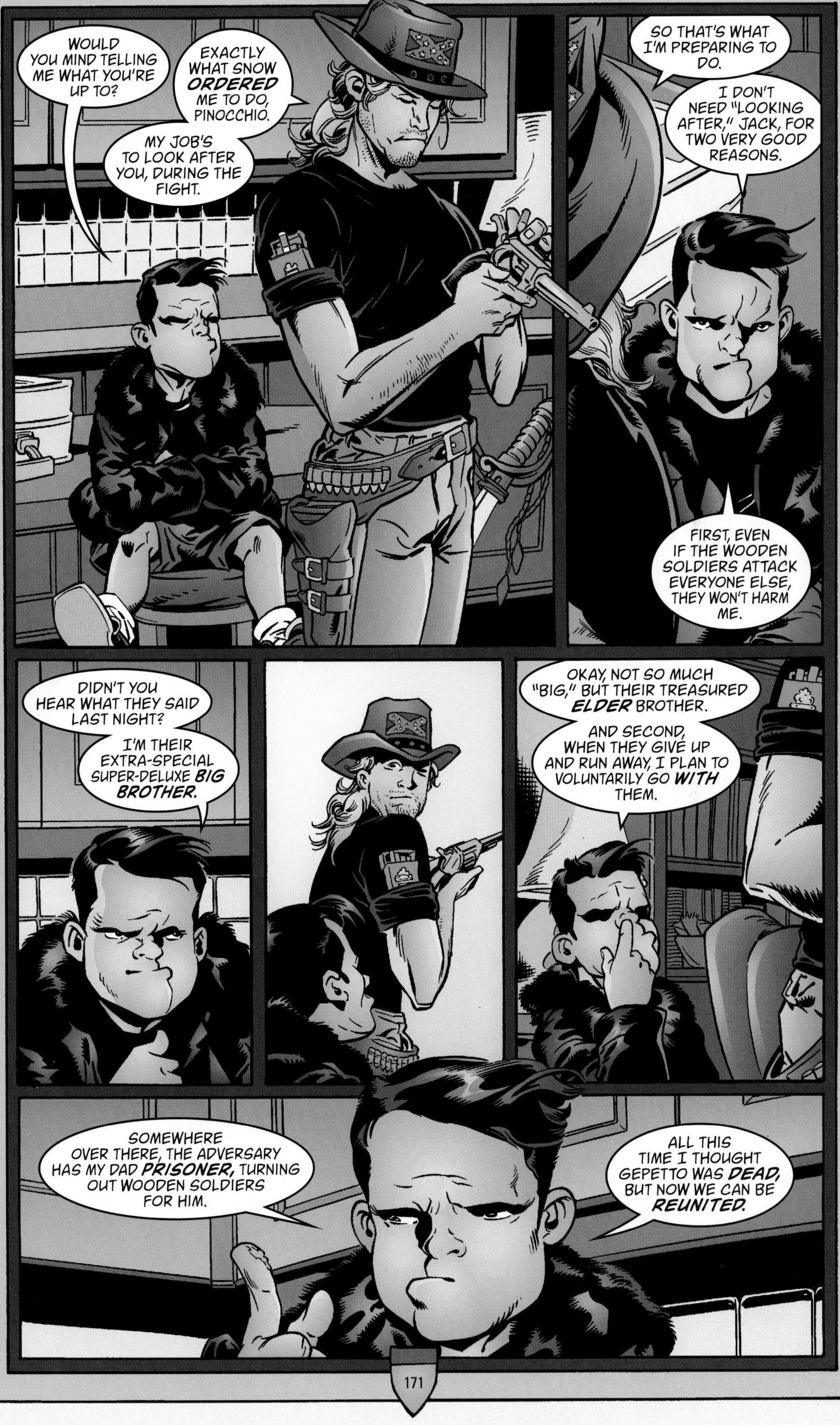

WOULD YOU MIND TELLING ME WHAT YOU'RE UP TO?
EXACTLY WHAT SNOW ORDERED ME TO DO, PINOCCHIO.
MY JOB'S TO LOOK AFTER YOU, DURING THE FIGHT.
SO THAT'S WHAT I'M PREPARING TO DO.
I DON'T NEED "LOOKING AFTER," JACK, FOR TWO VERY GOOD REASONS.
FIRST, EVEN IF THE WOODEN SOLDIERS ATTACK EVERYONE ELSE, THEY WON'T HARM ME.
DIDN'T YOU HEAR WHAT THEY SAID LAST NIGHT?
I'M THEIR EXTRA-SPECIAL SUPER-DELUXE BIG BROTHER.
OKAY, NOT SO MUCH "BIG," BUT THEIR TREASURED ELDER BROTHER.
AND SECOND, WHEN THEY GIVE UP AND RUN AWAY, I PLAN TO VOLUNTARILY GO WITH THEM.
SOMEWHERE OVER THERE, THE ADVERSARY HAS MY DAD PRISONER, TURNING OUT WOODEN SOLDIERS FOR HIM.
ALL THIS TIME I THOUGHT GEPETTO WAS DEAD, BUT NOW WE CAN BE REUNITED.

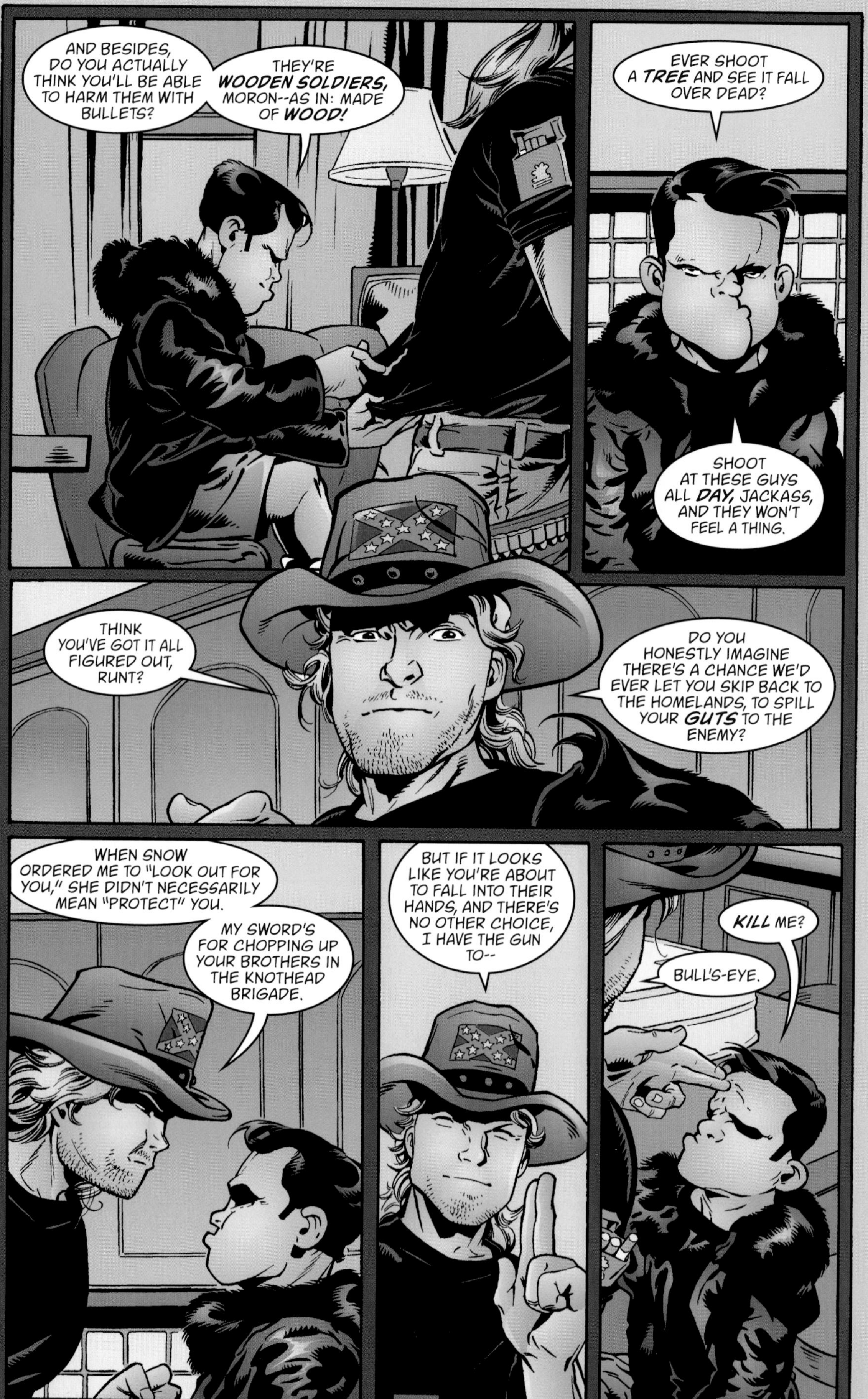
AND BESIDES, DO YOU ACTUALLY THINK YOU'LL BE ABLE TO HARM THEM WITH BULLETS?
THEY'RE **WOODEN SOLDIERS,** MORON--AS IN: MADE OF **WOOD!**
EVER SHOOT A **TREE** AND SEE IT FALL OVER DEAD?
SHOOT AT THESE GUYS ALL **DAY,** JACKASS, AND THEY WON'T FEEL A THING.
THINK YOU'VE GOT IT ALL FIGURED OUT, RUNT?
DO YOU HONESTLY IMAGINE THERE'S A CHANCE WE'D EVER LET YOU SKIP BACK TO THE HOMELANDS, TO SPILL YOUR **GUTS** TO THE ENEMY?
WHEN SNOW ORDERED ME TO "LOOK OUT FOR YOU," SHE DIDN'T NECESSARILY MEAN "PROTECT" YOU.
MY SWORD'S FOR CHOPPING UP YOUR BROTHERS IN THE KNOTHEAD BRIGADE.
BUT IF IT LOOKS LIKE YOU'RE ABOUT TO FALL INTO THEIR HANDS, AND THERE'S NO OTHER CHOICE, I HAVE THE GUN TO--
KILL ME?
BULL'S-EYE.

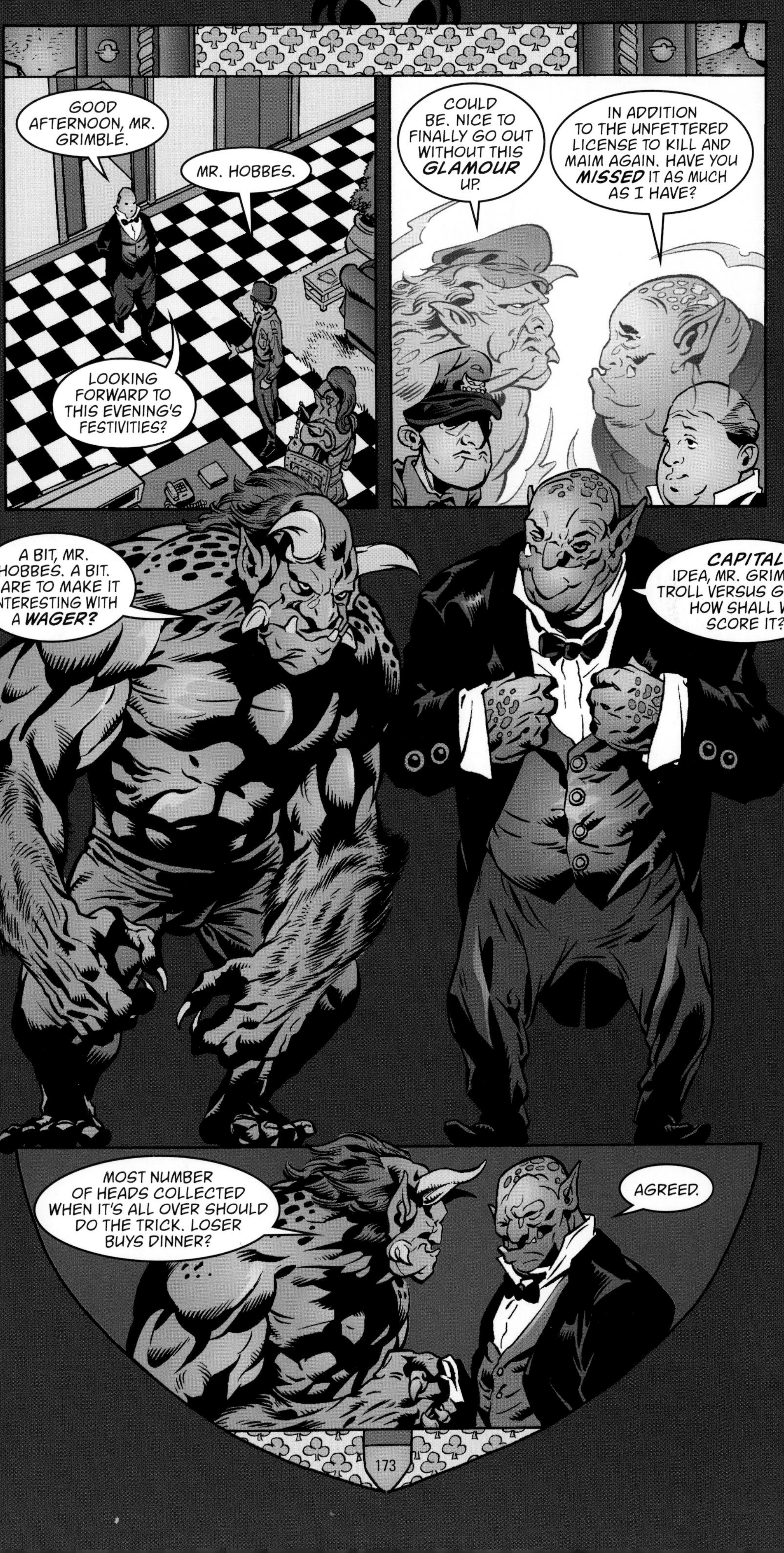
GOOD AFTERNOON, MR. GRIMBLE.
MR. HOBBES.
LOOKING FORWARD TO THIS EVENING'S FESTIVITIES?
COULD BE. NICE TO FINALLY GO OUT WITHOUT THIS GLAMOUR UP.
IN ADDITION TO THE UNFETTERED LICENSE TO KILL AND MAIM AGAIN. HAVE YOU MISSED IT AS MUCH AS I HAVE?
A BIT, MR. HOBBES. A BIT. CARE TO MAKE IT INTERESTING WITH A WAGER?
CAPITAL IDEA, MR. GRIMBLE. TROLL VERSUS GOBLIN. HOW SHALL WE SCORE IT?
MOST NUMBER OF HEADS COLLECTED WHEN IT'S ALL OVER SHOULD DO THE TRICK. LOSER BUYS DINNER?
AGREED.

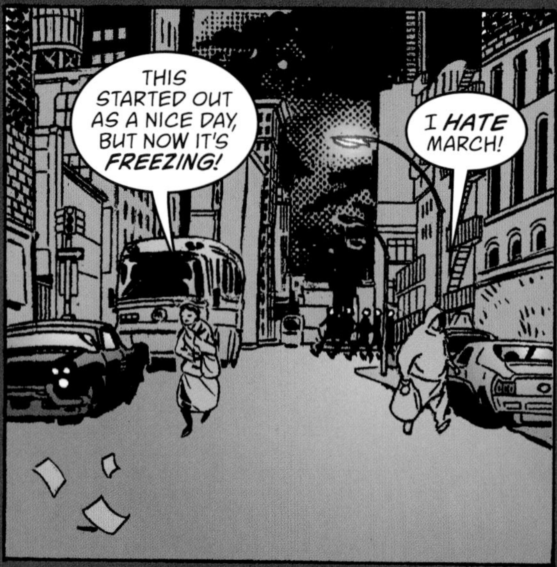
THIS STARTED OUT AS A NICE DAY, BUT NOW IT'S FREEZING!
I HATE MARCH!

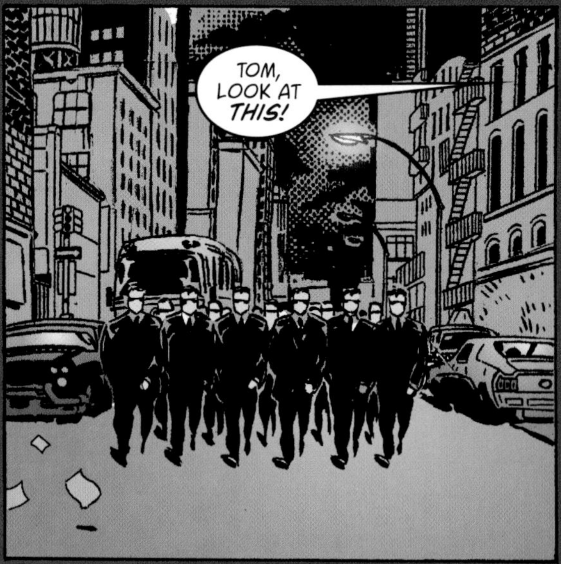
TOM, LOOK AT THIS!

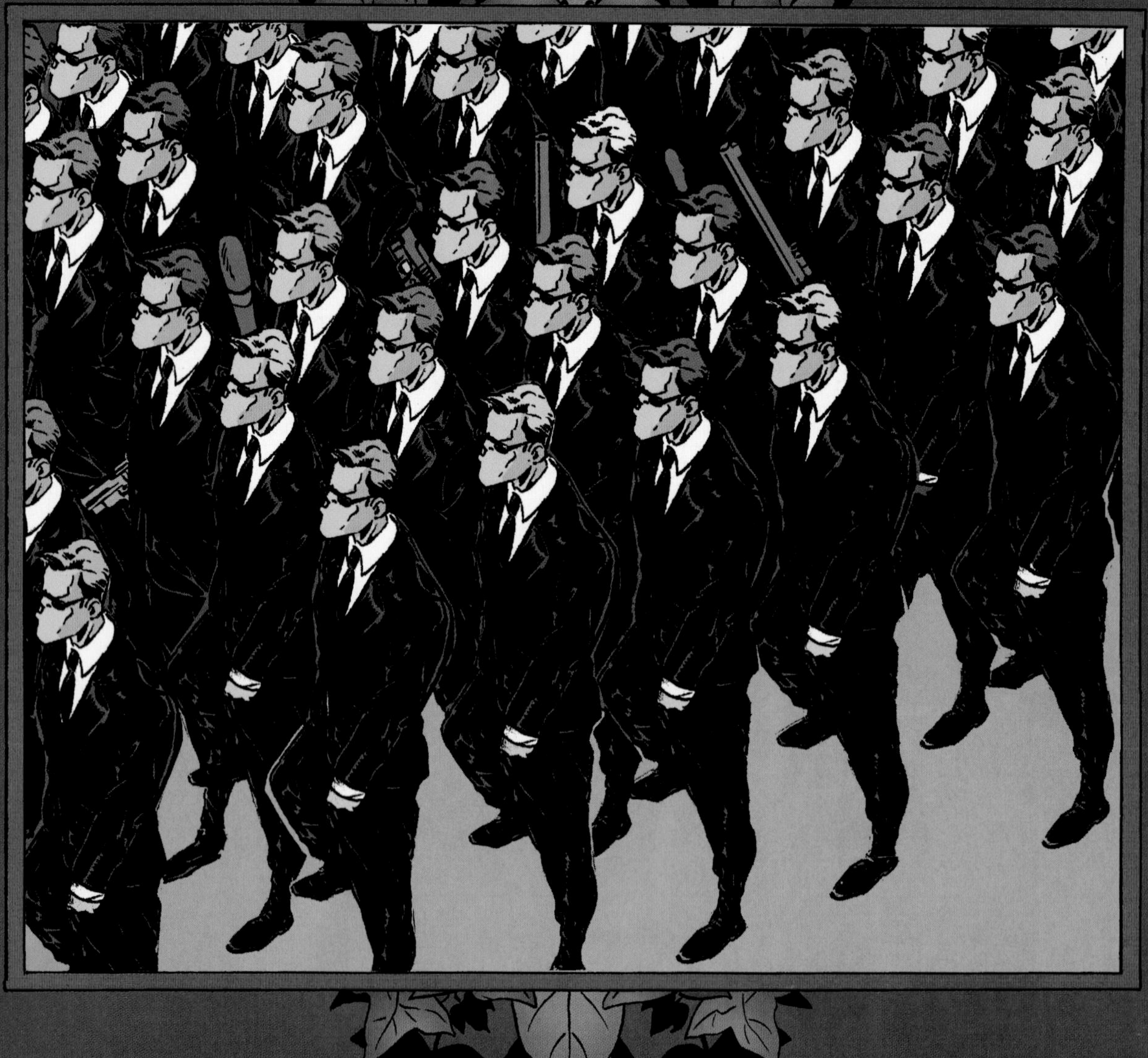

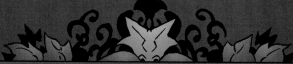

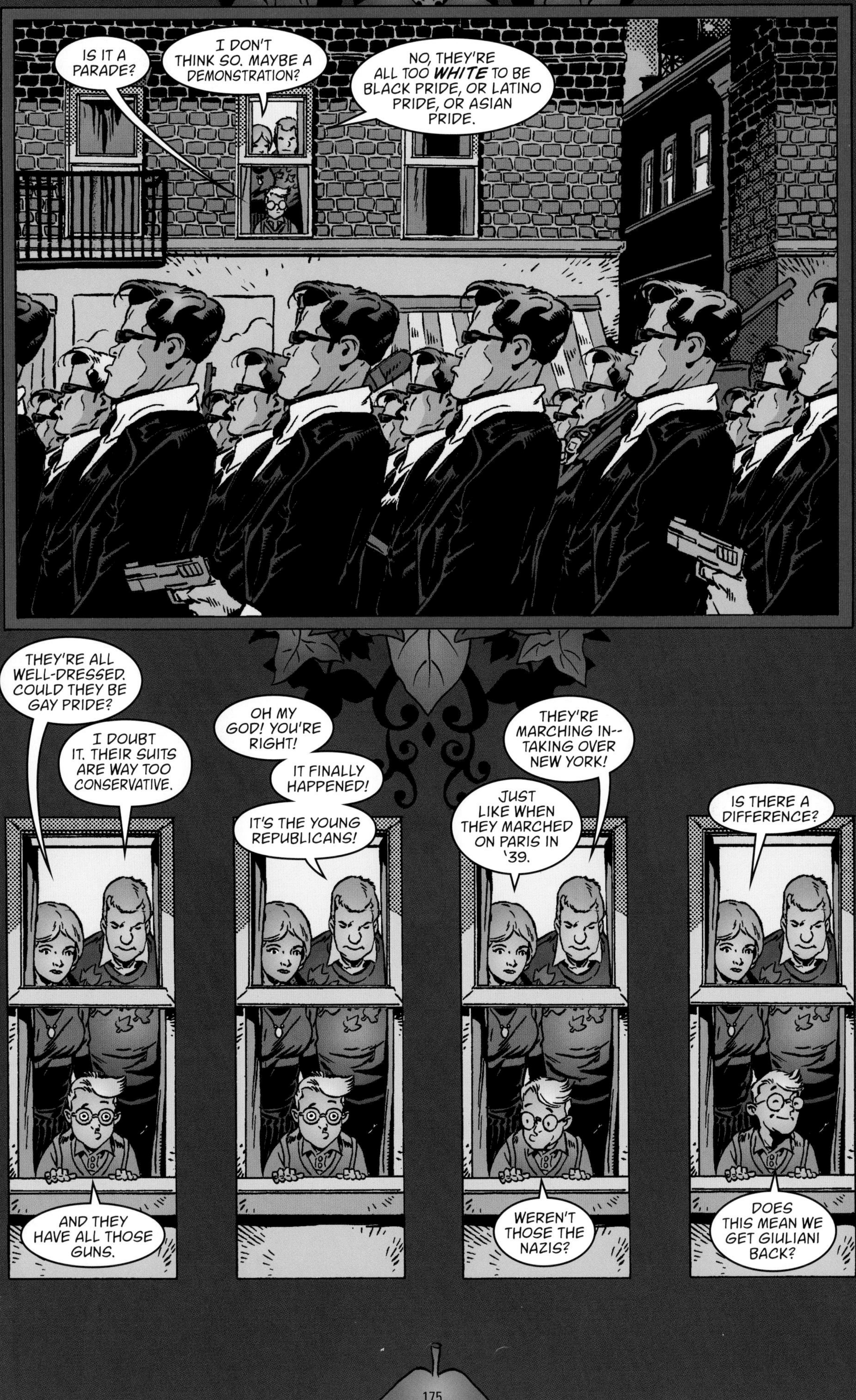
IS IT A PARADE?
I DON'T THINK SO. MAYBE A DEMONSTRATION?
NO, THEY'RE ALL TOO WHITE TO BE BLACK PRIDE, OR LATINO PRIDE, OR ASIAN PRIDE.
THEY'RE ALL WELL-DRESSED. COULD THEY BE GAY PRIDE?
I DOUBT IT. THEIR SUITS ARE WAY TOO CONSERVATIVE.
AND THEY HAVE ALL THOSE GUNS.
OH MY GOD! YOU'RE RIGHT!
IT FINALLY HAPPENED!
IT'S THE YOUNG REPUBLICANS!
THEY'RE MARCHING IN--TAKING OVER NEW YORK!
JUST LIKE WHEN THEY MARCHED ON PARIS IN '39.
WEREN'T THOSE THE NAZIS?
IS THERE A DIFFERENCE?
DOES THIS MEAN WE GET GIULIANI BACK?

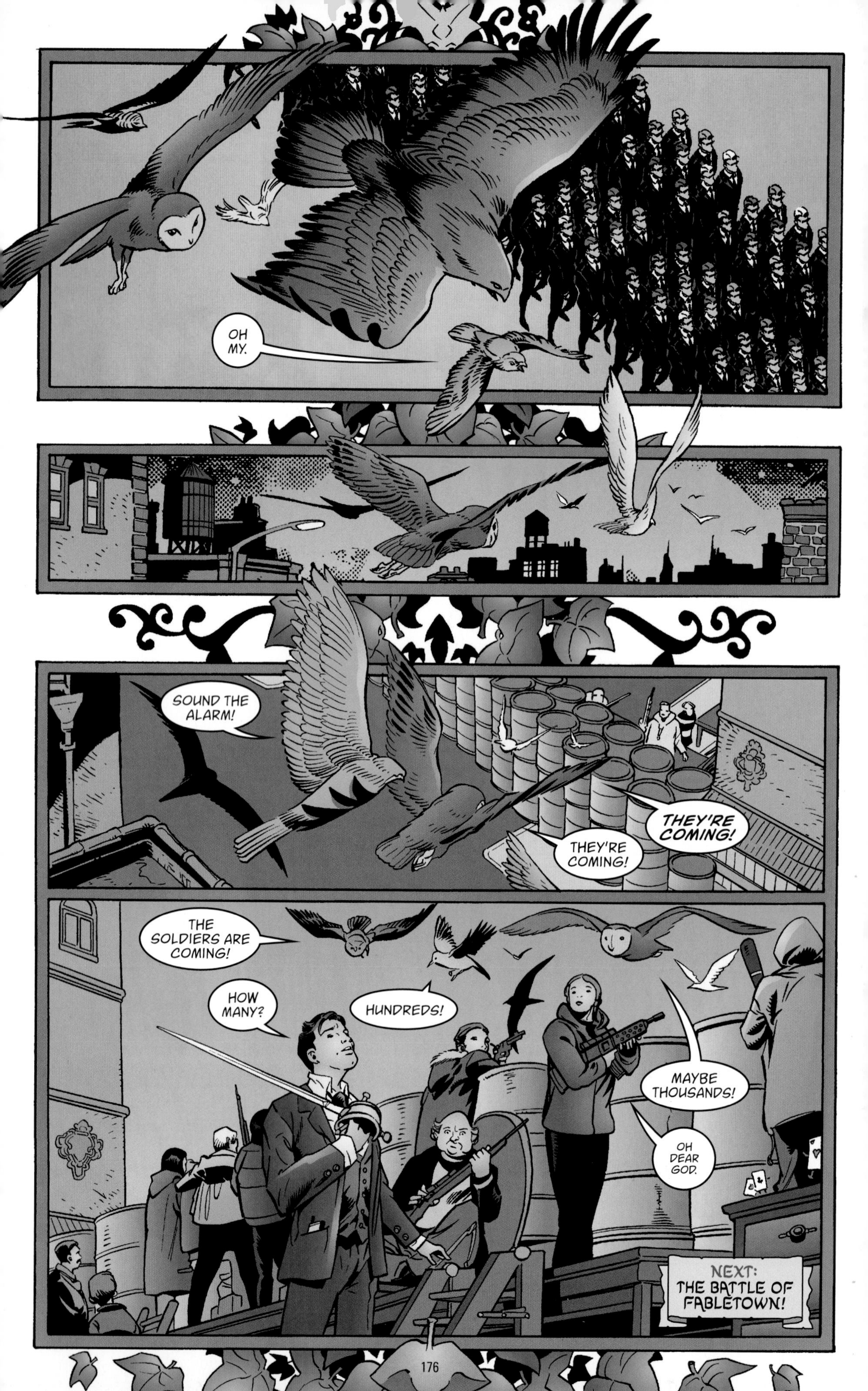
OH MY.
SOUND THE ALARM!
THEY'RE COMING!
THEY'RE COMING!
THE SOLDIERS ARE COMING!
HOW MANY?
HUNDREDS!
MAYBE THOUSANDS!
OH DEAR GOD.
NEXT: THE BATTLE OF FABLETOWN!

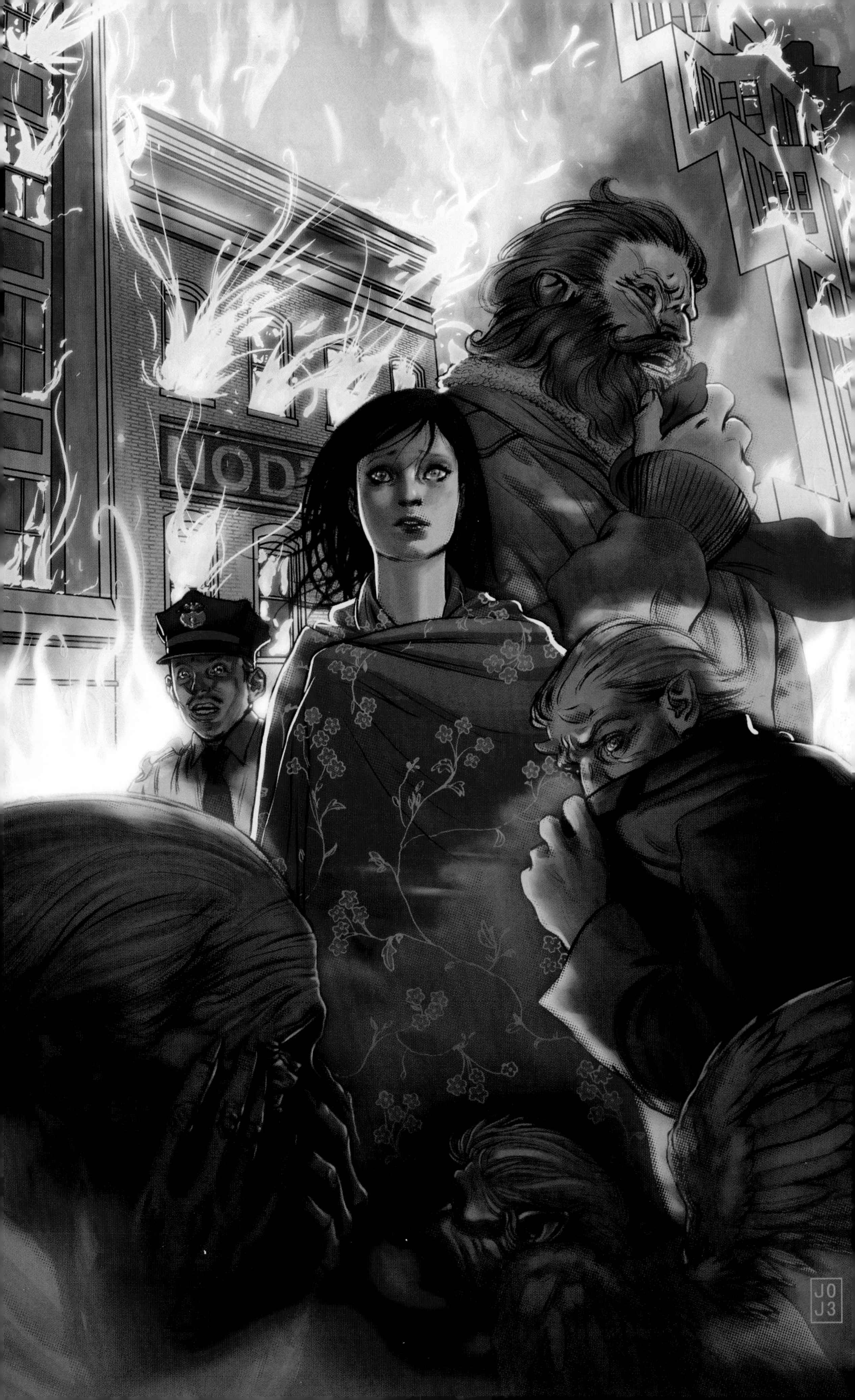
NOD

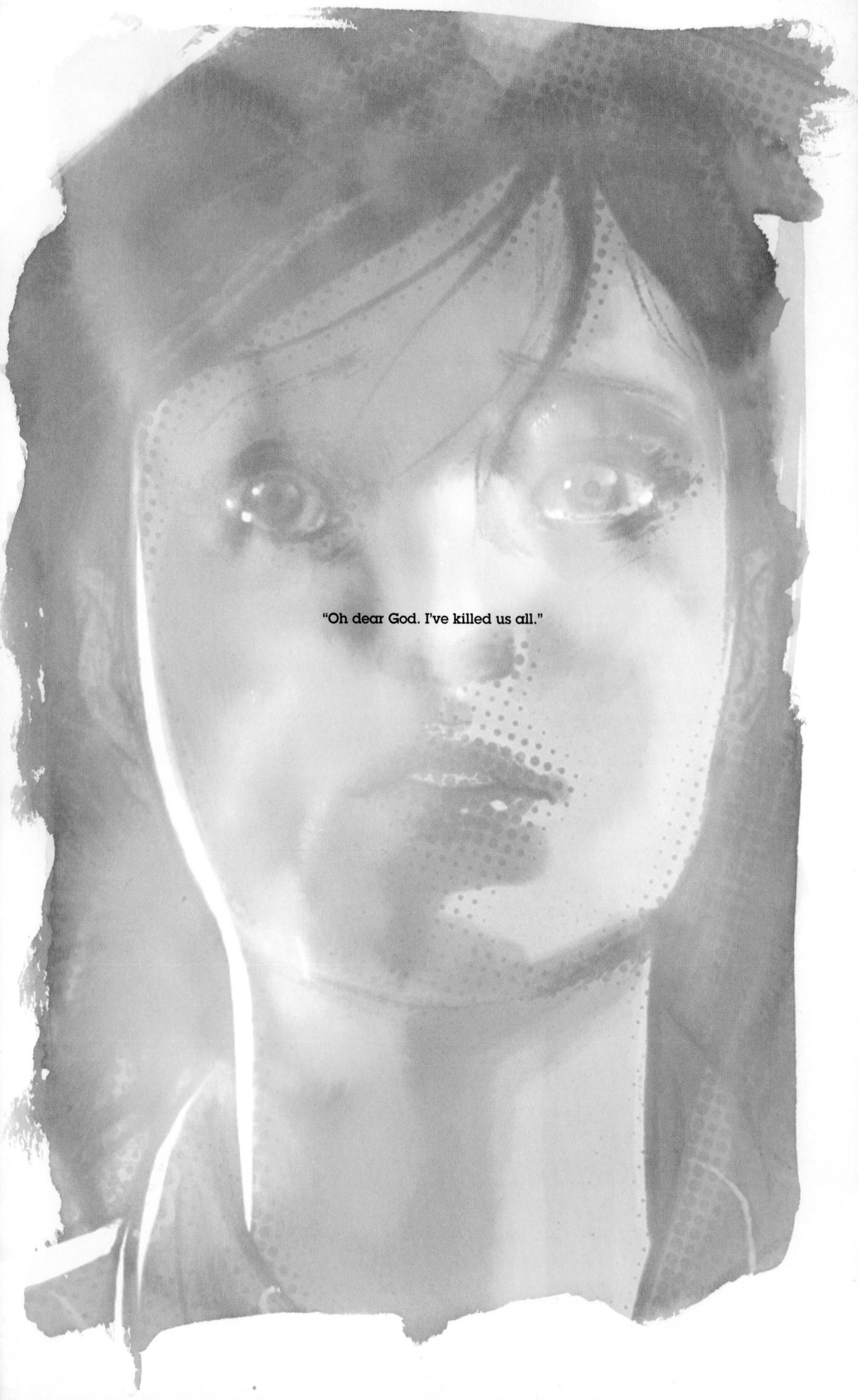
"Oh dear God. I've killed us all."

THE BATTLE OF FABLETOWN

CHAPTER SEVEN ○ MARCH OF THE WOODEN SOLDIERS

BILL WILLINGHAM writer/creator
MARK BUCKINGHAM penciller
STEVE LEIALOHA inker
DANIEL VOZZO color/seps
TODD KLEIN lettering
JAMES JEAN cover art
MARIAH HUEHNER assistant editor
SHELLY BOND editor

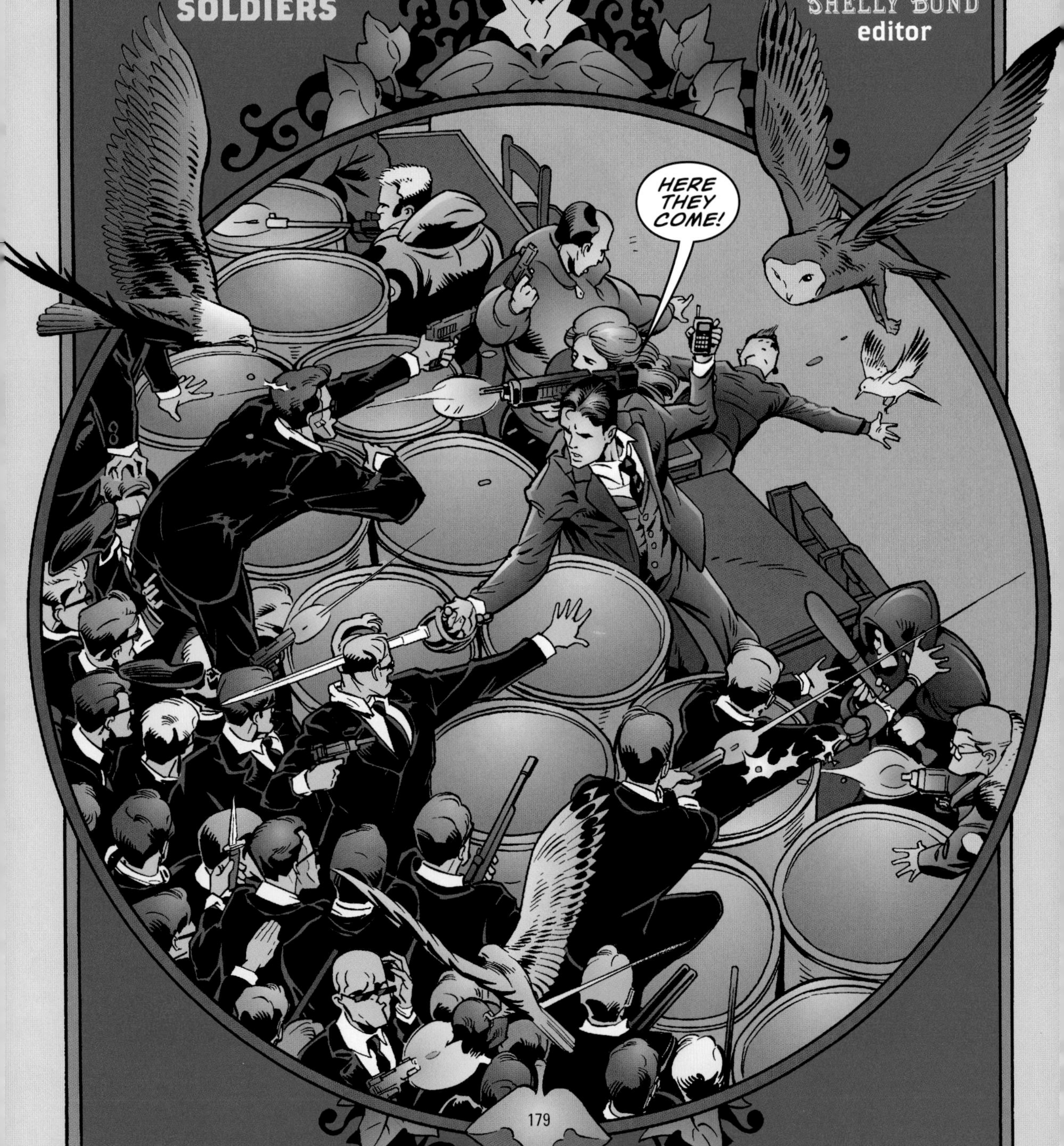

HERE THEY COME!

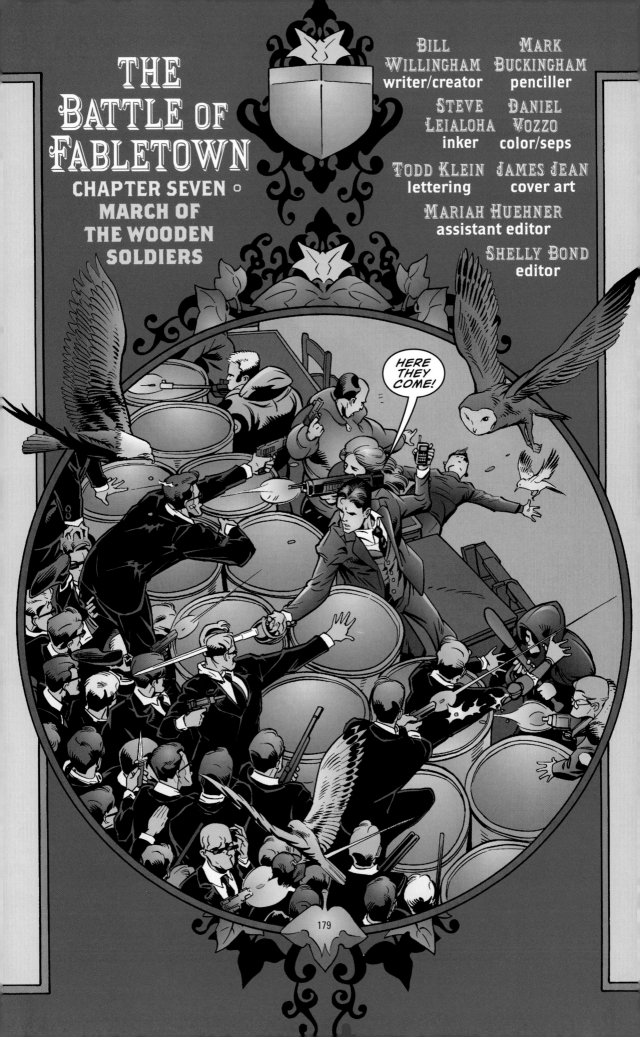

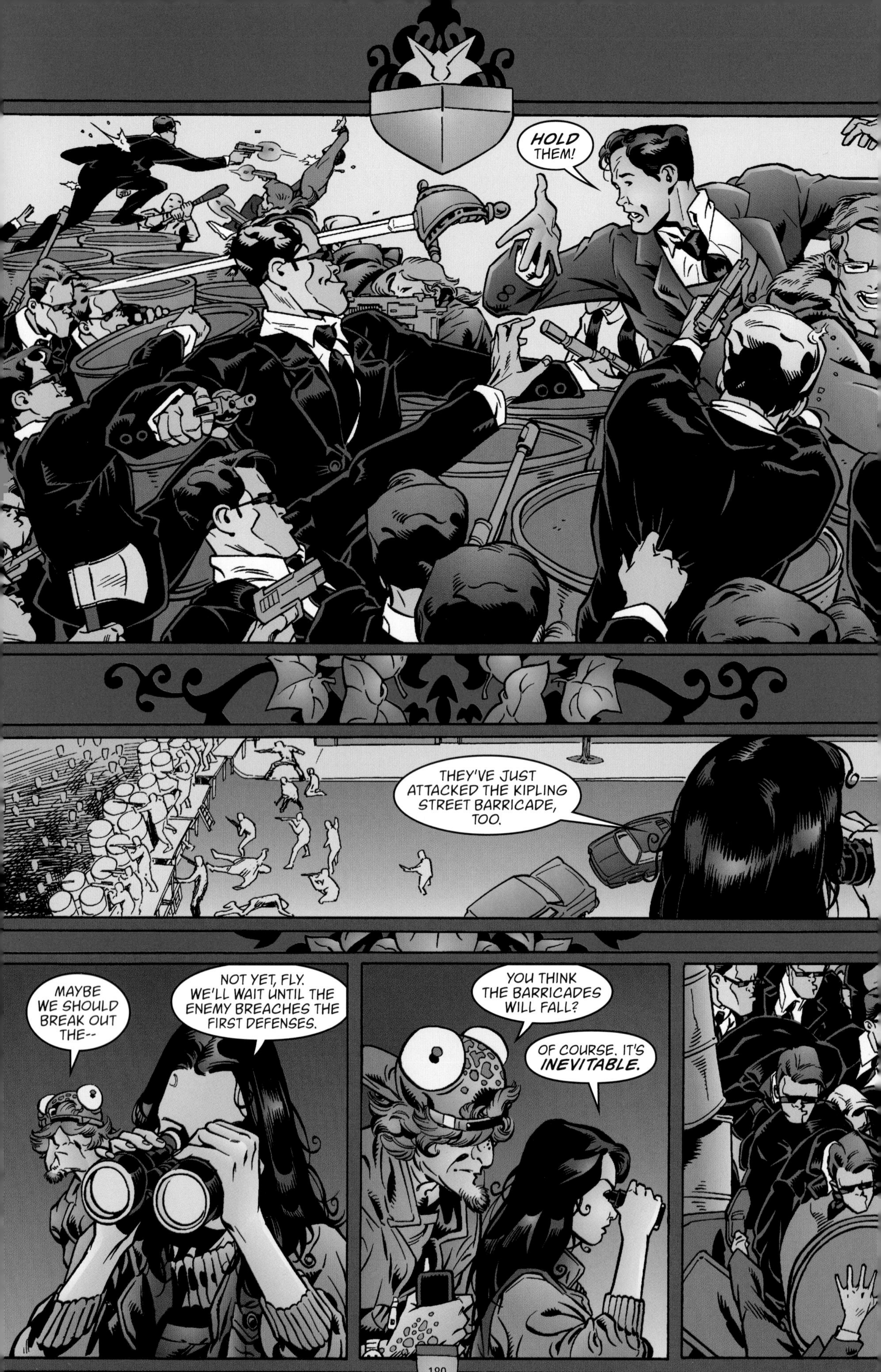
HOLD THEM!
THEY'VE JUST ATTACKED THE KIPLING STREET BARRICADE, TOO.
MAYBE WE SHOULD BREAK OUT THE--
NOT YET, FLY. WE'LL WAIT UNTIL THE ENEMY BREACHES THE FIRST DEFENSES.
YOU THINK THE BARRICADES WILL FALL?
OF COURSE. IT'S *INEVITABLE.*

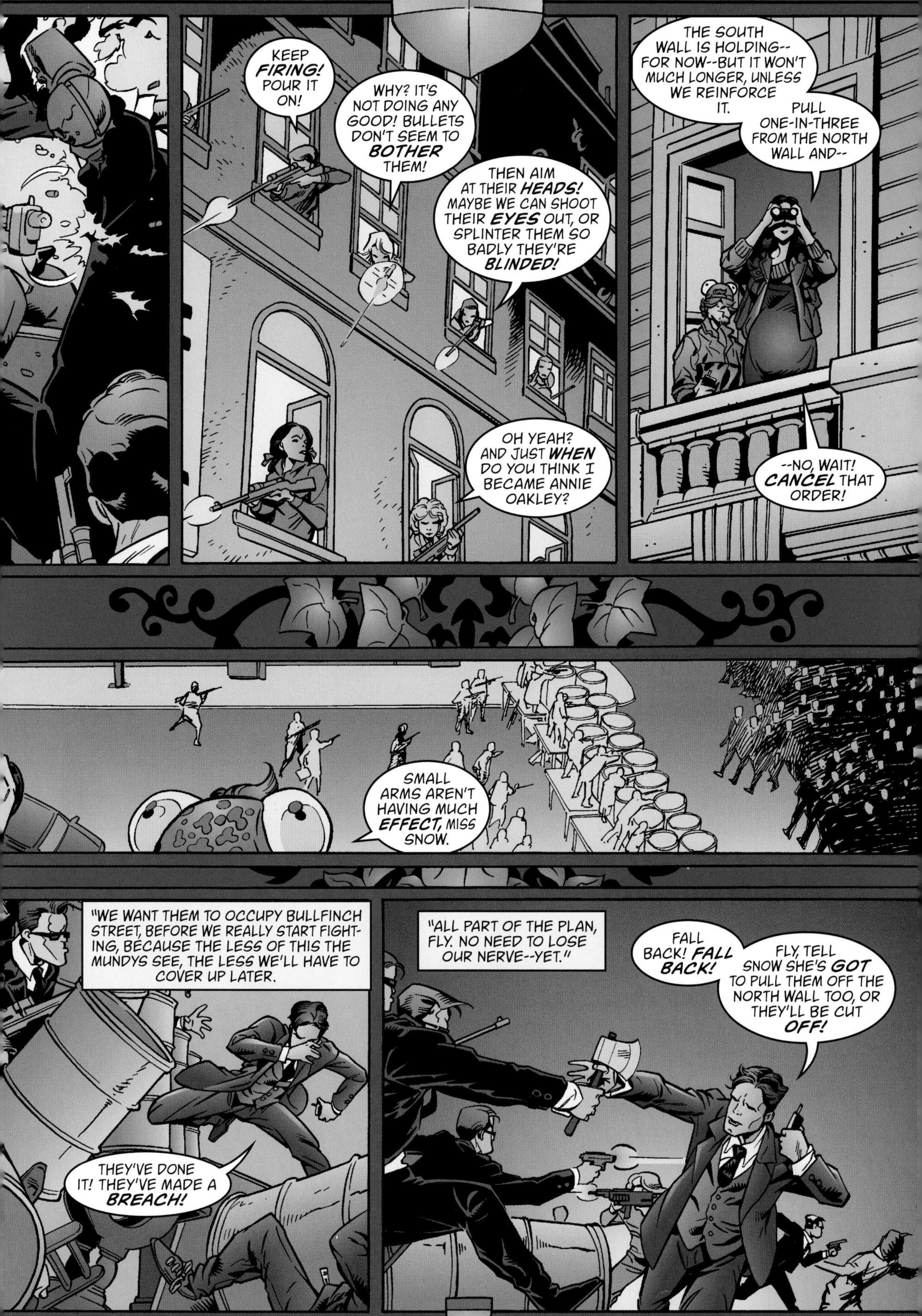
KEEP FIRING! POUR IT ON!
WHY? IT'S NOT DOING ANY GOOD! BULLETS DON'T SEEM TO BOTHER THEM!
THEN AIM AT THEIR HEADS! MAYBE WE CAN SHOOT THEIR EYES OUT, OR SPLINTER THEM SO BADLY THEY'RE BLINDED!
OH YEAH? AND JUST WHEN DO YOU THINK I BECAME ANNIE OAKLEY?
THE SOUTH WALL IS HOLDING--FOR NOW--BUT IT WON'T MUCH LONGER, UNLESS WE REINFORCE IT.
PULL ONE-IN-THREE FROM THE NORTH WALL AND--
--NO, WAIT! CANCEL THAT ORDER!
SMALL ARMS AREN'T HAVING MUCH EFFECT, MISS SNOW.
"WE WANT THEM TO OCCUPY BULLFINCH STREET, BEFORE WE REALLY START FIGHTING, BECAUSE THE LESS OF THIS THE MUNDYS SEE, THE LESS WE'LL HAVE TO COVER UP LATER.
THEY'VE DONE IT! THEY'VE MADE A BREACH!
"ALL PART OF THE PLAN, FLY. NO NEED TO LOSE OUR NERVE--YET."
FALL BACK! FALL BACK!
FLY, TELL SNOW SHE'S GOT TO PULL THEM OFF THE NORTH WALL TOO, OR THEY'LL BE CUT OFF!

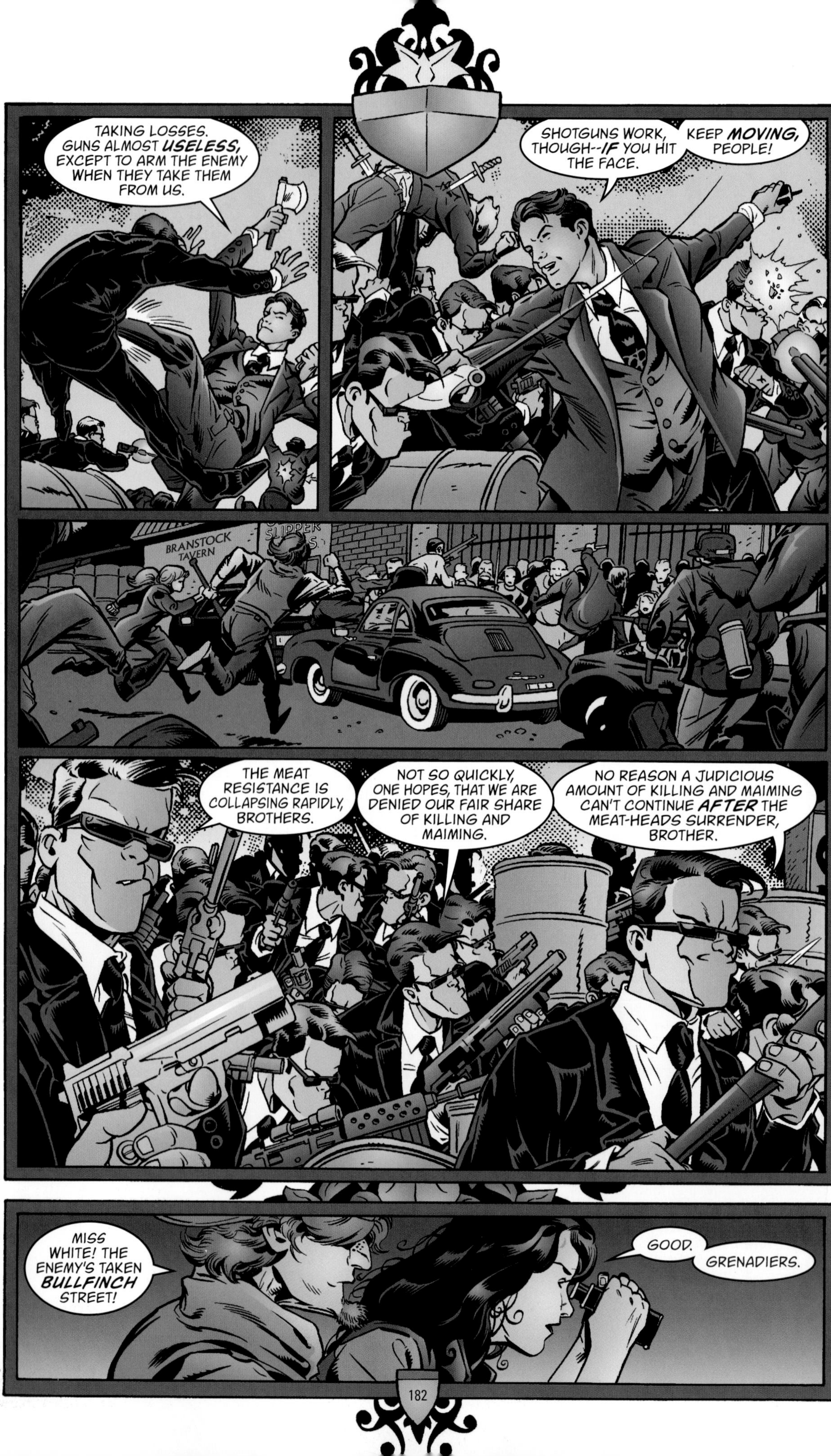

TAKING LOSSES. GUNS ALMOST USELESS, EXCEPT TO ARM THE ENEMY WHEN THEY TAKE THEM FROM US.
SHOTGUNS WORK, THOUGH--IF YOU HIT THE FACE.
KEEP MOVING, PEOPLE!
BRANSTOCK TAVERN
THE MEAT RESISTANCE IS COLLAPSING RAPIDLY, BROTHERS.
NOT SO QUICKLY, ONE HOPES, THAT WE ARE DENIED OUR FAIR SHARE OF KILLING AND MAIMING.
NO REASON A JUDICIOUS AMOUNT OF KILLING AND MAIMING CAN'T CONTINUE AFTER THE MEAT-HEADS SURRENDER, BROTHER.
MISS WHITE! THE ENEMY'S TAKEN BULLFINCH STREET!
GOOD.
GRENADIERS.

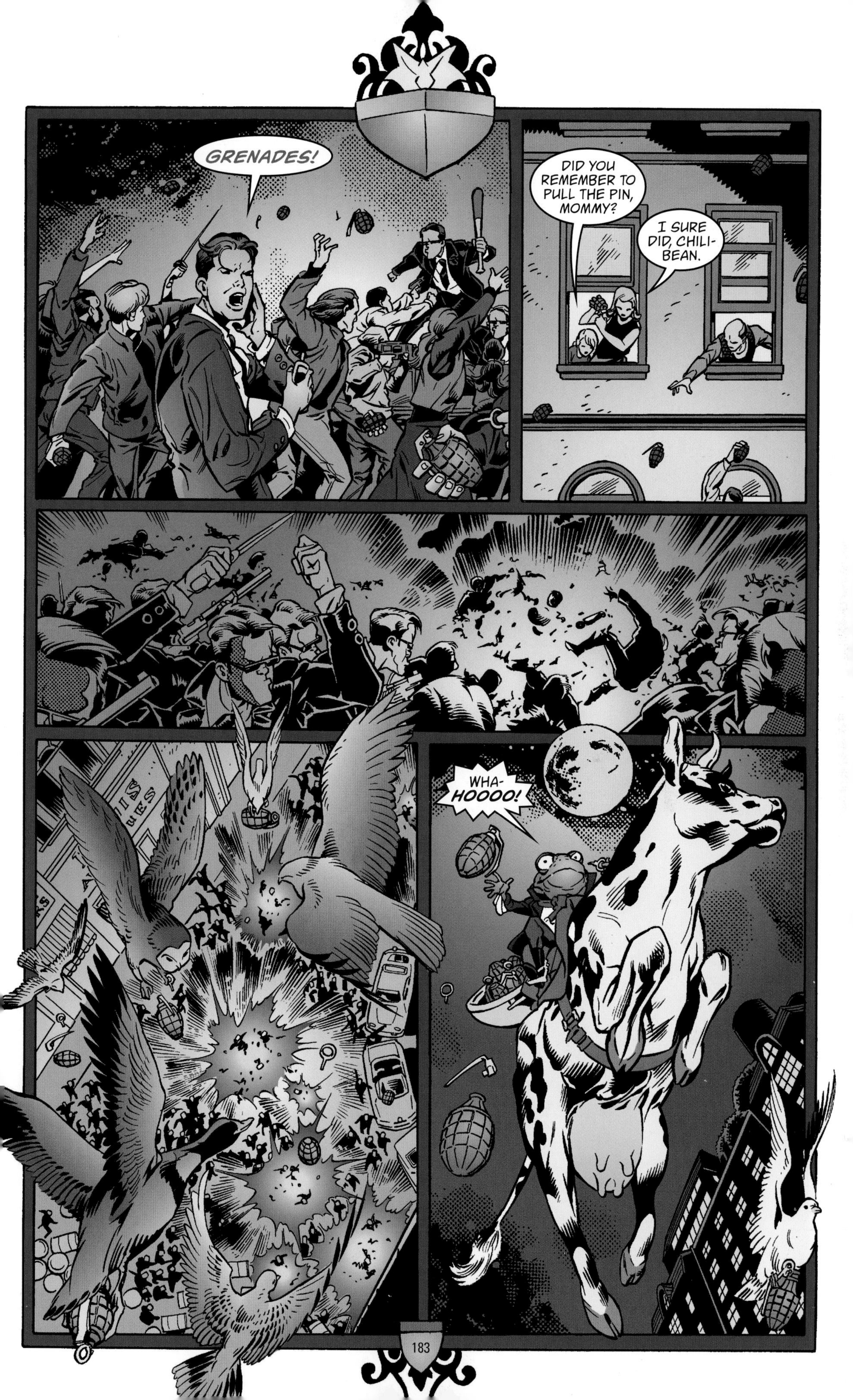
GRENADES!
DID YOU REMEMBER TO PULL THE PIN, MOMMY?
I SURE DID, CHILI-BEAN.
WHA-HOOOO!

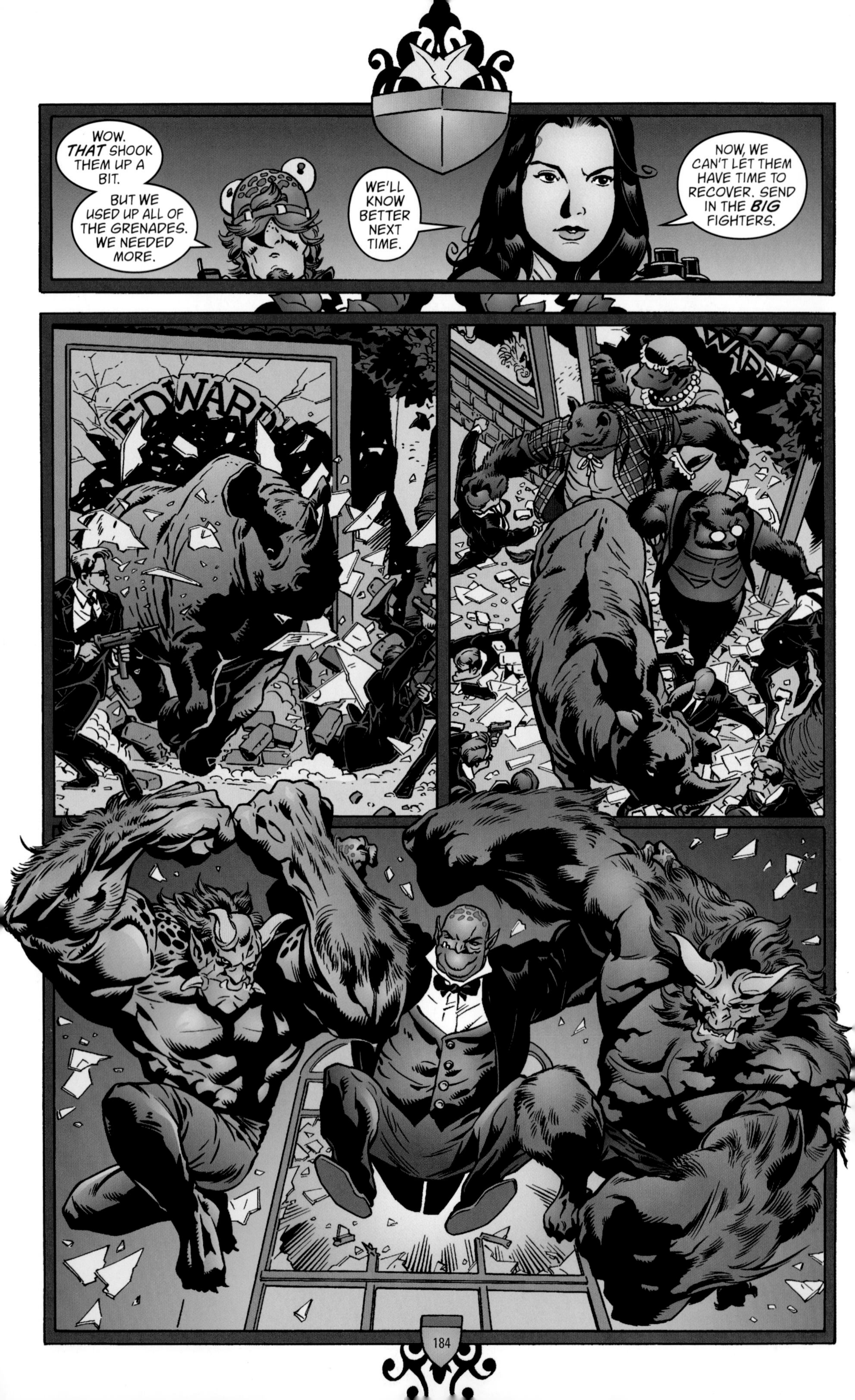
WOW. THAT SHOOK THEM UP A BIT.
BUT WE USED UP ALL OF THE GRENADES. WE NEEDED MORE.
WE'LL KNOW BETTER NEXT TIME.
NOW, WE CAN'T LET THEM HAVE TIME TO RECOVER. SEND IN THE BIG FIGHTERS.
EDWARD

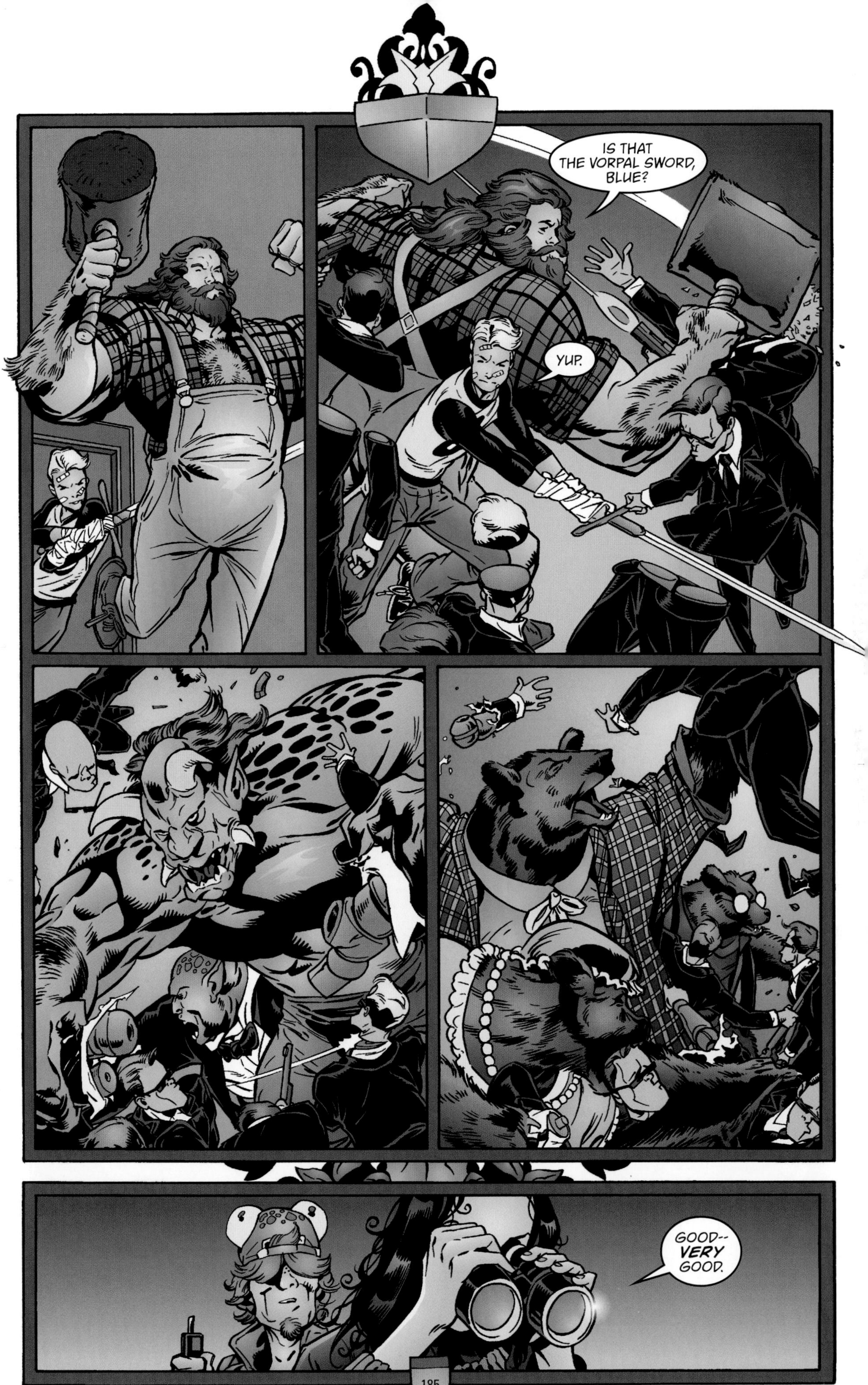
IS THAT THE VORPAL SWORD, BLUE?
YUP.
GOOD-- VERY GOOD.

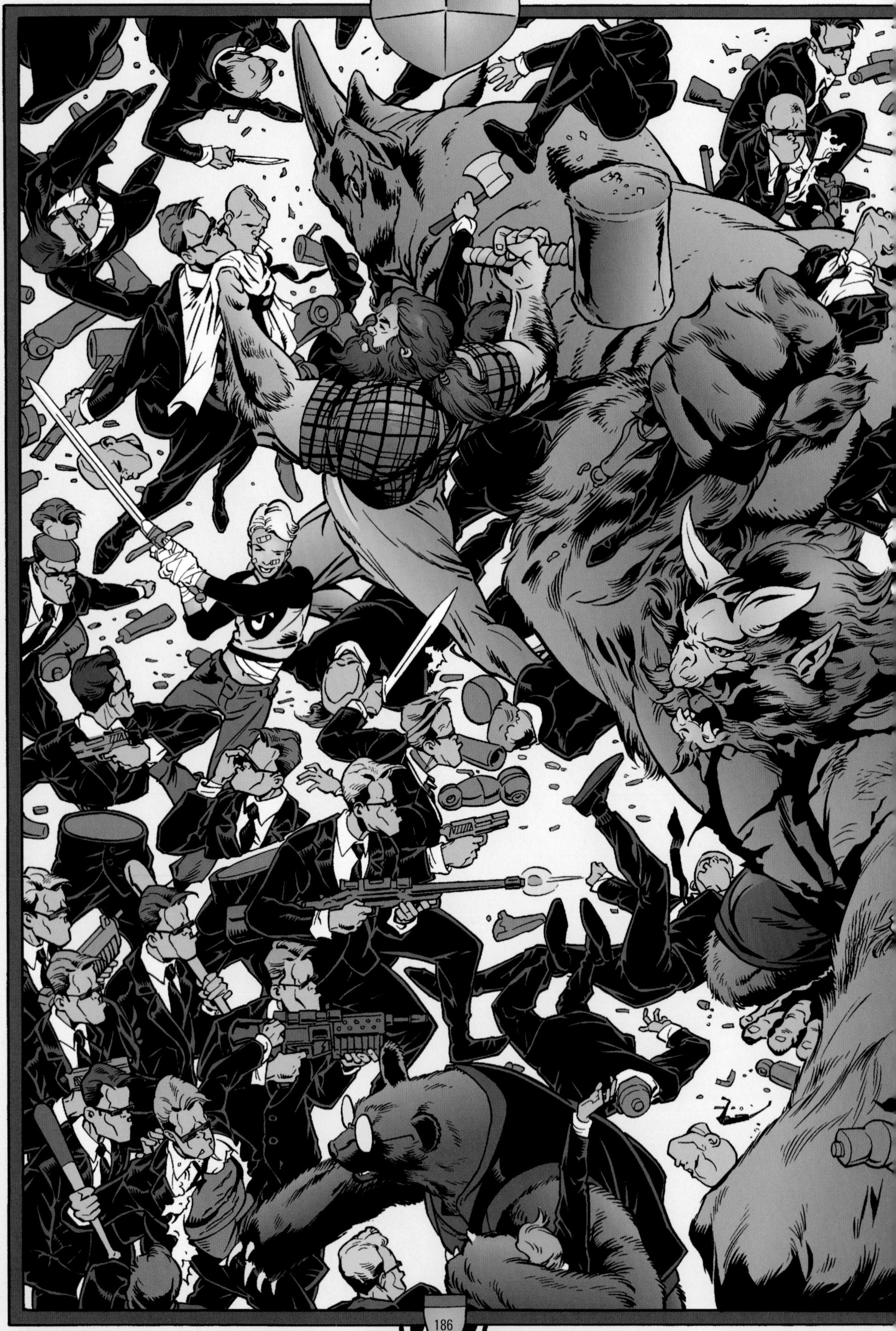

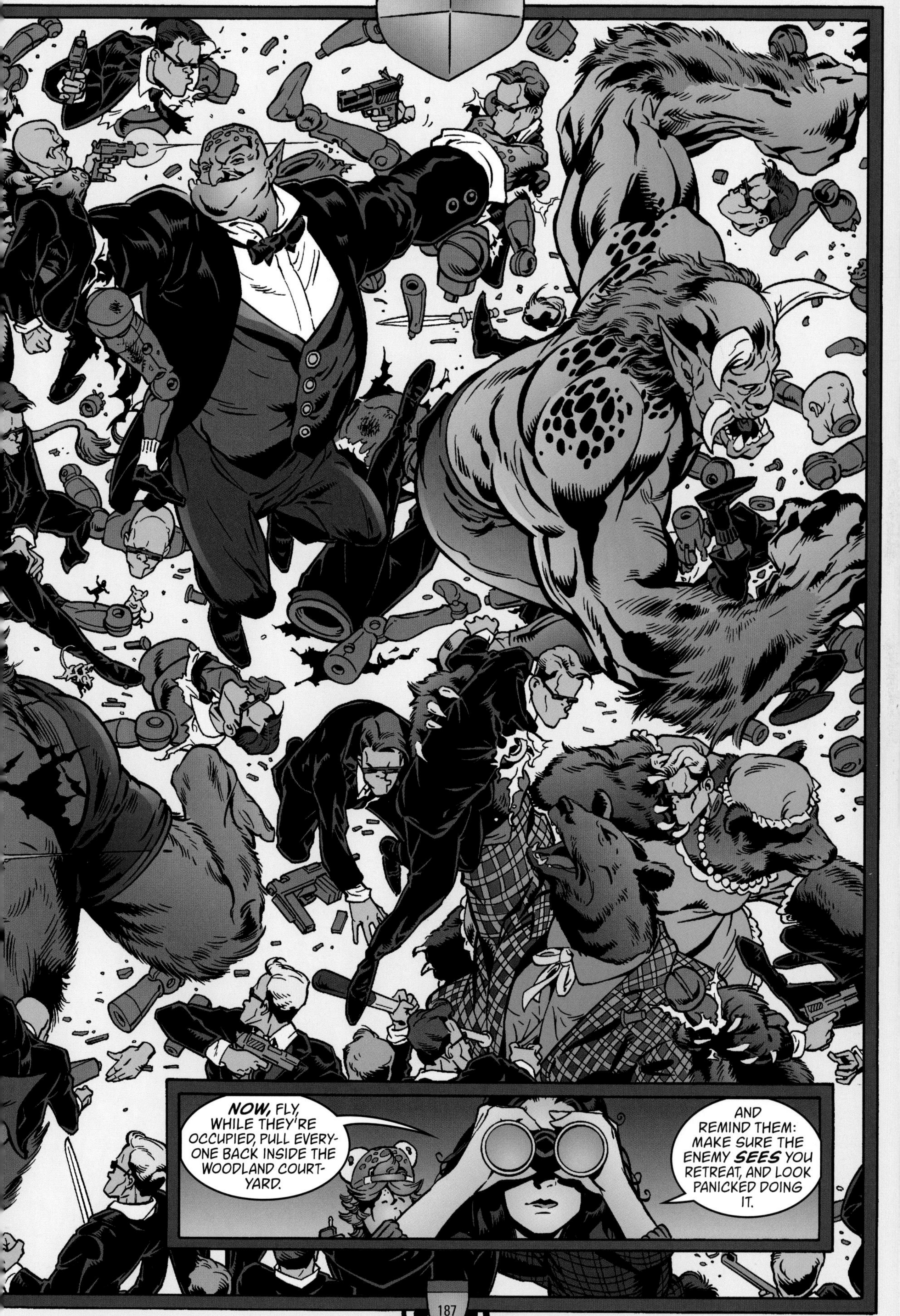
NOW, FLY, WHILE THEY'RE OCCUPIED, PULL EVERYONE BACK INSIDE THE WOODLAND COURTYARD.
AND REMIND THEM: MAKE SURE THE ENEMY SEES YOU RETREAT, AND LOOK PANICKED DOING IT.

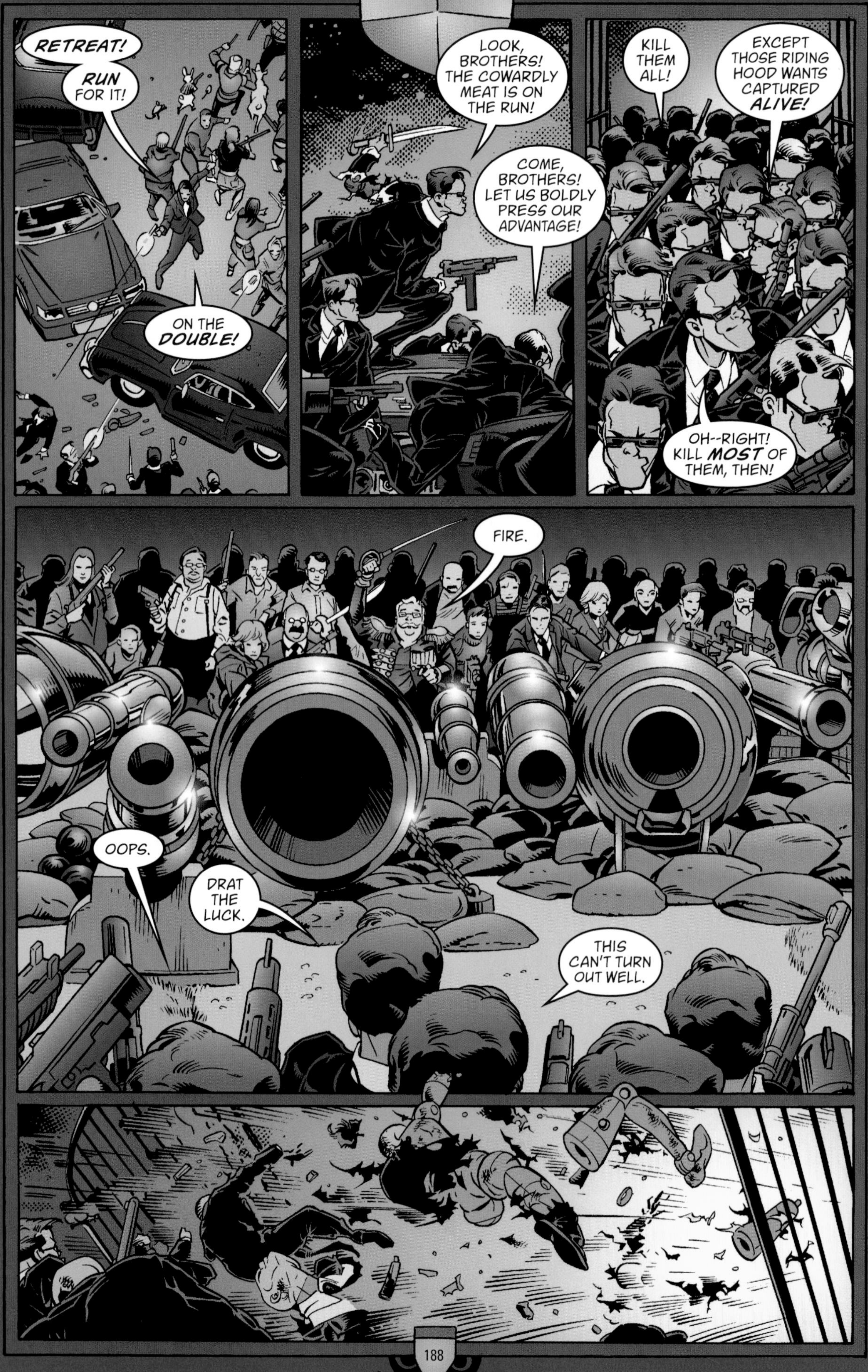
RETREAT!
RUN FOR IT!
ON THE DOUBLE!
LOOK, BROTHERS! THE COWARDLY MEAT IS ON THE RUN!
COME, BROTHERS! LET US BOLDLY PRESS OUR ADVANTAGE!
KILL THEM ALL!
EXCEPT THOSE RIDING HOOD WANTS CAPTURED ALIVE!
OH--RIGHT! KILL MOST OF THEM, THEN!
FIRE.
OOPS.
DRAT THE LUCK.
THIS CAN'T TURN OUT WELL.

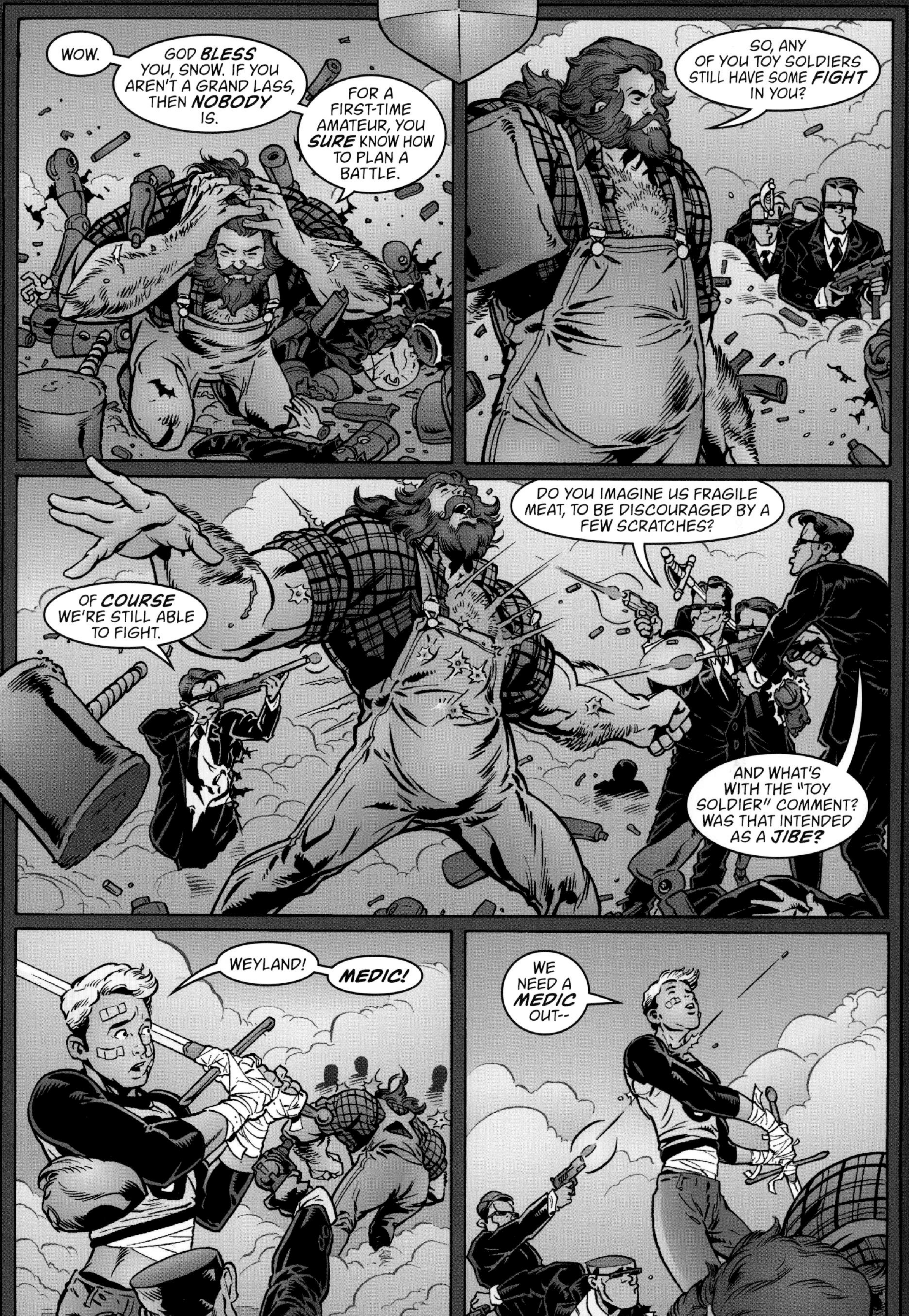
WOW.
GOD BLESS YOU, SNOW. IF YOU AREN'T A GRAND LASS, THEN NOBODY IS.
FOR A FIRST-TIME AMATEUR, YOU SURE KNOW HOW TO PLAN A BATTLE.
SO, ANY OF YOU TOY SOLDIERS STILL HAVE SOME FIGHT IN YOU?
OF COURSE WE'RE STILL ABLE TO FIGHT.
DO YOU IMAGINE US FRAGILE MEAT, TO BE DISCOURAGED BY A FEW SCRATCHES?
AND WHAT'S WITH THE "TOY SOLDIER" COMMENT? WAS THAT INTENDED AS A JIBE?
WEYLAND!
MEDIC!
WE NEED A MEDIC OUT--

LET US *THROUGH*, PLEASE!

MAKE A *HOLE!*

LET ME *GO*, JACKASS! I WANT TO SEE WHAT'S HAPPENING!

TOO BAD, PINOCCHIO. YOU'RE GOING TO STAY INSIDE HERE WHERE IT'S *SAFE.*

YOU SHOULD BE OUT THERE, TOO.

AND YET HERE I REMAIN.

COWARD.

PUNK.

DOCTOR SWINEHEART! THIS ONE'S WOUNDED BAD!

BUSINESS OFFICE

S. WHITE

WHERE DO YOU WANT HIM?

BUSINESS OFFICE

S. WH

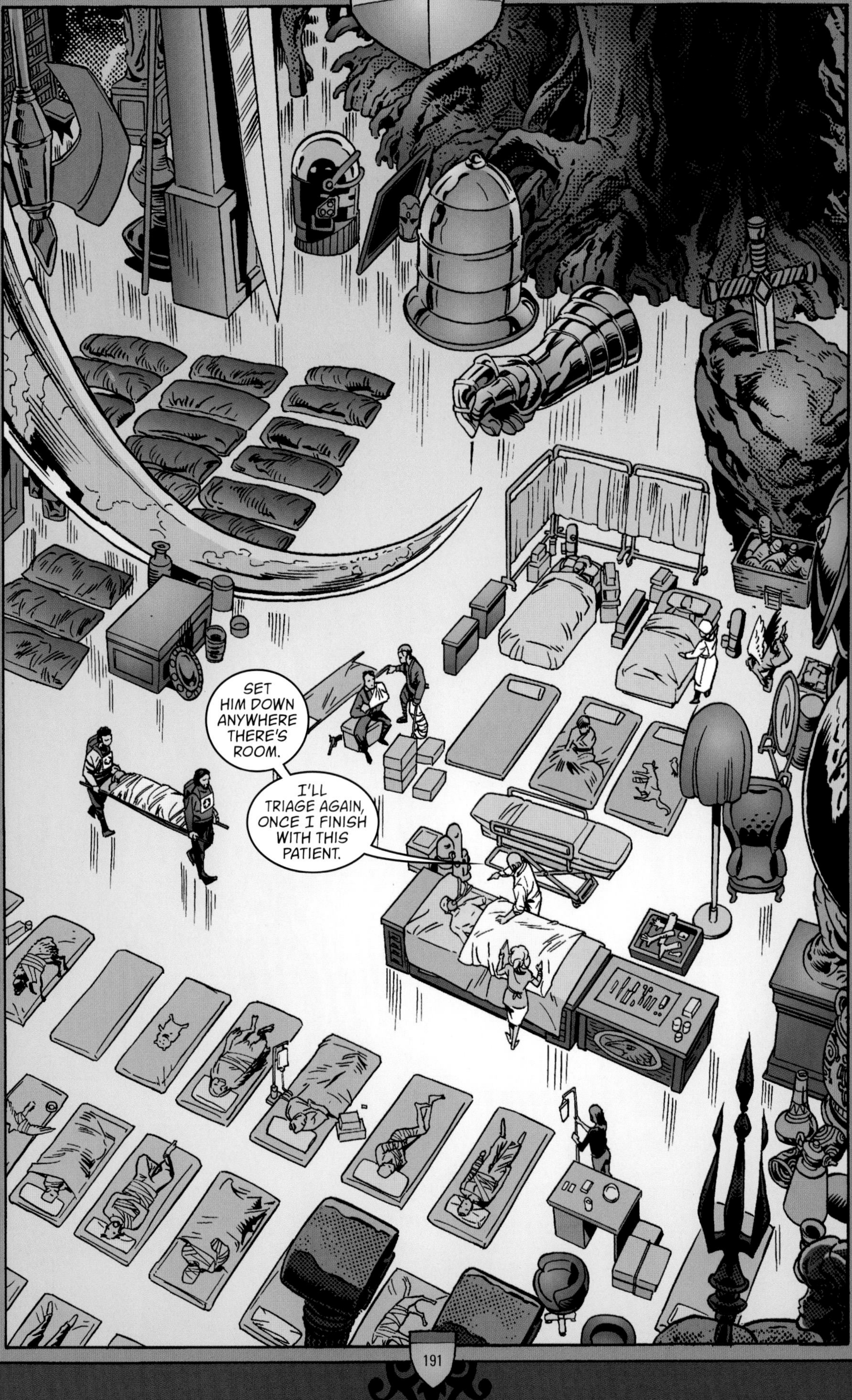
SET HIM DOWN ANYWHERE THERE'S ROOM.
I'LL TRIAGE AGAIN, ONCE I FINISH WITH THIS PATIENT.

WELL, *THAT'S* CLEVER.

WHAT?

"SOME OF THE WOODEN SOLDIERS ARE SALVAGING BODY PARTS FROM THEIR FALLEN COMRADES TO ASSEMBLE *NEW* SOLDIERS."

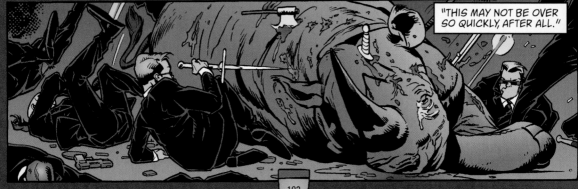

"THIS MAY NOT BE OVER SO QUICKLY, AFTER ALL."

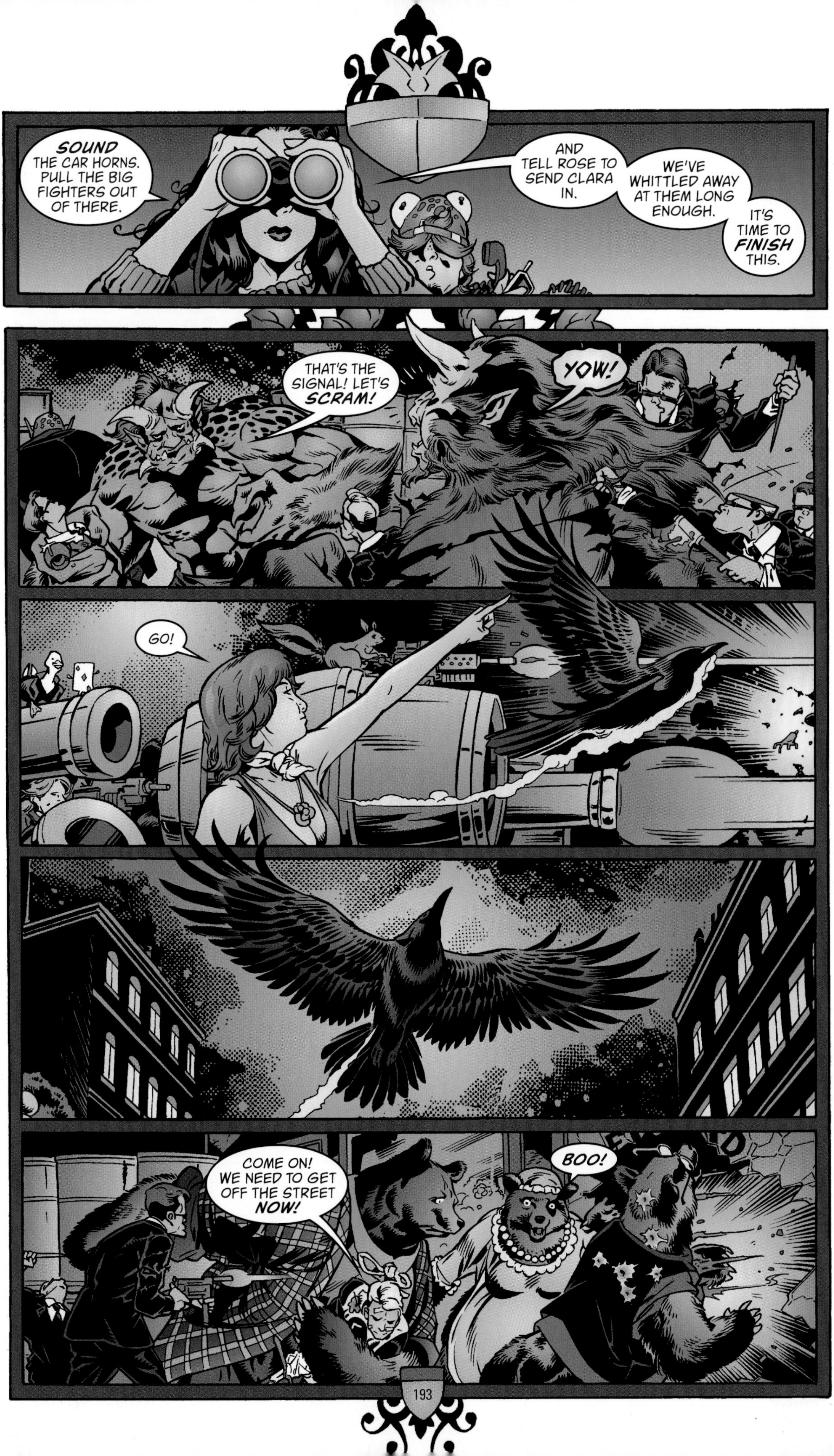
SOUND THE CAR HORNS. PULL THE BIG FIGHTERS OUT OF THERE.
AND TELL ROSE TO SEND CLARA IN.
WE'VE WHITTLED AWAY AT THEM LONG ENOUGH.
IT'S TIME TO FINISH THIS.
THAT'S THE SIGNAL! LET'S SCRAM!
YOW!
GO!
COME ON! WE NEED TO GET OFF THE STREET NOW!
BOO!

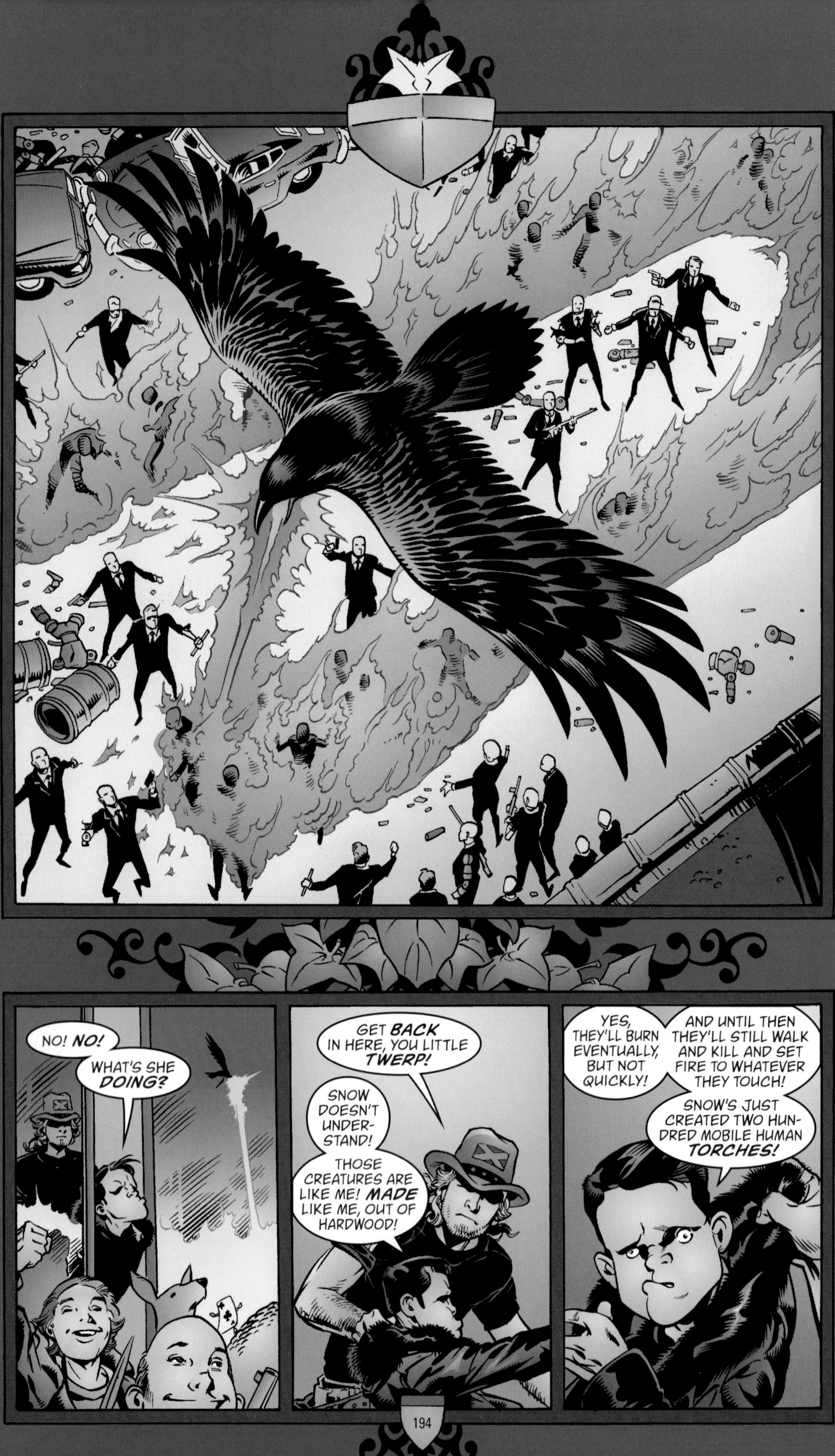
NO! NO!
WHAT'S SHE DOING?
GET BACK IN HERE, YOU LITTLE TWERP!
SNOW DOESN'T UNDER-STAND!
THOSE CREATURES ARE LIKE ME! MADE LIKE ME, OUT OF HARDWOOD!
YES, THEY'LL BURN EVENTUALLY, BUT NOT QUICKLY!
AND UNTIL THEN THEY'LL STILL WALK AND KILL AND SET FIRE TO WHATEVER THEY TOUCH!
SNOW'S JUST CREATED TWO HUN-DRED MOBILE HUMAN TORCHES!

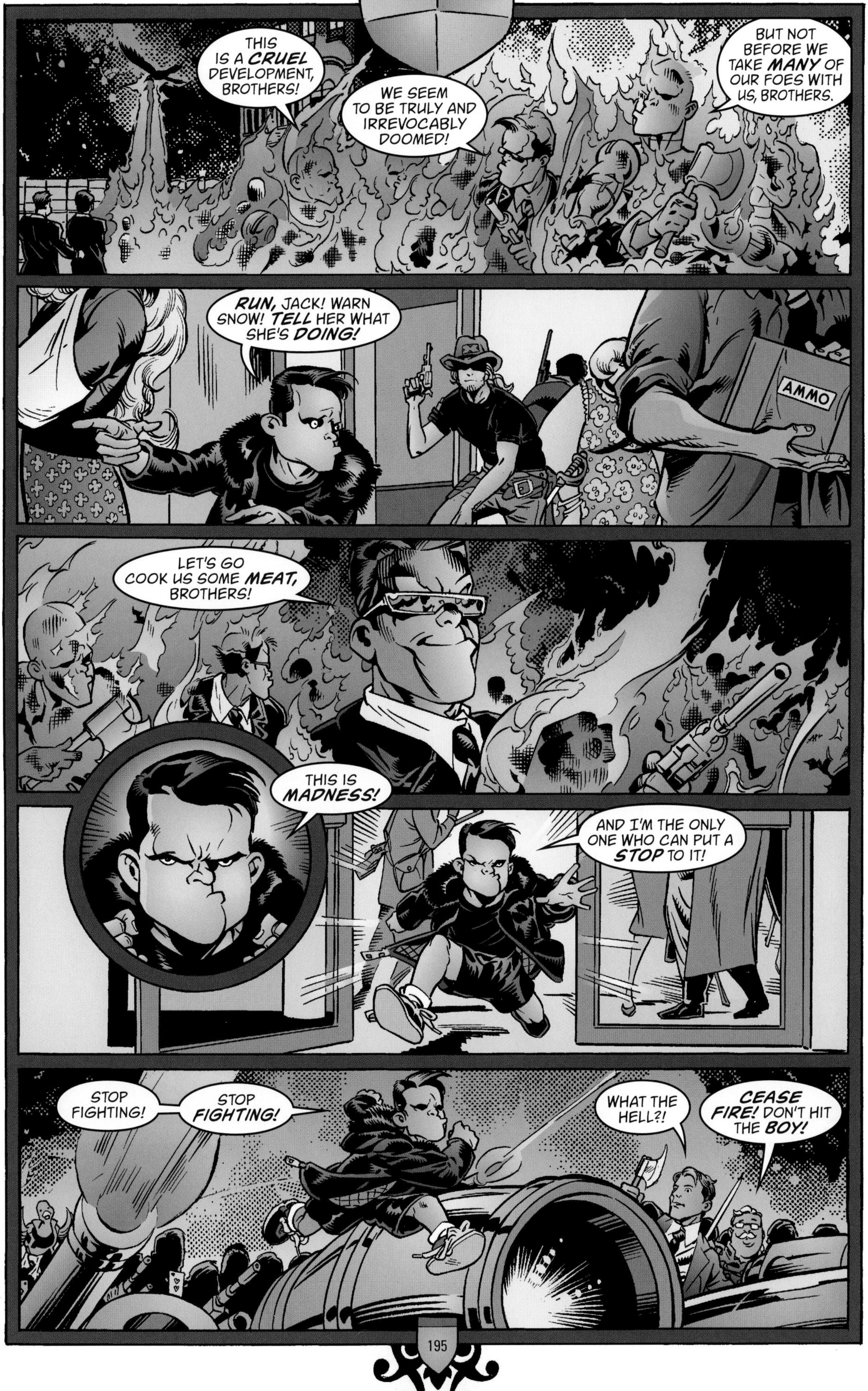
THIS IS A CRUEL DEVELOPMENT, BROTHERS!
WE SEEM TO BE TRULY AND IRREVOCABLY DOOMED!
BUT NOT BEFORE WE TAKE MANY OF OUR FOES WITH US, BROTHERS.
RUN, JACK! WARN SNOW! TELL HER WHAT SHE'S DOING!
AMMO
LET'S GO COOK US SOME MEAT, BROTHERS!
THIS IS MADNESS!
AND I'M THE ONLY ONE WHO CAN PUT A STOP TO IT!
STOP FIGHTING!
STOP FIGHTING!
WHAT THE HELL?!
CEASE FIRE! DON'T HIT THE BOY!

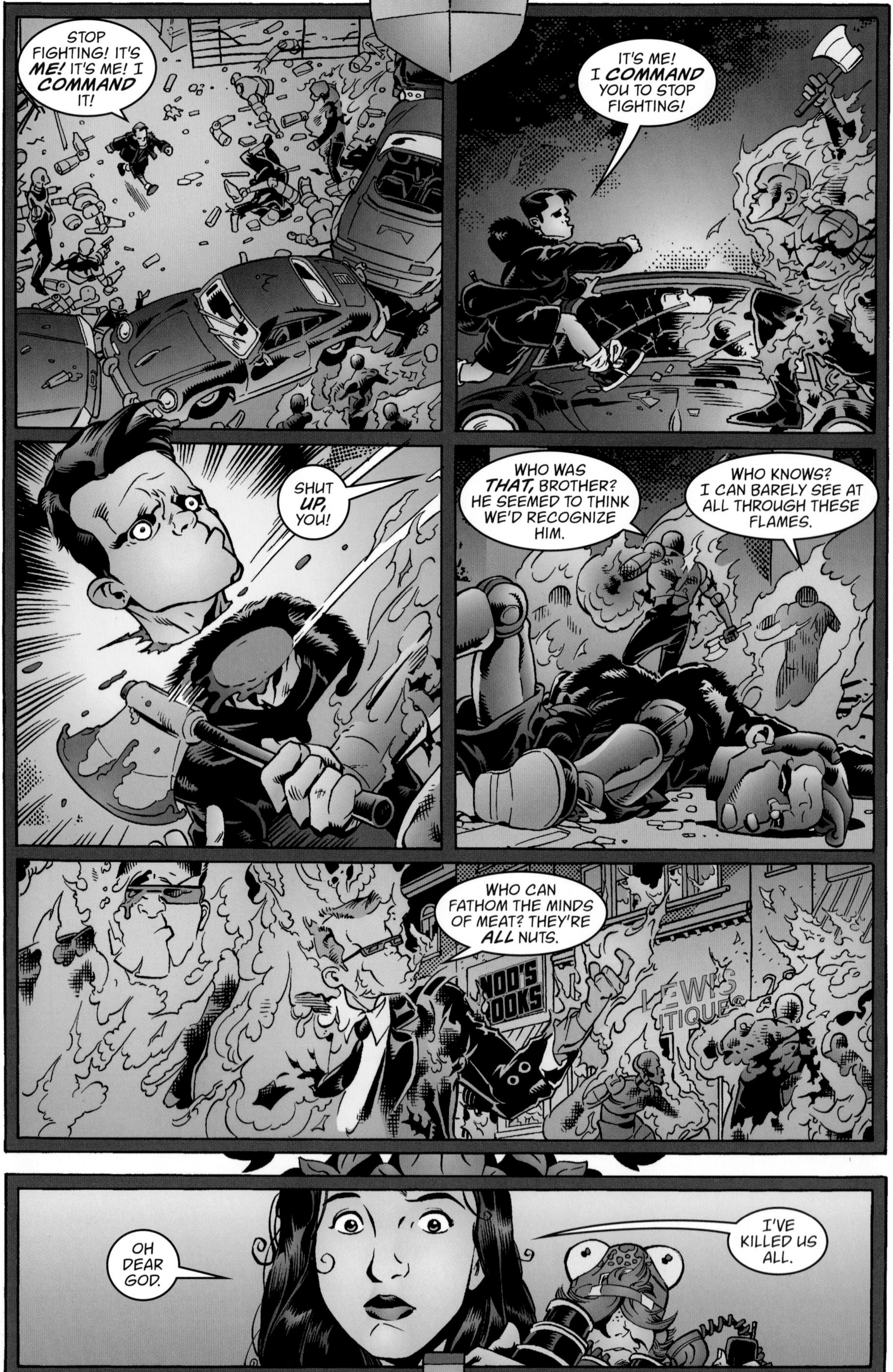
STOP FIGHTING! IT'S ME! IT'S ME! I COMMAND IT!
IT'S ME! I COMMAND YOU TO STOP FIGHTING!
SHUT UP, YOU!
WHO WAS THAT, BROTHER? HE SEEMED TO THINK WE'D RECOGNIZE HIM.
WHO KNOWS? I CAN BARELY SEE AT ALL THROUGH THESE FLAMES.
WHO CAN FATHOM THE MINDS OF MEAT? THEY'RE ALL NUTS.
OH DEAR GOD.
I'VE KILLED US ALL.

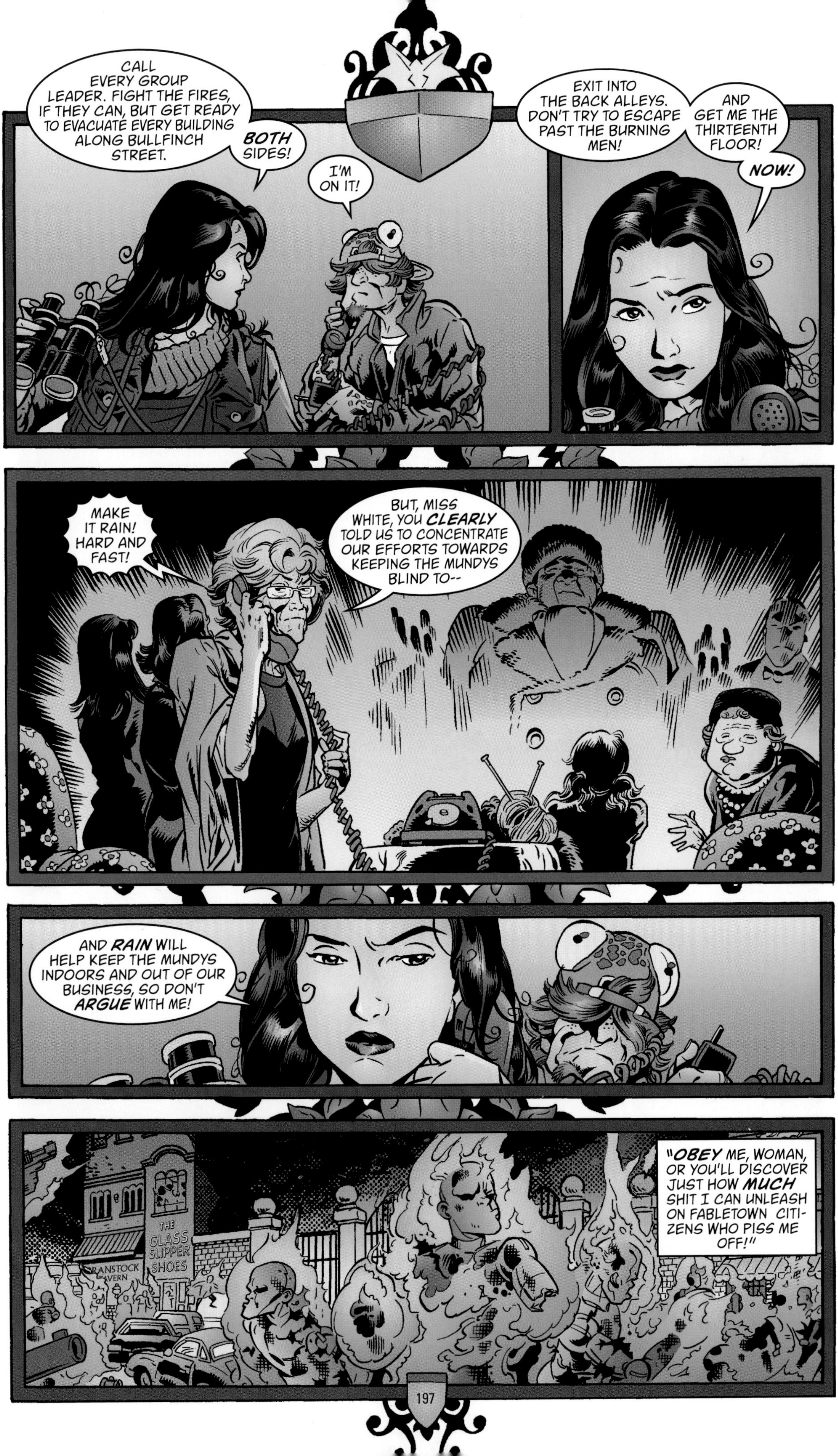
CALL EVERY GROUP LEADER. FIGHT THE FIRES, IF THEY CAN, BUT GET READY TO EVACUATE EVERY BUILDING ALONG BULLFINCH STREET.
BOTH SIDES!
I'M ON IT!
EXIT INTO THE BACK ALLEYS. DON'T TRY TO ESCAPE PAST THE BURNING MEN!
AND GET ME THE THIRTEENTH FLOOR!
NOW!
MAKE IT RAIN! HARD AND FAST!
BUT, MISS WHITE, YOU CLEARLY TOLD US TO CONCENTRATE OUR EFFORTS TOWARDS KEEPING THE MUNDYS BLIND TO--
AND RAIN WILL HELP KEEP THE MUNDYS INDOORS AND OUT OF OUR BUSINESS, SO DON'T ARGUE WITH ME!
THE GLASS SLIPPER SHOES
"OBEY ME, WOMAN, OR YOU'LL DISCOVER JUST HOW MUCH SHIT I CAN UNLEASH ON FABLETOWN CITIZENS WHO PISS ME OFF!"

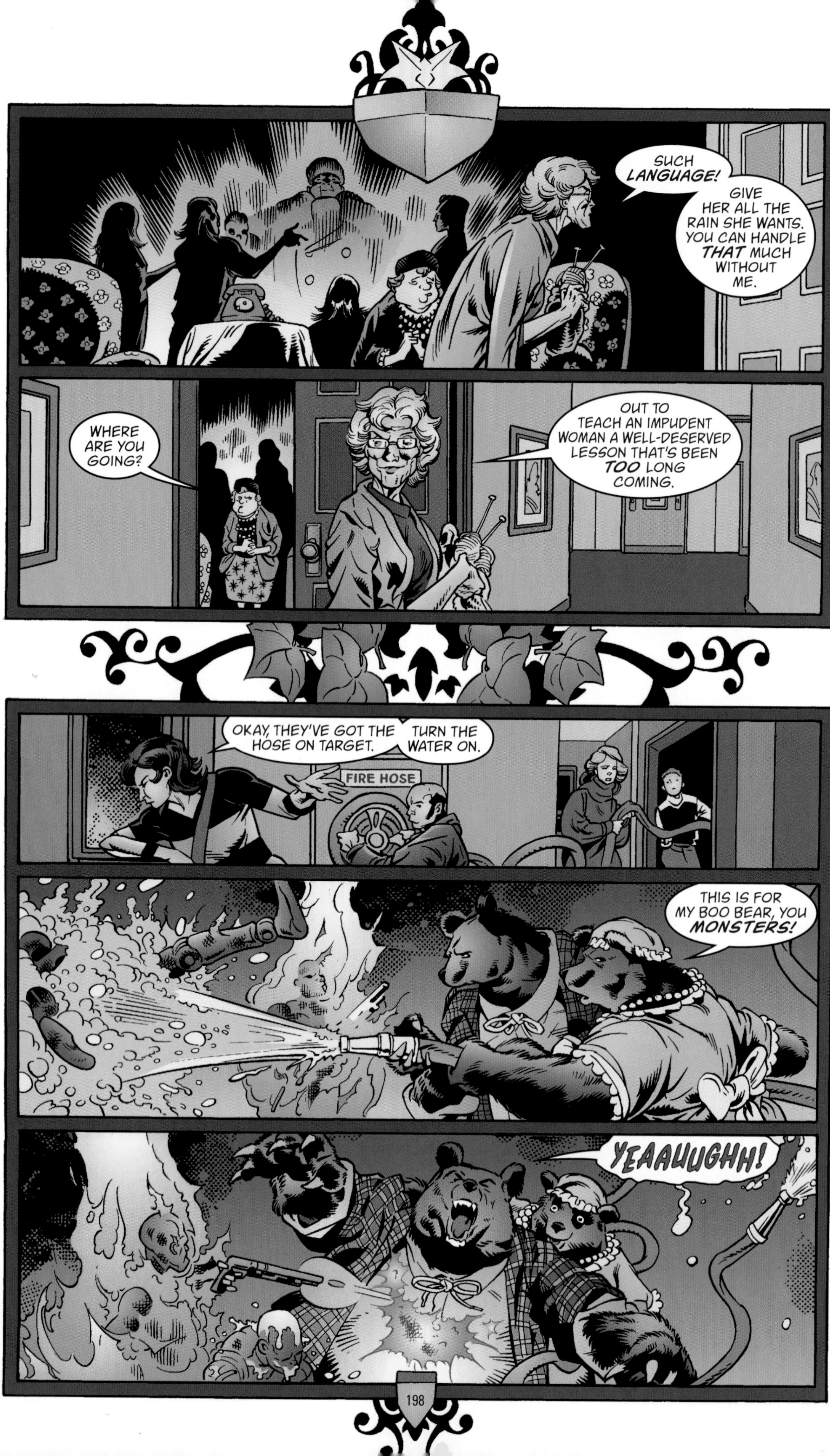
SUCH LANGUAGE!
GIVE HER ALL THE RAIN SHE WANTS. YOU CAN HANDLE THAT MUCH WITHOUT ME.
WHERE ARE YOU GOING?
OUT TO TEACH AN IMPUDENT WOMAN A WELL-DESERVED LESSON THAT'S BEEN TOO LONG COMING.
OKAY, THEY'VE GOT THE HOSE ON TARGET.
TURN THE WATER ON.
FIRE HOSE
THIS IS FOR MY BOO BEAR, YOU MONSTERS!
YEAAUUGHH!

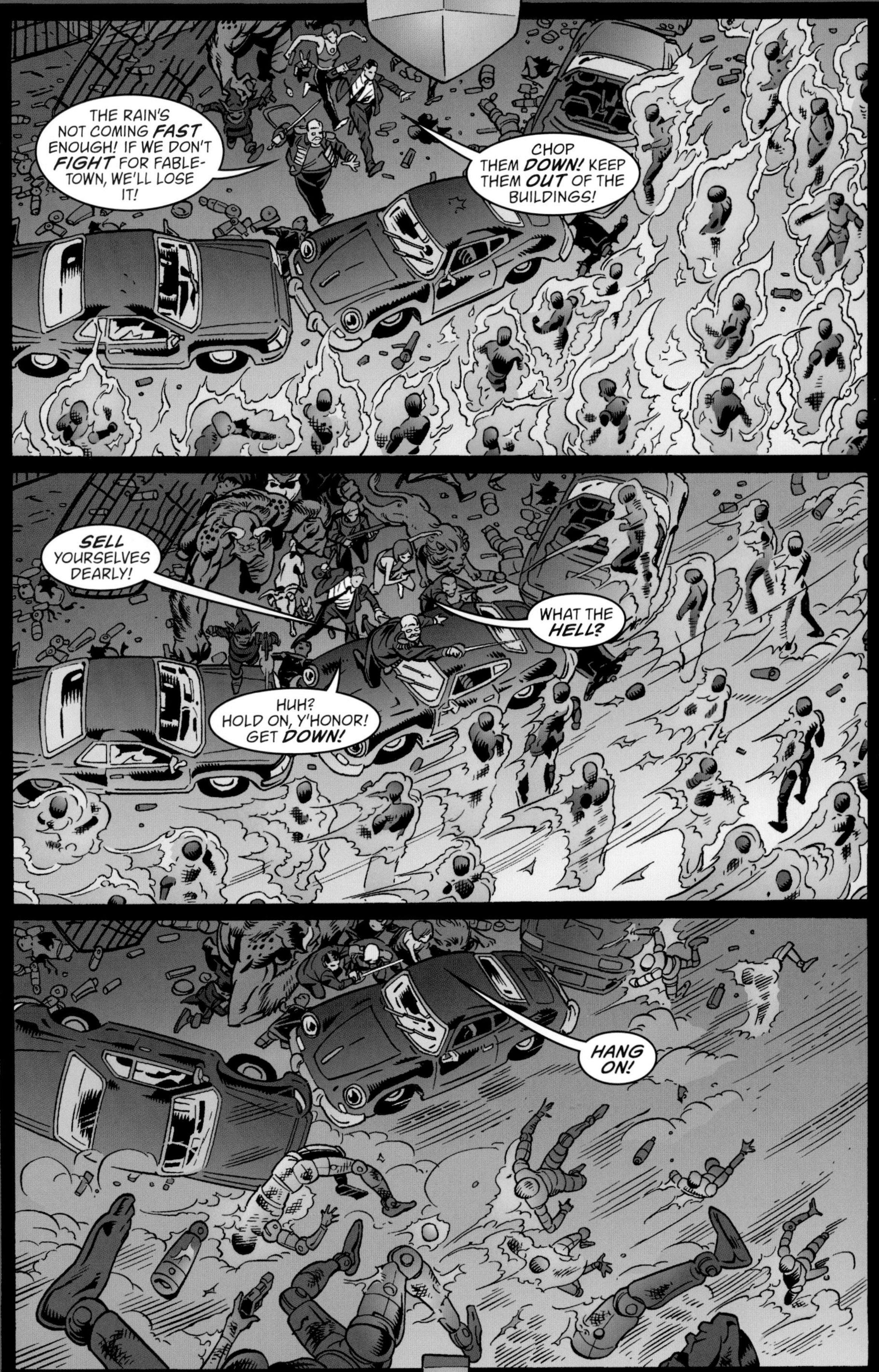
THE RAIN'S NOT COMING FAST ENOUGH! IF WE DON'T FIGHT FOR FABLE-TOWN, WE'LL LOSE IT!
CHOP THEM DOWN! KEEP THEM OUT OF THE BUILDINGS!
SELL YOURSELVES DEARLY!
WHAT THE HELL?
HUH? HOLD ON, Y'HONOR! GET DOWN!
HANG ON!

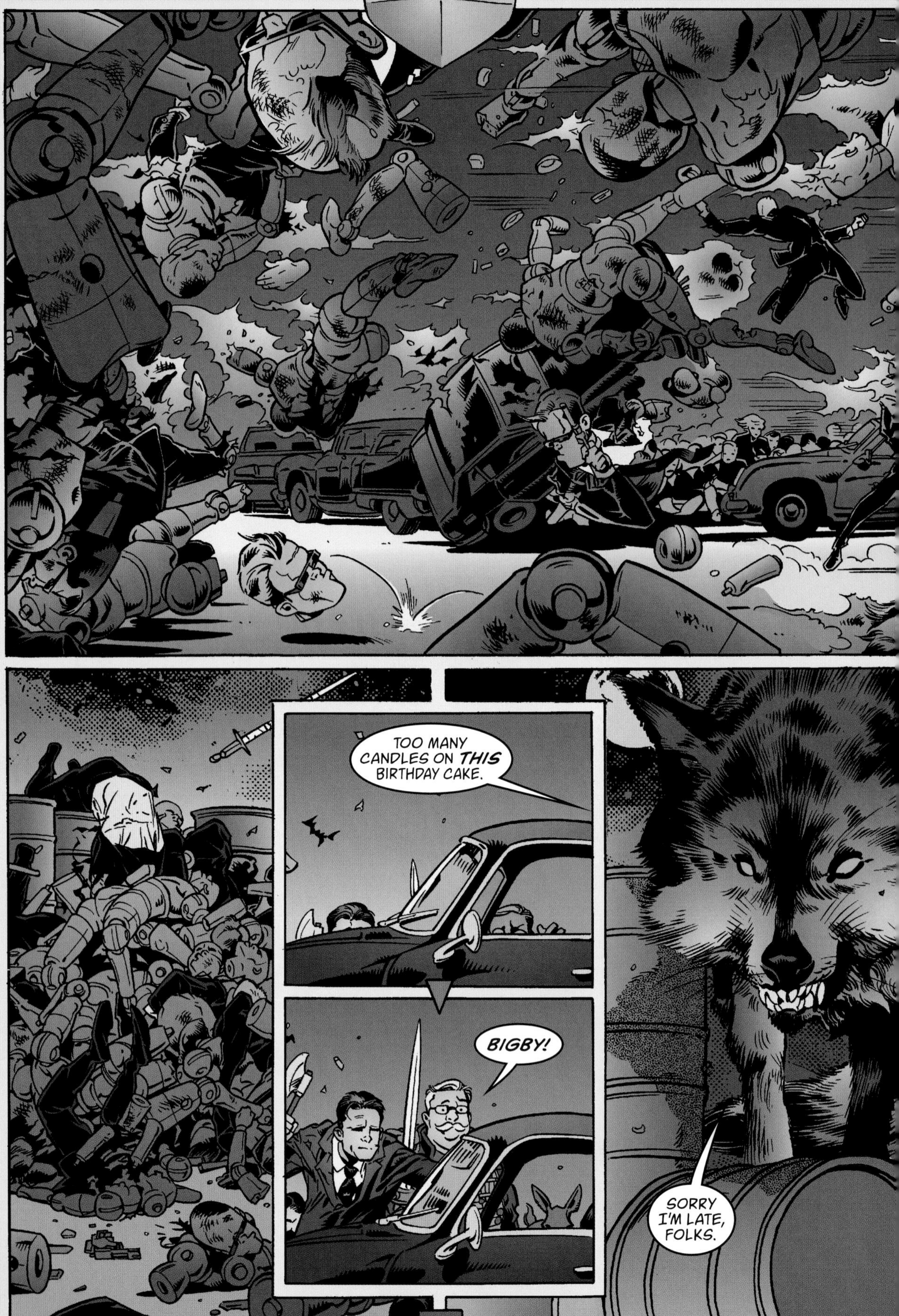
TOO MANY CANDLES ON THIS BIRTHDAY CAKE.
BIGBY!
SORRY I'M LATE, FOLKS.

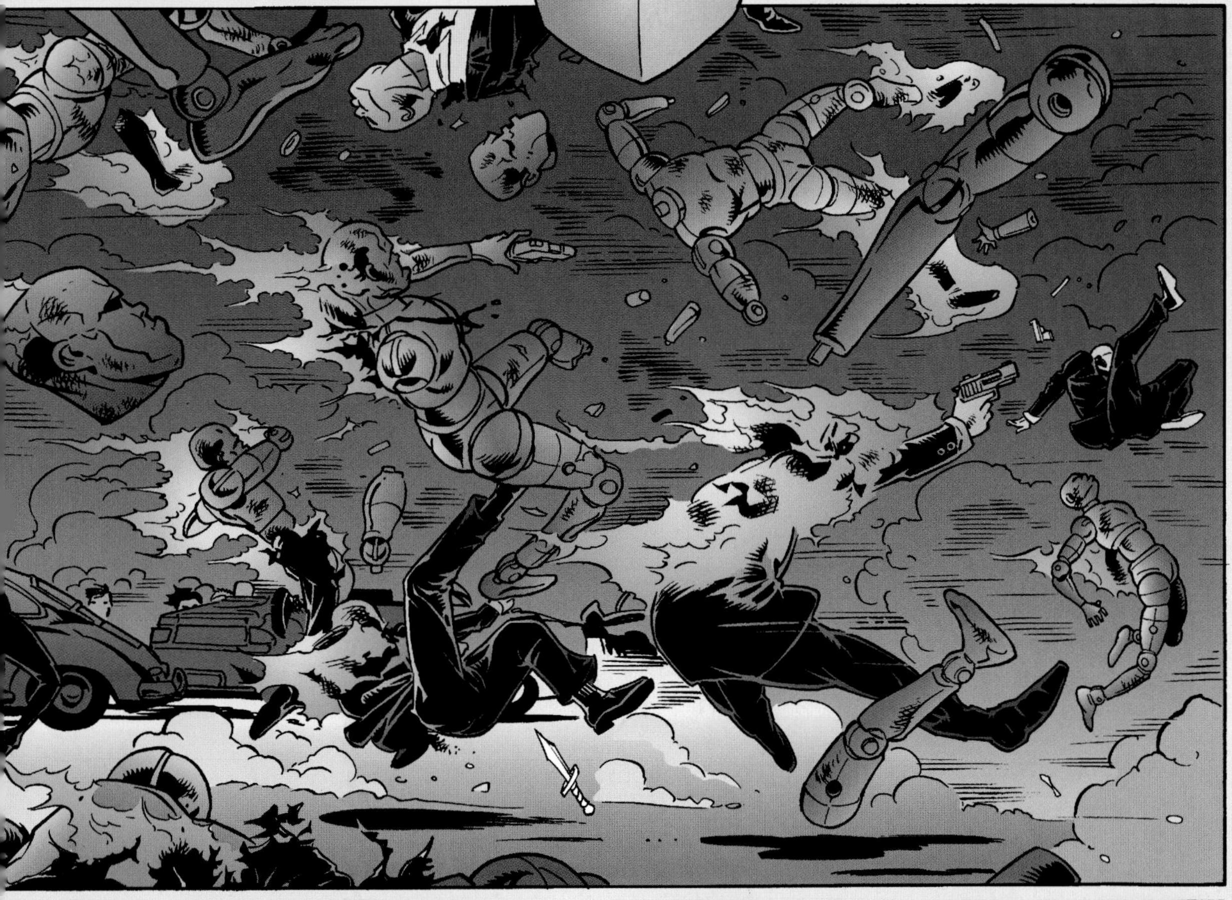

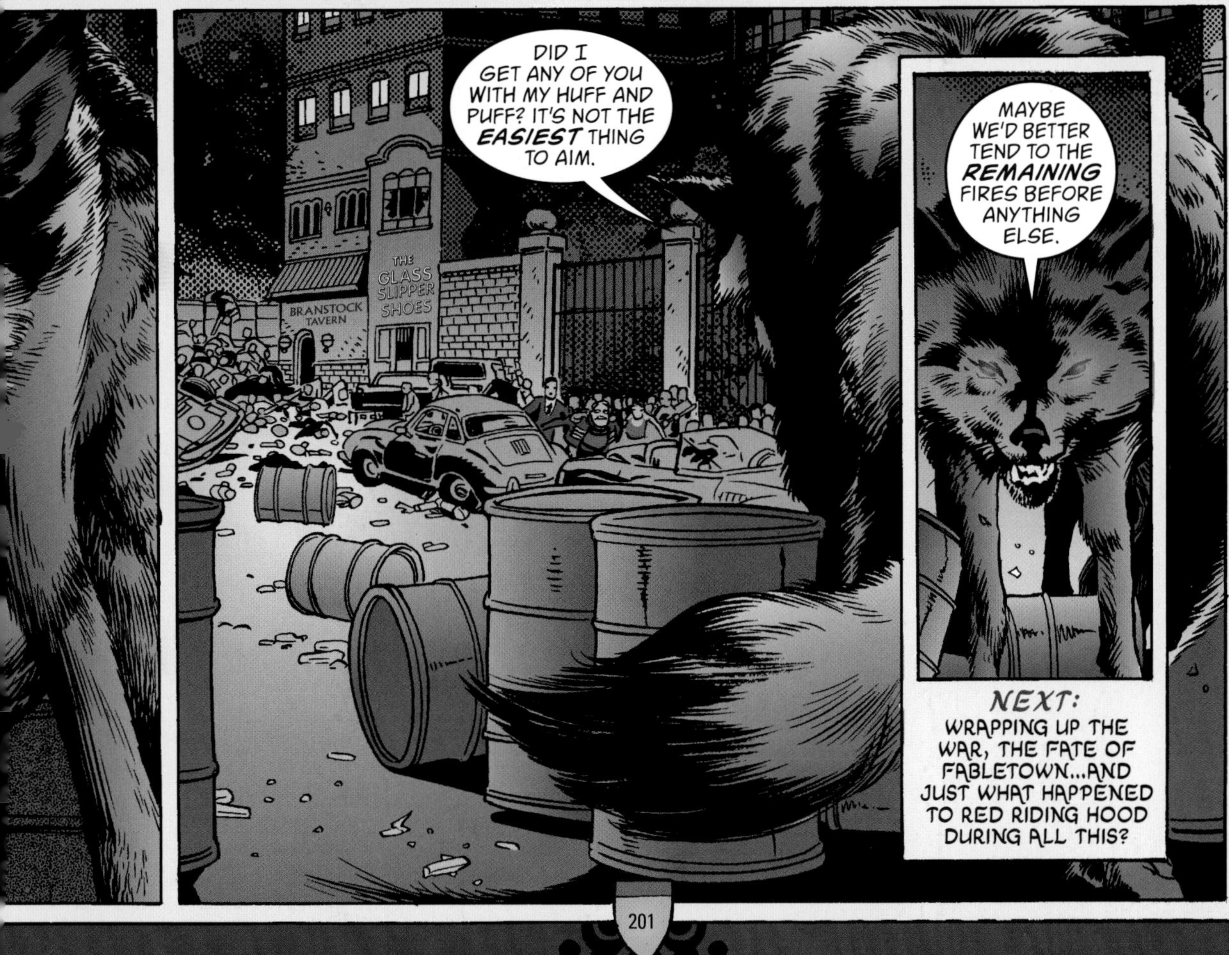
DID I GET ANY OF YOU WITH MY HUFF AND PUFF? IT'S NOT THE EASIEST THING TO AIM.
MAYBE WE'D BETTER TEND TO THE REMAINING FIRES BEFORE ANYTHING ELSE.
NEXT:
WRAPPING UP THE WAR, THE FATE OF FABLETOWN...AND JUST WHAT HAPPENED TO RED RIDING HOOD DURING ALL THIS?
THE GLASS SLIPPER SHOES
BRANSTOCK TAVERN

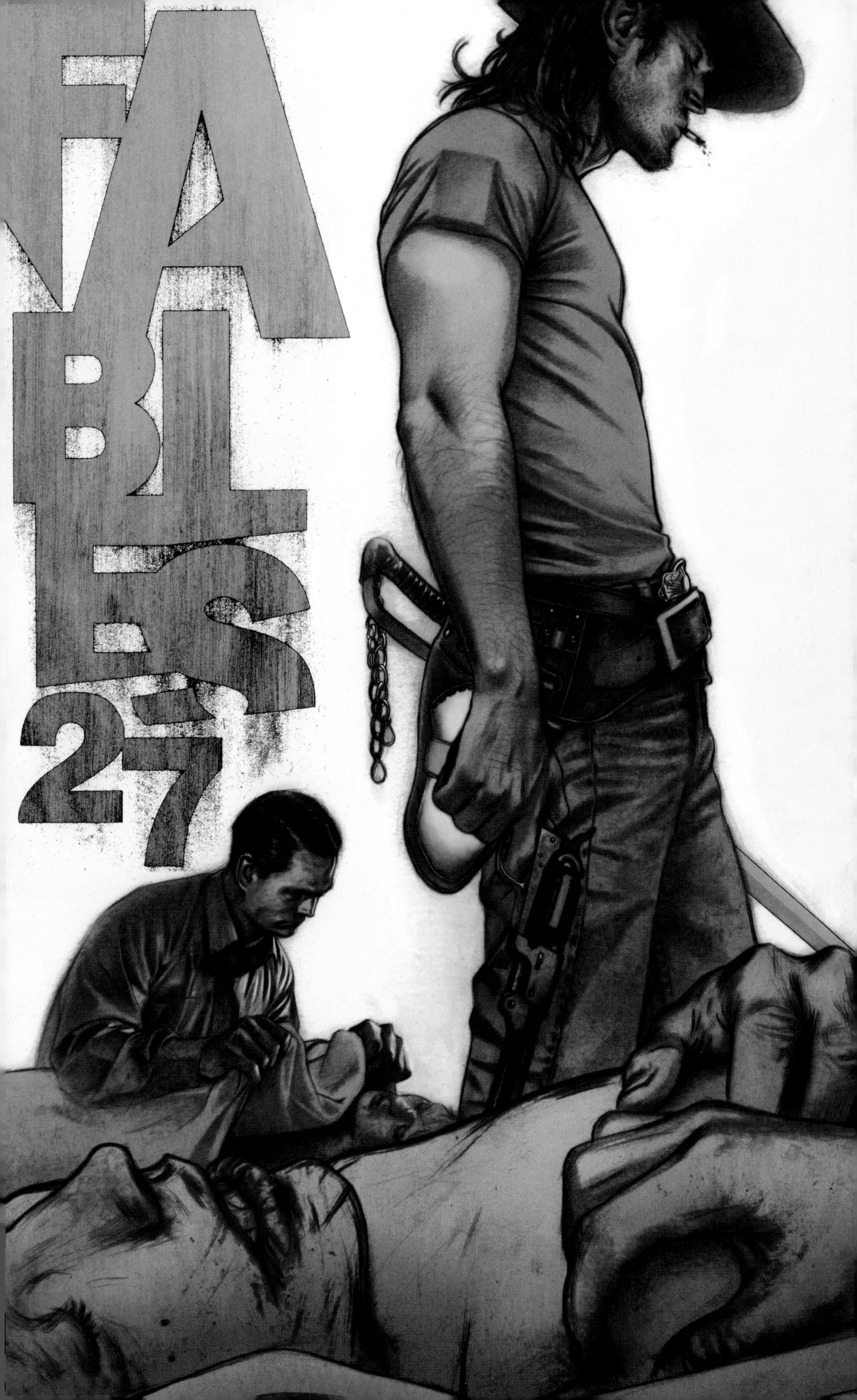
FABLES
27

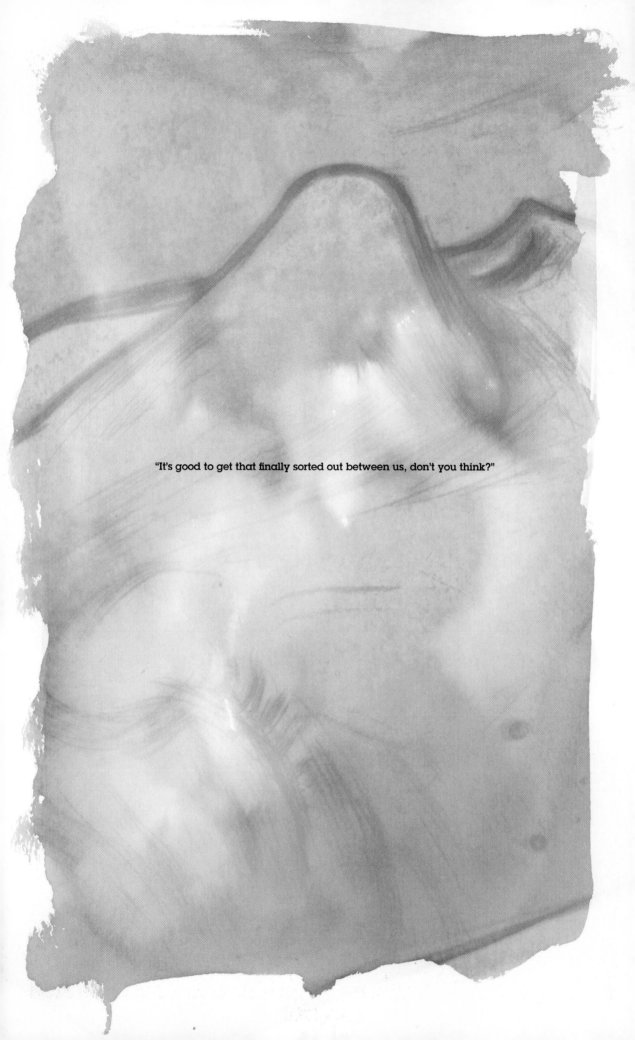

"It's good to get that finally sorted out between us, don't you think?"

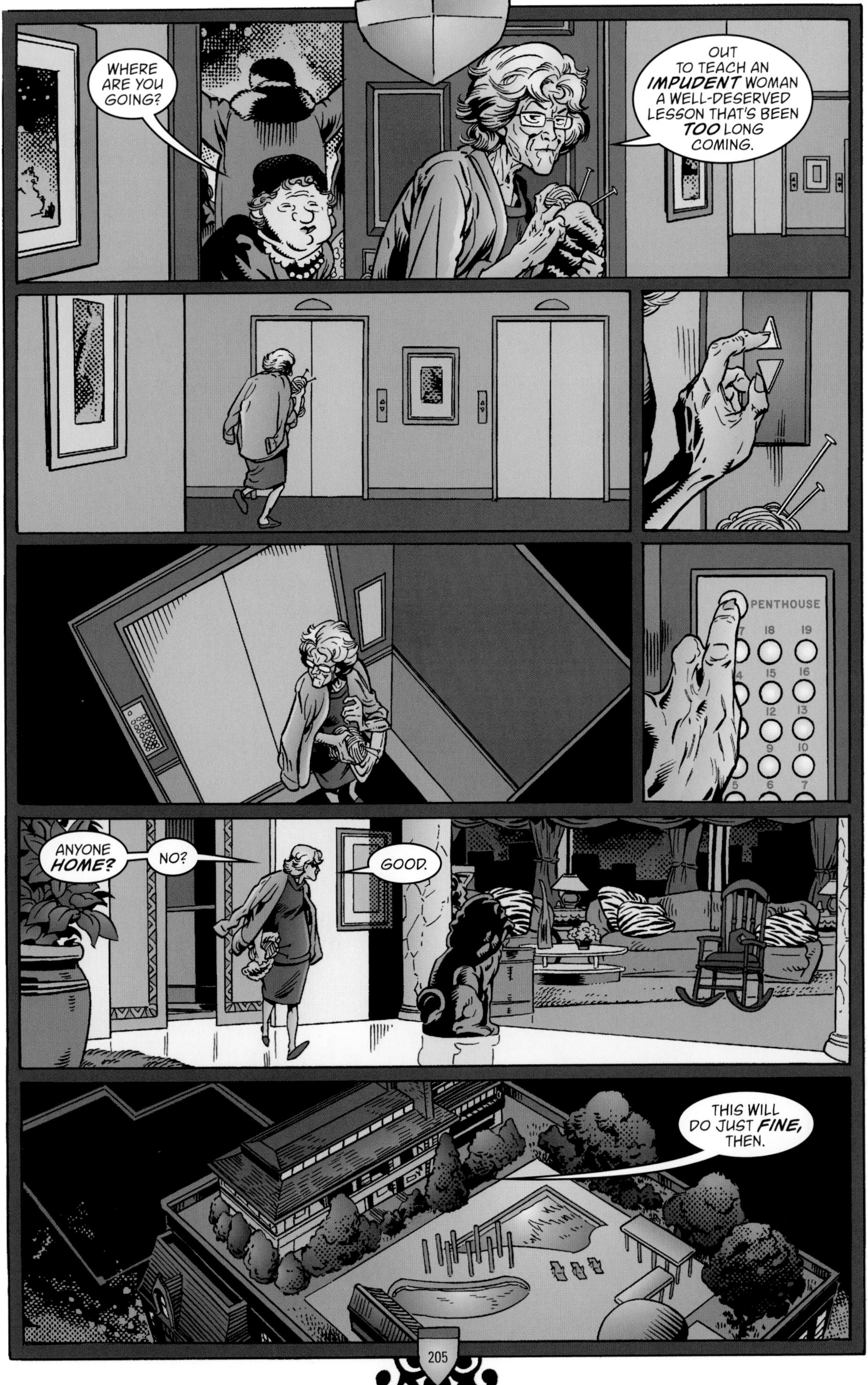
WHERE ARE YOU GOING?
OUT TO TEACH AN IMPUDENT WOMAN A WELL-DESERVED LESSON THAT'S BEEN TOO LONG COMING.
PENTHOUSE
ANYONE HOME?
NO?
GOOD.
THIS WILL DO JUST FINE, THEN.

IN LIKE A LION – OUT ON THE LAM

CHAPTER EIGHT ○ MARCH OF THE WOODEN SOLDIERS

BILL WILLINGHAM writer/creator
MARK BUCKINGHAM penciller
STEVE LEIALOHA inker
DANIEL VOZZO color/seps
TODD KLEIN lettering
JAMES JEAN cover art
MARIAH HUEHNER assistant editor
SHELLY BOND editor

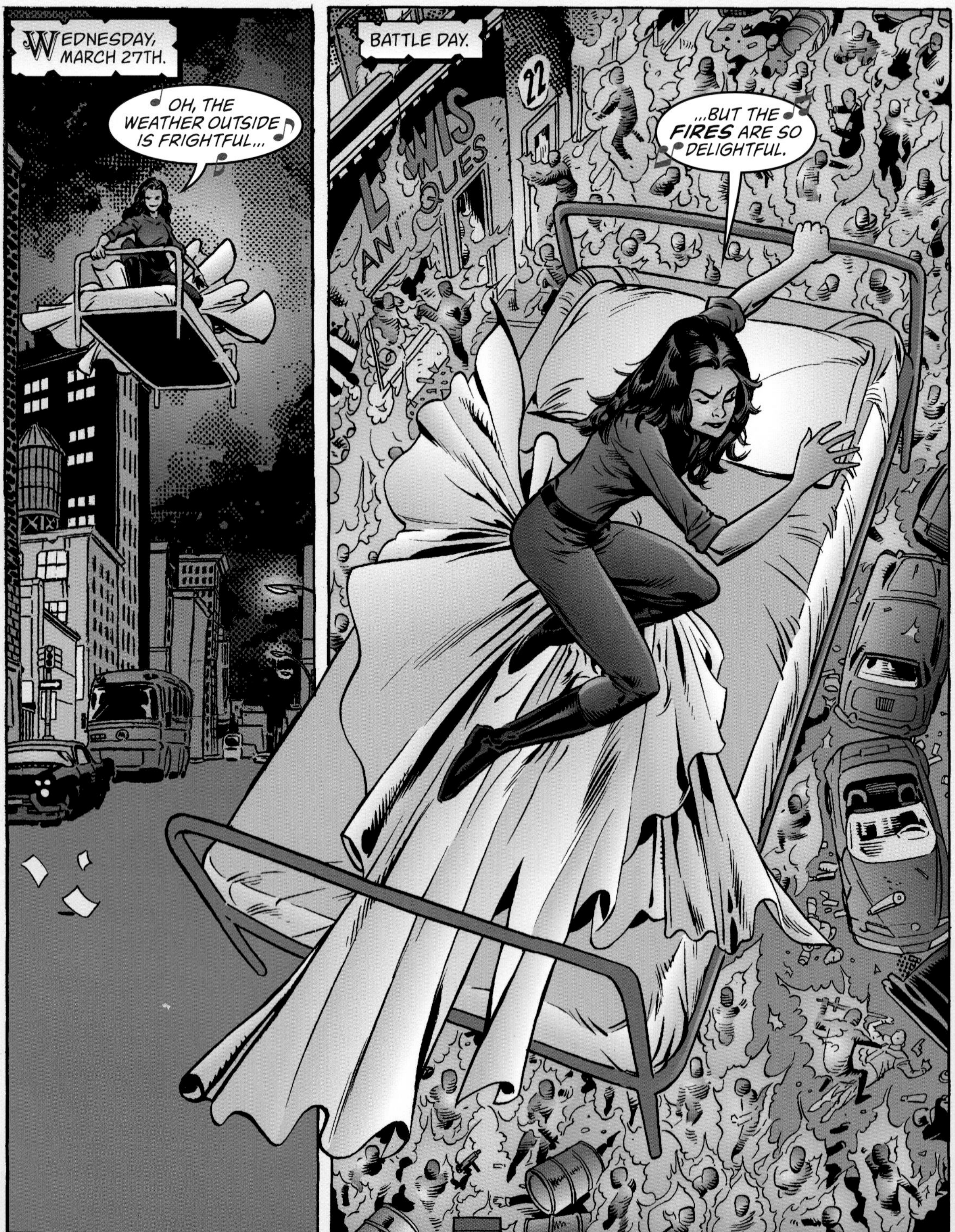

WEDNESDAY, MARCH 27TH.
OH, THE WEATHER OUTSIDE IS FRIGHTFUL...
BATTLE DAY.
...BUT THE FIRES ARE SO DELIGHTFUL.

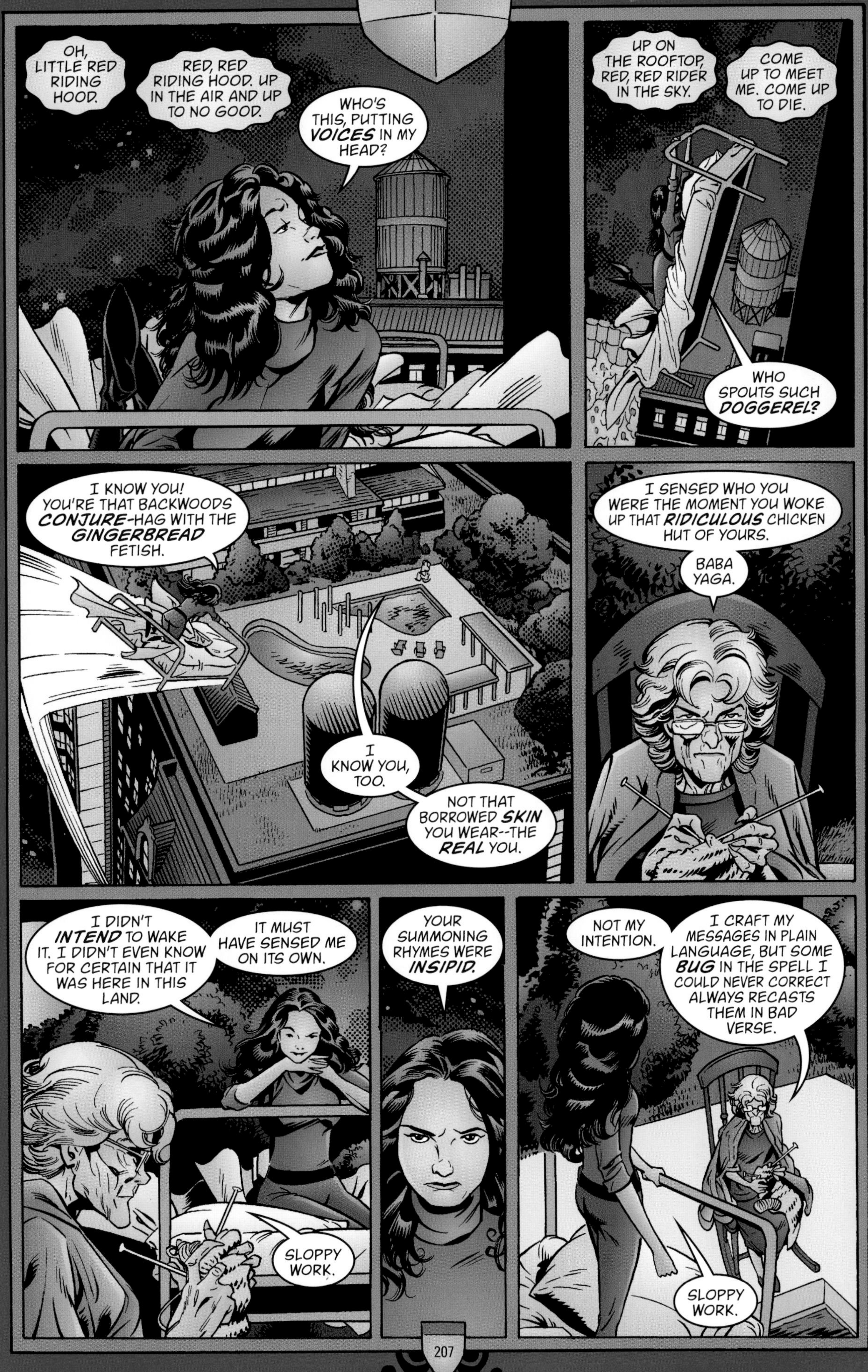
OH, LITTLE RED RIDING HOOD.
RED, RED RIDING HOOD. UP IN THE AIR AND UP TO NO GOOD.
WHO'S THIS, PUTTING VOICES IN MY HEAD?
UP ON THE ROOFTOP, RED, RED RIDER IN THE SKY.
COME UP TO MEET ME. COME UP TO DIE.
WHO SPOUTS SUCH DOGGEREL?
I KNOW YOU! YOU'RE THAT BACKWOODS CONJURE-HAG WITH THE GINGERBREAD FETISH.
I KNOW YOU, TOO.
NOT THAT BORROWED SKIN YOU WEAR--THE REAL YOU.
I SENSED WHO YOU WERE THE MOMENT YOU WOKE UP THAT RIDICULOUS CHICKEN HUT OF YOURS.
BABA YAGA.
I DIDN'T INTEND TO WAKE IT. I DIDN'T EVEN KNOW FOR CERTAIN THAT IT WAS HERE IN THIS LAND.
IT MUST HAVE SENSED ME ON ITS OWN.
SLOPPY WORK.
YOUR SUMMONING RHYMES WERE INSIPID.
NOT MY INTENTION.
I CRAFT MY MESSAGES IN PLAIN LANGUAGE, BUT SOME BUG IN THE SPELL I COULD NEVER CORRECT ALWAYS RECASTS THEM IN BAD VERSE.
SLOPPY WORK.

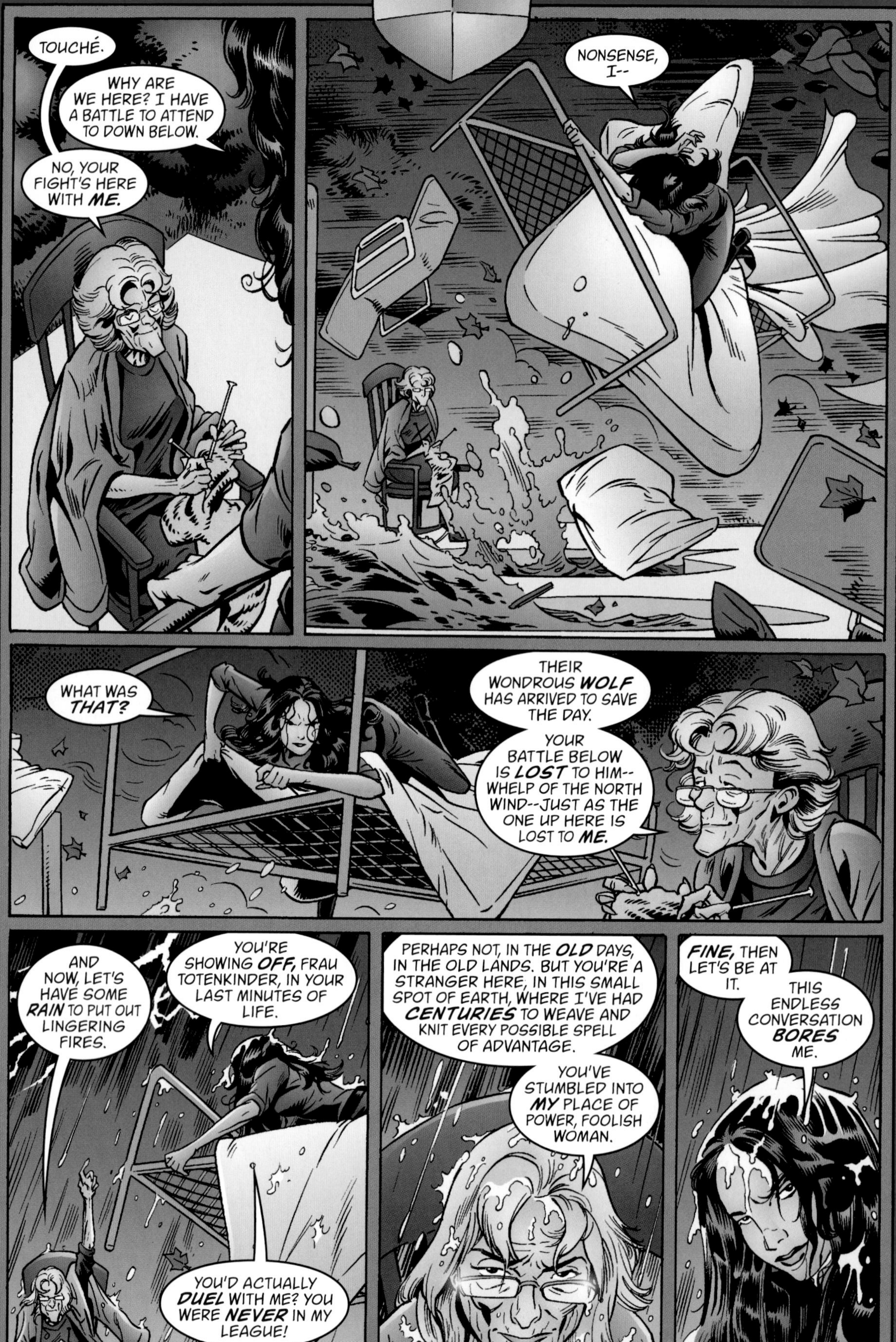

TOUCHÉ.
WHY ARE WE HERE? I HAVE A BATTLE TO ATTEND TO DOWN BELOW.
NO, YOUR FIGHT'S HERE WITH ME.
NONSENSE, I--
WHAT WAS THAT?
THEIR WONDROUS WOLF HAS ARRIVED TO SAVE THE DAY.
YOUR BATTLE BELOW IS LOST TO HIM-- WHELP OF THE NORTH WIND--JUST AS THE ONE UP HERE IS LOST TO ME.
AND NOW, LET'S HAVE SOME RAIN TO PUT OUT LINGERING FIRES.
YOU'RE SHOWING OFF, FRAU TOTENKINDER, IN YOUR LAST MINUTES OF LIFE.
YOU'D ACTUALLY DUEL WITH ME? YOU WERE NEVER IN MY LEAGUE!
PERHAPS NOT, IN THE OLD DAYS, IN THE OLD LANDS. BUT YOU'RE A STRANGER HERE, IN THIS SMALL SPOT OF EARTH, WHERE I'VE HAD CENTURIES TO WEAVE AND KNIT EVERY POSSIBLE SPELL OF ADVANTAGE.
YOU'VE STUMBLED INTO MY PLACE OF POWER, FOOLISH WOMAN.
FINE, THEN LET'S BE AT IT.
THIS ENDLESS CONVERSATION BORES ME.

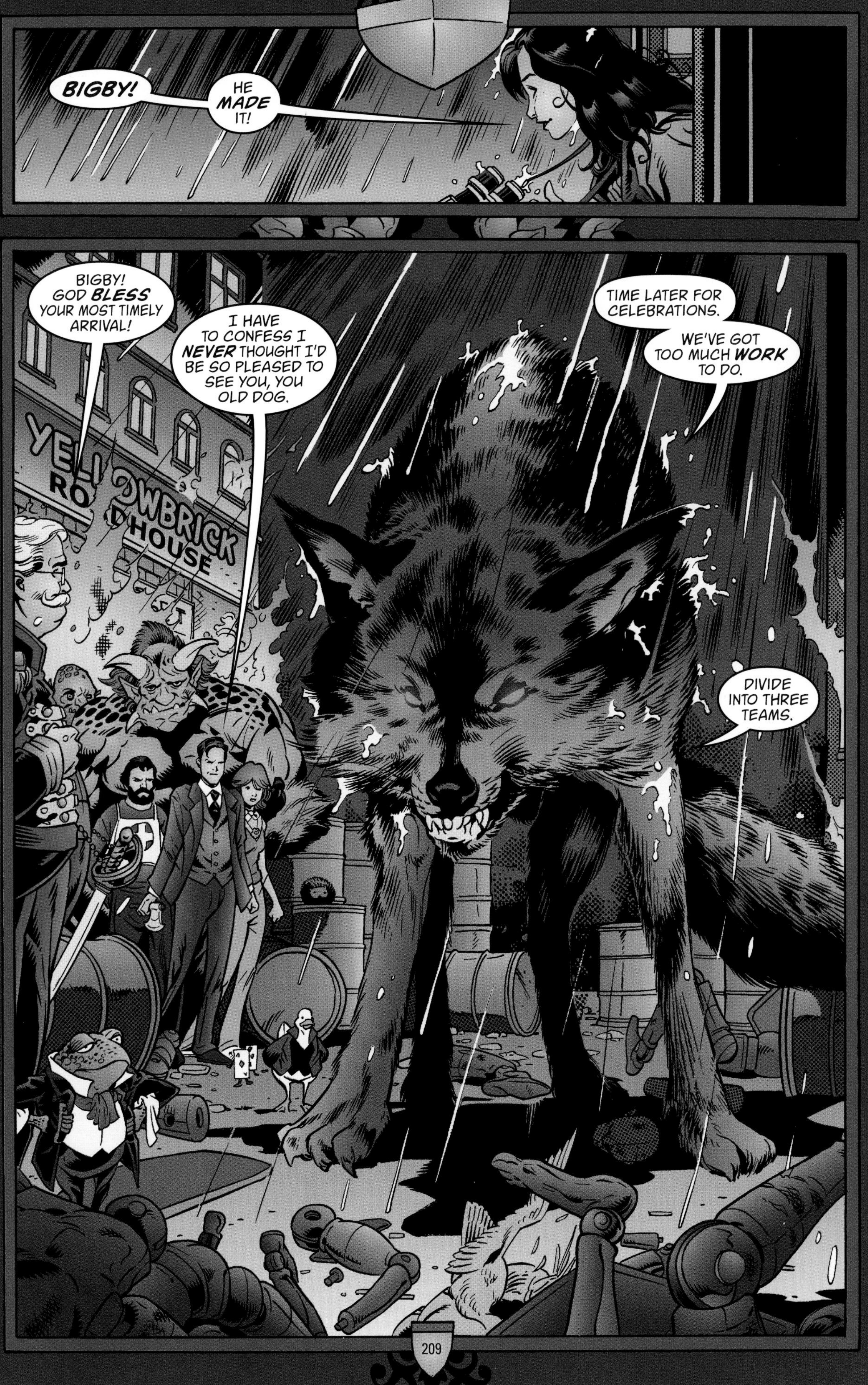
BIGBY!
HE MADE IT!
BIGBY! GOD BLESS YOUR MOST TIMELY ARRIVAL!
I HAVE TO CONFESS I NEVER THOUGHT I'D BE SO PLEASED TO SEE YOU, YOU OLD DOG.
TIME LATER FOR CELEBRATIONS.
WE'VE GOT TOO MUCH WORK TO DO.
DIVIDE INTO THREE TEAMS.
YELLOWBRICK ROADHOUSE

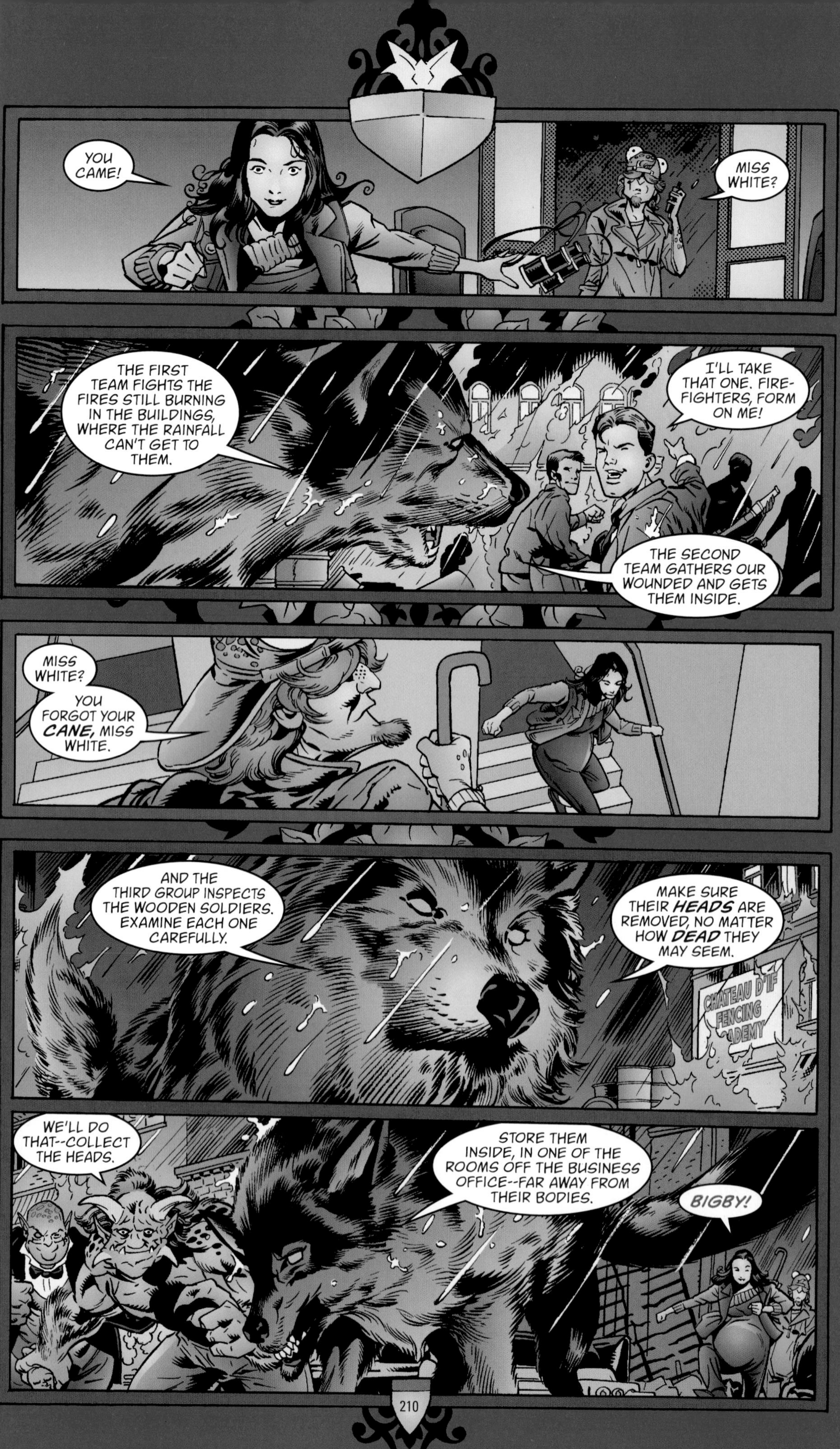

YOU CAME!
MISS WHITE?
THE FIRST TEAM FIGHTS THE FIRES STILL BURNING IN THE BUILDINGS, WHERE THE RAINFALL CAN'T GET TO THEM.
I'LL TAKE THAT ONE. FIRE-FIGHTERS, FORM ON ME!
THE SECOND TEAM GATHERS OUR WOUNDED AND GETS THEM INSIDE.
MISS WHITE?
YOU FORGOT YOUR CANE, MISS WHITE.
AND THE THIRD GROUP INSPECTS THE WOODEN SOLDIERS. EXAMINE EACH ONE CAREFULLY.
MAKE SURE THEIR HEADS ARE REMOVED, NO MATTER HOW DEAD THEY MAY SEEM.
CHATEAU D'IF FENCING ADEMY
WE'LL DO THAT--COLLECT THE HEADS.
STORE THEM INSIDE, IN ONE OF THE ROOMS OFF THE BUSINESS OFFICE--FAR AWAY FROM THEIR BODIES.
BIGBY!

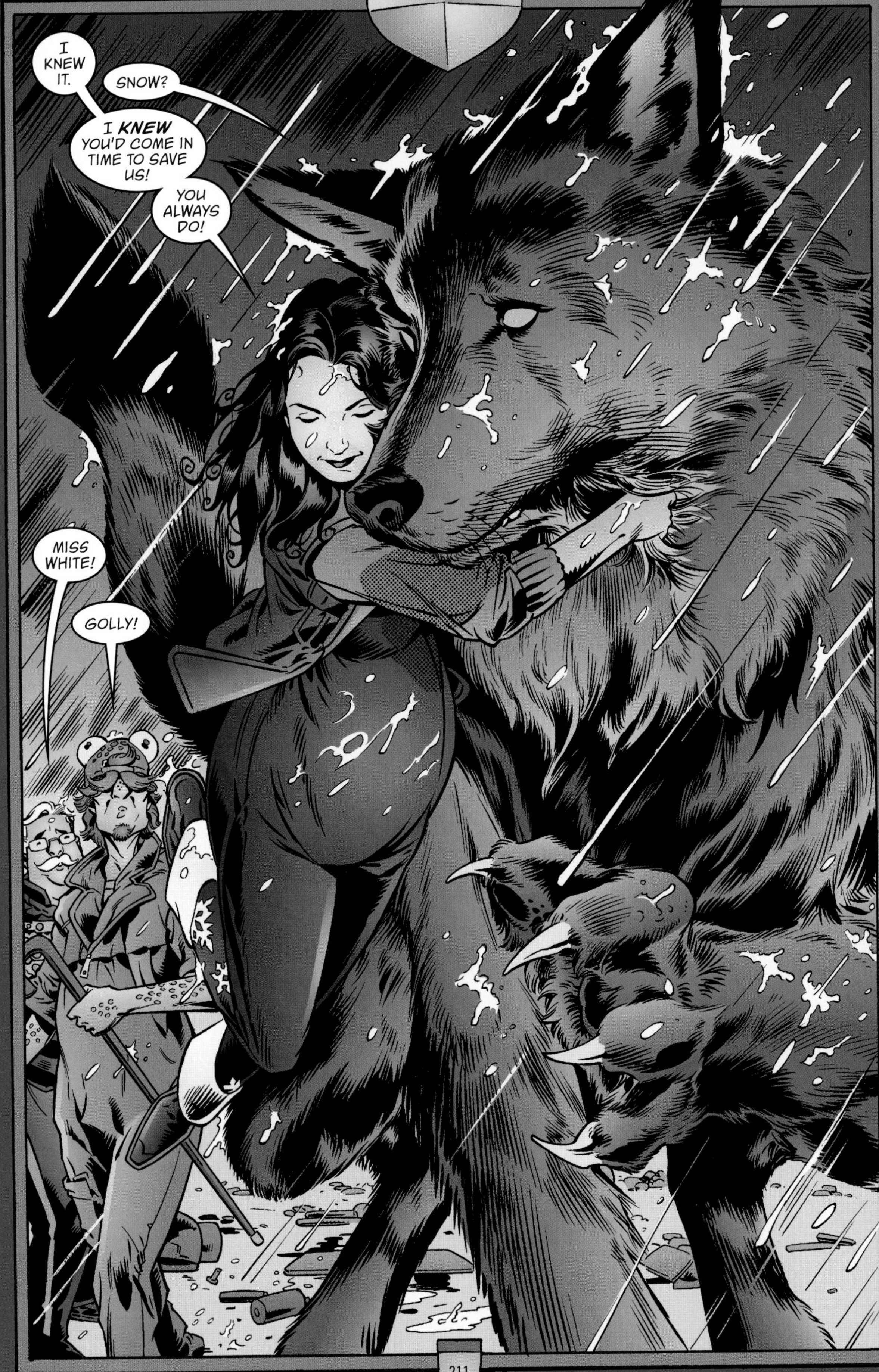
I KNEW IT.
SNOW?
I KNEW YOU'D COME IN TIME TO SAVE US!
YOU ALWAYS DO!
MISS WHITE!
GOLLY!

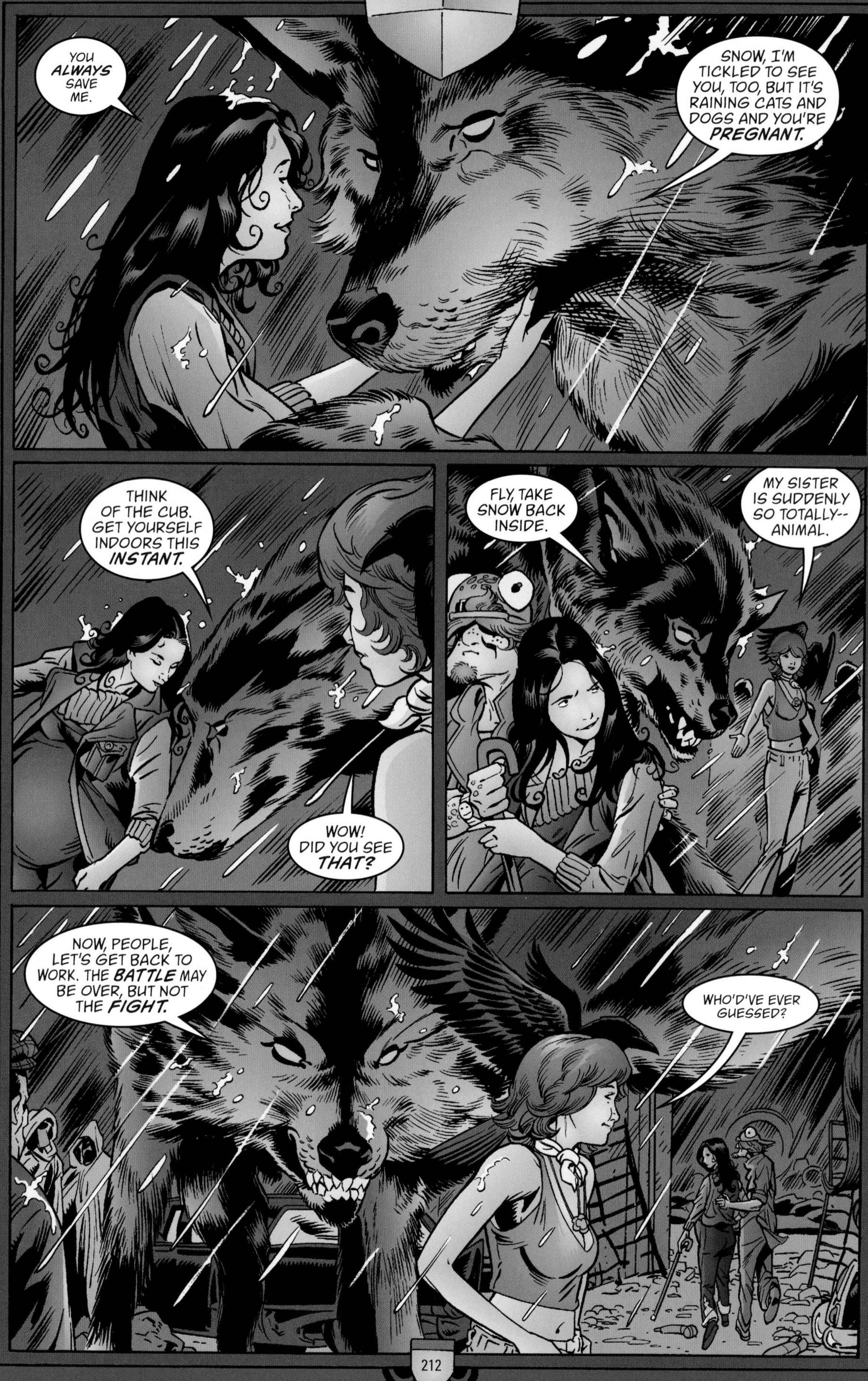
YOU ALWAYS SAVE ME.
SNOW, I'M TICKLED TO SEE YOU, TOO, BUT IT'S RAINING CATS AND DOGS AND YOU'RE PREGNANT.
THINK OF THE CUB. GET YOURSELF INDOORS THIS INSTANT.
WOW! DID YOU SEE THAT?
FLY, TAKE SNOW BACK INSIDE.
MY SISTER IS SUDDENLY SO TOTALLY-- ANIMAL.
NOW, PEOPLE, LET'S GET BACK TO WORK. THE BATTLE MAY BE OVER, BUT NOT THE FIGHT.
WHO'D'VE EVER GUESSED?

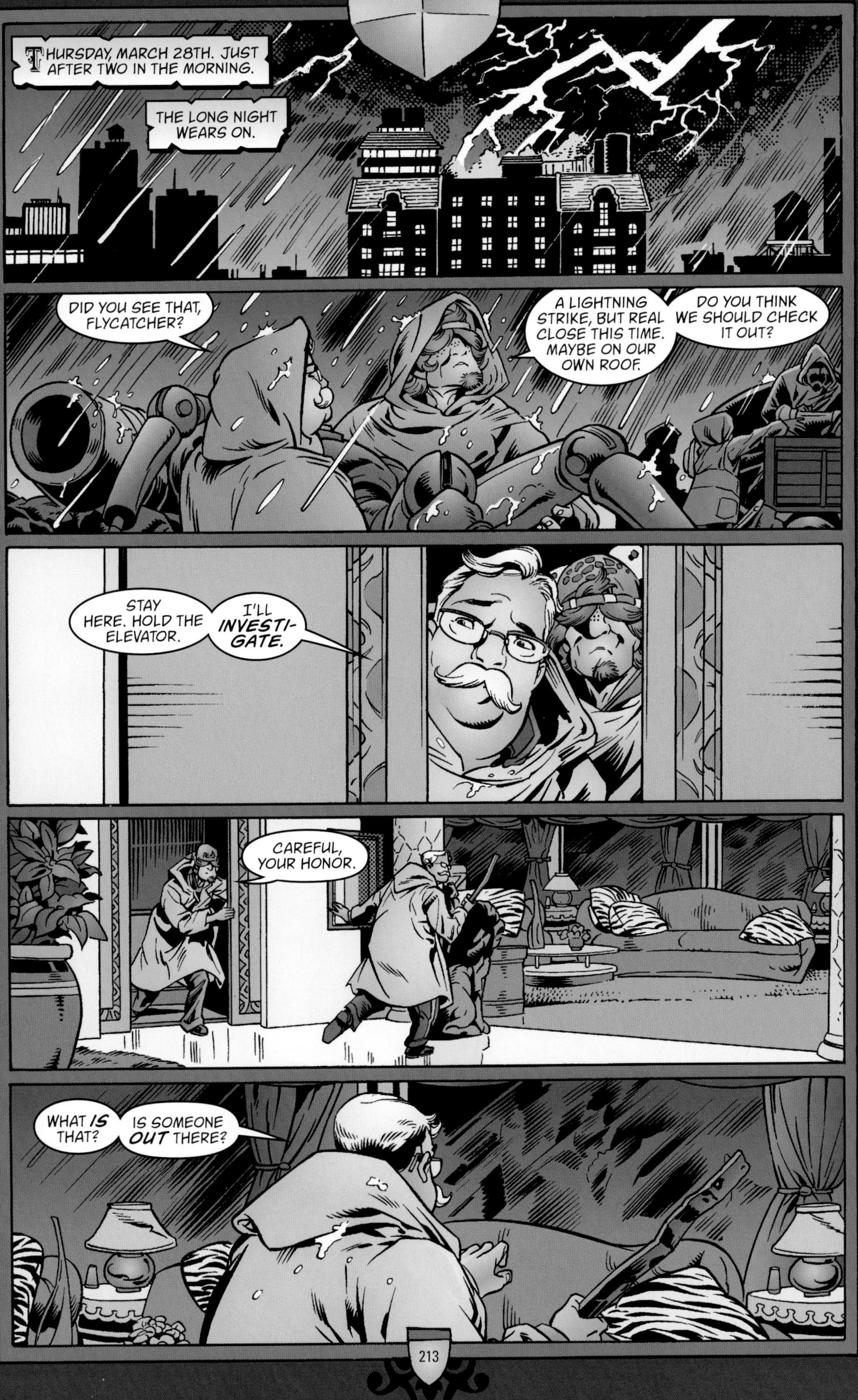
THURSDAY, MARCH 28TH. JUST AFTER TWO IN THE MORNING.
THE LONG NIGHT WEARS ON.
DID YOU SEE THAT, FLYCATCHER?
A LIGHTNING STRIKE, BUT REAL CLOSE THIS TIME. MAYBE ON OUR OWN ROOF.
DO YOU THINK WE SHOULD CHECK IT OUT?
STAY HERE. HOLD THE ELEVATOR.
I'LL INVESTIGATE.
CAREFUL, YOUR HONOR.
WHAT IS THAT?
IS SOMEONE OUT THERE?

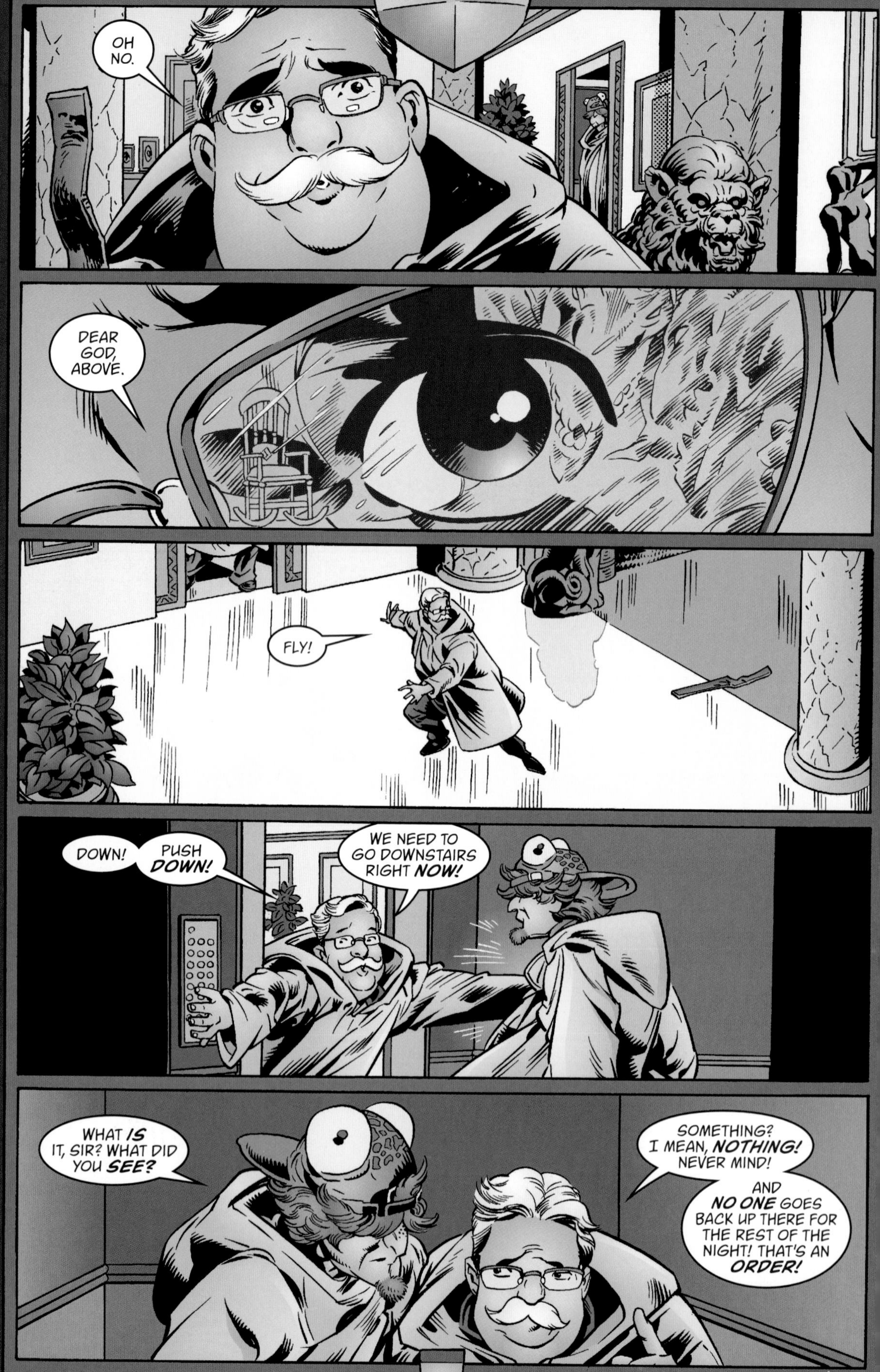
OH NO.
DEAR GOD, ABOVE.
FLY!
DOWN!
PUSH DOWN!
WE NEED TO GO DOWNSTAIRS RIGHT NOW!
WHAT IS IT, SIR? WHAT DID YOU SEE?
SOMETHING? I MEAN, NOTHING! NEVER MIND!
AND NO ONE GOES BACK UP THERE FOR THE REST OF THE NIGHT! THAT'S AN ORDER!

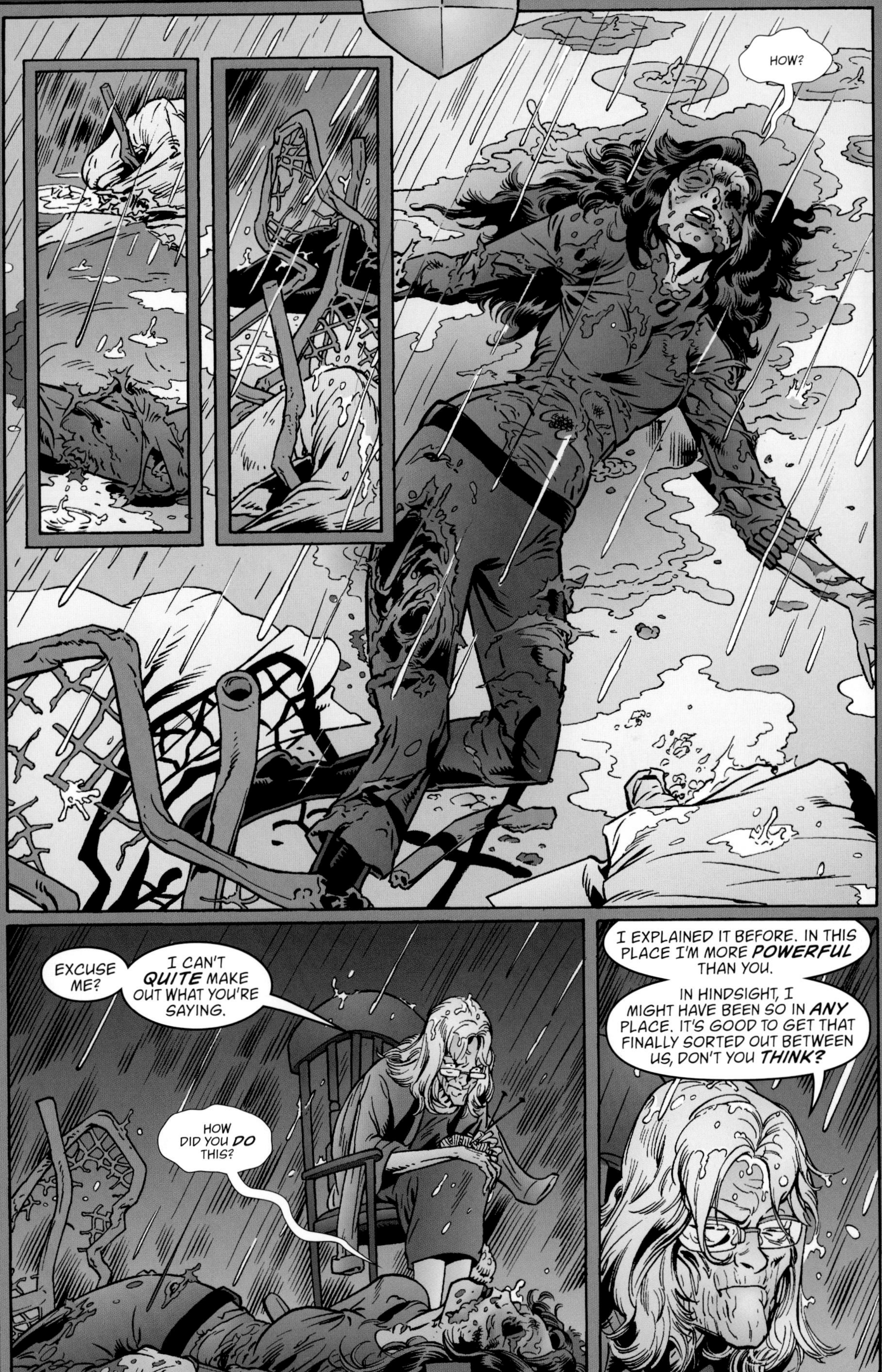
HOW?
EXCUSE ME?
I CAN'T QUITE MAKE OUT WHAT YOU'RE SAYING.
HOW DID YOU DO THIS?
I EXPLAINED IT BEFORE. IN THIS PLACE I'M MORE POWERFUL THAN YOU.
IN HINDSIGHT, I MIGHT HAVE BEEN SO IN ANY PLACE. IT'S GOOD TO GET THAT FINALLY SORTED OUT BETWEEN US, DON'T YOU THINK?

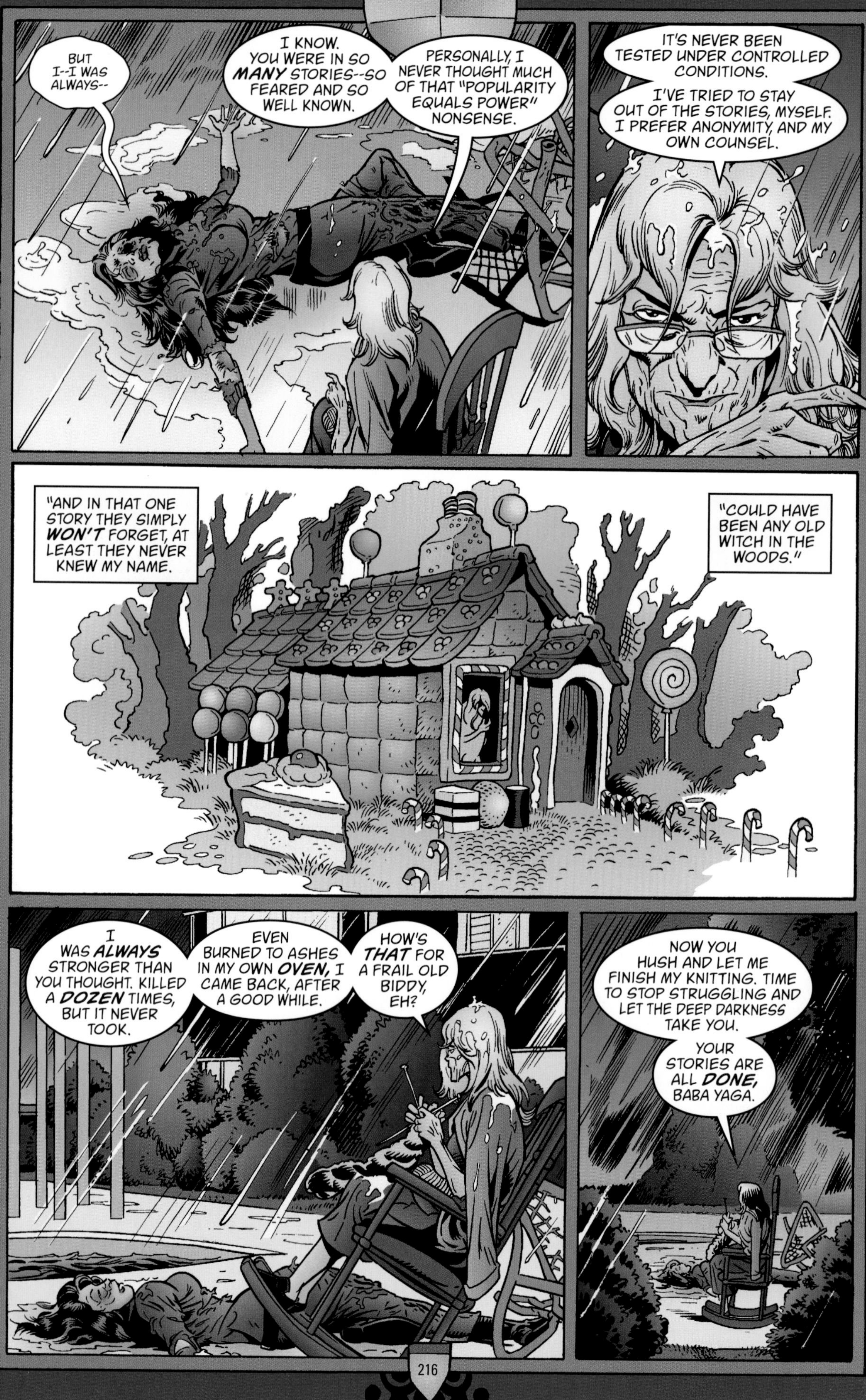
BUT I--I WAS ALWAYS--
I KNOW. YOU WERE IN SO MANY STORIES--SO FEARED AND SO WELL KNOWN.
PERSONALLY, I NEVER THOUGHT MUCH OF THAT "POPULARITY EQUALS POWER" NONSENSE.
IT'S NEVER BEEN TESTED UNDER CONTROLLED CONDITIONS.
I'VE TRIED TO STAY OUT OF THE STORIES, MYSELF. I PREFER ANONYMITY, AND MY OWN COUNSEL.
"AND IN THAT ONE STORY THEY SIMPLY WON'T FORGET, AT LEAST THEY NEVER KNEW MY NAME.
"COULD HAVE BEEN ANY OLD WITCH IN THE WOODS."
I WAS ALWAYS STRONGER THAN YOU THOUGHT. KILLED A DOZEN TIMES, BUT IT NEVER TOOK.
EVEN BURNED TO ASHES IN MY OWN OVEN, I CAME BACK, AFTER A GOOD WHILE.
HOW'S THAT FOR A FRAIL OLD BIDDY, EH?
NOW YOU HUSH AND LET ME FINISH MY KNITTING. TIME TO STOP STRUGGLING AND LET THE DEEP DARKNESS TAKE YOU.
YOUR STORIES ARE ALL DONE, BABA YAGA.

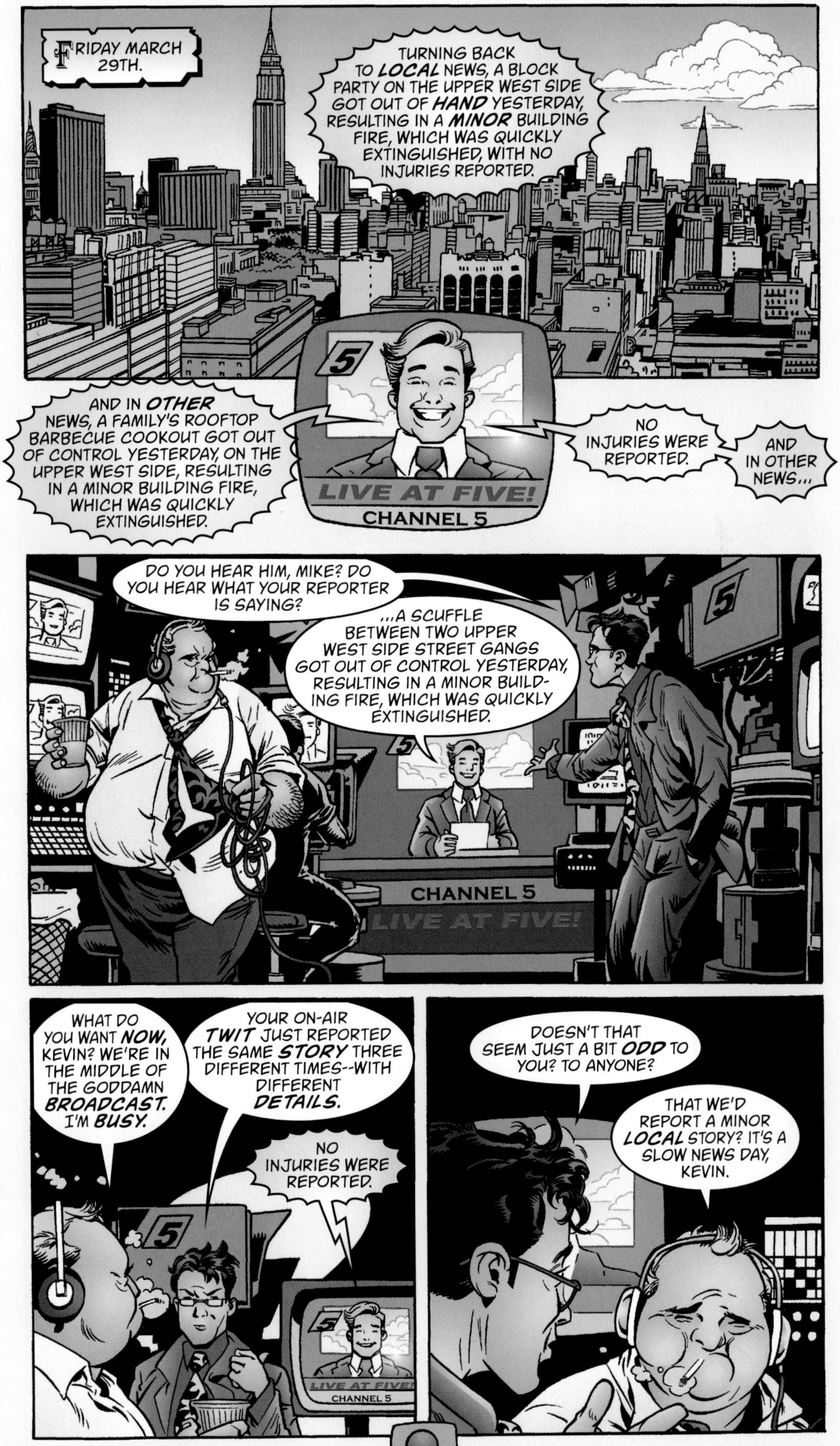
FRIDAY MARCH 29TH.
TURNING BACK TO LOCAL NEWS, A BLOCK PARTY ON THE UPPER WEST SIDE GOT OUT OF HAND YESTERDAY, RESULTING IN A MINOR BUILDING FIRE, WHICH WAS QUICKLY EXTINGUISHED, WITH NO INJURIES REPORTED.
AND IN OTHER NEWS, A FAMILY'S ROOFTOP BARBECUE COOKOUT GOT OUT OF CONTROL YESTERDAY, ON THE UPPER WEST SIDE, RESULTING IN A MINOR BUILDING FIRE, WHICH WAS QUICKLY EXTINGUISHED.
5
LIVE AT FIVE!
CHANNEL 5
NO INJURIES WERE REPORTED.
AND IN OTHER NEWS...
DO YOU HEAR HIM, MIKE? DO YOU HEAR WHAT YOUR REPORTER IS SAYING?
...A SCUFFLE BETWEEN TWO UPPER WEST SIDE STREET GANGS GOT OUT OF CONTROL YESTERDAY, RESULTING IN A MINOR BUILDING FIRE, WHICH WAS QUICKLY EXTINGUISHED.
CHANNEL 5
LIVE AT FIVE!
WHAT DO YOU WANT NOW, KEVIN? WE'RE IN THE MIDDLE OF THE GODDAMN BROADCAST. I'M BUSY.
YOUR ON-AIR TWIT JUST REPORTED THE SAME STORY THREE DIFFERENT TIMES--WITH DIFFERENT DETAILS.
NO INJURIES WERE REPORTED.
LIVE AT FIVE!
CHANNEL 5
DOESN'T THAT SEEM JUST A BIT ODD TO YOU? TO ANYONE?
THAT WE'D REPORT A MINOR LOCAL STORY? IT'S A SLOW NEWS DAY, KEVIN.

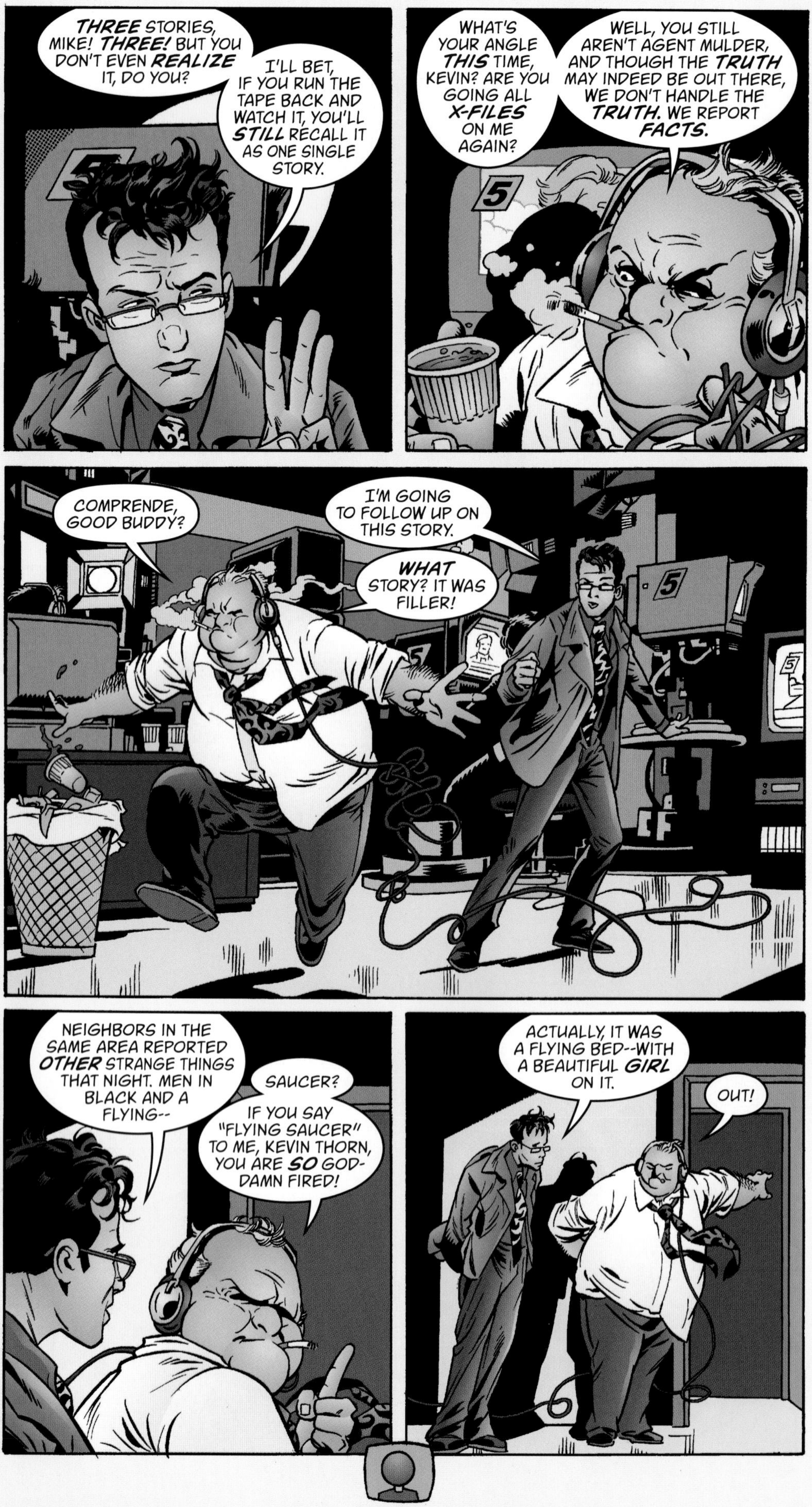
THREE STORIES, MIKE! THREE! BUT YOU DON'T EVEN REALIZE IT, DO YOU?
I'LL BET, IF YOU RUN THE TAPE BACK AND WATCH IT, YOU'LL STILL RECALL IT AS ONE SINGLE STORY.
WHAT'S YOUR ANGLE THIS TIME, KEVIN? ARE YOU GOING ALL X-FILES ON ME AGAIN?
WELL, YOU STILL AREN'T AGENT MULDER, AND THOUGH THE TRUTH MAY INDEED BE OUT THERE, WE DON'T HANDLE THE TRUTH. WE REPORT FACTS.
COMPRENDE, GOOD BUDDY?
I'M GOING TO FOLLOW UP ON THIS STORY.
WHAT STORY? IT WAS FILLER!
NEIGHBORS IN THE SAME AREA REPORTED OTHER STRANGE THINGS THAT NIGHT. MEN IN BLACK AND A FLYING--
SAUCER?
IF YOU SAY "FLYING SAUCER" TO ME, KEVIN THORN, YOU ARE SO GOD-DAMN FIRED!
ACTUALLY, IT WAS A FLYING BED--WITH A BEAUTIFUL GIRL ON IT.
OUT!

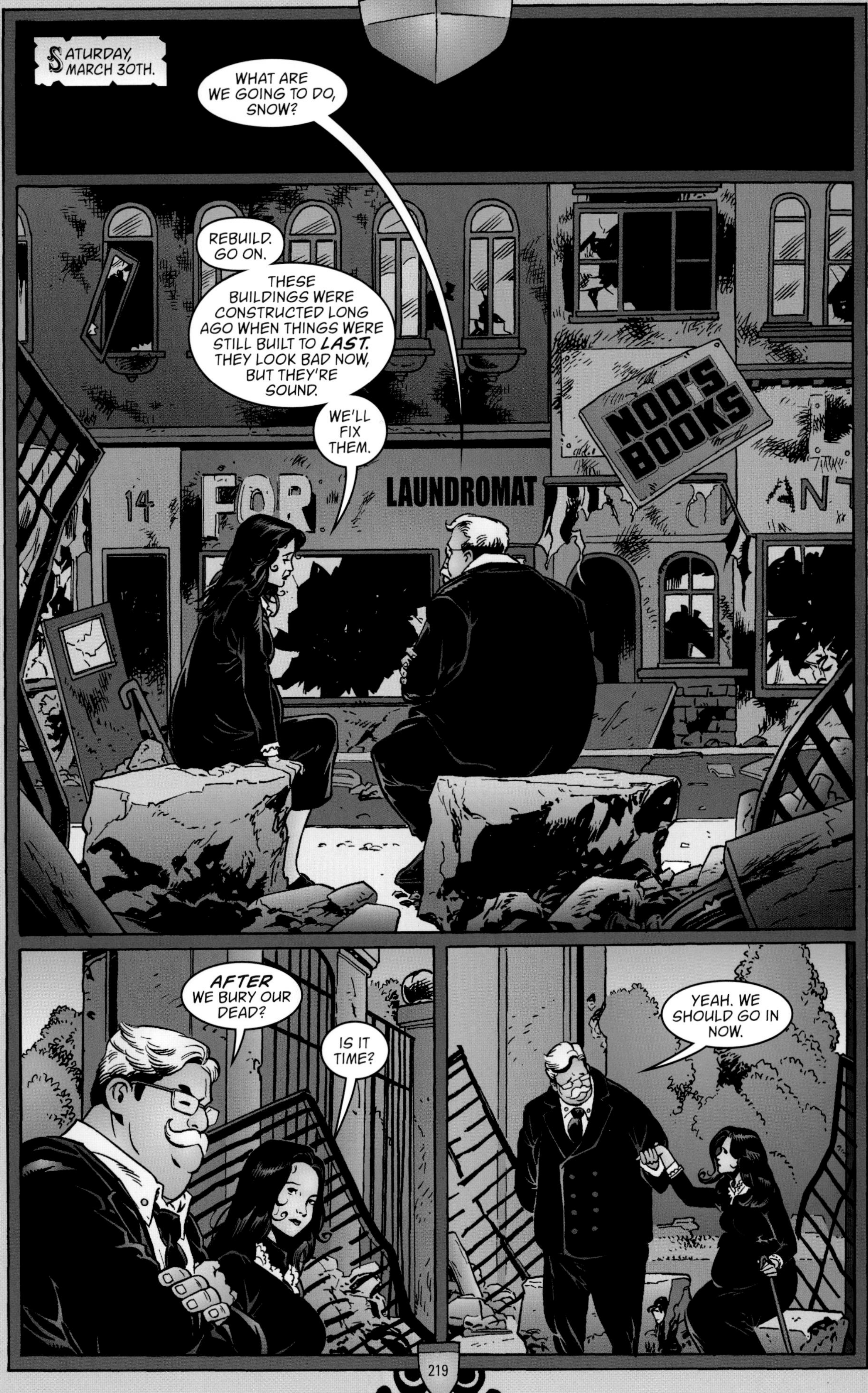
SATURDAY, MARCH 30TH.
WHAT ARE WE GOING TO DO, SNOW?
REBUILD. GO ON.
THESE BUILDINGS WERE CONSTRUCTED LONG AGO WHEN THINGS WERE STILL BUILT TO *LAST.* THEY LOOK BAD NOW, BUT THEY'RE SOUND.
WE'LL FIX THEM.
14
FOR
LAUNDROMAT
NOD'S BOOKS
AFTER WE BURY OUR DEAD?
IS IT TIME?
YEAH. WE SHOULD GO IN NOW.

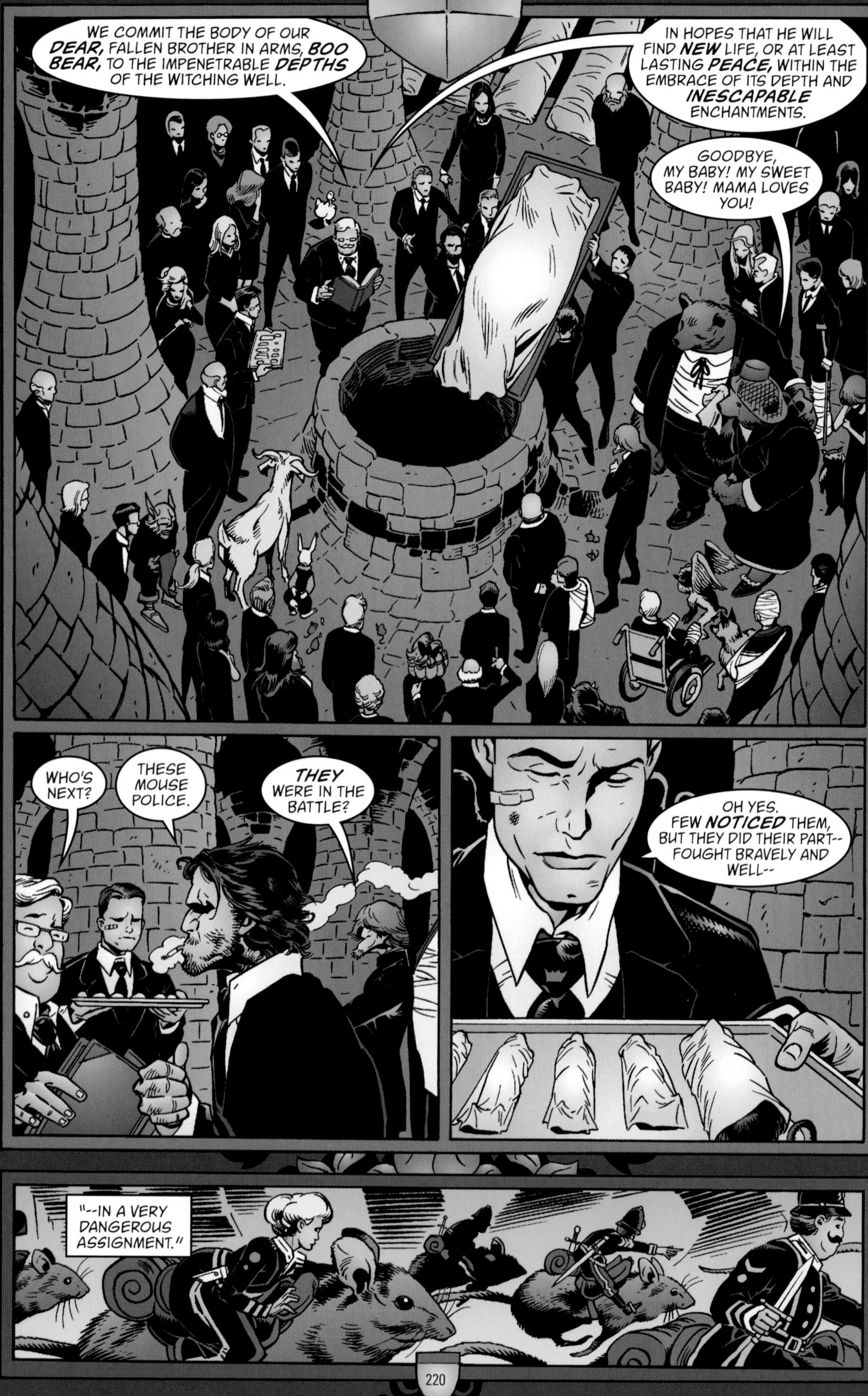

WE COMMIT THE BODY OF OUR DEAR, FALLEN BROTHER IN ARMS, BOO BEAR, TO THE IMPENETRABLE DEPTHS OF THE WITCHING WELL.
IN HOPES THAT HE WILL FIND NEW LIFE, OR AT LEAST LASTING PEACE, WITHIN THE EMBRACE OF ITS DEPTH AND INESCAPABLE ENCHANTMENTS.
GOODBYE, MY BABY! MY SWEET BABY! MAMA LOVES YOU!
WHO'S NEXT?
THESE MOUSE POLICE.
THEY WERE IN THE BATTLE?
OH YES. FEW NOTICED THEM, BUT THEY DID THEIR PART-- FOUGHT BRAVELY AND WELL--
"--IN A VERY DANGEROUS ASSIGNMENT."

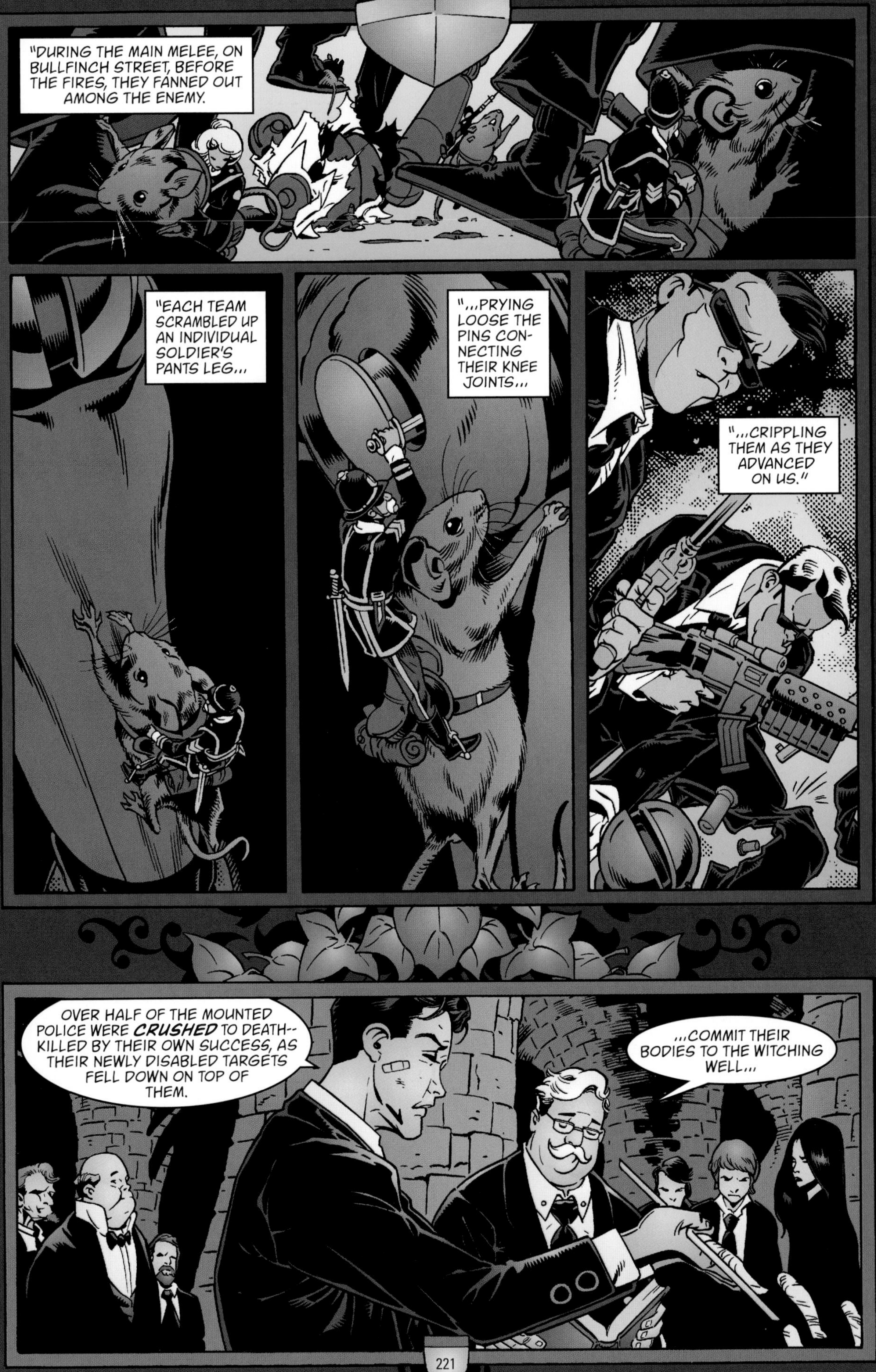
"DURING THE MAIN MELEE, ON BULLFINCH STREET, BEFORE THE FIRES, THEY FANNED OUT AMONG THE ENEMY.
"EACH TEAM SCRAMBLED UP AN INDIVIDUAL SOLDIER'S PANTS LEG...
"...PRYING LOOSE THE PINS CONNECTING THEIR KNEE JOINTS...
"...CRIPPLING THEM AS THEY ADVANCED ON US."
OVER HALF OF THE MOUNTED POLICE WERE CRUSHED TO DEATH-- KILLED BY THEIR OWN SUCCESS, AS THEIR NEWLY DISABLED TARGETS FELL DOWN ON TOP OF THEM.
...COMMIT THEIR BODIES TO THE WITCHING WELL...

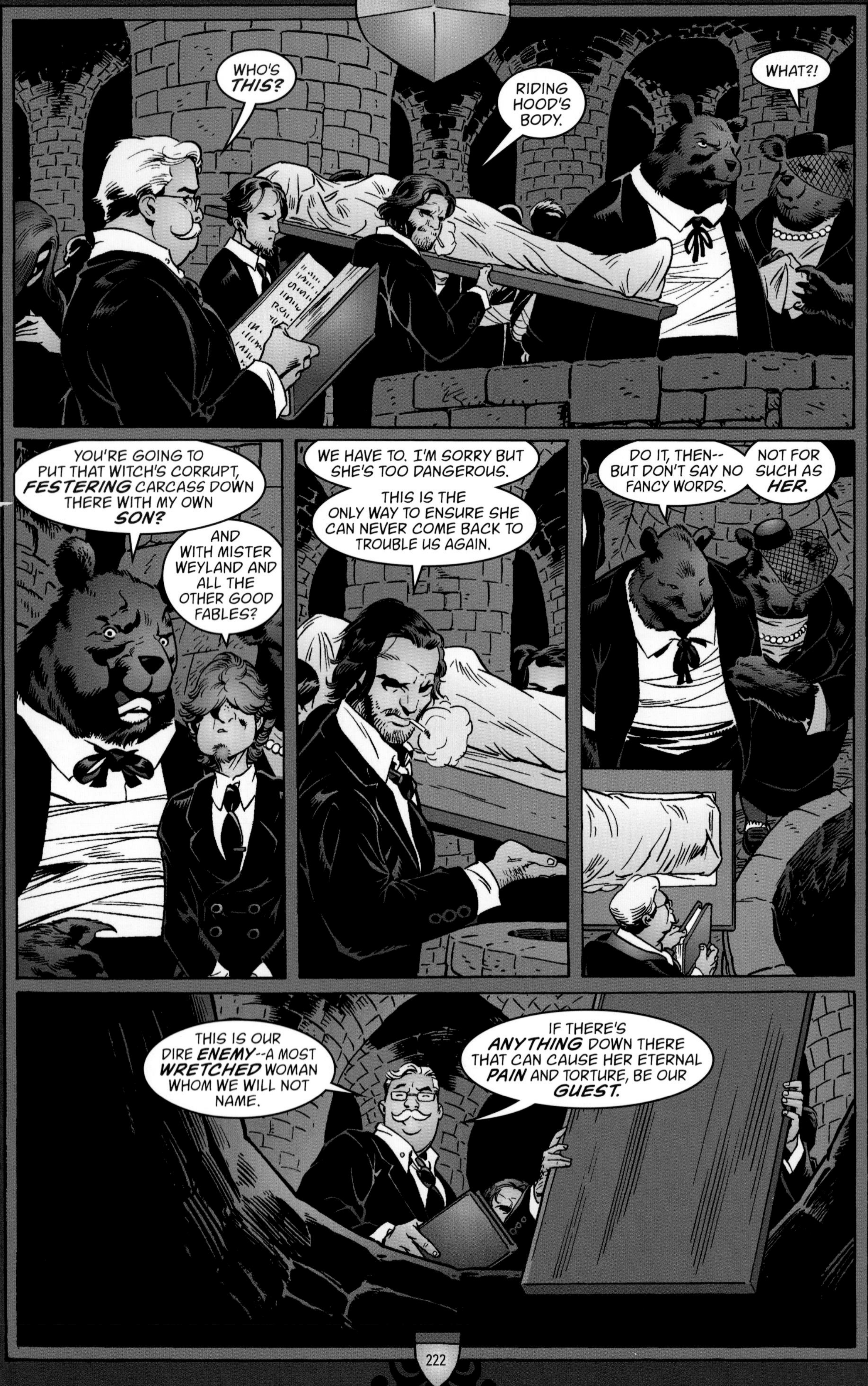
WHO'S THIS?
RIDING HOOD'S BODY.
WHAT?!
YOU'RE GOING TO PUT THAT WITCH'S CORRUPT, FESTERING CARCASS DOWN THERE WITH MY OWN SON?
AND WITH MISTER WEYLAND AND ALL THE OTHER GOOD FABLES?
WE HAVE TO. I'M SORRY BUT SHE'S TOO DANGEROUS.
THIS IS THE ONLY WAY TO ENSURE SHE CAN NEVER COME BACK TO TROUBLE US AGAIN.
DO IT, THEN-- BUT DON'T SAY NO FANCY WORDS.
NOT FOR SUCH AS HER.
THIS IS OUR DIRE ENEMY--A MOST WRETCHED WOMAN WHOM WE WILL NOT NAME.
IF THERE'S ANYTHING DOWN THERE THAT CAN CAUSE HER ETERNAL PAIN AND TORTURE, BE OUR GUEST.

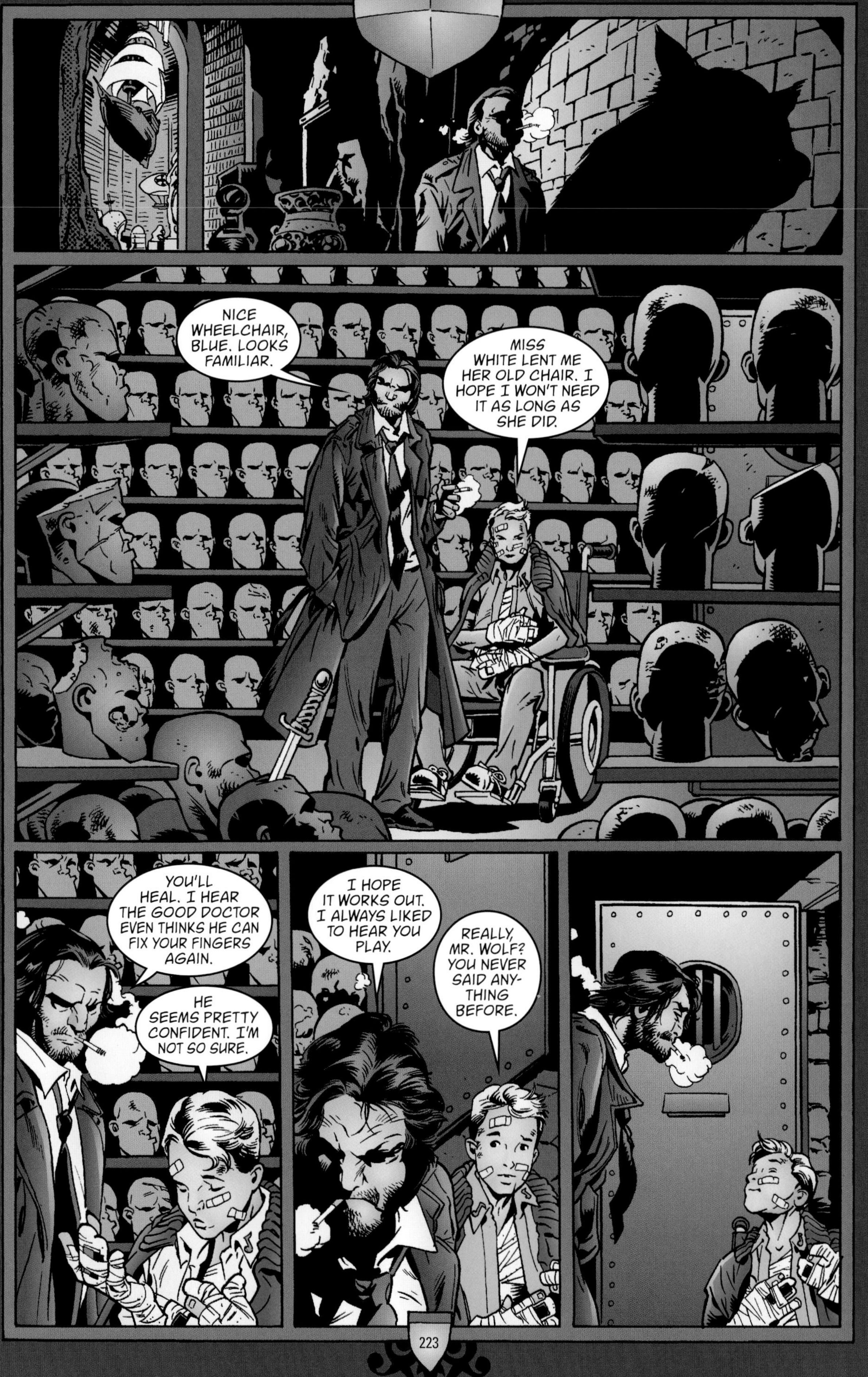
NICE WHEELCHAIR, BLUE. LOOKS FAMILIAR.
MISS WHITE LENT ME HER OLD CHAIR. I HOPE I WON'T NEED IT AS LONG AS SHE DID.
YOU'LL HEAL. I HEAR THE GOOD DOCTOR EVEN THINKS HE CAN FIX YOUR FINGERS AGAIN.
HE SEEMS PRETTY CONFIDENT. I'M NOT SO SURE.
I HOPE IT WORKS OUT. I ALWAYS LIKED TO HEAR YOU PLAY.
REALLY, MR. WOLF? YOU NEVER SAID ANY-THING BEFORE.

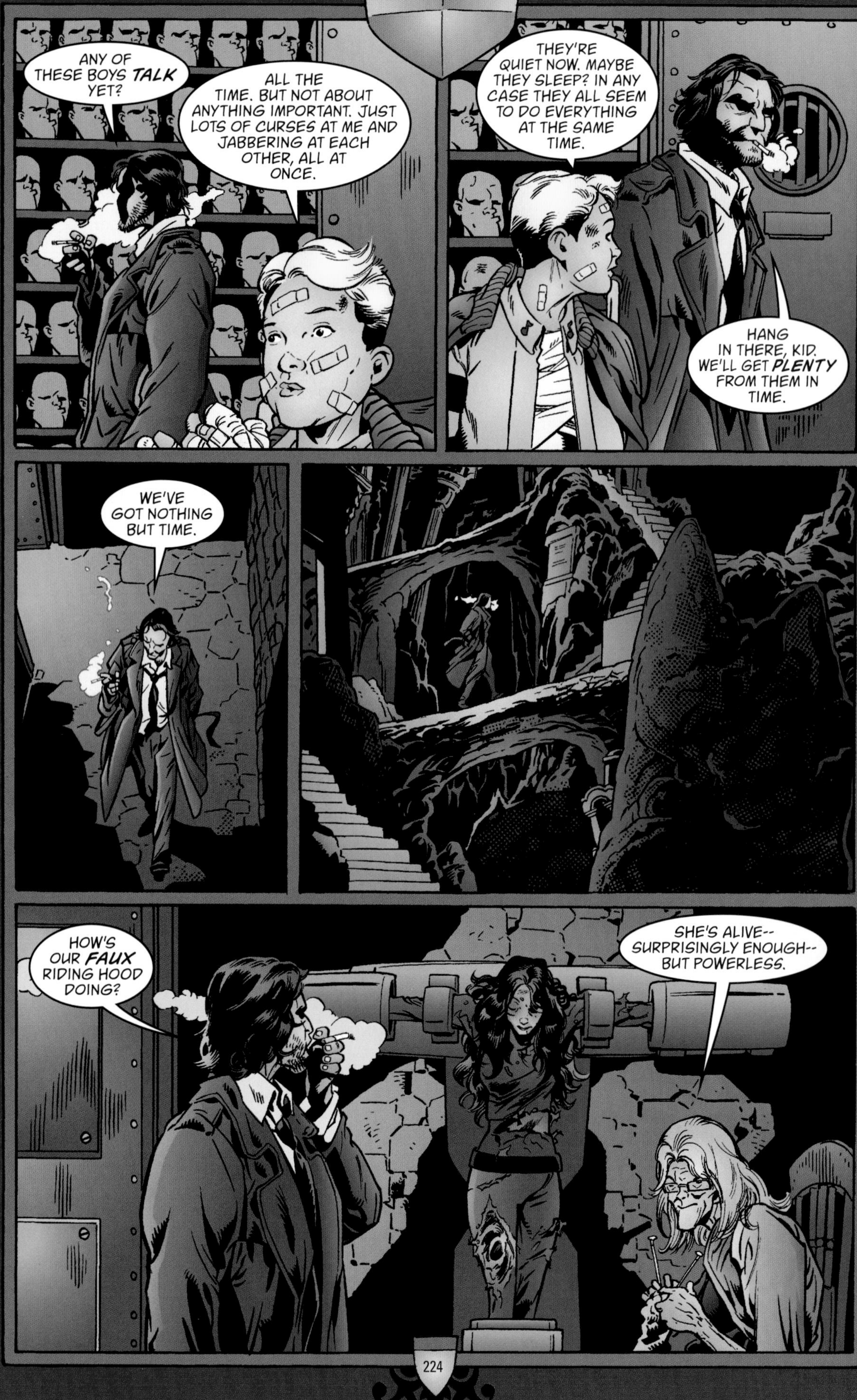
ANY OF THESE BOYS TALK YET?
ALL THE TIME. BUT NOT ABOUT ANYTHING IMPORTANT. JUST LOTS OF CURSES AT ME AND JABBERING AT EACH OTHER, ALL AT ONCE.
THEY'RE QUIET NOW. MAYBE THEY SLEEP? IN ANY CASE THEY ALL SEEM TO DO EVERYTHING AT THE SAME TIME.
HANG IN THERE, KID. WE'LL GET PLENTY FROM THEM IN TIME.
WE'VE GOT NOTHING BUT TIME.
HOW'S OUR FAUX RIDING HOOD DOING?
SHE'S ALIVE-- SURPRISINGLY ENOUGH-- BUT POWERLESS.

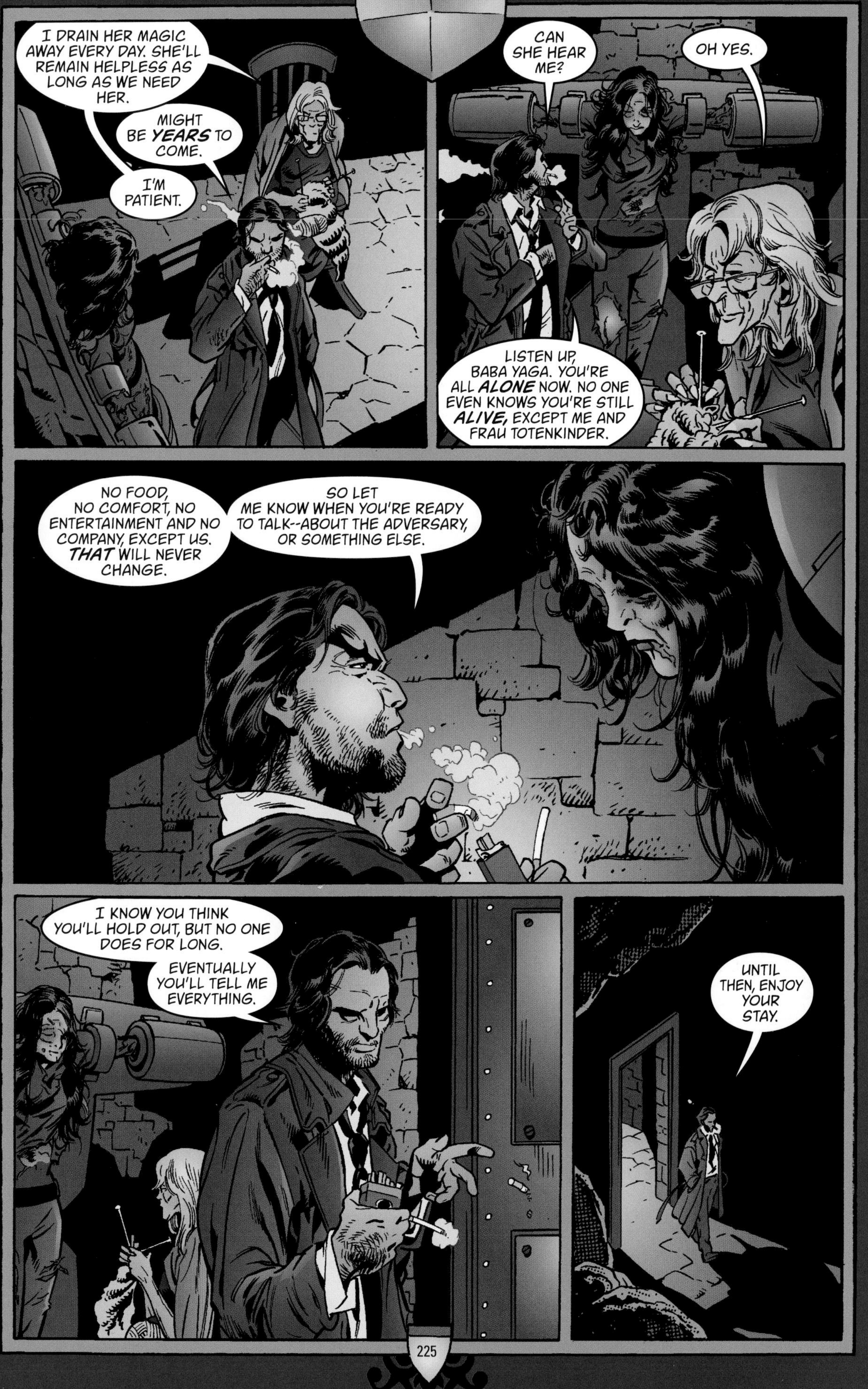

I DRAIN HER MAGIC AWAY EVERY DAY. SHE'LL REMAIN HELPLESS AS LONG AS WE NEED HER.
MIGHT BE YEARS TO COME.
I'M PATIENT.
CAN SHE HEAR ME?
OH YES.
LISTEN UP, BABA YAGA. YOU'RE ALL ALONE NOW. NO ONE EVEN KNOWS YOU'RE STILL ALIVE, EXCEPT ME AND FRAU TOTENKINDER.
NO FOOD, NO COMFORT, NO ENTERTAINMENT AND NO COMPANY, EXCEPT US. THAT WILL NEVER CHANGE.
SO LET ME KNOW WHEN YOU'RE READY TO TALK--ABOUT THE ADVERSARY, OR SOMETHING ELSE.
I KNOW YOU THINK YOU'LL HOLD OUT, BUT NO ONE DOES FOR LONG.
EVENTUALLY YOU'LL TELL ME EVERYTHING.
UNTIL THEN, ENJOY YOUR STAY.

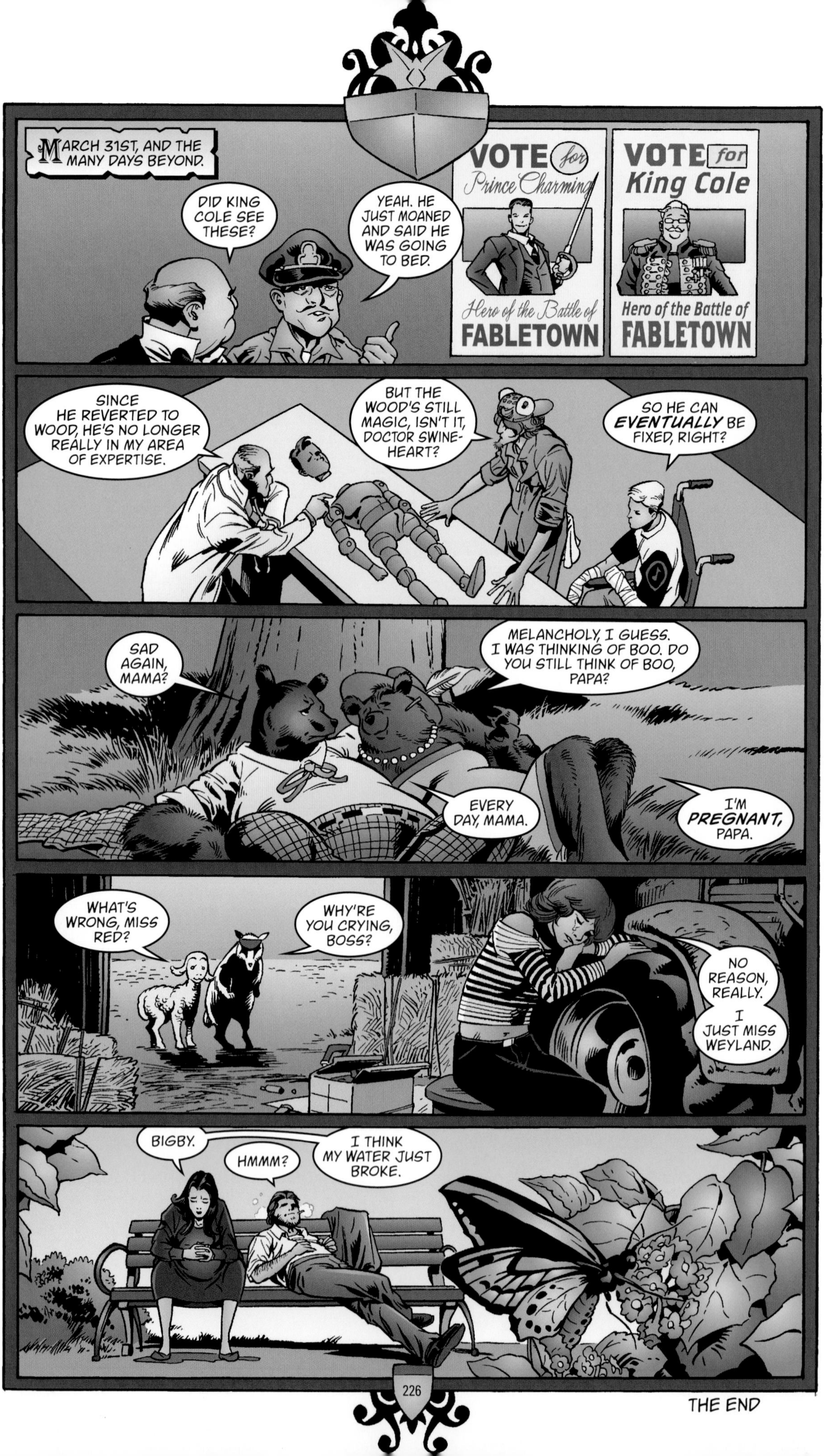
MARCH 31ST, AND THE MANY DAYS BEYOND.
DID KING COLE SEE THESE?
YEAH. HE JUST MOANED AND SAID HE WAS GOING TO BED.
VOTE for Prince Charming
Hero of the Battle of FABLETOWN
VOTE for King Cole
Hero of the Battle of FABLETOWN
SINCE HE REVERTED TO WOOD, HE'S NO LONGER REALLY IN MY AREA OF EXPERTISE.
BUT THE WOOD'S STILL MAGIC, ISN'T IT, DOCTOR SWINE-HEART?
SO HE CAN EVENTUALLY BE FIXED, RIGHT?
SAD AGAIN, MAMA?
MELANCHOLY, I GUESS. I WAS THINKING OF BOO. DO YOU STILL THINK OF BOO, PAPA?
EVERY DAY, MAMA.
I'M PREGNANT, PAPA.
WHAT'S WRONG, MISS RED?
WHY'RE YOU CRYING, BOSS?
NO REASON, REALLY.
I JUST MISS WEYLAND.
BIGBY.
HMMM?
I THINK MY WATER JUST BROKE.

THE END

Treasures from the Woodland Vaults

Below and following pages: Details and preliminary designs by Mark Buckingham for the Bigby Wolf and Snow White Statue, sculpted by Jim Maddox and released by DC Direct in 2007.

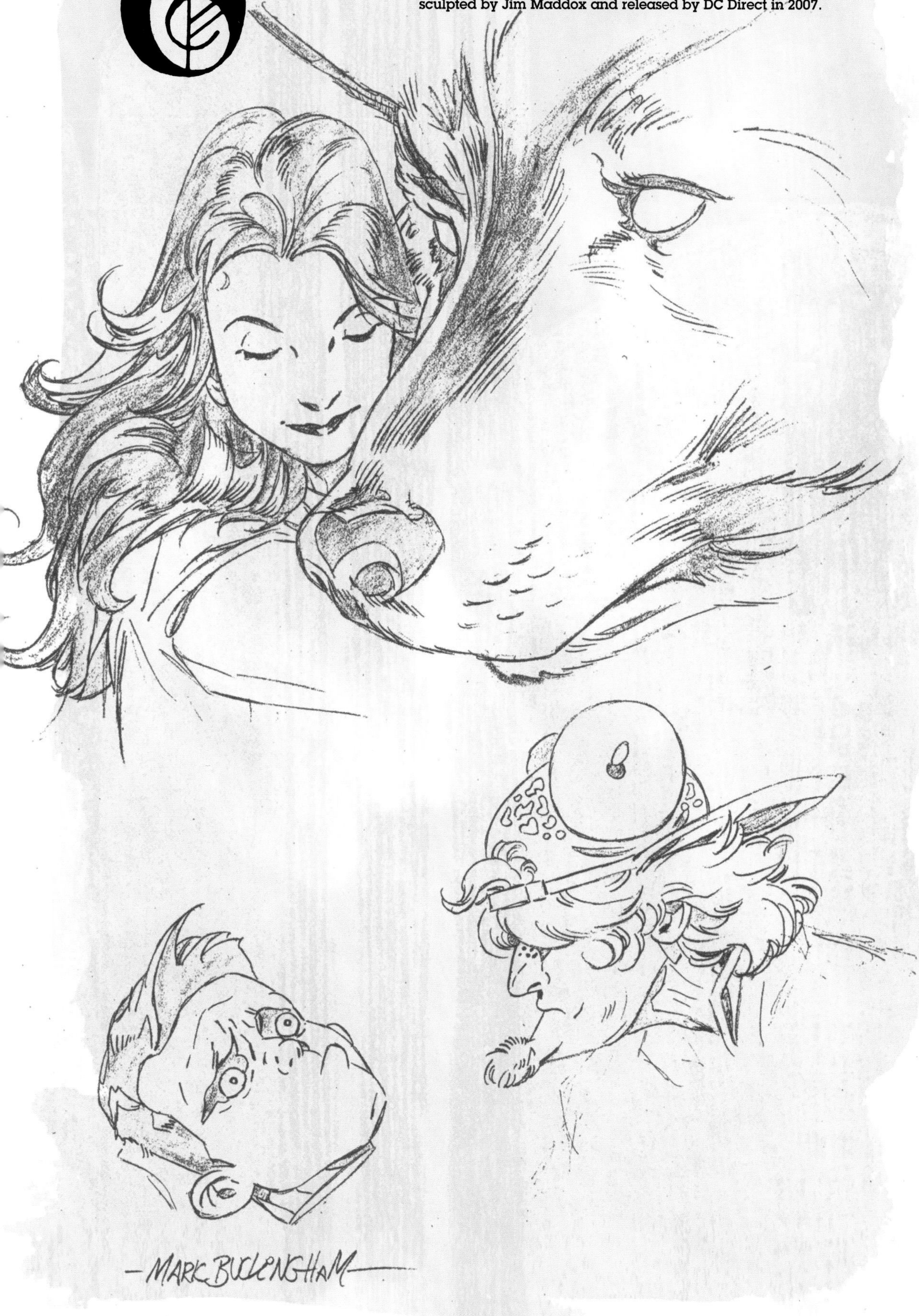

MARK BUCKINGHAM

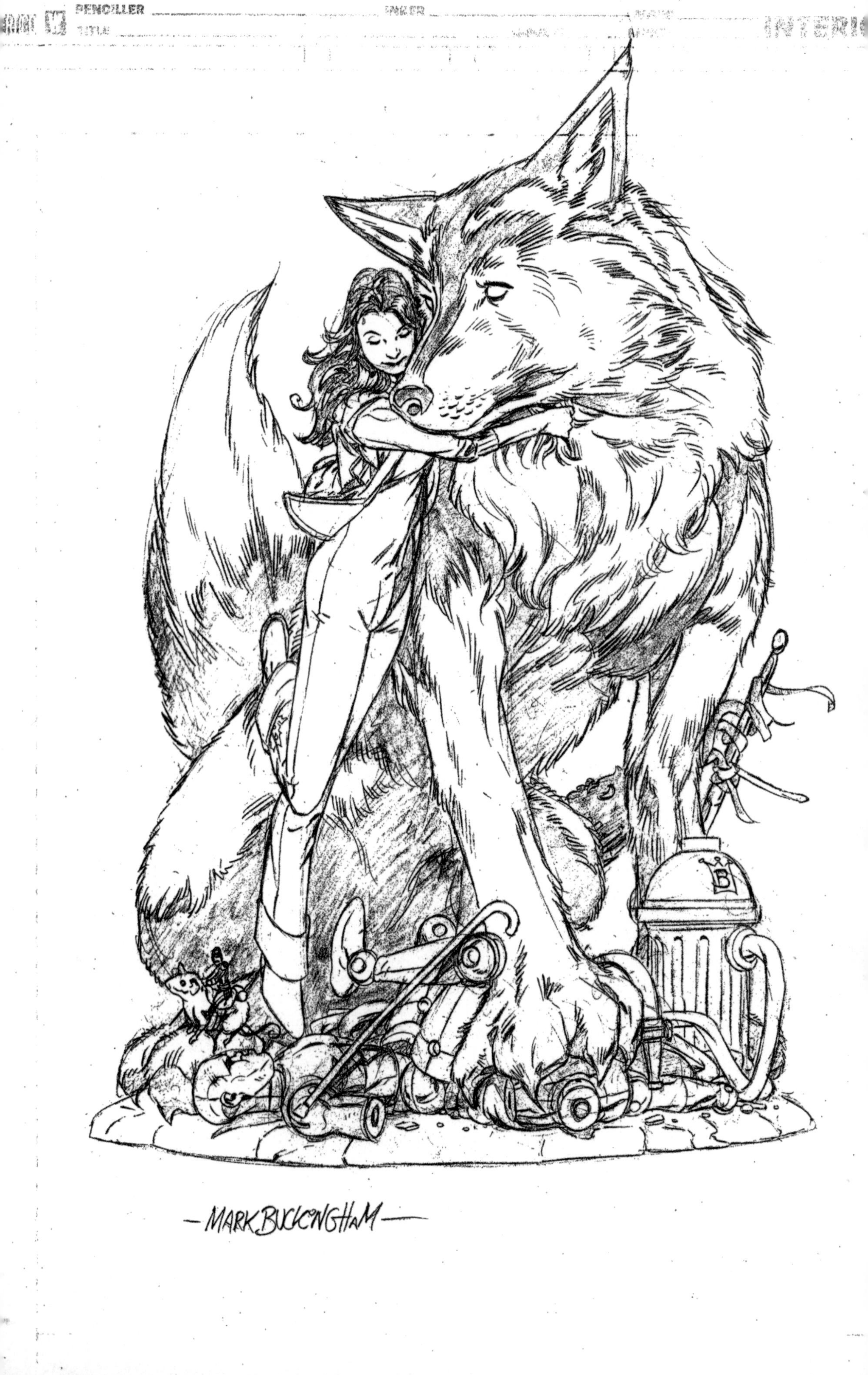
PENCILLER
INKER
TITLE
MARK BUCKINGHAM

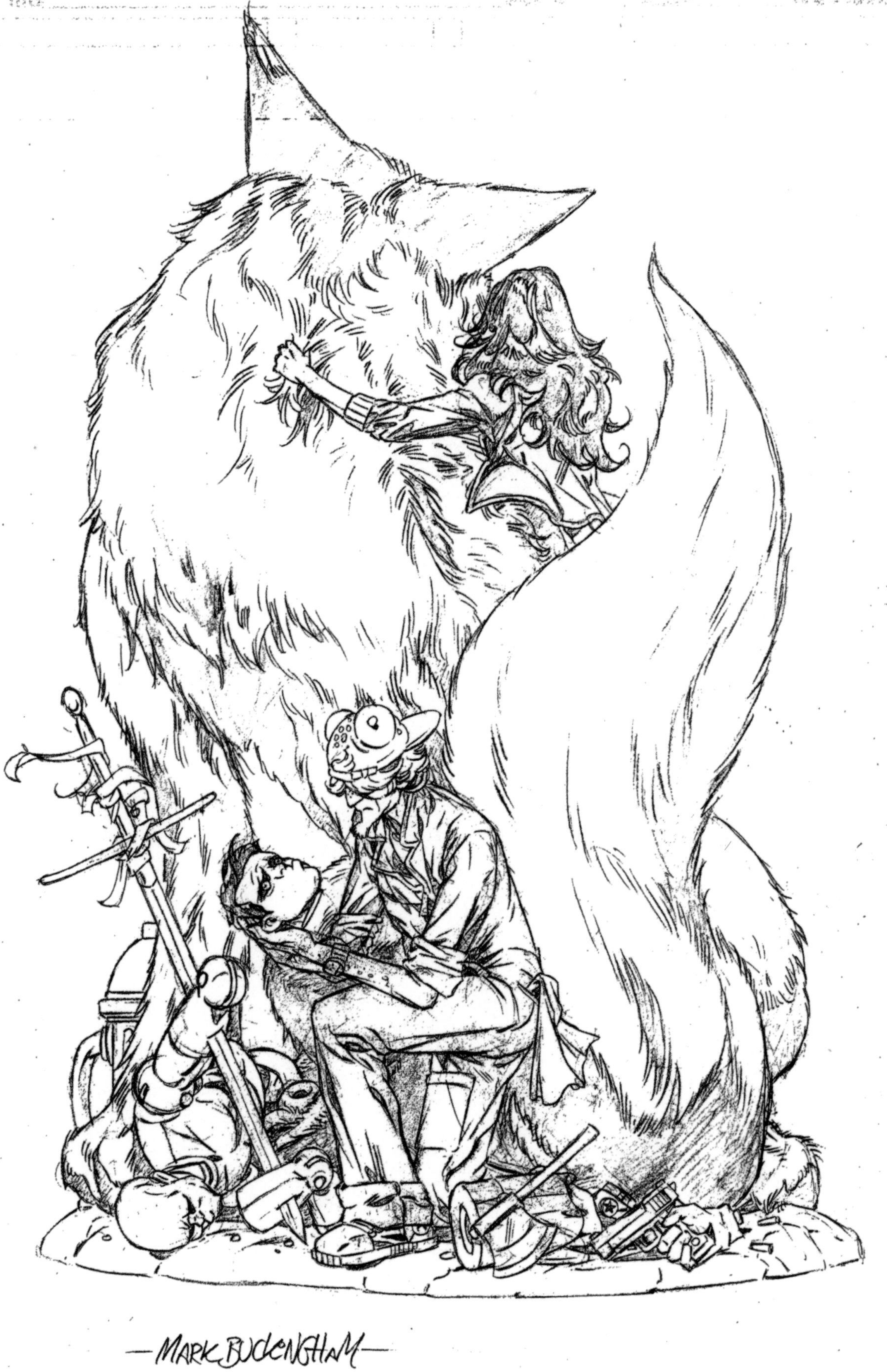
MARK BUCKINGHAM

Below: Pencils by Mark Buckingham for the climactic battle spread from FABLES #26.

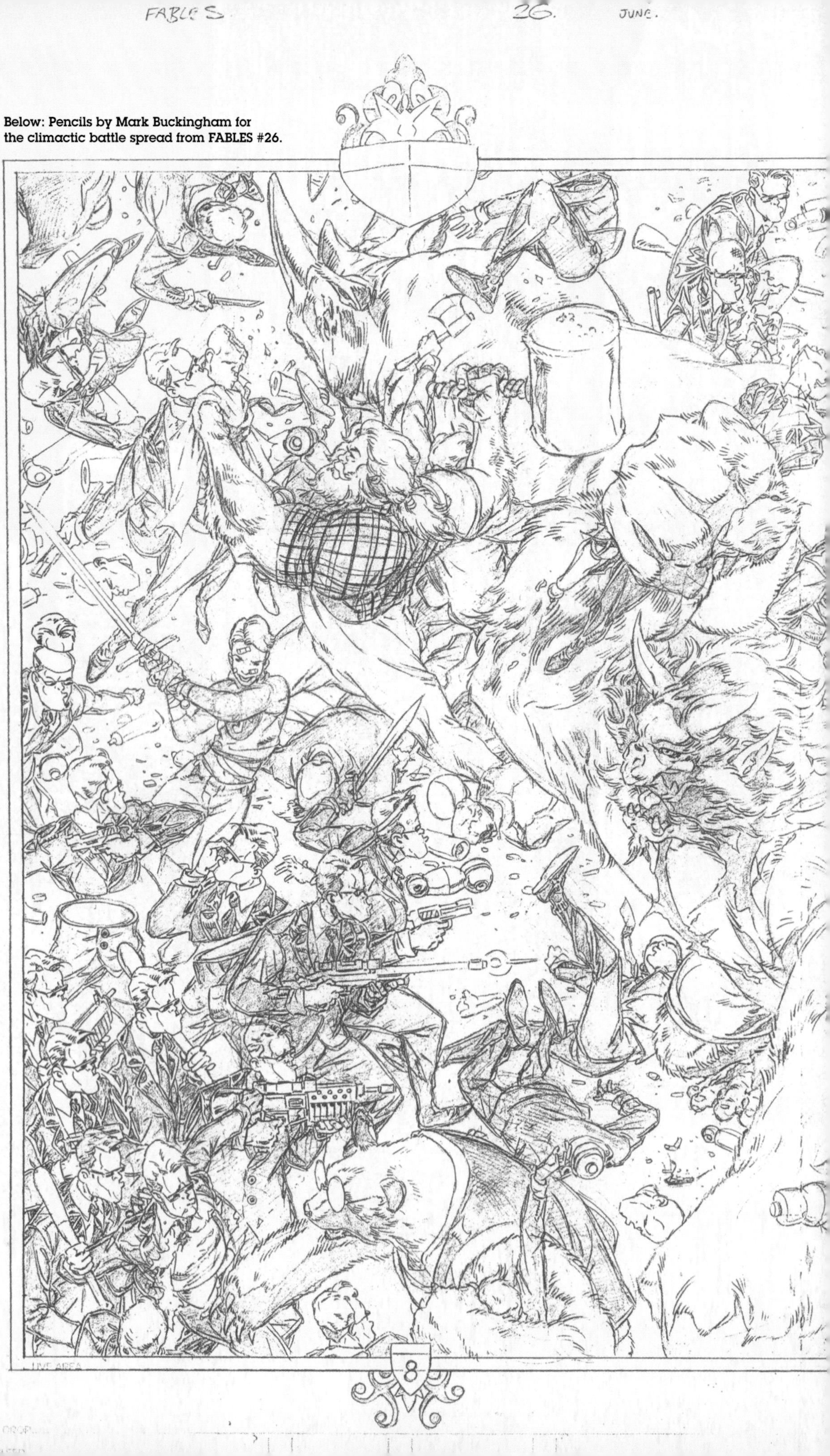
FABLES
26.
JUNE.
8

26. JUNE.

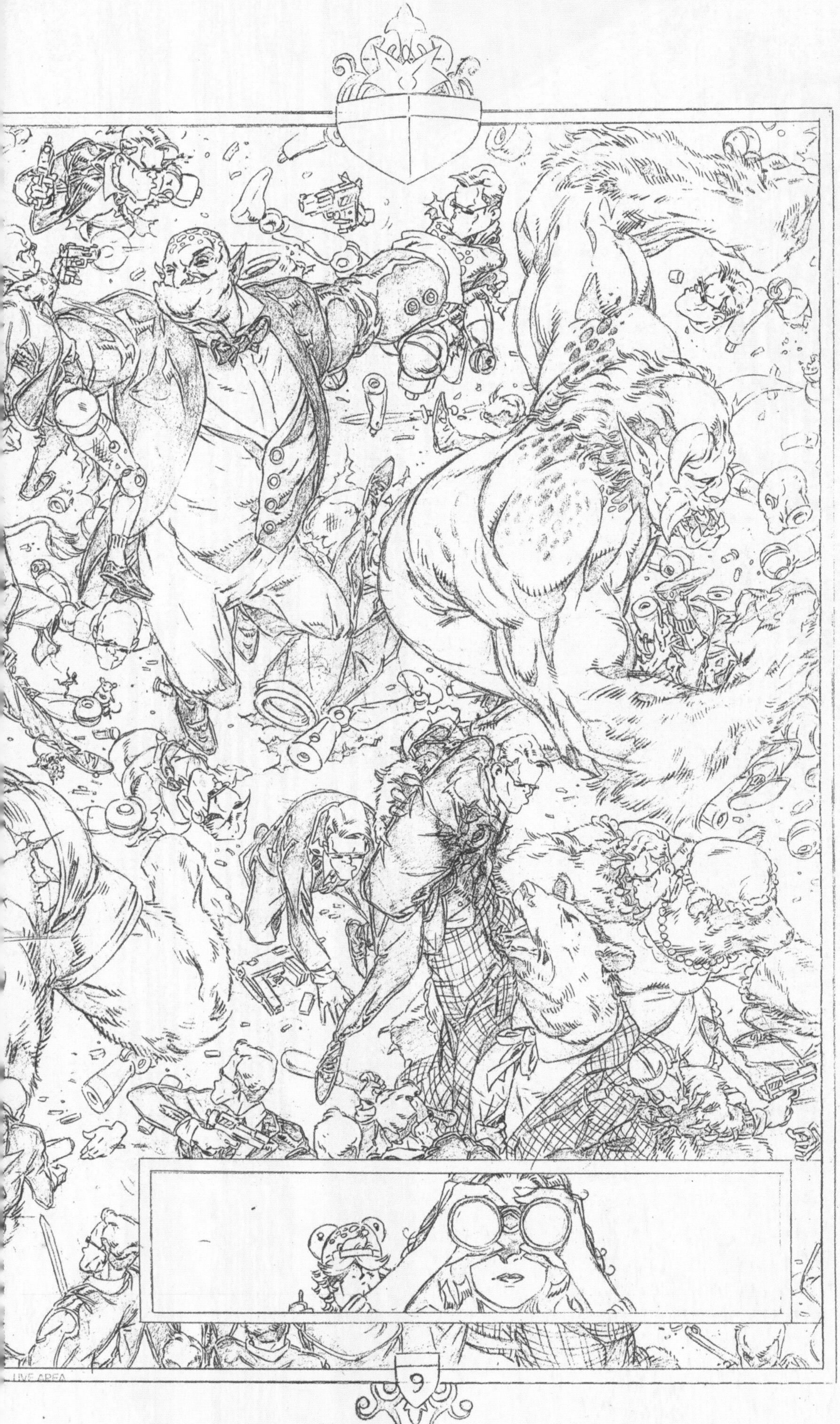
LIVE AREA
9